Information Technology

&

Environmental Management

INFORMATION TECHNOLOGY
&
ENVIRONMENTAL MANAGEMENT

Editor
Dr. Jagbir Singh

MD Publications Pvt Ltd
New Delhi
www.mdppl.com

Proceedings of the International Conference on Biodiversity, Environment and Sustainability Challenges for Future held on 4 to 6 September, 2008 at School of Environment Studies, University of Delhi (North Campus), Organised by Swami Shraddhanand College, University of Delhi, Alipur, Delhi -110036 and supported by the following agencies:

- UGC, New Delhi
- All India Foundation for Peace and Disaster Management, New Delhi.
- DST
- Delhi Pollution Control Committee
- Ministry of Environment, Delhi
- CSIR, New Delhi
- Maharastra Bank.
- ICCR
- MD Publications Pvt Ltd

Published by :

M D Publications Pvt Ltd
"M D House", 11, Darya Ganj,
New Delhi-110 002
Phone : +91-11-41563325 (Customer Service)
+91-11-41562846 (Editorial)
E-mail (orders) : **contact@mdppl.com**
Website : **www.mdppl.com**

ISBN : 978-81-7533-149-5

Price : Rs. 795.00

Published and Printed by Mrs. Rajni Gupta on behalf of
M D Publications Pvt Ltd at Printext

Preface

Life on Planet Earth has reached a crisis point. The very word "bio" means life and almost synonymous with it is energy and having polluted the world so badly in the last 200 years, we now need to look at ways of using clean renewable forms of energy. Water is the great sustainer of life in all its forms and we need to clean up the rivers of the world.

The International Conference on Biodiversity, Environment and Sustainability being held at Delhi University, India from September 4-6, 2008 will be presenting the newest and best ideas on an holistic approach in preserving the treasured information of the ancient use of Herbs grown in the Himalayas, used in agriculture and animal husbandry, together with the problem of water, soil, energy, tourism and terrorism, urbanization and air pollution.

This Conference promises to be the new nucleus of ideas for the future sustainability of our planet and we have to make governments realize their responsibility, and to remind them of the saying

"Not to know is bad - not to wish to know is even worse."

The world belongs to every living creature in it.

September, 2008

Dr. Jagbir Singh
Convener-ICBESCF 2008
&
Head, Department of Geography
Swami Shraddhanand College,
University of Delhi

Acknowledgements

The impetus of many encouraging minds from all over the world, as well as here in India, have merged to bring the most modern ideas together with almost a Tsunami wave of Knowledge to offer solutions to the world's most pressing problems involving Biodiversity, the Environment and its Sustainability. These are our challenges for the future and for the success of this Conference to be held at the school of Environmental Studies, University of Delhi Sept. 4-6-2008. I would like to acknowledge with gratitude the following people. Firstly I would like to express my heartfelt thanks to Dr. J.L. Bhat, Principal, Swami Shraddhanand College, who ones again has given me great inspiration and encouragement in making this Conference possible.

My thanks go to Mr. J.K. Dadoo, Secretary to the Dept. of Environment, Govt. of NCT, Delhi, who has taken a very keen interest in this conference and for providing funds for the conference, I am very grateful to him. I am also indebted to Prof. M.S.S. Rawat, Prof. Harjeet Singh, Ms. Joan S. Gilmour and also my students Ms. Babita, Rekha, Nidhi, Manju, Meenakshi, Mr. Sunil and Amandeep. Without the great enthusiastic team effort of all concerned, this conference would not have been possible.

Dr. Jagbir Singh
Convener-ICBESCF-2008
&
Head, Department of Geography
Swami Shraddhanand College,
University of Delhi

Acknowledgement

[illegible]

[illegible]

[illegible]

Content

1

Dam Safety Management

Christopher Lawson

Introduction

There are approximately 45,000 large dams (dams higher than 15 metres) in the world and more than two thirds of these dams were built in the last fifty years. In developing countries, dam construction is imperative to economical growth. In India, prior to Independence in 1947, there were fewer than 300 large dams. By the year 2000 the number had grown to over 4000, and more than half of these dams were built between 1971 and 1989. India ranks third in the world in dam building, behind the US and China. While some of these dams were built primarily for flood control, water supply, and hydroelectric power generation, the primary purpose of most Indian dams (96 per cent) remains irrigation. In fact, large dam construction has been the main form of investment in irrigation undertaken by the Indian government.

Dams are essential elements of a nation's infrastructure. However, the public risk in case of failure is great; large and increasing numbers of downstream lives and property are placed at risk. There are many people concerned with dam safety, however, the legal and moral responsibility for dam safety rests with the dam owner.

Each dam is unique in design and construction. However, the structural performance cannot be fully tested before the dam is set in operation. Structural problems due to design shortcomings, construction or material deficiencies or poor site conditions may not be apparent for many years and can escalate rapidly due to the dynamic nature of water impounded by the dam.

Dams can fail suddenly, with very little warning. Flooding is the most likely result of a dam failure. Knowing the risk of dam failure ahead of time and advance planning can reduce the risk of serious injury or loss of life.

Dams require ongoing surveillance and maintenance in order to keep them in an operational condition and to maintain their structural integrity and safety.

There are many lessons to be learnt from past dam incidents and failures. The lessons and incidents from the past are repeated in dam engineering seminars and papers to explain why dam safety programmes are essential to safeguard life and property.

There is a need for legislation to reduce the risk of dam failure:

- St Francis Dam in California failed on the night of 12 March 1928. Flood water killed 450 people. In 1929, the State of California enacted Dam Safety legislation.
- The failure of the Eigiau Dam in Wales on 2 November 1925 killed 16 people. In 1930, the United Kingdom passed dam safety legislation.
- Major disasters as at Malpasset (France – 1959), Vaiont (Italy – 1963) and Baldwin Hills (United States – 1963) resulted in many countries enacting new or revised laws for dam safety.

Surveillance programmes and vigilant site personnel can provide early warning of disasters and reduce the loss of life:

- Baldwin Hills Dam, Los Angeles was built in 1951 and failed in 1963. At 11.15am, the dam caretaker noticed unusually high seepage flows. When the dam failed at 3.38pm, 1,600 people had been evacuated from the downstream area. Five people died.
- Fountenelle Dam, USA nearly failed on 6 May 1965 due to excessive seepage. Quick action by the operations personnel in draining the reservoir averted a disaster.

A disaster can result if surveillance programmes are not effective or are "non existent":

- Vaiont Dam, Italy, completed in 1961, was overtopped by a wave in 1963 causing a massive landslide. The surveillance programme was found to be inadequate and 2,600 people died. Seven engineers were charged and three received gaol terms.
- A mine tailings dam near Starva, Italy failed on 19 July 1985 killing 279 people. There was no surveillance programme. The mine managers received gaol terms.

The following are just some of the hundreds of significant dam failures that have occurred around the world in the last few decades:

- Kanthale Dam in Sri Lanka -An 18 metres high embankment dam, originally built in the 7th Century and restored in 1875, failed in 1986 killing 129 people due to the failure of an outlet structure.
- Teton Dam in Ohio, USA - 93 metres high. This dam failed during commissioning in 1976 killing 14 people due to a piping failure initiated by the design and construction deficiencies.
- Banqiao and Shimantan Dams in China - Banqiao Dam was a 118 metres high dam built in the early 1950s and failed in 1975, due to design and construction deficiencies, causing the failure of the Shimantan Dam downstream and the loss of more than 18,000 lives. Details of the death toll were not released until 2005.
- Gouhou Dam in Qinghai Province, China – 71 metres high concrete-faced rockfill dam built in 1988 failed in August 1993 due to internal erosion and piping, killing more than 300 people.

The International Committee of Large Dams (ICOLD) has determined that the three major categories of dam failure are overtopping by flood, foundation defects and piping. For earthen dams, the major cause of failure was piping or seepage. For concrete dams, the major causes of failure were associated with foundations. Overtopping was a significant cause of dam failure in cases where there was an inadequate spillway.

It is now widely accepted that it simply costs too much to address the effects of emergencies only after they happen. The traditional approach of emergency response and restoration of communities must therefore be supported by emergency mitigation. Promoting a risk management approach for safer sustainable communities, mitigation is defined as any sustained action taken to reduce or eliminate a long-term risk to life and property from a hazardous event.

Hazard and Risk in Dam Safety Management

It is convenient to classify dams according to the hazard and risk presented by the dam. Hazard is the potential for loss of life, property and services. Risk is independent of the hazard category and is the probability of an adverse event occurring. The hazard category of the dam can change from low to high during the life of the dam.

The hazard potential of a dam is a qualitative assessment based on experienced judgement.

Hazard classification is used to categorise dams according to the degree of hazard potential and there are various systems adopted by dam authorities around the world.

The table below is an example of a four level hazard classification system.

Table 1: Potential Impact Categories for Dams in Terms of Failure Consequences. (After New Zealand Society on Large Dams)

Potential Impact Category	Potential Incremental Consequences of Failure	
	Life	**Socio-economic, Financial, and Environmental**
High	Fatalities	Catastrophic damages
Medium	A few fatalities are possible	Major damages
Low	No fatalities expected	Moderate damages
Very Low	No fatalities owner's property	minimal damages beyond

The hazard category determines the dam design criteria and the frequencies associated with inspection, monitoring, operation and maintenance. Emergency management and the formulation of emergency action plans are also determined by the hazard category.

A survey of the topography and population downstream of the dam combined with a computer simulated dam-break analysis is necessary to assess accurately and predict the consequences of dam failure.

Dam Safety Management Programme

It is the role of governments to enact legislation to protect the community. Dam safety legislation is necessary in order to establish regulatory authorities with the necessary powers to ensure that dam owners undertake appropriate dam safety management.

The objective of dam safety management is to protect life, property and the environment. The objective can be achieved by implementing and maintaining an appropriate dam safety programme that recognises the causes and possible impacts of dam failure and sets out a programme of several elements that include short term and long term actions.

A properly prepared Dam Safety Management Programme will contain elements and actions that:

- Ensure that current industrial standards are adopted for the investigation, design, construction, operation and maintenance of the dam.
- Prepare action plans to manage incidents.
- Provide a surveillance programme that monitors the operating status of the dam.
- Undertake regular safety reviews of the dam.
- Outline the responsibilities for dam safety.
- Provide dam safety training to the dam's management and operators.
- Ensure that appropriate funds and resources are available to maintain the programme.

Quality management can play an important role in assuring the effectiveness of the dam safety management programme through formalised procedures and documentation.

Many international and national non-government organisations (International Committee on Large Dams, Australian National Committee on Large Dams and New Zealand Society on Large Dams) have developed guidelines to assist in the preparation of Dam Safety Management Programmes.

The important interrelated elements of a Dam Safety Management Programme are:

Routine Dam Inspections

Regular visual inspections of dams are necessary in order to identify any adverse conditions that may affect the normal operation of the dam. Inspections are carried out by trained dam operators at frequencies relevant to the hazard category, of the dam. Any unusual sightings are brought to the attention of a qualified dams engineer. Special inspections are carried out by a dams engineer following unusual events such as earthquakes and floods. All inspections should have a check-list or form of reporting that documents the results of the inspection and provides conclusions and recommendations for remedial works or further investigations.

Dam Monitoring

Dam monitoring uses embedded and/or surface instrumentation at the dam to compare the actual performance of a dam with its intended design performance. A variety of instrumentation such as water level recorders, rain gauges, inclinometers, v-notch weirs, settlement gauges, piezometers, crack meters, pressure gauges, seismographs etc. can be used to monitor the performance of a dam.

The frequency of monitoring also relates to the hazard category of the dam. A dam with a high hazard category requires more instrumentation and a higher frequency of monitoring.

Operation and Maintenance

The proper and scheduled operation and maintenance of a dam is important to ensure the ongoing safe performance of the dam and ancillary equipment. Operational preparedness of the dam's critical equipment can be achieved only with a regular operational and maintenance programme and operational preparedness testing.

The preparation of Operation and Maintenance manuals includes routine and emergency operating procedures and preventative maintenance schedules to cover routine operation and the exercising of valves and equipment and condition based maintenance to replace worn components or coatings.

Safety Reviews

A safety review of a dam's performance is usually conducted every 10 to 15 years or when routine inspections raise concerns about the dam's performance. The safety review will assess the integrity of the dam against current accepted engineering design standards. Deficiencies identified by the review will be recommended for remedial action to the dam owner.

Dam Manager and Operator Training

Effective competency based dam safety training covering all aspects of dam safety management can be provided on-the-job or in the classroom for managers, operators and maintenance staff.

Dam Remedial Works

Regular surveillance, monitoring, operation and maintenance can identify deficiencies in a dam that may warrant immediate attention, further investigation and a possible safety review. Risk assessment techniques can be used to assist the selection of appropriate remedial actions.

Emergency Management Planning

Emergency management planning is the responsibility of the dam owner and such plans should be put in place for dams that have the potential to put lives at risk in the event of an emergency or a disaster.

Emergency Action Plans

When a dam is found to place lives at risk in the downstream community, emergency action plans are developed by authorities responsible for the evacuation of the downstream community in the event of a dam failure. The action plans use flood inundation maps, provided by the dam owner from dam-break studies, showing the extent of inundation caused by dam failure. The maps provide useful information relating to access and egress from the flood inundation area and enable the authorities to prepare evacuation plans.

Dam Safety Emergency Plans (DSEP)

GIS and GPS techniques can be used to provide information of the area downstream of a dam for consideration of the effects of a hypothetical dam failure. Computer dam-break software, originally produced by the American National Weather Service, can be used to simulate the effects of different dam failure mechanisms and also uses flood routing techniques to model the extent of flood inundation downstream of a failed dam. The flood inundation map enables authorities to identify the potential lives and property at risk and also verifies the hazard classification for the dam.

The preparation of the DSEP includes a notification flow chart, similar to that shown in figure 1 below, for the various emergency scenarios identifying who to be notified in order of priority, notification timing and method of notification (eg. telephone, mobile phone, fax, radio, satellite phone etc.). Dam safety emergency plans should exist for all dams where there is a potential for a loss of life in the event of dam failure. The plans identify the emergency conditions that could compromise the safety of a dam. They also describe procedures to be followed by the dam owner to respond to and mitigate the emergency conditions at the dam and to liaise with authorities responsible for emergency activities downstream of the dam.

References

1. Australian National Committee on Large Dams Inc., (2003), Guidelines on Dam Safety Management.
2. British Columbia Dam Safety Regulation (2000) - B.C. Reg.44/2000.
3. FEMA, US Department of Homeland Security (2004), Federal Guidelines for Dam Safety, Hazard Potential Classification System for Dams.
4. New Zealand Society on Large Dams, New Zealand Dam Safety Guidelines November 2000 Issue #2.

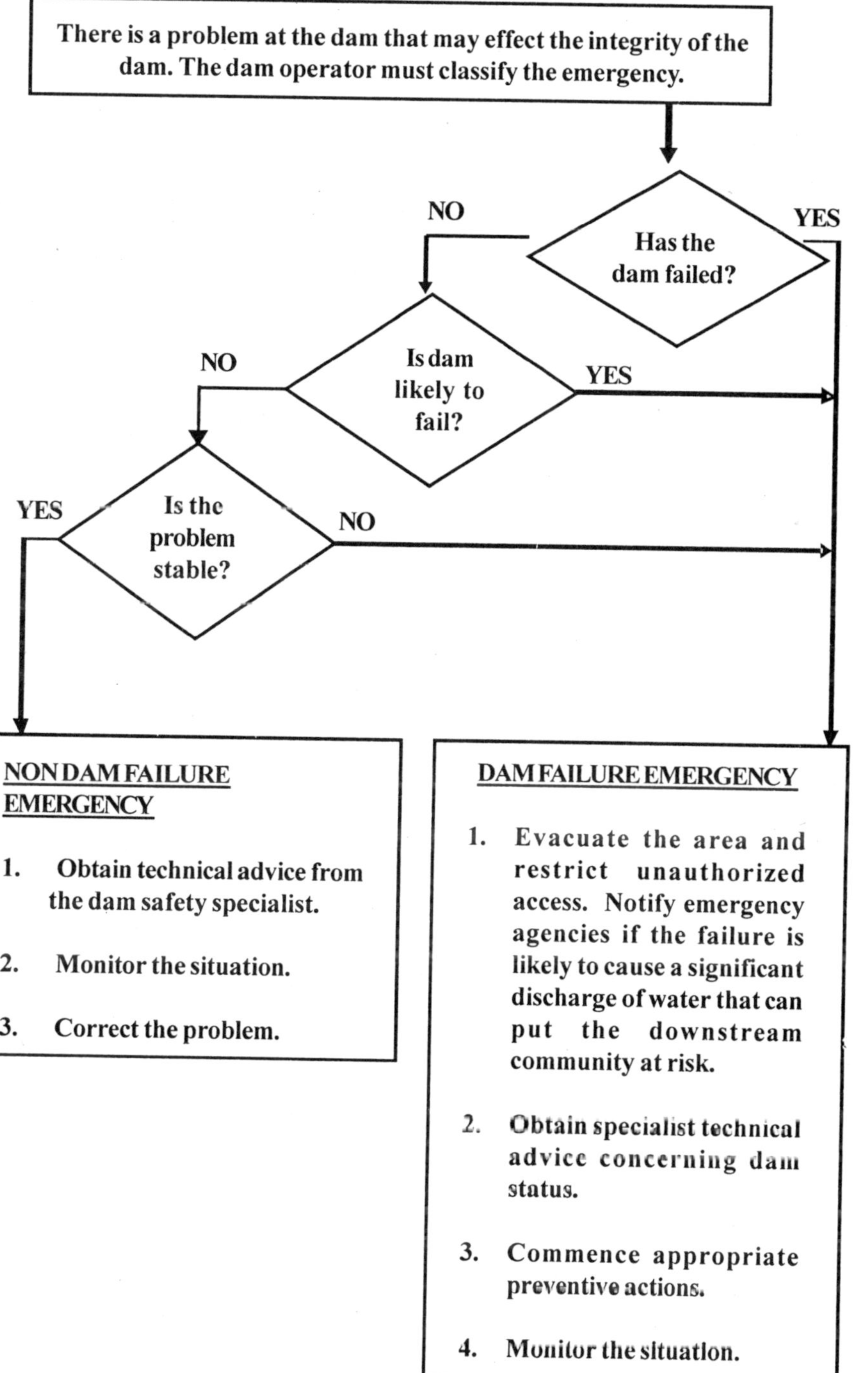

Fig. 1. DSEP Notification Flow Chart

2

Carbon Credit Cards
Greening the Globe

Dr Gursharan Singh Kainth

Introduction

The burning of fossil fuels is a major source of industrial GHGs emissions, especially for the power, cement, steel, textile and fertilizer industries. The major greenhouse gases (GHGs) emitted by these industries are carbon dioxide (CO_2), methane (CH_4), nitrous oxide (N_2O), hydro fluorocarbons (HFCs), Per fluorocarbons (PFCs) and Sulphur hexafluoride (SF_6) which will increase the atmosphere's ability to trap infrared energy and thus affect the climate. The concept of carbon credits came into existence as a result of an increasing awareness of the need for controlling emissions.

This tradable permit system is one of the policy instruments that have shown to be environmentally effective in the industrial sector, as long as there are reasonable levels of predictability over the initial allocation mechanism and long term price. Every Annex-I country has been assigned the amount of emission which is to be reduced by the concerned country. It also implies that a country is permitted to emit the remaining amount. This emission amount of allowance is actually one kind of carbon credit. The total amount is then subdivided into certain units expressed in terms of the carbon equivalent. Each unit gives the owner the right to emit one metric ton of carbon dioxide or other equivalent of GHGs. There is, however, another variant of carbon credit. This variant of carbon credit is to be earned by a country by investing some amount of money in such projects known as carbon projects which will emit lesser amounts of GHGs. This exchange may take place within the economy or it may take the form of international transactions. Accordingly, there are two types of carbon trading, namely, ***emission* trading** or ***cap-and-trade*** and ***offset*** trading or ***base-line-and credit*** trading. Credit cards are generated by enterprises in the developing world that shift to cleaner technologies and thereby save on energy consumption, consequently reducing their GHGs emissions.

Carbon trading is the name given to the exchange of emission permits, alternatively known as carbon credit. It is an emission allowance which was originally allocated or auctioned by the national administrators of a cap-and-trade programme or it can offset emissions. Such offsetting and mitigating activities can occur in any developing county which has ratified the Kyoto Protocol and has a national agreement in place to validate its carbon project through one of the UNFCCC's approved mechanisms. Once approved, these units are termed as ***Certified Emission Reductions*** (CERs). The Protocol allows these projects to be constructed and credited in advance of the Kyoto trading period. The Kyoto Protocol, provides for three mechanisms that enable countries or operators in developed countries to acquire GHG reduction credits.

1. ***Under Joint Implementation,*** a developed country with relatively high costs of domestic GHG reductions would set up a project in another developed country.

2. Under the ***Clean Development Mechanism*** (CDM) a developed country can sponsor a GHGs reduction project in a developing country where the cost of the GHG reduction project activities is usually much lower, but the atmospheric effect is globally equivalent. The developed country would be given credits for meeting its emission reduction targets, while the developing countries would receive the capital investment and clean technology or beneficial change in land use.

3. Under ***International Emissions Trading*** (IET) countries can trade in the international carbon credit market to cover their shortfall in allowances. Countries with surplus credit can sell them to countries with capped emission commitments under the Kyoto Protocol.

These carbon projects can be created by a national government or by an operator within the country. In reality, most of the transactions are not performed by national governments directly but by the operators who have been set quotas by their country. For trading purpose, one allowance of CER is considered equivalent to one metric tonne of CO_2 emissions. These allowances can be sold privately or on the international market at the prevailing market rates. These trades were settled internationally and hence allow allowances to be transferred between countries. Each international transfer is validated by the NFCCC. Each transfer within the European Union is additionally validated by the European Commission.

Climate exchanges have been established in order to provide spot market in allowances, as well as future and optional markets to help discover a market price and maintain liquidity. Carbon prices are generally quoted in Euros per tonne of carbondioxide or its equivalent (CO_2e). Other GHGs can be traded also, but are quoted as standard multiples of CO_2 with respect to their global warming potential. Currently there are six exchanges trading in carbon allowances, namely, European Climate Exchange; Nord Pool; Power Next; Multi Commodity Exchange and the National Commodity and Derivative Exchange. Recently, Nord Pool listed a contract to trade offsets generated by a CDM carbon project. Many companies now engage in emissions abatement, offsetting and sequestration programmes in order to generate credits that can be sold on.

Carbon trading is becoming popular day by day. The volume of carbon trade is increasing at a faster rate. The global carbon market has grown from USD 33 billion globally in 2006 to USD 60 billion in 2007 and is bound to grow even further as participation increases from other countries that have not so far ratified to the Kyoto Protocol. As per World Bank estimates, in the Carbon Finance unit, the volume of carbon trade through an Emission trading route only had shown a 240 per cent increase in 2005 over the previous year. Barclays Capital predicts that "Carbon will be the world's biggest commodity market and it could become the world's biggest market overall". As the deadline for meeting the Kyoto Protocol draws nearer, prices can be expected to rise as countries/companies save credits to meet strict targets in the future. India is well ahead in establishing a full companies fledged system in operationalizing CDM through the ***Designated National Authority*** (DNA)-Ministry of Forest and Environment,but this is not a good sign. The Kyoto Protocol was signed to reduce GHG emissions but this flexibility mechanism allows, especially the main culprits, to skip their reduction by spending some money. Moreover funds are invested in carbon projects which are meaningless from the view of emission reduction. Such projects only create a false sense of emission reduction and thereby jeopardize the ultimate objectives of the entire exercise. The time is now to fight climate change. We have to level with the public that there has to be a price on carbon emissions. Apparently, there should be a tax on carbon emissions. The belief is that by starting a carbon emissions tax, it would help reduce emissions and encourage companies and others to use renewable energy sources. These people in the fossil fuel industry should be prosecuted. Ecological Internet supports a global carbon market that is well regulated, but not as a replacement for carbon taxes, which will address the issue of pricing carbon more quickly, effectively and simply. While short-term politics favours markets, taxes would be better in the long-term because industry needs certainty for investments. A government committing to painful taxes signals the seriousness of its intentions.

Japan, the world's second-most populous country, rejected in April 2008 an international proposal to replace national limits on carbon dioxide pollution set by Kyoto with targets for individual industries, taking sides against Japan and the U.S. in how to curb global warming. India is opposed to suggestions by the world's two largest economies Japan and US to adopt a so called "bottom-up, sectoral approach" devised by Japan in its bid to lead the crafting of a successor to Kyoto.

Indian Scenario

India was the fourth largest emitter of carbon dioxide in 2004, according to the United Nations Development Programme's Human Development Report 2007-2008, after the U.S., China and Russia. India comes under the third category of signatories to UNFCCC. India signed and ratified the Protocol in August 2002 and has emerged as a world leader in reduction of GHGs by adopting ***Clean Development Mechanisms*** (CDM's) in the past few years. Even though India has no mitigation commitments under the Kyoto Protocol, India has the largest number of projects under the CDM of the Kyoto Protocol mooted to encourage investments in developing countries by promoting the transfer of environmentally-friendly technologies. The major CDM projects are located in Rajasthan, Andhra Pradesh, Maharashtra, Karnataka, Himachal Pradesh and the Punjab. One third of the total CDM projects registered with UNFCCC are from India. In

2007, a total of 160 new projects were registered with UNFCCC. As a consequence, Indian industry managed to generate over 27 million carbon credits. Indian projects receive further impetus by way of investments and finance from developed nations who are potential buyers of CERs. Till November 2007, 828 CDM projects have been registered in 48 countries. Three waste to energy projects are to be undertaken shortly at three of Delhi's sanitary landfills, namely at Timarpur, Okhla and Ghazipur, and all three are fine examples under CDM.

Other than Industries and transportation, the major sources of GHG emissions are the paddy fields, enteric fermentation from cattle and buffaloes and the municipal solid waste. The emission from paddy fields can be reduced through a special irrigation strategy and appropriate choice of cultivars, whereas the enteric fermentation emission can also be reduced through proper feed management. In recent days, the third source of emission, that is, Municipal Solid Waste (MSW) dumping grounds are emerging as a potential CDM activity despite being provided least attention till date. At present there are no Sanitary Landfill sites in India. MSW is simply dumped without any treatment into land (depressions, ditches or soaked ponds) or on the outskirts of the city in an unscientific manner with no compliance of regulations. The waste in the dumping ground undergoes various anaerobic reactions producing offensive odorous gases such as CO_2, CH_4, H_2S and Mercaptans, which foster harmful pathogens and lead to environmental, social and public health issues. Moreover, the existing dumping grounds are full and overflowing beyond capacity. It is difficult to get new dumping yards, and if at all available, they are far away from the city which adds to exorbitant transportation costs. As per estimate of CPCB the cumulative requirement of land for MSW disposal would reach around 169.6 km^2 by 2047 as against 20.2 km^2 in 1997. Moreover, various technologies/processes available to reduce the amount of MSW are unviable for existing dumping grounds due to various reasons such as the segregation of MSW etc.

Currently, India is one of the largest suppliers of carbon credit cards in the world with a whopping 29 million carbon credit cards and another 139 million in the pipelines. India is leading developing nations in carbon credits, expecting over 2.27 billion US dollars by selling certified emissions reduction units (CER) from approximately 300 Clean Development Mechanism (CDM) projects, according to the Designated National Authority (DNA) - India's Ministry of Environment and Forests. There is a great opportunity awaiting India in carbon trading which is estimated to go up to $100 billion by 2010. In the new regime, the country would emerge as one of the largest beneficiaries accounting for one fourth of the world carbon trade. The countries like US, Germany, Japan and China are likely to be the biggest buyers of carbon credits which are beneficial for India to a great extent. Hence MSW dumping grounds can be huge prospects for CDM projects in India. The utilization of MSW dumping grounds for energy production would mean a favourable and useful solution to the existing MSW disposal problem. Such projects can be executed using a Public-Private Partnership approach in which both the parties can invest and share the benefits. Investment and operating costs are recovered through the sale of CER. Such types of projects would not only be beneficial for the Government bodies and stakeholders but also for the general public. The collaborative action by governments, the community and individuals could combat climate change.

Low CER rates, non-enforcement of rich nation`s renewable energy investment commitments in poor nations, lack of transparency in the CDM quantification process and several other irregularities are cited in the CDM market. The CDM, one of three mechanisms of the Kyoto Protocol, allows Annex-I or industrialized nations to buy emission reduction units, called CERs, from non- Annex developing countries. Annex. I rich nations can then count these credits towards their GHG emission targets. The principle is to help rich nations reduce the cost of meeting their reduction targets by 2012 whilst mitigating climate change and helping the developing nations. There are six greenhouse gases (GHGs), carbon dioxide, methane, nitrous oxide, hydro fluorocarbons, per fluorocarbons and sulphur hexafluoride. One ton of carbon dioxide, or its equivalent of the other five gases makes one CER. As per the CDM rules, the emission reductions should benefit sustainable development, help alleviate poverty, create clean technology in a carbon-less economy and produce local benefits among others but not a single one of India's 252 CDM projects, as per the United Nations Environmental Programme, deals with afforestation, agriculture or even rural development. The majority of that number is energy-efficiency projects from industries. Since renewable energy technologies are given tax rebates as an incentive by the Indian government, industry is now quick to catch on to the double benefit of harnessing a CDM deal. With a history of renewable energy ventures falling by the wayside once this rebate has been used, the CDM's real contribution to development in India is a debatable one. Awareness on CDM in India also continues to remain poor. "The Protocol says Annex-I countries are to invest capital in renewable energy technology to be able to gain their CO_2 offsets, but this is neither happening, nor is there any mechanism to enforce this. Further, the CDM was to be between Annex-I and developing country parties. But Annex-I governments with their clout have now entered the scene, making small industries in developing countries unable to negotiate their own terms or prices with giant partners. This is just a 'charitable' way of seeing the current situation. We are selling off our assets without pinning a real value on our CO_2 ton, and checking to see whether our sustainable development is real or not. Rich nations are holding the power and dictating terms to developing nations. Apparently, there is a clear nexus between the WTO and the CDM process evolving but it is hoped that the market will allow CER rates to find their own level as per market driven forces. The small community and rural development projects being left out are unable to sell their small numbers of carbon offsets. The process of training various departments on 'bundling' small projects together should be initiated for raising skills and awareness amongst those in this sector. Another phenomenon in the market is an increasing number of 'Type 2' CDM deals between parties who do not fall under targets. The scenario, in type 2 deals, is fraught with irregularities and poor execution, over which even the World Bank has expressed concern. "The voluntary market lacks an internationally agreed, standardized protocol for engagement, leaving investors, buyers, project developers, verifiers and others to proceed on an ad hoc basis", according to the World Bank's Carbon Finance Unit. India, the world's fourth-largest emitter of carbon dioxide, plans to form eight commissions to promote solar power, energy efficiency and water conservation as it seeks to mitigate damage from the changing climate. Each of the eight panels will have an institutional structure consisting of government departments, industrial experts, academics and citizen representatives, the government said. Each so-called mission will devise a state-funded plan and have authority to carry it out. The missions include developing efficient building technologies, better Waste Management conserving water and sustaining the environment of the Himalayas.

India, China and other developing nations have asked industrialized countries to carry the burden of reducing CO_2 and other greenhouse gases through adopting emission targets by 2020. They also seek aid and technology to cut their own CO_2 output. India has resisted adopting limits so that its economy can grow enough to eliminate poverty. About 34 per cent of the nation's 1.1 billion people live on less than $1 a day, the UN has estimated. This does demonstrate that we are prepared to be responsible global citizens and join others in a collaborative effort to deal with climate change. Sustainable development has to be supported by both financial resources and technological resources. Until that happens, how does one expect the developing countries to take up quantitative restrictions?

India relies heavily on coal for power generation as it is so abundantly available. The coal-based plants account for a large part of the country's carbon dioxide emissions. India's commitment is to ensure that its per-capita emissions of green-house gases do not exceed those of developed nations but the new action plan makes no commitment to cutting overall emissions. Despite mounting international pressure, India has refused to make any specific commitments so far on reducing green-house gas emissions, pointing out that its per-capita emissions are a fraction of those in rich nations. Convergence of per-capita emissions in emissions from developed and developing countries" can be the only basis for any global agreement on climate change. India feels that developed countries have a larger responsibility to cut emissions. In terms of our development and growth today, we are already emitting emissions than the developed world did at the time it was growing, which means that our energy intensity is lower than theirs at the time of growth. Developed countries say developing nations like India must reduce emissions because it is one of the world's top polluters. India, a country of one-billion-plus people, needs to use more energy to power its growing economy and lift its people out of poverty.

References

1. Mankiw, N.G. (2007) : One Answer to Global Warming : A new Tax. *The New York Times*. September 16, 2007
2. Wintour, . (2006) : Miliband plans carbon trading "credit cards" for everyone. *The Guardian*. December 11, 2006

3

Spatial Modelling for Reducing Earthquake Disaster Damages in Iran

H. AGHAMOHAMMADI , A. RANJBAR , R. NOURJOU AND D. MOLAEI

Introduction

Earthquakes are one of the natural disasters but once happened, cause many problems and difficulties in the economical, environmental and human life sphere so earthquake Disaster Management is necessary for decreasing these problems which affect decision making under disaster conditions. Because most data related to earthquake disaster has spatial properties, the GIS can be used for better planning and decision making in earthquake Disaster Management. The Disaster Management cycle can be divided into two sections; after an earthquake and before an earthquake. Before an earthquake, a section is divided into three phases: planning, mitigation, preparedness, and after an earthquake, a section is divided into two phases: response and recovery [1]. In some countries such as Iran, disaster experiences show that the managing and decision making before an earthquake is more effective than doing some activity after an earthquake which has occured so therefore the pre-disaster phase is much more important [2].

We said that the Disaster Management cycle was divided into three phases. In the planning phase we assess the potential of a disaster occurrence and if there be any Earthquake disaster risk, we should go to the mitigation phase.The purpose of this phase is to plan for creating a resistant urban plan against an earthquake [3-4]. In the preparedness phase, we create a necessary preparedness against an earthquake (e.g. we store food and water in a special place).

One of the most important tasks which must be done for creating a resistance urban plan against an earthquake, is to enter earthquake zoning rules in urban planning [5]. We designed and implemented two efficient models. The first model is applied to check the land suitability with related application and the second model estimates any road obstruction with respect to damaged buildings debris.

Model of Checking Land Suitability with Related Application

In this stage, with respect to the kind of application, the different geological properties of the region and an earthquake model have been designed, which can answer the following question.

Does each land use with respect to an earthquake risk agree with the related parcel?

We can then identify which applications are exposed to danger, and after that we can decide how we can create a stable situation for moving the application. Another case of using this model is to give authorization to different applications. The case study is divided into four sites based on geological and earthquake properties as given at Table 1.

Table 1: Site Classification Based on Geological and Earthquake Properties.

Site Code	Site Characteristics
Site A	- Very low probability subsidence of soil
Site B	- Low probability subsidence of soil
Site C	- Medium probability subsidence of soil - Having a liquefaction potential - Distance of sites from fault between 300 and 500 meters
Site D	- High probability subsidence of soil - Having a liquefaction potential - Having a landslide potential - Distance of sites from fault less than 300 meters

Using JICA approach [6], probability map of subsidence, liquefaction, landslide and distance of active/ fault provided consideration of the above criteria. It is necessary to mention that the determination of the geological and earthquake properties, spatial modelling and layer composition have been done in a GIS environment. According to the suitability matrix [7] that has been shown in figure 1 the amount of land suitability for each application was checked based on its location.

Obstruction Zoning Model

However, roads are important for the rescue activation. Their obstruction is one of the more important problems for rescue in an earthquake situation [8-9-10]. Road obstruction models are developed based on probability approaches [8] or empirical approaches [4]. An empirical model has been developed using observations of the Manjil Earthquake in 1990 [4]. In this model is respect to a building`s height, road widths and materials which were used in the close structures, We were able to produce a map for representing danger for a road obstruction in three levels which we called low coefficient of danger, medium coefficient of danger and high coefficient of danger. Therefore, we can then decide about the resistance of buildings, widening of roads and

Land use \ Site	A	B	C	D
One Floor residential	suitable	suitable	suitable	unsuitable
2 & 3 Floor residential	suitable	suitable	un suitable	unsuitable
More than 4 Floor residential	suitable	unsuitable	unsuitable	unsuitable
Commercial	suitable	unsuitable	unsuitable	unsuitable
Educational	suitable	unsuitable	unsuitable	unsuitable
Religious	suitable	unsuitable	unsuitable	unsuitable
Medical	suitable	unsuitable	unsuitable	unsuitable
Official	suitable	unsuitable	unsuitable	unsuitable
Culture & Sport	suitable	unsuitable	unsuitable	unsuitable
Lifeline establishment	suitable	unsuitable	unsuitable	unsuitable
Industrial	suitable	unsuitable	unsuitable	unsuitable
Entertainment	suitable	suitable	suitable	suitable

Fig. 1. Suitability matrix

assigning authorization for construction.This model is based on the width of roads, height of blocks and materials. The coefficient of danger that was mentioned in table 2 and 3, are pulsed together. If the result is two o three, the obstruction danger is low. If it is equal to four and five, the obstruction danger is medium, and for six, seven and eight, we have a high obstruction danger.

Table 2: Danger Coefficient with Respect to Proportion of Width to Height.

Proportion of width to height	Coefficient of danger
$w/h < 0.5$	4
$0.5 < w/h < 1$	3
$1 < w/h < 2$	2
$w/h => 2$	1

Table 3: Danger Coefficient with Respect to Proportion of Width to Height.

Material Type	Coefficient of danger
Weak	4
Semi strong	3
Strong	2
There is no block	1

Case Study and Result

A part of Tehran that is called FARAHZAD was recognized as suitable because of the closing to active faults, and it has a high potential for destruction. This region is considered as a case study and models were done on it, because of the large volume of output. We just represent some of them in figure 2, 3 and 4.

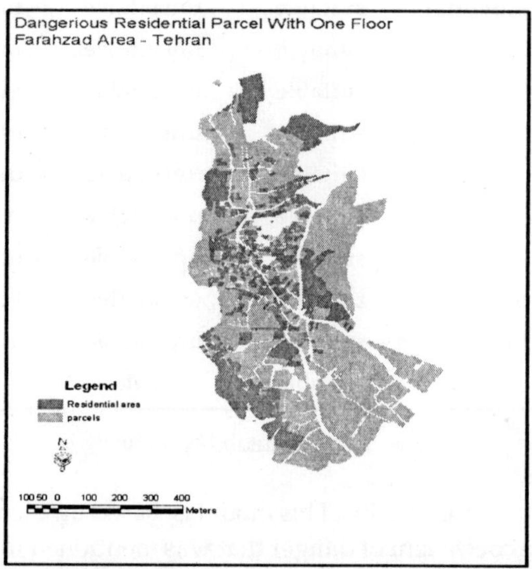

Fig. 2. Map of One Floor Residential Building that is in Danger from an Earthquake.

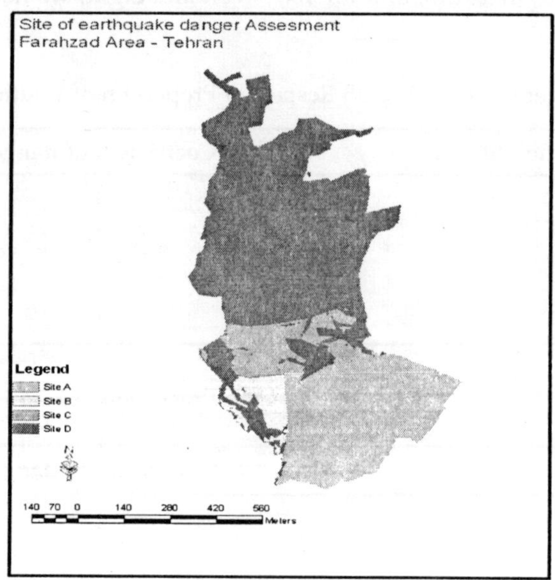

Fig. 3. Map of Different Sites have been Divided Based on Geological Properties and Earthquake Danger.

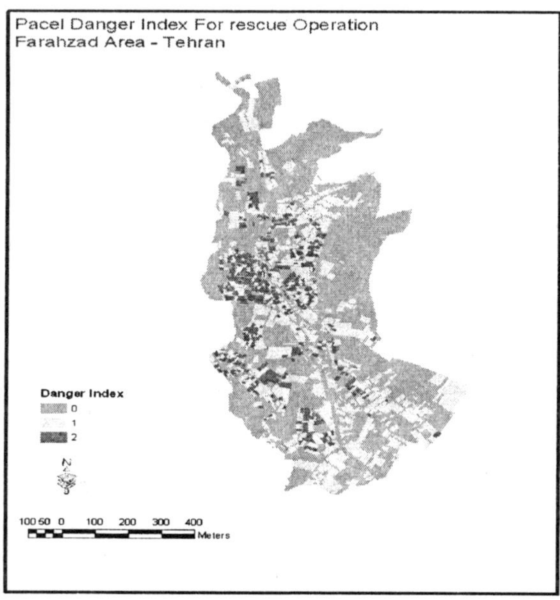

Fig. 4. Map of Road Obstruction.

Conclusion

With respect to the harmful effects of earthquakes on human societies, Disaster Management is a very important problem.GIS as a science and technology for managing, representing, retrieving, saving and modelling of spatial and non-spatial data, is an efficient tool for decision making and planning for earthquake Disaster Management.

Using some models in a GIS environment, we can help to have a resistance city against earthquakes. For example, if we use the results on our case study, we will be able to reduce earthquake damage. Finally, design and implementation of GIS is necessary for reducing the effects of an earthquake in Iran.

References

1. Aghamohammadi H., (2005) Design and Implementation of a GIS System for Decreasing Earthquake Disaster Damages, M.Sc. thesis, K.N.Toosi University of Iran.
2. Bahraini H., (1996). Land Use Planning In Seismic Regions (in Persian), Bonyade Maskan Press.
3. Franchin P., Lupoi A. and Pinto P. E., (2006). On The Role of Road Networks in Reducing Human Losses After Earthquakes, Journal of Earthquake Engineering, Vol. 10, No. 2.
4. Goretti A. and Sarli V., (2006). Road Network and Damaged Buildings in Urban Areas: Short and Long-term Interaction, Bulletin of Earthquake engineering, 4: 159-175.

5. HAZUS-FEMA, (2004). Technical Manual, "Multi-hazard Loss Estimation Methodology, Earthquake Model", HAZUS-MH MR1, Washington D.C.

6. Japan International Cooperation Agency (JICA), (2000). The Study on Seismic Microzoning of the Greater Tehran Area in the Islamic Republic of Iran, Final Report, Main Report, SSF JR 00-186.

7. Kiremidjin A., Moore J., Fan Y. Y., Yazlali O., Basoz N. and Williams M., (2007). Seismic Risk Assessment of Transportation Network Systems, Journal of Earthquake Engineering, 11: 371-382

8. Lekkas E. L., (2002). the Role of Earthquake-Related Effects in Urban Complexes, Natural Hazards, 25: 23–35.

9. Oliveira C. S., Roca A. and Goula (eds.) X., (2008). Assessing and Managing Earthquake Risk, Springer.

10. Oosterom P.V, Zlataneva S. and Fendel E. M., (2005). Geo-Information for Disaster Management, Springer.

4

Environment Laws and Regional Policies

PUNEET PABBY

Introduction

Environmental pollution has become one of the chief threats to the survival of mankind the world over. The rat race for development without concern for its environmental costs has led to a disturbance of the delicate, ecological balance between the living and non-living components of the biosphere. The unfavourable conditions created by man's reckless interference with nature not only threaten the survival of mankind, but also of other living organisms.[1]

The major environmental concerns of India today are air pollution resulting from industrial and domestic effluents, soil erosion, deforestation, desertification and loss of wildlife because of the imprudent and unplanned use of the land and its resources, the ugly landscape of the urban sprawl and city which seem to result from a burgeoning population.The protection of the environment presents a most fundamental challenge to the nation's desire to industrialise faster, to be self-sufficient in food and to be capable by fulfilling certain basic needs for a growing population.

Industrialists fear that if environmental laws are made to be too strict, investment in the sector will decline and foreign investors will be discouraged. They want pollution control standards established through a dialogue between the industry and the government, rather than unilaterally.

There is a widely shared feeling that compared with the grimface of the environmental damage, the response from administrative or governmental agencies is far from adequate. In fact, in the eyes of the common man, governmental functionaries and political executives are often suspected to be active collaborators of those who are destroying environmental resources for narrow and selfish gains.

The modern state is an administrative state. Administration has come to wield enormous importance in the contemporary states. The future of mankind for its very survival depends significantly on the successful functioning of an administrative system.[2]

In the field of environment protection too, the administrative system is entrusted with crucial responsibilities. To discharge these responsibilities effectively, the administrative system has to perceive properly the threats and causes of environmental pollution and should respond effectively both in devising and operational strategies to prevent further environmental decay. The crucial ingredients required to solve problems by an effective bureaucratic response team are structural conduciveness, clarity with an adequate comprehension of perception, autonomy of operation and behavioural congeniality.

The response of the governmental and legal systems also keep the hope alive that India will be able to generate a social mechanism to avert environmental disasters and lead the way for many other countries towards sustainable development. The silver lining on the horizon in recent times is the use of law for enforcing environmental protection and human rights.[3] Environmental policy is a subject of keen social, political and scientific interest in contemporary times. This interest is largely on account of the increasing levels of pollution and eco-degradation threatening the very survival of mankind. India is one of the very few countries which has enshrined in its constitution a commitment to environmental protection and improvement. Initially, the Indian constitution did not make any direct reference to environmental protection as such. This perhaps, was on account of the fact that the policy makers who were largely responsible for earlier environmental issues then, did not have to assume the proportion of the environmental degradation which is serious enough to compel them to engage their attention to such a widespread disaster today.

The 42nd Constitutional (Amendment) Act casts a fundamental duty for the protection of the environment on every citizen in the following words "It shall be the duty of every citizen of India to protect and improve the natural environment including the forest, rivers and wild life and to have compassion for living creatures" (Indian Constitutional Law). The Directive Principle of State Policy provides for a certain directive to the state regarding the protection and improvement of the environment under Article 48-A which states:

"The states shall endeavour to protect and improve the environment and to safeguard the forests and wildlife of the country" (Indian Constitutional Law). In addition to Article 48-A, Article 47 provides for the improvement of public health, the forests and wildlife of the country (Indian Constitutional Law).

The Constitution thus, makes a two -fold provision. On the one hand, it gives directive to the state for the protection and improvement of the environment and on the other, it casts a duty on every citizen to help in the preservation of the natural environment. These provisions are indicative of the policy maker's awareness of a contemporary problem and of the need for providing a constitutional base at local levels. When these provisions came up for consideration in both houses of parliament, a general concern was expressed by a cross-section of members about the deteriorating environment.

Laws Governing the Environment

The legal sanctions to protect different segments of the environment such as land, water, and air are incorporated into a multiplicity of laws enacted in the country. There are multitudes of laws in India which directly or indirectly relate to environmental protection.

General Laws

The general laws are in the nature of enactments which incidentally afford a scope for environmental protection even while subserving some general purposes or objectives. These laws contain provisions meant to protect the environment and to punish its polluters.

1. The Indian Penal Code
2. The Code of Criminal Procedure
3. The Police Act
4. The Code of Civil Procedure
5. The Specific Relief Act
6. The Factories Act
7. The Insecticide Act
8. The Motor Vehicles Act
9. The Pesticide Act

Most of these general laws are essentially punitive in nature and they do not have much sway in preventing the damage to the environment. Further, the procedural requirements under these laws are such that they make relief to the victim difficult. It is an account of these factors that special laws are required for a more effective protection of the environment.

Special Laws

There are a number of laws that are specially enacted or are aimed at pollution prevention and environmental improvement. They are:

1. The Wildlife (Protection) Act, 1972
2. The Water (Prevention and Control of Pollution) Act, 1974
3. The Water (Prevention and Control of Pollution) Act, 1981
4. The Forest (Conservation) Act, 1980
5. The Environment Protection Act, 1986
6. The Motor Vehicle Act, 1988
7. The National Environmental Tribunal Act, 1995

The list of the above enactment laws does not exhaust the catalogues of special laws relating to environmental protection and pollution prevention.

If law making alone were to be the answer to the environmental crisis and to address the question of wholesomeness of the environment,then India should figure as a front ranking nation among the committer of nations. The authorities under various Acts are entrusted with numerous responsibilities but they are not entrusted with commensurate power to carry out the same, Under The Water and Air Pollution Control Acts, the powers of the Pollution Control Board were leeringly advisory in nature. The only measure of control they could exercise was in issuing consent certificates, which were deemed to be given after the expiry of four months, in the Water Act and merely on application in the Air Act.

There is a considerable overlapping of powers of various authorities. In addition to the Pollution Control Boards created by the Water Act and Air Acts, there are local authorities like the Municipalities and Municipal Corporations which are empowered to issue industrial licenses. On account of this, even if the Boards refuse consent certificates the same can be obtained from the Municipalities. Most of the Boards that are already set up lack adequate infrastructure and funds to ensure effective implementation of the laws. The single most important factor accounting for the poor implementation of pollution control programmes in developing countries is the limited availability of funds.[4] The existing groups of environmentalists and consumer right activists are not powerful enough to pressurise the policy makers and implementing agencies in the cause for the environment. The parties in power are also not likely to win any more votes on account of their efforts in the direction of environmental improvement. Low public awareness is also to be blamed for this sorry state of affairs. The Environmental (Protection) Act, 1986 rightly purports to inculcate environmental ethics in every citizen and designs to take appropriate steps for the protection and improvement of the environment. Under this Act, a person cannot directly file a petition in court on a question of the environment. One is required to give a notice of not less than sixty days to the Central Government of his intention to make a complaint. One can go to the court only if the government does not act on the notice of this period. It may be submitted that such provisions impede rather than serve the cause of environmental protection. The role of the environmentalist and other voluntary bodies has being curtailed rather than enhanced. Public interest litigation cases will suffer a big setback under the provisions of the Act. In fact the Act has taken one step forward and two steps backward. The Act smacks of over centralisation of powers in central government which is not conducive to protection of the environment. The Act smacks of the over centralisation of power in the central government which is not conducive to the protection of environment. Environmental justice is entrusted to bureaucratic machinery which has a dysfunctional passion for the files but not for people.[5] It may be added that there is a dire need for imparting citizen education which inculcates and nurtures a culture in the human beings to protect the nature and environment while it is true that legislation itself needs to be strengthened their and simplified for its proper implementation. Needless to say legislation alone cannot be effective unless the enforcement machinery is not fully geared up.[6]

Area for Future Research

The investigator to identify certain areas for future investigation:

1) An analysis of co-ordination among and communication between various departments, agencies and bodies working for the conservation, preservation of the environment.

2) An analysis of the various models of administrative structures which could be effective in executing policies relating to the environment.

3) An analysis of the socio-economic and ecological input of environmental preservation on a national development.

Improvement in Environmental Legislation

There is a need for having a fresh and comprehensive environmental legislation in order to achieve a desired result. It would not be of much use because it is ridden with a number of loopholes and lacunae which provides a cover to people who wish to hood-wink environmental laws and molest the environment.

1) Legislation regarding the location of projects in the proximity of national parks, natural sanctuaries or monuments should be strictly enforced to save them.

2) An annual report on the state of the environment should be brought out and it should be given due publicity with the insertion of a relevant provision in environmental laws.

3) In order to provide support and strength to governmental agencies, the non-governmental organisations must be encouraged and given legal reorganisation to combat the menace of environmental pollution.

The National Environmental Tribunal Act which is the outcome of the Indian Governments participation in a UN Conference on Environment and Development held at Rio de Janeiro in June 1992 remains dormant. Under this act any which victim would be able to receive compensation from the neglect or wrongful act of any person causing loss or damage to property or the environment but the tribunal is non-existent.

Next, the task of concern is the absence of a legislative framework for the identification and disposal of electronic waste. It is a big issues in environmental degradation. The lack of a legal framework means that India become a dumping ground for waste generated by a host of electrical and electronic gadgets. At present e-waste, like a host of other waste is recycled by the informal sector, which poses a health hazard to the people working in such units and a danger to the environment. The absence of legislation ensures that large hardware companies which abide by all the, norms govern the disposal of e-waste in the country. It is a praiseworthy step of good performance of green guidelines in 2006-07 that are well followed and adapted in practical manner. The Ministry of Environment and Forest is planning to introduce an

Environment Tribunal Bill, which envisages the setting up of "Green Courts". It is pertinent to mention that poor performance in the area of environmental is due to the inadequacy of scientific know how in our country. Our poor record in area of environmental legislation science has reflected in the areas of environmental legislation in India and is a clear case of poor science leading to poor legislation. The public awareness is almost always directly proportional to the literacy and in some of the literate states, like Kerala, the people are more responsible and concerned towards environmental issues than many other states.

The government is drafting a legislation to establish a National Environmental Tribunal (NET) to view the policies passed by the government on environmental protection laws, water, air, wildlife or prevention of cruelty to animals. No other court to law or authority would have as much jurisdiction as that of the tribunal. The draft would be modified on law commission recommendations. The tribunal can take cognisance of any order passed by a central, state or public authority and it is a welcome step towards the improvement of regional policies on the environment.[7] Members of the public are the victims of pollution. It is necessary to safeguard their interest. Surprisingly, in Indian law the principle of public participation seems to have been not considered at all.

Suggestions

1) Formulation of a comprehensive environmental code.
2) Judicial innovation - moving the courts to the scene of a disaster.
3) Waiver of court fees.
4) Principle of 'Polluter Says' and 'Pollution Caution' be applied.
5) Rehabilitation in terms of family and health relief.
6) The Department of the environment should present the state of the environment and report annually to the public.
7) The Public should have the right to sue the polluter.
8) There should be separate environmental courts in the country observed as by the Hon'ble Supreme Court in M.C. Mehta's case.
9) Legal aid and advise to sufferers of environmental degradation.
10) Establishment of an independent apex body with its branches in all the states and union territories to audit the state of the environment.[8]

References

1. Environmental Protection Laws, The Hindu Survey of the Environment.
2. Environmental Protection Laws. D. Geetha

3. Environmental Pollution, Legislative Control and Role of Judicial, Ranbir Singh.
4. Environmental Law: Limitation and Potential for Liberation, Upendra Baxi.
5. Indian Environmental Policies: A Review.
6. Indian Journal of Environmental Protection.
7. Pollution and the Environmental Law.
8. The Global Environment: A New Hope for Mankind.

5

Chemical Hazard And Hazardous Waste

Namrata Sood

Introduction

We are consuming like never before, and more of us shall join this race for possessing material things in various forms. The fundamental law is, that the more you consume the more your appetite will increase and therefore the more you will waste. The race makes us akin to rats, rabbits and lower mammals. We throw away in the surroundings what we cannot manage. The unused inventories, bio toxins related materials, bio medical residues, used cars, batteries and even ships are being disposed of recklessly in the oceans and on the land.

This consumption orientated modern society generates large amounts of waste. Plastics, pesticides, medicines, paints, oils, batteries, gasoline, metals, leather and textiles are some of the major consumer products, their production and manufacture of which, results in the generation of large amount of hazardous waste. By virtue of their toxic, corrosive, inflammable and infectious and non-biodegradable nature and their improper disposal, poses a serious threat to human and eco health. Generally, the term hazardous waste excludes radioactive and municipal solid waste. By virtue of its toxic nature, its generation, collection, treatment, transport storage and disposal are all full of risks and they require special treatment and safe disposal. The problem has to be tackled in a synergic way and includes scientific, technical and legal ways, not only at a country level but also at a global level.

The rich and powerful keep their surroundings neat and cosy at the cost of the health and discomfort of their lesser mortals. About a tenth of all the hazardous waste generated around the world each year crosses natural frontiers. A large proportion of this hazardous waste has gone and is still going on from industrialized countries to developing countries where disposal costs are lower.

The global concern regarding unscrupulous production, transmigration and the disposal of man-made waste goes back many decades. The Industrial revolution, petroleum decades and the new era of information technology have one thing in common viz. all produce huge quantities of hazardous waste. Agriculture also is increasingly becoming an industry and exposes masses of hazardous chemicals. The defense inventories, radioactive material used for peaceful purposes have also contributed to the stocks of extremely hazardous waste.

The earth is soon going to throw up its arms. We are soon approaching the grand finale of this rat race where there shall be no winners and nobody will be left to cheer or grieve. It will be incorrect to state that there is no activity on the environmental front. There is a loose international consensus on issues relating to the environment. The global norms for environmental law include the sovereign rights of nations, liability to consult, monitor and co-operate common but differentiated responsibilities, citizen's rights to a decent and healthy environment, polluter pays principle, public trust doctrine, cooperation of civil society in environmental governance, principles of inter and intra generational equity and sustainable development.

Hazardous Waste

Indian Scenario

India is one among the few countries where environmental protection has been given a constitutional status with Articles 48A and 51A(g). Prior to the 42nd constitutional amendment, the environment was being regulated by a public nuisance provisions of the Indian Penal Code, the Easement Act. However in the following years legislative and judicial reforms have, to some extent, diluted this attack. A large number of acts and rules were enacted by the parliament, state legislature and local bodies regarding environmental protection. Apart from this the various judgements provided by the Supreme Court of India and different High Courts made Article 21 of the Constitution of the India Right to Life include the waste right to a clean and healthy environment also.

Very soon after the adoption of the Basel Convention, the Government Of India in the year 1989 brought under the delegated legislation provisions under S.3 of the Environment Protection Act, 1986, the Hazardous Waste (Management and Handling) Rule of 1989. The Rule derives its mandate from the Basel Convention and imitates the phraseology to the extent of plagiarism. Provisions were made for the storage, disposal labelling, recording , transporting, importing, exporting, testing and recycling of hazardous waste. The rule initiated a fee based permit raj without providing enough for community participation, voluntary disclosure and certain incentives for deducing the quality and hazardousness of the waste. The rules have provided for an environmental impact assessment for industries dealing with hazardous substances.

The 1989 Rule together with the subsequent amendment rule notification brought out in the years 2000 and 2003 contain a total of 21 rules in 8 schedules and 13 forms. The applicability clause in rule 2 exempts waste water and exhaust gases, waste arising out of the operation of ships beyond five kilometres, radioactive waste, biomedical waste, municipal and solid waste, and lead acid batteries from the scope of the application of the rules as they are subject to regulations under different enactments.

Secondly, the amendment definition of Hazardous Waste, includes within the ambit of hazardous waste generated through 36 processes, a list of waste which also constitutes a limit of concentration together with the applicability of imports and exports also. The definition carves out a distinction between indigenously generated and hazardous waste subjects for the transboundary movements. The new definition shows a significant improvement over the original one which specified hazardous waste to mean only 18 waste streams and their regulatory quantities.

Rule 3 includes the definition disposal, environmentally sound management of hazardous waste, hazardous wastes sites, illegal traffic and transboundary movement.

Rule 4 makes the occupier and the operator of a facility responsible for the collection, reception, treatment, storage and disposal of hazardous waste.

Rule 4A The occupier and operator of a facility are duty bound to take adequate steps while handling hazardous waste to-(i) Contain contaminants and prevent accidents and limit their consequences on humans and the environment; and (ii) provide for persons working on the site with information, training and equipment necessary to ensure their safety.

Rule 5 Grants authorisation for handling hazardous waste.

Rule 6 Power to suspend or cancel an authorisation.

Power vests in the State Pollution Control Board or Committee that they may cancel an authorisation issued under these rules or suspend it for such period as they think fit, if in their opinion, the authorised person has failed to comply with any of the conditions of the authorisation or with any provisions of the act or these rules, after giving the authorised person an opportunity to show cause after recording the reasons therefore.

Rule 7 Packaging, labelling and transport of hazardous waste.

The occupier or operator of a facility shall ensure that the hazardous waste is in packages, based on their composition in a manner suitable for handling, storing and transporting and that the labelling and packaging shall be easily visible and be able to withstand physical conditions and climatic factors, while being transported.

Rule 8 Disposal Sites.

The occupier or operator of a facility or any association of occupiers, shall be jointly and severely responsible for identifying sites for establishing the facility for treatment, storage and disposal of hazardous waste.

Rule 9 Provides the Records and returns.

Rule 10 Reporting of an Accident with reporting and follow-up.

Role of the Supreme Court in India

The Supreme Court of India yet again wore the executive hat in 1997 when it formed a high powered committee to give recommendations and set guidelines for the entire ambit of activities relating to hazardous waste. The Research Foundation for science (an N.G.O) had filed a public interest litigation against the Union of India regarding a blatant disregard to the provisions of the treaty signed by the Government at the Basel Convention. It was informed that out of 76 items mentioned as hazardous in the Basel Convention, only 29 were prohibited on Indian soil and for them also a lethargic government had failed to issue the notification. The Supreme Court was informed of large quantities of waste oil entering India under the disguise of petroleum due to the absence of adequate testing facilities. The stockpiles of hazardous waste which entered the country on pretext of recycling and reuse, were lying unnoticed. The Indian hazardous waste management regime had failed in many courts.

In this case , the Supreme Court of India had also given directions "with effect from today no authorization/permission would be given to any authority for the import which has already been banned by the central government or by any order made by any court or any authority. With effect from today, no import would be made or permitted by any person of any hazardous waste which has already been banned under the Basel Convention or to be banned hereafter with effect from the date specified therein." Here the second direction may be interpreted as giving effect to the Basel ban amendment. It is important to mention that this amendment has not been ratified by the Government of India.

Again the court realized the gravity of the situation with reference to the indigenous practice generated and imported hazardous waste gave directions for the constitution of an appropriate committee to ensure that the necessary work is done to arrest the further growth of this problem. Following the directions the MOEF constituted on High Power Committee to oversee the strict and faithful implementation of relevant rules and regulations on the management of hazardous waste.

In the year 2001 the HPC submitted its report to court and the court in 2003 gave effect to several recommodations.

"The provisions of a covenant which elucidates and goes to effectuate the fundamental rights guaranteed by our constitution can be relied upon by the courts as facets of those fundamental rights and hence enforceable as such. The Basel Convention, it cannot be doubted effectuates the fundamental right guaranteed under Article 21 of the constitution. The right to information and community participation for the protection of the environment and human health is a right which flows from Article 21."

The Supreme Court in its order has shown its concern regarding the abysmal state of the management of hazardous waste and issued directions to the executive to put its house in order. The order which runs into pages primarily emphasizes the principles of good governance such as rule of law, transparency, accountability, community participation, effective state institutions and respect for human life and well being in the management of hazardous waste. It also reiterates the commitment to international obligations and promotes time bound monitored targets on the following:

1. Developing fully equipped laboratories at ports and by the Customs Authorities.

2. Notification of items classified as hazardous as in the Basel Convention.
3. Establishment of hazardous waste landfills.
4. Addressing problems of occupational hazards.
5. Re export or destroy illegally imported hazardous waste (waste oil) and punish offenders.
6. Integration of policies and synergizing efforts.
7. Augmentation of resources for hazardous Waste Management.
8. Emphasis on IEC and advocacy.
9. Research and Development on clean technologies and safe disposal.
10. Imposing an excess on industries generating hazardous waste.
11. Strengthening of the CPCB to form a National Environment Protection Agency.
12. Import and exports to be environmentally compliant.
13. Ban on PVC plastic scrap, used edible oil, etc.
14. Increase in industrial compliance .
15. Close monitoring of recycling industries.
16. Strengthening of state pollution control boards.
17. Auction of hazardous waste only to firms having environmentally sound management facilities.
18. Constant vigil against industries using Indian soils for dirt technologies.
19. Monitoring of incinerator facilities.
20. Road map for the ship scrapping industry.
21. Monitoring interstate movements of hazardous waste.
22. Inventory of hazardous waste and dumping sites.
23. National plan for the rehabilitation of hazardous waste dumping sites
24. National policy document on hazardous waste.
25. Fresh look at legislations and regulations.

The court accepted the recommendation of the HPC with regard to ship breaking activities. Adhering to the precautionary principle, CPCB guidelines and taking the working conditions of the workmen.

The court converted the standing committee of these MOEF on issues pertaining to hazardous wastes and other related areas into a monitoring committee to oversee that the directions of this court are timely implemented. The court also gives directions to the MOEF to prepare a policy document on hazardous waste in a time bound manner. With reference to the breaking up of the Clemenceau,the French decommissioned aircraft carrier in the year 2006, the SC refused the ship entry into entering the Indian Exclusive Economic Zone, but due to the media hype, and stiff public opposition the ship was recalled back but still the matter is in sub-judice, but one thing is certain only, for the intervention of the SC the matter would not have been solved so amicably. Overall the SC in the above mentioned cases gave really a judicial push and punch to the regulatory authorities and made the Indian law to large extent compatible with the Basel Convention.

Then the higher judiciary often wore the executive hat for matters concerning the environment. Through case law, they brought in the principles of absolute liability,the polluter pays principle, precautionary principle, public trust doctrine, etc. in Indian environmental jurisprudence. The courts have reiterated the extension of A21 of the constitution to include the right to a wholesome environment. The SC has been quite proactive in cases relating to hazardous waste. The Delhi HC in 1996 imposed certain restrictions on the import of waste containing lead and zinc. In various orders relating to public interest litigation by the green lawyer Mr.M.C Mehta all the hazardous industries were removed from Delhi. In the year 2003 the CPCB has formulated a draft national policy on hazardous waste management and circulated the same in the year 2004. The policy document contains a hazardous waste management scenario, the Basel Convention, regulatory framework, provisions in hazardous waste management, waste avoidance, waste minimization, recycling of hazardous waste the safe disposal of hazardous waste generated, setting up of common facilities, interstate transportation, etc. The policy is yet to get the nod of approval from the MOEF, Government of India.

Chemical Hazard

Chemicals are the most common and significant health hazard. They can be hazardous for numerous reasons and combine with other chemicals to make new hazards. All hazards must be taken into account when using and storing chemicals.

The degree of hazard associated with a particular chemical will depend on the

- physical property,
- its toxicity,
- the way its used and
- the environment in which it is encountered.

Physical Classification

Chemicals may be found in

- Solid,
- Liquid,
- Aerosol,
- Gas and Vapor form.

The danger varies according to the form of the chemical and the other properties discussed earlier.

A. Solids

Not all forms of a chemical nature pose a health hazard. For eg: a lead pipe is not a significant health hazard. However the lead can become a human health hazard if the pipe is sanded or welded, producing lead dust or fumes. The dust or fumes can become airborne and can be inhaled or it can leach into water and be ingested. Fuming solids emit toxic vapors that may be inhaled. Some solids are not hazardous alone but become hazardous when they come into contact with other chemicals(eg: acid in contact with iron can release hydrogen gas).

B. Aerosols

Is a term used to describe fine particles suspended in air, eg: dust, fumes, mist, fog, smoke, smog. Knowing how various aerosols are generated will help you anticipate where aerosol hazards may exist in the field. Aerosol may be a hazards to the eye, skin and respiratory system.

C. Liquids

Many liquids are hazardous when they come in contact with the skin. They either damage the skin or they are easily absorbed through the skin. It is important to remember that chemicals that damage or be absorbed through the skin will have this effect on all the skin and not just the hands. The degree of hazard associated with a liquid depends on its characteristics and how it is handled. In the last 50 years, a number of new chemicals have increased exponentially. Chemicals are released into the environment through the air, water and ground.

Chemical exposure- routes of entry

- Inhalation
    i. Breathe 20,000-25,000 times per day
    ii. At rest- inhale 10,000 to 14,000 litres of air per day
- Absorption- skin
- Ingestion-digestive track
- Injection-typically through sharps

Types of chemical exposure

i. Acute-short term

ii. Chronic-over a long period of time

iii. Chemical exposure may or may not result in an adverse impact, depending on the amount of the exposure(i.e., the dose).

"Dosis facit venenum"- THE DOSE MAKES THE POISON

"all substances are poisonous; there is none which is not a poison. The right dose differentiates a poison..."

M.C. Mehta v. Union of India

One of the most tragic cases of a chemical hazard has been the "Oleum Gas Leak Case". It has been discussed in detail here:

Facts

The case came up before the five-judge bench of the Supreme Court after a three-judge bench had referred it to a higher bench because certain questions of seminal importance and high constitutional significance were raised in the course of arguments when the writ petition was originally heard.

1. The Bench of three Judges permitted Shriram Foods and Fertiliser Industries (hereinafter referred to as Shriram) to restart its power plant for the manufacture of caustic chlorine including its by-products and recovery plants like soap, glycerine and technical hard oil, subject to the conditions set out in the Judgment.

2. The main issue in the original writ petition which was filed in order to obtain a direction for closure of the various units of Shriram on the ground that they were hazardous to the community.

3. But while the writ petition was pending, there was an escape of oleum gas from one of the units of Shriram on 4th and 6th December, 1985 and applications were filed by the Delhi Legal Aid & Advice Board and the Delhi Bar Association for an award of compensation to the persons who had suffered harm on account of the escape of oleum gas.

4. The Court thought that these applications for compensation raised certain important issues and those issues should be addressed by a constitutional bench.

Judgment

The first question which requires to be considered is as to what is the scope and ambit of the jurisdiction of this Court under Article 32 ?

The Court wholly endorsed what had been stated by Bhagwati, J. in Bandhua Mukti Morcha v. Union of India and Ors. as regards to the true scope and ambit of Article 32. It may now be taken as well settled that Article 32 does not confer power merely on this Court to issue a direction, order or writ for enforcement of the fundamental rights but it also lays a constitutional obligation on this Court to protect the fundamental rights of the people and for that purpose this Court has all incidental and ancillary powers including the power to forge new remedies and fashion new strategies designed to enforce the fundamental rights. The next question which arises for consideration on these applications for compensation is whether Article 21 is available against Shriram which is owned by Delhi Cloth Mills Limited, a public company limited by shares and which is engaged in an industry vital to public interest and with a potential to affect the life and health of the people. The issue of availability of Article 21 against a private corporation engaged in an activity which has the potential to affect the life and health of the people, was vehemently argued by counsel for the applicants and Shriram.

The Court traced the evolution of the Doctrine of State Action to ascertain whether the defendants, in this case they fall under the definition of the term "state", as provided under Article 12, or not. The Court also looked into the Industrial Policy of the Government. Under the Industrial Policy Resolution of 1956, industries were classified into three categories having regard to the part which the State would play in each of them. The first category was to be the exclusive responsibility of the State. The second category comprised those industries which would be progressively State owned and in which the State would therefore generally take the initiative in establishing new undertakings but in which private enterprise would also be expected to supplement the effort of the State by promoting and developing undertakings either on its own or with State participation. The third category would include all the remaining industries and their future development which would be left generally to the initiative and enterprise of the private sector.[2] If an analysis of the declarations in the Policy Resolutions and the Act be undertaken, we find that the activity of producing chemicals and fertilisers is deemed by the State to be an industry of vital public interest, whose public import necessitates that the activity should be ultimately carried out by the State itself, in the interim period with State support and under State control and private corporations, may also be permitted to supplement the State effort. The argument of the applicants on the basis of this premise was that in view of this declared industrial policy of the State, even private corporations manufacturing chemicals and fertilisers can be said to be engaged in activities which are so fundamental to the Society as to be necessarily considered government functions.

Issue of Absolute Liability

On the question of developing a new doctrine to attach liability the court commented that; We must deal also with one other question which was seriously debated before us and that question is as to what is the measure of liability of an enterprise which is engaged in a hazardous or inherently dangerous industry, if by reason of an accident occurring in such industry, persons die or are injured? Does the rule in Rylands v. Fletcher apply or is there any other principle on which the liability can be determined? The rule in Rylands v. Fletcher was evolved in the year

1866 and it provides that a person who for his own purposes brings on to his land and collects and keeps there anything likely to do mischief if it escapes, must keep it at his peril and if he fails to do so, is prima facie liable for the damage which is the natural consequence of its escape. The liability under this rule is strict and it is no defence that the thing escaped without that person's wilful act, default or neglect or even that he had no knowledge of its existence. This rule laid down a principle of liability that if a person who brings onto his land and collects and keeps there anything likely to do harm and such thing escapes and does damage to another, he is liable to compensate for the damage caused. Of course, this rule applies only to a non-natural user of the land and it does not apply to things naturally on the land or where the escape is due to an act of God and an act of a stranger or the default of the person injured or where the thing which escapes is present by the consent of the person injured or in certain cases where there is statutory authority.[3]

This rule evolved in the 19th Century, at a time when all these developments of science and technology had not taken place, cannot afford any guidance in evolving any standard of liability consistent with the constitutional norms and the needs of the present day economy and social structure. We need not feel inhibited by this rule which was evolved in this context of a totally different kind of economy. Law has to grow in order to satisfy the needs of the fast changing society and keep abreast with the economical developments taking place in the country.

We cannot allow our judicial thinking to be constricted by reference to the law as it prevails in England or for that matter of that in any other foreign country. We are of the view that an enterprise which is engaged in a hazardous or inherently dangerous industry which poses a potential threat to the health and safety of the persons working in the factory and residing in the surrounding areas, owes an absolute duty to the community to ensure that no harm results to anyone on account of a hazardous or a material of an inherently dangerous nature of the activity which it has been undertaken.

The enterprise must be held to be under an obligation to provide that the hazardous or inherently dangerous activity in which it is engaged must be conducted with the highest standards of safety and if any harm results on account of such activity, the enterprise must be absolutely liable to compensate for such harm and it should be no answer to the enterprise to say that it had taken all reasonable care and that the harm occurred without any negligence on its part. We would therefore hold that where an enterprise is engaged in a hazardous or inherently dangerous activity and harm results to anyone on account of an accident in the operation of such hazardous or inherently dangerous activity resulting, for example, in escape of toxic gas, the enterprise is strictly and absolutely liable to compensate all those who have been affected by the accident and such liability is not subject to any of the exceptions which operate vis-à-vis the principle of strict liability under the rule in Rylands v. Fletcher. We would also like to point out that the measure of compensation in the kind of cases to which we referred in the preceding paragraph must be co-related to the magnitude and capacity of the enterprise because such compensation must have a deterrent effect. The larger and more prosperous the enterprise, the greater must be the amount of compensation payable by it for the harm caused on account of an accident in the carrying out of the hazardous or inherently dangerous activity by the enterprise.[4]

Order of the Court

The Supreme Court made the following observation:

Since we are not deciding the question as to whether Shriram is an authority within the meaning of Article 12 so as to be subjected to the discipline of the fundamental right under Article 21, we do not think it would be justified in setting up a special machinery for investigation of the claims for compensation made by those who allege that they have been the victims of an oleum gas escape, but we would direct that the Delhi Legal Aid and Advice Board take up the cases of all those who have claimed to have suffered on account of oleum gas and to file actions on their behalf in the appropriate court for claiming compensation against Shriram. Such actions claiming compensation may be filed by the Delhi Legal Aid and Advice Board within two months from today and the Delhi Administration is directed to provide the necessary funds to the Delhi Legal Aid and Advisary Board for the purpose of filing and prosecuting such actions. Thus the High Court was directed to nominate one or more Judges as may be necessary for the purpose of trying such actions so that they may be disposed of expeditiously.

Conclusion

The environmental issues like ozone depletion, bio safety and climate change get more publicity, budgetary support, attention of the governments and civil society mainly due to their international appeal. The issue of climate change is advocated and not hazardous waste as the developed nations are convinced that always it could be thrown into somebody else's backyard. Chemical hazards are of a more immediate and contemporary concern, than hazardous waste. The increasing stockpile of hazardous waste is mainly a result of chemical waste and needs a strong policy initiative for mitigating its ill effects and saving the vastly poor, ignorant and susceptible population to the possible harm caused by it. Economical measures like the polluter pays principle have been suggested as a catalyst for change. One of the most cited Indian success stories is that of an eco industrial networking accomplished by the Narod Industrial Estate in Gujarat. The estate has a large number of industries emitting hazardous waste. The company established a waste minimization cycle and eco industrial network. The company has come out with a model of clean technology and sound environmental practices. There is a huge problem lying outside the canvass of large industries located in the industrial estate. The hazardous waste and chemical waste which results in chemical hazards remains unchecked and recorded in the small scale industries, tiny industries and households. Chemical waste which is released from industries into rivers, landfill and is also emitted as fumes, adds to the amount of the pollution levels in the environment. In one of the severe cases of environmental pollution, untreated chemical waste was being released into the river. This water was being used by eleven villages for irrigation, bathing, washing, cooking and drinking. The water was highly contaminated due to the chemical waste and because of that the water had turned red and the chemical had seeped into the soil and contaminated the ground water as well. Thus, this shows that due to the carelessness of industrialists, the rural population is being affected.

If steps are not taken soon to keep a check on industries and to treat chemical and hazardous waste properly, then this could cause a mass destruction of the environment by increasing the level of pollution to the land, water and air.

References

- *M.C. Mehta v. Union of India,* AIR 1997 SC 734. (per Kuldip Singh, J.).
- **See also** the explanation for the principle of absolute liability in *M.C. Mehta* v. *Union of India (Oleum Gas* case), AIR 1987 SC 965, and its subsequent application in *Indian Council for Enviro-Legal Action v. Union of India,* (1996) 3 SCC 212.

1. paras 8 and 9
2. ^ para 21-24
3. ^ Para 31
4. ^ para 32

6

National Action Plan on Climate Change
Issues and Perspectives

STELLINA JOLLY AND AMIT JAIN

Introduction

While the world's climate has always varied naturally, the vast majority of scientists now believe that rising concentrations of "greenhouse gases" in the earth's atmosphere, resulting from economical and demographic growth over the last two centuries since the industrial revolution, are overriding this natural variability and leading to irreversible climatic changes.[1] Today, Climate change has become one of the most important global environmental challenges, with implications for food production, water supply, health, energy, etc. It has been defined by various authorities. It is defined as a "statistically significant variation in either the mean state of the climate or in its variability, persisting for an extended period [2]. Further, the United Nations Framework Convention on Climate (UNFCC) states that a climatic change is a variation in the climate, which can be attributed to human activity, either directly or indirectly, and stresses that it must be in addition to a natural variation being experienced during the same time period.[3]

There has always been a controversy regarding whether climate change is happening or not. The IPCC report considered to be the most authentic one, leaves no doubt in our minds regarding the gradual and exponential occurrence of climate change. Its report of 2001, shows that the earth warmed between 1900 and 1940, then subsequently cooled between 1941 and 1965, but surface temperatures have been warming ever since[4] . This data is believed to be the most authentic when describing the state of the global climate. This almost indicates that global warming is occurring.[5] This has now given an end to the debate on whether climate change is happening or not.

The climatic change which is giving humanity a real challenge is due mainly to the anthropogenic activities of human beings. In the report of the IPCC "Climate change represents

[1] http://www.cdmindia.com/India %20CDM%20Potential.pdf

[2] Houghton, Global warming:The complete briefing,2001

[3] Framework Convention on Climate Change, United Nations, New York.,1992

[4] Inter Government Panel on Climate Change Report 2001

[5] http://www.climate-change.me.uk/html/is_climate_change_happening_.html

opportunities and risks for human development". The areas where climate change could produce opportunities include:-

- Expansion of agriculture into areas previously limited by temperature, but only if adequate soils are present.
- As the arctic ice thins, areas will be accessible for surface navigation that were previously inaccessible.
- Heating demand and mortality from the cold in winter could decrease due to milder weather. [6]

Generally, the opportunities which we gain out of climate change, are much less and its negative fallouts are more. While northern regions could actually benefit from global warming by the expansion of arable lands and a decreased need for heating, tropical zones will suffer most from droughts, a loss of water resources and the expansion of epidemics. Higher sea levels, due to the polar melting process, will affect most low-lying developing countries like Bangladesh and small island states.[7] Additionally, to make matters worse, Greenhouse gasses are not local environmental pollutants and thus there is no domestic incentive to reduce their emissions. They arise in all sections of an economy, which means that an efficient climatic policy has to be cross-sectoral.

Climate Change : International Legal Framework

Climate change emerged on the political agenda in the mid-1980s with the increasing scientific evidence of human interference in the global climatic system and with a growing public concern about the environment. In 1988 the United Nations Environment Programme (UNEP) and the World Meteorological Organizations (WMO) established the Intergovernmental Panel on Climate Change (IPCC) to provide policy makers with authoritative scientific information.[8] The UN General Assembly responded to this by launching negotiations to formulate an International Treaty on global climatic protection, which resulted in the completion of the United Nations Framework Convention on Climate Change (UNFCCC) in May 1992,[9] which laid the framework for the eventual stabilization of greenhouse gases in the atmosphere, recognizing the common

---

[6] http://www.climate-change.me.uk/html/climate_change_impacts.html

[7] Henry Willis, Earths future climate.Oxford University Press, p 24

[8] The Intergovernmental Panel on Climate Change (IPCC) has been established by WMO and UNEP to assess scientific, technical and socio- economic information relevant to the understanding of climate change, its potential impacts and options for adaptation and mitigation. It is currently finalizing its Fourth Assessment Report "Climate Change 2007". http://www.ipcc.ch/(last visited on 8-02-2007 at 10.20am)

[9] The Convention on Climate Change sets an overall framework for intergovernmental efforts to tackle the challenge posed by climate change. It recognizes that the climatic system is a shared resource whose stability can be affected by industrial and other emissions of carbondioxide and other greenhouse gases. The Convention enjoys near universal membership, with 189 countries having ratified. The Convention entered into force on 21 March 1994.http://unfccc.int/essential_background/convention/items/2627.php/(last visited on 18-02-2007 at 10.45am)

but differentiated responsibilities and respective capabilities, and social and economical conditions. The Convention came into force in 1994. Subsequently, the 1997 Kyoto protocol, which came into force in 2005, reasserted the importance of stabilizing greenhouse gas concentrations in the atmosphere and adhering to sustainable developmental principles. The Protocol laid out guidelines and rules regarding the extent to which a participating industrialized country should reduce its emissions of six greenhouse gases - carbondioxide, methane, nitrous oxide, chlorofluorocarbon, hydrofluorocarbons and per fluorocarbons. It requires industrialized countries (listed as Annex B countries in the Protocol) to reduce their greenhouse gas emissions by a weighted average of 5.2%, based on the 1990 greenhouse gas emissions. The reduction is to be achieved by the end of the five-year period, 2008 to 2012. The Kyoto Protocol does not require the developing countries to reduce their greenhouse gas emissions[10]. However the Kyoto Protocol has been a partial success. Major GHG countries have not signed Kyoto Protocol.

India and Climate Change

India is concerned about climate change since this phenomenon might have substantial adverse impacts on them. Not all possible consequences of climatic change are yet fully understood, but the three main 'categories' of impacts are those on agriculture, the rise in the sea level leading to the submergence of coastal areas, as well as the increased frequency of extreme events.[11] Each of these pose serious threats to India. In a study done by Kumar and Parikh they examined the impact of climatic change on agricultural crop yields, GDP and welfare. They estimated that: without considering the carbondioxide, fertilization effects yield losses for rice and wheat which vary between 32 and 40%, and 41 and 52%, respectively;[12] Large-scale mass departure from coastal zones is anticipated due to the submergence of coastlines after sea levels have risen. This will produce in terms of legal language, large masses of environmental refugees especially from low-lying delta regions in poor countries. Similarly, the intrusion of sea-water in the ground water can affect the agricultural production drastically. Parts of India dependent on coastal fishery and agriculture, are likely to be adversely affected. Large areas in Mumbai and West Bengal are threatened by the submergence of coastal areas.

However, these are long term issues. The overriding immediate concern for India should be the fast pace at which negotiations are taking place on the climatic front. India's main energy resource is coal. With the threat of climate change, India is called upon to change its energy strategy based on coal, its most abundant resource, and to use other energy resources like oil, gas, renewable and nuclear energy instead which may turn out to be expensive. Thus, an immediate issue is to come up with a better negotiational strategy so that we have more freedom to decide on which type of energy we use, how we generate power, how we can reduce methane

---

[10] Current Science, VOL. 90, NO. 3, 10 FEBRUARY 2006

[11] Jyoti Parikh, Climate change: Indias Perceptions policies and possibilities , OECD

[12] Kumar, K.S. Kavi and Jyoti Parikh, "Climate change impacts on Indian agriculture: The Ricardian approach" in Dinar et.al., Measuring the impacts of Climate Change on Indian Agriculture, World Bank Technical Paper No.402, 1998.

emissions by agricultural practices or forestry and so on. Negotiations are important for us as a means of reducing or postponing future vulnerability by getting the developed countries to reduce their emissions.

Climate Change: Indian Response to the National Action Plan on Climate Change

India has released a national climatic change action plan. NAPCC is an important step in the direction of achieving sustainable development. The NAPCC has laid down a national strategy on climate change with regard to the adaptation and mitigation of greenhouse gas emissions, both domestically and in the context of global arrangements under the United Nations Framework Convention on Climate Change (UNFCCC). Sustainable development is the key theme running through the breadth of the plan. The action plan does not set target reduction of greenhouse gas emissions but seeks to promote sustainable development through the use of clean technologies. India has been under pressure from several quarters over its climatic change policy. The document will help bolster the country's argument that it is ready to take an array of 'no-regret' actions — steps towards a low carbon economy that does not come at the cost of its poverty alleviation and growth targets. The Action plan focuses on eight core areas and prescribes the development of technologies to reduce carbon and other greenhouse gas emissions.[13] These eight focus areas include :

National Solar Mission:

The NAPCC aims to promote the development and use of solar energy for power generation and other uses with the ultimate objective of making solar energy as available options compared with other fossil fuel based energy options. The plan covers various areas. It emphasises:

- It aims at increasing the use of solar thermal technologies, especially in urban areas. Industry, and commercial establishments;
- Aims to increase the production of photovoltaics to 1000 MW/year;
- More importantly it aims to produce at least 1000 MW of solar thermal power generation.

National Mission for Enhanced Energy Efficiency:

One of the immediate concerns of India regarding climatic change relates to its energy strategy. Expectantly the plan recommends:

- Encouraging energy consumption decreases in large energy-consuming Industries, and providing them with a mechanism for companies and industries to trade energy-saving certificates;
- Provision of tax reduction and incentives for less energy consumption.; and
- Special emphasis on public-private partnerships to reduce energy consumption through demand-side managerial programmes in the municipal, buildings and agricultural sectors.

[13] National Action Plan on Climate Change, Government of India

National Mission on Sustainable Habitat:

Under this mission, urban areas were given special focus. The plan emphasises the use of efficient energy as a core aspect of urban planning. The plan stresses on

- Extending the existing Energy Conservation Building Code;
- Special emphasis is given to Waste Management and its recycling as a method of decreasing carbon emissions and help urban surroundings.
- To decrease the transport pollution, the plan intends to strengthen the enforcement of efficient fuel usage and production of fuel efficient vehicles.[14]

National Water Mission:

With the water scarcity projected to worsen as a result of climatic changes, the plan sets a goal of a 20% "improvement in water use efficiency" through pricing and other measures.[15]

National Mission for Sustaining the Himalayan Ecosystem:

The Himalayan ecosystem is one of the most affected and is facing a threat of degradation due to anthropogenic activities. One of the immediate concerns of the climatic change in the Himalayan region is the expected receding of glaciers which is the foremost source of the water supply in the region. The plan aims to conserve the biodiversity both in terms of flora and fauna, forest cover, and in preserving the soils , and other ecological values in the Himalayan region.[16]

National Mission for a "Green India":

An increase in green areas is the key counter to the threat of climatic changes. The plan aims to increase the forest cover from 23% to 33%. It also plans to convert 6 million hectares of degraded forest land by afforestation.[17]

The National Mission for Sustainable Agriculture:

One of the worst affected areas of climatic change in the long run will be the agriculture of India which accounts for around 27% of the GDP. In the field of agriculture, the emphasis is on developing climate resilient crops, expansion of weather insurance mechanisms and most sophisticated climate friendly agricultural practices. [18]

National Mission on Strategic Knowledge for Climatic Change:

To gain a better understanding of climate science, impacts and challenges, the plan envisions a new Climate Science Research Fund, improved climate modelling and increased

---

[14] Id

[15] Id

[16] Id

[17] Id

[18] Id

international collaboration. It also encourages private sector initiatives to develop adaptation and mitigation technologies through venturous capital funds.

The implementation of the plan rests with the respective ministries. They are directed to develop objectives, implementation strategies, time line's monitoring and evaluation criteria. This will be submitted to the Prime Minister's Council on Climate Change. The Council will periodically review and monitor the progress of missions. To be able to estimate progress, appropriate indicators and methodologies will be developed to assess both avoided emissions and adaptation benefits.

Critical Evaluation

The plan in a way marks a new direction in India's climatic policy. It brings about a more coherent and systematic approach to climatic changes and thereby aims to achieve sustainable development. It contains certain positive salient features. The plan will definitely give a boost to India's suitability at the global level to augment our bargaining control with the developed nations, especially for providing clean technologies at cheaper rates. For the first time the plan chalks out an *institutional structure* for future action overseen by the Council on Climate Change headed by the Prime Minister.[19] If we analyse the plan, we do not commit to specific emission reduction targets or energy efficiency targets. Instead it states that India's per capita of GHG emissions would at no point exceed that of the developed countries. [20]The underlying principle behind this seems to be the fact that India's per capita emission is just above one tonne compared with the average per capita emission of other nations, but this will attract flak from western developed nations. Though India's stand is motivated by its developmental needs like tackling poverty and giving boost to industrialisation, the stand does not go with India's image of a responsible player and nation in world affairs.

India's NAPCC is saturated with grandiose but blurred goals and how these superficial goals will be translated into reality, is clearly missing in the strategy from the plan. Further clear targets in the form of medium and long term goals and a well thought out time table is clearly absent from the plan.The NAPCC fails to estimate the few quantitative targets except in one or two cases. The plan lays down that to be able to estimate progress, appropriate indicators and methodologies will be developed to assess both avoided emissions and adaptation benefits. It is left to various ministries to come out with strategies, milestones etc. which will be submitted to, Council on Climate but such a mechanism will not ensure co-ordination between the different departments, which is very important for the success of any plan.

Even the eight missions which are the focus area under the plan, many suffer from certain serious shortcomings. For instance at present, 80% of most of our energy comes from the burning of fossil fuels which is a major source of GHGs. The action plan gives emphasis to the production of solar energy and aims to increase its share. What is to be noted is the fact that the identification of nuclear energy is missing from the plan and this is quite noticeable in the wake of our

[19] Id

[20] Id

prospective nuclear deal with the U.S. government. At present the contribution from nuclear energy constitutes only around 3%. It is imperative that the nuclear energy programme should be given a prominence if India has to overcome its energy crisis and also due to the environmental details. Another area neglected is wind energy which also has tremendous potential and its scope has been assessed at 45,000 MW.[21] There is no emphasis on developing technologies to tap both these sources of energy. On conventional power generation, NAPCC discusses various options at length particularly as to the introduction of available new technologies but little on increasing energy generation efficiencies in existing plants. Similarly, in the mission regarding habitat, there are lots of homilies to promoting public transport, better urban planning and paying attention to the water supply and sanitation but, apart from recounting estimates from the National Energy Map of India, that energy savings could be as much as 30 per cent in new residential and 40 per cent in new commercial buildings and that substantial savings could be garnered by shifts to public transportation and inter-modal shifts from road to rail. Again, there are again no targets.[22] The plan relies on labelling, tax policies and credit mechanisms but no mandating or regulatory measures.[23]Throughout the plan, an action plan needs to set various goals in place. For instance the plan states that the Tenth Plan promise of a 100 per cent water supply and a 75 per cent sewerage/sanitation service in urban areas should be achieved but does not say how much was achieved. This sort of stand is felt throughout the document. The plan does not lay down in each field what the present scenario is or what are the existing technologies and legislative provisions or how many targets from earlier plans have been achieved.

Further regarding Municipal solid Waste Management. The plan takes pride in mentioning that Municipal Solid Waste (MSW) Management should be considered a public asset or an environmental service to be provided by the government but it simply forgets its business sense and the profitability behind it. Further, there is nothing new in the plan of increasing forest cover from 23% to 33%. The existing environmental policy already contains provisions for it. The plan merely reiterates the existing mechanisms. Similarly, the issues of the Intellectual property issue which evokes fierce debate under any climate related discourse also does not find much prominence.

Conclusion

It is to be hoped that in the undertaking of "the NAPCC that it will continue to evolve" has not been forgotten and that it does not remain in the letter of the law only and for these reasons, there is an urgent need for the NAPCC to be thrown open for wider consultations with stakeholders including corporates, NGOs, the general public and especially the youth etc.. Informed public opinion and mass campaigns and the civil society should endeavour to restructure the Climate Action Plan towards meeting the double and balancing goals of climatic

[21] P P Sangal, India Climate Change Action Plan

[22] India's Climate Action Plan: Many points, No direction by Peoples democracy.

[23] Id

change alleviation and sustainable development. To conclude, we should not forget the fact that at the current rate of emissions, the world would be hitting a disastrous threshold limit of 550 PPM of carbon emissions in less than a decade, if measures are not taken now on a stern footing. India, being a great democracy and world leader, must take a responsible stance for the future.

References

1. BioCarbon Fund—http:/www.biocarbondfund.org
2. International CDM resource base:
   http://www.geogr.ku.dk/project/rened/international@20resource@base.htm
3. India's climate Action Plan: Many Points, NO Direction by People's democracy. Vol. XXXII, No. 26, 06, 2008.
4. Jyoti K. Parikh and Kirit Parikh, CLIMATE CHANGE : INDIA'S PERCEPTIONS, POSITIONS, POLICIES AND POSSIBILITIES, OECD 2002.
5. Murthy, N.S., Manoj Panda and Jyoti Parikh (1977a)
   "Economic Development, Poverty Reduction and Carbon Emissions in India", *Energy Economics*
6. Mitra A.P. (Ed.), (1992)
   Global Change: Greenhouse Gas Emissions in India – 1991 Methane Campaign, Scientific Report No. 2, NPL, Publication and Information Directorate, CSIR, New Delhi, India, June 1992.
7. United Nations Framework Convention on Climate Change (UNFCCC) –
   http:/cdm.undfccc.int.

7

Multivariate Statistical Analysis of Sediment Pollution in the Savitri River Basin of the Mahad Industrial Area

P. B. LOKHANDE AND H. A. MUJAWAR

Introduction

An environmental assessment is increasingly employing sediment rather than a water analysis to assess the heavy metal contamination of rivers[1]. The level of contamination of the sediment is closely linked to the health of the ecosystem as a whole and it is an indicator of an environmental disaster. Sediments are both potential sources and carriers of pollutants, especially metals, resulting in their transfer from the sediment to the biota[2].

The Savitri River is the largest river system in the Konkan region with a fast economical growth and an increasing population in the area. The annual discharge of industrial wastewater and sewage water has risen. Consequently, the inputs of pollutants, particularly heavy metals, to the local aquatic environment have greatly increased. The objectives of the present study are: (1) to evaluate heavy metal enrichment in sediment profiles using the appropriate reference element ascertained by statistical correlation and principal component analysis, and (2) to examine the accumulation of heavy metals in sediments by the baseline model of linear regression and other physico-chemical components.

As sediments are the major depositories for particle bound metals in rivers, sediment health is critical in maintaining the ecological quality[3]. Sediment analysis provides an economical and reliable assessment procedure for catchment management and is increasingly being employed in the early phases of environmental assessment of aquatic systems[4]. At present there are no clear and unambiguous guidelines or agreed European standards for metal concentrations in rivers or floodplain sediments as there are for metal concentrations in surface and ground waters.[9-12] The concentration of trace elements in natural sediment is largely determined by the inorganic material resulting from the physical and chemical weathering of landmasses, thus natural variability exists between different sediment samples.[13-17]

Catchment has a wide variety of other polluting inputs along its length, including pharmaceutical, chemical and light engineering operations and a number of treated and untreated sewerage inputs[18]. Agriculture and forestry also contribute to diffuse pollution loads, as sediment contamination is a useful indicator of ecosystem health and an inventory of the sediment contamination throughout the whole catchment area was carried out as a part of an ongoing river restoration programme. The aims of this study were (i) To identify the key sources of heavy metals in the Savitri River catchment; (ii) To assess the overall health of the substrate for biota and fisheries; and (iii) To evaluate the usefulness of sediment inventories in identifying key biological and chemical sampling stations for river basin management.

The problems of data reduction and interpretation, characteristic change in water quality parameters and indicator parameters and identification can be approached through the use of the principal component analysis (PCA), principal factor analysis (PFA) and cluster analysis[25-26]. In recent years, the PCA and PFA techniques have been applied to a variety of environmental applications, including the evaluation of groundwater monitoring wells and hydrographs, the examination of spatial and temporal patterns of surface water quality, the identification of chemical species related to hydrological conditions and the assessment of environmental quality indicators.[5,8,22,24]

Sample Area and Locations

In this study, the Savitri River basin was selected for the sampling. The Savitri River catchment area is located in the Konkan region of Maharashtra. The surface water runoff carries the inorganic material and discharge into the river. Mostly, the iron and manganese ore deposits are predominant in the catchment area. Natural abundance of different constituents that are carried by the surface water are deposited in the Savitri River sediments. This natural abundance is mostly influenced by anthropogenic sources like industrial and domestic activities. The change in the chemical composition, structure, size and texture shows the long-term effect on the aquatic flora and fauna life.

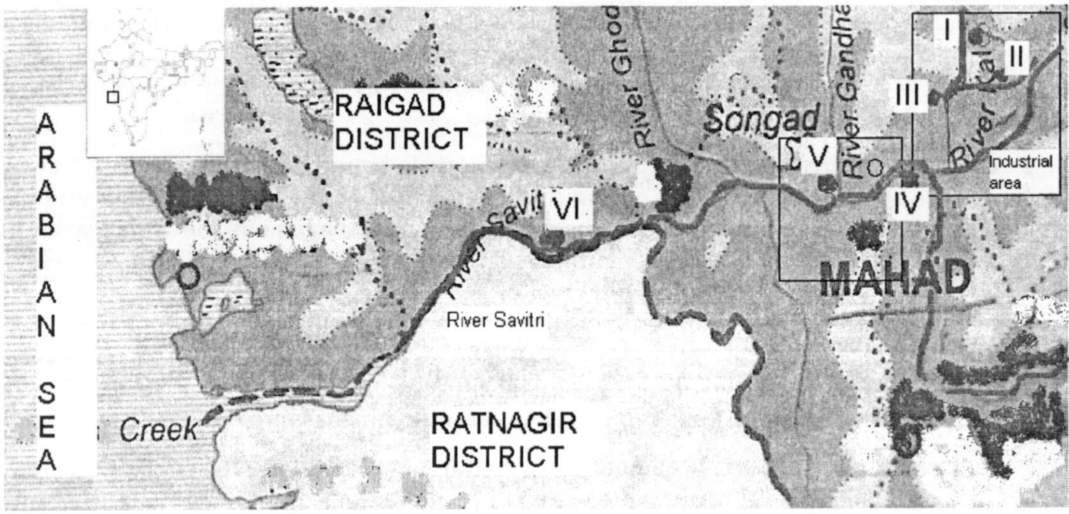

Fig. 1. Sampling locations of sediment in Savitri river basin.

The sampling locations were selected on the basis of a study of point and non point sources of pollutants and the preparation of maps. Sampling locations are the same as the water sampling points.

Materials and Methods

Sampling

The sampling of a sediment sample is a difficult task because at the time of sampling, the water may dissolve and remove the sediment constituents and we would not be able to collect the right sample. Precautions were taken when collecting the sample. A special apparatus was used for sampling. After sampling, the samples were collected in polyethylene bags and wrapped and transported to the laboratory for analysis. Samples were collected during the winter and summer season of Oct.2005 to May 2007. Due to heavy rainfall and flooding in the river, samples were not collected in the monsoon (rainy) season.

Analysis of Sediments

Soil sediments were dried at a temperature of 90 °C in the oven. 2gm of sample were dissolved in the 100ml-distilled water and filtered through Whatman filter paper No 41.The pH balance and conductance of this filtered water were measured. The known weight of sediment (100gm) was dissolved in 1 litre water and boiled to get the maximum desired constituents into the water. Alkaline metals were analyzed on a flame photometer, the anions were determined on an Ion chromatography and heavy metals on an atomic absorption spectrophotometer by following the procedure given in the APHA.

Results and Discussion

Soil Texture

Particle size distribution (of the mineral fraction) is a fundamental characteristic of any soil or sediment. It can provide a valuable insight into the origins of particular archaeological contexts and is useful in the characterization of sedimentary sequences. Physical characteristics of the dredged material must be determined in order to help assess the impact of disposal on the benthic environment and the water column at the disposal site. This is the first step in the overall process of sediment characterization, and also helps to identify appropriate control and reference sediments for biological tests. In addition, physical analyses can be helpful in evaluating the results of analyses and tests conducted later in the characterization process. The sediments at most of the sampling sites consisted primarily of sand (>76%).

Physico-Chemical Analysis

Chemical analysis provides information about the chemicals present in the dredged material that, if biologically available, could cause toxicity and/or be bioaccumulated. This information is valuable for an exposure assessment and for deciding which of the contaminants present in the dredged material, are good to measure in tissue samples.

pH balance and Conductance

The pH balance of a soil/sediment is critically important in terms of the preservation of various natural materials and artifacts (e.g. bone, mollusca and many metals which rapidly decompose in acidic conditions), and this also affects the retention of phosphate. It is important therefore to have some knowledge of the pH balance of soils and specific contexts on archaeological sites. The pH balance is determined on a 1:2.5 (air-dry soil weight: volume of water) soil suspension using a pH meter with a pH probe (combined glass electrode and calomel half cells). pH of the sediments ranged from 5.7 to 7.1 and the conductance of the sediment from 2.7 to 22, as the locations are under the influence of the low and high tides of estuarine water.

Anions in Sediments

Ions were analyzed on an Ion chromatograph. The concentration of fluoride in the sediments was at an appreciable quantity, which was ranging from 0.4-12 ppm. Sampling site VI shows the highest concentration of fluorides in sediments during the summer season but they were much less (0.4) at location IV during the winter season.The chloride concentration range was 58 to 725 ppm and highest at location VI. The Bromide concentration range was 0.4 to 2.8 ppm and nitrate 4 to 23 ppm. The values of sulphate were observed to be higher than the other anions, so the metal sulphates were present in the sediments.Their concentration was ranging from 32 ppm at location IV to 374 ppm at location VI.

Metals

Sodium, potassium, magnesium and calcium are usually considered major metals in nature. Sodium concentration in the sediments was analysed and detected in the range of 23 to 988 ppm. The concentration of Potassium was observed in the range of 0.2 to 1.9 ppm. The Na and K are both important nutrients. In agriculture and human pathology, the ratio of sodium to total cations is of importance, because it can affect soil permeability.

Ca and Mg concentration in sediments were ranging from 10 and 5 ppm to 288 and 189 ppm respectively. Iron ore deposit is abundant in the Savitri River catchment area and that was influenced on the composition by the iron in the sediment. Iron concentration was found to be very high and ranging from 214 to 435 ppm whereas Magnesium ranges were from 5 to 189 ppm. Manganese is an essential element for plants and hence it was included in certain fertilizers. Manganese cations are more toxic than the anionic form and Mn(II) is more toxic than Mn(III). In this study, Manganese was found to be at an appreciable quantity and concentration was ranging from 36 to 102 mg/l.

Heavy metal contamination in sediments was detected for metals Cd, Cr, Ni, Zn, Cu and Hg. The term heavy metal includes both essential and nonessential trace metals that may be toxic to living things, depending on their own properties, availabilities and their level of concentrations.

Table 1: Metals and anions in the sediment of Savitri River basin. (Metals and anions in ppm, Condt. in mmhos)

		Winter 2005	Sampling locations					Winter 2006	Sampling locations				
Sr. No		I	II	III	IV	V	VI	I	II	III	IV	V	VI
1	pH	6.2	6.6	6.4	7.1	6.3	6.2	6.2	6.5	6.4	7	6.2	6
2	Condt.	12.3	12	13	2.7	17.2	19.1	12.4	11.5	14	3.7	18	20.1
3	Fluoride	3.5	3.2	3.3	0.4	5.8	9.3	3.8	3.4	3.7	0.4	6.2	9.8
4	Chloride	506	430	456	58	670	694	518	442	478	62	681	710
5	Bromide	1.2	1.2	1.3	0.5	1.4	1.6	1.2	1.2	1.3	0.5	1.6	1.8
6	Nitrate	12.3	12.3	12	4	14	15	13.1	12.3	13.4	4	17	19
7	Sulphate	98	102	103	32	228	316	112	98	107	33	234	324
8	Na	140	130	140	23	876	945	145	145	144	22	883	953
9	K	1	1.1	1	0.2	1.4	1.4	1	1.1	1	0.2	1.5	1.6
10	Ca	104	110	109	10	205	245	110	108	114	13	218	256
11	Mg	56	88	86	5	125	146	63	78	86	6	131	154
12	Fe	345	340	352	214	389	396	336	341	345	214	384	396
13	Mn	45	48	48	36	78	83	50	51	52	33	82	88
14	Cd	0.02	0.02	0.02	0.01	0.04	0.05	0.02	0.02	0.02	0.01	0.04	0.06
15	Cu	1.6	1.5	1.5	0.8	1.8	1.9	1.6	1.5	1.6	0.8	1.9	2.1
16	Cr	0.32	0.32	0.31	0.1	0.49	0.52	0.32	0.32	0.32	0.1	0.52	0.64
17	Zn	0.7	0.6	0.7	0.12	0.8	0.89	0.7	0.6	0.7	0.1	0.8	0.9
18	Ni	0.23	0.22	0.23	0.02	0.31	0.34	0.23	0.22	0.23	0.02	0.33	0.35
19	Hg	0.5	0.5	0.6	0.08	0.9	1.2	0.5	0.5	0.6	0.07	1.1	1.4
Sr. No		Summer 2006							Summer 2007				
1	pH	6.1	6.3	6.2	6.9	5.8	5.8	6	6.2	6	6.9	5.7	5.7
2	Condt.	15	14.6	15.3	4.2	20.1	21.4	15.1	14.8	15.6	4.5	21	22
3	Fluoride	3.9	3.8	3.9	0.6	7.1	10.1	4.2	4.1	4.3	0.6	7.6	12
4	Chloride	578	569	584	78	694	715	581	584	584	82	702	725
5	Bromide	1.2	1.2	1.3	0.5	1.8	2.4	1.2	1.2	1.3	0.5	1.9	2.8
6	Nitrate	14.2	14.2	14.9	4	19	22	14.5	14.6	14.9	5	23	28
7	Sulphate	117	102	113	38	243	334	210	213	213	42	258	374
8	Na	160	160	162	28	893	965	174	178	178	35	905	988
9	K	1	1.1	1	0.2	1.5	1.6	1	1.2	1.2	0.3	1.8	1.9
10	Ca	116	116	118	15	228	263	129	132	136	18	239	288
11	Mg	69	72	88	7	146	166	70	72	92	9	178	189
12	Fe	346	348	348	214	395	405	368	372	374	238	416	435
13	Mn	50	51	52	32	86	96	53	60	63	38	88	102
14	Cd	0.02	0.02	0.03	0.01	0.04	0.07	0.02	0.02	0.03	0.01	0.05	0.08
15	Cu	1.6	1.5	1.6	0.8	1.8	2.2	1.7	1.5	1.7	0.8	1.9	2.5
16	Cr	0.32	0.32	0.32	0.1	0.56	0.66	0.32	0.34	0.36	0.1	0.7	0.78
17	Zn	0.8	0.6	0.8	0.1	0.9	1.1	0.8	0.6	0.8	0.1	1	1.3
18	Ni	0.23	0.22	0.23	0.02	0.33	0.39	0.24	0.22	0.28	0.02	0.41	0.49
19	Hg	0.5	0.6	0.5	0.05	1.1	1.5	0.5	0.6	0.5	0.05	1.2	1.8

High concentration of heavy metals are present in urban and industrial areas, and can lead to a bad effect on health when they are taken in through drinking water or accumulated through the food chain. Heavy metal concentrates were found to be higher during the summer season and the range of Cd, Cr, Ni, Zn, Cu and Hg concentrates were observed to be from 0.01 to 0.08 ppm, 0.8 to 2.5 ppm, 0.1 to 0.78 ppm, 0.1 to 1.3 ppm, 0.02 to 0.49 and 0.05 to 1.8 ppm.

Changes in the concentration of chemical parameters

The present changes in the concentration of the different physico chemical parameters in the sediment with a comparison of an earlier year to the next year ie. 2005-06 to 2006-07 were calculated for all the three seasons.

Winter Season

The percent change in the concentration of contaminants in the sediment during the winter season is shown in Fig.2. The highest variation in the concentration of the parameter was observed at location VI for the nitrate, Cd, K, Cr, and Hg. A negative change was observed at location II and IV for Mg, Mn, and Zn. At location IV Ca and Mg showed 10 to 20 % increase in concentration with respect to an earlier year.

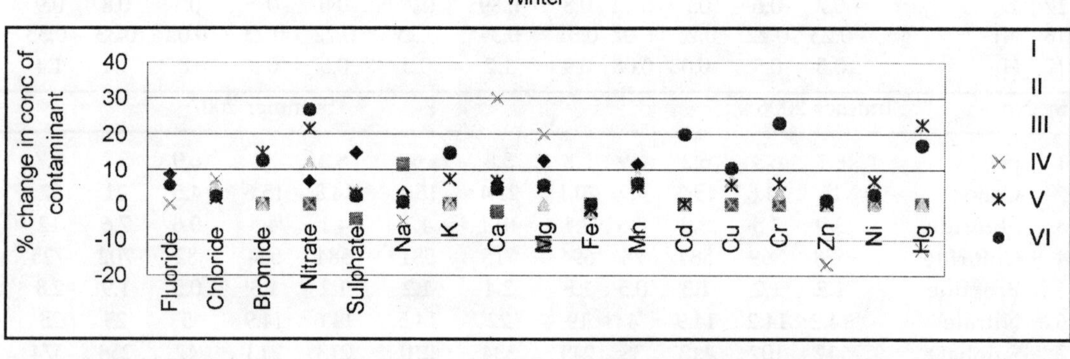

Fig. 2. Percent change in concentration of metals and anions in the next year with respect to an earlier year during the winter season.

Summer Season

Changes in the nature of a graph during the summer season were observed for the % change in the concentration of contaminants in the sediment and shown in fig.3. Very few changes in concentration of contaminants of the sediment were observed during the summer season except sulphate, which had shown more than a 100% variation at locations II and III. Other parameters shows 0 to 20 % change in concentration of contaminants and no negative values.

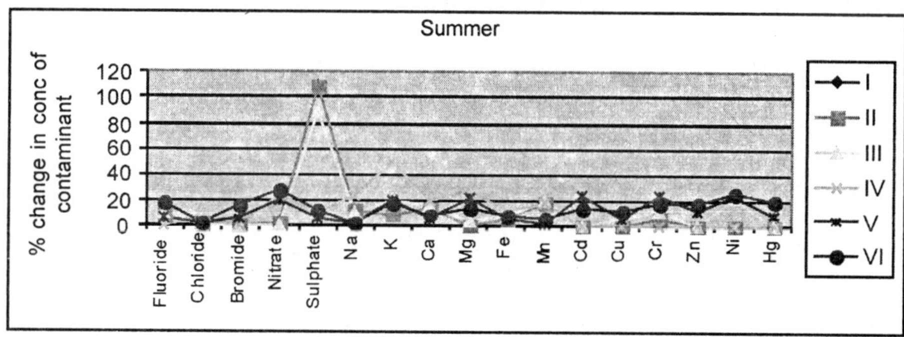

Fig. 3. Percent changes in the concentration of metals and anions for the next year with respect to an earlier year during the summer season.

Multivariate Statistical Analysis

Multivariate Statistical Analysis is an advanced technique to process large data set into a simpler form. The statistics XL software is used for statistical analysis.

Correlation Matrix

Correlation coefficient matrix among the concentration of sediments is shown in the Table 2. A very high correlation was observed among the different parameters which showed the correlation coefficient values to be higher than 0.9. Sodium had a correlation coefficient value 0.720 for Cl^-, 0.725 for Zn, 0.782 for Cu, 0.724 for Fe, 0.720 for chloride and 0.767 for nitrate.

Table 2: Correlation matrix of metals and anions in the sediment.

	F^-	Cl^-	Br^-	NO_3^-	SO_4^{--}	Na	K	Ca	Mg	Fe	Mn	Cd	Cu	Cr	Zn	Ni	Hg
Fluoride	1.000																
Chloride	0.841	1.000															
Bromide	0.951	0.846	1.000														
Nitrate	0.913	0.901	0.969	1.000													
Sulphate	0.960	0.828	0.889	0.870	1.000												
Na	0.905	0.720	0.818	0.767	0.894	1.000											
K	0.909	0.949	0.928	0.957	0.881	0.816	1.000										
Ca	0.975	0.904	0.937	0.924	0.955	0.931	0.958	1.000									
Mg	0.950	0.884	0.947	0.938	0.911	0.901	0.965	0.981	1.000								
Fe	0.859	0.980	0.886	0.929	0.849	0.724	0.975	0.916	0.915	1.000							
Mn	0.961	0.826	0.921	0.896	0.959	0.959	0.914	0.979	0.961	0.846	1.000						
Cd	0.970	0.738	0.935	0.873	0.927	0.910	0.844	0.931	0.920	0.765	0.952	1.000					
Cu	0.934	0.942	0.954	0.955	0.893	0.782	0.960	0.946	0.935	0.957	0.890	0.875	1.000	0.941			
Cr	0.966	0.872	0.961	0.954	0.927	0.911	0.962	0.983	0.981	0.900	0.971	0.942	0.941	1.000			
Zn	0.893	0.946	0.940	0.958	0.847	0.725	0.944	0.912	0.918	0.961	0.848	0.828	0.981	0.914	1.000		
Ni	0.931	0.943	0.957	0.970	0.893	0.815	0.986	0.961	0.968	0.969	0.915	0.875	0.983	0.967	0.977	1.000	
Hg	0.986	0.831	0.963	0.921	0.936	0.924	0.922	0.977	0.964	0.857	0.970	0.965	0.928	0.980	0.881	0.935	1.000

Principle Component Analysis (PCA)

A principle component loading of PC1 and PC2 for different parameters is shown in Fig. 5 and the scree plot of Eigenvalues for 17 components is shown in Fig. 4. PC1 shows a positive loading to all the parameters with values more than 0.9.

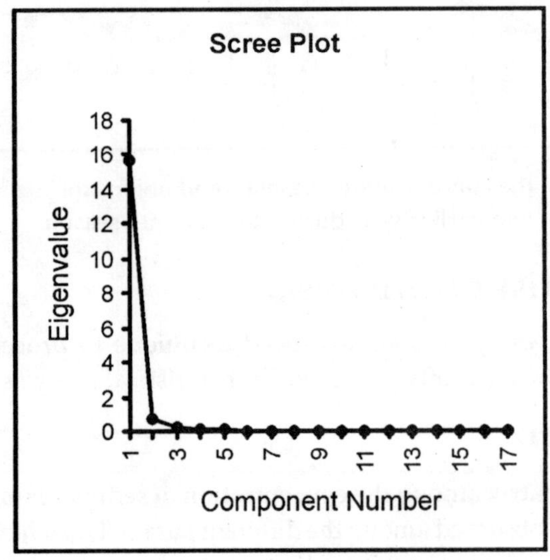

Fig. 4. Scree plot of eigenvalues vs component number of sediment analysis.

The PC2 loading shows a negative loading for chloride, Nitrate, K, Fe, Cu, Zn, Ni, and a poor positive load with other parameters. The scree plot indicates a change in the graph after the second and third components.

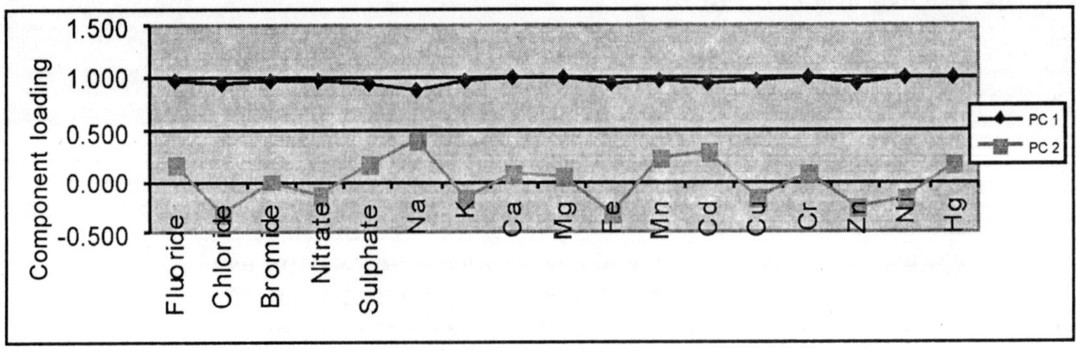

Fig. 5. Component loading of parameters in sediment.

Factor Analysis

Varimax rotated factor loadings were calculated (Table 3). Rotation was completed in eight iterations after normalization. Factor 1 shows Eigenvalues 15.6 and 92.15 percent of total variance. All the parameters are positively loaded in factor 1 whereas they are negatively loaded in factor 3. Zn, Fe and chloride show the higher values of factor loading. Sodium has a factor loading value of 0.917.

Table 3: Varimax rotated factor loading of metals and anions.

Variable	Factor 1	Factor 2	Factor 3
Fluoride	0.539	0.745	-0.362
Chloride	0.891	0.421	-0.104
Bromide	0.613	0.591	-0.516
Nitrate	0.725	0.502	-0.440
Sulphate	0.534	0.769	-0.225
Na	0.364	0.917	-0.094
K	0.790	0.554	-0.221
Ca	0.639	0.739	-0.210
Mg	0.648	0.691	-0.269
Fe	0.882	0.428	-0.176
Mn	0.515	0.818	-0.228
Cd	0.392	0.794	-0.449
Cu	0.766	0.512	-0.361
Cr	0.615	0.710	-0.319
Zn	0.813	0.421	-0.378
Ni	0.772	0.545	-0.313
Hg	0.531	0.757	-0.361
Eigenvalue	15.666	0.766	0.238
% of Var.	92.152	4.504	1.398
Cum. %	92.152	96.656	98.054

Cluster Analysis

The dendrogram of the cluster analysis of the sample location for the winter and summer season is shown in Fig. 6. The location V and VI clusters are in one group and the others are in another group. Location IV has a cluster for the summer and the winter season. A similar characteristic location has clusters in one group and the distance between the two different groups shows how these are similar.

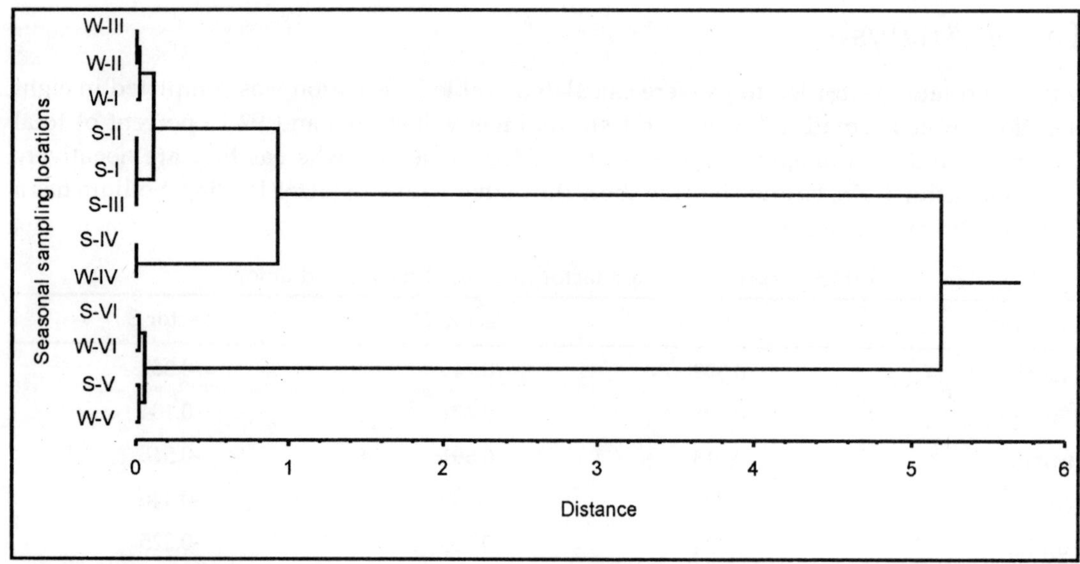

Fig. 6. Dendrogram of cluster analysis of a sample location for the winter and summer season

Conclusion

As sediments are the major depositories for particle bound metals in rivers, sediment health is critical in maintaining an ecological quality and they are indicators of an environmental disaster. The Savitri River catchment area is located in the Konkan region of Maharashtra. Samples were collected during the winter and summer season from Oct.2005 to May 2007. Heavy metal contamination in sediments was detected for metals Cd, Cr, Ni, Zn, Cu and Hg. PC2 shows a negative loading for chloride, Nitrate, K, Fe, Cu, Zn, Ni and gave a poor positive load with other parameters. The scree plot indicates changes in the graph after the second and third components.

References

1. Adams, W.J., Kimberley, R.A. and Barnett, J.W. (1992). Sediment quality and aquatic life assessment. Environmental Science and Technology 26, 1865 – 75.
2. Alargasmi R. (1988). A study of some metals in the Mandovi Estuary sediment, Goa. M.Sc. Thesis (Mumbai University)
3. Birch, G.F., Taylor, S.E. and Matthai, C. (2001). Small scale spatial and temporal variance in the concentration of heavy metals in aquatic sediments: a review and some new concepts. Environmental Pollution 113, 357 - 72.
4. Brady N., (1990). The nature and properties of soil. 10th Edn., MacMillan New York.
5. Chaosheng Zhang, (2006). Using Multivariate analysis and GIS to identify pollutants and their spatial pattern in urban soils in Galway, Ireland. Environmental Pollution, 142, 501-515.

6. Datta, D. and Subramanian, V. (1998). Distribution and fractionation of heavy metals in the surface sediments of the Ganges, Brahmaputra, Meghna river system in the Bengal Basin. Environmental Geology, 36, 93 - 101.

7. Garlaschi et al. (1985). Trace metals in sediments of Mapocha river, Chile. Engr, Tech, Letters. 6, 405-414.

8. Gangopadhyay S., Gupta, A. S., Nachabe, M. H. (2001). Evaluation of groundwater monitoring network by principal component analysis. Ground water, 39(2), 181-191

9. Herr, C. and Gray, N.F. (1997b). Metal contamination of riverine sediments below the Avoca Mines, southeast Ireland. Environmental Geochemistry and Health 19, 73 - 82.

10. Ingole S. (1988). An analysis of heavy metals and petroleum hydrocarbons from the sediments of Ambo river estuary. M.Sc. Thesis, Mumbai University.

8

Environmental Depletion, Climate Change and Urbanisation

Finding a Balanced Breakthrough

PRATEEK DESAI AND ARVIND GIRIRAJ

Introduction

Ancient Indian culture specifies through Rig-Veda that the Universe consists of five basic elements earth, air, fire, water and space called Panchabhootha. India has a tradition of protecting and worshipping nature since time immemorial and hence the land, trees and environment were placed on a high pedestal. The human activity was governed by the various positions of the sun and the moon. Our houses and buildings where built after taking into account the weather conditions and the awareness regarding the nature and the ecological equilibrium, which was considered to protect the environment. It is evident from history that man has been struggling endlessly to manage his environment in order to improve his well-being. Presently because of industrial, scientific and technological revolutions, the struggling capacity of man has increased the exploiting of the natural resources beyond his control by military emissions, nuclear explosions, and hazardous industrial emissions etc.

The UN Conference on the human environment (1972) stated that many parts of the earth are affected by dangerous levels of the pollution of water, air, earth etc. These are the major and undesirable sources for disturbances to the ecological balance. The biosphere destruction, depletion of irreplaceable resources and gross deficiencies are harming the physical, mental and social health of man. Taking this as a basis, the world community signed the Stockholm declaration of 1972 for the prevention and protection of the human environment for the first time. India, being a representative to the declaration took a decision to take appropriate steps for the preservation of its natural resources including the preservation of the quality of air to control air pollution. In this regard India enacted in legislation The Air (Prevention and Control of Pollution) Act 1981.The Act provided provisions relating to the protection of the quality of air and to control all forms of pollution, which were the result of industrial and vehicular emissions. However human activities also contribute to the air pollution like traffic, heating, use of domestic fuel etc. effecting human health, animal life, vegetation and property. Apart form this, the Environment (protection) Act 1986 was passed by our parliament for protecting the environment at all levels. The fact that the rapid urbanization is causing pollution has made the efforts of parliament, environmentalists and others determined to prevent the same.

In spite of all this there should be a sustainable development, to sustain the quality of the environment. This paper examines in detail the developments and their impacts on the environment and sustainable development paying special attention to relevant issues. It specifies natural and socio economic characteristics of urban systems, which are taken into account for defining environmentally sustainable developments in cities.

Urbanization

"Urbanization" is the expansion of a city, namely the proportion of the total population or area in urban localities or areas (cities and towns), or the increase of this proportion over time. It can thus represent a level of urban living relative to the total population or area, or the rate at which the urban proportion is increasing. Both can be expressed in percentage terms, the rate of change as a percentage per year, decade or period between censuses. For instance, the United States or the United Kingdom have a far higher urbanization level than China, India or Nigeria, but a far slower annual urbanization rate, since far fewer of the population are rural dwellers in the process of moving to town. Los Angeles is a great example of urbanization. The rate of urbanization over time is distinct from the rate of urban growth, which is the rate at which the urban population or area increases in a given period relative to its own size at the start of that period. The urbanization rate represents the increase in the proportion of urbanization over the period. In terms of a geographical place, urbanization means increased spatial scale and/or density of settlement and/or business and other activities in the area over time. The process could occur either as a natural expansion of the existing population (usually not a major factor since urban reproduction tends to be lower than rural), the transformation of peripheral population from rural to urban, incoming migration, or a combination of these. In either case, urbanization has profound effects on the ecology of a region and on its economy.

Rapid urbanization is expected to continue without any hurdles. Projections show that over half of the world's population have been living in urban areas since 2005. An estimate is that by the year 2025 more than half of the world's population will live in mega cities. This hyper urbanizational trends and the concentration of urban pollution in the big cities are developing to bring not only the problems of resource limitations, but are adding new problems as well. Urbanization has both direct and indirect impacts on the human environment.

The development of metropolitan areas at all the sub-regional or even the regional level is important for the economical development and plays a dominant role in future land use. At the same time, the protection of the landscape and natural parks and forests in metropolitan areas will require a strict land use plan and in some cases ownership of such common land by governmental organizations. Hence economical, social and environmental aspects have to be included in a comprehensive urban infra-structural plan for the Sustainable Development.

Sustainable Development

Sustainable Development has been practiced by many cultures, but the industrialized world first became interested in the concept in the 1960s. Many credit Rachel Carson and her book

"The Silent Spring "(1962, Penguin Books) as the catalyst for the worldwide acknowledgment of environmental problems. In the following years a number of publications including Paul Erlich's Population Bomb (1968, Buccaneer Books) and the Club of Rome's Limits to Growth (1972, Pan Books) drew attention to Global Developmental issues.

In 1987, Sustainable Development was defined by the world commission on the Environment and Development (in the Brundtland Report) as "development that meets the needs of the present without compromising the ability of the future generations to meet their own needs". Unfortunately this definition remained vague and little guidance was offered on how countries could develop coherent sustainable development polices. The concept of Sustainable Development was first given prominence at the UNCED.[1] The Earth Summit in Rio in 1992, followed the notion of Sustainable Development and it rapidly gained wide credibility and encouraged a greater awareness of the major environmental problems and disparities in the world. That global companies are engaged in a wholesale migration of polluting industries to developing countries has no basis in fact. Pollution control is a very small component of the cost of production in any industry, so globalization requires sustainable development strategies to entitle everybody to have a decent standard of living.

There is a common understanding that sustainable development implies a better balance between economical, social and environmental goals in policy formation as well as a long-term perspective about the consequences of today's activities such as industrialization and urbanization etc. Sustainable Development is capturing the attention of planners, politicians and business leaders. Within the academic sphere, its study is increasingly breaching disciplinary boundaries to become a focus of attention for natural and social scientists alike in studying such a key concept,and it is vital that there be a clear definition of what it means, how it is applied on the ground and the influence it exerts upon people's perception of changes to the physical environment, economical activity and society.

Substitutes for Natural Resources

The basic assumption on which our model is grounded concerns the existence of a private good, which can be consumed as a substitute for the free access environmental resource; in order to face the deterioration of the natural resource, economical agents may substitute consumption patterns and economical activities requiring a high availability of the environmental resource with consumption patterns and economical activities less affected by environmental deterioration. Within this context, the increase in their labour input in sector x may be interpreted as a self-protection choice, enabling them to alleviate the negative consequences generated by the scarcity of natural resources.

The possibility of substituting natural resources with an increase in the activity level in sector x has essentially been contemplated in many of the above mentioned works. For example, we can consider Matsuyama's model; in this model, the possibility of substitution is made certain by foreign trade, which, through the export of the goods produced in sector x and the

[1] United Nations Conference on Environment and Development

import of agricultural goods, allows a reduction of the damages generated by the low productivity of the domestic agricultural sector.

Substitution possibilities are various and those concerning the agricultural sector constitute only a portion of them. For example, let's consider the tourism sector; an economy can derive consistent revenues from such a sector, which, ceteris paribus, possesses a greater growth potential, the higher the endowment of the environmental resources is. However, the revenues derived from the tourism sector can be substituted by the revenues produced by any other economical activity. Other substitution possibilities are associated with the consumption of environmental resources as final goods rather than as intermediate goods. In this case, the scarcity of environmental resources can make "environment intensive" consumption patterns comparatively less attractive than those based on the consumption of private goods, which are less likely to experience the negative effects derived from environmental deterioration.

The main focus of our model will concern the transformation of consumption patterns generated by environmental deterioration[2]. The notion that environmental deterioration may alter consumption patterns causing them to become more dependent on the consumption of private goods rather than on the consumption of free access environmental resources is shared by several works on the subject of environmental defensive expenditures.[3] Here are some traditional examples. Mineral water may substitute spring water or tap water. Medicines may mitigate the effects of respiratory diseases caused by air pollution. Individuals may react to the deterioration of the seaside near home by going to a less deteriorated seaside area by car or by boat. They may build a swimming pool in their gardens. They may purchase houses in exclusive areas at the seaside or buy holiday-packages in tropical paradises. Individuals may defend themselves from external sources of noise by installing sound-proofing devices, and so on. However, the general insight provided by this said literature is that individual reactions to environmental deterioration can be diverse and are likely to influence deeply the consumption patterns of the future thereby increasing the consumption of private and expensive goods as opposed to free access environmental resources. Urban life offers an illustrative example of the said substitution mechanism. Cities are often characterized by the scarcity of a free access environment and at the same time, they are able to supply a considerable variety of private and expensive consumption opportunities [see e.g. Hueting (1980), Antoci and Bartolini (1999, 2004), Bartolini e Bonatti (2002)]. The scarcity of areas where individuals can meet away from the dangers of city traffic brings on additional expenses for childcare [baby-sitters, playgrounds, etc.], as well as for the leisure of adults. To a degree, the reason for the constant increase in the

[2] However, this model can be modified easily in a two-sector model - the sector x and the agricultural or tourism sector - in which the natural resources enter as intermediate goods.

[3] [see e.g. Hueting (1980), Shibata and Winrich (1983), Leipert (1989), Shogren and Crocker (1993), Antoci (1996), Antoci and Bartolini (1999, 2004), Bartolini e Bonatti (2002)].

consumption of "home entertainment" in an industralized society can indeed be found in the substitution mechanism as previously defined.[4]

In our model, individual substitutive consumption made with the aim of facing environmental deterioration generates negative externalities on all the other agents, as it further leads environmental deterioration. This context has been examined by Shogren and Croker (1991), who demonstrate that if the self-protecting choices of an economical agent "transfer" the environmental damage on to other economical agents, and if the economical agents do not coordinate themselves, then the self-protecting choices are enforced beyond the socially optimal level.[5] However, Shogren and Croker analyse a static model and do not develop their model in order to further examine the consequences that an "excess" of self-protecting choices may determine on economical growth, should the self-protecting choices involve the consumption of private goods and services. In our model we expand Shogren and Croker's work in this direction.

Beltratti (1996) analyses a model wherein environmental goods and private goods are substituted. Such models differ from ours for two main reasons. The first one relates to the fact that in Beltratti's model, decisions are made by a social planner; therefore, there are no positive nor negative externalities, and consequently, such a model is not likely to examine the cumulative effect determined by the interaction between positive and negative externalities, as we do in our model. The second reason is that Beltratti analyses a model in which the produced goods may be accumulated in order to become capital and in which the labour input is generously given. In this context, an increase in the substituted consumption in the instant of time of the reference cannot be achieved increasing the labour input and therefore it completely weighs on the accumulation of capital, which is reduced; as a consequence, environmental deterioration inhibits growth in Beltratti's model.[6] The idea that environmental negative externalities can be an engine of economical growth was first introduced, in a mathematical model, by Antoci

[4] A phenomenon that is in many instances considered a consequence of environmental deterioration and is often associated with a radical transformation of consumption patterns, is rural exodus. With urbanization, consumption patterns tend to become market-oriented. The resources that were freely accessible in rural communities become accessible only through purchase on the market of substituted goods and, therefore, through entry into the labour market [see e.g. Humphries (1990), Myers (1997), Epstein and Jezeph (2001)].

[5] The distinction between self-protecting options that "transfer" negative externalities on to other economical agents and options that instead "filter" them has been introduced by Bird (1987).

[6] It is correct to emphasize the fact that Beltratti's model focusses on proving that in the event of a substituted consumption, the optimal co-evolution* of capital and environmental deterioration may not give rise to the environmental Kuznets' curve.

[7] The idea that negative externalities derived from economical growth may, in their turn, "fuel" the growth process through the enforcement of defensive consumption has been contemplated by economic literature at least since Hirsh's famous work (1976). However, it was only recently that this idea was introduced in mathematical models.

(1996) and Antoci and Bartolini (1997, 1999).[7] In these works, the selection process of labour inputs and of consumption patterns is analysed in an evolutionary game context without accumulation of assets. Antoci and Bartolini (1994) contain a further development of such models. Bartolini e Bonatti (2003) have analysed the dynamics of the accumulation of physical capital in an economy where agents possess perfect foresight and they have shown that it is possible to have an undesirable economical growth generated by negative externalities even assuming that the economical agents are perfectly rational.[8]

Institutional Sustainability

Institutional sustainability can strengthen institutional structure but does it continue to deliver the results of the technical co-operation to the ultimate end-users? The results may not be sustainable if, for example the planning unit strengthened by the technical cooperation ceases to have access to top-management or is not provided with adequate resources for the effective performance after the technical co-operation was terminated. Note that institutional sustainability can also be linked to the concept of social sustainability, and of how social structures and institutions can sustain the interventions.

Economical and Financial Sustainability

Can the results of the technical co-operation continue to yield an economical benefit after the technical co-operation is withdrawn? For e.g.: The benefits from the introduction of new crops may not be sustained, if the constraints to marketing the crops are not resolved. Similarly, economical (as distinct from financial) sustainability may be at risk, if the end-users continue to depend on heavily subsidized activities and inputs.

Ecological Sustainability

Are the benefits to be generated by the technical co-operation likely to lead to a deterioration in the physical environment (thus indirectly contributing to a fall in production) or to the well-being of the groups targeted and their society? Out of all these three types Ecological Sustainability is more related to the environmental issues.

Factors Which are Contributing to the Urban Pollution

Pollution may be defined as the contamination of the environment in such a way that it creates hazards or potential hazards to health and the well being of living and non-living beings. An air pollutant means any solid, liquid or gaseous substance including noise present in the atmosphere in such concentrations as may be or tend to be injurious to human beings or other

[8] Antoci, Sacco e Vanin (2004) analyse a model wherein economic agents possess perfect foresight and accumulate physical and social capital; in such model, economic agents may face the negative externalities generated by a low level of social capital, by increasing their consumption of private goods. Within this context, the authors point out some of the mechanisms through which the accumulation of physical capital and the accumulation of social capital may end up being in conflict.

living creatures or plants or property or the environment. Air pollution means the presence in the atmosphere of any air pollutant. Air pollution affects adversely man and material, flora and fauna, humans by breathing problems, skin, blood, eyes and lungs. The Urbanization process is deteriorating natural resources by increasing pollution. Due to the emissions of hazardous chemicals from neighbouring industries or refineries and from vehicular pollution, the Taj Mahal[9] at Agra, India, is changing its colour from white to a yellowish colour.

The polluter pays principle applies to air pollution, as well as to greenhouse emissions. The right to human safety in the environment is indirectly approved in the M.C.Mehta case. In M.C.Mehta v. Union of India[10], the Supreme Court directed the company manufacturing hazardous and lethal chemicals and gases posing danger to the health and life of the workmen and people living in its neighborhood to take all necessary safety measures before reopening the plant. The second M.C.Mehta v. Union of India[11] modified some of the conditions for the environmental protection of life by adopting an absolute liability principle. To encourage Sustainable Development the costs of pollution and environmental damage must be weighed against the benefits. Diesel engines are a very significant source of pollution, which is considered to be the most dangerous of all common air pollutants. Sustainable policies need to be developed in order to reduce the impact of this toxic pollution on our health.

Population Growth

Population growth is the key factor for the environmental pollution. The increase in the population demands additional requirements for food products, goods and commodities etc. The population increase has given rise to overcrowding, noise, insects, rodents, air pollutants and street filth. These factors in turn affect the human health. In thickly populated cities like Delhi, Mumbai etc. the serious problem is air pollution with a deficiency of oxygen in the environment. Water is essential for our survival; the demand for it is growing with the increase in the population. The technology for extracting ground water is so advanced that we neglect to harness surface water. We continue to exploit ground water resources despite realizing that it is limited. We are polluting the rivers and also marine waters extremely by discharging the sewerage and hazardous waste into them. It is evident from MC Mehta Vs Union of India[12] that the Ganga pollution was caused extensively by an over population problem.

Poverty often promotes environmental destruction as poorer people rely heavily upon the extraction of natural resources. At the same time environmental degradation worsens poverty, resulting in a vicious cycle of environmental degradation and human suffering. Combating poverty is an important step in the struggle to protect the environment for a Sustainable Development. The areas with the most rapid human population growth and highest population density generally harbour the highest diversity of species. A variety of strategies are currently being used to balance population growth, economical development and environmental health

[9] MC Mehta Vs Union of India AIR 1997 SC 734

[10] AIR 1987 SC 965[11] AIR 1987 SC 982

[12] AIR 1988 SC 1115

in order to attain Sustainable Development. The strategies include changing farming practices, providing new kinds of tourism and designing more environmentally suitable conditions.

Industrialization

Man has been inventing new things and methods, in order to meet his requirements or to raise his standards of living but he has been carrying on the various activities by exploiting natural resources. Due to the the rapid industrialization process, the release of noxious and hazardous substances into the atmosphere has created a lot of hazards. When smoke and dust combine with water vapor, they form smog, which is very dangerous to human life. On December 4, 1984, due to the release of poisonous gases (MIC) from the Union Carbide Corporation India Ltd, thousands of people died, which was described as the world's greatest gas disaster and it happened in Bhopal. Global warming, ozone depletion, acid rains etc. are the results of industrialization.

In Vellore Citizen's Welfare Forum v. Union of India[13], the petitioner filed a writ petition by the PIL[14] drawing the attention of the court towards the pollution caused by an enormous discharge of untreated effluent by the tanneries and other industries in the State of Tamil Nadu. It was argued that due to the discharge of untreated effluent, the river water became unfit for consumption and the physio-chemical properties of the soil are no longer suitable for agricultural purposes. The court held that while such industries are of vital importance for the country's progress as they generate foreign exchange and provide employment avenues, they must have regard to the pollution caused by them,as the principle of Sustainable Development has to be adopted as a balancing concept between ecology and the development. The court held that the Precautionary Principle and the Polluter Pays Principle combine to form Sustainable Development and have been accepted as part of the law of the land for these two principles. The court directed the closure of these industries unless they install pollution control devices. A pollution fine shall be recovered in arrears of land revenues. The Court suggested constituting a special bench to be called the 'Green bench' of the Madras High Court to deal with these and other similar environmental cases.

Transport

Transportation is the single largest contributor of air pollution. In urban areas it is contributing to forty five per cent of the world's air pollution, in the form of pollution from road vehicles, railways, aircraft modes of transport, combusting ships and other combustions of fuel i.e., diesel and petrol. The number of air pollutants discharged into the atmosphere, affect people with various chemical infections and reactions decreasing people's age span. Transportation also accounts for man-made ozone.

Efforts are being made all over the world to increase the Sustainable Development patterns in the areas of transportation. Hence sustainable transportation is a part of a broader strategy

[13] (1996) 5 SCC 647

[14] Public Interest Litigation

of transportation and land use planning for sustainability. The various strategies for increasing transportation sustainability include demand management, operational management, pricing policies, vehicle technology improvement, clean fuels, integrated land use and transportation planning. In developed nations, special attention is being given to the sustainability of current and emerging land use and transportation patterns. This reflects both the significant impacts that current patterns of transportation have on the environment and the interaction between transportation, land use and activity systems.

Globalization

The rapid growth of technology due to inventions has increased, making people prefer more luxuries. The multinationals are instruments of foreign direct investments facilitating capital inflow. They are the principle vehicles for the transfer of the host country in the international trade and markets through their already established global networks. The multinational corporations impose upon the developing countries products and ideas which have originated in the developed countries and they also change the consumption patterns of the people. For globalization, rapid industrialization and urbanization are the major contributory factors for the exploitation of the natural resources and environmental pollution in the developing country.

Housing and Building

Expansions and improvement of housing due to industries in cities is causing the rise in the demand for shelter thus increasing slum pollution. This kind of pollution is hazardous to the environment and as well affects the public health and other living organisms. To combat this problem, green building techniques must be followed when planning housing and building activities. These "Green" building techniques like energy efficiency, improved indoor air quality, green material selection and sensitive site development provide a higher level of comfort and livability, reduce utility bills and add value to the Sustainable Development.

Food Supply

Due to the increase in the urban population, the maintenance of very low levels of consumption of food rich in proteins, minerals and vitamins, is becoming very difficult unless there is a major improvement in the technologies of production, processing and transporting of them. The prices are in consistent with the great majority of urban residents. Highly efficient food security prediction and warning systems should be established which would include forecasts of natural conditions on agricultural production to help in monitoring the growth of the food production environments. Hence emphasis should be paid to the monitoring of factors like soil fertility, soil and water erosion, and the state of pollution in the agricultural environment. The quality of the environment for food production should be improved to ensure the production of contaminated free food. Food storage, processing and distribution should be improved at all levels. The use of pesticides and non-degradable plastic films should be strictly controlled, and the use of low residue, less toxic pesticides and degradable films should be encouraged for all Sustainable Development. The protection and rational utilization of natural resources has become necessary for the Sustainable Development.

Water and Electricity

Water and energy are the two most important factors necessary for the development of any country, especially the developing one. Therefore, the developmental approach nowadays in the prevailing competitive environment, should take a hard look at the water and power needs at the planning stage itself, along with their effective monitoring during the implementation stage for sustainability. The utilization of the existing infrastructure that was already developed should be maximized through regular technological improvements as well as innovative skills. The acute shortage of water is causing unhygienic conditions thereby causing various health problems to mankind. Due to the shortage of water, the contents of the oxygen in the air is decreasing on account of non-plantation.

Peace and Security

Urbanization requires political and administrative management of a very high order, which ensures an adequate access to the most basic needs like food and water. Progressive improvements must go to the essential services in housing and for increasing gainful opportunities of employment, sustainable development and proper management is required.

Noise Pollution

Noise is an unwanted, undesired, unpleasant sound and sound is hazardous to human health. The sources of noise pollution vary from industries, loud speakers, automobiles, aircrafts, trains, construction work, radio, television, even domestic usages like grinder, cooker etc. In India we have no specific statutes relating to noise pollution.

However certain provisions are provided as under:

- The Environmental (Protection) Act 1986
- Motor vehicles Act- 1988 and Rules framed there under
- Chapter 3 of the Factories Act- 1948
- Sections 268 and 298 of IPC 1860
- Articles 39 (E), 47, 48-A, 49 and 51(G) of the Constitution.

One deterrent to high-density living is urban noise pollution. Sustainable cities may need to take effective measures to discourage noise pollution from traffic, domestic and customary usages.

Suggestions

- Sustainable development should be given more importance.
- Improve the human settlement.
- Enhance environmental patterns especially in schools and in all other educational institutions.
- Integrated planning, management and implementation of environmental standards by the central and state Governments.
- Vehicle emissions should be controlled by new technologies developed by new intellects.
- Promoting local empowerment.
- Impose strict duties upon the citizens for protecting environmental pollution.
- Working out options for recycling industrial hazardous substances with new technology or their disposal with a minimum of environmental pollution.

Conclusion

The Constitution of India confers a fundamental right[15] on the human being for the freedom of equality and adequate conditions of life. However, by destroying the natural environment, man is committing matricide, thus destroying the mother earth. In the consciousness of development, man cannot destroy the ecology, nor can be degrade the environment and injure the health of himself and that of his fellow human being. Hence appropriate steps regulating the environment should be the aim of every citizen. The issue of the urban environment and Sustainable Development is a complex one. Often environmental and developmental matters are intertwined and on holistic understanding of them is necessary in order to achieve the goal of Sustainability. Therefore, protecting the environment for future generations and assuring safe and healthy surroundings for all, preserving natural resources and promoting recycling and the use of renewable resources, should take care of the sustainable development in the context of urbanization. Global sustainability issues such as climatic changes demand global solutions. Governments of developed and developing countries need to formulate and implement policies and programme's to integrate and address Sustainable Developmental issues in the national research and innovation system. The implications of Sustainable Development mean that they can be effectively addressed only through international co-operation in developing, accessing and diffusing appropriate knowledge and technology, especially for developing countries. International co-operation to develop appropriate technologies for Sustainable Development should start with the identification of local needs. The precautionary approach is applied by states according to their capabilities. Where there is a threat of serious or irreversible damage, lack of full scientific certainty shall not be used as a reason for postponing cost-effective measures to prevent environmental degradation.

---

[15] 51-A (g)

References

1. Antoci, Angelo, Environmental Resources Depletion and Interplay Between Negative and Positive Externalities in a Growth Model (January 2005). FEEM Working Paper No. 09.05.

2. Antoci A., Bartolini S., (1999), Negative Externalities as the Engine of Growth in an Envolutionary Context, Working paper 83.99 FEEM, Milan.

3. Bartolini S., Bonatti L., (2003), Undesirable Growth in a Model with Capital Accumulation and Environmental Assets, Environment and Development Economics 8, 11-30.

4. Bird J., (1987), The Transferability and Depletability of Externalities, Journal of Environmental Economics and Manaement 14, 54-57.

5. United Nations Conference on Environment and Development—Rio de Janerio, Brazil.

9

Fragile Ecosystem
The Concern of the Present World

MILITA HALDAR

Introduction

There has been at present, an increasing concern regarding the growth rate of more and more fragile ecosystem zones in India due to the undue interference of human beings in the natural functioning of the ecosystem which is the smallest unit of the biosphere that has all the characteristics to sustain life. It is one of the most complex systems running in the environment that plays an important role in sustaining the abiotic component on one hand and the biotic component and its waste on the other. The ecosystem's interconnected and interdependent system brings about a competition and co-action between the two predefined components. There at the same time the external forces of the ecosystem either pamper or hamper the growth of these components and often tend to bring about a change in the ecosystem by altering the two

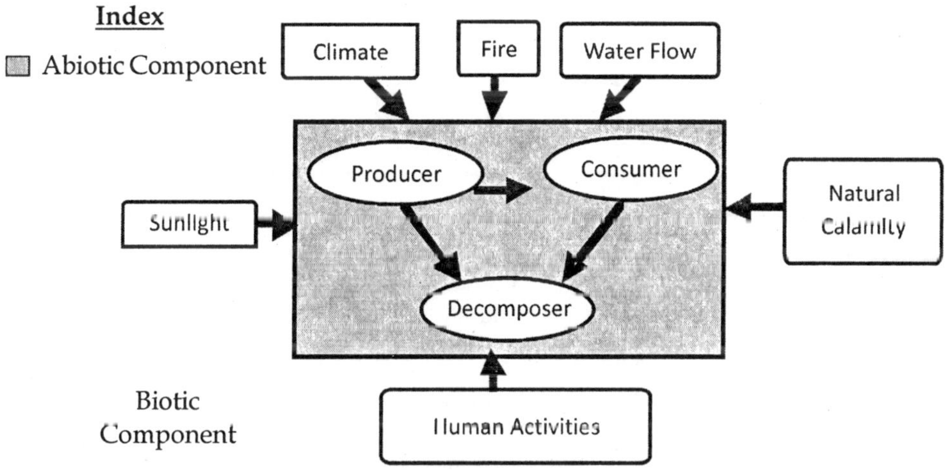

Fig. 1. Functioning of the Ecosystem

components. This overall functioning of the ecosystem is then regulated by the inbuilt self regulating mechanism or the homeostatic mechanism of the ecosystem. The homeostatic ability helps to regulate any of the changes brought in the natural ecosystem or the environmental system by the external forces of the ecosystem. This change is counterbalanced by the positive or the negative responses of the system. When the system counteracts the deviations in the system then the condition is known as a negative response and it leads the mechanism back to its ideal situation. The positive feedback of the ecosystem adds to the stress condition and tends to take the system away from the optimal condition. The two modes of responses of the homeostasis mechanism delimit the condition of equilibrium and the condition of disequilibrium. *Many ecosystems are especially vulnerable to change, the cause of which could include their location, extent, biodiversity and linkages with other ecosystems.*

The external forces as a whole or partially, can bring about a change in any of the biotic components. This change would also be visible on the other biotic and often the abiotic components too, all because of the fact that all these components of the ecosystem are so intimately co-related to each other. The change brought in by the physical environmental processes on the earth's surface, occur in such a way that the equilibrium of the ecosystem is maintained through the negative feedback mechanism, only if man does not interfere in the natural state of physical environmental processes. Now, man has emerged as a very important geomorphic agent and is capable of changing the earth's surface at a much faster rate than many of the natural processes. Various changes in the natural ecosystem and its functioning have highlighted the active role played by the conscious mind of man in changing the physical environment and thus generating a new geological epoch. This pertinent penetration of humans in the ecosystem has bought about a disequilibrium condition giving rise to a state where the ecosystem cannot support or sustain the components that depend upon it, resulting in a chaotic condition of natural catastrophes. This wide chain of change can lead to the formation of a FRAGILE ECOSYSTEM.

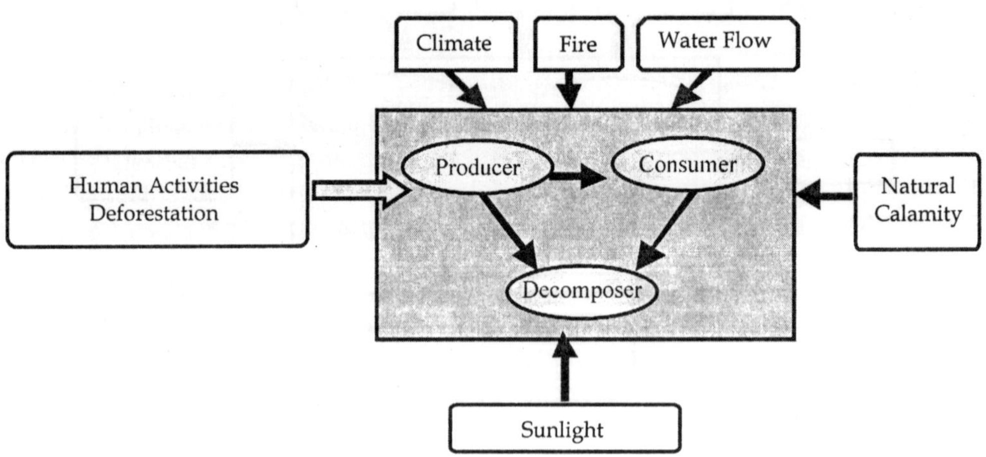

Fig. 2. Cause and impact of an external change on the ecosystem

What is a fragile ecosystem? A fragile ecosystem is an ecosystem or community which lacks resilience or which is so heavily impacted by an 'un-natural' (human?) event that it changes in an unexpected and undesirable way leading to the conditions that are often termed as natural catastrophes. However, if a disturbing event occurs which exceeds the tolerance of the community, a major change may result. Such an example would be the combination of two extreme events; perhaps drought and wildfire, which can shift a rainforest community to dense, simple, low diversity kunai grassland. Any definitions of fragility must be relative to the normal disturbance regime which that community would be expected to encounter. Disturbance regimes cover a spectrum which include small frequent events and everything up to extreme uncommon events. These can be considered statistically as in the concept of a 1:100 flood, drought or bushfire and it is obvious that a community which suffers such an event will change. Therefore all communities and ecosystems are vulnerable or fragile to some extent. Recognizing the limits is the key to understanding and management.

Fragility and resilience are often linked to bio-diversity and the concepts of an ecosystem maturity but these relationships are not nearly as clear as many texts would indicate. For example, rainforests are species-rich ecosystems which are commonly seen as being very complex, very old (mature) and very fragile and thus it is assumed that even the removal of a few species might significantly change them.

Nature of Problem

The fragile ecosystem, as can be claimed, is the price paid by humans for the incessant development done at the cost of natural destruction .The human impact upon the ecosystem, of which he is a part, has been increasing, as in the case of the great Himalayas some parts of which also feature among the fragile ecosystem. For centuries, this ecosystem has remained delicately balanced, and has been responsible for the tremendous biodiversity of the Himalayas. Only in recent years has the ecosystem been disturbed in various parts due to processes both man-made and natural.

Man has also been responsible to a large extent for some of the environmental problems faced by the mountains. Striving for industrialization, modernization and the so-called higher standard of living, man has disturbed the natural ecosystems of many parts of the world. The Himalayas have been no exception. Over the centuries, pilgrims and explorers have visited the mountains. However, in the past, their numbers were few and the Himalayan ecosystem, fragile as it is, was able to cope with the effects of human exploration in the areas, but today, the story is different. In the last few decades, an intricate network of roads has been built into the mountains, which have made some of the most remote areas more easily accessible. This has translated into a tremendous increase in the numbers of people who visit the mountains every year. The Himalayas are now being exploited to the hilt in many areas, to provide materials for the growing number of forest-based industries. Thus, it is not surprising that environmental problems have emerged in the Himalayan region also. The frequent occurrence of landslides is one indicator that speaks for the case that emphasises the weak resilient power of the Himalayan ecosystem against the change brought to it in its local ecosystem. Thereby the resultant affect of the disadvantageous advances made by man for his development against the resilient power of the environment, has backfired and now the scientist and technology are realizing that what they are using for their development is rendered useless against the might of nature.

The fragile ecosystem has now become a matter of great concern for the present scientists and researchers and the condition is still deteriorating with man's ever increasing needs. The consequences that have come up regarding the fragile ecosystem have added to the woes of man and have further aggravated the problem. The causes that can be headed as having a resultant impact upon the resilient power of the ecosystem are-

- **Population Growth.** The rapid rate of an ever-increasing world population, and the increasing gap between the developed and the developing regions, the increasing proportion of the urban- rural population etc. are the basic and root causes of all sorts of environmental degradation and ecological imbalance because an increase in the population means more exploitation of natural resources which means an inauguration of new environmental problems.

Table 1: Population Growth in India since 1901.

Census Year	Population (in lakhs)
1901	2384.0
1911	2520.9
1921	2513.2
1931	2789.8
1941	3186.6
1951	3610.9
1961	4392.3
1971	5481.6
1981	6833.3
1991	8463.0
2001	10270.1

The ever increasing population places greater demands on the finite resources of the earth. The rate of exploitation of the natural resources has increased more rapidly than that of the rate of the population growth. This has caused and is causing exhaustion of certain valuable non-renewable resources.

Overpopulation is another problem so intimately related with the ever growing human population which also results in an economical poverty because all the resources are utilized to meet the bare necessity of the people. This results in an unbalanced exploitation of natural resources that has further changed large areas of natural landscape into vast wastelands and thus has caused several severe environmental problems such as the accelerated rate of soil erosion, floods, droughts etc. Thus it is obvious that overpopulation is the root cause of environmental degradation and ecological imbalance. It is high time for science and technology to be so developed that we could be able to feed the ever growing population and use the available resources scientifically and effectively.

- **Intensive Industrialization.** During the past several hundred years, humans have begun to industrialize rapidly. In many cases, they have added capabilities which have been used to manipulate natural things for human benefit, often at the expense of other things, specifically the environment. On the other hand, technological advancement has required that humans come to a better understanding of the world, bringing with them a greater potential to do good, to manipulate things for the benefit of the planet.

  Even though industrialization has opened new dimensions for human development, the development has been at the cost of an adverse impact upon the environment; though the impact of industrialization at first upon the environment was not so immediately noticeable, because in many cases the ill-impact of industrialization was slow, but with the passing of time, industrialization at many places has changed the overall character of natural systems and the chain effects have sometime become suicidal for the human society. The majority of problems which the impact of industrialization has caused are related to pollution and environmental degradation.

  The release of toxic elements into the environment through the application of chemical fertilizers etc has affected the food chain and food web of the ecosystem. Similarly the release of toxic gases in the atmosphere has changed the composition of air; the burning of hydrocarbon fuels has increased the concentration of CO_2 in the atmosphere. The rapid rate of industrialization has also aggravated several of the problems like deforestation over the utilization and pollution of the water resources. Thus, industrialization as a whole has played an important role in bringing a disadvantageous change in the environment and at the same time the presence of industries in fragile zones of the ecosystem has also altered the unstable physical and biological entities of the already imbalanced ecosystem.

- **Unplanned Urbanization.** As the rate of industrialization is increasing, the problem of urbanization is also increasing with it too. Urbanization means a phenomenal increase in the concentration of the human population in a limited space. The rapidly expanding cities face the twin challenges of an exploding population and scarce resources and suffer from a number of environmental problems including poor urban infrastructure (inadequate housing, polluted water, growing problems of solid waste collection and disposal), congestion, overcrowding, uncontrolled and conflicting land use, unabated pollution and poor maintenance as well as the over-exploitation of already depleted resources. Increasing urbanization increases pressure on the resources as it has been in the case of the over use of groundwater for domestic and industrial use. Excessive withdrawal of groundwater results in the formation of large cavities below the ground surface. The development of such cavities causes the collapse of the ground surface and thus inflicts great damage to human health and wealth. The cases of land subsidence due to the withdrawal of groundwater have occurred all over the world e.g. Houston (Texas, U.S.A. subsidence of land by 0.3m to 1.0m). The development of urban centres and their related problems have either further changed the fragile zones (e.g. hilly areas) or are gradually changing the more stable ecosystems to fragile ecosystems.

- **Intensive Agriculture.** The Green Revolution is synonymous with the development in agriculture and has depended on the application of scientific techniques, advanced technologies, uses of chemical fertilizers, pesticides, expansion of irrigation activities etc. The adoption of these techniques in farming gave a few years of a bumper harvest in Punjab and the surrounding areas, but later on, crop failures were reported in many areas despite the liberal use of NPK. This resulted mainly from micronutrient deficiencies caused by the rapid and continuous removal of micronutrients by the 'HYVs' and the replenishment of the macro nutrients only. Plants need these micronutrients more than NPK and the high yielding varieties extract micronutrients from the soil at a very rapid rate, creating deficiencies of zinc, iron, copper, manganese etc. The impact is either a gradual decrease in the production of the food grain or the food production does not increase in comparison with the amount of chemical fertilizers that are put in the field as is evident from the following data:

Table 2: Co-relation of fertilizer input and total food production.

Year	Consumption of Chemical Fertilizer(in lakh metric ton)	Total food grain production(in lakh metric ton)
2003-04	64.26	444.64
2004-05	64.77	399.97
2005-06	67.14	405.28
2006-07	73.04	416.27
2007-08	73.37	419.64

Furthermore a micro nutrient imbalance decreased the production in the Punjab, the food bowl of India, as zinc deficiency (a micro nutrient) in the Punjab had reduced yields of rice, wheat and maize by up to 3.9 tonnes, 1.98 tonnes and 3.8 tonnes per hectare respectively. Intensive agriculture required intensive irrigation as it had been known that agriculture in India was a gamble of monsoonal winds. This increase in water use through irrigation had also resulted in a destabilization of the water balance in the region of the Punjab, as the alluvial soils of the Punjab have a very negligible slope. All these factors related with the new era of agriculture result into changes in the abiotic and biotic structure of the environment, the changes that were often irreparable as desertification, salination etc. The change gave way to a natural system that was different from the previous condition which was not able to support the dependent component, specifically the human being.

- **Extensive Exploitation of Available Natural Resources.** Over exploitation of natural resources in some cases leads to exhaustion, particularly by excessive forestry, fishing and hunting. This over exploitation occurs due to an overpopulation in some areas, and at the same time the ever increasing demand for these resources and the development of international trade are the other major factors.

  The over exploitation of the natural resources has triggered various problems correlated to it. Often exploitation of some resources requires extraction (as in the case of mining) that creates further pressure on the environment in the form of pollution as for a tiny ring, when miners dig up 30 tonnes of rock and sprinkle it with diluted cyanide to extract the yellow metal. This extra pressure on land leaves it tenuous as the extracted part of the natural ecosystem is not replenished and the act of extraction goes on and gradually the ecosystem is unable to sustain the demand and often gives up, by giving a positive feedback to the change, resulting in the decline of the abiotic structure and death of the biotic structure. Altogether, the eco as a system declines to work in coordination.

- **Unscientific Method of Resource Use.** The ways in which the resources are being utilized often dictates the future availability of these resources. The resource utilization pattern in most of the developing and often in the developed countries too, is not up to the mark. This unscientific resource utilization has actuated several ecological problems also.

  As in the Himalayas, the ecologically fragile and economically underdeveloped region of India, with geo-environmental constraints imposes severe limitations on the level of resource productivity. Consequently, subsistence agriculture constitutes the main source of livelihood in the region. The rapid growth of the population has brought about extensive land-use changes in the region, mainly through the extension of cultivation and large-scale deforestation. This irrational land transformation process has not only disrupted the ecological balance of the Himalayan watersheds through reduced groundwater recharge, increased run-off and soil erosion, but has also adversely affected the ecology and economy of the adjoining Indo-Gangetic plains by recurrent floods and decreased irrigation potential.

The resultant impact of the problems are-

- **Lowering of the water table.** The growing population, rapid industrialization and intensive irrigation have been the major factors that have resulted in the decrease of the water table, as the exploitation rate of the water is higher then the rate by which it is being replenished either by the natural method or man made methods.

Table 3: Decreasing water table level of some of the prominent areas of Lucknow reflects the aftermath of a growing population.

AREA	MAY 2003 (IN METRE)	MAY 2006 (IN METRE)	MAY 2009 (EXPECTED TABLE IN METRE)
Indira Nagar	21.49	24.62	27.75
Nirala Nagar	26.30	28.45	30.60
Aliganj	16.06	18.02	20.00
Gomti Nagar	15.45	20.45	25.45
Mahanagar	24.05	26.53	29.01
New Hyderabad	19.21	20.77	21.70
Vikas Nagar	22.06	24.77	27.48
Lucknow Univ.	24.95	26.98	29.01

The going down of the water table has triggered several problems related to it, as the occurrence of warm land, land subsidence or cracks on the land surface have increased in many areas in northern India: the area of perennial rivers. The decrease in the moisture content has left the areas affected with severe soil erosion and they have also adversely affected the food production.

- **Pollution.** Pollution has been the end product of many of the human activities that have created a lot of changes in the ecosystem. The causes that have been the factors of the pollution are also the motive behind the development of the fragile ecosystem and pollution as the end result, has been playing a decisive role in further degrading the already frail ecosystem.

- **Decline in the Availability of Resources.** There is a growing imbalance between the demands of human population and the resources that support human life. Fresh water, land, finite resources like fossil energy are depleting very fast because of the increased pressure to meet the growing demand of an expanding population. According to a study, most replacement of eroded agricultural land is now coming from marginal and forest land. We are gradually losing the much needed resources to the need of development as many of the resources are non- renewable in nature.The decline in the availability of the resources has further stressed the condition as the demand for the resources have often been seen going up resulting in conflict over the declining natural resources.

- **High Price Rise.** With the passing of time and the dwindling available resources, the demand of the available resources is rising at a very fast rate. Natural resources as known are limited in supply and the reinforcement of these limited resources takes a very long time, to develop. Still, with the passing of time and the dawn of the new era, pollution and the over exploitation of the limited resources have further limited the availability of these resources for human beings. The resultant impact of this has been that the price attached to these natural resources has further increased as the demand of these resources has not subsided as man is dependent upon many of these resources for his survival and has not been able to cut down on the demand of many available natural resources. The demand and supply of natural resources and the over exploitation of these, have become a vicious circle.

- **Regular Occurrence of Natural and Man Made Disasters.** The change in the ecosystem brought in by the external forces often tends to instigate the rate of disasters, as the environment is not able to resist the changes caused by its weak resilient power. Often the changes which start a chain of activities as the external forces role in modifying the environment, often do not stop and that leads to a further decline of the resilient power and the occurrence of the disaster becomes more regular.

- **Poverty.** Depleting natural resources and an increasing demand of the same resource, have created a big scarcity of the resources. The price rise of the most essential resources has laid more stress on the economical condition of the people, as the region is often affected by change and is unable to support the people depending upon it. As desertification the resultant impact of land degradation has left many farmers landless and poverty stricken because the infertility of the soil is unable to produce good or any amount of any crop.

Study Area

Bundelkhand, the study area of my paper, occupies almost 70,000 square kilometers of the central plains in India. The Bundelkhand stretches over twelve districts of northern Madhya Pradesh (MP) and five districts of southern Uttar Pradesh. Bounded to the north by the Yamuna River and to the south by the hills of the Vindhyan Plateau, the region presents a unique set of geological and geographical characteristics which have had a profound effect on the human development in the region, as well as on the country, as a whole.

The impact of human activity on the region has until now been unsustainable. Bundelkhand has been seen as a region suffering from acute ecological degradation, as logging and mining activities over the past several centuries have denuded the landscape and facilitated the erosion of the fragile soils. Additional population and livestock pressures, which are already high, have only served to aggravate the problem. Expanding ravine lands, especially in the northern area, are already threatening local farmland and can have serious consequences on the socio-economic condition of the natives.

Access to abundant water resources has always been one of the major environmental concerns in the region. Irregular rainfall has often led to either drought or flood conditions with consequent effects on the natural and human environment. The increasing dependence on groundwater resources has led to a lowering of the groundwater table in places where withdrawals have exceeded recharge. The decline in groundwater levels has further undermined water security in the region and accelerated desertification and erosion. It has been noticed that out of 822 development blocks in 71 districts of the state, the ground water level in over 450 blocks was found to be in the category of the seriously affected, the scenario giving sleepless nights to the state authorities as told by the SGWD authorities. In a joint survey by the Central Ground Water Department and the SGWD recently showed that the situation of ground water in 22 development blocks of 13 districts was found to be 'over-exploited' and 'critical', whereas, the water level in 75 development blocks of 29 districts was 'semi-critical'. In a worse scenario, this year, ground water level in 38 blocks was found to be 'over-exploited' and 'critical' while in 88 blocks, the level is in the category of 'semi-critical'. The over exploitation of the water resources at present has erupted another major problem of crack formation on the fragile land of Bundelkhand. It was first reported in the dailies in 2007 on 11 August that 5 km away from the village Jigni of the district Rath 'the earth had cracked to the length of 350m and it was about 2.5 feet to 8 feet broad and 35 to 60 feet deep. The incident was again noticed this year i.e. 2008 in the month of June when 18 regions of Bundelkhand reported land cracks.There were 13 in Hamirpur and 5 in the Jalaun district. The cracks and land subsidence were noticed after the region received an unprecedented first shower after four years of drought at the end of June and the beginning of July. This was basically due to the fact as quoted by P N Razdan, Senior Deputy Director General, GSI, northern region. "Since Bundelkhand received deficient rainfall for the last four to five years, excessive exploitation of groundwater over this period has created a tension in the aquifer. Now, with the sudden recharge of water due to incessant rains, fissures have opened up." The formation of cracks has further laid stress upon the drought affected region of Bundelkhand and a proof of its turning into a fragile zone of India.

Major Findings

The analysis of the report published in the dailies and news being highlighted in the media spoke of the fact that undue pressure or the practicing of the unsustainable methods of debilitating had an unenviable effect on human beings and a debilitating impact upon the ecosystem. The weak homeostatic mechanism of the fragile ecosystem has given way to various problems.

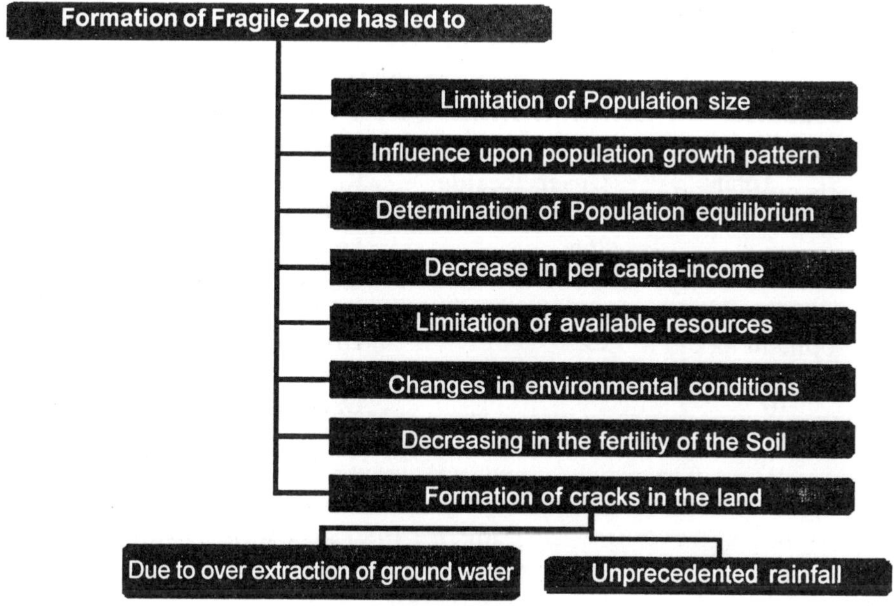

Fig. 3. Problems of fragile zone

- The impact of a fragile zone on the population structure of the affected area has been mainly due to the *out-migration* of the people specifically young male members of the family in search of jobs to support their families and this has lead to a change in the population structure and sex ratio of the region; as the population basically consists of old, female and children.
- As the areas affected were mainly the rural areas where farming is the main source of income the formation of fragile zones has affected the production and in return the per-capita income, of the people.
- Limitation of available resources has been due mainly to the over-exploitation of the resources. In Bundelkhand it has been mainly the extraction of ground water without proper replenishment of the same which has led to an over exploitation of the same. For the irrigation purpose of irrigation, further limiting the available resource. *Overuse, encroachment* and *improper management* of the water resources have had an impounding impact upon the available resources.
- *The excessive extraction* of water led to the formation of cracks as told by Ms.Vibhuti Rai a professor with the Lucknow University's geology department. "Owing to the loss of groundwater, the soil at the affected sites has lost its cohesive property that tends to keep it intact. With the loss of this property, the soil is not able to bind with the water molecules. This resulted in the cracks." But later on, after a heavy spell of rainfall the condition did

Dry repositories

Most water bodies in Bundelkhand (UP) are in disrepair

Water Sources	Total	Unserviceable	Reasons
Wells	486	266	Less rainfall, low impounding of water in wells, no maintenance
Ponds	56	29	Drying up, encroachment
Rivers	6	4	Drying up, no dredging and ouverts/misuse
Drains	26	25	Disrepair, embankments, encroachments and disrepair

Source: Study on Bundelkhand's water repositories by CASA

Fig. 4.

improve but the improvement came with problems of land crack and land subsidence this time due to the opening of the *fissures*.

- The fertility of the soil was also affected due to removal of the top most layer of the soil by the *wind erosion*. This was basically due to the fact that the soil had lost its moisture content. This also had an impact on the turbidity of the water bodies due to the deposition of the soil in the water bodies.

Methods that can be adopted for a gainful development can be:

- Practising a rain harvesting method for the replenishment of the ground water.
- Adopt soil and moisture conservation measures terracing, bunding etc.
- Review of the progress of the implementation of ongoing schemes and programmes connected with the conservation and development of land resources and soils.
- Enhance people's participation in fragile ecosystem development programmes by creating mass awareness. This can be effectively achieved by strategically evolving a layout for future education based on experiences of best practices to safeguard the fragile ecosystems from the different parts of the world.

Sustainable Method

It mainly and basically emphasizes meeting the needs of the present without compromising those of the future. To attain this goal, appropriate technology should be adopted to attain the goal of sustainable development that would further help in combating the problem.

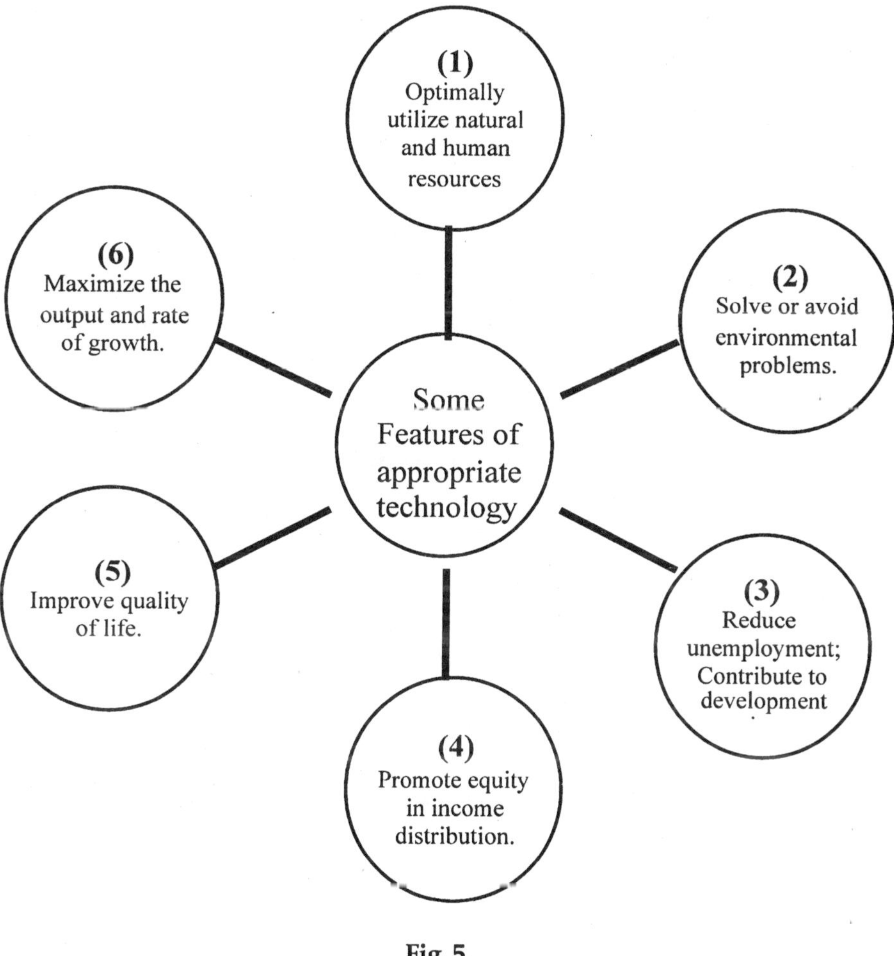

Fig. 5.

This technological strand of environmental movement strives for a working synthesis of the different mediums of resource exploitation i.e. agriculture, industry etc. A change in the technological approach in these sectors can have a direct and lasting impact in sustaining the degrading environment.As in the solution of every problem so in the solution of the problem of a fragile ecosystem, the government and the general masses have to come together in framing and implementing the precise managerial methods. Together we have done and together we can.

Conclusion

Many policies have been framed and many policies are being framed to combat the problem of the growth of a fragile zone but the framing of the policies has been faulty. One such policy of the government is a massive plantation drive in the Bundelkhand region with an estimated expenditure of over Rs. 450 crore by the forestery department. It is all set to go down the drain for the simple reason that the entire exercise is being undertaken in an unplanned and unscientific manner. As before, the plantation of saplings has been planted with no proper soil analysis undertaken, and secondly the saplings selected do not suit the rock terrain of Bundelkhand as the suitable species was that of a eucalyptus, babul, jatropah etc but the species identified were khera, mango, bakain. Therefore there is an urgent need to think and plan emphatically and scientifically for the proper management of the affected area. Now is the time to protect this because region it is on the verge of losing its resilient power, and before it becomes too late for a land to sustain the needs of human beings. On an average, the environmental management should include (i) adoption of methods that can curtail and regulate the changes that have been taking place in the environment and (ii) judicious and gainful utilization of natural resources for socio-economical development [i.e. sustainable development].

References

1. Aplin, *et. al* (1995), *Global Environmental Crises: An Australian Perspective,* Oxford University Press.
2. Cunningham WP & Saigo BW (1992), *Environmental Science: A Global concern, Second Edition.* Wm. C. Brown Publishers, IA., USA.
3. Primack, R.B., (1993), *Essentials of Conservation Biology,* Sinauer Asociates inc. Publishing, Mass., USA.
4. Planning Commision, Government of India, *Study on Bundelkhan.* Available at http://planningcommision.nic.in/.
5. White, I.D.,.Mottershead, D.N., & Harrison, S.J., (1992), *Environmental Systems: An Introductory Text, second edition,* Chapman & Hall, London.

10

Meeting the Challenges of the Booming Tourism Sector in Mauritius

Foolmaun Rajendra Kumar, Chamilall Dinkar Sharma, Priya Thaunoo-Chady, Moonawwara Begum Outim and Amit Jheengut

Introduction

The Republic of Mauritius is a democratic and prosperous small island state whose entire population of 1.2 million inhabitants, has ancestral origins from Europe, Africa, India and China. Mauritius achieved independence in 1968 in the wake of the silent revolution without violence and with very little opposition. Successive political masters have kept all the island's myriad communities in peace and this has been instrumental in working successfully towards the country's economical and social welfare. The Mauritian society is a fast changing one as it emerges from a developing country into a newly developed country with inevitable and apparent changes in our lifestyles, consumption and production patterns. The standard of living in Mauritius is now ranked with the developed countries and there is greater access to health care, education, domestic water supply and other facilities. Moreover, Mauritius is engaging in internationally inspired developments in line with the Millennium Development Goals whilst struggling to survive in the global market.

Indeed Mauritius has stepped into the 21st century with important economical challenges especially with the 36% reduction in the guaranteed price of sugars.The dismantling of the multi-fibre agreement and the rising price of petroleum products has culminated in increasing our economical vulnerability. The Mauritian Government has prepared an economical restructuring plan to consolidate the existing pillars of the economy and to develop new areas of growth such as the Integrated Resort Scheme, Pharmaceutical products, Information and Communication Technology, Marine Industry, better Medical facilities and Tourism.

The Government of Mauritius, as well as the private sector, is fully conscious that the long-term socio-economical success of the country is not possible without environmental sustainability; environmental concerns have been placed high on the developmental agenda. Programmes or projects which are to be implemented are being considered carefully to focus on growth, poverty alleviation, environmental management, gender and governance issues. It is clear that the condition of the environment is a key driver for creativity, innovation and competitiveness across the world and investment in environmental sustainability leads to higher competitiveness. The potential for growth in the tourism industry and associated Integrated Resort Schemes (IRS) and projects exist and in this line, it is of crucial importance that the preservation and protection of the natural resources and environmental qualities that nurture this industry, be safeguarded so that the country can have that competitive edge.

Furthermore, as a Small Island Developing State (SIDS), Mauritius is constrained in its development by a multiplicity of factors such as: small domestic market, limited resources, limited arable land, ecological fragility, proneness to natural disasters such as cyclones, rising sea-levels, tsunamis, high infrastructure costs, narrow production base, high costs of transport to export to overseas markets and a heavy dependence on international trade. Moreover, the island's fragile ecosystem is threatened with a host of environmental issues such as solid waste disposal, biodiversity loss, degradation of coastal zones, fresh water pollution, air pollution, hazardous waste disposal, mainly resulting from unprecedented economic, social development, industrialization, and unsustainable production and consumption patterns.

Though various concrete measures have been taken to remedy or curb down the environmental pollution, a considerable effort still needs yet to be deployed. Environmental issues are frequently complex and contested. Research, invention, innovation and adaptation are all required. None is possible without a clear understanding of the ecological and policy issues and the different linkages involved. Without a firm, educated basis of knowledge and understanding, progress on environmental issues becomes haphazard, uncertain and unlikely. In fact, the ability of Mauritius to meet environmental threats is inextricably linked with the priority it places on effective environmental education. One of the key areas to be tackled on the agenda for the sustainable management of the environmental assets, national heritage and natural resources, includes mass sensitization and public awareness raising on environmental issues so as to inculcate environmental stewardship at all levels of society and sections of the economy.

Environmental education for Sustainable Development plays a key role in raising awareness and bringing about a change in attitudes, values and behaviour. It can help the citizens of Mauritius to achieve the vision of a sustainable society with a sustainable natural environment as a pre-requisite. All sections of society, not just those with formal education, are stakeholders in EESD. As UNESCO has established the period from 2005 to 2014 as the 'Decade of Education for Sustainable Development', there are opportunities for the Ministry of Education and Human Resources, which is responsible for the formal level of education, to reorient the education system so that values inherent in sustainable development are integrated into all aspects of learning, so that an increased quality of teaching and learning is fostered, resulting in a positive change in behaviour.

Pressures of Tourism on Environmental Sectors

Tourism is holding its growth in Mauritius at a time when the price of sugar is falling and our textile industry is facing competition with emerging market operators like Bangladesh, Madagascar, China, Kenya and Sri Lanka. However, if not properly planned and managed, tourism could significantly degrade the environment through the following main pressures:

Land Resources

Mauritius is densely populated and has a limited area of land suitable for development. The current pattern of land use is illustrated below:

High quality land, particularly in prime coastal areas, is scarce and is sought after by a variety of competing users. Land planning failures in the past, coupled with an inadequate control of development, have led to the admixture of incompatible development, encroachment into environmentally sensitive areas, backfilling of wetlands and the conversion of prime agricultural land. With the coming of two million tourists on the island, there will be a high demand for land for the construction of hotels, integrated resorts, bungalows and therefore a high pressure on land resources. It is feared that the pressure to build more hotels will require the conversion of prime agricultural land which will lead to rocketing prices for land thus making it unaffordable for middle and low income Mauritian citizens to have land for their own housing estates.

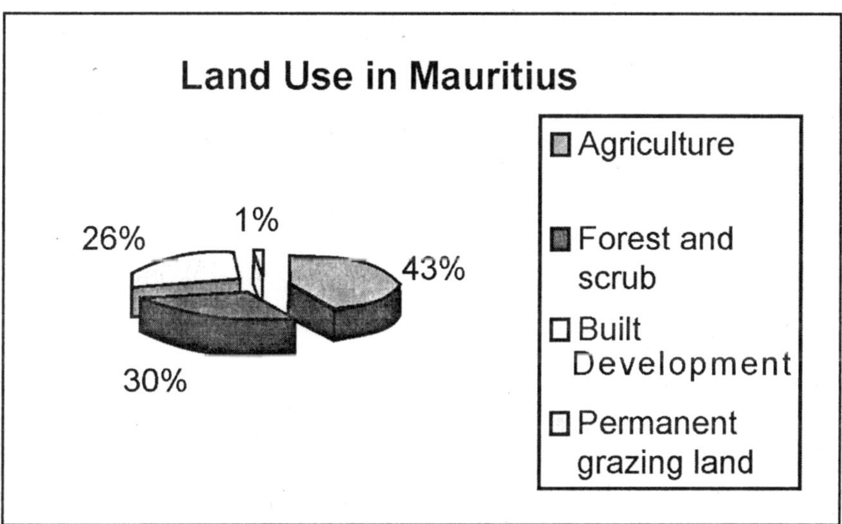

Water Resources

The present usable freshwater potential has been estimated at 1 300 Mm^3 per year (equivalent to 1 083 m^3/person/year) and as such, Mauritius can be classified within the class of countries suffering water stress and scarcity (UNDP, 1998). Added to the already high population density and the heavy demand for irrigation and the industrial sector, the tourism sector will definitely intensify the water stress, especially when we know that the target set by the Government is to welcome 2 million tourists by 2015.

The projected total demand for water by 2030 is 1200 Mm^3 per year. This is in excess of projected supplies and close to utilizing a renewable freshwater potential of 1 300 Mm^3 per year. Though the potential yield from existing water resources is achieved, this would still leave the country in a water stress by UN standards (Anon, 2005). These conditions of water stress and scarcity would restrict economical and social development and pose a serious overall challenge for water management. In addition, there will be a problem of an uneven distribution of water to the general population and a need for this problem also to be tackled.

In order to sustain an economical development and improve the quality of life, water management will become an increasing problem for the future challenge and it is feared that climate change with a sea level rise, would make the situation worse. Moreover, the Mauritius Island faces periodic drought, making it a continual challenge for the Central Water Authority to provide water to all the sectors namely household, industrial, agricultural and the tourist industry. Inadequate and insufficient storage facilities, outdated infrastructure and leakages are the main constraints for the development of this sector and this has to be addressed urgently by the Government.Although water supply networks have already been extended across the whole island, it is not expected that the increasing demands for water will be fully met. In this line, to be able to fulfil the water requirement, substantial investment in the rehabilitation and renewal of old distribution mains in towns and for some provision for new resources, treatment capacity, storage facilities and water mains to provide an acceptable year round service to the whole population, is required.

Energy Resources

Mauritius imports its fossil fuels, which is the main primary commercial energy. The cost, source and usage of energy has become a major concern for the Small Island Developing States and warrants careful energy planning. In 2003, 77% of the total energy requirement was met from imported fuels, while the remaining 23% was supplied from indigenous sources, hydro and bagasse principally. Programmes for expanding renewable energy sources are not keeping pace with the increasing demand.Energy management covers energy supply and energy demand. Sectoral use of energy is dominated by the growth in transport with its impact on air pollution. The increase in vehicles is also associated with the increase in CO_2 emissions, more traffic congestion and longer travel times.The major challenge facing Mauritius is therefore the additional energy resources which need to be supplied to the targeted tourism industry in terms of the energy requirement by the additional hotels, villas, traffic etc.

Coastal Zone

Coastal and marine resources are of vital importance to the socio-economic development. The coastal zone of Mauritius is under growing pressure from both sea based and land based activities. Increasingly over the last thirty years, with the development of international tourism through long haul jet airlines, the coastal zone has experienced a very rapid development and mounting ecological pressure. Moreover, development associated with the expansion of tourism has resulted in the construction of a large number of jetties, slipways, piers and breakwaters around the island for fishing boats, pleasure boats and yachts. Numerous groins and sea walls have been privately built in front of beachfront hotels and private villas to protect the beaches from erosion, but evidence suggests that these structures promote rather than inhibit, beach erosion, leaving uprooted trees, exposed roots and visibly narrowing beaches.

The targeted 2 million tourists will imply construction of additional hotels, villas, jetties, slipways etc. It will equally imply more beach games, pleasures and leisure sport activities within the lagoon.

Solid Waste

Rapid economical growth achieved through industrialization and urbanization, coupled with a general improvement in the standard of living, has contributed significantly to the quantities of waste being produced. Today, some 1 200 tonnes of solid waste is generated daily (1 kg waste per capita) and the cost of the collection, transportation and disposal costs around US $ 19 million annually. The only disposal route of solid waste is via the sole landfill which is currently reaching capacity. Owing to land scarcity and to numerous complaints from inhabitants residing near the landfill area, selection for an alternative landfill site has become almost impractical. Thus the government is confronted with a serious problem regarding the disposal of the waste. With the targeted 2 million tourists, the government should cater for the additional waste from these tourists. The Government will not only have to put in place additional waste disposal facilities but will also need a further deployment of resources for the collection, transportation and disposal of the waste.

Biodiversity

The flora and fauna of Mauritius evolved through millions of years of isolation into a unique biological resource. Much has disappeared over the past 400 years of human settlement and much of the remainder is threatened and vulnerable. Only 1.6% of the total land area contains original native species as constant pressure for land development has resulted in the clearing of the natural ecosystem.Though bold measures have been initiated, it is still feared that the development of land in order to accommodate 2 million tourists may further contribute to the loss of our biodiversity. One way perhaps to surmount this problem, would be to promote ecotourism, which will ensure the protection of our flora and fauna.

Advantages of the Tourist Industry

Tourism is one of the world's largest industries and one of the fastest growing economic sectors. This industry is presently the third pillar of the Economy after the EPZ manufacturing sector and agriculture and has been a key factor in the development of Mauritius.

The tourist industry, without any doubt, is a major provider of job opportunities both in terms of direct and indirect employment. For example, the arts and crafts industries are also flourishing parallel to the tourist sector. According to the available statistics, this sector seems to be the most promising in terms of job creation at the moment. With the increasing number of tourists visiting the island, the sector is viewed as a major foreign exchange earner which in turn provides the possibility for other development in the country. In view of providing up to date facilities for the tourists, the Government in collaboration with private sectors, has hastened the development of the infrastructure such as roads, recreational areas, improvement of beaches and a sewerage system which is also benefiting the local population. In addition to these positive attributes of Tourism on the island, the inflow of tourists may be regarded as beneficial since it allows an exchange of cultural views, ideas and experiences between foreigners and locals. Regular contacts with tourists from different parts of the world, also help the locals to develop their language and communication skills.

Impacts of the Tourist Industry

In December 2007, the New York Times, the largest paper circulated in America included 'Mauritius in its list of the **50 most interesting destination to go to in 2008'**. Indeed, the number of tourists visiting the island has been constantly increasing for the past few years and the Government of Mauritius is putting all its effort into being able to welcome 2 million tourists annually by the year 2015. However, the economical and touristic boom are both threatening the very beauty that makes Mauritius such an attractive place in which to work and live. Recently, the National Geographic Traveller Magazine sounded a warning bell about the impact of such development on Mauritius and other islands and countries around the world. A panel of 522 experts rated the SIDS and found that the majority of them are under stress as far as environmental issues are concerned being given that small island states are more vulnerable. Mauritius was rated '*moderate trouble, with a mixture of positives and negatives*'.A study carried out by the Ministry of Tourism in 1998, revealed that Mauritians had shown their concern for the fact that the majority of the hotels are along the coast line thus hampering the access of the Mauritians themselves to their own quality beaches.

Recently some Non Governmental Organizations have started raising their voices against the allocation of the best beaches for the construction of hotels and bungalows by the private sectors. The pressure on such sites has become so high that there has been a dramatic increase in the land values, making it quite impossible for locals to acquire such land.From the environmental point of view, hotels and bungalows are considered as a major source of noise pollution emanating especially from live music being played as entertainment.

Conclusion

The Government should undertake a study to determine the Ecological Footprint of the Tourist Industry as it is at present and also for the forecasted 2 million tourists which have been set as a target with a carrying capacity for the Tourist Industry to see if it can withstand the number without having a major environmental impact. This will be used as a tool by the Government, as far as the policy decisions are concerned, relating to the Tourist Industry in Mauritius for the future.

References

1. Human Development Reports (UNDP)—1988, http://hdr.undp.org/en/reports/global/hdr1998/

11

Mining As an Environmental Hazard

HELINA JOLLY

Introduction

Mining is second only to agriculture as the world's oldest and most important industry. Mining is an integral part of human society. Human civilizations are held strongly by the pillars of mining and minerals. The socio-economical evolution of mining and human culture is depicted well by the nomenclature of these epochs: Stone Age, Bronze Age, Iron Age and it is also a sequence that shows the increasing complexity of society's relationship with mining. The contribution of mining has played a big part in the development of civilization, more than is usually recognized by the average citizen. In fact, products of the mineral industry pervade the lives of all members of our industrialized society, but this dependence is not a green signal for the industry to break and bend laws. India being one of the developing countries is struggling hard to maintain its clean environment image. Any development which is not based on the principles of Sustainable Development will put the survival of the people of our nation at stake. The permanent damage caused by the mining industry will resonate in the spheres of biodiversity, health and natural resources. This, in the long run will disfigure the beautiful faces of development.

History of Mining

Mining began with the Paleolithic people, perhaps 300,000 years ago, during the Stone Age, when flint implements were sought for agricultural and construction purposes. Primitive miners first extracted and fashioned the stone raw materials that they needed from deposits at the surface, but by the beginning of the New Stone Age (c. 40,000 BC), they began to mine underground as well. Early people relied upon wood, bone, stone, and ceramics to fashion tools, weapons, and utensils. Civilization was advanced by the discovery of abundant supplies of high-quality flint in northern France and in the chalk beds of southern England. The culture and civilizations advanced and along with that, human needs also increased. Man learned the secrets of smelting and metallurgy, just as food metals became a part of human life. Then came the greatest revolution in human culture, the Industrial Revolution. The machine age, introduced by the Industrial Revolution of the late 18th century, also required minerals as raw materials and as a source of energy. Industrial power thus became a measure of political and military power, and the exploration for attainable mineral resources extended to nearly all parts of the world. Nation's economies became interdependent. The final result was that political and commercial control over mineral resources and their distribution played a leading role both in the maintenance and destruction of world peace. The mining industry also opened new venues of employment too. The economical development that started in the Neolithic periods has led to the modern developments which had their base fixed on minerals.

Indian Scenario of Mining and Related Industry

An overview of the Indian mining sector can be summarized by the following details. Mining leases occupy about 0.7 million hectares which is 0.21 per cent of the total land mass of the country. It consists of four fuel minerals, 11 metallic, 53 nonmetallic and 22 minor minerals. It operates more than 3100 mines which consist of 572 coal mines, 2500 metalliferrous mines and a score of other small mines. The Indian mining industry gives employment to about 1.1 million people. The following column gives the percentage contribution of India in the world resources.

The export value of the minerals and contribution to GDP (Gross Development Product)

In Million Tonnes		
India's Resources as a % of World Resources	**Key Resources**	**India Resources**
10	Coal (including lignite)	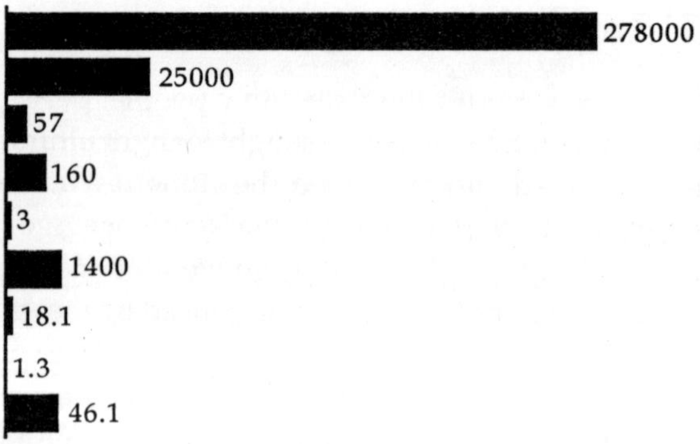 278000 25000 57 160 3 1400 18.1 1.3 46.1
13	Iron Ore	
7	Chromite	
3	Manganese Ore	
0.3	Copper	
4	Bauxite	
11	Kaolin	
1	Lead	
30	Ilmenite	

Mining Industry - GDP Contribution

	2002-03	2003-04	2004-05	2005-06	2006-07
GDP growth rate of Country	3.8%	8.5%	7.5%	9.0%	9.4%
GDP growth rate of Country	8.8%	3.1%	7.5%	3.6%	5.1%
GDP growth rate of Country	2.8%	2.5%	3.0%	2.8%	2.7%

Source: Compiled from Planning commission reports

Mineral Production and Export Value

	2002-03	2003-04	2004-05	2005-06	2006-07
Coal	341	361	383	407	430
Bauxite (000 tonnes)	9867	10957	11964	12335	13075
Iron Ore	99	121	146	154	172
Chromite (000 tonnes)	3069	3199	3621	3423	4101
Copper (000 tonnes)	152	143	137	124	115

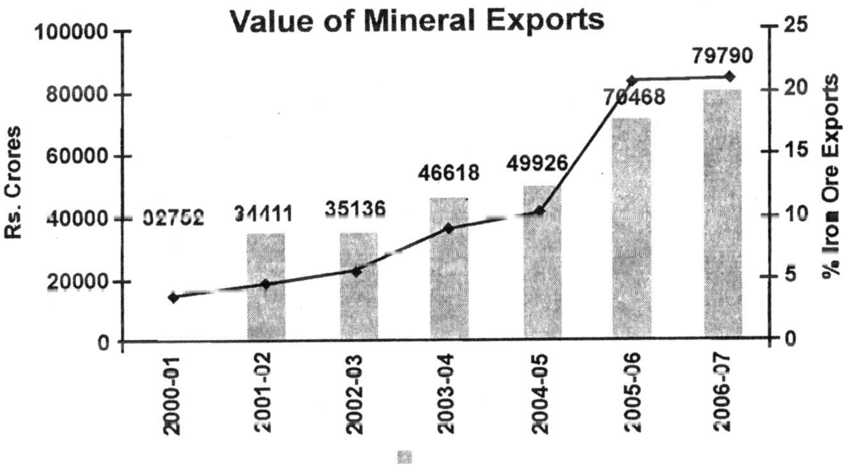

• Source: Annual Reports Ministry of Mines

The Total Value of Mineral Production for the period 2006-07 is estimated to be Rs. 87866 crores, a 4.67% increase over the previous year. Fuel Mineral including coal, oil and lignite accounts for 72% of the total value of mineral production. Iron ore exports account for 21% of the total export value for the year 2006-07. As Indian mining moves into the 21st century with new technologies and innovations, we are witness to an unparalleled growth in the industry.

Reasons for the Sudden Boom in Mining Industry

The new breed of human beings(*Homo sapiens sapiens*) with highly developed grey and white matter has the principles of selfishness lining their mind. We human beings have locked ourselves into highly consumptive lifestyles which is one of the most important reasons for the sudden boom in the mining industry. Demand promotes any product , the direct relation of supply and demand explains the reason for the flourishing of the mining industries. The modern man has turned so much more consumption friendly that he is putting his own survival at stake. Apart from that the mining industry is one of the largest industries providing employment to almost 59% of the population of the world . Studies conducted by economists, mineral specialists, and geologists throughout the world came up with some disturbing data. 50% of all newly mined gold is taken from native lands. It accounts for 10% of the world's energy consumption. India, the leading consumer of gold in the world , accounts for 800 metric tonnes per year. In the United States, over 50 billion beverage cans are wasted each year- that is a quarter of a million in scrap metal valued at $750 million.We busy and ambitious humans do not have time to ponder on these details.

Mining in General

The world's first mining textbook, *De Re Metallica,* by Georgius Agricola in 1556, contains an excellent description of the destruction caused by mining in Germany. To study the impacts of mining, we need to analyze the methods of carrying out mining.The initial steps of mining include the indentification of the ore deposit and bringing it to the surface.It is cheaper to blast away the soil and rock surface rather than digging with an undershaft. This is what results is open pits that obliterate the surrounding landscape and open up vast craters.These produce waste rubble . Globally , two thirds of all metals are mined in open pits and that figure is rising.Once the mineral is obtained it has to be processed.Depending on the mineral, the processing varies producing immense quantities of waste.It is because the amount of mineral, even in the high grade mineral ore is just a few fractions compared with the ore.All this waste is then discarded into various sources like seas and rivers, thus producing a vicious cycle of pollution and polluted materials.The Mining industry is one of the leading industries that emits toxic waste materials.These include heavy metals like Arsenic, Mercury, Selenium and Lead.

The Hazards of Mining can be Direct or Indirect

It was only in the last two decades that public concern has been raised for the environmental problems associated with this industry.The most severe environmental hazards commonly occur adjacent to a mining operation and those most likely affected are the employees.Some of the hazards are direct and so all countries have a stringent legislation and control to safeguard mine workers. This normally protects the general public , either directly or indirectly.There are many hazardous aspects of mining but even then, sometimes the public safety can be endangered on occasions through negligence or unusual or unforeseen circumstances. Some of them can be sudden failure in the reservoir , waste dumps. Eg: Aberfan disaster in south Wales.

The use of explosives in mining causes the accidental release of toxic effluent due to unforeseen reasons into regions of human habitation.Other than these, mining has also many indirect effects on the wellbeing of human beings. In spite of studies, only little is known about the long term effects of exposure to some aspects of mining. Air and water pollution caused by the uncontrolled emission of toxic materials which are byproducts of mining cause some of the long term hazards and have developed due to the over exposure to noise and dust. One of the other indirect effects is the damage to property, crops and livestock. Nowadays new problems are arising due to the over exploitation of the resources resulting in the exhaustion of ores. Some of the environmental hazards due to mining can drain out the national capital like river, forest, and wildlife. These issues have to be studied more carefully for heading a country towards sustainable development.

1. Effects of mining in the bio- cultural diversity: Extinctions happen by evolution about 10,000 times faster than natural replacement. Natural species represent a living library of options for adapting to local and global environmental changes, on which future generations depend. Humans have already destroyed one quarter of all bird species in the past 2000 years. Extinction now proceeds at the rate of 1,000 and is expected to rise to10,000 species per year, or 3-30 per day! Most will be insects because they comprise 98% of all species. A normal extinction rate is 1 out of 5000 mammals every 200 years, but since 1600, at least 484 animals and 654 plants have become extinct, mostly on islands and in lakes. Mammals die out 40x faster, birds 1000x than normal. 1% of all birds and mammals become extinct in the 20th century. Many experts think that 30-50% of all species will become extinct in the 21st century, based on calculations of habitat loss. Mining has been happening on a large scale in areas of the country which are ecologically sensitive . It is found to effect the population of many endangered species of plant and animals. An overlay of the forest and mineral maps of our country India, show that almost all of the major concentrations of bauxite, coal and iron are concentrated in forest areas. Some of the areas affected by mining are the western ghats, eastern ghats, Aravallis and the western Himalayas. They are destroying the catchment areas providing the water security to millions of people. At least 90% of wildlife sanctuaries and national parks are threatened. Mining in these areas is also affecting the culturally and economically fragile areas. The fact that there is an overlap between our forest reserves and mining areas, compounds the situation. Culturally and economically, fragile communities residing in these areas, including the adivasis or the tribal groups, are seriously affected by mining.

   Some of the mining is or will be causing permanant damage to Indian diversity both from a cultural and a biological viewpoint. The marble mines of Rajasthan the coal mines of Meghalaya and the iron ore mines of Karnataka come under this category.

2. Effects of mining in the hydrosphere: Water is one of the most important abiotic factors required for the survival of organisms. The disposal of the mining waste into the river's ecosystem has been one of the common ways followed by the mining sector of India. This lead to the clogging and poisoning of the aquatic ecosystems. 20% of the known species are marine, but they comprise 80% of the phyla. Many marine species (bacteria, viruses, etc.) have been poorly studied. Several lifestyles are totally absent on land, such as filterfeeding. Marine foodwebs are more complex than terrestrial ones. There is less spatial complexity (trees/coral), less variation (temperature, etc) thus more sensitivity to environmental changes. The basic nature of water, that of dissolving many chemicals, makes water pollution a threat to marine organisms. Since nutrients in the ocean are naturally hard to come by, many marine organisms are capable of concentrating these, including human-made chemicals. The chemistry of pollution reacts with the chemistry of life. This also affects the wetland biodiversity of the area too. Mining industrial practices, the illegal dumping of waste into the oceans affects the marine biology too. Through mining and soil erosion, humans moved 42 billion tonnes of earth, compared with volcanoes above and under water, 44 billion. By 1980, mining moved more rock than natural erosion worldwide. Mining creates a profound disturbance to the soil and subsoil. It causes mud to run off into rivers. Minerals, once safely locked underground, now become exposed and poison the environment. Mines in areas of high rainfall are more likely to encounter water quality problems. One of the most common causes of tailings in dam failures is "overtopping," or overflow during high rainfall. According to ICOLD, the major reason for tailings impoundment failures in the past 60 years has been "lack of control of the hydrological regime," particularly in flood-prone areas (ICOLD, 2001: 31). High rainfall may also interact with waste and ore piles at a mine site, creating acid drainage and the release of toxic metal sand reagents. Rainfall is highest in the tropics and temperate coastal zones. Mining in other areas may also result in serious water quality problems.

3. Health hazards of mining: **Physical hazards** Traumatic injury remains a significant problem and ranges from the trivial to the fatal [3,4]. Common causes of fatal injury include rock fall, fires, explosions, mobile equipment accidents, falls from height, entrapment and electrocution. Less common but recognized causes of fatal injury include flooding of underground workings, wet-fill release from collapsed bulkheads and air blast from block caving failure. The systematic application of risk management techniques has contributed to a substantial decline in injury frequency rates in developed nations. Further improvement, however, is required to reach rates tolerable to the broader community. Noise is almost ubiquitous in mining. It is generated by drilling, blasting, cutting, materials handling, ventilation, crushing, conveying and ore processing. Controlling noise has proven difficult in mining and noise-induced hearing loss remains common. Heat and humidity are encountered in tropical locations and in deep underground mines, where the virgin rock temperatures and air temperatures increase with depth, due principally to the geothermal gradient and auto-compression of the air column . Fatal heat stroke has been a significant problem in the South African deep underground gold mines and heat exhaustion remains a contemporary problem in deep

underground mining . Malaria rubra, colloquially also known as 'mucker's mange' is problematic in deep underground mines. Whole body vibration commonly experienced whilst operating mobile equipment, such as load-haul-dump units, trucks, scrapers and diggers. This can cause or exacerbate pre-existing spinal disorders. Poorly maintained roads and vehicles contribute to the problem. Hand-arm vibration syndrome is also encountered with the use of vibrating tools such as air leg rock drills. Radon exposure in underground mining has increased the risk of lung cancer, but is now generally controlled by mine ventilation. Solar ultraviolet exposures in surface mining operations are likely to contribute to the occurrence of squamous cell and basal cell carcinomas, although this is an inference drawn from studies of outdoor workers in other industries. Occupations involving substantial outdoor work appear not to be associated with an increased risk of melanoma. Infra-red exposures in pyrometallurgical processes contribute to heat stress and may induce cataracts. Electromagnetic fields are encountered in electrolytic smelting and refining processes. Barometric pressure is elevated in deep underground mines and reduced at high altitude mines in South America. Chronic intermittent hypoxia at altitude has been reported to induce physiological adaptations and symptoms of benign acute mountain sickness (AMS) in mine workers . High altitude pulmonary oedema (HAPO) and high altitude cerebral oedema (HACO) were not seen. Increased barometric pressures in deep mines increase air temperatures, increase convective heat exchange and reduce sweat evaporation rates.

Chemical hazards: Crystalline silica has long been a serious hazard in mining, with the risk of silicosis at its worst during dry drilling late in the nineteenth century [38]. Silicosis has been subject to considerable investigation. Axial water-fed rock drills, wet techniques, ventilation, enclosed cabins and respiratory protection have largely controlled silicosis in developed nations. However, silicosis remains a problem in developing nations and silico-tuberculosis is rampant in Africa, where the high prevalence of HIV infection among miners increases the risk. Prolonged exposure to crystalline silica can also cause chronic obstructive pulmonary disease. There is some evidence for accelerated silicosis in rheumatoid arthritis and of renal disease following prolonged silica exposure. There is also now good evidence that prolonged exposure to crystalline silica increases the risk of lung cancer. Coal dust has also been a serious hazard in mining, causing coal workers' pneumoconiosis or 'black lung' and chronic obstructive pulmonary disease . The risks have now been largely controlled in developed nations by dust suppression, ventilation and respiratory protection. Vigilance is, however, required to maintain effective control. Although largely historic in the developed world, the mining and milling of asbestos has caused a legacy of asbestos-related diseases, which continue to occur today. Diesel particulate exposures occur in underground mines because of diesel powered mobile equipment, used primarily for drilling and haulage. Diesel particulate is an IARC Group 2A and is a probable human carcinogen and several epidemiological studies from other industries suggest that there is an excess risk of lung cancer . Control measures include the use of low sulphur diesel fuel, engine maintenance and mine ventilation. Arsenic is sometimes a contaminant of metal ores and has been commercially extracted during copper smelting with an accompanying risk of lung cancer.

Exposures to nickel compounds in some nickel refineries have been reported to increase the risk of lung cancer and nasal sinus cancer. However, these risks have declined substantially with improving hygiene. Several other metal ores, including those of lead, cadmium, manganese, platinum and cobalt, present health hazards. The risks are usually greatest during metallurgical processing, when air concentrations exceed those experienced during mining of the ore. Appropriate control measures are required. Exposures to coal tar pitch volatiles in the Soderberg aluminium smelters have been reported to increase the risk of lung cancer and bladder cancer. Occupational asthma has also been a problem in the pot rooms of aluminium smelters. Coal dust and methane gas explosions in underground coal mines remain a serious risk requiring comprehensive monitoring and management. Some underground coal mines also have problems with carbon dioxide and hydrogen sulphide gas. Cyanide is used as a solvent for metals such as copper and gold in hydrometallurgical processes. Exposure to hydrogen cyanide gas can occur during a cyanide solution.

Biological hazards: The risk of tropical diseases such as malaria and dengue fever is substantial at some remote mining locations. Leptospirosis and ankylostomiasis were common in mines, but eradication of rats and improved sanitation has controlled these hazards effectively in the developed world. Cooling towers are commonly found on mine sites. Regular microbiological analysis of the water is necessary to detect *Legionella* contamination or high concentrations of other heterotrophic microorganisms.

Ergonomic hazards: Although mining has become increasingly mechanized, there is still a substantial amount of manual handling. Cumulative trauma disorders continue to constitute the largest category of occupational diseases in mining and often result in prolonged disability. Overhead work is common underground, during ground support and during the suspension of pipes and electrical cables. This can cause or exacerbate shoulder disorders. Broken ground is often encountered and can cause ankle and knee injuries. Most mines operate 24 h per day, 7 days per week, so shiftwork is very common. There has generally been a trend towards 12 h shifts in recent years. Fatigue in relation to shiftwork has been subject to considerable investigation in the industry. Sleep deficiencies which might be expected in hot locations, have been shown to cause impairments of cognitive and motor performance among drivers from other industries. The remote control of mobile equipment in underground mining has been introduced to reduce the risk of fatal injuries from rock falls. This has required attention to cognitive ergonomic issues, many of which are similar to those found in metallurgical plant control rooms. Proximity safety devices have also been developed.

Psychosocial hazards: Drug and alcohol abuse has been a difficult issue to deal with in mining, but policies and procedures are now in place in most large mining operations. Debate continues about how to measure psychophysical impairment. Nevertheless, mining operations commonly require the measurement of urinary drug metabolites and breath or blood alcohol on pre-employment and following accidents. Remote locations are common in mining. Massive ore-bodies, such as those at Mount Isa in Queensland, Australia that have been mined for 80 years, justify the establishment of a city. Contemporary finds, however, tend to be smaller and do not justify the establishment of permanent townships. As a result, there has been a trend towards 'fly-in-fly-out' operations, with mine employees separated from their families and communities during work periods. Expatriate placements are also common in mining and the associated psychosocial hazards have been reviewed recently . Unfortunately, fatal and severe traumatic injuries continue to occur in mining and often have a profound impact on morale. Post-traumatic stress disorders are sometimes developed in witnesses, colleagues and managers. Registered managers often feel personally responsible for such injuries, even in the absence of negligence, and face the ordeal of government inquiries and legal proceedings. Many of the contemporary and emerging issues are common to the practice of occupational medicine in all industries. Risk management and sustainability have become central to the way companies operate and occupational health needs to be integrated into these systems. Multinationals are developing global corporate occupational health and hygiene standards, which require core components compatible with local legislative requirements. Effective health surveillance and biological monitoring require sophisticated information technology systems that are only now being adequately developed.

We are faced with the paradox of increasing intolerance of occupational and environmental health risks, at a time when they are declining rapidly.This emphasizes the need for more effective risk communication. The provision of medical services at remote locations is problematic, with difficulty in attracting and retaining appropriately trained staff. Few have the desired mix of occupational health and emergency medical skills and maintaining these skills at remote locations is difficult. There is a tendency to outsource non-core functions, including occupational medicine. Epidemiological studies are needed to understand the relationship between genetic markers and the risks of diseases.

Controversy

Controversy 1: Uranium mining in Andhra Pradesh

UCIL united corporation of India Ltd is working on the extraction and mining of uranium from four mines in Andhra Pradesh. There are many controversies relating to it. The controversies are because the location of the project sites near the Nagarjuna Sagar dam supplying water for irrigation, the Akkampalli reservoir point at which drinking water is channelled to Hyderabad and the Rajiv Gandhi Tiger sanctuary. These problems have been topics of debates and discussions quite often.

Controversy 2: Rajsamand Lake

This beautiful historical lake built by the king of the Mewar dynasty on the Gomati river is in the verge of death due to the mining of marble in the nearby area. The main purpose of the lake was to protect wildlife and to provide employment to people besides creating recreational facilities, but the sudden boom in the marble industry has adversely impacted on most water bodies in the area. Mining is the largest sector providing employment second to agriculture. It has also damaged the fragile hills of Aravillis. The long term effects of mining on health and environment have yet to be studied.

SUGGESTIONS TO IMPROVE: The hue and cry over this sensitive issue is falling on deaf ears. How can the unspoken agony of the animals and common people shatter the penned laws of money and power? When money and power has bureaucracy's eye folded, the judiciary can only fold its hands and see what happens. This largest sector has not been a threat only to human lives but it has also disturbed the fragile relations and beauty of the biodiversity. Some of the suggestions can be as follows:

1. Legal suggestions: Ecologically sensitive areas, which are disturbed by mining activities must be identified and those areas which may be affected in the future must also be brought under surveillance and necessary measures must be taken by the Govt of each country to do something about it.

2. EIA - Environmental Impact Assessment and legal proceedings must be properly managed and they should be transparent. They should be applicable to all types and sizes of mining under the environmental and industrial acts.

3. The areas which are negatively affected by mining also include biodiversity rich areas like water catchments. They must be properly safeguarded and laws regarding proper use of land and water must be implemented.

4. Mine affected areas which are ecologically fragile must be identified , categorized and restoration proceedings must begin soon before they are destroyed.

5. Proper disposal of hazardous waste and chemicals in the various processes of mining must be regulated.

6. Human rights must be properly respected , the legal considerations for the Tribals and other indigenous communities must be preserved . The Tribal areas, particularly 'scheduled areas' must be protected from being mine grounds.

7. That a sudden ban in the mining industry must always be framed properly with an action plan, to provide a safe and sustainable livelihood for the labour affected by the stopping of the activities of these industries.

8. Attitude of the people: As told by economists, the demand and supply are proportionally related . When people stop buying metals and minerals just for their lucrative greed then the demand of these mining industries also stops. People should make the best use of their mobiles and computers. They should develop an awareness to follow up the discarded electronic gadget. People should say no to dirty gold, where the waste of mining is diaposed of or dumbed down causing health hazards.

9. The recycling of minerals should be promoted. This saves not only the exploitation of natural resources like minerals but it also saves energy and coal which is the major source of energy for this industry.

Conclusion

The developed countries have developed methods of disposing of waste materials related to mining by sending the waste often to developing countries. The use of advanced technology like GIS in determining the potential area of minerals, can help in studying the biodiversity of that area well and so an early assessment can be done. This also helps in rehabilitating the tribal people. This planet is not the private property of the human race. Other organisms also have equal right to live here with dignity. Developing nations like India with a large population still struggle to meet the clean environment image. All it requires is a simple thought of improving efficiency so that we do not have to put our 'national capital' – rivers, forests, lakes etc. at stake for uplifting our economic capital.

References

1. Down to earth
2. Environmental Impact of Mining- C.G Down and J. Stocks
3. Survey of environment -2004, 2005, 2006, 2007 THE HINDU
4. The Ecologist Asia

References

12

Nanotechnology
Opportunities and Risks for Humans and the Environment

MANISH VASHISHTHA

Introduction

Nanotechnology is regarded as one of the key technologies of the future and associated with high expectations by Politicians, scientists and economists.The term of "nanotechnology" is defined as the manufacturing, analysis and use of structures – for example particles, layers or tubes of less than 100 nanometers (nm) in at least one dimension. Artificially produced nano-sized particles and nanoscale system components have new properties which are of importance to the development of new products and applications. Such new properties of materials and substances result from the special properties of surfaces and interfaces and, in part, from the geometric shape of the material.

Based on the available literature data[1], it has been assumed that in the decades to come, nanotechnology will have a strong influence on essential industries such as the automotive, chemical and pharmaceutical industries as well as mechanical engineering, medicine, biotechnology and environmental engineering, and that it has a potential for fundamentally changing whole fields of technology. In the opinion of a great number of experts, nanotechnology has a positive potential not only for economical development, but considerable improvement is also expected with regard to the protection of the environment and human health. Thus, nanotechnology development may increase the efficiency of resources and improve the overall performance of environmental protection.

However, despite the vehement development of nanotechnology in recent years and an increasing number of products made by means of nanotechnology, knowledge about the exposure of humans and the environment to nano-sized particles has been very scarce so far. Questions arising as to the implications of the exposure to nanoparticles for humans and the environment have not yet been sufficiently elucidated. Due to the novel properties of nanoparticles, the technological development should therefore be accompanied by a corresponding risk assessment in order to identify and subsequently avoid potential damage and cost caused by the new technology, a procedure that has meanwhile become common for other new technologies.

The discussion about the opportunities and risks of nanotechnology should take place in an unemotional and objective atmosphere beyond technoscepticism and technomania.

In the following paper a summary of the knowledge gained so far on opportunities and risks of nanotechnology is presented. This outline considers both the potential benefits for the environment to be expected from this innovative technology, mainly in the fields of the conservation of resources, energy efficiency and health protection, and the potential adverse effects on the environment and possible health risks, as well as approaches to reduce such adverse effects.

Development and Application Fields of Nanotechnology Products

Based on the information available[2], nanotechnology is going to provide a great number of innovative developments in different technological fields and for a number of applications and branches of industry. Although the development and market penetration of many nanotechnological methods and products is still at a very early stage, a number of products and production methods are already commercially available or on their way to appear in the market (see Table). The various fields of their application are:

- Surface functionalization and refinement (for example, thermal and chemical protective coatings, nanometer-thin coatings for computer hard disks, biocidal coatings);
- Catalysis, chemical and material synthesis (for example, catalytic nanoparticles, catalytic motor vehicle exhaust gas converters, nanoporous filters, nanoreactors);
- Energy conversion and use (for example, dye-sensitized solar cells, fuel cells, batteries/accumulators with a higher capacity, LEDs);
- Construction (for example, plastic materials containing nanofillers, new metallic compounds with improved mechanical and thermal properties, improvement of properties of construction materials by means of concrete additives);
- Nanosensors (for example, magnetic field sensors, optical sensors, biosensors (lab-on-a-chip systems));
- Data processing and transmission (for example, organic light-emitting diodes (OLEDs), electronic components having nanometer dimensions); and
- Life sciences (for example, use of nanobiotechnology in analysis and diagnostics, targeted transport of active substances (drug delivery systems), biocompatible artificial implants).

From the angles of environmental and health protection, it has to be taken into account that nanoparticles are either firmly embedded in a matrix or used in free form. No information has been available so far on the release of originally firmly embedded nanoparticles from products due to ageing or degradation processes. Based on the current state of knowledge, considerable release from these products may hardly be expected because, as a rule, the nanoparticles are firmly fixed to layers or dispersions.

At present, major economic importance is attributed to *inorganic nanoparticles* from metal and other oxides (particularly silicon dioxide, cerium oxide, titanium dioxide, aluminium oxide).Their main uses are in electronics, pharmacy, medicine, cosmetics and chemistry/ catalysis, e.g.

- Titanium oxide and zinc oxide particles as UV absorbers in sun blockers;
- Gold particles as markers in medicine and for biological rapid assays; and
- Aluminium oxide particles as a porous base layer for catalytic motor-vehicle exhaust gas converters.

Carbon particles of current economic relevance include carbon black and special carbon blacks used for example as fillers in rubber and as pigments (toner). A great economic potential in the future is expected for carbon nanotubes (CNTs) - above all for their use in sensor technology and electronics, such as TV and PC flat-panel displays.

Organic nanoparticles such as polymer nanoparticles and nanotechnology-based active substances may optimize the physiological activity of pharmaceuticals, cosmetics, plant protection products, or foods and the technical properties of substances, for example, in paints and printing inks. A high potential for added value is expected above all for binders used in normal and glossy paints, for adhesive tapes and coating systems for textiles, wood and leather.

For *nanolayer systems*, there are a great number of possible uses expected to have a high market potential, such as

- Hard coatings (for scratch resistance);
- Tribological coatings (for wear protection);
- Anti-fogging coatings (for example, self-cleaning surfaces for glass or textiles);
- Antireflective coatings (for example, to increase the efficiency of solar cells);
- Anticorrosive coatings.

Due to the potential environmental and health effects of nanoparticles, special attention should be paid above all to those products and production processes which are suspected of releasing nanoparticles. These include cosmetic products, biocides, processes of environmental rehabilitation and the production of nanoparticles proper.

The current state of development and the uses of nanotechnology products have been listed in the table below:

	Already available on the market	**Awaiting marketability**	**Under development**	**Existing as concept**
Chemistry	Inorganic nanoparticles Carbon black Polymer dispersions Micronized active substances Surface refinement Easy-to-clean coatings	Chemical sensors Nano-layered silicates Organic semiconductors Dendrimers Aerogels Polymer nanocomposites Glossy paints	CNT composite materials Highly efficient hydrogen storage systems	Self-healing materials
Automotive engineering	Fillers for car tyres Components with hard coatings Antireflective coatings Scratch-resistant paints	Nanopigments Magnetoelectronic sensors Fuel cell Nanocomposites Fuel additives Anti-fogging coating Polymer windscreens	Thermoelectric waste heat recovery	Smart paints Ferrofluid shock absorbers
Electronics	GMR HDD	CMOS electronics <100nm Polymer electronics FRAM MRAM	PC RAM Molecular electronics RTD Millipede	DNA computing Spintronics
Optical industry	White LED	Ultra precision optics OLED	CNT FED Quantum cryptography EUVL optics Quantum dot laser Photonic crystals]	
Life sciences	Biochips Sun protection	Antimicrobials Magnetic hyperthermia Drug delivery Contrast media	Biosensors Lab-on-a-chip Tissue engineering	Neuronal coupling to artificial systems Biomolecular motors
Environmental engineering	Membranes for sewage treatment	Catalytic exhaust gas converters	Filter systems to collect ultrafine particulates Products for treatment of groundwater and soil	

Legend: GMR HDD: giant magneto resistance head hard disk drive. CMOS: complementary metal oxide semiconductor; FRAM: ferroelectric random access memory; MRAM: magnetic random access memory; PC RAM: personal computer random access memory; RTD: resistance temperature detector; DNA: deoxyribonucleic acid; LED: light-emitting diode; OLED: organic light-emitting diode; CNT-FED: carbon nanotube field emission display; EUVL: extreme ultraviolet lithography

Potential Benefits for the Environment

With the help of nanotechnology and nanotechnological products, it is possible to increase the efficiency of the use of raw materials and energy over the life cycle of a product and thus reduce the emission of pollutants as well as energy consumption. Below, a number of examples have been listed.

Economical use of raw materials by means of miniaturization

- Owing to their low weight, nanotechnology-based sensors are very energy-efficient to operate. Such sensors are developed predominantly for biomedical and military purposes. Future opportunities are also expected for environmental applications such as the optimized and specific detection of biological and chemical contaminants.
- Raw materials can be saved by means of a reduction of coating and layer thicknesses: for nanoscale coating and catalyzer materials, for light-weight construction materials optimized by means of nanoparticles, for wear-resistant and low-friction surfaces in mechanical engineering and highly specific membranes used in biotechnology.

Saving of energy owing to reduced weight or optimized function

- Nanotechnology can help improve water quality. Applications include seawater desalination by means of nanotechnology-based flow-through capacitors (FTC). This technology may reduce the energy consumption by more than 99% of that needed for conventional methods such as reverse osmosis or distillation.
- The energy efficiency achieved by the use of nanotechnology-based light-emitting diodes (LEDs) for lighting is three to five times higher than that of a conventional energy-saving lamp.
- Nanotechnology serves to develop a more efficient use of renewable energies. Examples include the so-called organic solar cells and dye-sensitized solar cells. Organic solar cells (photoactive layers consisting of organic material) are more efficient in light absorption than inorganic solar cell material and therefore, the layer thickness required is considerably less. Dye-sensitized solar cells can achieve a higher efficiency of light capture by means of nanofine distribution of a light-absorbing dye. Improved solar cells for low power applications such as mobile telephones or laptop computers are currently being developed to become marketable soon.
- Silicon dioxide and carbon black nanoparticles are being added to modern car tyre materials for reinforcement. They reduce rolling resistance and thus help achieve a fuel saving of up to 10%.

Improvement of the treatment efficiency of filter systems

- In the future, the so-called inverse nanotechnology (techniques to remove nanoparticles) will play an important role in sewage treatment. Thus, agents of disease such as viruses can be removed from pre-treated sewage by using nanoporous membranes, thus preventing these agents from spreading into the environment. It is already in operation in municipal sewage treatment works in Germany.
- Research activities have demonstrated that nanoporous membranes and filters are also suitable to remove contaminants and to separate by-products from gaseous and liquid media.
- Nanotechnology can optimize exhaust emission control in motor vehicles. Currently, nanoporous particle filters are being developed which are intended to collect nanoscale soot particles from exhaust gases.

Health protection from therapeutic applications

- In the field of health care, the special properties of nanomaterials can be used to enable therapeutics to cross the blood-brain barrier (for example, in the treatment of meningitis).

Reduction of the use, or replacement of dangerous substances

- A number of nanomaterials can also be useful in the prevention of infections and in pest control, e.g. by means of ultrathin biocidal polymer coatings on permanent catheters or textiles. A biocidal substance such as silver which is released in controlled quantities over an extended period may be added to nanoporous oxide layers (e.g. silicon dioxide). Thus, toxic organic biocides can be replaced. Wood preservatives containing nanoparticulate silver for a more efficient prevention of fungal and bacterial growth are already commercially available on foreign markets.
- In metal corrosion protection, a use of paint coatings containing chromium (VI) which are harmful to health and the environment will no longer be necessary where surfaces have a nanotechnology-based finish.
- Targeted control of reactions with the help of nanocatalysts will result in a reduction of by-products being hazardous to the environment in a better yield (more efficient utilization of resources).

Research into the potential benefits for environmental relief is needed above all with regard to the problems listed below, which have to be tackled on the basis of defined products and methods.

- Which are the impacts of nanotechnology on the energy and raw material input?
- Which nanomaterials are suitable for an efficient treatment of contaminated groundwater and exhaust air?
- What will happen to such materials in the environment and what are their effects on the latter?

Potential Impact on Humans and the Environment: Possible Risks, Exposure and Persistence

Due to the increasing use of synthetic nanoparticles, also an increasing introduction of such particles into the environmental media, i.e. soil, water and air, has to be expected in the future. Similar to larger airborne particulates, nanoparticles form during technological as well as natural processes, such as volcanic eruptions or forest fires. Naturally produced nanoparticles vary considerably as to their shape, composition and size. In contrast, manufactured, i.e."deliberately" produced nanoparticles are of a uniform design to comply with the desired properties. Studies involving naturally formed ultrafine particulates or those produced by combustion, permit estimates concerning the behaviour and impact of the nanoparticles on the environment. However, these estimates are insufficient to assess reliably the risks carried by manufactured nanoparticles. The broad application of nanotechnology and the great differences existing between the various nanomaterials require a differentiated evaluation of possible risks for the environment and human health.

At present,the labelling of products with regard to the quantities of nanoparticles contained is not required by law. Users are unable to find out whether or not a product contains such particles. Therefore, a specific investigation to establish the origin and presence of certain nanomaterials in the environment is difficult.

The highest risks for humans and the environment are associated with nanomaterials contained in products in the form of free particles. As long as nanoparticles remain firmly embedded in materials, hardly any risk should be expected. However, it has to be clarified in these cases whether and in which form, nanomaterials can be released into the environment during the production process, the use of the product, due to ageing and degradation, as well as during the disposal and recycling processes. Of course, also in the case of nanomaterials, an environmental risk assessment should take into account their entire life cycle.

The assessment of the risk involved in nanoparticles will decisively depend on the form in which these materials come into contact with humans and the environment. In this respect, important open questions still to be answered include the following: How stable and persistent are these forms? Do they decompose or agglomerate? Are they soluble in water? Will they interact with other nanoparticles, chemicals, or surfaces? Are they degradable, and how will their properties change during degradation?

Because of their size, nanoparticles may cross barriers by the airborne route, also by adherence to aerosols.

Nanoparticles can penetrate into live cells. Therefore, they have a potential to accumulate in organisms and thus, also in the food chain.

No data is available so far on the degradation of organic nanomaterials in the environment. No indications can be found of a degradation of carbon nanomaterials (fullerenes and nanotubes), which are being produced in major quantities already today.

Health aspects of nanosized particles

So far, there has hardly been any research into potential health risks posed by nanotechnology-based products already available on the market, such as cosmetics. Classic routes of exposure of the body are through the respiratory tract by inhalation, through the skin by absorption and through the mouth by ingestion, or a combination of these routes.

In contrast to larger particles, nanoparticles can reach the alveolar region of the lungs. Because of their low size, they are removed only insufficiently by the alveolar macrophages. This may result in inflammatory processes in the lungs. Transfer from the pulmonary alveoli to the circulatory system has been demonstrated, with smaller particles entering the bloodstream more readily.

With regard to dermal absorption, two pathways are conceivable, on principle: Firstly, particles can enter the skin through the upper layer of the skin and secondly, through the hair roots. However, knowledge is insufficient so far both with regard to intact and pre-damaged skin. It has also remained unclear whether toxic substances possibly adhering to the particles may enter the body by the dermal route of exposure. Investigation into the importance of this route of exposure should be given priority since nanoparticles are already contained in a great number of skin care products.

The European project NANODERM is dedicated to research into open questions and the development of suitable examination methods, with a particular focus on the penetration of titanium dioxide nanoparticles through the skin. In addition to the deliberate uptake of nanoparticles through the mouth (e.g. as ingredients of pharmaceutical products), also an unintentional oral ingestion, e.g. through food additives should be considered.

On principle, insoluble particles can be absorbed through the intestine and thus enter the lymphatic system. From there, such particles may enter the blood circulation and spread over the body. However, no studies are available at present that would provide sufficient information about the assessment of possible risks involved in the ingestion of nanoparticles.

The relative importance of the individual routes of exposure cannot be described in quantitative terms at present. At any rate, much importance will have to be attributed to the influence of the respective conditions of exposure. It is, however, understood that particles entering the body via the blood stream may be transported to a number of organs (heart, liver, spleen, kidneys, bone marrow).

Studies have indicated that nanoparticles are capable of crossing biological barriers such as the blood-brain barrier. Also, it has to be assumed that a transfer of nanoparticles through the placenta into the foetus is possible. Irrespective of the chances of a specific utilization of these mechanisms for therapeutic purposes, they may also involve risks.

The distribution of nanoparticles in the body seems to depend on their size, form and substance properties. Biodegradable nanoparticles are metabolized and excreted. However, little is known so far about the behaviour of non-degradable nanoparticles. It has to be assumed that accumulation will take place predominantly in the organs of detoxification. Whether or not a risk may arise from such accumulation of particles in the body has not yet been sufficiently examined.

Ecotoxicological aspects

There are still only a few scientific studies available on the impact of nanoparticles on the environment. However, it has to be assumed that due to their special properties, nanoparticles will definitely pose a risk for the environment.

Up to the present, only a few organisms in aquatic ecosystems have been studied. Thus, water fleas (*Daphnia*) may die already at a relatively low concentration of C_{60} molecules (buckminsterfullerenes) and nanoscale titanium dioxide in the water, depending on the type of administration. Experiments performed in young large mouth bass (*Micropterus salmoides*) have revealed that C_{60} nanoparticles are absorbed by these fish through their gills. They overcome the blood-brain barrier and cause damage to the brain already at low concentrations. In zebrafish (*Danio rerio*) embryos, carbon nanotubes were shown to cause a delay in the hatching of the offspring. Furthermore, the bactericidal activity of some nanomaterials could produce adverse effects in sewage treatment works and cause a change in the composition of the microbial population of the water.

Likewise, studies of the impact of nanoparticles on soil ecosystems are missing almost completely. As far as mammals are concerned, the results of laboratory studies modelling the impacts on human health can be extrapolated to wildlife animals also. No studies are available so far that would refer to other vertebrates or invertebrates. Experiments using aluminium nanoparticles have revealed a reduced growth of the roots of a number of crops (e.g. maize, cucumber, soya, carrot). Such effects were not produced by larger aluminium particles. Due to their biocidal action, i.e. their ability to kill bacteria, nanoparticles may interfere with the composition of the microbial population in the soil.

Need for information

So far, sufficient information is lacking for a reliable and comprehensive risk assessment. It should be the aim to assign nanoparticles to classes characterized by similar effects and define suitable reference parameters (e.g. mass, particle count, surface area) in order to achieve a comparable evaluation of results. Suitable methods of measurement are to be developed and optimized to determine exposure in order to be able to record the parameters required for an assessment. Methods to establish ecotoxicity and toxicity for humans and testing strategies have to be examined and optimized as to their suitability for the evaluation of nanoparticles regarding their special properties and possible new endpoints. A preferential task to be accomplished within a short period of time consists in the recording of the production and consumption of the variety of nanoparticles involved using suitable information systems and an undertaking by manufacturers to provide information. To this aim it is required that companies engaged in manufacturing and trade, submit any information available on the behaviour of nanoparticles with regard to possible exposure and their fate in the environment.

A preferential need for research and information has become apparent above all in the following fields:

- Information on uses and applications of nanoparticles:

Exposure scenarios covering the life cycle of nanoparticles;

- Information on relief potentials:

Investigation into the impact of nanotechnology on raw material and energy input

- Information on the release of nanoparticles:

The testing of products that are already commercially available or will soon be placed on the market, such as cosmetics, household products, biocides; coatings for textiles and materials coming into contact with foods;

- Assessment of impact:

Investigations into persistence and bioaccumulation of nanoparticles;

Development and optimization of suitable metrological methods to identify any exposure of humans and the environment;

- Identification of relevant parameters for characterization and classification as well as for an assessment of the effects of nanoparticles;

Development of suitable testing methods and strategies to identify ecotoxicological and health implications; determination of dose-effect relationships for the different routes of exposure.

Summary and Recommendations for Action

Nanotechnology does not only promise positive effects in economical terms. There is a wide range of applications of nanotechnology that have, or suggest to have potential benefits for environmental relief. If these potentials are utilized on a large scale by means of specific promotion of such environmentally beneficial nanotechnologies, a marked reduction of the exploitation of environmental assets and in some cases, also of adverse effects on health can be achieved. The scientific community is determined to promote nanotechnology and needs more in-depth information:

1. In order to substantiate their positive potential, nanotechnological methods and products have to be evaluated as to their advantages for the environment as compared with conventional alternatives.
2. Like the opportunities, attention has to be given to the risks associated with this technology. Given the very dynamic development of technology and the indications of very serious implications and possible risks for human health and the environment that may arise from nanotechnology, there is an urgent need to identify and assess such risks. In spite of the increasing numbers of scientific studies, there are still considerable gaps as far as information is concerned, so that there is a great need for further research.

References

1. Ministry for Environment and Water Conservation, Agriculture and Consumer Protection of the federal Land of North Rhine-Westphalia, Federal Ministry for the Environment, Nature Conservation and Nuclear Safety, and Federal Environment Agency (2006, in press): Municipal Wastewater Treatment Using Membrane Technology.

2. Oberdörster, G., E. Oberdörster, et al. (2005). "Nanotoxicology: An Emerging Discipline Evolving from Studies of Ultrafine Particles." Environmental Health Perspectives 113(7): 823-839.

3. Scientific Committee on Emerging and Newly Identified Health Risks (SCENIHR) Opinion on the appropriateness of existing methodologies to assess the potential risks associated with engineered and adventitious products of nanotechnologies, EU Commission.

4. The Royal Society and The Royal Academy of Engineering (2004) Nanoscience and nanotechnologies: opportunities and uncertainties July 2004.

5. U.S. Environmental Protection Agency (2005): External Review Draft: Nanotechnology White Paper.

13

The Role of the Judiciary in Environmental Governance

SHASHANK MANISH, SUDHIR KUMAR AND SUNIL CHOUDHARY

Introduction

The Rule of Law is eloquently symbolized in the image of the blindfolded maiden holding aloft evenly balanced scales. The blindfold and the scales signify the very essence of the Rule of Law: that all parties are equal before the law and that justice must be dispensed without fear or favor, in an even-handed way.

Legal historians have amply demonstrated the intrinsic linkage between legal developments and the historical settings in which they take place. The concept of the Rule of Law is no exception. It is grounded in the ideas of justice, fairness and inclusiveness discussed by Aristotle; in the rules of war addressed in the ancient Indian epics Mahabharata and Ramayana; in the foundations of religious thought such as the Ten Commandments and the Dharma Chakra; and in seminal historical documents such as the Magna Carta, which embodied the principle that government itself is bound to abide by the law. Since then, philosophers and jurists from all corners of the world have moulded the philosophical underpinnings and judicial content of the Rule of Law. Today, the Rule of Law is the foundation of good governance. This requires adherence to constitutional supremacy, recognition that government and the governed are equal before the law, acknowledgment that government itself is limited by the law and cannot engage in any arbitrary exercise of power, and recognition that individuals are endowed with certain inalienable rights that cannot be denied even by legitimately constituted governments.

Concepts of the role of the judiciary and the limits of its functions are similarly anchored in the fertile western intellectual thought of the seventeenth and eighteenth centuries and have been depicted in the writings of Count Montesquieu, who in 1748 wrote, "There is no liberty, if the judicial power be not separated from the legislative and executive. Were it joined with the legislative, the life and liberty of the subject would be exposed to arbitrary control; for the judge would then be the legislator. Were it joined to the executive power, the judge might behave with all the violence of an oppressor." Modern constitutionalism is firmly anchored in this concept of the separation of powers. Another fundamental notion that is intimately connected with these principles is the rights of the individual, which is eloquently expressed in the Indian Constitution. It states that all men are created equal and that among their inalienable rights are the "rights to life, liberty and the pursuit of happiness."

These rights of the individual are today expressed as Human Rights. They were initially set out in the Universal Declaration of Human Rights, which itself is mankind's response to the unparalleled horrors of complete and widespread denial of human dignity and life, which took place during one of the darkest chapters of human history.

The Mindset of the Judiciary

Governance is the process of decision-making. It is the sum of the many ways in which individuals and institutions manage their common affairs. It is undergirded by fundamental notions of inclusiveness, transparency and accountability, which themselves are ways of realizing the ideals of democracy, justice and fairness.As described by the recent report "Decisions for the Earth," which was developed by UNDP, UNEP, the World Bank and the World Resources Institute, studies of environmental governance address how decisions concerning the environment are made and who participates in the decision making process. The Report aptly links the process and the participants by stating: "how we decide and who gets to decide, often determines what we decide."

The environment transcends sectors and mediums to encompass intangibles such as culture, values, lifestyles, and consumption patterns. It is a dimension of almost every human activity. The interconnectivity and interdependence of all these components of the environment have far reaching implications for judicial thinking and decision making and, consequently, for the development of environmental jurisprudence. Even those cases that are not specifically identified as "environmental" often have implications for ecosystem protection. Narrowly-defined cases may impact a wider community – a nation, a region, or even the whole world. The broad spectrum of issues encompassed by the term "environmental governance" is detailed in the report by UNDP, UNEP, World Bank, and World Resources Institute, which identifies seven broad elements of environmental governance:[1]

1. Institutions and Laws:
    - Who makes and enforces the rules for using natural resources?
    - What are the rules and the penalties for breaking them?
    - Who resolves disputes?
2. Participation Rights and Representation:
    - How can the public influence or contest the rules over natural resources?
    - Who represents those who use or depend on natural resources when decisions on these resources are made?
3. Authority Level:
    - At what level or scale - local, regional, national, international - does the authority over resources reside?

4. Accountability and Transparency:
   - How do those who control and manage natural resources answer for their decisions, and to whom?
   - How open to scrutiny is the decision-making process?
5. Property Rights and Tenure:
   - Who owns a natural resource or has the legal right to control it?
6. Markets and Financial Flows:
   - How do financial practices, economic policies, and market behaviour influence authority over natural resources?
7. Science and Risk:
   - How are ecological and social sciences incorporated into decisions on natural resource use to reduce risks to people and ecosystems and identify new opportunities?

These elements reveal that environmental governance does not exclusively involve decisions made by governments. The series of questions raised above demonstrates a much more diffuse level of responsibility for global environmental governance.

The environment is a dimension of almost every human activity, perhaps even of every human decision. These range in significance from the simple act of dropping a ticket in the street to the complex activities involved in major developmental projects. The more one reflects on the root causes of environmental pollution and natural resources depletion, the conclusion is inescapable that the "mindset" in which human decisions are made—from the simplest to the most complex—is the key to properly understanding those decisions. This is equally true for judicial decision making.

Environmental jurisprudence, especially over the past three or four decades, provides illuminating evidence of the rise of proactive judicial engagement in resolving disputes that require a delicate balancing of competing and compelling interests. For example, judges have attempted to balance promoting the well-being of people and alleviating poverty and preserving the integrity of the environment and advancing the imperatives of economical development.

Principles of Environmental Governance

The following Principles, accordingly, guide the activities of different sectors in relation to India's National Environment Policy (NEP). The NEP is a comprehensive document covering all concerned sectors and stakeholders. Each of these principles has an established genealogy in policy pronouncements, jurisprudence, international environmental law, or international State practice:

i. **Human Beings are at the Centre of Sustainable Developmental Concerns:**
   Human beings are at the centre of concerns for sustainable development. They are entitled to a healthy and productive life in harmony with nature.

ii. **The Right to Development:**

The right to development must be fulfilled so as to meet developmental and environmental needs equitably for the present and future generations.

iii. **Environmental Conservation is an Integral Part of the Developmental Process:**

In order to achieve sustainable development, environmental conservation should be constituted as an integral part of the developmental process and cannot be considered in isolation from it.

iv. **The Precautionary Approach:**

Where there are credible threats of a serious or irreversible nature to damage the key environmental resources, lack of full scientific certainty shall not be used as a reason for postponing cost-effective measures to prevent environmental degradation.

v. **Economical Efficiency:**

In various public actions for environmental conservation, economical efficiency would be realized. This principle requires that the services of environmental resources be given an economical value, at for or with the other goods and services, in an analysis of alternative courses of action.

Further implications of this principle are as follows:

a) **"Polluter Pays:**

Impacts of acts of production and consumption of one party may be visited on third parties who do not have a direct economical nexus with the original act. Such impacts are termed "externalities". If the costs (or benefits) of the externalities are not re-visited on the party responsible for the original act, the resulting level of the entire sequence of production or consumption, and externality, is inefficient. In such a situation, economical efficiency may be restored by making the perpetrator of the externality bear the cost (or benefit) of the same.

b) **Cost Minimization:**

Where the environmental benefits of a course of action cannot, for methodological or conceptual reasons, be imputed economical value (as in the case of "Incomparable Entities"), in any event the economical costs of realizing the benefits should be minimized. Efficiency of resource - use may also be accomplished by the use of policy instruments that create incentives to minimize wasteful use and consumption of natural resources. The principle of efficiency also applies to issues of environmental governance by streamlining processes and procedures in order to minimize costs and delays.

vi. **Entities with "Incomparable" Values:**

Significant risks to human health, life and environmental life-support systems, besides certain other unique natural and man-made entities, which may impact the well-being broadly conceived of a large number of persons may be considered as "Incomparable" in that individuals or societies would not accept these risks for compensation in money or conventional goods and services. A conventional economial cost-benefit calculus would not, accordingly, apply in their case, and such entities would have priority in allocation of societal resources for their conservation without consideration of direct or immediate economical benefit.

vii. Equity:

The cardinal principle of equity or justice requires that human beings cannot be treated differently based on irrelevant differences between the Equity norms but must be distinguished according to the context, i.e. "procedural equity", relating to fair rules for the allocation of entitlements and obligations and "end-result equity", relating to fair outcomes in terms of the distribution of entitlements and obligations. Each context, in addition, must be distinguished in terms of "intra-generational equity", relating to justice within societies and in particular providing space for the participation of underprivileged, and "inter-generational equity." Equity in the context of this policy refers to both equity in entitlements, and participation of the relevant stakeholders, in processes of decision-making and the overuse of environmental resources.

viii. Legal Liability:

The present environmental redressal mechanism is predominantly based on doctrines of criminal liability, which has not proved sufficiently effective, and needs to be supplemented. Civil liability for environmental damage would deter environmentally harmful actions, and compensate the victims of environmental damage. Conceptually, the principle of legal liability may be viewed as an embodiment in legal doctrine of the "polluter pays" approach, derived from the principle of economical efficiency. The following alternative approaches to civil liability may apply:

a) **Fault Based Liability**

In a fault based liability regime, a party is held liable if it breaches a pre-existing legal duty, for example, an environmental standard.

b) **Strict Liability**

Strict liability imposes an obligation to compensate the victim for damage resulting from action or failure to take action, which may not necessarily constitute a breach of any law or duty of care.

ix. Public Trust Doctrine:

The State is not an absolute owner, but a trustee of all natural resources, which are by nature meant for public use and enjoyment, subject to reasonable conditions, necessary to protect the legitimate interest of a large number of people, or for matters of a strategic national interest.

x. Decentralization:

Decentralization involves ceding or the transferring of power from a Central Authority to State and Local Authorities, in order to empower public authorities having jurisdiction at the spatial level at which salient environmental issues are to be addressed.

xi. Integration:

Integration refers to the inclusion of environmental considerations in sectoral policymaking, the integration of the social and natural sciences in environmentally related policy research, and the strengthening of relevant linkages among various agencies at the Central, State, and Local Self- Governments where the environmental policies are to be implemented.

xii. Environmental Standard Setting:

Environmental standards must reflect on the economical and the socially developed situations, in which they apply. Standards adopted in one society or situation may have unacceptable economic and social costs in another society or context, if implemented without considering the consequences.

xiii. Preventive Action:

It is preferable to prevent environmental damage from occurring in the first place, rather than attempting to restore degraded environmental resources after the damage.

xiv. Environmental Offsetting:

There is a general obligation to protect threatened or endangered species and natural systems that are of special importance to sustaining life, providing livelihoods, or general well-being. If, for exceptional reasons of overriding public interest, such protection cannot be provided in particular cases, cost-effective offsetting measures must be undertaken by the proponents of the activity. It must aim to restore the lost environmental service produced to the same public in question.

Categories of Environmental Governance

In order to address local to global concerns, environmental governance could broadly be categorized at the following three levels:

1. International Environmental Governance – looking after global environmental issues through multilateral environmental agreements. In order to address the global environmental concerns (climate change, conservation of biodiversity, desertification and management of persistent organic pollutants etc) a number of multilateral environmental agreements (MEAs) are in place. Most of these agreements were initiated under the auspices of the United Nations Environment Programme (UNEP). After negotiations, these MEAs have their own independent existence by way of their separate Secretariats providing necessary programmatic support. The Conference of Parties (COP) in case of Conventions and Meeting of Parties (MOP) for Protocols are the supreme bodies consisting of all Parties providing overall direction and guidance to such international agreements. India is a party to most of these multilateral environmental agreements.

2. National Environmental Governance – a set of legislative and policy measures at the national level governing environmental issues. These national policy measures could be in response to either fulfilling international environmental commitments or fulfilling the same according to the national environmental priorities. The Ozone Depleting Substances

(Regulation) Rules in India are in response to the country's obligation under the Montreal Protocol while the Environment Protection Act, the Forest Conservation and the Air and Water Pollution (Prevention) Acts are driven by national environmental requirements. In case of large countries such as India, an intermediate level of provincial / state level is also often in place. The Constitution of India prescribes protection and improvement of the natural environment including forests, lakes, rivers and wildlife and to have compassion for living creatures, as one of the fundamental duties of every citizen of India. As a directive principle of the state policy, Article 48A of the Constitution states that the State shall endeavour to protect and improve the environment and safeguard the forests and wildlife of the country. The Public Interest Litigation (PIL) is a unique feature of the Indian judicial system. In fact, an independent Judiciary has been exceptionally effective in the area of environment by achieving a greater degree of compliance with the laws and upholding the rights of citizens to an acceptable quality of water and air. A diverse developing society such as India provides numerous challenges in the economical, social, political, cultural and environmental arenas. As a major developing country, India has a well-developed body of environmental laws. The volume of these laws is gradually growing, bringing more and more aspects into its fold. However, much more needs to be done in India regarding the compliance with and enforcement of these laws and regulations. It has been an endeavour in India to apply the principles of good governance (transparency, rationality, accountability, reduction in time and costs, participation and regulatory independence) to the management and regulation of the use of environmental resources.

3. Local Environmental Governance - dealing with local environmental issues and the sharing of property rights over local natural resources. Devolution of power to people through constitutional amendments, in the nineties, is already showing remarkable results in a number of areas. By transferring the managerial powers of 29 sectors of economy to village councils and allowing them to raise resources through taxation, the first major step in empowering people to manage their resources has already been taken. The steps contemplated for the future are,the sharing of state and central revenue with village councils and their direct involvement in the management of social sector activities and the village infrastructure. Moving beyond the elected representatives of village councils, a number of initiatives for the management of natural resources seek direct involvement of the whole village, for example, Joint Forest Management, Watershed Development Committees and Participatory Irrigation Management to mention but a few. Clearly the emerging strategy is to empower people to manage their resources to establish sustainable livelihoods. The important thing is to understand that the poor are not the problem. They are part of the solution.

Judiciaries and Sustainable Development

Courts also have played a crucial role in advancing the Principles contained in the Stockholm and Rio Declarations. They have produced numerous decisions that have contributed to balancing environmental and developmental considerations, promoting natural resources conservation and sustainable use, achieving equity and justice, and, overall, implementing the goals of sustainable development.

The principle of sustainable development has been discussed by the International Court of Justice, in the Hungary- Slovak Republic case on the Gabcikovo-Nagymaros Project. At the national level, judiciaries throughout the world have made significant contributions to the progressive development of this body of law. The following is a brief overview of these legal developments:

- Continuous mandamus in the corpus of international and national law; invocation of the extraordinary jurisdiction of the Supreme Court in environmental matters; public participation, including substantive and procedural matters relating to public interest litigation[2];
- Limits of the concepts of "aggrieved person" and "locus standi" in regard to environmental damage[3];
- Interpretation of the Right to Life in Constitutions as including the right to a healthy environment in which the right to life itself may be enjoyed; inter-generational and intra-generational equity; court commissions to ascertain facts and an authoritative assessment of the scientific and technical aspects of environment and developmental issues;[4]
- Public's right to information; obligation for continuous environmental impact assessment[5];
- Application of the public trust doctrine in regard to natural resources and the environment[6];
- Approaches to judicial reasoning on environmental matters and the importance of promoting public awareness and environmental education at secondary and tertiary levels[7] ;

The following is intended to provide a flavour of the manner in which judges around the world have given judicial recognition to the Principles of the Rio Declaration on Environment and Development.

Sovereignty and Jurisdiction

In 1997 the International Court of Justice (ICJ) prevented Hungary from suspending and abandoning the works of the Gabcikovo-Nagymaros Barrage System. In issuing its opinion, the ICJ stated that the "existence of the general obligation of States to ensure that activities within their jurisdiction and control respect the environment of other States or of areas beyond national control is now part of the corpus of international law relating to the environment."[8]

Inter-generational Equity

In forbidding limestone mining operations in the Himalayan foothills, the Supreme Court of India took into account the interests of future generations in the unique legacy of the Himalayan ecosystem, requested to them by past generations.[9] Similarly, the need to "defend and improve the human environment for present and future generations" was considered by the Court in ordering the closure of several tanneries, despite the unemployment resulting from such an order.[10] Likewise, the Philippines' judiciary agreed to afford legal standing to a group of petitioners that sued on behalf of future generations. The Court determined that every generation has a responsibility to the next to preserve nature for the full and healthful enjoyment of its ecology.[11]

Access to Information

In South Africa, applicants were granted the right to require information on how the construction of a developmental project in an area in which they intended to build a holiday house would affect the environment.[12] Uganda's judiciary stated that every citizen has a right of access to information in the possession of the State.[13] From a different perspective, the Ukrainian judiciary stated that an applicant for a project with environmental consequences should announce the findings of the state environmental expert body on the proposed project through the mass media.[14] The Supreme Court of India, in response to a petitioner's request for issuing a court directive on the importance of public information in environmental matters, called on cinemas and video parlours to project environmental messages and films about environmental issues and requested that radio companies make programmes on the environment and pollution. [15]

Public Participation

In Chile, the judiciary upheld the standing of a party that challenged the validity of a resolution that admitted the technical viability of a project that—according to the same resolution—did not fulfil the requirements for its environmental viability.[16]

The Supreme Court of Bangladesh granted legal standing to the representative of an environmental association that challenged the implementation of a flood control plan. The original court had dismissed the petition by establishing that the petitioner was not an "aggrieved person" within the meaning of the Constitution. However, on appeal, a standing was granted by treating the association as a "person aggrieved" within the meaning of the Constitution "because the cause it bonafide espouses, both in respect of fundamental rights and constitutional remedies, is a cause of an indeterminate number of people in respect of a subject matter of great public concern."[17]

Likewise, the Supreme Court of Nepal granted a standing to a petitioner who complained that the construction of a building on the banks of the Rani Pokhari destroyed the beauty of an historical and archaeological site and sought orders to stop the construction as well as demolish all the structures already constructed. The court held that 1) it was an obligation of the Nepalese government to apply the commitments it made under The Convention for the Protection of the World Cultural and Natural Heritage 1972 and 2) every individual was entitled to show concern for public property and "public rights" in terms of Art 88(2) of the Constitution of the Kingdom of Nepal of 1990.[18]

Precautionary Principle

In a recent decision, Argentina's judiciary ordered the temporary suspension of a project that sought to build an electricity grid above a human settlement. By finding support within Argentina's environmental legal framework and other international instruments, this decision ordered the defendant to present a report on the probable negative effects that the resulting electromagnetic fields could have on human health, as well as how they could be prevented.[19] In a similar case, the Supreme Court of Pakistan accepted the need to apply the precautionary principle and appointed a commissioner to study the likelihood of adverse effects of a proposed electricity grid on local residents.[20]

A Colombian administrative tribunal called on the national government to end spraying over illicit drug crops until scientific studies on the effects of the chemicals used on human health were carried out.[21] When confronted with an action that sought to stop industries from discharging untreated effluent into agricultural fields, the Supreme Court of India called upon the government to create an authority that would address polluting industries. After announcing that the precautionary principle had become International Customary Law, the Court recommended that the announced authority consider this principle.[22] Australia's judiciary has explicitly recognized the binding force of the precautionary principle. The Land and Environment Court of New South Wales stated that the lack of full scientific certainty should not be used as a reason for postponing measures that avoid potential threats.[23]

When asked to deny the construction of a power station because of its negative impact on the Earth's atmosphere (greenhouse effect), a magistrates' court in Australia held that the precautionary principle does not give a special preference to the consideration of greenhouse impacts above developmental projects that demonstrate the capacity to address environmental concerns.[24]

Polluter Pays

The polluter pays principle has been recognized within the jurisdiction of the Supreme Court of India, which has held that "along with the precautionary principle- the polluter pays principle is a part of customary international law."[25] Following similar reasoning, the Supreme Court of India held a company liable for the diversion of a stream and ordered payment of compensation to restore damages to the environment, invoking the Polluter Pays Principle.[26]

Conclusion

Judicial decisions are prone to a less efficacious enforcement in the area of corporate environmental management. When Courts, by way of remedial action, prescribe compensation to be paid, very few corporate bodies actually end up paying the amount. This is due to the poor enforcement, low inclination and most often, the inability to pay these enormous sums. Such a situation leaves the people affected helpless, with no remedy. It also leads to instances of the concerned Government being directed to pay the compensation in certain cases, such as the Union Carbide. This only means an additional burden on the taxpayers indirectly. Very often, the errant corporation escapes with little or no liability. It is also seen that most cases involving environmental mismanagement by large corporations involve attempts to settle the dispute through compromises, such as the Bhopal Gas case. There may be instances of inequitable solutions reached, which disadvantage only the affected parties. Moreover, this cannot be an advisable precedent as corporations would then manipulate this loop hole and continue their pollution of the environment. In addition to the practical inability of enforcement, the judiciary often places an overemphasis on the constitutional origins of the right to the environment through Article 21. This approach has the effect of encouraging the emerging, yet vague, concept to the detriment of more specific domestic legislations on the point. Moreover quite often the Court has to invoke its inherent power to suit a situation that does not strictly fall under the various legislations. This makes the entire process unpredictable and uncertain. This area of law requires precise judicial precedents to be laid down, which are capable of checking damage caused by industrial disasters. It is submitted that the judiciary has a very limited role to play in the scheme of corporate environmental management. It seeks to enforce only what is laid down by the Central Government and the various legislations.

However, an area of corporate environmental management requires constant innovations and flexibility to suit the situation. This ability, due to the nature of the judicial function as a law enforcer, does not lie with the judiciary. There is thus a need to conceive of a scheme of corporate environmental management in India, which is not entirely judicially based. It is proposed that the scheme involve codes for industrial activity to be followed by corporate entities, backed by legislation and checked by the judiciary.

References

1. Dr Mohiuddin Farooque v Bangladesh, Represented by the Secretary, Ministry of Irrigation, Water Resources & Flood Control & Ors : 48 DLR 19 96, Supreme Court of Bangladesh.
2. Kajing Tubfk & Ors v Ekran BHD & Ors, Originating Summons No. 55 (21 June 1995) High Court Kuala Lumpur; Movement Social de Petit Camp/Valentina v Ministry of the Environment and Quality of Life, Mauritius Environment Appeal Tribunal (Cause No. 2/94).
3. MC Mehta v Kamal Nath & Ors, Supreme Court of India (1997) Supreme Court Cases 388; Juan Antonio Oposa and Others V. The Honourable Fulgencio S. Factoran and another, G.R.No: 101083, Supreme Court of the Philippines.
4. MC Mehta v Kamal Nath & Ors, Supreme Court of India (1997) Supreme Court Cases 388; corporate responsibility and liability (Charan Lal Sahu v Union of India (Bhopal Case II) AIR 1990 Supreme Court 1480.
5. MC Mehta v Union of India & Ors , Supreme Court of India, Writ Petition Civil No 860 of 1991.
6. MC Mehta v Union of India & Ors, AIR 1988 Supreme Court 1037; Rural Litigation and Entitlement Kendera v State of UP, AIR 1988 SC 2187; The Environmental Foundation Limited & Ors v The Attorney General & Ors, Supreme Court of Sri Lanka SC, Application No 128/91.
7. WRI 2003.

14

A must for a Healthier World

Realms of Environmental Education and Awareness

ROHIT DHINGRA, RANJEETA AND RAKHI

Introduction

Environmental education is a learning process that increases people's knowledge and awareness about the environment and associated challenges, develops the necessary skills and expertise to address the challenges and fosters attitudes, motivations and commitments to make informed decisions and take responsible action (UNESCO, Tbilisi Declaration, 1978). It may also be referred to an organized effort to teach about how the natural environment functions and particularly, how human beings can manage their behaviour and ecosystems in order to live sustainably. The term is quite often used to imply education within the school system, from primary to post-secondary. However, it is sometimes used more broadly to include all efforts to educate the public and other audiences, including printed matter, websites, media campaigns, etc.

The environment is considered as the sum total of all conditions and influences that effect our development or the effects of the development of any living organism. Human beings can play a very crucial role in preserving and improving the environment which has become the necessity of the hour and very important for our coming future. The acceleration of various sets of developmental activities is degrading our environment [1] The shortage of the natural resources is threatening the sustained productivity of the economy, economical production and other activities. The quality of the environment is also affected by the overloading of the natural sinks with the waste and pollutants. These environmental consequences are neglected in the name of profits and higher incomes. This is not only affecting our environment but indirectly it affects our health. Environmental damage can also undermine future attainments and productivity if the factors of production are adversely affected. Therefore, for a sustainable economical development, every country needs to follow a stringent environmental policy where people will be responsible for ensuring long-term development, sustainability and suitability of efforts, and the ultimate success of projects at mobilizing local resources for meeting local needs and concerns. Education is critical for promoting sustainable development and improving the capacity of people to address environmental and developmental issues. It is also critical for achieving environmental and ethical awareness, values and attitudes, skills and behaviour consistent with sustainable development [2].

Environment and Educational Institutes

Environmental education has been considered an additional or elective subject, generally in many schools both at primary and high school level. At the elementary school level, environmental education can take the form of a science enrichment curriculum, natural history field trips, community service projects and the participation of outdoor science schools. In secondary school, the environmental curriculum can be a focused subject within the sciences or as a part of student interest groups or clubs. At the undergraduate and graduate level, it can be considered in its own field within education, environmental studies, environmental science and policy, ecology, or human/cultural ecology programmes [3].

It is crucial that education be placed at the centre of this developmental arena where environmental education must be accepted as the prerequisite for sustainable development. The education can be basic in nature having the broadest coverage with a general orientation where values have a higher impact. This approach is consistent with the prescriptions of the Agenda 21, as finalized by UNCED: "A major priority is to reorient education towards sustainable development by improving each country's capacity to address environment and development in its environmental programmes, particularly in basic learning. This is indispensable for enabling people to adapt to a swiftly changing world and to develop an ethical awareness consistent with the sustainable use of natural resources. Education should, in all disciplines, address the dynamics of the physical/biological and socioeconomical environment and human development, including spiritual development."

Education needs to be regarded as an investment as this plays a vital role in the economical growth of any country which transforms it into an asset in the coming future. Education is the source of knowledge, values and skills which are necessary for the development and building of any nation. Education helps in achieving goals which are laid down in advance. The end goal of environmental education is the transformation of the environment according to nature's law. It is the comprehensive study which includes all the relationships between human beings and their impact which is an independent field of study. Environmental education starts from the primary school level and is prevalent at the higher levels of our educational systems i.e. universities and research institutes. Generally we call this nature study and conservation education but all are the same in principle as behind all of them, the aim is to save the environment from artificial changes brought on by us. Environmental education is both theoretical and practical as it is learning how to manage and improve the relationship between human society and the environment in an integrated and sustainable way [4].

Environmental education also entails practising in decision-making and self-formulating a code of behaviour about issues concerning environmental quality. One of the landmarks in the history of environmental education is the Stockholm Conference on Human Environment, organized by the UNESCO in 1972. Thereafter UNESCO launched the International Environmental Education Programme (IEEP) in the year 1975. The activities under the IEEP in the first phase culminated in the organization of the first inter governmental conference on "Environmental Education" at Tbilisi (USSR) in 1977. This specified the nature and scope of environmental education and also laid down the aims and objectives as well as the repertoire of strategies to be adopted at the national and international levels (Bhushan S et al 1990). The conference resolved that environmental education should consider the environment in its totality i.e. natural and built, technological, social, economical, political, cultural, historical, moral, aesthetic, etc.

Postulates are

1. Environmental Education is considered as a continuous, life long process that begins at the preschool level and continues through all formal and unformed states.
2. Environmental Education is interdisciplinary in its approach and draws on the specific content of each discipline to give it a holistic and balanced perspective.
3. It examines major environmental issues from local, regional, national and international points of view so that students receive insight into environmental conditions in other geographical areas.
4. The focus on current and potential environmental situations while taking into account the historical perspectives.
5. This promotes the values and necessity of local, national and international cooperation in the prevention and solution of environmental problems.
6. These enable learners to have a role in planning their learning experience and provide them with an opportunity for making decisions and accepting their consequences.
7. The relative environmental sensitivity, knowledge, problem solving skills and clarification of values pertaining to different ages, but with special emphasis on environmental sensitivity to the learner's own community, is important in the early years.
8. This will help learners discover the symptoms and real causes of environmental problems.
9. This will emphasize the complexity of environmental problems and will help the need to develop critical thinking and problem solving skills.
10. This will utilize diverse learning environments and a broad array of educational approaches to teach learning about the environment, emphasizing practical experience [5].

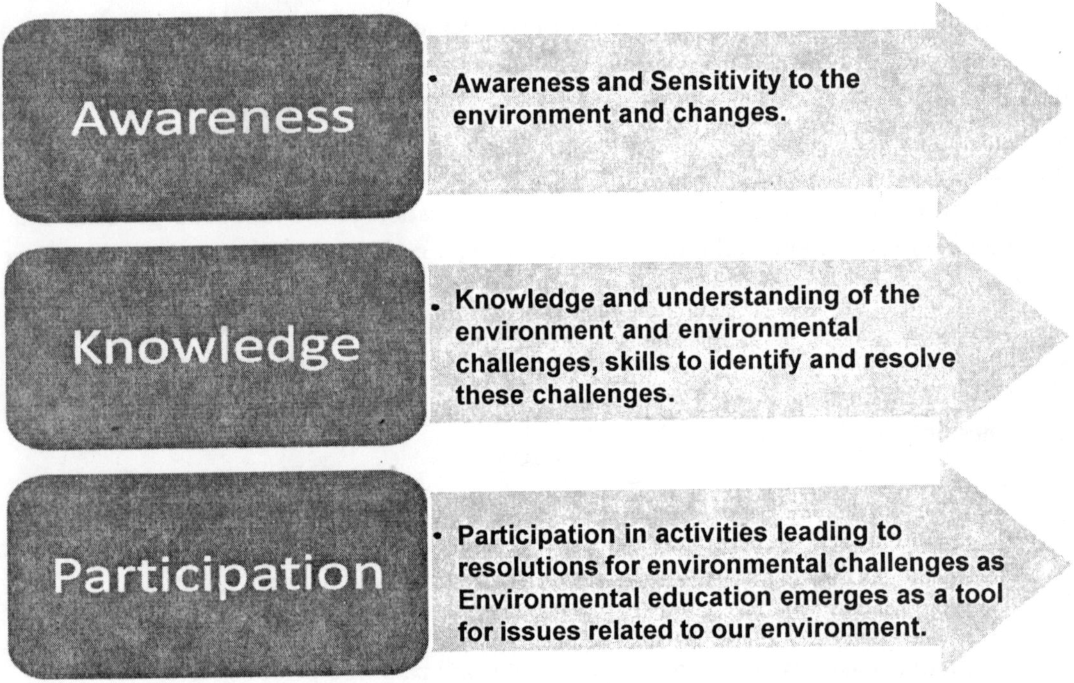

Awareness

- Awareness and Sensitivity to the environment and changes.

Knowledge

- Knowledge and understanding of the environment and environmental challenges, skills to identify and resolve these challenges.

Participation

- Participation in activities leading to resolutions for environmental challenges as Environmental education emerges as a tool for issues related to our environment.

Fig. 1. Model Representing Components of Environmental Education.

Need for Environmental Education

Awareness through education is one of the most effective ways for saving our environment. We can define the environment that was given to us by nature as pure air, water and soil as these are the essential elements for life to sustain and continue at its pace. Hence we can say that for enhancing and preserving the environment, education is very important. Education is the only way by which people can be made aware. Environmental education has been in vogue since human beings have been interacting with the world around them and teaching their children to do the same. Rural people everywhere have a good perception of their surrounding natural systems and a deep reverence for them. We have passed our understanding and our values from generation to generation through written and oral communication,but the underlying reasons for doing things and the ways of doing them have changed over time [2]. There are historical reasons for environmental education. People acquire basic environmental knowledge in order to grow food, find water and protect themselves from the climate. We still need the knowledge of science and technology to shape and perpetuate the modern world. However, a more complete and constructive reason for environmental education has emerged out of the combination of all the other reasons.

Reasons for Developing Environmental Education

1. Developing the critical thinking skills needed to make responsible decisions on behalf of our natural resources so that it builds creative thinking skills and abilities.

2. Present strategies to care for the environment around us for now and for future generations.

3. On an increasingly urban planet, it helps us gain an understanding of interactions between human society and the environment, and it also provides learners with the confidence to voice personal opinions and beliefs.

4. Develops teamwork skills for problem solving and expands traditional classroom lessons into ones that will reach multiple learning styles where it easily integrates into all different subject areas [1].

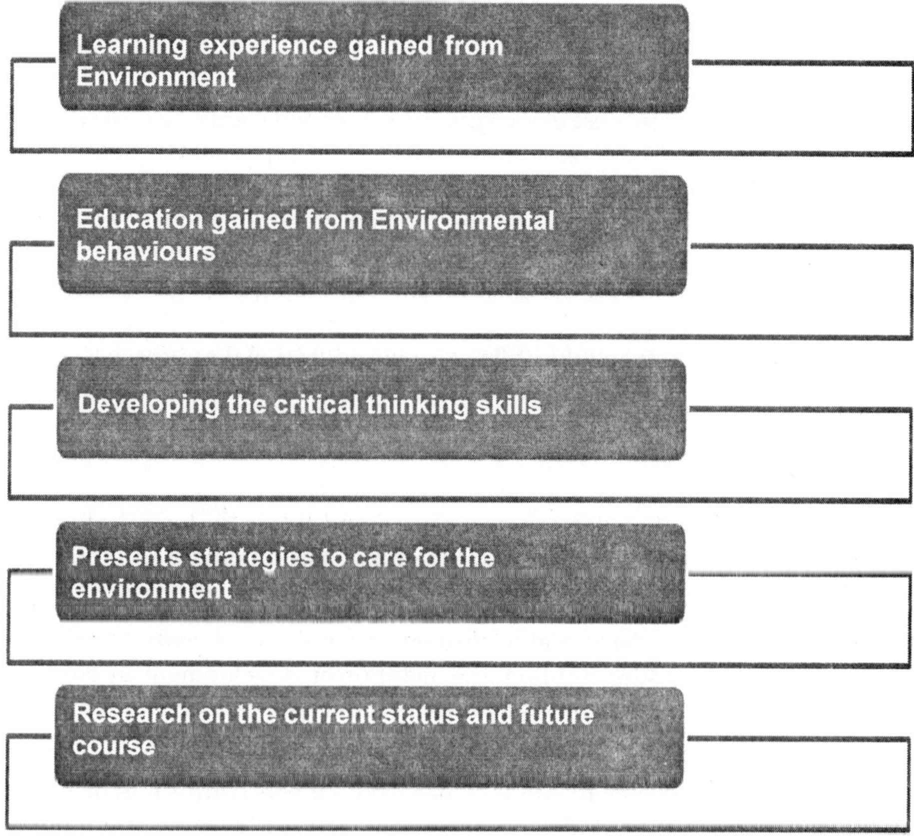

Fig. 2. Reasoning Model Based on Environmental Studies.

History and Current Trends

One of the current trends within environmental education seeks to move from an approach of ideology and activism to one that allows students to make informed decisions and take action based on experience as well as data. Within this process, environmental curriculae have progressively been integrated into governmental educational standards. Some environmental educators find this movement distressing and move away from the original political and activist approach to environmental education, while others find this approach more valid and accessible.

Overall there is a movement that has progressed since the relatively recent founding (1960s) of the idea of environmental education in industrial societies, which has transported the participant from nature appreciation and awareness to education for an ecologically sustainable future. This trend may be viewed as a microcosm of how many environmental education programmes seek to first engage with participants through developing a sense of appreciating nature which is then translated into actions that affect conservation and sustainability [3].

Training Objectives and Methodology

Environmental Education is a process of recognizing values and clarifying concepts in order to develop skills and added tools necessary to understand and appreciate the inter-relationship among man, his culture and his bio-physical surroundings. It creates an overall perspective, which acknowledges the fact that the natural environment and the man-made environment are interdependent. It should consider the environment in its totality and should be a continuous lifelong process beginning at the pre-school level and continuing through all stages. It should be inter-disciplinary and examine major environmental issues from local, national and international points of view. It should utilize various educational approaches to teach and learn about the environment with stress on practical activities and first-hand experience. It is through this process of education that people can be sensitized about the environmental issues.

Training Objectives:

1. Development of educational/teaching materials and aids in the formal education sector to encourage non-governmental organizations, mass media and other concerned organizations for promoting awareness among the people at all levels.
2. To promote environmental education through existing educational/scientific/research institutions and to ensure training and manpower development in environmental education and to mobilize people's awareness for the preservation and conservation of the environment.
3. The programme conducted initiatives which were launched are a part of a scheme and fall into the category of Formal and Non-Formal sectors.Where the programmes under Formal Environmental Education are environmental Education in the School System, Environmental Appreciation Courses and Environmental concepts in the Management

and Business Studies, the programmes under Non-Formal Environmental Education are the National Environmental Awareness Campaign (NEAC) and Eco-clubs (NGC), Mass Awareness.

4. To develop mechanisms and institutions for enhancing outreach activities through Nature Clubs of India; Eco club and Interpretation programmes to increase the presence and influence of environmental education in formal education systems at the primary and higher levels through policy advocacy with the Central Boards and the National Council for Education and Research Training.
5. To develop implemention of comprehensive teacher training programmes that include the recapitulation and implementation of environmental sensitization programmes or modules for key target groups.
6. To advocate research on EE in the formal education to enhance impacts on policies related to the increased focus on EE and to integrate ESD into the training of India's future educators through the National EE Guideline implementation.

To achieve the above objectives, the Ministry has been implementing several schemes and programmes. Some of the major schemes implemented for imparting environmental education and for the creation of environmental awareness among the general public.

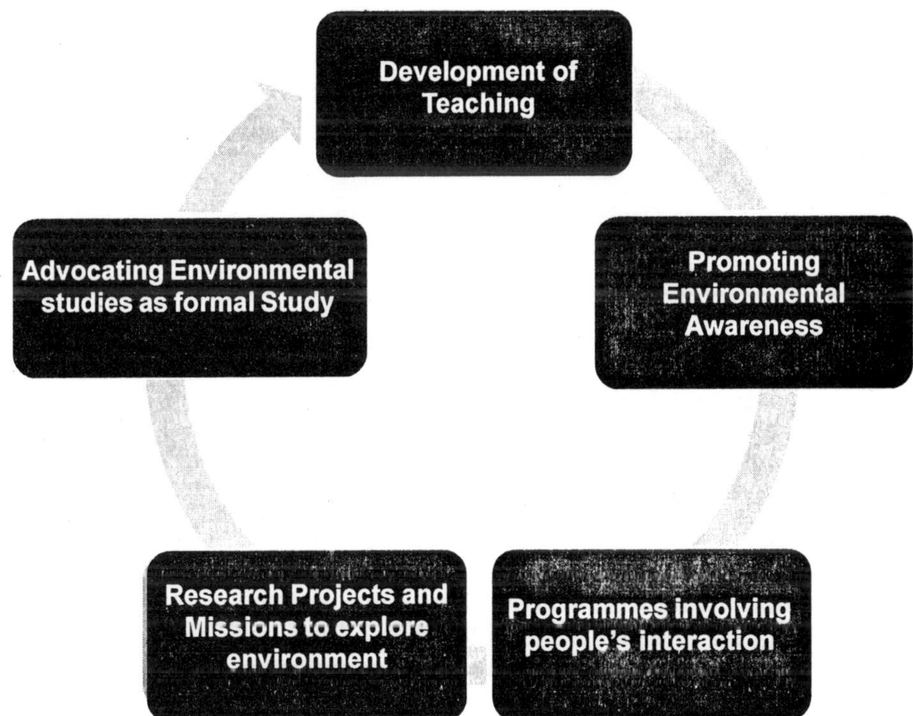

Fig. 3. Training Model for Environmental Education Awareness.

Awareness Programmes

Despite great efforts to spread environmental awareness by the government of many countries through the medium of several schemes like funds for research projects and scholarships for further study in environmental issues, it has been felt that a large population, especially in rural areas, is still left out. The best way to reach out to them and make them aware of the environmental problems is through media, particularly the electronic media. "Mass Awareness" has therefore been identified as one of the thrust areas of the Ministry, not only to intensify the efforts already being made in this direction but also to launch new initiatives. The Media plays a very important role on the awareness programmes as they telecast environmentally based programmes and information commercials. Professional Media agencies which are hired to assist the environment related ministry in carrying out the campaign, also play a major role. To encourage individual efforts in producing films/documentaries on environmentally/wildlife related themes in the country, the government has to sponsor these initiatives [5] through separate departments which are aimed at creating environmental awareness among children. These include environmental quizzes (both written as well as televised), organizational activities for observation of special occasions such as earth day, special programmes for children, etc. These proposals which are received throughout the year from various NGOs and other agencies, are considered on merit, as and when received, and are supported. For example, such programmes are:

1. An International or National written Environmental Quiz programme, Debating contests aimed at environmental issues where students from other countries need to be invited as this will help in spreading the message of environmental education throughout the world where this will prove to be a great success in sensitizing the children about environmental issues. Written environmental quiz programmes in different regional languages are being started. The winners of a written quiz would participate in a televised quiz programme [8].
2. Awareness activities / events by NGOs, academic institutions etc. on the occasion of special Environment days like Earth Day etc.

Our Purposed Model and Flow of Events

The whole concept of sustainability, participation and education needs to be evaluated in the light of certain assumptions. The first prerequisite is the provision of environmental data in a structured and presentable format. It is the foundation stone for any concerted action on environmental issues. The furnishing of such data will help in causal analysis of the facts, i.e., to find out the cause and effect relationship between predators and the final outcome. The results, thus obtained, need to be presented in the form of information sheets for further evaluation. This, in turn, calls for the dissemination of the information for the general public in order to understand the complex linkages to achieve sustainable development [6]. Once disseminated, it will lead to a gaining in knowledge with further acknowledgement of the interconnections and the cause-effect of environmental problems. This will boost mass awareness about environmental issues, thereby strengthening capacity- building in participatory activities. Environmental education, which is mostly informal, is in fact the broad categorization of the acknowledgement of mass awareness, unless formally taught as a part of curriculum. Education and consciousness will ultimately translate into public participation culminating into the adoption of specific environmental actions. The follow-up of each action will again help in generation of data and results for future planning. Thus appraisal is as important as participation to maintain the cyclical flow of events that may lead to promote sustainable development.

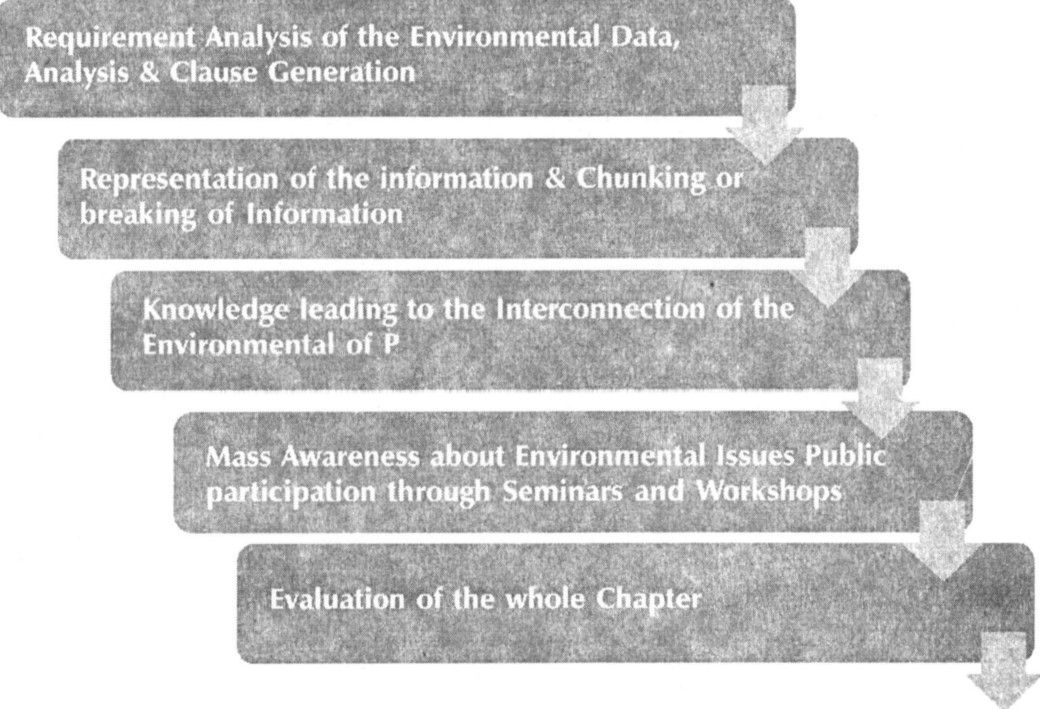

Fig. 4. Purposed Model / Flow chart for Environment Studies.

Conclusion

We have tried to discuss the ever increasing and pressing need for environmental education through the medium of a research paper where we have put various issues associated with environmental studies such as the importance, need and classification of education as the highlights. Our idea is for tackling the issues associated with the environment as we need education in the form of training or studies at every level of our educational system. Environmental education should be flawless as only then we can succeed in our objective. We have proposed a model that is based on the analysis and designing of policies for sound environmental education. Our efforts will help the research community to understand these problems in a better way.

References

1. Centre for Environmental Education < http://www.ceeindia.org/cee/index.html>
2. Centre of Environment Studies < http://hpuniv.nic.in/envstu.htm>Centre of Environment Studies < http://hpuniv.nic.in/envstu.htm>
3. Environment Education Division < http://envfor.nic.in/divisions/ee/ee.html>
4. Environment Education Program< http://www.wwfindia.org/about_wwf/what_we_do/education/index.cfm>
5. Environmental Studies by Shriram Institute of Industrial Research < http://www.shriraminstitute.org/environment1.html>
6. Environmental studies< http://en.wikipedia.org/wiki/Environmental_studies
7. Moral Development and the Social Environment by By Georg Lind, Hans A. Hartmann, Roland Wakenhut
8. Moral Development and the Social Environment by By Georg Lind, Hans A. Hartmann, Roland Wakenhut
9. Science, technology, society and environment education< http://en.wikipedia.org/wiki/Science%2C_technology%2C_society_and_environment_education >

15
Urbanization Ecology and Health Issues

VIKAS KUMAR AND PRASHANT KUMAR MISHRA

Introduction

Our planet is increasingly urban. Approximately 50% of the world's people now live in urban areas. In many regions of the world, the rate of urbanization is declining; however, individual cities, metropolitan regions, and urban areas continue to grow (in number, extent and population). In this context, urban ecology is an important approach to environmental science and sustainable development. People throughout the world practise urban ecology. These people are motivated by a desire to create healthy human ecosystems and liveable communities in which to live, work, and play. In this paper, we will study some of these people, projects, and places. Key questions: What is an urban ecosystem? Are cities sustainable environments? What are civic stakeholders, local communities, and global societies doing to ensure that urban and urbanizing landscapes are healthy and desirable places for today's world?

The world's population is anticipated to increase from 6.1 billion to 8.1 billion over the next 25 years, with urban expansion expected to accommodate nearly all of this population increase. By 2030, inhabitants of urban areas are expected to account for approximately 60% of the world's population. This pattern of population increase is expected in Australia, as it is in other parts of the world. The benefits we derive from our cities have come at a considerable environmental cost. Rivers and streams around the world have been profoundly changed by human activity and urbanization, despite our increasing awareness of the link between stream health and human health. However, streams in urban areas have received relatively little scientific attention when compared with systems in natural (minimally disturbed) or rural areas.

Cities are where human civilization began; where the world's great universities, libraries, cathedrals and museums are found. They have been the centre of scientific discovery and technological innovation, of commerce and literacy. However, even in ancient times, cities were also congested – metropolitan Rome and Carthage each had nearly one million inhabitants.

There has been a major shift of the population over the previous century. At the beginning of the 20th century, most of the world's population lived in rural areas; now more than half live in urban areas. The migration of people to urban areas has been fuelled in a large part by the hope for a better quality of a life than that afforded in a labour-intensive rural existence. It is projected that within 25 years, more than two-third of the global populations will live in cities.

There are now 23 "megacities" in which each has populations over 10 million. Many are located in developing countries which do not have adequate infrastructures in place to meet even the basic needs of rapidly growing populations. In many large cities around the world, air quality, sanitation and access to clean water are serious concerns. Therefore, there has been an increased attention and study of these burgeoning urban ecosystems.

There is also a wide array of environmental benefits to growing cities. In the U.S., for example, while most of the population lives in urban areas, only five per cent of the land is occupied by cities, paved roads, and the built environment, leaving much land for crops, pasture, or intact natural habitat. Across the globe, urban populations also tend to have fewer children than those in rural areas, since children are not required for subsistence labour. Finally, various systems which we have come to depend on – energy, communication, sanitation, and transportation – can be more efficient in urban areas; designs for future urban development are continuing to increase the effectiveness of these systems.

Urbanization - Impacts

1. The Concept of Urbanization

Urbanisation is the physical growth of urban areas into rural or natural land as a result of population in-migration to an existing urban area. Effects include a change in density and administration services. While the exact definition and population size of urbanized areas varies among different countries, urbanization is attributed to the growth of cities. Urbanization is also defined by the United Nations as the movement of people from rural to urban areas with a population growth equating to urban migration. The UN projects that half the world's population will live in urban areas at the end of 2008.

Urbanization also refers to a general increase in population and the amount of industrialization of a settlement. It includes an increase in the number and extent of cities. It symbolizes the movement of people from rural to urban areas. Urbanization happens because of the increase in the extent and density of urban areas. The density of population in urban areas increases because of the migration of people from less industrialized regions to more industrialized areas.

2. Causes of Urbanization

Urbanization occurs naturally from individual and corporate efforts to reduce expense in commuting and transportation while improving opportunities for jobs, education, housing, and transportation. Living in cities permits individuals and families to take advantage of the opportunities of proximity, diversity, marketplace competition and cultral activities.

People move into cities to seek economical opportunities. In rural areas, often on small family farms, it is difficult to improve one's standard of living beyond basic sustenance. Farm living is dependent on unpredictable environmental conditions, and in times of drought, flood or pestilence, survival becomes extremely problematic.

Cities, in contrast, are known to be places where money and wealth are centralised. Cities are where fortunes are made and where social mobility is possible. Businesses, which generate jobs and capital, are usually located in urban areas. Whether the source is trade or tourism, it is also through the cities that foreign money flows into a country.

These conditions are heightened during times of change from a pre-industrial society to an industrial one. It is at this time that many new commercial enterprises are made possible, thus creating new jobs in cities. It is also a result of industrialisation that farms become more mechanised, putting many labourers out of work.

3. Effects of Urbanization

Urbanization brings with it several consequences - both adverse and beneficial. They impact on social and environmental areas.

Adverse Effects of Urbanization

There is an increasing competition for facilities due to the high standard of living in urban areas, which has triggered several negative effects. Many people including farmers who move to cities in search of a better life end up as casual labourers as they lack adequate education. This leads to one of the worst problems of urbanization - the growth of slums.

Slums

They are urban areas that are heavily populated with substandard housing and very poor living conditions. As a result several problems arise.

- ***Land Insecurity*** - Slums are usually located on land which is not owned by the slum dwellers. They can be evicted at any time by the landowners.
- ***Poor living conditions*** - Crowding and lack of sanitation are the main problems. This contributes to the outbreak of diseases. Utilities such as water, electricity and sewage disposal are also scarce.
- ***Unemployment*** - Since the number of people competing for jobs is more than the jobs available, unemployment is an inevitable problem.
- ***Crime*** - Slum conditions make maintenance of law and order difficult.The patrolling of slums is not a priority of law enforcing officers. Unemployment and poverty force people into anti-social activities. Slums become a breeding ground for criminal activities.

Environmental Impacts of Urbanization

- ***Temperature*** - Due to factors such as paving over formerly vegetated land, an increasing number of residences and high-rise apartments and industries, contribute drastically to temperature increases.

- *Air pollution* - Factories and automobiles are symbols of urbanization. Due to harmful emissions of gasses and smoke from factories and vehicles, air pollution occurs. Current research shows high amounts of suspended particulate matter in the air, particularly in cities, which contributes to allergies and respiratory problems thereby becoming a huge health hazard.
- *Water issues* - When urbanization takes place, water cycles change as the cities have more precipitation than surrounding areas. Due to the dumping of sewage from factories into water bodies, water pollution occurs which can lead to outbreaks of epidemics.
- *Destruction of Habitats* - To make an area urbanized, a lot of forested areas are destroyed. Usually these areas would have been habitats to many birds and animals.

Benefits of Urbanization

Although urbanization has its drawbacks, it also has its benefits.

- *Efficiency* - Cities are extremely efficient. Less effort is needed to supply basic amenities such as fresh water and electricity. Research and recycling programmes are possible only in cities. In most cities flats are in vogue today. Many people can be accommodated within a small land area.
- *Convenience* - Access to education, health, social services and cultural activities is more available to people in cities than in villages. Life in cities is much more advanced, sophisticated and comfortable, compared with life in villages. Cities have advanced communication and transport networks.
- *Concentration of resources* - Since major human settlements were established near natural resources from ancient times, a lot of resources are available in and around cities. A lot of facilities to exploit these resources also exist only in cities.
- *Educational facilities* - Schools, colleges and universities are established in cities to develop human resources. A variety of educational courses and fields are available offering students a wide choice for their future careers.
- *Social integration* - People of many castes and religions live and work together in cities, which creates a better understanding and harmony and helps breakdown social and cultural barriers.
- *Improvements in economy* - High-tech industries earn valuable foreign exchange money and a lot of money for a country in the stock markets.

Causal Factors behind Urbanization

General

The major reasons for increasing the urban population are rural to urban migration, including international migration to a lesser extent, and the re-classification or expansion of existing city boundaries to include populations that were hitherto classified as being residential outside the city limits. These are estimated to contribute about 60 per cent of the region's urban growth, while a natural increase counts for some 40 per cent.

Rural -Urban Migration

Primary driving forces of rural-urban migration include the opportunities and services offered in urban areas – especially jobs and education, while in some cases, conflict, land degradation and exhaustion of natural resources in rural areas are also important.The patterns of rural-urban migration may be city-specific, reflecting, among other things, changes in the city's economical base, labour market and age structure. They also reflect social, economic and political changes within the region and nation and are influenced by economical factors in the surrounding and distant rural areas, such as landowning structure, agricultural practices and crop prices, and overall rural productivity. Most evidence suggests that increasing the income and level of education of rural populations accelerates migration and this phenomenon, coupled with the greater access to urban areas, has led to an inevitable increase in rural populations seeking employment opportunities in urban areas.

Links to Globalization

The steady increase in the level of urbanization reflects the fact that the size of the world's economy has grown many times and has also changed from one dominated by relatively closed national economies or trading blocks to one where most countries have more open economies and where production and the services it needs, including financial services, are increasingly integrated internationally. These trends appear to be strengthening, reinforced especially by the freer and faster flows of information and knowledge under the impact of new information technologies. Technology has increased the already dominant economic role and importance of urban areas worldwide, indicating the growing importance of cities in the global economy.

Mismanagement

It is often pointed out that many urban environmental problems are the result of poor management, poor planning and the absence of coherent urban policies rather than of urbanization itself. The problem of urbanization has significantly been exacerbated by inappropriate incentive systems, such as the "growth-first" strategy adopted by the Governments of many countries in the region, especially in developing countries. In order to attract investment, industrial promotion policies are designed to offer privileges and incentive packages, including low-taxes, lax regulations and a subsidized infrastructure, targeting urban areas. Industrial growth, combined with an adequate infrastructure, inappropriate pricing of resources and services, and an inadequate institutional mechanism to ensure environmental protection, further accelerates environmental degradation in urban areas. The 'land market' factors that accounted for exacerbating urbanization problems include inappropriate regulation, lack of tenure security, inadequate infrastructure capacity, inadequate information, inadequate pricing and taxation, and weak institutions and poorly coordinated actors in the land market. All these factors necessitate significant improvements in overall urban governance to reduce and bypass the urbanization problems effectively.

Urbanisation and Problems Related to Health

The World Health Organization (WHO) Commission on Social Determinants of Health (CSDH) has posed a provocative question for public health: "Why do we keep treating people for illnesses only to send them back to the conditions that created the illness in the first place?"[1] For the WHO Centre for Health Development (WHO Kobe Centre), hub of the Commission's Knowledge Network on Urban Settings (KNUS), this represents a challenge to the public health sector not only to acknowledge the pervasiveness of urban poverty as a critical pathway to ill health and health inequities, but to address this as an urgent public health issue affecting a billion people living in informal settlements, or "slums."[2]

People who live in informal settlements are often systematically excluded from opportunities, decent employment, security, capacity, and empowerment[3] that would enable them to gain better control over their health and lives. As noted in the *Interim Report by the Millennium Development Goals (MDG) Task Force*, this focusses on improving the lives of urban slum dwellers:

Much of urban poverty is not because of distance from infrastructure and services but from exclusion. They are excluded from the attributes of urban life that remain a monopoly of a privileged minority—political voice, secure good-quality housing, safety and the rule of law, good education, health services, decent transport, adequate incomes, access to goods and services, credit—in short, the attributes of full citizenship.[4]

The issue of urban poverty is not new, but it is often narrowly viewed as an economical issue that is best addressed by economical policies and interventions. Urban poverty today, as driven by globalization and rapid uncontrolled urbanization, also needs to be recognized as a social, political, and cultural process that has profound impacts on public health. Exclusion of the urban poor from the benefits of urban life fosters discontent and political unrest. Within the broader context of health and human development, rapid urbanization of poverty and ill health have been characterized as a new human security threat.

Rapid uncontrolled urbanization results from the interaction between global and local forces. The interconnectedness of cities through trade, business, industry, tourism, international travel, information technology, and media is reshaping social determinants of

---

[1] UN-HABITAT defines "slum" as: "A heavily populated urban area characterized by substandard housing and squalor.

[2] These numbers are based on country reports from UN-HABITAT in 2001, which were subsequently organized as WHO regional statistics.

[3] Former WHO Director-General Dr. J. W. Lee stated at the launch of the WHO Commission for Social Determinants of Health that social determinants of health are the conditions in which people live and work. They are the "causes behind the causes" of ill health. (http://www.medicalnewstoday.com/medicalnews.php?newsid=21561 accessed 21 February 2007).

[4] Knowledge Network on Urban Settings.

health that are manifest at the city level. On the other hand, local and national governance capacity in relation to health systems, housing, transport, property rights, migration, land use policy, working conditions, and employment may be unable to cope with the speed of change brought about by the global economical restructuring. Inequity in cities that leads to urban poverty, and poor health, therefore, are also products of global and local forces in the urban setting. Public health can play an important role in ameliorating urban poverty through social processes (participation, social capital, social accountability, and social inclusion) that influence urban governance at multiple nodes of power. Addressing urban poverty as an urgent public health issue opens a policy space for fairer health opportunities and healthier and more equitable cities.

Understanding the Role of Public Health in an Urbanizing World

The Knowledge Network on Urban Settings has worked with researchers, local communities, academia, developmental organizations, donors, and practitioners from local, national, regional and global organizations to distill what is known about social determinants, health and health inequities in urban settings.

While KNUS[4] research is ongoing, the following findings are of particular relevance to public health:

- The urban poor do not "wait" for governments or organizations to act on their behalf. They have the desire and resourcefulness to find ways to improve their shelters, access running water, produce food, organize child care, educate themselves and their children, and protect each other amid extreme poverty.[5]
- While poor communities are severely affected by violence, it is important to recognize the wealth of untapped social resources within informal settlements. One case study from the favelas of Brazil notes the presence of "social networks, trust, solidarity and mutual support, celebration, cultural life, local businesses, informal activities on education, recreation, sports, religion, politics, and much more."
- Uncontrolled, rapid urbanization and the unravelling of the traditional social fabric deepen inequity and give rise to alternative governance structures such as gangs (which target impoverished youth) and paramilitary organizations (known to recruit children for warfare). People who live in informal settlements are at a higher risk of exposure to crime and violence.
- Since 2000, the world's fastest growing urban areas are also those where there are increasing concentrations of informal settlements. This has profound consequences for

[5] Chitekwe B, Mitlin D. The urban poor under threat and in struggle: options for urban development in Zimbabwe, 1995-2000. Environ Urban. 2001;13(85):85-101

public health strategies to control communicable (HIV-AIDS, TB, H5N1 virus, dengue, and other vector-borne diseases), as well as non-communicable (obesity, diabetes, cancer, chronic heart disease, stroke, hypertension) diseases, mental health and conditions that are associated with urban life (road traffic injuries, urban violence, obesity, and unsafe settlements).

- Urban poverty has been narrowly framed as an economical developmental issue. Unless a broader developmental perspective is used, policies, programmes, measurements, evaluations, and strategies – as well as the "actors" and "stakeholders" who are expected to take action – will fail to engage fully the social, cultural, environmental, and health dimensions of urbanization and urban poverty.
- Improving local urban governance as a strategy for alleviating urban poverty (as exemplified by the work of UN-HABITAT) has created a new policy space for linking development to health and vice-versa, but this space has not been effectively used by the public health sector as a means of shaping healthier public policy in the majority of cities.
- Given the high concentration of national resources in cities, it is often assumed that city dwellers have a better access to services including health care, and that poor people in urban settings are therefore better off than their rural counterparts. This is where the issue of equity emerges as crucial for the urban poor, who, in fact, grapple with complex and debilitating challenges: inability to pay for goods and services, lack of social support systems, unhealthy and unsafe living and working conditions, exposure to crime and violence, limited food choices, discrimination, isolation and powerlessness.
- Despite the obvious linkage between urban poverty and ill health and the potential impact on the rest of the population, the health sector in many countries continues to define narrowly its role as that of finding ways to improve access to services and improve the financing of health care services for the poor. Although important, this is far from sufficient.

Public Health: A Rallying Point for Equity in Cities

The need for intersectional action and policy to address social determinants of health is not a new concept. The challenges and difficulties of mobilizing intersectional support for policy and resources are known. In its review of 80 case studies, KNUS has discovered that "health" can unite individuals, communities, institutions, leaders, donors, and politicians from divergent sectors, even in complex and hostile contexts where structural determinants of health are deep and divisive. Some of the case studies are highlighted below.

While debate and discourse inevitably arise on methods, terminology, resources, and priorities for achieving better health, invoking health as a social goal and the imperative for "fairer health opportunities for all" has been a powerful lever for addressing social determinants of health in urban settings. The research and analysis also point to the critical importance of social processes in achieving more equitable health outcomes. Preliminary findings from the thematic papers of KNUS[4] suggest that:

- Integrated interventions that *support community action through participation and empowerment* (urban primary health care Healthy Cities Community-Based Initiatives, Sustainable Cities Local Agenda 21 sites Cities Without Slums and many other integrated approaches) have been shown to reduce health risks, improve health outcomes, and promote better quality of life[6];
- Where integrated interventions are further linked to better urban governance (local government accountability, local capacity building in support of decentralization, land use policy, participatory budgeting, urban planning and design, sustainable food systems), a healthier social environment is possible;
- Where "change agents," "catalysts," and "facilitators" have stepped in to mobilize communities toward public health action and ultimately to influence intersectoral policy and mobilize resources for health equity (national urban renewal programmes, agricultural policy, national housing policy linked to urban development), bringing interventions to scale is more likely; and
- Networked governance where urban poor communities and other organized groups (e.g., Shack Dwellers International) work with local or national government agencies such as the Community Organizations Development Institute of Thailand and the Committee of Resource Organizations of Mumbai[7], India and international alliances or organizations like the Alliance of Healthy Cities, European Healthy Cities Network, Network of Healthy Municipalities, Cities Alliance, UN-HABITAT and WHO, demonstrates the power of harnessing social processes created by the interconnectedness of cities. Taking the principles of empowerment and participation a step further through city-to-city learning is a means of transforming global power relations and overcoming the structures that perpetuate urban poverty.

Sharpening the Focus on Social Processes

Primary health care and its emphasis on community action and a social process in the urban setting is a key strategy in achieving better health equity for the urban poor. Sharpening the focus on social processes throughout the entire public health arena paves the way for scaling up interventions that work.

The case studies of KNUS describe a range of actions that contribute to strengthening and supporting the role of public health:

---

[6] UN-HABITAT. The Challenge of Slums: Global Report on Human Settlements. U.S. & UK: Earthscan; 2003.

[7] Palnitker S. *New culture of urban sanitation, Mumbai (CORO)*. Available at: http://www.archidev.org/article.php3?id_article=391.

1. Engaging in political processes (budget hearings, elections, lobbying, campaigns) that impact on social determinants such as violence prevention, employment, child development, and gender equity;
2. Strengthening "bonding" and "bridging" social capital by facilitating dialogue among stakeholders across sectors and within hierarchies;
3. Using a "healthy settings approach";
4. Engaging communities through participation and use of empowering processes;
5. Engaging in intersectional policy debates on no health equity drivers (e.g., transportation, land use policy, land tenure, human rights);
6. Using existing networks to advance policy issues (local, national, regional, international);
7. Advocating for social and financial accountability at all levels;
8. Recognizing the links between mental health and well-being and public places, community spaces, parks and gardens where social cohesion and the expression of diversity are simultaneously nurtured through cultural activities, art, recreation, sports and play;
9. Using local data (intra-urban health differentials) and local situations to articulate the links between health and other sectors such as transportation, housing, and public services that impact on social determinants;
10. Supporting regulations that protect people, especially vulnerable or exposed groups, from threats and hazards (in workplaces, communities, schools).

Conclusion

Social capital, as part of social processes, is a critical means of changing power relations in cities. Public health can provide the "glue" to link, network and bind the growing groups of poor and marginalized populations to nodes of power.

The urban setting is a social determinant of health in itself. Public health gains in disease prevention and control in our cities can unravel easily with the growth of physical and social environments of extreme deprivation. In an interconnected world, our cities can continue to be "engines of economic growth and "centres of culture". The question is whether public health can use the interconnectedness of cities as a positive pathway to enhancing equity in health between and among cities and nations.

A variety of options in terms of policy responses and tools to cope effectively with the urbanization transition has been proposed and discussed for several decades. These options may be categorized in the following four strategic steps.

a) National planning to control urbanization to manageable levels.
b) Regional / Urban planning to guide urbanization to manageable situation.
c) Intra-urban management to cope with urbanization problems.
d) Participation, Partnership and Governance.

Local and national governments and multilateral organizations are all grappling with the challenges of urbanization. Urban health risks and concerns involve many different sectors, including health, environment, housing, energy, transportation, urban planning, and others. Two main policy implications are highlighted: the need for systematic and useful urban health statistics on a disaggregated, i.e., intra-urban, basis, and the need for more effective partnering across sectors. The humanitarian and economic imperative to create livable and sustainable cities must drive us to seek and successfully overcome challenges and capitalize on opportunities. Good urban planning and governance, exchange of best practice models and the determination and leadership of stakeholders across disciplines, sectors, communities and countries will be critical.

References

1. Burris S, Hancock T, Herzog A, Lin V. Emerging strategies for healthy urban governance. *J Urban Health*. 2007 (In press). DOI 10.1007/s11524-007-9174-6.
2. Garau P, Sclar ED. Interim Report of the Millennium Development Goal Task Force 8 on Improving the Lives of Slum Dwellers. New York: United Nations; 2004.
3. IDEA. *Democracy and Human Security*. In: Democracy, Conflict and Human Security: further reading. Stockholm, International Institute for Democracy and Electorate Assistance, 2006:22
4. Kawachi I, Wamala SP. Poverty and Inequalities in a Globalized World. In: Kawachi I, Wamala SP, eds. Globalization and Health. New York: Oxford University Press; 2006:122–137.
5. Marmot M. *Social Determinants of Health. First Meeting of the Social Determinants of Health for the Asia Network*. Tokyo, Asia Network, 2006.
6. PAHO. Gender ,Health, and Development in the Americas:Basic Indicators 2005. Washington DC: Panamerican Health Organisation; 2005.
7. UNFPA. *Urbanization: A Majority in Cities*. Available at:http://www.unfpa.org/pds/urbanization.htm.
8. UN-HABITAT. Urbanization, Urban Population and Urban Slum Dwellers, in Financing Urban Shelter: Global Report on Human Settlements 2005. U.S. & UK.: Earthscan; 2005.
9. UN-HABITAT Features. *The Urban Penalty: The Poor Die Young*. United Nations Human Settlements Programme; Available at: http://www.unhabitat.org/documents/media_centre/sowcr2006/SOWCR%2022.pdf..
10. UN-HABITAT. The Challenge of Slums: Global Report on Human Settlements. U.S. & UK: Earthscan; 2003.
11. UN-HABITAT Features. What are slums and why do they exist? United Nations Human Settlements Programme, 2003.
12. Wallerstein C. Tuberculosis ravages Philippines slums. Br Med J. 14 August 1999;319(7202):402.

[illegible]

References

[illegible]

16

Energy Environment in Agriculture in Jhajjar District of Haryana

DR. MOHINDER SINGH KADAYAN

Introduction

Energy has been a dynamic force in the growth and development of human society from human energy to wood energy and later to the use of animal power, fossil fuels, nuclear energy, and now renewables such as solar, wind, etc. The evolution of energy use is the story of control over energy sources to serve man. In the world economy today, the level of energy consumption has become an indicator of a country's modernization. This has led not only to a substantial growth in the demand for energy but also resulted in environmental degradation. Energy is obtained by exploiting a wide variety of resources which are utilized in various activities by human beings. Agriculture, one of the antique occupations of human beings has always been the source of energy consumption since the advent of sedentary life.

Agriculture today utilizing modern technology, consumes various types of energy, i.e. commercial energy or conventional energy in the form of oil and electricity; non-commercial energy in the form of crop residue, animal residue, animal power and man power, mechanical energy in the form of machines such as tractors, thrashers, crushers etc. and chemical energy in the form of fertilizers and pesticides. Depending upon the nature or use of energy products, energy could be direct or indirect. The products of oil, gas and electricity are used directly while indirect energy consumption is in the form of seeds, fertilizers, chemicals, materials and human and bullock labour.

In India, out of the total consumption of energy, 65 per cent is met through commercial sources, and 35 per cent through non-commercial sources. Our per capita consumption of commercial energy is about one-eighth of the world's average. Table 1 shows sectoral and temporal variations in the consumption of commercial energy in India. It shows that the agricultural sector has registered a decline in the consumption of commercial energy, i.e. from 9.4 per cent in 1979-80 to 7.1 per cent in 1999-2000. In 2009-10 it is projected that the share would further fall to 4.8 per cent as the other sectors of the economy like industry and transport, are gaining importance day by day.

Table 1: Sector-wise Commercial Energy Consumption in India.
(in Percentage)

Sector	1979-80	1999-2000	2004-05	2009-10 (Projected)
Household	15.7	18.4	20.7	21.4
Agriculture	9.4	7.1	5.7	4.8
Industry	38.2	49.5	48.2	47.3
Transport	32.8	23.6	23.9	24.8
Others	3.9	1.4	1.5	1.7
Total	100.0	100.0	100.0	100.0

Source : 1. Tata Energy Research Institute, New Delhi, 2005-06
2. Planning Commission, Government of India

There are a lot of spatio-temporal variations in the use of energy at all levels, i.e. international, national, regional, local as well as sectoral. Although there has been a phenomenal increase in agricultural production due to the adoption of new strateges for agricultural development, the gains are confined to specific areas. In the present paper a modest attempt has been made to examine the energy environment in agriculture in the Jhajjar district of Haryana.

The Study Area

Jhajjar is one of the districts of Haryana which came into existance w.e.f. 15th July, 1997 and it is geographically located between 28°19' 30" to 28°50' 21" north latitude and 76°16 36" to 76°57' 41" east longitude covering an area of 1,834 sq. km. It supports 8,80,072 persons with a density of 480 persons per sq.km. Jhajjar with 22.16 per cent of its population residing in urban areas is one of the less urbanized districts in the state. The sex ratio (847 per 1000 male) too is quite low in the district. The district has a literacy rate of 72.38 per cent, which is above the state average. Likewise, the female literacy (59.65 per cent) too, is more than the state as such.

The district enjoys a sub-humid climate with an average temperature of 29°C and about 6 cm average annual rainfall. The soil of the district, mainly in the north-east, is fertile alluvium suitable for cultivation but in the south-west sandy plains and sand dunes are also present. Agriculture is the base of the economy and more than 80 per cent of its total area is under cultivation and about 60 per cent of it is irrigated. The major *kharif* crops grown in the area are jowar and bajra, while the major *rabi* crops are wheat and mustard.

Aim and Objectives

Although there are varied aims and objectives, the main objectives of the study are :

(i) To find out the agricultural operation-wise and source-wise energy use per unit area.

(ii) To find out the crop-wise energy input and output and their relationship per unit area.

Research Design and Methodology

Since the authentic data of energy use in agriculture at micro level is not available, the study is entirely based on primary data collected at the farmer level. Based on the purposive sampling technique, 7 villages being representative of the Jhajjar district and having a high level of agricultural advancement, have been selected from the 5 community development blocks. The name of the sample villages selected are Mahandipur (from block Bahadurgarh), Jondhi and Boria (Jhajjar), Bakra (Beri), Sundrehti and Karoda (Matenhail) and Sarola (Sahlawas) (Fig.1). From each sample village roughly 10 per cent of the total households amounting to 143 households were selected keeping in view the tractor operated farms and size of holdings and further the heads of all the 143 selected households were interviewed according to a well-structured questionnaire which mainly included the use of energy in selected agricultural operations, in selected crops, yields of crops and other relevant Information.

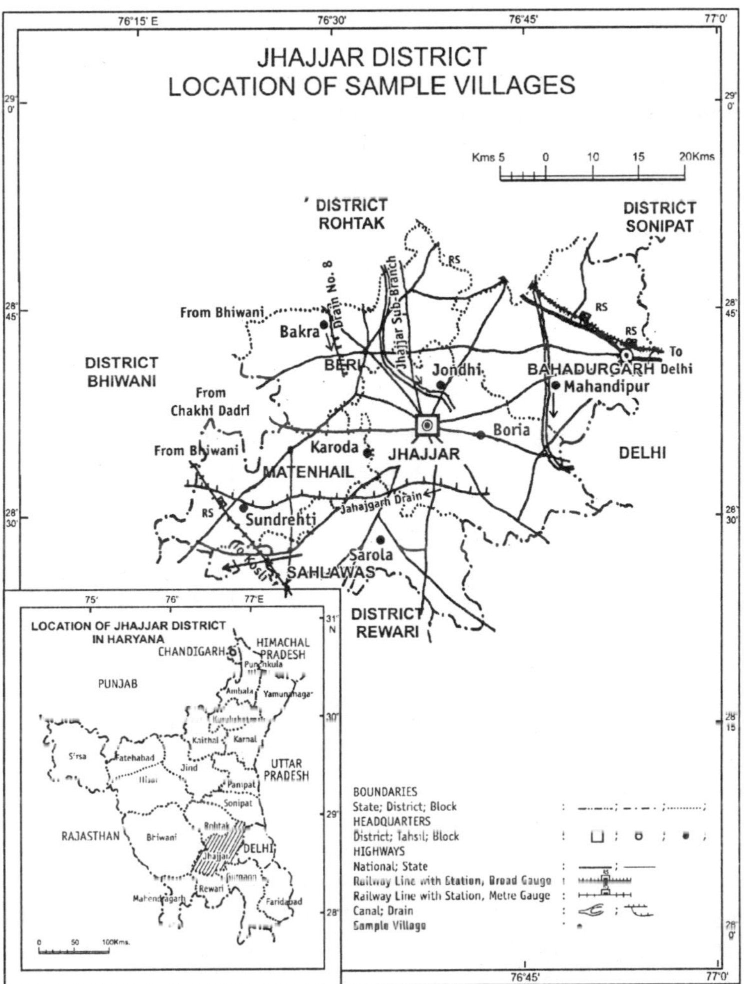

Fig. 1

Agriculture is a very complex primary activity in its practice, production and organization. Hence,the generation of data in the of use of energy in agriculture is very complicated and complex. However, following seven main agricultural operations, although there may be a few more,these have been taken to assess the use of energy:

(a) Field preparation
(b) Sowing
(c) Irrigation
(d) Fertilizer application
(e) Harvesting and transporation
(f) Threshing and winnowing
(g) Marketing process.

Similarly out of many sources of energy the following five major sources of energy have been considered:

(a) Human
(b) Diesel
(c) Chemical Fertilizers
(d) Seeds
(e) Tractor

Since various sources of energy used in agriculture are of varied type and nature, they cannot be aggregated. Hence, all these sources of energy have been converted into kilo calories with the help of a standard conversion table (Tata Energy Research Institute-1987) (Table2).

Table 2: Energy Equivalents for different Inputs and Outputs.

Category	Energy Equivalents
Man	470 K.Cal / hr
Diesel	9,400 K.Cal / ltr
Tractor (30 hp)	19,230 K.Cal / hr
Elect. Tubewell (20 hp)	12,820 K.Cal /hr
Diesel Pump Set (7.5 hp)	4,807.5 K.Cal / hr
Nitrogen (Fertilizer)	14,325 K.Cal / kg
Phosphate (Fertilizer)	2,650 K.Cal / kg
Potash (Fertilizer)	1,600 K.Cal / kg
Seeds and Outputs : Cereals (wheat and bajra)	3,510 K.Cal / kg
Oil-seed (mustard seeds)	5,970 K.Cal / kg

Source: Tata Energy Research Institute, 1987-88, **TERI Energy Data**

Directory and Yearbook, New Delhi.

Based on this conversion the total energy used per hectare by each respondent is calculated and finally the average energy use in agriculture in kilo calories per hectare for each sample village is calculated by dividing the total energy used per hectare of all the selected respondents by the total number of selected respondents of the same village. Likewise, agricultural productivity has been measured in terms of kilo calories per hectare and the average agricultural productivity per hectare in selected crops is calculated for each sample village by dividing the total agricultural productivity of all the selected respondents by the total number of selected respondents of the same village. The crop-wise energy input : output ratio specially in bajra (*kharif*), wheat and mustard (*rabi*) is also worked out for the sample villages.

Agricultural Operation-wise Use of Energy

There are various stages in the production of agricultural commodities, and in each stage energy is consumed, but its use is not uniform in all the stages of agricultural operations. Hence, an attempt has been made in the present study to find out the details on the variations in their energy consumption. There are mainly seven stages of the requirements of energy sources or power in agricultural production; viz., field preparation, sowing, irrigation, fertilizer application, harvesting and transportation, threshing and winnowing and the marketing process. For the assessment of energy use in agriculture, firstly the entire energy use by an individual respondent in different agricultural operations is converted into kilo calories and has been added together to get his total energy consumption in a comparable unit. Finally, to find out the average k.cal./hect. the total energy consumption in different agricultural operations in a sample village is divided by the total number of respondents taken from that village. The agricultural operation-wise use of energy in the Jhajjar district is presented in table 3.

Table 3 : Agricultural Operation-wise use of Energy in Sample Villages of Jhajjar District.
(Average k.cal./hect.)

Sample Village	Agricultural Operation						
	Field Preparation	Sowing	Irrigation	Fertilizer Application	Harvesting and Transportation	Threshing and Winnowing	Marketing Process
Mahandipur	6,59,609	6,28,846	24,38,660	50,89,525	4,13,060	3,29,880	1,46,039
Jondhi	6,32,835	6,21,412	16,69,243	58,15,816	3,74,833	3,14,463	1,46,039
Boria	7,30,195	11,40,646	17,60,530	46,67,741	3,65,542	3,29,880	1,46,039
Bakra	5,67,118	6,25,806	14,60,588	56,60,441	4,49,162	2,72,098	1,46,039
Sundrehti	5,04,156	7,65,985	25,03,865	33,61,826	2,99,441	3,48,887	3,40,757
Karoda	5,11,136	6,38,084	22,95,210	60,68,555	4,78,706	3,98,728	1,75,246
Sarola	9,24,914	6,68,886	23,47,373	31,02,566	4,02,707	3,14,463	1,53,341
Total	46,09,963	50,89,665	1,44,75,469	3,37,66,470	27,83,481	23,08,399	12,53,500
Average Jhajjar District	6,58,566	7,27,095	20,67,924	48,23,781	3,97,640	3,29,771	1,79,071

Table 3 depicts that the use of energy varies according to various agricultural operations. Fertilizer application, being the prime agricultural input in such a semi-arid agricultural system where several crops require urea (nitrogen) and Di Ammonium Phosphate (DAP) as their main chemical fertilizers, is the main user of energy amounting to an average of 46,80,924 k.cal./hect. in the Jhajjar district followed by an irrigation amounting on an average of 20,67,924 k.cal./hect. in the district, while the marketing process consumes an average of 1,79,071 k.cal./hect. which falls at the lowest level in all of the agricultural operations. The average energy consumption in the case of sowing, field preparation, harvesting and transportation, and the threshing and winnowing process is, 7,27,095, 6,58,566, 3,97,640 and 3,29,771 k.cal./hect. respectively in the district.

Source-wise Use of Energy

In order to have an in-depth understanding of the patterns of energy use in agriculture in the study area, the source-wise average use of the energy has been reckoned at k.cal./hect. for all the sample villages of the district. Although there are various sources of energy used in agriculture in the district, the major ones are human, diesel, chemical fertilizer, seeds and tractor. A brief account of each one of these is given in table 4.

Table 4: Source-wise use of Energy in Sample Villages of Jhajjar District (Average k.cal./hect.).

Sample	Source of Energy				
Village	Human	Diesel	Chemical Fertilizers	Seeds	Tractor
Mahandipur	4,91,444	22,21,480	50,33,525	4,71,847	14,87,323
Jondhi	4,33,084	15,20,585	58,07,334	4,28,480	13,85,158
Boria	4,31,806	16,03,742	46,14,065	4,76,184	20,14,776
Bakra	4,82,153	13,30,512	55,57,387	4,68,808	13,42,392
Sundrehti	4,80,817	22,80,878	33,09,658	5,51,205	15,82,359
Karoda	5,14,613	20,90,805	50,14,066	4,73,144	14,73,067
Sarola	5,25,472	21,38,323	30,47,730	5,03,946	16,98,779
Total	33,59,389	1,31,86,325	3,23,83,765	33,73,614	1,09,83,854
Average Jhajjar District	4,79,912	18,83,760	46,26,252	4,81,944	15,69,122

Table 4 shows that there are a lot of variations in the source-wise energy use in the study area. The sources of energy indicate that chemical fertilizers, diesel, and tractor are the major sources of energy accounting an average of 46,26,252, 18,83,760, and 15,69,122 k.cal./hect. respectively in the district. The other sources of energy used are seeds and human accounting for an average of 4,81,944 and 4,79,912 k.cal./hect respectively in the district. Fertilizer application and irrigation are the major agricultural operations which together use 74.65 per cent of the total energy in the district. The other operations like sowing, field preparation, harvesting and transportation, threshing and winnowing, and the marketing process consume 25.35 per cent of the total energy. Among these operations sowing and field preparation together consume 15.33 per cent of the total energy in the district.

Crop-wise Energy Input and Output and their Relationship

The crops grown in the Jhajjar district are divided into two main categories, viz. *kharif* and *rabi*. From these categories three dominating crops, i.e., bajra (*kharif*), wheat and mustard (*rabi*) are taken into account to find out the average energy input and output in k.cal./hect. and further the input : output ratio of these crops is calculated which is presented in table 5.

Table 5 : Crop-wise Energy Input and Output and their Relationship in Sample Villages of Jhajjar District (Average k.cal./hect.).

Sample Village	Bajra (kharif)			Wheat (rabi)			Mustard (rabi)		
	Input	Output	Input Output Ratio	Input	Output	Input: Output Ratio	Input	Output	Input: Output Ratio
Mahandipur	16,78,361	52,04,031	0.32	47,23,654	1,30,10,078	0.36	33,03,604	1,03,26,517	0.31
Jondhi	18,40,361	43,36,692	0.42	48,49,480	1,25,76,408	0.38	28,84,800	95,88,909	0.30
Boria	9,58,740	43,36,692	0.22	57,32,931	1,21,42,739	0.47	24,48,902	95,88,909	0.25
Bakra	11,31,460	39,03,023	0.28	42,99,875	1,17,09,070	0.36	37,49,917	88,51,301	0.42
Sundrehti	11,73,414	39,03,023	0.30	47,48,393	1,12,75,401	0.42	22,83,110	88,51,301	0.25
Karoda	9,74,110	39,03,023	0.24	54,72,347	1,08,41,731	0.50	31,19,238	88,51,301	0.35
Sarola	10,10,607	34,69,354	0.29	46,83,418	1,04,08,062	0.44	22,20,225	73,76,084	0.30
Total	87,67,053	2,90,55,838	2.07	3,45,10,098	8,19,63,489	2.93	2,00,09,796	6,34,34,322	2.18
Average Jhajjar District	12,52,436	41,50,834	0.30	49,30,014	1,17,09,069	0.42	28,58,542	90,62,046	0.31

Table 5 depicts that all the crops are energy efficient in the Jhajjar district. The energy input : output ratio is below 1.00 which exhibits the energy efficiency of the crops. Among the crops, the input : output ratio of bajra, and mustard is 0.30 and 0.31 respectively which are lower than the wheat ratio. It describes that these crops are more energy efficient than the wheat crop or they consume less energy but yield higher returns. The highest input : output ratio of 0.42 is found in wheat in the district which describes that it consumes more energy but gives a lower return. Therefore the growing of bajra and mustard crops in the district is more economical than wheat. The variations in energy efficiency in various crops in the region is mainly due to the lack of irrigational facilities, and physical factors.

An increase in agricultural productivity can never be imagined in the absence of higher doses of energy as the agricultural productivity of a region is the result of a number of factors like land productivity, the use of various forms of agricultural inputs such as irrigation, fertilizers, high yielding varieties of seeds, pesticides, machinery etc. Since all these factors which are energy conducive are not equitably available in all the regions, there exists variations in agricultural productivity.

Suggestions

As a key to reducing hunger, poverty and minimizing harmful environmental impacts on agriculture, the following guidelines have been suggested for achieving a sustainable agricultural system in the area.

(i) Integrated and balanced use of available water sources, surface and ground water, should be made.

(ii) Dryland farming should be introduced by giving more emphasis to grow bajra, pulses and mustard crops in the area.

(iii) Increase the use of organic manures, solar, wind, and biomass energy to grow and process crops.

(iv) Mixed cropping should be praticised wherever possible.

(v) High yielding and disease resistant plant varieties should be introduced.

(vi) Exotic varieties should be introduced only after due consideration of long-term impacts.

(vii) Increase the use of biological pest control and integrated pest management.

(viii) Learn sustainable forms of crop growing from successful traditional farmers, and transmit knowledge to other farmers.

Conclusion

Taking a rational view of all these facts, it may be conceded that the use of HYV of seeds of various crops, the use of chemical fertilizers along with bio-fertilizers, extension of irrigation facilities, both surface and groundwater, and proper soil and water management would go a long way in raising the production of foodgrains in the Jhajjar district. Stress must also be given on the selective adaptation of technology based upon ecological considerations to ensure maximum benefits in the long run.

References

1. Anjaneyulu, Y., 2005 : **Introduction to Environmental Science**, B.S. Publications, Hyderabad.
2. **C.D. Block-wise Primary Census Abstract, Rohtak, 2001-02,** Economic and Statistical Organization, Planning Department, Haryana, 2003.
3. Dhingra, I.C., 2003: **The Indian Economy-Environment and Policy**, Sultan Chand and Sons, New Delhi.
4. **District Statistical Abstract, Rohtak, 2002-03**, Economic and Statistical Organization, Planning Department, Haryana, 2004.
5. **Economic Survey, 2004-05**, and various other issues, Government of India, Ministry of Finance, Economic Division, New Delhi.

6. Gupta, S.P., 1992: **Statistical Methods**, Sultan Chand and Sons, New Delhi.
7. **Haryana District Gazetters, Rohtak, 2001**, Haryana Gazetteers Organization, Revenue Department, Chandigarh.
8. Kadayan, M.S., 1989 : **Impact of Irrigation on Agricultural Land Use in Haryana State (1971-72 to 1980-81)**, M.A. Dissertation, Department of Geography, Maharshi Dayanand University, Rohtak, Haryana.
9. Kadayan, M.S., 1993 : **Energy Use in Agriculture in Block Sonipat**, M.Phil. Dissertation, Department of Geography, University of Delhi, Delhi.
10. Kadayan, M.S., 2003 : **Impact of Energy Use on Paddy Productivity in Agasteewaram Block of District Kanniyakumari, Tamil Nadu**, Survey Report, Department of Geography, B.R. Ambedkar College, University of Delhi, Delhi.
11. Kadayan, M.S., 2006 : **Impact of Energy Use on Agricultural Productivity in Rohtak District**, Ph.D. Thesis, Department of Geography, University of Delhi, Delhi.
12. Kadayan, M.S., 2007 : "Global Warming Challenges for Food Security in India", in Singh, J. (ed.) **Disaster Management : Future Challenges and Opportunities**, I.K. International Publishing House Pvt. Ltd., New Delhi.

17

Global Warming
An Upcoming Disaster for the World

Amit Laddha and Arijit Roy Choudhury

Introduction

Man is both creature and moulder of his environment, which gives him physical sustenance and affords him the opportunity for intellectual, moral, social and spiritual growth. In the long and tortuous evolution of the human race on this planet, a stage has been reached when, through the rapid acceleration of science and technology, man has acquired the power to transform his environment in countless ways and on an unprecedented scale. Both aspects of man's environment, the natural and the man-made, are essential to his well-being and to the enjoyment of basic human rights, the main one being the right to life itself.

Due to the advancement of science and technology, man is creating not only a better world in which to live, but is knowingly or unknowingly also creating a world in which the life of each human being is going to be dissolved. On one side man is going to outerspace, which shows the enormous advancement of science and technology but on the other side man is also creating nuclear bombs, which shows not only the advancement of science and technology but that this advancement is creating problems for future generations to live in this world.

Understanding Global Warming

Global warming is one of the greatest threats to long term human survival. Our future will depend on how each of us responds today, to the rising carbon dioxide levels. The greatest changes will come not from governmental decisions, statistics or graphs on global warming, but from consumer choices, which will in turn drive business activity. Global warming represents the greatest new market opportunity for decades and will drive business investment for several generations.

Climatic change is any substantial change in Earth's climate that lasts for an extended period of time. Global warming refers to a climatic change that causes an increase in the average temperature of the lower atmosphere. Global warming can have many different causes, but it is most commonly associated with human interference, specifically the release of excessive amounts of greenhouse gases.

According to the report of IPCC, humans have brought on the global warming that has caused the extreme hurricanes, and that the 21st century will see even more of them. The portion of this study that has blamed humans was a result of expert opinions more so than a product of research.

Effects of Global Warming

Due to the change of climate which is the result of global warming, droughts affect crops and livestock production, sea levels are rising, glaciers are melting, floods and landslides are prevalent and destructive storms prevail.

Some impacts from increasing temperatures are already happening.

- Ice is melting worldwide, especially at the Earth's poles. This includes mountain glaciers, ice sheets covering West Antarctica and Greenland, and Arctic sea ice.
- The decline of the Adélie penguins on Antarctica, where their numbers have fallen from 32,000 breeding pairs to 11,000 in 30 years.
- Rising sea levels have become faster over the last century. Sea levels are expected to rise between 7 and 23 inches (18 and 59 centimeters) by the end of the century, and continue to melt at the poles and this could add between 4 and 8 inches (10 to 20 centimeters).
- Some butterflies, foxes and alpine plants have moved farther north or to higher, cooler areas. Species that depend on one another may become out of sync. For example, plants could bloom earlier before the pollinating insects become active. Global warming is pushing a reported 2000 species towards the poles. The climate is becoming warmer in the habitats which the plants and animals occupy.
- Precipitation (rain and snowfall) on an average have increased across the globe.
- Spruce bark beetles have boomed in Alaska thanks to 20 years of warm summers. The insects have chewed up 4 million acres of spruce trees.

Economical Aspects

Global warming is big business. Some economists argue that a warmer climate could benefit certain crops and the farming communities. However, property insurers are predicting that worsening storms caused by global warming could eventually bankrupt the insurance industry. Insurance companies are now trying to form strategic alliances, and pool resources, which could cover severe economical loss from climatic changes.

In addition, the costs to implement a worldwide plan to cut the production of CO_2 and other gases, which contribute to global warming, would cost approximately 3 percent of the World's total GDP. However, there is a dispute as to whether the industrialized world should be responsible for the main economical contributions to clean up this planet. It is important to realize that many less industrialized nations are unable to afford actions to prevent an increase in CO_2, and the fact that they have no incentive to reduce the carbon emissions that cause the "greenhouse" effect. Several less industrialized nations argue that the developed world was allowed to use nature in creating welfare, and that it is now morally right for them to be paying what has been taken. I believe that funds dedicated to the former Cold War should be used for world ecology.

Effect of Global Warming in India

Surveys have shown that the quantity of monsoons in India has increased in the last 50 years, and for some, the monsoonal rains can be seen as either a huge advantage or an equally large disadvantage. Although the average rainfall amount has not increased, the number of heavier monsoons has increased since the 1950s.

Surveys have recently discovered a trend within annual monsoon measurements toward fewer, more extreme downpours — and this raises the concern of more potential floods and other natural disasters. Monsoons are needed to nourish crops and supply water for farming communities, but too much of the monsoon rains can devastate crops and livestock as well — a delicate balance is always required.

Surveys also show that heavy and very heavy rain downpours over central India have increased significantly since the 1950s ... also, the magnitude of the very heavy events in a given year has shown a clear increasing trend."

Surveys show that "As the weak and moderate events decrease, their contribution to the mean decreased while the increasing number of heavy and very heavy events make an increasing contribution to the mean ... these two opposing contributions roughly balance each other out and keep the mean unchanged."

The average — although remaining unchanged — still does not preclude that area from the potential for extreme downpours and flooding, which can end up being catastrophic.

Effect of Global Warming in the Polar Regions

- Arctic air temperatures increased by about 5°C in the 20th century - ten times faster than the global-mean surface temperature - while Arctic sea-surface temperatures have risen by 1°C over the past 20 years.
- In the Northern Hemisphere, the spring and summer sea-ice cover decreased by about 10 to 15% from the 1950s to the year 2000; sea-ice extent in the Nordic seas has shrunken by about 30% over the last 130 years.
- Arctic sea-ice thickness declined by about 40% during late summer and early autumn in the last three decades of the 20th century.
- Alaska's boreal forests have been expanding northward by some 100 kilometers for every one degree Celsius of temperature rise.

- Precipitation has increased over the Antarctic; the Antarctic Peninsula has experienced a marked warming trend over the past 50 years, while the rest of the continent also seems to have warmed.
- Surface waters of the Southern Ocean have warmed and become less saline; the water flowing from the Atlantic into the Arctic Ocean has also warmed, and the water in the Beaufort Sea has become less saline.
- The major seal breeding grounds in the Bering Sea have seen fur-seal pup numbers fall by half between the 1950s and the 1980s.

Effects on Wildlife and Ecosystems

- In the Alps, some plant species have been migrating upwards by one to four metres per decade; some plants previously found only on mountaintops have now disappeared.
- Butterflies, dragonflies, moths, beetles and other insects are now living at higher latitudes and altitudes, where previously it was too cold for them to survive; migratory birds arrive earlier in the spring and depart later in the autumn, and many birds and amphibians are reproducing earlier.
- Cold- and cool-water fish are losing suitable habitat; warm-water fish are expanding their ranges in both the northern and the southern hemispheres.
- Some bird species in Europe, North America, and Latin America are breeding earlier in the season; in Europe, egglaying has advanced over the last 23 years; in the UK, 20 of 65 species, including long-distant migrants, advanced their egg-laying dates by an average of eight days between 1971 and 1995.
- Remarkable species such as the tiny golden frog living in Costa Rica's misty forests are becoming extinct because their habitat has become drier.
- Changes in climatic variables have increased the frequency and intensity of pest and disease outbreaks as the related organisms shift their ranges poleward or to higher elevations.
- Across Europe, the growing season in controlled mixed-species gardens lengthened by 10.8 days from 1959 to 1993; separate studies of 46 plant and tree species in the US show that they are flowering earlier because of higher spring temperatures.
- Almost two thirds of the glaciers in the Himalayan and Tienshan mountains have retreated in the past decade; Andean glaciers have also receded dramatically in the past several decades.

Effect on Sea Level

- Vast expanses of the oceans have warmed over the past 50 years; globally, sea-surface temperatures have risen in line with land temperatures.

● The global mean sea level has risen by 10 - 20 cm during the 20th century – ten times faster than the rate for the previous three thousand years.

● More water is evaporating from the sea surface; this has likely resulted in total atmospheric water vapour increasing by several percent per decade over many regions of the Northern Hemisphere.

● Seventy per cent of sandy shorelines have retreated over the past 100 years; 20 - 30 percent are stable, while less than 10 percent are advancing.

● Seawater is seeping into freshwater aquifers and intruding into estuaries in low-lying coastal areas around the world, particularly on low-lying islands.

New Environmental Conditions could Affect Food Security

The effects of global warming on agriculture will vary widely both from region to region and from place to place. Changes in local and regional temperatures, precipitation, soil moisture, sunshine and cloudiness, and extreme events such as storms and hail will all have an influence. Other important variables will include the species and cultivars (variety) being farmed, soil properties, pests and pathogens and air quality. In general, the temperate mid-latitudes are expected to receive more rain with global warming. However, mid-continental areas such as the US grain belt and vast areas of Asia are likely to dry, as will much of Australia. Less rain, warmer temperatures and greater evapotranspiration could reduce agricultural yields by a third or more in these areas. Even though increased CO_2 concentrations can stimulate crop growth and yield, these benefits may not always overcome the adverse effect of excessive heat and drought. In the tropics, many crops are already near their maximum temperature tolerance, and farmers are often unable to irrigate because water supplies are inadequate. Where dryland agriculture relies solely on rain – as in sub-Saharan Africa – yields would decrease generally with even minimal increases in temperature. More extremes and a shift in precipitation zones could worsen food security in Africa. While climatic change could be linked to local or regional food shortages, the world as a whole would still grow enough food to satisfy demand if global temperatures rise by less than 2.5° C.

Environmental Changes will Harm Human Health

The World Health Organization (WHO) defines health as "a state of complete physical, mental and social well-being and not merely the absence of disease or infirmity". Global climate change will have a wide range of affects on human health as so defined. Overall, the negative effects are expected to outweigh the positive ones. New patterns of heat waves and cold snaps, floods and droughts, and local pollution and allergens would affect health directly. Indirect effects will result from changes to ecological and social systems. Such impacts will include changes in infectious diseases, freshwater supplies, local food production, population movements and economical activities.

Studies of the health impacts associated with climate variability (particularly those related to El Niño events) have provided new evidence of the sensitivity of human welfare and health to climate, particularly regarding vector- and water-borne diseases such as dengue and cholera.

The increased frequency and intensity of heat waves could lead to more deaths and serious illnesses, especially amongst the elderly and urban poor. Hotter conditions would be exacerbated by greater humidity and urban air pollution. Studies suggest that a number of US cities would experience an average of several hundred extra deaths each summer. More frequent and intense storms, floods, droughts and cyclones will also harm human health. These natural hazards can lead directly to death, injury and mental stress. Indirect effects would result from the loss of shelter, contamination of water supplies, reduced food supplies, heightened risk of infectious disease epidemics (such as diarrhoea and respiratory disease), damage to health service's infrastructure and the displacement of people. In recent years, major climate-related disasters have had serious consequences for human health, including Hurricane Mitch, which devastated Central America in 1998, as well as floods in China, Bangladesh, Europe, Venezuela and Mozambique. Climate change will undermine air quality in cities. Higher temperatures (possibly accompanied by more ultraviolet radiation) will promote the formation of surface ozone, a pollutant that harms human respiratory health as well as plants. Higher temperatures and changes in precipitation and climatic variability would alter, and in some cases extend, the geographical range and seasonality of vector-borne diseases. Climate change may affect the marine environment in ways that would worsen the risk of biotoxin poisoning from consuming fish and shellfish. Biotoxins associated with warmer waters, such as ciguatera in the tropics, could extend their range to higher latitudes. Warmer seas will also encourage more toxic blooms of algae which can be linked to human poisoning. Declining water quantity and quality would cause more cases of diarrhoea. With some 790 million people currently undernourished, changes in food supply resulting from climate change could be affected.

Conservation of Environment: International Perspective

➢ ***Rio. (1992 Earth Summit)***

According to this summit most of the world's governments signed on to documents that fulfil an environmental agenda. The global-warming scare was accepted as real enough, even by the representatives of the United States, to justify early programmes to suppress consumption of carbon fuels. Also accepted was the general theme that nature has a higher priority than humanity—which severely restricts logging, mining, oil search, and other instruments of economical development and despite a qualified U.S. stand on the Biodiversity Treaty, most governments went along with the notion that private-property rights to technology can be overridden in the new ecological order.

➢ ***Kyoto protocol***

The Kyoto Protocol is an international agreement reached in 1997 in Kyoto, Japan to address the problems of climate change. The Kyoto Protocol commits 38 industrialized countries to cut their greenhouse gas emissions. The Canadian government ratified the Kyoto Protocol in December 2002, and has a target of reducing greenhouse gas emissions to six percent below their 1990 levels by 2012.

This Protocol sets legally binding targets for developed countries to reduce greenhouse emissions within 7 years, to about 5% below 1990 levels. To reach this goal, countries must put greenhouse emission controls on their largest polluters, which are corporations and militaries. Productivity will be maintained only if the polluters seek cleaner, renewable alternative energies to replace fossil fuel (gas) energy. Solar, wind and geothermal energy are examples of these renewable sources.

The Future of the Kyoto Protocol: The Kyoto Protocol became legally effective after obtaining support from countries representing 55% of worldwide greenhouse gas pollution. The agreement expires in 2012. It's likely that a new agreement will be proposed in 2012. However, if the US does not sign on, and instead chooses to pander to profits and business lobbyists, then the agreement will likely fall apart.

Work done by Different Environmental Agencies

The Environmental Protection Agency, Consad Research Corporation, NRCM, and IPCC are just a few of the environmental research companies studying global warming. In a recent study completed by the IPCC the prediction that global warming will have a significant impact on coastal communities was founded. Global warming is melting the ice on the Earth's surface. Places such as the Antarctica, Greenland, Alaska, Alps, Andes, and the Rockies are seeing an increase in their receding glaciers. Glaciers around the world are receding around one foot to one mile per year. The melting water is flowing into our water systems increasing the elevation of seawater. The IPCC found that seawater levels have increased 4-5 inches since 1900. They are also predicting that sea levels will rise at least 2.5 feet by 2100. The U.S. Environmental Protection Agency reported that the twentieth century was the hottest in the last thousand years, that the nine hottest years on record have all occurred since 1987, and that 1998 was the hottest year ever.

Recommendations

Firstly, for controlling Global Warming it is necessary that there should be cooperation of government. This cooperation of government with its citizens and companies and with other countries should aim to grow research and experimentation on the long-term effects of climatic change. A research should be done into the fact of how will climate change affect our rainforests and the world's major bodies of water like the oceans, lakes, rivers, and the livelihood of people who are depending on them? Addressing all such environmental issues is desperately needed to tackle the effect of global warming. It is also necessary on our part that we should start reducing carbon emissions and emissions of other greenhouse gases, and teach people about climatic change issues and what practical solutions can be done. Our future generations will judge us by how we respond to global warming.

Each country has to map out how much carbon dioxide and greenhouse gas it produces and emits into the atmosphere and in the same way it has to decide how much greening of the environment, through reforestation in the rural areas and the planting of plants and trees in urban areas, is needed to neutralize these harmful gases emitted into the air. Once these gases are in the atmosphere, they stay there for a long time thus trapping the heat in the lower atmosphere and radiating some of it back to earth. With huge amounts of carbon dioxide and greenhouse gases in the atmosphere it would increase the global surface temperature, thus higher sea levels, melting the north and South Pole glaciers or causing drought, and disrupting not only the natural balance of the world's climate but the ecological balance of the environment as well.

Through environmental awareness, every individual can help in his own little way to combat global warming. Every little thing we can do at home in the use of gas emitting equipment or vehicles will help. We need to minimize their use if we cannot totally avoid them. Any equipment or vehicle using oil and gas produces carbon dioxide. Greenhouse gas is emitted by compressor-run equipment like air- conditioning units, refrigeration and freezing units, etc. which need to be reduced because of the effect they can bring to our ozone layer.

These gases are the most devastating global warming gases, which remain in the atmosphere for a long time. Energy efficient appliances should be encouraged and by saving energy, this will help reduce gas emissions of power plant generators generating electricity. So it is better to discard inefficient equipment and switch off the appliances, lights and compressor-run equipment when not in use. If we are going somewhere not far from our home, try walking. It is not only a good exercise but it will help to save the environment also from deteriorating.

It is also necessary that we should decrease the use of our car. Besides saving money on gas, oil, tyres, parts, and repairs, we can help reduce greenhouse gases. The Supreme Court in California has proposed stricter regulations on car emissions. CO_2 emissions from cars are just part of the pollution problem creating the greenhouse effect. The burning of fossil fuels and land use are creating changes in the carbon dioxide levels. With the burning of fossil fuels, car emissions, and lack of plant life in some areas the carbon dioxide will keep increasing. To prevent this increase we are trying to create environmentally friendly cars, establishing stricter regulations on current automobiles, replanting forests and changing to natural gases to avoid burning fossil fuels.

For the controlling of Global Warming it is also necessary to follow the following environmental policy of **"Reduce.... Reuse...Recycle."** Reuse of anything is the easiest and best way to recycle. Save containers, bags, everything that you may be able to use again in the future. Also, use cloth towels and napkins instead of paper ones, and use rechargeable batteries instead of disposable ones. Furthermore, we can reduce the need to recycle paper by getting off the junk mail lists. Recycling is only effective when we buy products made from recycled materials. People should try to buy quality products that can be used for a long time, buy products with minimal packaging, and not buy disposable products. We certainly have to make-up our minds whether our success as an individual should not be based on the quantity of our consumption, or on the quality of our natural environment. Now, the time has come to examine our moral values. Examine our attitudes as they relate to our natural world.

Unfortunately, the imbalance which we have created between our lives and the Earth is already showing the signs of disaster. "Earth in the Balance" is moving to the Earth in imbalance, which, in the long run will cease to exist. Remember, we are all in the greenhouse together, nobody can stop the world and get off.

Conclusion

Today the whole world is focussed on the challenge of reducing greenhouse gas emissions. This makes sense that unless we start cutting emissions soon, atmospheric concentrations of heat-trapping gases will continue to rise, making the impacts described above that much more likely and severe. The future of global warming will be shaped by emotion rather than science. In providing the safeguards to stop global warming municipal government has to take the initiative. The threat of global warming is a global problem and the nations should forget their personal interest and work in cooperation with other countries to stop this growing threat. The U.S.A., being the largest emitter of greenhouse gases, should cooperate with other countries in reducing greenhouse gases and should sign the Kyoto protocol forgetting their personal benefit. In developing countries like India there are not many municipal legislations but seeing the international crisis towards global warming, new policies should be formulated to prevent global warming.

Since much of the blame for global warming will be laid on the wealthiest nations by the poorest, and on the poorest nations by the wealthiest, the stage is set for some of the most dangerous conflicts our world has ever seen. Many governments will come to see global warming as an urgent issue of national security, far more serious than the threat from terrorism.

Thus, it can be concluded that if we don't stop this monster from growing, it would be very soon that it engulfs the whole world within it.

References

1. Connor, Steve (September 23, 2008). "Exclusive: The methane time bomb". The Independant. Retrieved on 2008-10-03.
2. Earth Summit at Rio: Politics, Economics, and the Environment, The Environmental History, Jan 2000 by Wirth, John D.
3. Forster, Piers; *et al.* (2007-02-05). "Changes in Atmospheric Constituents and in Radiative Forcing" (PDF). *Climate Change 2007: The Physical Science Basis. Contribution of Working Group I to the Fourth Assessment Report of the Intergovernmental Panel on Climate Change* 188-193. Intergovernmental Panel on Climate Change. Retrieved on 2007-09-17.
4. Jaschek, C. & Jaschek, M. (1992) Astron. Astrophys., 95, p. 535.
5. James P. Kennett, Kevin G. Cannariato, Ingrid L. Hendy, and Richard J. Behl, (2003) *Methane Hydrates in Quaternary Climate Change: The Clathrate Gun Hypothesis*, Washington, DC: American Geophysical Union.
6. Kiehl, J. T.; Kevin E. Trenberth (February 1997). "Earth's Annual Global Mean Energy Budget" (PDF). *Bulletin of the American Meteorological Society* 78 (2): 197–208.
7. Prentice, I. Colin; *et al.* (2001-01-20). "3.7.3.3 SRES scenarios and their implications for future CO_2 concentration". *Climate Change 2001: The Scientific Basis. Contribution of Working Group I to the Third Assessment Report of the Intergovernmental Panel on Climate Change*. Intergovernmental Panel on Climate Change. Retrieved on 2007-04-28.
8. Richard Black (April 3, 2008). "'No Sun link' to climate change", BBC News Online

18

Sustainable Development and Environmental Responsibilities

ANKUSH BHADORIYA AND DHARMENDRA SINGH MOHTA

Introduction

Sustainable development: Enjoying the Earth's resources without jeopardising the welfare of future generations - James Jones, Bishop of Liverpool (2003)

The word environment is a broad spectrum which brings within it a hygienic atmosphere and an ecological balance. Saving this planet Earth is now of the utmost concern for the entire humanity. The world is witnessing a global crisis of environmental degradation. The future of the earth is entirely linked with a sustainable development that may take place in various countries, both developed and developing. They have to adopt a visionary approach in consistent with the needs of man and the earth. There is a human threat to air, water and land. Environmental degradation is seriously threatening the economical and social progress of the country and that our future generations may discover that life support systems have been damaged beyond repair. The post-independent India was concerned with equity and growth and the environmental concern was added only as a third dimension. Thousands of people migrated to cities in search of jobs and basic living conditions. This resulted in massive increases in the population in the cities. The concern for poor and needy people was voiced by the then Prime Minister, Mrs. Indira Gandhi at the *United Nations Conference on the Human Environment held at Stockholm* on 14th June, 1972. In this paper the authors would like to discuss the relationship between sustainable development and environmental responsibilities, which are two sides of the same coin. The definite shape which was given to the significance of sustainable development was given by the world commission on the environment, which was known as *"our common future"* where it was defined as development that meets the needs of the present without compromising the ability of the future generations to meet their own needs".

Sustainable development implies using renewable natural resources in a manner which does not eliminate or degrade them, or otherwise diminish their usefulness for future generations.

Sustainable Development as a Global Principle

Sustainable development is no 'backwater' of a topic; it raises some of the most fundamental issues currently facing the international community. This part of the paper puts light on the development of law over this topic at an international scenario and how it affected India's national law. While the World Commission on Environment and Development (known as the Brundtland Report) spoke of sustainable development in eloquent terms in 1987, the issue came to the fore in 1992. It was in this year that leaders at the Earth Summit built upon the framework of the Brundtland Report to create agreements and conventions on critical issues such as Climate Change, Desertification and De-forestation. The Earth Summit also drafted a broad action strategy, known as Agenda 21, as the work plan for Environment and Developmental issues for the coming decades. As the ILA New Delhi Declaration again notes, at another point, 'sustainable development is a matter of common concern both to developing and industrialised countries'. In more emotive language, the 2002 Johannesburg Declaration on Sustainable Development states *'we risk the entrenchment of [...] global disparities and unless we act in a manner that fundamentally changes their lives the poor of the world may lose confidence in their representatives and the democratic systems to which we remain committed, seeing their representatives as nothing more than sounding brass or tinkling cymbals*[1]

The role of the international *legal* system in promoting sustainable development has been a central, if ambiguous, element of this political process since the notion of sustainable development was first introduced. The World Commission on Environment and Development noted, early on, that '*[h]uman laws must be reformulated to keep human activities in harmony with the unchanging and universal laws of nature*[2]'. In particular, the aim should be 'to strengthen and extend the application of existing laws and international agreements in support of sustainable development'[3]. The role of international law in achieving sustainable development has been a theme throughout the intergovernmental discussions on sustainable development.

As Professor McGoldrick has noted, *the critical importance of sustainable development is that it is an integrationist principle...The relative weighting of economic, environmental and human right's*

[1] Paragraph 15 (UN Doc. A/CONF.199/20 (2002)).

[2] World Commission on Environment and Development (WCED), Our Common Future (Oxford, Oxford University Press, 1987) 43.

[3] World Commission on Environment and Development (WCED), Our Common Future (Oxford, Oxford University Press, 1987) 388

norms has become increasingly complex[4]'. The importance of this principle to sustainable development has also been supported by a number of decisions of international tribunals[5].

Sustainable Development Environmental Responsibility: Position of Indian Law

After the liberalization and era of globalization the shortcomings of the executive in coping with the pressures on the environment brought about by change in the country's economical policies, had thrust the responsibility of environmental protection upon the judiciary. This has meant that in India, the Judiciary in some instances, has had to exercise its role not only as an interpreter of the law but also has had to take upon itself the role of constantly monitoring and implementating necessities through a series of public interest litigations that have been initiated in various courts. However, in the defiance of the executive, it must be said that India has actively participated in several multilateral treaties and has been active in admitting its commitments to the environment in accordance with the general principles of *International Law while incorporating them into its national laws.* India's commitment to the concept of sustainable development, in contrast, is a part of the vision reflected by our Constitution makers in various provisions of the Indian Constitution. The Forty-Second Amendment to the Indian Constitution in 1976 introduced principles of environmental protection in an explicit manner into the Constitution through Articles 48A and 51A(g). Article 48A, part of the Directive Principles of State Policy[6], obligated the State to protect and improve the environment. On the other hand, Article 51A(g) obligated citizens to undertake the same responsibilities.[7] As far as legislative power was concerned, the Amendment also moved the subjects of "forests" and "protection of wild animals and birds" from the State List to the Concurrent List.[8] The Stockholm conference is honoured by references in the Air Act and the Environment Act - a result of effective applications of Article 253 of the Constitution, which gives the Parliament (India's central

---

[4] D. McGoldrick, 'Sustainable Development and Human Rights: An Integrated Approach ' 45 International and Comparative Law Quarterly (1996) 818.

[5] See Case Concerning Gabèíkovo-Nagymaros Project (Hungary Slovakia) ICJ Report (1997) 7, 140: 'This need to reconcile economical development with protection of the environment is aptly expressed in the concept of sustainable development' and United States - Import Prohibition of Certain Shrimp and Shrimp Products (Shrimp-Turtle case) WT/DS58/AB/R, 12 October 1998 paragraph 153: 'We note once more that this language demonstrates a recognition by WTO negotiators that optimal use of the world's resources should be made in accordance with the objective of sustainable development. As this preambular language reflects the intentions of negotiators of the WTO Agreement, we believe it must add colour, texture and shading to our interpretation of the agreements annexed to the WTOAgreement, in this case, the GATT 1994'.

[6] Article 48A: "The State shall endeavour to protect and improve the environment and to safeguard the forests and wildlife of the country." For a discussion of the legislative debate behind the origin of the amended Article,

[7]Article 51A(g): "to protect and improve the natural environment including forests, lakes, rivers and wild life, and to have compassion for living creatures;"

legislature) the power to make laws implementing India's international obligations, as well as any decision made at an international conference, association or other body.[9] The concept of sustainable development has over the years become multi-dimensional, in that it encompasses within itself the concerns of economical growth, social & cultural growth, scientific growth and above all environmental protection. In its nascent form, Stockholm Declaration on the Human Environment of 1972, the First Principle proclaimed a common conviction of States that man bears a "solemn responsibility to protect and improve the environment for present and future generations". The Fifth Principle of the said Declaration contemplated employment of non-renewable resources in such a manner as to guard against the danger of their future exhaustion and ensure that benefits thereof are shared by all mankind. It is inherent in this Principle that all the States are expected to adopt an integrated and coordinated approach to the development planning so as to ensure that development is compatible with the need to protect and improve the environment.

The concept of Sustainable Development attempts to balance the scales between the quantity of development and the quality of the environment, the effort being to ensure that the development does not disturb the delicate equilibrium. It thus deals with two types of equity; firstly, the equity for human generations yet to come, whose interests are not represented by standard economical analysis or by market forces that discount the future, and secondly, the equity for people living now who do not have equal access to natural resources. The conflict between the two kinds of equities has given rise to International treaty obligations, some of which have been incorporated into municipal law and by most of which India feels itself bound to abide. International environmental law has been heavily influenced by considerations relating to the protection of the rights of future generations. Over the years, there has been a paradigm shift from rights-based approaches to a concentration on duties, standards and enforcements. It now seems to be universally accepted that pollution need not always be the inevitable consequence of industrial activity or of activity involving the use of natural resources. Courts in various jurisdictions have shown an increased inclination to lean in favour of the right of the society as a whole against the adverse impact on the environment when it comes in conflict with economic well-being of an individual or the State.

---

[8] The Seventh Schedule of the Constitution delineates legislative power between the Centre and the States. List I (the Union List) comprises subjects over which only the Centre shall legislate. List II (the State List) comprises subjects over which only the State shall legislate. List III (the Concurrent List) contains subjects over which both entities may legislate, subject to a preference for the Centre pursuant to the doctrine of "occupied field".

[9] It has been pointed out that the Parliament has the power to legislate on virtually any subject in the State List by virtue of Entry 13 of the Union List, which covers participation in international conferences and the implementation of decisions made at the conferences. see Shyam Divan and Armin Rosencranz, Environmental Law and Policy in India: Cases, Materials and Statutes, 2nd Edition, Oxford University Press, New Delhi, 2001, pp.45-46.

The development of Indian environmental law has happened, for the most part, over the last three decades, with a significant level of polarization around the latter half of this period. The development of the law in this area has seen a considerable share of initiative by the Indian judiciary, particularly the higher judiciary, consisting of the Supreme Court of India and the High Courts of the States. Legislative schemes and initiatives have been created in most areas involving the environment, albeit with some degree of overlap. The role of the administration, although a critical factor in the success of any environmental managerial programme, has seen its share of problems of scale and definition. The essence of the existing law relating to the environment has developed through legislative and judicial initiative.[10] Since the latter is responsible for the most recent developments, this paper will attempt to lay the foundation for understanding through a discussion of legislation and administrative rules, and then detail development of the law and environmental principles through the discussion of judicial decisions. It is possible to suggest with conviction that the beginnings of Indian environmental law were sown at the United Nations Conference on the Human Environment held at Stockholm in 1972, where India was a participant, leading to some sort of realization that a framework of laws was necessary to deal with environmental hazards that would result from the stage of development that India was entering in the 1970s.[11] Prior to this phase, Indian environmental law mainly consisted of claims made against tortuous actions such as nuisance or negligence. *The Water (Prevention and Control of Pollution) Act of 1974 gave the statute book its first real foundation for environmental protection. Other major enactments followed in 1980 (The Forest (Conservation) Act), 1981 (The Air (Prevention and Control of Pollution) Act[12], and 1986 (The Environment (Protection) Act).*

The judiciary, in their quest for innovate solutions to environmental matters within the framework of public interest litigation, looked to constitutional provisions to provide the court with the necessary jurisdiction to address specific issues. Furthermore, Article 142 afforded the Supreme Court considerable power to mould its decisions in order that complete justice could be done. As the Supreme Court is the final authority as far as matters of constitutional interpretation are concerned, it assumes a sort of primal position in the Indian environmental

---

[10] With few exceptions such as Environment Impact Assessment (1994), Coastal Regulation Zone Notification (1991), and the Joint Forest Management Programme, the wealth of Indian Environmental Management stems from legislative and judicial actions. However, the Ministry of Environment and Forests is the nodal agency for virtually all environmental managerial processes set up by the legislature.

[11] This is in contrast to laws in countries such as England, which were sometimes a direct result of some mass environmental disaster; for example, the Clean Air Act of 1956 was the outcome of the deadly smog that killed over 4000 people in London in 1962. (The Act has since been replaced by the Clean Air Act of 1993). See Harish Salve, "Justice between Generations: Environment and Social Justice", Supreme But Not Infallible: Essays in Honour of the Supreme Court of India, Oxford University Press, New Delhi, 2000, pp.360-380. Salve adds: "In the fullness of time, political upheavals brought home the realization that freedom can survive only if it honours basic human rights and is founded on principles of natural justice."

[12] See the Preamble to the Act for a specific reference to the Stockholm conference.

legal system. For example, the fundamental right contained in Article 21[13] is often cited as the violated right, albeit in a variety of ways. We can proudly proclaim that Judiciary in India has been ahead of the pack having played a pro-active role in the matters involving environment for over two decades now. The Supreme Court has read the right to life enshrined in Article 21 as inclusive of right to a clean environment.

Development of Environmental Law Principles

Virtually leading the International judicial trends on the subject, the Indian Judiciary has consistently refused to be the prisoner of the strict jurisdictional rule of "recognized legal interest" by going beyond the traditional concept of locus standi and has encouraged environmental issues concerning the community as a whole to be raised for judicial redress through the mechanism of public interest litigation. The Supreme Court rather gave a clarion call to the other branches of the State to lend a helping hand to the Court to meet the challenge by setting up an Environment Court and making available expert advice on the issues being increasingly raised concerning environmental pollution and ecological destruction having a bearing on the material basis of the livelihood of millions of poor people.

The Court has successfully isolated specific environmental law principles upon the interpretation of Indian statutes and the Constitution, combined with a liberal view towards ensuring social justice and the protection of human rights. The principles have often found reflection in the Constitution in some form, and are usually justified even when not explicitly mentioned in the concerned statute. There have been also occasions when the judiciary has prioritized the environment over development, when the situation demanded an immediate and specific policy structure.[14]

The Precautionary Principle

Beginning with **Vellore Citizens' Welfare Forum v. Union of India**[15], the Supreme Court has explicitly recognized the precautionary principle as a principle of Indian environmental law. More recently, in A.P. Pollution Control Board v. M.V. Nayudu[16], the Court discussed the development of the precautionary principle[17]. Furthermore, in the Narmada case[18], the Court explained that "When there is a state of uncertainty due to the lack of data or material about the extent of damage or pollution likely to be caused, then, in order to maintain the ecological

---

[13] Article 21: "No person shall be deprived of his life or personal liberty except according to procedure established by law".

[14] See for example M.C. Mehta v. Union of India, (1987) 4 SCC 463. The Court held: " life, public health and ecology has priority over unemployment and loss of revenue problem."

[15] AIR 1996 SC 2715

[16] AIR 1999 SC 812

[17] See also S. Jagannath v. Union of India (Shrimp Culture case), AIR 1997 SC 811

[18] Narmada Bachao Andolan v. Union of India, AIR 2000 SC 3751

balance, the *burden of proof that the said balance will be maintained must necessarily be on the industry or the unit which is likely to cause pollution*."[19]

The "Polluter Pays" Principle

The Supreme Court has come to sustain a position where it calculates environmental damages not on the basis of a claim put forward by either party, but through an examination of the situation by the Court, keeping in mind factors such as the deterrent nature of the award.[20] However, it held recently that the power under Article 32 to award damages, or even exemplary damages to compensate environmental harm, would not extend to the levy of a pollution fine.[21] The "polluter pays" rule has also been recognized as a fundamental objective of government policy to prevent and control pollution.[22]

Sustainable Development and Inter-generational Equity

What is meant by the phrase "sustainable development"? The definition which is used most often comes from the report of the Brundtland Commission, in which it was suggested that the phrase covered "*development that meets the needs of the present without compromising the ability of future generations to meet their own needs.*" However, different levels of societies have their own concept of sustainable development and the object that is to be achieved by it. For instance, for rich countries, sustainable development may mean steady reductions in wasteful levels of the consumption of energy and other natural resources through improvements in efficiency, and through changes in life style, while in poorer countries, sustainable development would mean the commitment of resources toward continued improvement in living standards.

Sustainable development means that the richness of the earth's biodiversity would be conserved for future generations by greatly slowing and, if possible, halting extinctions, habitat and ecosystem destruction, and also by not risking significant alternations of the global environment that might - by an increase in sea level or changing rainfall and vegetation patterns or increasing ultraviolet radiation - alter the opportunities available for future generations.

---

[19] See also P. Leelakrishnan, "Environmental Law", Annual Survey of Indian Law, Volume XXXVI, 2000, pp. 252-

[20] See also the explanation for the principle of absolute liability in M.C. Mehta v. Union of India (Oleum Gas case), AIR 1987 SC 965, and its subsequent application in Indian Council for Enviro-Legal Action v. Union of India, (1996) 3 SCC 212.

[21] See M.C. Mehta v. Kamal Nath, AIR 2000 SC 1997.

[22] Ministry of Environment and Forests, Government of India, "Policy Statement for Abatement of Pollution", para 3.3, February 26, 1992.

How has this phrase been understood in India? Perhaps the answer lies in the decision of the Supreme Court in **Narmada Bachao Andolan v. Union of India**[23] wherein it was observed that "*Sustainable development means what type or extent of development can take place, which can be sustained by nature/ecology with or without mitigation.*" In this context, development primarily meant material or economical progress. Being a developing country, economical progress is essential; at the same time, care has to be taken of the environment. Thus, the question that squarely arises is: How can sustainable development, with economical progress and without environmental regression, be ensured within the Indian legal framework? This can be achieved through the implementation of good legislation. The courts have attempted to provide a balanced view of priorities while deciding environmental matters. As India is a developing country, certain ecological sacrifices are deemed necessary, while keeping in mind the nature of the environment in that area, which is critical to the community. This is in order that future generations may benefit from policies and laws that further environmental as well as developmental goals. This ethical mix is termed sustainable development, and has also been recognized by the Supreme Court in the *Taj Trapezium* case.[24]

In the *State of Himachal Pradesh* v. *Ganesh Wood Products*[25], the Supreme Court invalidated forest-based industry, recognizing the principle of inter-generational equity as being central to the conservation of forest resources and sustainable development.[26]

Holistic Adjudication

The Supreme Court, in recent years, has been adopting a holistic approach towards environmental matters. This is usually done through detailed orders that are issued from time to time, while Committees appointed by the Court monitor the ground situation. The origin of this tendency may be seen in cases such as *Ratlam*[27] and *Olga Tellis*[28].

Judicial Attitude to Policy

To a substantial extent, the courts have had to fill in the gaps and doubt left by the absence of a clear governmental policy. However, there have been occasions when the court has considered it appropriate to disregard the policy and proceed with a decision that better accommodates constitutional values.[29] At other times, the Court has stated that it is not in the public interest to require the Court to delve into those areas that are the function of the executive.[30]

---

[23] 2000 (10) SCC 664 at p.727

[24] M.C. Mehta v. Union of India, AIR 1997 SC 734. (per Kuldip Singh, J.).

[25] AIR 1996 SC 149

[26] .See also Indian Council for Enviro-Legal Action v. Union of India (CRZ Notification case), (1996) 5 SCC 281. The Court noted that the principle would be violated if there were a substantial adverse ecological effect caused by industry.

[27] Municipal Council, Ratlam v. Vardhichand, AIR 1980 SC 1622.

[28] Olga Tellis v. Bombay Municipal Corporation, AIR 1986 SC 180.

The Right to Livelihood

In certain cases, the judiciary has to choose between the preservation of environmental resources in state, and the right of communities to extract value out of those resources. To facilitate this choice, the courts have evolved a right to livelihood[31] for communities affected by new state-run conservation initiatives. A clear position on this issue is not immediately forthcoming, as the decision depends heavily upon the factual matrix of each dispute.[32] The Court has also observed the environment-development debate, and stated that the most desirous position is a harmonious form of co-existence of these ends.[33]

The Doctrine of Public Trust

To further justify and perhaps extract state initiative to conserve natural resources, the Court enunciated Professor Joseph Sax's doctrine of public trust, obligating conservation by the state. In *M.C. Mehta* v. *Kamal Nath*[34], the Court held that the state, as a trustee of all natural resources, was under a legal duty to protect them, and that the resources were meant for public use and could not be transferred to private ownership.

Conclusion

In India, sustainable development is generally perceived as rooted in the firm realization on the part of the judiciary that the bounties of nature, liable to be tapped for purposes of present needs for development and growth, have to be protected at the same time against permanent damage for the sake of posterity. This is a challenge and yet an opportunity. It requires besides appropriate legislation an effective enforcement and generation of public awareness through various agencies including educational institutions, NGOs and local bodies that can bring about community participation.

We have a plethora of laws governing the subject. What seems to be lacking is, however, proper enforcement of various laws. The responsibility of enforcement of these laws made for the welfare of the future of the community is not that of the State agencies alone. It is here that the community participation becomes important. It is here where the industry, in particular the

---

[29] See for example Sachidanand Pandey v. State of West Bengal (Calcutta Taj Hotel case), AIR 1987 SC 1109. The Court permitted the construction of a hotel near land belonging to the Calcutta Zoological Garden, stating that tourism was important to the economical progress of the country, thereby underlining the constant controversy between development and the environment.

[30] See supra n.28 at 3828.

[31] See Olga Tellis v. Bombay Municipal Corporation, AIR 1986 SC 180.

[32] For decisions on either side, see supra n.22 and Animal and Environment Legal Defence Fund v. Union of India, JT 1997 (3) SC 298. The former returned a decision in favour of conservation, and the latter stated that conservation, though not secondary, must factor community livelihood and quality of life into ecologically oriented efforts. See also Banawasi Seva Ashram v. State of Uttar Pradesh, AIR 1992 SC 920.

[33] See Indian Council for Enviro-Legal Action v. Union of India

, AIR 1995 SC 2252; Indian Council for Enviro-Legal Action v. Union of India, (1996) 5 SCC 281.

[34] (1997) 1 SCC 388

private sector, has a larger role to play. It is now universally recognized that it is possible to make development and environment protection compatible by following certain sustainable strategies which steadfastly avoid use of such technology, or engagement in such activity, as causes permanent damage to the environment. In evolving sustainable strategies, care is required to be taken to bring about, amongst others, population stabilization, efficient use of natural resources, waste reduction, pollution prevention, integrated environmental systems management, determining environmental limits perception and attitudinal changes at social and cultural levels etc. Since, 'Sustainable Development' would always require integration of social, ecological and economic objectives, each player in the economic activity will have to address him to the concerns. Industry is one of the most important players in this activity. The concept of sustainable development has thus evolved into a legal term that refers to process, principles and objectives as well as to a large body of International Agreements on Environment Economics and Civil and Political Rights. Supreme Court of India in recent years has been adopting a holistic approach towards environmental matters. For this, it would issue detailed orders or directions and appoint committees to monitor the enforcement thereof. It has applied the principle of "Polluter Pays" by interpreting it as the absolute liability for harm to the environment extending not only to compensate the victims of pollution but also the cost of environmental degradation. The concerns of economical development in a sustainable mode include putting in place regulatory mechanisms. Thus, the arrangement of environmental management is composed of a harmonious blend of initiatives from the legislature, the executive, and the judiciary. The higher judiciary plays a rather stalwart role owing to its unique position and power, and due to the circumstances of inefficiency within the executive and the existence of a skeletal legislative framework. The principles of Indian environmental law are resident in the judicial interpretation of laws and the Constitution, and encompass several internationally recognized principles, thereby providing some semblance of consistency between domestic and global environmental standards.

References

1. Abraham, C. M.; "Environmental Jurisprudence In India" Martinus Nijhoff, 1999.
2. D. McGoldrick, 'Sustainable Development and Human Rights: An Integrated Approach' 45 International and Comparative Law Quarterly (1996).
3. Global Environmental Outlook, United Nations Environment Program (UNEP), Oxford University Press, 1999.
4. Leelakrishnan, P. ;"Environmental Law In India", 2nd Edition Eastern Book Company, 2004.
5. Leelakrishnan P. "Environmental Law", Annual Survey of Indian Law, Volume XXXVI, 2000, pp. 252-257
6. Ministry of Environment and Forests, Government of India, "Policy Statement for Abatement of Pollution", February 26, 1992.
7. Singh, R.B. And Misra, Suresh; "Environmental Law In India : Issues and Responses", Vedams Books (P) Ltd. 1996.
8. World Commission on Environment and Development (WCED), Our common future (Oxford: Oxford University Press, 1987).

19

Urban Water Problems and their Solutions
A Case Study of Delhi

Sheel Kumar

Introduction

Water is extremely useful to man, providing a basic necessity of a human being's comfort, in addition to being a necessity for animals and plants. Furthermore, it is necessary that the water required must be good and it should not contain unwanted impurities or harmful chemical compounds or bacteria in it. Therefore, in order to ensure the availability of a sufficient quantity of good quality water, it becomes almost imperative in a modern society, to plan and build suitable water supply schemes, which may provide potable water to the various sections of the community in accordance with their demands and requirements. The provision of such a scheme shall help not only in supplying safe water to the people for drinking, cooking, bathing, washing etc., but it will also keep the diseases away and promote better health. It would also help in supplying water for fountains, gardens, etc., thus, helping in maintaining better sanitation and beautification of surroundings. Besides promoting overall hygiene and public health, it shall ensure safety against fire by supplying a sufficient quantity of water to extinguish one. The existence of such a water supply scheme shall further help in attracting industries (since industries require large amounts of water) and will thereby help in the industrialization and modernization of society, consequently reducing unemployment and ensuring better living standards. Such schemes shall help in promoting wealth and welfare to the entire community as a whole, because water is precious for all living beings. In the present 21st century, total water withdrawals have risen continuously with total water consumption increasing dramatically since 1960. Water consumed as a percentage of water-withdrawn rose between 1960 and 2000. There are 425 bgd (billion gallons per day) being withdrawn from surface and ground water sources and 135 bgd are being consumed. It shows the huge amount of ground water wastage throughout the world and even in India and Indian cities.

About 90% of the precipitation falling over the landmass is of oceanic origin and 10% is from the land source obtained through the process of evaporation from the water bodies. The evapo-transpiration from the soil and vegetation shows that the water resource occupies a special place among the other natural resources. Water is the most widely distributed substance on our planet. It is available almost everywhere and plays a vital role in both the environment and human life (Postel, 1985). Water occurs in abundance in nature but the availability of fresh water is limited. About 71% of the total area of the earth is a water body, whereas the rest is landmass. It may be interesting to note that approximately 96.50% of terrestrial water is confined to the oceans and fresh water reserves account for only 2.53%. The other 0.97% of the total water resources of the earth, being brackish or ocean water is neither potable nor suitable for plant life.

Approximately 71% of the earth's surface is covered with water. Current estimates indicate that the total volume of water on the earth is about 1.4 x 10 km^3, of which 97.3% is ocean water. The balance, 2.7% is fresh water. At any given time, 77.2% of the fresh water is frozen in the polar ice caps and in the glaciers in various parts of world, and thus, for all practical purposes, is unavailable for human consumption or for vegetation. Ninety percent of this ice is in the Antarctica, and the remainder for the most part, is contained in the Greenland ice caps (Charney and Woodard, 1984).

Ground water and soil moisture constitute 22.4% of global fresh water, but nearly two-thirds of this lies deeper than 750 metres below ground level. About 0.1% of this reserve (13,000 cubic kilometer) participates in the hydrological cycle in an average year, mostly through the contribution to a stream flow. Nearly 30% of the total stream flow is contributed by groundwater. Lakes contain about 200,000 cubic kilometres of fresh water, which is about four times the overage annual run off from all land areas. In contrast, artificial lakes store more than 11% of the yearly run off (about 5,000 cubic kilometer). Lakes, the atmosphere and streams contain only 0.4% of fresh water, or 0.01% of the total volume of water. This tiny fraction is vitally important in sustaining life on this planet (Bourne, 1984).

The tremendously dynamic nature of the hydrological cycle can be demonstrated by two simple facts. Firstly, even though the mean annual precipitation of the earth is about 973 mm, the water content of the atmosphere at any given instant is only 0.001% of the total water of the earth, and if by some means this entire vapour can be precipitated, it would cover the earth's surface to a depth of only about 25mm. Secondly, withstanding a large discharge of the major givers, the amount of water contained in the world's rivers at any instant is relatively small. Thus, the important factor to consider in water resource planning and management is not the actual quantity of water in a channel at any time but rather its flow through the channel over time (Chiconie and Ramamurthy, 1986).

The pricing policies, water laws and institutions encourage inefficiency and wastage of water. It may be noted that the investment in water efficiency, re-cycling and conservation technologies would yield more usable water per unit of money when compared with conventional water supply projects (Postel, 1985). Drinkable water receives a high priority in water resource allocation; agriculture is the largest sector of water consumption. In the developing countries, it accounts for about 90% of the total water consumed (Sinha, 1991). The development of water resources, viewed as the key to economical growth and prosperity, expand virtually unchecked across the world. The severe problem of drinking water experienced in recent times by most of the developing countries has led to the declaration of 1981-1990 as the

"Decade of Drinking Water and Sanitation" by the United Nations, because the provision of a safe and convenient water supply and basic sanitation services is of paramount importance to the health of the people in developing countries (Reddy, 1998). On the basis of a report in India, the Seventh Five-Year Plan aimed at providing safe drinking water to all sections of society besides raising the per capita norms of the water supply from 40-70 litres per day, but the recent evidence indicates that the achievements of the plan are far below the targets of the objective of providing -drinking water to all section of respondents. According to some estimates in urban areas, only 72% of the population receive safe drinking water (or tap water) and the coverage of poor (below poverty line population) is still lower at 66% (Kundu, 1991).

Research Problem

The walled city Delhi is situated on the banks of the river Yamuna and the city is mainly supplied by surface water from the Yamuna and the dam on the Beas, which is a tributary of the river Indus. Delhi has no right on the Yamuna and is, therefore, largely dependent upon its neighbours, especially during the summer months. Underground water represents only approximately 11 per cent of Delhi's water resources.

Table 1: Estimation of the Supply and Demand Gap for Water in Delhi.

Year	1991	2001	2001 low option	2001 high option
Population (million)	94	137	12.8	14.0
Consumption Norm1 (lppd) (by DDA)	363	363	363	363
Consumption Norm 2 (lppd (by DWSSDU)	318	318	318	318
Estimated Consumption (lppd)	227	248	–	–
Current Production (mld)	2,137	2,728	–	–
Required Production 1 (mld)	3,412.2	3,993	4,646.4	5,082
Deficit with Norm 1 (mld)	1,275.2	1,265	–	–
Required Production 2 (mld)	2,989.2	3,498	4,070.4	4,452
Deficit with Norm 2 (mld)	852.2	770	–	–

Sources: Author's calculation based on DDA and DWSSDU reports.

This norm is based on the following per capita water requirement: domestic consumption (225 lppd), shops and industries (47 lppd), horticulture (35lppd) and floating population (52 lppd).

In 1996, the optimum production was assessed at 2,728 mld (millions of litres per day) with a daily average of 2,634 mld. The Drinking Water Supply and Sewage Disposal Unit (DWSSDU) made very determined efforts to increase water production. Since 1961, water production has multiplied six times and despite a growth in population, there has been an increase in the average per capita consumption of only (166 lppd in 1961, 221 lppd in 1981 and 248 lppd in 1996). Officially today, water consumption is estimated at approximately 250 lppd a high consumption level comparable with developed countries. However, the DWB considers that there is a production deficit as high as 700 mld, (CSE,2001).

Two consumption norms have been utilized to project the required production. The first, defined by the Delhi Development Authority (DDA, 1992), is 363 lppd' and the second used by the DWSSDU, is 318 lppd. Table 1 displays the difference between the actual and the required amount of the DWSSDU while a leakage percentage has been introduced in the third capita consumption and it is calculated by simply dividing the optimum total production by the number of inhabitants, which explains the surprisingly high figure of 250 lppd. However, physical loss, underestimated at 20 per cent by the DWSSDU, should be taken into consideration. The calculations of Table 1, reveal that the DWSSDU and the average consumption underestimated the production deficit which was over estimated. With a 30 percent loss, the average per capita consumption is reduced from 248 lppd to 173 litre per person day (lppd). Further, even with the unlikely possibility of a low demographic growth, Delhi's water production in the year 2001 should increase at least 1.5 times. This will require not only an increase in its production capacity but also an improvement in the effectiveness of the distribution network.

In addition, underground water resources are limited and diminishing. The Central Ground Water Board conducted studies in Delhi that revealed that sub-soil water has become polluted. Moreover, the water table levels decreased by 2 to 4 m (up to a maximum of 8 m) between 1983 and 1994 (Kittu et al., 1996; Sikka, 1995). Groundwater represents an important extra source of water for Delhi. In order to increase its production, the DWSSDU was planning to increase the number and the yield of its rainy wells. These studies, therefore, imply that there is an urgent need to develop policies to protect this resource. Unfortunately, it is especially difficult to establish the private tube wells dug by households and the industrial sector for their own supply. Similarly, many water tanker and bottled water companies are using and selling groundwater. The lack of rules and regulations related to private or individual extraction of groundwater aggravates this situation even more.

As far as surface water is concerned, the absence of right on the Yamuna is a major concern for the Delhi government. Delhi can use only a share released by Haryana from the Tajewala dam situated 250 km upstream from Wazirabad. The construction of three new dams (Tehri, Kishau and Renuka) aiming at augmenting water resources are either underway or envisaged in the long term and today Delhi has to negotiate regularly with the neighbouring states to get a higher allocation of water from the Yamuna.

The water supplied in Delhi is treated and therefore supposedly safe. However, risks of water contamination during its distribution are extremely high because of the state of disrepair of the main lines and the high percentage of leakage. The high level of pollution of the Yamuna led the Supreme Court to order the DWSSDU to install sufficient wastewater treatment plants before the end of 1997. Therefore, the quality of groundwater is also doubtful as the wells are situated on the banks of the Yamuna. The DWSSDU completely stopped supplying water from shallow wells after the 1988 cholera epidemic that broke out in many resettlement colonies. The publication of a book on the pollution of the river Yamuna by the Centre for Science and Environment brought the problem of unsafe water to the forefront again. Besides, in March 1997, the Government Accounts Office blamed the Delhi Water Board for deficiencies in water treatment (such as incorrect dosage of chemical added). The municipal authorities who till date claim that they supply perfectly safe water, were obliged to acknowledge partly this shortcoming.

The city of Delhi is perpetually in the grip of a water crisis, more so during the dry season when serious water shortages afflict the city. A large number of residents depend on groundwater to augment the municipal supply. Delhi has no right over the Yamuna and is supplied by surface water from the Yamuna and the dam on the Beas River from its neighbouring states. The population of Delhi, according to the 2001 census, was 13.42 million, which is expected to cross 20 million by 2011. Against the present requirement of about 3324 million litres/day (mld), the installed capacity is only 2634 mld.

Although the average water consumption in Delhi is estimated at 240 litres per capita per day (lpcd), the highest in India, the figure is not indicative of an adequate supply to every resident since the water supply in Delhi is far from being uniformly distributed. The New Delhi Municipal Corporation (NDMC) and the Delhi Contonment areas get an average supply of above 450 lpcd, while areas in the Narela and Mehrauli zones get less than 35 lpcd (CSE, 2001). The gap between the supply and demand of water has resulted in large-scale developments of groundwater. This has led to serious problems with both the quantity and quality of the groundwater.

Of the water supplied by the municipality, 11 percent of it comes out from groundwater extraction, because a large number of private tube-wells dug by households and the industrial sector for their own supply are unaccounted for in the official figures (Jairaj, 1995). Many water tanker and bottled water companies are drawing and selling groundwater. The unplanned and uncontrolled extraction of groundwater, has disturbed the hydrological balance, leading to a decline in the productivity of wells, a rise in energy requirement and the deterioration in the quality of water.

There has been a widespread drop in the groundwater table in the entire region of Delhi, especially in the south and southwestern localities of Delhi. It has been assessed that the water table has been sharply depleted by 2 to 8 m in the past five decades. The lack of regulation related to the private or individual extraction of groundwater aggravates this situation (CSE, 2001). In addition to the overexploitation of groundwater, the uncontrolled disposal of effluents and sewage in the city has contaminated the groundwater to alarming levels. Studies conducted by the Central Ground Water Board in Delhi indicate that groundwater in most parts of Delhi is contaminated with fluoride and nitrate and it has been suggested that the available water of the region is unfit for drinking purposes.

The situation of the water supply in Delhi provides an ideal ground for study. According to the official figures, the average per capita consumption of water in Delhi is estimated at about 250 litres per person per day which is the highest in all of the Indian cities. Newspapers in the

Capital regularly report the water related problems about the water supply in various localities of the city. If one wants to sort out the reason for Delhi's distribution problems, one finds that the problem lies more in inefficient management of the supply network rather than in a scarcity of water resources. The study on the consequences of unreliability has affected the entire population. The comparison of behavioural patterns, techno-economic and socio-cultural factors is responsible between households with a 24 hour's water supply and households with an intermittent and irregular supply. Delhi, for the understanding of the problems between households also has this problem due to the rapid growth of population and thus it always has a water scarcity in summer and in the late winter season.

The main objective of the present research study is to examine the viability of technological adoptions in reducing the demand of water. In order to achieve the above-mentioned objective, the following hypothesis has been formulated showing the techno-economic and socio-cultural factors affecting water consumption.

Study Area

Delhi lies between 28° 24' 17" to 28° 53' North latitude and 76° 50' 24" to 77° 20' 37" East longitude. It has an area of 1483 km^2. Its greatest length is 51.90 km and its width is 48.48 km and it has 685.34 km^2 urban area and 797.6 km^2. a rural are. It has 209 villages and 29 census towns and 3 municipal bodies (a) NDMC, which serves 3,01,297 people (b) Delhi Cantonment Board which serves 94,393 people (c) MCD which serves 94,20, 644 people of Delhi. There is an area of 42.74 km^2 under NDMC, 49.97 km^2 for the area under the Delhi Cantonment Board and a 1397.29 km^2 area under the MCD. There are 7,050 people per square kilometer density in the NDMC area.

Delhi is bounded by two states; Haryana in the north, west and south and Uttar Pradesh in the east. It has fourth rank among the union territories. The normal annual rainfall of Delhi is 467.1 mm. July, August and September receive the maximum rainfall of nearly 80% of the total, but in a regional context all six blocks vary in the total rainfall receiving annually. The area selected for the case study is the Delhi urban area. It is a densely populated built up area and this area was settled for settlement before 1981. It came in the urban area of Delhi in the 1981 census. Four localities which have been chosen as the samples, based on economical activities or on the income and living standards, are: (1) High Income Group - Model Town, (2) Middle-income Group - Timarpur, (3) Low-income Group - Azadpur, (4) Below the poverty line or Slum group - Wazirpur (*jhuggi cluster*).

Study Findings

The population of Delhi is increasing very rapidly, because here per day 877 persons were added to Delhi's population during the 1981-1991 decade and in the decade 1991-2001 it rose by up to 1195 new born daily. It shows the very rapid increase in the population. Forest areas in Delhi are declining day by day. The net sown area is also declining day by day due to the urban expansion or rapid urbanization.

The use of Underground water can solve the drinking water problem of Delhi and also balance and equalise the demand and supply of water in the area for all seasons. The second option of conserving water is to use buckets and mugs for all purposes. It may also reduce water wastage by up to 60%. Finally, the water harvesting technique is also important to maintain the balance between the demand and supply of underground water. It is because if the underground water is exploited more, there will not be any replenishment of water, resulting in the lowering of underground water levels (deficit) rapidly, which may produce a water crisis in the future. Thus, it is also important to conserve water. Only a few people are familiar with the traditional methods of water conservation. So, this factor is too weak to conserve the water because it requires more space in the city and space is not available even for houses, so then how can it be successful in Delhi. The use of MCD water for cooking and drinking purposes is a very weak factor among all the variables.

In all, revenues from water supplies do not cover even the working expenses, let alone the capital costs. In study areas, the shortages are both in terms of quantity and quality. These shortages have led to the development of water markets and HIG pay a much higher price for water, when compared with Azadpur and Wazirpur. The per capita water use (lpcd) in the actual situation is much less than WHO norms as well as per capita water supplies provided by PHED. The per capita use levels are considerably lower in water shortage conditions where supply regulations are severe. Slum people and low-income groups are more dependent on stand posts/hand pumps where supply levels are low, unreliable and of poor quality. They also spend more in terms of indirect costs of water, i.e. walking distances and spending time for fetching water.

The price of water appears to be an important demand management variable in the absence of technological factors. The household level also supports the above argument. The pricing is of an elastic nature and determines water use initially, altering the consumption (Water use) pattern at the household level. This also indicates that price can be used as a demand management variable, without sacrificing the quality aspects.

The capacity, utilisation and distribution of service connection would result in a higher per capita consumption of water due to the absence of effective distribution systems. As the size of the household increases, the per capita demand tends to decline. Contrary to general belief households are willing to pay substantially higher prices (double the present price) for an improvement of water supplies. Therefore, willingness to pay is not a handicap for charging higher prices.

The general assumption is that a household is willing to pay about 5 percent of its expenses towards water. However, the WTP bids may not fully reflect the ability of the households, as the lower income group households are willing to pay a larger proportion of their household expenses towards water. Therefore, in the event of ad-hoc or blanket pricing policies, these households may bear a disproportionately higher burden. In these areas the shortages are both in terms of quality and quantity. These shortages have led to the development of water markets and HIG pay a much higher price for water, when compared with Azadpur and Wazirpur.

Suggestions

Water resources planning and management has been a neglected area in India as well as other developing countries. As a result, the paucity of water is increasingly felt by all the sectors in most of these countries. The situation is more severe in the case of municipal water supplies. For instance, despite the best efforts of national and international organisations to provide basic amenities like drinking water and sanitation to all sections of the population, most of the developing countries, including India, failed to fulfil their objectives during the international decade 1981-91. The situation is no better in other sectors like agriculture and industry. However, the drinking water problems are obviously more strident as they affect directly our well-being. The main reason behind this state of affairs is the philosophy of supply side management to be followed, to the neglect of demand side aspect, by policy makers.

Unless the demand regulation is given importance in the water resource planning and management, it would be difficult to meet the demands of the increasing population, either in terms of water or food, in the event of increasing water shortages coupled with mounting financial constraints. Demand regulating includes the conservation of water, enhancing the productivity of water etc., through following an appropriate price policy and adopting technologies fostered with suitable institutions. In this study, the issue of water resources planning has been addressed from the demand side. The main focus of the study is on analysing the factors influencing the demand for urban residential water in Delhi. The analysis was carried out at the household level as well as the aggregate (town) level. Further, the willingness and ability of the households to pay for water is also estimated and an attempt is also made to estimate the current demand for water to various sectors like municipal and industrial. The shortages and financial aspects of water supply schemes and the distribution aspects of water supplies between HIG, MIG and LIG slum income groups was analysed. The analyses were carried out at a local level and the data pertain to the year 2001-2002. As the present study focuses on the strident aspects of the residential water demand, especially in urban areas, it would be important to suggest some strategies for future improvement. The important policy implications that flow from the present study are as follows:

Apart from the constraints of supply expansion, the major problem that leads to water shortages is the wastage through distribution and transmission losses and the inefficient distribution network presently existing. As to how the wastage of water can be calculated proves to be very expensive and the investments in leak detection and leak proofing must prove to be more productive.

The average consumption levels do not cross 100 locations of supply conditions (irrespective) and income groups indicate that the actual consumption levels are below the fixed (WHO) norms (i.e.150-200 LPCD). Therefore, in order to achieve the distributive objective and maximum coverage, the present consumption levels should be taken into account.

Even the investment required for improving the supply network is substantial and hence resource availability is the major constraint in this regard. One of the important outcomes of the study is that resources can be generated through the proper pricing of water. In this context, it may be suggested that water pricing should at least cover the working expenses in the short run and they should cover at least partially, the capital costs in the long run.

Pricing of water on a cost basis is essential because it helps not only in resource generation but also results in an efficient usage of water and discourages wastage of water. It is often observed that the decision makers permit shortages and allocate water by a no-price means of supply regulation when the existing capacity is on the verge of full utilisation. Though this has become a norm in most of the developing countries, supply regulation is considered to be an unsatisfactory permanent policy. Therefore, pricing policies should follow the marginal cost pricing. Marginal cost pricing requires that pricing should be equal to short run marginal cost, when capacity is less than fully utilised, but, if the demand increases and the existing capacity becomes fully utilised, the price should be raised to ration existing capacity (Saunders and Withford, 1976).

Table 2: Extent of Water Saving Through Various Techniques.

	Device	Water Use	% of Saving Over Conventional Methods
A	Conventional	13	32
B	Common low-flush	4	79
C	Wash Down	2	89
	Shower Heads (litres/minute)		
A	Conventional	19	
B	Common low flow	11	42
C	Flow Limiting Cloth Washers (litres/use)	7	63
A	Conventional	100	17
B	Wash recycle	80	50
	Faucets (Taps) (litres/minute)		
A	Conventional	12	
B	Common low flow	10	17
C	Flow Limiting	6	50

Source: Postel, 1985

At present, marginal amounts of water are being recycled and reused in India. The experience of other countries indicates a greater potential for recycling and reuse. Therefore, investments in this regard would be productive. Though the present study does not directly address the impact of technological factors on conserving water, one should not underestimate the potential of these devices. It is observed that water saving household appliances such as toilet flushes, showerheads, clothes, dish washers, etc., can reduce water consumption by 50-70 percent without affecting the quality of life. The following table (II and III) gives the extent of water saving by various devices.

Table 3 Adoption of Technology and Urban Residential Water Requirement Norms

Items	Present Consumption Norm (IPCD)	I	II	III
Drinking	5.00	5.00	5.00	5.00
Cooking	5.00	5.00	5.00	5.00
Bathing	55.00	31.90	20.35	6.05
Clothes Washing	20.00	16.60	10.00	10.00
Utensils Washing	10.00	10.00	10.00	10.00
House Cleaning	10.00	10.00	10.00	10.00
Flushing of toilets etc.	30.00	20.40	6.30	3.30
Total	135.00	98.90	66.65	49.35
	73%	49%	37%	

Source: G.S. Birde and J.S. Birde (1990)

Using this information we can estimate the extent of water saving in the urban areas. For this purpose, we have used the item-wise water consumption data and estimated the requirements with new techniques. Simulations are worked out for different techniques in each category. The estimates indicate that water saving devices can reduce consumption norms drastically.

In fact, with the latest water saving devices, the water requirement norms can be fixed as low as 50 litres per day as against the prevailing 135 litre per day. This results in the increase of water productivity to the tune of 273 percent. On the whole, extents of water savings ranging from 27 percent to 62 percent are depending on the types of technology adopted. Therefore, it is clear that through technology, the quality of life can be maintained if not enhanced, with lower water supplies.

Though the extent of water saving through improved devices is substantial, the adoption of these devices needs legislative and institutional support. Therefore, policy makers should bring in the necessary legislation in order to enforce the adoption. Most of these devices need little convincing at the consumer level as they are cost effective and energy saving. Therefore, the stress should be at the manufacturing level, discouraging the production of conventional devices and encouraging the modern devices. On the other hand, as in the United States, the municipal authorities should consider this aspect while giving permission to new constructions. Moreover, the adoption of water saving devices would automatically take place once proper pricing policies are followed.

Need for Water Harvesting

The annual rainfall over India is computed to be 1,170 mm (46 inches). This is higher compared with the global average of 800mm (32 inches). However, this rainfall occurs during short spells of high intensity. Because of such intensities and short duration of heavy rain, most of the rain falling on the surface tends to flow away rapidly, leaving very little for the recharge of groundwater. This makes most parts of India experience a lack of water even for domestic use. Ironically, even Cherrapunji, which receives about 11,000 mm of rainfall annually, suffers from an acute shortage of drinking water. This is because the rainwater is not conserved and is allowed to drain away. Thus it does not matter how much rain we get we don't capture or harvest it. This highlights the need to implement measures to ensure that the rain falling over a region is tapped as fully as possible through water harvesting, either by recharging it into the groundwater aquifers of storing it for direct use. Delhi has an annual average rainfall of 611.8 mm. However, recharge to groundwater is limited because of the decreasing availability of permeable soil surfaces due to the existence of roads and buildings. As a result, a poor recharge and heavy extraction of groundwater levels in Delhi have declined by as much as 8 metres in the past decade. Groundwater can be a sustainable source of water only if it is ensured that recharging an equal amount of rainwater into the ground compensates for the amount of water withdrawn from the groundwater aquifers. Water harvesting provides the means to recharge the groundwater, thereby maintaining the balanced situation of the resource.

Rainwater harvesting has a huge potential in Delhi. The illustrative calculation for the water harvesting potential for a single building can be applied to the city also as a whole. With an area of 1486 sq. km., the rainwater harvesting potential of Delhi comes to be about 907 billion litres annually. This is equal to about 270 days of water requirement for the entire city. The entire annual rainfall is received over a period of 27 days, 80 percent of which falls in the period between July to September. The rainwater therefore has to be harvested during this short period. It is well known that water is precious for all living beings and that it is a 'free' gift of nature. Therefore, there is an equal right of all beings to consume it, but there are certain mis-conceptions, i.e. water is unlimited, water is a common resource, earth is a watery planet so there is lots of water on it etc. Human beings are misusing this natural resource and if sudden action is not being taken, then it may be a warring situation to fetch water to quench our thirst. For quenching the thirst, poor people are unable to purchase safe drinking water, so their inequality has come into commerce. Rich people can afford the cost of bottled drinking water easily but the poor or middle class family cannot afford the high cost of safe drinking water.

Conclusion

There is a need of water harvesting to avoid the water scarcity and also to change our water-consuming behaviour. It is a necessity to change our practice of daily water use in order to conserve and preserve the groundwater as well as the rain water and the MCD supplied water. If the commuters show an irresponsibility regarding the conservation of water, then it may be a crisis for even drinking water in the future and then the saying with come true that, **"Water, water everywhere, but not a drop to drink"**.

References

1. Banerjee, B. (1999), *Use and Misuse of Water*, Geographical Review of India, Vol. 60, No.3. June.

2. Banerjee, B. (1997), *Population Expansion, Food Security and Sustainable Development*, Geographical Review of India, Vol. 59, No. 1, pp 1-10, Calcutta.

3. Bourne, P.G. et. al. (1984), *Water and Sanitation, Economic and Sociological Perspectives*, Academic Press Inc. London, pp. 2-19,70-91.

4. Biswas, A.K. ed. (1990), *Environmentally Sound Water Management*, Oxford University Press, Delhi.

5. Biswas, A.K. ed. (1978), *United Nations Water Conference Summary and Main Documents*, Vol. 2, Water Development, Supply and Management Series, Pergamon Press, Oxford.

6. Birdie, G.S. and Birdie, J.S., (1990), *Water Supply and Sanitary Engineering*, (4th Edition) Dhanpat Rai and Sons, Delhi, pp 79.

7. Charney, A.H. and Woodard, C. (1984), *A Test of Consumer Demand Respondent of Water Prices: Comment*, Land Economics, Volume 60, No.4, November.

8. Chicoine, D. and Ramamurthy, G. (1986), *'Water Demand Estimation Under Block Rate Pricing - A Simultaneous Equation Approach*, Water Resource Research, Vol.22, No.6, June, pp-859-863.

9. Council of Environmental Quality (CEQ), (1990), *The Global 2000 Report to the President*, Vol.1. Washington, D.C., Government Printing Office, pp.1.

10. Centre for Science and Environment, (2001), *A Water Harvesting Manual For Urban Areas: Case Studies from Delhi*, Age of Enlightenment Publications (Printer), Faridabad.

11. Jain, A.K. (1990), *The Making of Metropolis: Planning and Growth of Delhi*, National Book Organization, Delhi.

12. Jairaj, B. (1995), *Regulating Ground Water of Delhi: Scope for Legal Intervention* Spatio-Economic Development Record, Vol.2, No.6, pp, 42-46 New Delhi.

13. Kundu, A. (1991), *Micro-Environment in Urban Planning Assess of Poor to Water Supply and Sanitation*, Economic and Political Weekly Vol. XXVI, No.37, Sept.

14. Kaczmarek, T. et.al. (1996), *Water Resources Management in the Face of Climatic/ Hydrologic Uncertainties*, Water Science and Technology Library, 18 Kluwer , Dordrecth, The Netherlands.

15. Kittu, N. et. al.(1996), *Ground Water Situation and Development Prospects in National Capital Region*, 22-23 November, Seminar Organized By INTACH, Water Resource of National Capital Region: Problems and Alternatives.

16. Kundu, A. (1993), *In the Name of Urban Poor: Access to Basic Amenities*, Sage Publication, New Delhi.

20

The Concept of Environment in Holy Tourism

A Case Study of Delhi

DR. AZKA KAMIL

Introduction

A tour to a holy place fulfils one's spiritual quest and brings one closer to the divine. Travel to such places provides an opportunity to be closer to nature as well. India is famous for its holy places which are spread throughout its length and breadth. Our mountains are not only famous for their loftiness and snow covered perennial peaks but also for their being abodes of the divine. If we seek after the nature of God, we must consider the nature of man and earth, and if we look at the earth, questions of divine purpose in its creation and of the role of mankind on it inevitably arise (Glacken, 1967). The environment has intrigued man to search for the supreme power and has also influenced his search. The present paper seeks to find the relationship between Geography (Environmental Geography) and Religion and also the role of environment in religious belief. It also brings out a case study on Delhi as a holy tourist site with respect to the role of the environment on religion and vice versa. Although Religion and Science run parallel to each other, they have influenced each other implicitly. The Cartographic representation of the world by the Greeks, which includes maps and diagrams, was shaped by religion. One of the prominent Greek geographers Anaximander made an inviolable spatial-order and it is the manifestation of religious principle. Issac (1965) emphasized Ecclesiastical as well as Biblical Geography, where the focus in the former was on mapping the spatial advance of Christianity in the world while the latter attempted to identify places and names mentioned in the Bible. The search for the remains of Noah's Ark is such an attempt. Nature was seen as divine since the birth of man; who gave due emphasis to the environment. Ellen Semple (1911) a proponent with a determined approach pointed out that the place which we inhabit determines various religious symbols. For example, to people inhabiting the colder region of the world, hell is a place of darkness and intense cold while to the inhabitants of equatorial regions hell is related to fire and heat. Later, a significant change was introduced by the works of Max Weber (1922) who called for examining religion's influence on social and religious structures instead of understanding the role of environment on religion. The emphasis on the landscape as altered by the people may be likened to the more possibilistic stance of the

Vidalian school of geography and Carl Saur's school of cultural geography in which the landscape is the primary object of research (Kong, 1990). The early 1960s witnessed a worldwide process of secularization that Buttner (1980) called for the incorporation of the process of secularization into the Geography of Religion, which was transformed to the Geography of Spiritual Attitudes. With this development authenticity of the historical sites was of less importance as long as they believed in the historical and religious geography of the holy place (Shachar and Shoval, 1999). In the twentieth century, consumerism and media has played a prominent role in highlighting a holy place. Mark Gottdiener (1997) has focused on the increased use of themed environment with its pervasive use of media culture, motifs that define an entire built up space and are clearly tied to commercial enterprises, characterize more and more the daily life in the westernized countries (Gottdiener,1997). This has resulted in the commercialising of the holy tourist sites and thus one questions the role that religion or the holy places play in safeguarding the environment or the role of environment in holy places.

In India too, environment plays a crucial role on religion, belief and values and vice versa Delhi is the political capital of India and a cosmopolitan city that reflects secularism. It is a lesser known venue for holy tourism, though thousands of inbound, internal and domestic tourists visit the not so popular holy sites. The religious places of all the four major religions co-exist harmoniously in the lap of Delhi, namely, Hinduism, Islam, Sikhism, Jainism, Buddhism and Christianity. There are several holy tourist spots like Jama Masjid , Hazrat Nizamuddin Darga, and Moth ki Masjid. Jama Masjid built by Shah Jahan was originally called a Masjid-e-Jahanuma. Hazrat Nizamuddin Aulia, an important Sufi mystic, attracts a dedicated following from all over. The tomb is also flanked by a mosque and graves of the great Sufi poet Amir Khusro and Jahanara, a daughter of the Moghul emperor Shah Jahan. An interesting legend is attached to the origin of the Moth ki Masjid, or the Lentil Mosque, of India. One day Sikandar Lodi gave a grain of moth (a type of lentil) to his loyal minister Miyan Bhuwa as a reward for fun. The witty minister planted the seed carefully year after year until it multiplied so many times that it could finally finance the construction of the mosque. He then went to the sovereign to ask his permission to build the mosque. The king was quite impressed. He then laid the foundation of Moth ki Masjid himself. There is an intrinsic relationship between Islam and the environment. In Islam God is the supreme, regulating the entire universe. The nature itself confirms that God is supreme and nothing is associated with God. So the nature gets accorded the status of a God-built guiding system and protection and respect to the environment is seen as service to Almighty. There are more than five hundred verses that invoke respect to environment into the conscience of the believers. The Holy book mentions to take utmost care of things that one's right hand possesses that is any flora, fauna or living being or nonliving things (mountains, rivers etc) under man's control. Also the emphasis to lead a simple life is a principle to avoid a wasteful squandering of the natural resources.

Chattarpur Temple is the seat of the Goddess Durga, also known as Parvati or Kali or Lalitha, the wife of Lord Shiva. Goddess Parvati is the mirror of Prakriti (Nature) as well as Shakti (Strength) and the Mother of the universe. All living beings of the Earth come from Nature, hence she is also known as Jagadamba. Lakshmi Narayan Mandir is dedicated to the Hindu deities Lord Vishnu and the Goddess Lakshmi. The lotus flower is a symbol of purity throughout India, and Delhi's Bahai Temple celebrates this in a unique architectural way. It was designed by Fariburz Sahba, an Iranian-born Canadian architect. The building incorporates the number nine – the highest digit and, in the Bahai faith, a symbol of unity. The sleek structure has two layers: nine white marble-covered petals that point to heaven, and nine petals that conceal the portals. It looks like a fantastic work of origami. The nine pools outside signify the green leaves of the lotus and cool the starkly elegant, usually silent marble interior. The ISKCON Temple is located at Hari Krishna Hill. A fine example of architecture, it sports 'Shikharas', rising to a height of 90-ft above ground level. One of the largest temple complexes in India, it also boasts of a Robot, which was built especially to enact and preach 'Gita'. In Hinduism, the God of earth, atmosphere, sky, water, fire and wind suggests an underlying ecological sensitivity within the Hindu tradition. Hinduism has long revered the flora and fauna; tulsi plant, neem tree, papal tree, tale of Shankuntalam, Asokan edicts. The modern chipko movement sanctifies all of the environment. Numerous Vedic hymns are associated with rivers and more than sixty are dedicated to R. Saraswati alone as a symbol of learning. Likewise,the Ganges plays an indispensable role in rituals. The architectural style of ancient monuments and temples reveal various flowers and animals engraved in them. The epic Mahabharata and Ramayana show reverence towards nature.

The Jain temple, also called Indraprastha Tirth Sumatinatha Jain Svetamber Temple, is painted with finely rendered murals and decorations covering the walls, arches, and ceilings. In Jainism life particles in earth, water, fire, microbes and plants each experience the world through the sense of touch. For Jains to hurt any living being is thickening one's karma, thus obstructing towards advancement and towards liberation and so there is a need to avoid activities associated with violence and follow a vegetarian diet. Jains hold an affinity for ideals of the environmental movement. The non violence movement so preached fosters respect to all life forms. Truthfulness and acceptance of interrelatedness of things checks waste and reflects on limited resources. The discipline of non possession questions the conspicuous consumption of material goods. However some exceptions remain, where a Jaina people will participate in planting an environmental activity but on the other hand, monks and nuns most likely would not plant trees because of the pain and harm to the earth due to digging. In Buddhism the life of Buddha talks at length of the closeness to the environment. The reference is made to the Sal tree at the time of his birth, the Rose and Apple tree where he meditated, the Bodhi tree where he attained enlightenment and the twin Sal tree, where he attained parinirvana. Buddhism emphasizes the harmonious interaction between us and nature.

The Cathedral Church of the Redemption and Church of the Sacred Heart, were both designed by Henry Medd. Lord Irwin, the then Viceroy, was so impressed by its high curved arches and subtle domes that it came to be known as 'Viceroy's Church'. In Christianity, Jesus refers to his followers as the salt of the earth which is not used for seasoning but rather as a means of preventing meat from spoiling. Therefore, it concludes that if the salting effect of the God fearing people is reduced then social decay and environmental degradation will increase.

Bangla Sahib Gurudwara by all means draws admiration to the distinctively ostentatious style. There is an interesting story associated with Majnu ka Tila Gurudwara. According to the tale, a Muslim hermit used to live on this hillock, during the reign of Sikander Lodhi. He used to row people across the River Yamuna free of charge. He so yearned for the glimpse of God that the local people called him 'Majnu'. It is said that he finally attained enlightenment by the blessings of Guru Nanak and became his devout disciple. Gurdwara Nanak Piao is dedicated to the first Sikh Guru, Sri Guru Nanak Dev. Guru Nanak used to distribute all these offerings to the poor and needy. Besides these, he used to offer food and water to the hungry and thirsty. This gave Nanak Piao Gurudwara its name. Gurdwara Rakab Ganj was built by Lakhi Banjara, the devotee who performed the last rites of the martyred Guru Teg Bahadur. Gurdwara Sis Ganj commemorates the martyrdom of Guru Tegh Bahadur. The Sikh Gurus have preached the human responsibility towards nature. Guru Nanak gave the status of mother to the earth. Sikhism follows a three year cycle and the name of the next cycle (1999) is the Cycle of Creation, thus emphasizing immense environmental practices in the temple. Sikhism highlights the awareness of the sacred relationship between humans and the environment. Humans create their surroundings as reflection of their inner state, thus the increasing barrenness of the earth reflects the spiritual emptiness within humans.

So there is a diffusion of environmental concern in every religion which gets implicitly as well as explicitly reflected.

References

1. Adhikari, S. 1995, Fundamentals of Geographic Thought, Chaitanya Publishing House, Allahabad.
2. Burgess and Gold, 1985, Geography, media and popular culture, Croom Helm.
3. Durkheim , E. 1976, The Elementary Forms of Religious Life, London, George Allen and Unwin.
4. Glacken, C.J. 1960, Changing ideas of the habitable world, Chicago, Chicago University press.
5. Gottdiener, Mark 2000, New Forms of Consumption; Consumers, Culture and Commodification, Rowan and Littlefield Publication.
6. Husain, M. 1999, Evolution of Geographical Thought, Rawat Publications.
7. Kong, L. 1990, Geography and Religion: Trends and prospects, Department of Geography, Human Geography, University of London, Vol 14.
8. Weber, 1905, The Protestant Ethic And Spirit of Capitalism.

http://environment.harvard.edu http://delhitourism.nic.in/index.aspx

21

Vermicompost from Crop Residues for Sustainable Agriculture

SURINDRA SUTHAR, SUSHMA SINGH AND PARVIN K. MOTIYAR

Introduction

The soil fertility level and the soil organic structure in natural systems are maintained over time through the addition of organic matter from litter fall and root mortality. However, in conventional agro-ecosystem conventional seed-based practices, such as tillage and crop biomass removal, can result in the deterioration of the soil structure and the loss of soil organic matter (Dalal and Mayer, 1986). The application of organic matter in the form of plant residue has long been known to improve the properties of soil, especially soil organic matter (Blevins and Frye, 1983). However, agriculture by-products e.g. animal dung, farmyard manure and crop residue are potential sources of plant nutrients. According to Lal (2005) the annual crop residue production in the world is estimated at 2.8 billion Mg of cereals, 305 million Mg of legumes, 108 million of oil crops, 373 million Mg of sugar crops and 170 million Mg of tubers. The integrated approaches

Table 1: Production and chemical characteristics of major crop residues.

Crop	Residue production in 2001 (10^6 Mg) (FAO, 2001)	Nutrient contents % (oven dry basis)		
		N	P_2O_5	K_2O
Rice straw	152	0.58	0.23	1.66
Wheat straw	214	0.49	0.25	1.28
Sorghum	43	0.40	0.23	2.17
Millet	37	0.65	0.75	2.50
Corn	138	0.59	0.31	1.31
Total pulses	66	1.60	0.15	2.00
Pigeon peas	6.65	1.10	0.58	1.28
Chickpea	5.05	1.19	-	1.25
Sugarcane	19	0.35	0.04	0.50
Oilseeds	70	-		-
Seed cotton	16	-	-	-

to utilize the crop residue for industrial, animal husbandry, crop production, bioenergy production, industrial development and soil amendment technology, may be a key component of sustainable environmental development. According to a conservative estimation, around 600 to 700 million tonnes (mt) of agricultural waste (including 272 mt of crop residue) is available in India every year, but most of it remains unutilized. The crop residues has a considerable amount of plant nutrient (Table 1), which may be converted into nutrient rich bio-fertilizer (vermicompost) for sustainable land restoration practices. The nutrient rich crop residue must be 'prepared' before it is used as a fertilizer and earthworms are the best candidates for this job. Although thermocomposting has been adopted as a basic tool for an on site waste decomposition, there are some disadvantages of traditional thermocomposting methods, such as the long duration of the process, frequent aeration required, loss of nutrients (e.g. gassing off of nitrogen) and a heterogeneous end product (Nair et al., 2006).

The decomposition of complex organic waste resources into odor free humus like substances through the action of the worms, is termed vermicomposting. However, vermicomposting is the stabilization of organic material involving the joint action of earthworms and microorganisms. Although microbes are responsible for the biochemical degradation of organic matter, earthworms are the important drivers of the process, conditioning the substrate and altering the biological activity. The vermicomposting process procures a better quality product than traditional composting system in terms of nutrient availability. Lorimor et al. (2001) concluded that compared with the conventional composting system (as commonly used in India to recycle organic waste), the vermicomposting often results in a mass reduction, a shorter time for processing and high levels of humus with reduced phytotoxicity in ready material i.e. vermicompost. There are several successful episodes of utilizing the potential of earthworms in stabilizations of anthropogenic waste generated from different industries (Elvira et al., 1998; Garg and Kaushik, 2005; Suthar, 2006; Suthar, 2007a b; Suthar, 2008a b; Suthar and Singh, 2008 a b c).

The aim of this study was to convert the crop residue into biofertilizer i.e. vermicompost using two composting earthworm species (*Eisenia fetida* and *Eudrilus eugeniae*), under laboratory conditions.

Materials and methods

Earthworm Culture and Organic Waste Collection

Eisenia fetida (Savigny) and *Eudrilus eugeniae* Kinberg of different age groups were obtained from stock culture. The post-harvesting residues e.g. chopped straw of wheat (*Triticum aestivum*), millet (*Pennisenum typhoides* and *Sorghum vulgare*) and pulses (*Vigna radiata*) was collected from a local agricultural farm. The cattle shed manure consisting of animal excreta, discarded cattle feed etc., cow dung (7.82 pH, 298 g kg^{-1} organic carbon, 5.72 g kg^{-1} total nitrogen, 2.32 g kg^{-1} phosphorous, and 5.62 g kg^{-1} potassium) and sheep manure (8.12 pH, 306 g kg^{-1} organic carbon, 12.02 g kg^{-1} total nitrogen, 5.42 g kg^{-1} phosphorous, and 10.56 g kg^{-1} potassium) was collected locally from a farm.

Preparation of Vermibeds and Composting Trial

The crop residues were dried at 60 °C in a hot air oven, chopped and sieved (< 2 mm). The crop residues were mixed with cattle dung in different ratios in order to produce different waste combinations (dry weight proportion in plastic containers) for laboratory screening of waste (Table 2). One treatment was composed of pure cattle shed manure. The mixed substrate material served as bedding as well as feed for the earthworms. For laboratory screening, plastic circular containers of an appropriate size (28 cm diameter and 30 cm in depth), with pierced lids for aeration, were used. Experimental beddings were kept in triplicate for each treatment, and another triplicate for each treatment without earthworms served as the experimental control (composting). All beddings were kept for 3 weeks prior to experimentation for thermal stabilization, initiation of microbial degradation and the softening of waste. Twenty four week old clitellated earthworms were collected from the stock culture and released into different containers containing one kg (on dry weight basis) of substrate material. The moisture level of substrates was maintained around 70 – 75 %, throughout the study period by the periodic sprinkling of an adequate quantity of tap water. Containers were placed in a humid and dark room at a temperature of 26.2 °C (SD = 0.4).

Table 2: Composition of treatment bedding used in this study.

Treatment	Composition (A + B)		
	(A) Crop residues	(B) Animal dung	Ratio of A & B
Millet straw + sheep manure	*Sorghum vulgare* + *Pennisenum typhoides*	Sheep manure	1:2
Pulse bran + wheat straw + cow dung	*Vigna radiata* + *Triticum aestivum*	Cow dung	1:2
Mixed crop residues + cow dung	Mixing of all types crop residue used in this study	Cow dung	1:1
Cattle shed manure	Discarded cattle feed (chopped green fodder and dry wheat straw) and animal dung	Cow dung	-

The important chemical parameters of substrate were measured in all the treatments before the introduction of earthworms and after each 30-day interval, up to 150 days. Some biological parameters of composting earthworm (biomass change, cocoon production, total mortality etc.) were studied in the vermicomposting sub system by the following method described by Suthar (2007 b, c).

Chemical Analysis

The pH balance was measured using a digital pH meter (Systronic made) in a 1/10 (w/v) aqueous solution (deionized water). Organic carbon was determined by the partial-oxidation method (Walkley and Black, 1934). Total Kjeldahl nitrogen (TKN) was measure by the following method as described by Jackson (1975). Available phosphorous was measured using the method described by Anderson and Ingram (Olsen et al., 1954). Exchangeable K was determined after extracting the sample using ammonium acetate (Simard, 1993) and analyzing with a Perkin-Elmer model 3110 double beam atomic absorption spectrophotometer (AAS).

Statistical Analysis

One-way ANOVA was used to analyze the significant differences between the treatments. Duncan's multiple-ranged test was also performed to identify the homogeneous type of the bedding material in respect to different parameters used in this study. A paired-sample *t*-test was performed between the control (compost without worms) and the experiment (vermicompost with earthworms) for different chemical parameters.

Results and Discussion

Potential of Earthworm in Organic Waste Mineralization

The vermicomposting caused drastic changes in the physico-chemical parameters of waste mixture as compared with their initial levels (Table 3). The pH balance was lower than their initial values in all treatments (Table 4). Comparatively, the pH balance was lower in vermicomposted material than control or composted (Table 5) material and the difference was also statistically significant (*t*-test, $P < 0.05$, for both earthworm species). The shift in the pH balance could be due to microbial decomposition during the process of vermicomposting. Haimi and Huhta (1986), while studying the vermicomposting of some organic residue, concluded that the lower pH balance in the end product (vermicompost) might be due to the production of CO_2 and organic acids by microbial decomposition, during the process of the vermicomposting.

Table 3: Chemical characteristics (g kg^{-1}) of different experimental beddings at start (mean ± SD, n = 3).

Bedding	pH	Organic C	Total N	Available P	Exchangeable K	C: N ratio
Millet straw + sheep manure	8.45 ± 0.03	477.10 ± 0.05	10.58 ± 0.09	5.03 ± 0.05	4.13 ± 0.03	45.09 ± 0.39
Pulse bran + wheat straw + cow dung	8.79 ± 0.02	437.40 ± 0.09	13.01 ± 0.10	5.98 ± 0.07	8.95 ± 0.07	33.62 ± 0.17
Mixed crop residues + cow dung	8.25 ± 0.03	356.48 ± 0.05	12.52 ± 0.09	6.87 ± 0.05	9.91± 0.14	28.47 ± 0.19
Cattle shed manure	8.89 ± 0.04	369.12 ± 0.02	12.61 ± 0.03	4.30 ± 0.09	4.32 ± 0.05	29.27 ± 0.07

* For bedding composition see text

Table 4: Nutrient content ((g kg^{-1}) of vermicomposts obtained form different vermibeds (mean ± SD, n = 3).

Waste mixture	pH	Organic C	Total N	Available P	Exchangeable K	C: N ratio
E. fetida						
Millet straw + sheep manure	7.76 ± 0.05	379.9 ± 2.9	26.7 ± 0.56	10.5 ± 0.44	8.9 ± 0.31	14.2 ± 0.37
Pulse bran + wheat straw + cow dung	7.95 ± 0.04	332.7 ± 3.1	27.1 ± 0.73	9.8 ± 0.11	12.7 ± 0.23	12.1 ± 0.40
Mixed crop residues + cow dung	7.62 ± 0.06	262.2 ± 2.8	31.7 ± 0.59	9.9 ± 0.11	9.6 ± 0.12	8.3 ± 0.24
Cattle shed manure	8. 09 ± 0.09	255.7 ± 2.5	24.9 ± 0.26	11.9 ± 0.13	14.6 ± 0.52	10.3 ± 0.19
E. eugeniae						
Millet straw + sheep manure	7.86 ± 0.06	384.7 ± 4.47	25.7 ± 0.33	9.6 ± 0.14	7.4 ± 0.09	15.0 ± 0.19
Pulse bran + wheat straw + cow dung	8.01 ± 0.05	338.7 ± 0.10	26.4 ± 0.17	9.6 ± 0.11	12.6 ± 0.07	12.8 ± 0.08
Mixed crop residues + cow dung	7.67 ± 0.04	267.2 ± 0.08	30.6 ± 0.06	9.5 ± 0.06	8.6 ± 0.16	8.7 ± 0.02
Cattle shed manure	8. 11 ± 0.11	269.7 ± 0.31	24.6 ± 0.51	11.7 ± 0.65	14.7 ± 0.10	10.7 ± 0.23

* For bedding composition see text Table 2 Description of vermibeds used for experimentations

Table 5: Physico-chemical properties (mean ± SD, n = 3) of composted material at the start of the experiment.

Bedding	pH	Organic C	Total N	Available P	Exchangeable K	C: N ratio
Millet straw + sheep manure	8.06 ± 0.02	8.06 ± 0.02	10.74 ± 0.13	7.34 ± 0.07	5.95 ± 0.06	34.6 ± 0.44
Pulse bran + wheat straw + cow dung	8.32 ± 0.05	8.32 ± 0.05	13.31 ± 0.06	8.17 ± 0.08	10.89 ± 0.10	24.6 ± 0.11
Mixed crop resi dues +cow dung	8.05 ± 0.03	8.05 ± 0.03	13.79 ± 0.07	6.77 ± 0.03	6.40 ± 0.05	19.1 ± 0.10
Cattle shed manure	8.59 ± 0.06	8.59 ± 0.06	13.42 ± 0.17	8.77 ± 0.28	11.69 ± 0.08	19.7 ± 0.25

It is also suggested that the mineralization of the nitrogen and phosphorous into nitrites/nitrates and orthophosphates and bioconversion of the organic material into intermediate species of the organic acids, lower the pH balance of the substrates. The earthworms alter the chemical properties of the substrates and indirectly promote microbial propagation and colonization, resulting in a more prominent mineralization rate in the vermicomposting beds than general composting (Suthar, 2007a).

The organic C content was lower in the final products than their initial levels in both composting and vermicomposting. According to Dominguez (2004), the vermicomposting is a combined operation of earthworm and microorganisms, in which the earthworm fragments and homogenizes the ingested material through muscular action of its foregut and also adds mucus and enzymes to ingested material, thereby increasing the surface area for the microbial action while, microorganisms perform the biochemical degradation of waste material providing some extra-cellular enzymes required for the organic waste decomposition within the worm's gut. Moreover, this biological mutuality caused C loss in the form of CO_2 from the substrates during the decomposition of the organic waste. The conversion of some part of organic fractions of waste into worm biomass can also reduce the C loss form the substrate (Suthar, 2007 a, b; Suthar, 2008 a c d). The difference in the C mineralization rate among different waste mixtures may be related to the quality of the crop residue and amendment material.

Total N was significantly higher in the end product (Table 4) than initial substrate material (Table 3). Both composting (Table 5) and vermicomposting showed a valuable increase in the TKN content, but the increase in the TKN was significantly higher (*t*-test; $P < 0.001$ for all) in vermicomposted material than control (composted without worms). Studies have revealed that earthworms also enhance the N-levels in the vermicomposting substrate by adding their excretory products, mucus, body fluid, enzymes and even through the decaying tissues of dead worms in the vermicomposting sub-system (Suthar, 2007c). The observed differences among different vermibeds for the final TKN content could be related to the quality of the substrate, used for worm feeding. The higher nitrogen content in vermicomposted material suggests its' potential use in plant production. The available P was higher in the end product than in the initial feed mixtures. There was a more manifold increase in the quantity of available P in the vermicomposted material than in the initial material. The difference between control and experimental bedding was statistically significant for both of the earthworm species (*t*-test; $P < 0.001$, for all). Earlier studies have revealed that during vermicomposting, the release of the available P content from organic waste is performed partly by earthworm gut phosphatases and further release of P might be attributed to the P-solubilizing microorganisms present in worm casts. Gosh et al. (1999) studied the transformation of P during vermicomposting and found higher contents of available P in the case of earthworm-inoculated organic waste. Satchell and Martein (1984) also found an increase of 25 % in P of paper waste sludge, after worm activity. They attributed this increase in P to direct action of worm gut enzymes and indirectly by the stimulation of the microflora. Recently Suthar (2008 a c) and Suthar and Singh (2008 e) claimed higher contents of available P in organic waste after inoculation with epigeic earthworms.

Table 6: Individual growth, cocoon production and mortality in composting earthworms during vermicomposting (mean ± SD, n = 3).

Waste mixture	Mean individual weight (mg)	Maximum individual weight achieved (mg)	Net weight gain (worm^{-1})	Growth rate (mg wt. worm^{-1} day^{-1})	Total population mortality in vermibeds (%)
E. fetida					
Millet straw + sheep manure	305.0 ± 1.9	643.1 ± 4.0a	338.1 ± 2.1a	2.82 ± 0.06 a	15.0 ± 2.9b
Pulse bran + wheat straw + cow dung	314.0 ± 2.3	477.4 ± 6.0b	430.4 ± 5.8b	3.59 ± 0.11 b	15.0 ± 2.9b
Mixed crop residues + cow dung	314.5 ± 3.4	802.4 ± 6.5c	487.9 ± 8.9c	5.42 ± 0.18 c	6.7 ± 1.7ab
Cattle shed manure	305.6 ± 1.8	864.7 ± 5.3d	559.1 ± 7.0 d	6.21 ±0.10 d	5.0 ± 2.9a
E. eugeniae					
Millet straw + sheep manure	305.3 ± 3.92	1044.6 ± 13.49 a	739.26 ± 9.6 a	6.16 ± 0.06 a	16.7 ± 7.6 a
Pulse bran + wheat straw + cow dung	310.0 ± 4.92	1147.4 ± 17.69 b	837.40 ± 12.8 b	6.98 ± 0.11 b	6.7 ± 7.6 a
Mixed crop residues + cow dung	316.3 ± 3.85	1211.5 ± 20.14 c	895.19 ± 16.3 c	9.94 ± 0.18 c	5.0 ± 2.7 a
Cattle shed manure	305.4 ± 4.32	1261.3 ± 7.0 d	955.84 ± 11.0 d	10.62 ±0.10 d	11.3 ± 8.0 a

Mean Value followed by different letters (a - d) is statistically different (ANOVA; Duncan's multiple-ranged test, $P < 0.05$)

The extractable K was higher in vermicomposted material than initial material in all vermibeds, and comparatively the potassium mineralization rate was higher in vermicomposting beds than in the composted material (*t*-test; $P < 0.001$ for all) (Table 4). According to Suthar (2008 d e), the earthworm converts the organic fraction of the waste into forms, which are more available to the plants. The increased label of exchangeable K in vermicompost was due to an earthworm mediate rapid waste decomposition in waste mixtures. It is suggested that the vermicomposting process accelerates the mineralization rate and subsequently enriches the end product with more available forms of plant nutrients. A similar pattern of K enhancement in vermicomposted material is well documented in the literature (Garg et al., 2006; Suthar, 2007b c; Suthar, 2008 a e).

The C: N ratios of substrate materials showed the drastic changes after 150 days of experimentation. The final C: N ratios of the vermicomposts were in the range of 8.3 – 15.0, at the end of the experiment. The parameter traditionally considered to determine the degree of maturity of compost and to define its agronomic quality is the C: N ratio. According to Morais and Queda (2003) a C: N ratio below 20 is indicative of acceptable maturity, while a ratio of 15 or lower is preferable for the agronomic use of composts. The vermicomposts obtained in this study showed tht the C: N ratio was within the preferred limit as described by Morais and Queda (2003), which further indicates the agronomic potential of ready vermicompost for crop production. In the vermicomposting sub system, there is a loss of carbon as carbon dioxide, due to the respiratory activities of the earthworms and associated microflora, and simultaneously there is an adding of nitrogen in the substrate material by the inoculated earthworms (through the production of mucus, enzymes and nitrogenous excrements). (Tripathi and Bhardwaj, 2004; Suthar, 2008 a,d).

Earthworm Production During Vermicomposting

As data presented in Table 5, the inoculated earthworms showed a considerable increase in their biomass, after 150 days of experimentations. However, there was a statistically significant difference among different vermibeds for the maximum individual biomass increase for both *E. fetida* (ANOVA: $F = 289.2$, $P < 0.001$) and *E. eugeniae* (ANOVA: $F = 158.4$, $P < 0.001$). The maximum individual biomass was 864.7 ± 5.3 mg for *E. fetida* and 1261.3 ± 7.0 mg for *E. eugeniae* in cattle shed manure vermibed, at the end. The net biomass gain was in the ranges of 338.1 ± 2.1 mg (millet straw + sheep manure) – 559.1 ± 7.0 (cattle shed manure) for *E. fetida* and 739.3 ± 9.6 mg (millet straw + sheep manure) – 955.8 mg (cattle shed manure). The ranges of growth rate in *E. fetida* (2.82 ± 0.06 mg - 6.21 ± 0.10 wt worm^{-1} day^{-1}) was slightly lower than the individual growth rate ranges in *E. eugeniae* (6.16 ± 0.06 mg – 10.6 ± 0.10 mg wt. worm^{-1} day^{-1}. The difference in both earthworm species for the maximum individual biomass and individual growth rate may be of a species-specific character. The quality of feedstock also influences the earthworm weight gain during vermicomposting. Suthar (2007 a) demonstrated a close relationship between the N content of feedstock and the earthworm growth rate in *Perionyx excavatus*. He suggested that the crop residue has a different palatability, particle size, protein and crude fibre content and that the polyphenols and related substances directly or indirectly influence the biological growth in composting earthworms during the vermicomposting process. In this study, the difference in the growth rate among different feed mixtures seems to be closely related to the feed quality. The studies have revealed that the presence of some growth retarding substances in plant-derived waste, directly affects the palatability and acceptability of food sources by earthworms in the waste decomposing sub-system.

There was a significant difference among vermibeds for the total cocoon production in both *E. fetida* and *E. eugeniae*. The cocoon production was in the range of 60.7 – 81.0 for *E. fetida* and 58 – 87.7 for *E. eugeniae*, at the end. The total cocoon production showed significant difference among different vermibeds and the highest cocoon production was in the cattle shed manure, whilst the millet straw + sheep manure vermibed showed the lowest cocoon numbers, at the end (Fig. 1a). The reproduction rate (cocoon worm^{-1}) ranged 3.59 ± 0.26 (millet straw + sheep

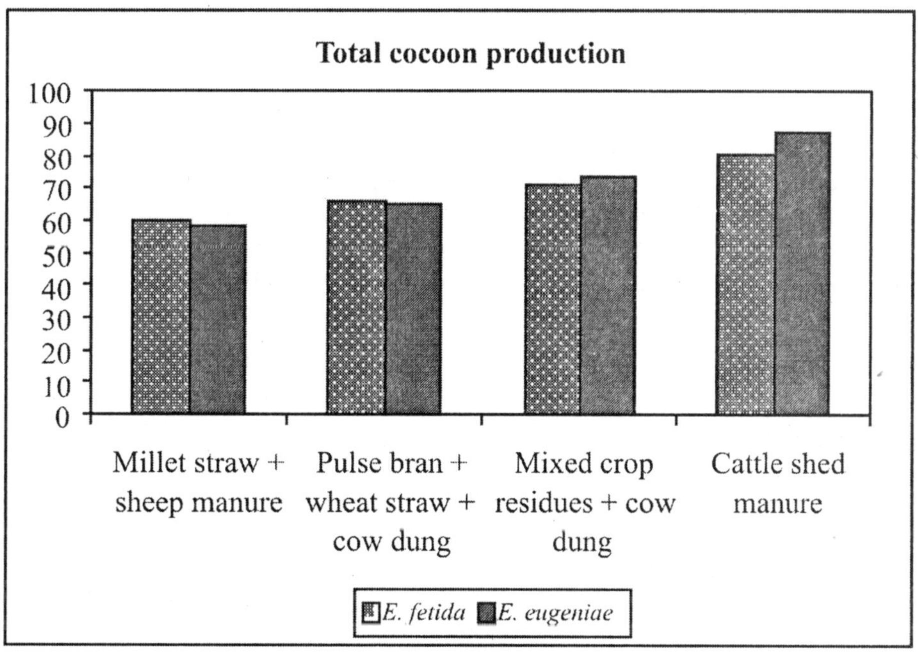

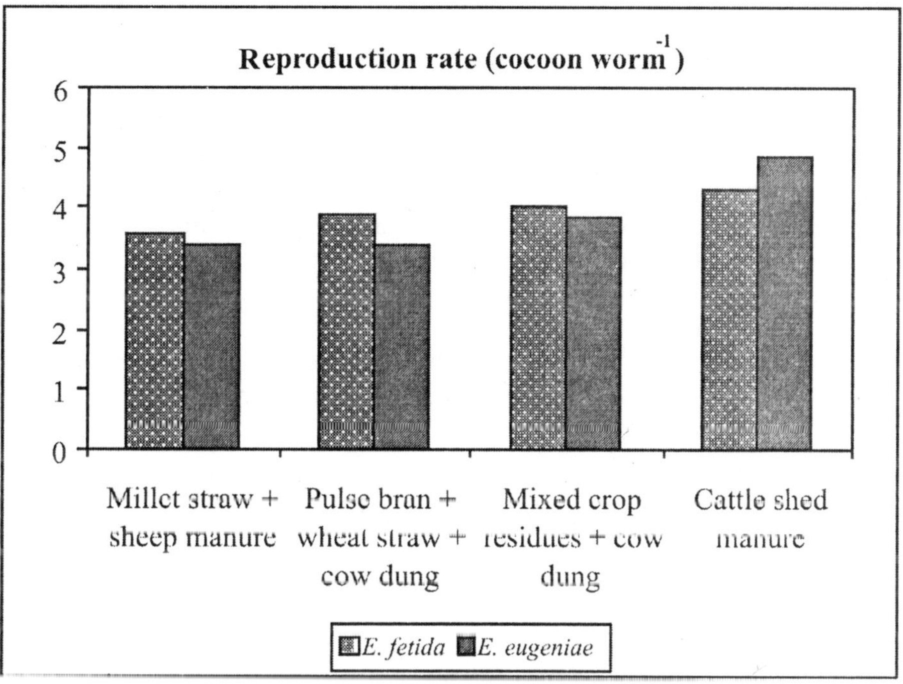

Fig. 1. Total cocoon production (a) and reproduction rate in earthworms during vermicomposting process.

manure) – 4.29 ± 0.39 (cattle shed manure) for *E. fetida* and 3.41 ± 0.01 (millet straw + sheep manure) – 4.82 ± 0.07 (cattle shed manure) for *E. eugeniae* (Fig. 1b). The factors relating to the growth of earthworms may also be considered in terms of physiochemical and nutrient characteristics of waste feed stocks. It is suggested that organic waste palatability for earthworms is directly related to the chemical nature of the organic waste, which consequently affects the cocoon production rate in earthworms. Suthar and Singh (2008 c) concluded that the important difference between the rates of cocoon production in the two organic wastes must be related to the quality of the waste. This study clearly suggests that crop residue could be a better substance for large-scale vermiculture practices after mixing them with a suitable bulking agent i.e. cattle dung.

There was a population mortality rate during vermicomposting, but the difference among vermibeds for mortality was not statistically significant for both earthworm species. The total population mortality rate ranged from a 5 % (cattle shed manure) – 15.0 % (millet straw + sheep manure and pulse bran + wheat straw + cow dung) for *E. fetida* and 5.0 % (mixed crop residues + cow dung) – 16.7 % (millet straw + sheep manure) for *E. eugeniae*. In general, the survival of earthworms in a waste decomposing sub-system depends mainly on the physical and initial chemical profile of the feedstuff (Suthar, 2006, 2007a). The production of toxic gases e.g. ammonia, nitrogen oxide, carbon dioxide etc. in vermireactors during waste mineralization may harm earthworms up to some extent or changes in the pH balance of the substrate media may also be responsible for an observed mortality rate in composting earthworms. It is suggested that the degradation process in vermibeds probably caused drastic changes in the microclimates of decomposing vermibeds, which consequently influenced the survival rate of the worms in vermibeds.

Conclusion

The feasibility of earthworms to decompose agricultural waste was studied by using a variety of combinations of waste under laboratory conditions. The vermicomposted material showed a more manifold increase in some important plant nutrients than simple composting, which suggests that the product can be used as a potential plant growth media. A considerable amount of worm biomass and cocoons were also produced in the different treatments. This study revealed that the vermicomposting technology could be used efficiently to combat the problem of agricultural waste management.

References

1. Blevins, R. L., Frye, W. W., (1993). Conservation tillage: an ecological approach to soil management. Adv. Agro. 41, 33 – 78.

2. Dalal, R. C., Mayer, R. J., (1986). Long-term trends in fertility under continuous cultivation and cereal cropping in Southern Queensland. III. Distribution and kinetics of soil organic carbon in particle size formation. Aus. J. Soil Res. 24, 293 – 300.

3. Dominguez, J., (2004). State-of-the art and new perspectives on vermicomposting research. In: Edwards CA (ed) Earthworm Ecology, 2nd ed., CRC Press, pp 401-424.

4. Elvira, C., Sampedro, L., Benitez, E., Nogales, R., (1998). Vermicomposting of sludges from paper mill and dairy industries with *Eisenia andrei*: A pilot scale study. Biores. Technol. 63, 205-211

5. Garg, P., Gupta, A., Satya, S., (2006). Vermicomposting of different types of waste using *Eisenia foetida*: A comparative study. Biores. Technol. 97, 391-395.

6. Garg, V. K., Kaushik, P., (2005). Vermistabilization of textile mill sludge spiked with poultry droppings by an epigeic earthworm *Eisenia foetida*. Biores. Tech. 96, 1063-1071.

7. Ghosh, M., Chattopadhyay, G. N., Baral, K., (1999). Transformation of phosphorus during vermicomposting. Biores. Tech. 69, 149-154.

8. Haimi, J., Huhta, V., (1986). Capacity of various organic residues to support adequate earthworm biomass for vermicomposting. Biol. Fertil. Soils 2, 23-27.

9. Jackson, M.L., (1975). Soil Chemical Analysis. Pranctice Hall of India, New Delhi.

10. Lal, R., (2005). World crop residues production and implications of its use as biofuel. Environment International 31, 575 -585.

11. Lorimor, J., Fulhage, C., Zhang, R., Funk, T., Sheffield, R., Sheppard, C., Newton, G.L., (2001). Manure management strategies/technologies. White paper on Animal Agriculture and the Environment for National Center for Manure and Animal Waste Management. MWPS, Ames, IA, 52 p.

22

Solid Waste Management Pertaining to Kitchen Waste

J. S. SUDARSAN AND DR. A. ABDUL RAHAMAN

Introduction

Agriculture is the major occupation in India, which is the life line basis for food production. About 80% of the population is involved in this field. Agriculture produces huge organic waste. In this ever-changing world, the technical advancement of waste utilization becomes imperative. Numerous waste from various agricultural fields poses huge pollution problems for the environment. This waste can be utilized for cattle feed, manure and compost production. For raising food production, soil fertility is a main factor, which can be raised by applying chemical fertilizers.But these fertilizers create a great threat to the environment so in using agricultural waste as a compost in place of chemical fertilizers can obtain a good yield as well as prevent pollution. A similar study is required on the waste generated in the restaurants. Huge waste is generated and dumped in the backyard and it produces an obnoxious smell and functions as a breeding ground for insects, particularly house flies and mosquitoes etc., further, the biological energy is also wasted. Hence converting this waste into good compost is the need of the hour. To achieve quick composting, scientists have been engaged in the utilization of the bacterial consortium for converting kitchen waste by composting. This project is an attempt in that direction.The conversion of kitchen waste into compost is renewable in nature.The banana, one of the most prominent crops in India, generates 7.77×10^6 tons of agro waste with 3.86×10^6 hectares under cultivation. Microbial conversion of an abundant supply of agricultural waste has become a subject of considerable interest as a renewable source of raw material for manure and composting sectors. Anaerobic bacterial consortiums are effective degraders of lingnocelluisoic complexes of agricultural waste.

Review of Literature

General

Although the decomposition of organic matter has been taking place in nature since life first appeared on earth, only recently have scientists attempted to control the process in order to make it more efficient. Left to itself, any organic matter will decompose by its biological action, but this process is slow and relatively inefficient, and for the decomposition to be complete, it may take a few months, or even years as in the case of other biological materials. In composting, this process is directly utilized for the agricultural waste disposal and the reclamation of organic waste materials by creating optimum conditions for the micro organisms participating in the process.

Composting

Composting is an application of a natural process of decay, the distinction being, that sufficient organic materials are gathered so that the heat produced accumulates. This has benefits for the speed of the process and achieves sterilization of potential pathogens. Composting is a controlled biological decomposition and a stabilization of organic substrates under conditions that are primarily aerobic and that allow the development of a thermophilic temperature as a result of biologically produced heat. It results in a final product, that has been sanitized and stabilized and is high in substances for humus which can be beneficially applied to land. Composting is driven by a succession of microbial processes. Broadly, the process is divided into four phase the-heating, thermophilic decomposition, mesophilic decomposition, curing. In the heating phase, microbial action in the presence of oxygen causes the temperatures in the compost mass to rise. While this occurs, there is a change in the microbial population from those which thrive at ambient temperatures to those which prefer elevated temperatures up to and around 70°C (Thermopiles). The action of the thermopiles maintains the high temperature. From the practical standpoint, this ensures that pathogens are destroyed and this results in a rapid waste treatment while very high temperature is generated in the compost. These are not particularly beneficial as very few organisms are able to function above 70°C. As the readily available source of energy declines, the compost pools and new population of mesopilic microbes preferring warm temperatures, become established. The compost remains warm and active and considerable degradation continues. Eventually all the readily degradable materials have been utilized. The temperature returns to an ambient one and the active compost process has ceased. At this stage, the compost is usually referred to as immature because it contains relatively high levels of ammonia and other compounds that are toxic to plants. Microbes are able to oxidize ammonia to nitrate but are not able to survive at an elevated temperature. During curing, these microbes recolonize and phytotoxic compounds are dissipated and stabilized.

The important factors affecting the decomposition of waste materials during the process of composting are temperature, nutrients present in the waste material, the pH balance of the waste material and the texture and moisture content of the waste.

Study Area

The study area for carrying out this experimental study was our university hostel. In our University, there are around 5000 students who stay in the hostel. For this study, we considered only the biodegradable waste from the canteen. Our normal canteen waste consists of vegetable, fruit peel, unutilized food parasols and all other kitchen refuse.The SRM university hostel is located inside our university campus. Our university is on the NH45 National Highway, nearly 40kms from Chennai city, Tamil Nadu, India.

Methodology

The common methodology used, for carrying out this study is anaerobic in-vessel composting.

Anaerobic Composition

In this matter, organic material is decomposed in the absence of atmospheric oxygen. Anaerobic bacteria, fungi and moulds bring about the decomposition of organic matter by a process of reduction. As in aerobic composting, the organism utilizes the nitrogen, phosphorus and other nutrients in developing self protoplasm, but reduces the organic nitrogen to organic acids and ammonia. The carbon from the organic compounds which is not utilized in the self protein, is liberated mainly in the form of methane. A small portion of carbon may be released as carbon-dioxide. Since the aerobic destruction of organic matter is a reduction process, the final product, humus is subject to some aerobic oxidation, and then put on the soil. This oxidation takes place rapidly. Left to it, any organic matter will decompose and for the decomposition to be completed, it may take a few months or even a year.

In-Vessel System

In this system, the waste is retained in a closed vessel and the composting process is carried out in the closed vessel type unit. The compost is retained within such a sort of vessel and the environmental and human impacts can therefore be tightly controlled and a huge quantity of waste can be handled.

- There are opportunities for strict monitoring.
- The thermal properties of the systems generally ensure rapid and sustained heating.
- Air delivery is well controlled.
- Systems are generally scalable.
- In-Vessel solutions are relatively capital intensive and total processing cost reflect this, but they offer the most comprehensive control and containment option.

Based on this concept, a prototype model has been developed, to carry out the experimental study of converting the kitchen waste into manure. The prototype model consists of a small vertical cylinder like setup which is having one inlet for sending the biodegradable solid waste and there will be one outlet at the bottom through which the treated waste sludge will be released out.

In the opposite side of the inlet pipe, there will be two openings.Through one opening, the gas will be released and it is controlled by pressure guards, and there will be another opening through which the slurry is injected.

We are planning to implement this prototype model in a large scale in our university campus by using the following methodology.

The prototype model will be loaded with biodung (leaves, kitchen refuse and peels of vegetables and fruits fermented with water in an enclosed space is called biodung). Garden waste can be added also to the mixture in an anaerobic atmosphere to create hydrocarbon methane along with organic fertilizer.The pH balance is maintained above 7 to 7.5. The maximum observed temperature inside the digester has been 43°C. Raw sewage along with liquor ammonia is added to maintain the pH level.

A Laboratory Test result obtained by C.R Doss et.al proved that the gas produced by using 2 litre of raw sewage mixed with 1.50 gms of kitchen garbage with 50gms of biodung gave 6.75 litres of biogas in 20 days. The temperature of the bath in which the experiment was conducted was maintained at 35°C.The gas burned with a blue flame upon ignition, signifying methane.

Results and Discussion

By using the above prototype model, 50Kg of minimum biodegradable waste from the kitchen has been treated. We analyzed the characteristics of the sludge produced by the degradation of this waste for a tenure of 1 month.

From this study, it is inferred that the sludge which is produced by this degradation is having a good humus value with a sufficient NPK content and the average result of the 50 samples are given below.

Bio-compost food waste	Actual results in%
Nitrogen as N	2.02
Phosphorus as P	0.67
Potassium as K	1.11
Iron as Fe	0.1
Zinc as Zn	0.48
Magnesium as Mg	0.05
Manganese as Mn	0.01
Boran as B	Not detected
Calcium as Ca	1.36

Nature and Value of Finished Compost

According to Bhoyer, finished compost is designated by the general name 'humus'. In general humus is characterized by the following features,

1. It is a dark brown to black in colour.

2. It is practically insoluble in water, although a part of it may go into colloidal suspension in pure water.
3. It contains a larger amount of carbon than do plants, animals and microbial bodies.
4. It contains a considerable nitrogen content of about 3% to 6%. In certain cases it may be 0.5 to 0.8%.
5. It contains the elements carbon and nitrogen in proportions which are close to 10:1
6. Humus is not in a static, but rather in a dynamic condition.
7. Humus serves as a source of energy for the development of various groups of microorganisms and it gives off a continuous stream of carbondioxide and ammonia.

By comparing the results with the above mentioned points, it is clear that the sludge produced from the process of in-vessel anaerobic composting, has sufficient humus and it can be used as manure.

Further it is confirmed that the production of inert gas is through the outlet provided in the upper most portion of the container with the help of a pressure gauge. From the smell inferred through the outlet, clearly indicates that it is a mixture of methane and other inert gases which can be used for domestic purposes. As this experiment was carried out in a prototype form, we are unable to produce large amount of gas, but if it be implemented on a large scale, we will be able to produce large amounts of gas.

Conclusion

At this juncture with heavy increase in the crude oil price and scarcity in the availability of LPG cylinders, the above mentioned composting process would be one of the best methodologies in solving the energy crisis. Kitchen waste along with sewage when utilized can bring the following benefits:

(1) It ushers a "Zero garbage" Zone in community living.

(2) It enables recovery of energy (Bio-Gas).

(3) It provides rich manure.

Bio-Gas technology is related to public Health, employment generation, energy, fertilizer environment and sanitation. It is a potential area for low energy and if it be confined with storage technology, it can be a great boon for mankind.

References

1. Bio-gas technology by K.C. Khandelwal, Tata McGraw Hill publications.
2. Bio-gas plant construction guidelines published by Vivekananda Kendra, Kanyakumari, Tamil Nadu.

3. Fry, John "Practical Building of Methane Power Plants" (1974), Chapel river press, England.
4. Journals: C.R Das and S.D Ghatnekar (1980), Replacement of cow dung by fermentation of Aquatic & Terrestrial Plants for use as Fuel, Fertilizer and Biogas Plant Feed, TERI Documentation Notes, Private Communication from TERI.
5. Metcalf and Eddy, Waste Water Engineering (1979). Tata McGraw Hill.
6. Methane digesters for fuel gas and fertilizers with complete instructions of two working models by L.John fray.
7. Proceedings of Nature solar Energy convention 1981, solar Energy society of India.
8. Practical hand book for bio gas managers published by regional centre for bio-gas development IIT Kharagpur.
9. Sudarsan J.S. paper on " Bio gasification of natural fuels" Proceedings of National workshop on recent trends in pollution control and Environmental conservation ENVIRON-TECH 2K4 JULY 15& 16 2004 at Bannari Amman Institute of Technology sathyamangalam Tamil Nadu India.
10. Solid and Liquid waste management in rural areas a technical notes published by Ministry of rural development in association with UNICEF.

23

Coliforms Bacterial Contamination of Drinking Water in Some Rural Areas of Northern Rajasthan

VIKRAM CHHIMPA, SURINDRA SUTHAR, RAJENDER K. BISHNOI, INDIRA SAHARN, VIKAS BENIWAL, VINOD CHHOKAR AND BHARAT PAREEK

Introduction

Poor water quality has appeared as a major threat for infant mortalities in developing countries. According to Ashbolt (2004) poor water quality, sanitation and hygiene account for some 1.7 million deaths a year world-wide (3.1 % of all deaths), mainly through infectious diarrhoea. Nine out of ten such deaths are in children and virtually all of the deaths are in the developing countries. However, a common health problem of drinking water includes the exposure to toxic organic substances, heavy metals, bacterial and other pathogens, increased nitrogen concentrations and other trace chemicals and micronutrients in drinking water resources.

The biological origin of contamination is considered a major problem of drinking water in developing countries. According to the WHO (1984) infectious diseases caused by pathogenic bacteria, viruses and protozoa or by parasites, are the most common and widespread health risks associated with drinking water. Walsh (1990) estimated that 10 major water-born diseases are responsible for over 28 billion disease episodes annually in developing countries. Ashbolt (2004) concluded that drinking water is a major source of microbial pathogens in developing regions, although poor sanitation and food source are integral to enteric pathogenic exposure. The bacterial contamination of water resources has appeared as a major threat in India because of the ill-maintained water pipelines and sewer lines.Open air defecation is rampant, the lack of disposal of human, animal and household waste, and the general lack of awareness of good sanitation and personal hygienic practices all contribute to an unnecessary pollution of the environment (Planning Commission, 2002). A large number of microorganisms present in water are responsible for causing diseases like cholera, typhoid, dysenteries, bacillary dysentery etc. (Ashbolt, 2004). The major pathogenic bacteria in drinking water of rural habitations are coliforms (Suthar et al., 2008). The coliforms include the members of the family *enterobacteriaceae* e.g. *Escherichia coli* (*E. coli*) *Enterobacter aerogenus*, *Salmonella* and *Klebsiella*. If such bacteria are not detectable in water in 100 ml, the water can be said to be potable water (Klein and Casida

1967). The major pathogenic bacteria responsible for waterborne disease is spread by the faecal-oral route, in which water may play an intermediate role.

In this study we analysed the quality of drinking water resources in respect to microbial contaminations, especially coliforms. A survey was conducted in some rural habitations of northern Rajasthan, India. The associability of the drinking water quality may provide some basic ideas about the load of water borne diseases in this area.

Materials and Methods

Study Site and Sampling

A total of 86 water samples were collected from 26 different villages/ towns. The sampling sites are located within the territory of the Hanumangarh district of Rajasthan, India Geographically the district is located between 28°44' to 29° 57' N and 73° 47' to 75° 31' E. The total human population of the district is about 1.58 million with a population density of 120 persons /km^2. Most of the population of this region inhabits rural areas (nearly 76.8 percent of the total population). The climate of this region is semi arid with extreme temperature conditions in summer (up to 45°C) and winter (up to 1°C). The site is influenced by the Indian southern-west or summer monsoon (June - September) and during winter (December - February) by Siberian anticyclones. The annual mean rainfall was recorded as 253.0 mm. The canal water is considered as a major source of potable water. Also,the public waste water supply is based on canal water.

Bacterial Enumeration, Isolation and Identification

The samples were collected in sterile capped containers by the following method as described by Greenberg et al., (1985). To avoid contaminations, disposable gloves were washed with HCl 1 N and were worn during the water sampling. The water containers were kept in large plastic airtight ice-cold containers and were transported to the microbiology laboratory within 6 h of their collection for the further processing. The work methodology used for whole bacterial analysis included: enumeration, isolation characterization and identification of microorganism following methods described by Williams (1989) and Aneja (2004). The enumeration of microbial populations was accomplished using a Total Viable Count (TVC) method (Williams, 1989). 10^{-6}, 10^{-7} and 10^{-8} dilutions were used from all the samples. 1ml of appropriate diluted suspension was transferred in petriplates and a molten agar medium (45°C) was added to each petriplate in replicates. Plates were incubated at 37°C for 24 hrs (Aneja, 2004). The isolation was completed by a serial dilution method, spreading and pour plate method as described in the enumeration technique on agar media (Aneja, 2004). The primary identification of the solates was carried out on the basis of their cultural characteristics on agar plates and microscopic observations, which formed the basis for the selection of biochemical tests to be performed (Secondary Identification) (Greenberg et al., 1985).

E. coli Detection and MPN Counting

To detect the total coliforms, especially the faecal coliforms *E. coli*, the specific media containing two substrates O-nitrophenyl-b-D-galactopyranoside (DNPG) and 4-methylumbelliferyl-b-D-galacuronidase (MUG) can be used (Tortora et al., 1988). 100 ml of samples were enriched overnight in 50 ml of a triple strength lauryl tryptose broth at 37 °C and streaked on sorbitol McConkey (SMAC) agar containing potassium tellurite. The sorbitol negative strains ($SMAC^{-}$) were tested for enzyme b-D- galacuronidase using MUG as the substrate. A colony of test isolate was applied to MUG impregnated filter paper; moistened with a drop of saline and incubated at 37 °C for 20 min. The absence of enzymes was indicated by the lack of fluorescence under UV light. The water samples, which showed the presence of coliforms, were further used to enumerate them using the Multiple Probable Number (MPN) test. The MPN test was to calculate the total numbers of coliforms in a water sample by the following method as described by Mackie and McCartney (1996).

Results and Discussion

The microbial load in water as measured through a standard plate count (SPC) was within the ranges of 8.3 ´ 10^4 to 28.3 ´ 10^4 in different localities of northern Rajasthan (Table 1). A total of 7 pathogenic bacterial species *Escherichia coli, Pseudomonas aeruginosa, Enterobacter aerogenosa, Klebsiella sp, Proteus vulgaris, Bacillus cereus* and *Staphylococcus aureus* were identified from drinking water samples in different habitations. The highest numbers of pathogenic bacterial species (5) were recorded from villages: *Ranjeetpura, Bhompura, Rawatsar, Jeevannagar, Mirzawali, Gandheli, Thalrka, Bropal* and *Manksar* (Table 1). The occurrence of pathogens and indicator organisms in the ground and surface water sources, depends on a number of factors, including intrinsic physical and chemical characteristics of the catchment area and the magnitude and range of human activities and animal sources that release pathogens into the environment (WHO, 1984). There are several emerging waterborne issues in developing countries and they relate mostly to unsafe drinking water, poor sanitation and inappropriate hygiene. The present members of the family *enterobacteriaceae* e.g. *Escherichia coli* (*E. coli*) *Enterobacter aerogenus, Salmonella* and *Klebsiella* in drinking water are of primary importance because these constitute a major part of coliform organisms in open water resources. These organisms generally live together in water different from other intestinal pathogens and, therefore, are easily detected compared with real pathogens. The coliform groups are present in water due to faecal contamination i.e. discharge of faeces by humans and other animals in water. In this study all three coliform bacteria (*E. coli, Enterobacter aerogenus,* and *Klebsiella* sp.) were detected in drinking water samples from *Silwala, rawatsar, Mirzawali, Gandheli* and *Manaksar* villages. The occurences of coliforms in drinking water indicate that drinking water sources of these areas are severely contaminated with human faecal material. According to Klein and Casida (1967) coliforms could be used as a water quality indicator and if such bacteria are not detectable in water in 100 ml, the water can be said to be potable water. As summarized in Table 2, *E. coli* appeared as the dominant bacterial species in drinking water samples and recorded from water samples of 19 villages, followed by *Klebsiella* and *Enterobacter aerogenosa.* However, the presence of coliforms shows the danger of faecal pollution and consequent the hazard of contracting disease through

Table 1: Incidences of bacterial stains in water sample in drinking water samples.

Village/ town	No. of samples	SPC*	TCC^m	Total pathogenic bacteria recorded
Salemgarh	3	21.3 ´ 10^4	32	3
Tibbi	6	19.3 ´ 10^4	38	4
Talwara	4	20.6 ´ 10^4	32	4
Silwala	3	19.3 ´ 10^4	32	4
Masitawali	3	21.6 ´ 10^4	31	4
Ranjeetpura	3	19.0 ´ 10^4	25	5
Pakki Dawali	3	20.3 ´ 10^4	32	4
Munda	3	28.3 ´ 10^4	31	4
Mohanmagria	4	13.0 ´ 10^4	28	3
Meharwala	3	24.6 ´ 10^4	41	4
Keharwala	4	15.0 ´ 10^4	31	4
Bhompura	3	23.0 ´ 10^4	32	5
Chaiya	3	19.3 ´ 10^4	32	4
Chahuwai	4	14.0 ´ 10^4	31	4
Rawatsar	5	22.0 ´ 10^4	28	5
Jeevannagar	4	21.3 ´ 10^4	32	5
Mirzawali	3	11.6 ´ 10^4	31	5
Bhurampura	3	9.3 ´ 10^4	26	4
Gandheli	4	7.3 ´ 10^4	32	5
Thalrka	4	7.3 ´ 10^4	38	5
Bropal	4	22.3 ´ 10^4	32	5
Sahrini	3	13.3 ´ 10^4	38	4
Rampura	4	8.6 ´ 10^4	32	4
Naiwala	4	8.3 ´ 10^4	25	3
Manksar	3	8.3 ´ 10^4	32	5
Sarekan	3	8.3 ´ 10^4	28	3
	93			

* Standard Plate Count, ^{m} Total coliform count (MPN index/ 100 ml)

pathogenic organisms. The disease-causing organisms (pathogens) transmitted via drinking water are predominantly of faecal origin. According to Trabulsi et al., (2002) a typical enteropathogenic *E. coli* starin is a leading cause of infantile diarrhoea in developing countries, whereas they are rare in industrialized countries. Some strains of *E. coli* produce toxins of two different kinds, a heat stable toxin (ST) and a heat-labile toxin (LT). Both toxins cause diarrhoea. Apart from this *E. coli* is also responsible for causing UTI, pulmonary infections, abscesses and skin-wound infections.

Table 2: Occurrences of coliforms in drinking water samples of different habitations.

Village/town	Coliforms bacteria		
	Escherichia coli	*Klebsiella sp*	*Enterobacter aerogenosa*
Salemgarh	+	-	+
Tibbi	+	+	-
Talwara	+	-	+
Silwala	+	+	+
Masitawali	+	+	-
Ranjeetpura	-	-	+
Pakki Dawali	+	-	+
Munda	-	+	-
Mohanmagria	-	+	+
Meharwala	+	-	+
Keharwala	-	+	-
Bhompura	+	+	+
Chaiya	+	-	+
Chahuwai	+	+	-
Rawatsar	+	+	+
Jeevannagar	+	+	-
Mirzawali	+	+	+
Bhurampura	-	+	-
Gandheli	+	-	+
Thalrka	+	+	-
Bropal	I	+	-
Sahrini	+	-	-
Rampura	+	-	-
Naïwala	-	+	-
Manksar	+	+	+
Sarekan	-	+	+
Total	19	17	14

The total coliform count (TTC^m) (^{m}= MPN index/ 100 ml) was recorded in the range of 41 (village *Meharwala*) and 25 (village *Naiwala*). As per the described limit of the WHO, all the potable water samples collected during this study were under the category of slightly polluted (if 100 *E. coli* in per litre) (Table 3). According to the WHO (1984) the presence of *E. coli* in water pollution can be used to measure the pollution status of potable water (Table 3).

Table 3: The pollution status of drinking water on the basis of E. coli contents (WHO, 1984).

E. coli in per litre	Water pollution status
10,000	Heavily polluted
1000	Polluted
100	Slightly polluted
10	Satisfactory
3 or less	Potable

In surface waters, potential pathogen sources include point sources such as municipal sewerage, as well as non-point sources, such as contaminated runoff from agriculture areas and areas with sanitation through onsite septic systems and latrines. In rural habitations, the open system for night soils elimination and washing of dirty hands in flowing canal water are common customs. Yan and Sadosway (2007) summarized the source of faecal bacteria in waterways. They concluded that faecal pollution of waterways could originate from wastewater treatment facilities, septic tanks, domestic-and wild-animal faeces, and pets. Moreover, the direct access of livestock to canal water in rural areas could be another important sources of potential pathogens in water. Pujari et al., (2007) suggested that on-site sanitation is increasingly adopted in India, which could be responsible for high levels of nitrates and bacterial contamination in drinking water sources. In rural areas, people prefer to eliminate night soils in open places especially in agriculture fields. In such conditions, there would be more possibilities for the contamination of drinking water resources through rainwater runoff mechanisms. According to a report by the Planning Commission, India (2002), the risk of water contamination resulting in water-borne disease is higher in rural areas under the following conditions: inadequate availability of water, poor quality of water at its source, ill-maintained water pipelines and sewer lines, open air defecation is rampant, lack of disposal of human, animal household waste, and a lack of awareness of good sanitation and personal hygienic practices. Out of these several features the last fact i.e. lack of awareness of good sanitation and personal hygienic practices seems to be more practical for rural areas of this region. Total results suggest that the drinking water of the Hanumangarh zone has low nutritional value due to the presence of coliforms. The increasing rate of infant mortality due to diarrhoea in rural areas of northern Rajasthan indicates the poor sanitation and hygienic conditions.

Conclusion

This study indicated that drinking water of this region contains a wide variety of enteropathogenic bacteria such as *E. coli, Enterobacter aerogenosa* and *Klebsiella* etc. The microbial load in drinking water as measured though a standard plate count (SPC) varied greatly 8.3′ 10^4 to 28.3′ 10^4 among different localities of the site studied. The data clearly suggests that people of this region are under a severe threat of water-related diseases and health risks. The continuous consumption of such polluted water could pose serious health risks, especially in infants.

References

1. Aneja, K.R. (2003). *Experiments in microbiology, plant pathology & biotechnology.* (4th edition) New Age International (P) Ltd. Pub. New Delhi.

2. Ashbolt, N.J. (2004). Microbial contamination of drinking water and disease outcome in developing regions. *Toxicology*, 198, 229-238.

3. Greenberg, A. E., Trussell, R.R. & Clescri, L.S. (1985). *Standard methods for the examination of wastewater.* 16th ed. APHA, AWWA, WPCF, New York, USA.

4. Klein, D.A. & Casida, L.E. (1967). *E. Coli* die out from normal soil as related to nutrient availability and the indigenous microflora. *Canadian Journal of Microbiology*, 13, 1456-1461.

5. Mackie, McCartney (1996). *Practical Medical Microbiology*. Colle, J.G., Fraser, A.G., Marmion, B.P. & Simmons, A. (Eds.). Churchill Livingstone, New York, USA., 14th ed.

6. Planning Commission (2001). *Report of the Screening Committee on Drinking Water Supply & Sanitation (Rural and Urban) for Tenth Five Year Plan*, Planning Commission, New Delhi, India.

7. Pujari, P.R., Nanoti, M., Nitnaware, V.C., Khare, L.A., Thacker, N.P. & Kelkar, P.S. (2007). Effect of on-site sanitation on groundwater contamination in basaltic environment- A case study from India. Environmental Monitoring & Assessment, DIO-10.1007/s10661-007-9616-3.

8. Suthar, S., Singh, S., Chhimpa, V., Bishnoi, R.K., Sharan, I., Mittal, N., Garg, V.K. (2008). The problem of safe drinking water in northern Rajasthan, India. In: Puranik et al. (Eds.), *Groundwater Resources: Conservation and Management* (Proc. 16th NSE, Hisar), 491-496.

9. Tortora, G.J., Funke, B.R., Case, C.I. (1988). *Microbiology: An introduction.* 3rd ed. Benjamin/ Cummings Publishing Co. Inc., California, USA.

24

Modelling the Participatory Discourse of Enhancing Player's Coping Capacity for Environmental Conflict Resolution

A Case Study

SUMAN RANJAN SENSARMA

Introduction

Concerning the idea of 'wilderness to be conserved' along with the Malthusian theory of population explosion, and Hardin's 'Tragedy of Commons', in 1989, Ives and Messserli postulated their hypothesis, i.e., 'Perceived Himalayan Crisis' which has been widely applied in policy making concerning the hill and forest area in India. In this related context we can find two distinct discourses in the forest policy. When local people are seen as basically destructive to their environment, the environment in question should preferably be managed by an outside agent, say for example the State government representing forest officials and wildlife wardens, as this type of approach is as a 'governance discourse'. Conversely, if local people with local knowledge are considered to be using their environment with care (if given the chance), then the protected areas are expected to be managed best by the forest dwellers themselves. This approach can be seen as 'a people oriented discourse'. More realistically, the negotiating outcome would be preferably a joint venture coordinated between the Forest Department and the local forest dwellers in collaboratively managing the forest. We call this approach 'participatory discourse' in the resource management.

The main focus of this paper is to address the necessity and possibility of resolving a resource management conflict by participatory discourse in a theoretical game domain. To participate, a player needs to have knowledge, capacity to represent their preferences and to execute their strategies. The paper intends to analyze the process of enhancing the coping capacity for yet undeveloped stakeholders to become complete players. The Graph Model for Conflict Resolution (GMCR), a game with a theoretical approach in conjunction with a social network approach, is used as an analytical tool to model and analyze the player's capacity building process in a game.

Background and Chronology of the Conflict

The proposed Rajaji national park comprises 825 sq. km of land, situated in the Shiwalik hills, and is representative of the Shiwalik ecosystem which lies between the Himalayas and the upper Gangetic plains. The park is known as an ecologically sensitive area and is the habitat of many endemic plant species, and also forms the North -West most range of the Asiatic elephants. The Van Gujjars are the pastoral nomads who have lived for centuries in deras, large thatched circular huts, throughout much of the park area as well as in the Shiwalik forest division to the west. The majorities of the Van Gujjars either migrate to the mountains for the summer and monsoon seasons or move to the shorter distances out of the park. Basically their livelihoods are based on raising buffaloes and selling milk. They utilize the forest fodder for their animals. In the periphery of the forest, the local villagers' livelihood is also based on the local resources. The confrontation arose in 1983, when the Rajaji area was declared as a proposed national park. The real conflict is centered around the forcible displacement of forest-based families from their traditional habitat and the disruption to their livelihoods. The major claim made by the State government is to clear the national park area from encroachment. The history and the chronology of the conflict are described here in different time periods in Table 1. The information is synthesized from many sources like the reports (RLEK, 1997; IPT, 2002; Gooch, 1998), newspaper articles and the field interview with the stakeholders.

Table 1: Chronology of the conflict.

Phase I

1983	Within the notification of the proposed Rajaji national park in 1983 and on the basis of Wildlife Protection Act, 1972, the Forest Department forced the Van Gujjars to move from the core of the forest in order to protect the fragile ecosystem.
1985	Pathri gujjar colony was constructed by the Uttar Pradesh Government.
1986	The GKMM (Ghad Kshetra Mukti Morcha), a local NGO has been involved with several issues at the village level including the land rights, grazing rights, corruption in government departments, oppression of women, education.
1988	In view of the Honorable Supreme court order efforts were made for rehabilitant Gujjar families outside of the Rajaji national park at Pathri. As a result, in 1988, 62 families selected their houses at Gujjar colony.
1989	In January 1989, the Van Gujjars filed a written petition in Hon'ble supreme court of India in which they opposed rehabilitation outside of the Rajaji national park.
1991-92	In 1991, several rounds of meeting were held with the Forest Department to try to resolve the crisis of access to bhabar grass.
1992	The conflict had escalated to September when the Forest Department forced the Van Gujjars to move from the park.

	The Van Gujjars brought the details of the case to the notice of the RLEK, a Dehradun based NGO.
1993	After the UN declaration, the Van Gujjars' conflict became a territory of national and global interest. The IPT (People's Tribunal on Environment and Human Rights) report declared on April 22, which recommended the setup of a multi-stakeholder platform to reduce the conflict.
1995	GKMSS has kept up the pressure on the Forest Department to find a suitable way to meet local resource requirements. In May 1995 the State responded by issuing an unprecedented order which has provided much hope in the region. The Forest Department succeeded in coaxing 65 Gujjar families to move to the Pathri rehabilitated colony.
	Phase II
1996	The issue attends the interest of, among others, a BBC film team as well as a team from a large German magazine Stern. The Wild Life Institute of India had launched a project called 'Building Partnerships For Biodiversity Conservation in RNP' with the help of the Ford Foundation, an international donor agent, and continued till March 2000. This project has provided money to create a participatory platform where all the stakeholders can share their views. In February, RLEK organized a national consultancy workshop and they presented the plan 'Community Forest Management in Protected Areas Van Gujjars-proposal for the Rajaji Area' with the close collaboration with the Van Gujjars and the peripheral forest dwellers. On September, some of the Van Gujjars' representatives met the U.S. representative from the World Bank at a workshop in Delhi to discuss the eco-development project being jointly funded by the Global Environmental Facility (GEF) and the World Bank for some Indian national parks. This meeting was later presented in the Indian media as 'probably the first time the World Bank sat down at the negotiation table directly with Indian forest dwellers.' The people of the villages took a decision of the possibility of establishing resource utilization forest committees through their several public meetings.
1998	Gujjars through RLEK went to the Human Rights Commission and alleged the human rights violation against them inside the RNP. A fresh census of the van Gujjar's families was carried out in which 1390 Van Gujjars were identified inside the RNP. A fresh rehabilitation scheme was prepared for them.

	The Human rights commission gave their consent order dated 15/03/99 and passed certain orders. The crux issues were, Van Gujjars living inside the forest area cannot be denied the rights which they have been enjoying since time immemorial viz. the right to lop and the right to graze their cattle. The forest authorities are not entitled to coerce the Van Gujjar families to move out of their habitation until their rights are legally determined in accordance with the law.
2000	On May 11, the Rajaji area came under the jurisdiction of a newly formed state Uttaranchal formerly Uttar Pradesh. On September 30, the Ministry of Environment and Forest (Central Government) again requested State/UT governments to consider the settlement order issued on 18th September, 1990 and to set up commission/committies at the District levels involving Revenue, Forest and Tribal welfare departments for the settlement of the disputed claims of tribal and forest dwellers.
2004	Another rehabilitation colony, Gandikatha, a few kilometers away from the park was built to rehabilitate 778 Gujjar families, but only 255 families moved and others opposed to move to this new location.
2005	Van Gujjars filed a written petition to the Lokayukta to take further action for the rehabilitation issue and their rights to local resources.
2006	Van Gujjars had complained to the Uttaranchal Lokayukta against the move by the State government to forcibly evict the nomadic community despite earlier orders by the National Human Rights Commission (NHRC). The Forest Rights bill passed.
2007-2008	Gujjars with the help of the local organization is struggling to execute their rights.

Graph Model for Conflict Resolution

GMCRII provides a simple strategic representation of conflict, with minimal information requirements that can be analyzed for a range of stability patterns that represent different styles of decision making in a real-world conflict. This is founded upon a mathematical framework utilizing concepts from a graph theory, set theory and logical reasoning. It represents a conflict as moving from one state to another state (the vertices of a graph) via transmissions (the arcs of the graph) controlled by the decision makers. Mathematically, this Let $N = \{1, 2, \ldots, n\}$ be the set of players and $K = \{k_1, k_2, \ldots, k_u\}$ be the set of states of the conflict, and n-tuple $\{D_i\}$ (i=1, 2..., n) be the set of directed graphs where $D_i = (K, V_i)$. Set of arcs V_i means player i's possible move between states. Let $k_l k_m$ be the arc from state k_l to state km. If, $k_l k_m \in V_i$ it implies that player i can move from state k_l to state k_m unilaterally. Payoff function P_i specifies player i's preference order for states. If $P_i(k_l) > P_i(k_m)$, player i prefers state k_l to state k_m. The Graph Model for Conflict Resolution (GMCR) is presented by 4-tuple $\{N, K, V, P\}$, where $N = \{1, 2, \ldots, n\}$, $K = \{1, 2, \ldots, k\}$, $\mathbf{V} = \{V_1, V_2, \ldots, V_n\}$ and $P = P_i / i \in N\}$.

One advantage of the graph model over more traditional game theoretical approaches is that it can represent irreversible moves. In such cases, a decision maker can unilaterally move from state *k* to state *q* but not from *q* to *k*.

Preferences in graph models are expressed in terms of a pair of binary relations $\{\succ i, \sim i\}$on S ,where $s_1 \succ s_2$ indicates that player *i* prefers s_1 to s_2, and $s_1 \sim s_2$ means that player *i* is indifferent between s_1 and s_2 (or equally prefers s_1 and s_2). Three subsets of the state S are defined as:

$\Phi_i^+ (s) = \{s_m: s_m \succ_i s\}$;all states that player *i* prefers to *s*.

$\Phi_i^- (s) = \{s_m: s \succ_i s_m\}$;all states that player *i* prefers *s* to.

$\Phi_i^= (s) \{s_m: s_m \sim_i s\}$; all states are indifferent to *s* for player *i*.

In the graph model, player *i*'s reachability list $R_i(s)$ from a given state *s*, contains all states that player *i* can move to in one step. $R_i(s)$ can be partitioned into three subsets using the above mentioned subsets of the state S:

$R_i^+ (s) = R_i(s) \cap (s)\, \Phi_i^+$; all unilateral improvements from *s* to player *i*.

$R_i^- (s) = R_i(s) \cap (s)\Phi_i^-$; all unilateral disimprovements from *s* to player *i*.

$R_i^= (s) = R_i(s) \cap (s)\Phi_i^=$; all equally preferred states reachable from state *s* by player *i*.

When a player does not have an incentive to move from a particular state, the state is called stable for the player, and the state is called equilibrium if it is stable for all the players.

$G = (S, (A_i: i \in N))$......... (1)

The main stability definitions currently used in graph model analysis include Nash Stability (Nash), General Metarationality (GMR), Symmetric Metarationality (SMR), Sequential Stability (SEQ), Limited Move Stability (L_h), and Non-Myopic Stability (NM).

Players Vs Actors

We claim that in game theory each player is ideally assumed to be complete to obtain three following capacities i.e., representability, knowledge, and executability. Representability describes the possibilities to depict player's own preferences in a game. Common knowledge refers that if all of the players know it (it is mutual knowledge) and all of the players know that the other players all know it, and that they know that all other players know that all other players know it, and so on. Another kind of knowledge is an external knowledge, which does not belong to the concerned players, but if an external actor provides the concerned players with some external knowledge that was not perceived and owned by the players, it becomes a shared knowledge. Executability refers to some capacity to transfer player's strategies into action. Without the knowledge and representability the player cannot achieve the executability of the strategy (Sensarma and Okada, 2007).

Depending on the extent to which these capacities are fulfilled by the players, we propose to categorize systematically the capacity status of the players, e.g., 'null player,' 'intermediate player' and 'complete player' in the game. The last is the ideal player obtaining the three capacities as assumed in the conventional game theory. Thus our concern is to find out how their status affects the structure of the game and subsequently their strategic choices. (Somewhat differently in the context of the cooperative game, Hart defines the null player as "a player i is a null player in (N,v) if $v(S \cup \{i\})=v(S)$ for all S". The axiom states that if i is a null player in (N,v) then j^i $(N,v)=0$). We define here a null player in a non-cooperative game as one lacking representability, complete knowledge and executability in the game. Null players cannot move unilaterally. They are forced to move along with their opponent players only. They have to see the game precisely to accept totally (mirror) their opponent's preference. A null player can become empowered to become an intermediate or complete player if he/she receives some complementary competence from a supportive actor. If the null player can obtain representability, and common knowledge with the rest of the players, he/she will become an intermediate player. But to become a complete player, he/she needs the capacity to execute his/her representative moves.

Here we note that actors are differentiated from players. An actor can be defined as an external stakeholder who can participate in the game only from outside and indirectly. Actors are, however, not players who can play the game openly. They serve to upgrade the status of a null player to become an intermediate and finally a complete player in terms of enhancing their representability capacity and common knowledge. The executability can also be provided by an actor with authority to do so (Sensarma and Okada, 2007).

In the following section, we elaborate the above idea illustrating a real world environmental conflict case, where a player`s coping capacity is modelled in the different stages using the GMCR in conjunction with a social network approach. The formation of preferences and player's strategies is modelled in a theoretical game form in conjunction with a social network approach. It has also shown that so far, more attention has to be paid to this kind of social network approach, and its strategic evolution in a theoretical game domain. Thus another aim is to enhance awareness producing a prototype method for highlighting this unexplored research. As Skyrms and Pemantle (2000) argued that, "the idea of a simultaneous evolution of strategy and social network appears to be almost completely unexplored."

Rajaji National Park Conflict: Modelling and Interpretation

Initial Stage (Phase I)

In the beginning of the conflict, the Van Gujjars and the peripheral forest dwellers were not able to represent their utility. They were the null players in this conflict. As a complete player, the Forest Department had the full power to play the game. The players were not interacting (connected) to each other and thus the null graph evolved with no vertices and no edges in the initial confrontation phase. Fig. 1 represents the null space of this confrontation discourse. Table 2 shows the options available to the players during this phase. Here, the Van Gujjars and the peripheral forest dwellers cannot move unilaterally from state k to state q and their common move is also nullified.

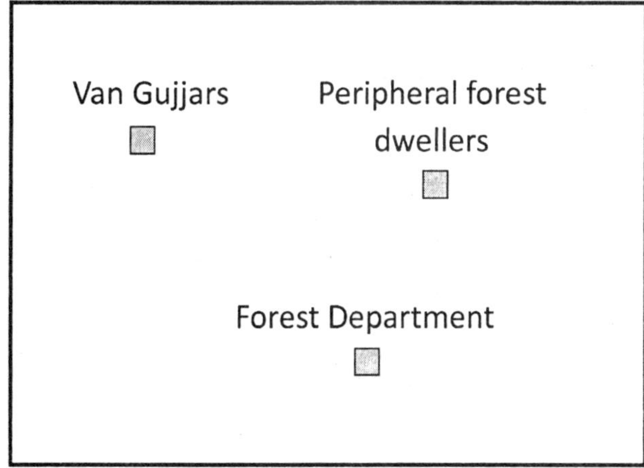

Fig. 1. Null graph in the initial stage .

Intermediate Stage (Phase I)

In 1992, the conflict had escalated during and the spring (September) when some of the Van Gujjars returned from their annual migration they were stopped by the Park authorities (Forest Department) at the boundary of the national park and asked to move to the Pathri resettlement colony and also those Van Gujjars, who were staying in the park area, had been forced by the Forest Department to put their thumb print on a piece of paper saying that they would not be allowed back in to the forest when they returned in autumn.

The Van Gujjars brought the details of the case to the notice of the RLEK, a Dehradun based NGO who organized the first meeting of the Van Gujjars to protest this incident. Since then, this NGO had started different development projects in cooperation with the Van Gujjars to strengthen their pastoral life and overall welfare. Another organization GKMM had been involved with several issues in the peripheral level, especially those involving dalits* and other backward classes, including land rights, grazing rights, corruption in government departments, oppression of women, education, but the ban worker issue has always been a primary one for the organization. Obviously the turn of the conflict was due to the emergence of actors supporting the former null players, the Van Gujjars and the peripheral forest dwellers. The actual game started when the null players began to interact with the other actors. These interactions are modelled as games. The payoff represents the stakeholder's gradation up to become a player. The RLEK serves to the Gujjars and the GKMM serves to the peripheral forest dwellers to become a player. Thus social network evolved through the involvement of different actors limited to different players, their strategy and link with others (Fig.2). The knowledge is provided by the external actors and consequently the Gujjars and the peripheral forest dwellers are able to represent their preferences due to the complements from their supportive actors, i.e., RLEK and the GKMM.

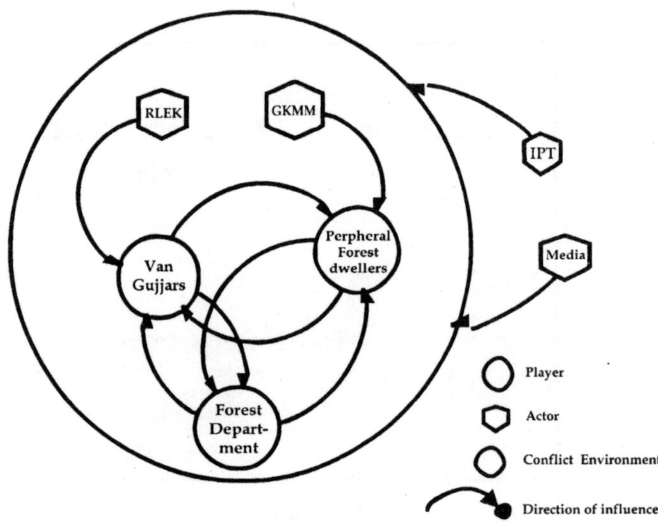

Fig. 2. Social network in the intermediate stage (Phase I).

The conflict is modelled as 3 players, i.e., the Van Gujjars, the peripheral forest dwellers and the Forest Department. In this stage, everyone is connected interacting as a decision maker with others and they have the following options: Opposing the rehabilitation (Van Gujjars), claiming the resource rights (peripheral forest dwellers), rehabilitating the Gujjars, and opposing the resource rights (Forest Department) (Table 2). Mathematically there are total 18 (2^4=18) possible states, but after removing all the infeasible states there are 9 feasible states in total (Table 3). Some states are infeasible because they are mutually exclusive. The number is reduced substantially by removing the infeasible states. In the Tables 2 and 3, 'Y' means 'Yes' and indicates that the option is taken for a corresponding state, and 'N' means 'No', that the option is not taken. Given this set of preferences, states 4, 6, 8 and 9 are the possible equilibria in this game. In equilibrium 4, both the Gujjars and the peripheral forest dwellers would be better off but the status quo state is unstable. Table 4 shows the reachability and the payoff functions of the players. The Van Gujjars and the peripheral forest dwellers reachability and payoffs represent the joint involvement with the supportive actor(s). Fig.3 shows the possible moves of the players in this phase in a state transitional graph. It represents players' possible strategies in a game.

Table 2: Players and their options (Phase I).

Players and their options	Status Quo State
Van Gujjars	
1. Opposing the rehabilitation Peripheral forest dwellers	Y
2. Claiming the resource rights Forest Department	Y
3. Rehabilitating the Gujjars	Y
4. Opposing the resource rights	Y

Table 3: Feasible states of the conflict (Phase I).

Options \ States		1	2	3	4	5	6	7	8	9
Van Gujjars	1	N	Y	N	Y	N	N	N	Y	N
Peripheral Forest Dwellers	2	N	N	Y	Y	N	Y	N	N	N
Forest Department	3	N	N	N	N	Y	Y	N	N	Y
	4	N	N	N	N	N	N	Y	Y	Y

In 1995, the IPT requested the former justice P.S.Poti to visit the Rajaji national park, where a series of consultation meetings were held with representatives of the local communities, the NGOs, the (former) field director of Rajaji and the other Forest Department officials, the Wild Life Institute of India and other organizations. Following this initiative the interim report was released by the IPT on April 22, 1995. The major focus of the IPT report was on the process of combining conservation with meeting local people's needs, including the creation of a multi-agency team to plan and manage the park. The IPT's role was more like a catalyst to reinforce the conflict to move on to a negotiation stage, i.e., phase II. The media also played a vital role to open up this discourse to a large public. A Swedish researcher wrote, media representations of the Van Gujjars pastoralists and the conflict over Rajaji has consequently been very important in changing the public image from one at the beginning of the conflict, where they were pictured as 'destroyer' of their forest environment to one which gained in importance during time, where they are seen as 'saviours' of the very same environment.

State	Van Gujjars		Peripheral Forest Dwellers		Forest Department	
k	S_1 (*k*)	P_1 (*k*)	S_2 (*k*)	P_2 (*k*)	S_3 (*k*)	P_3 (*k*)
1	2	5	3	5	5,7,9	4
2	1	8	4	6	8	2
3	4	6	1	8	6	3
4	3	9	2	9	Ø	1
5	Ø	2	6	4	1,7,9	8
6	Ø	3	5	7	3	7
7	8	4	Ø	2	1,5,9	6
8	7	7	Ø	3	2	5
9	Ø	1	Ø	1	1,5,7	9

Table 4: Reachability and payoffs of the RNP conflict (Phase I: Intermediate stage)*.

* Note: *K*= state number;$S_i(k)$ = reachable list for player *i* from state *k*;*Pi* (*K*) = payoff of player *i* for state *k*.

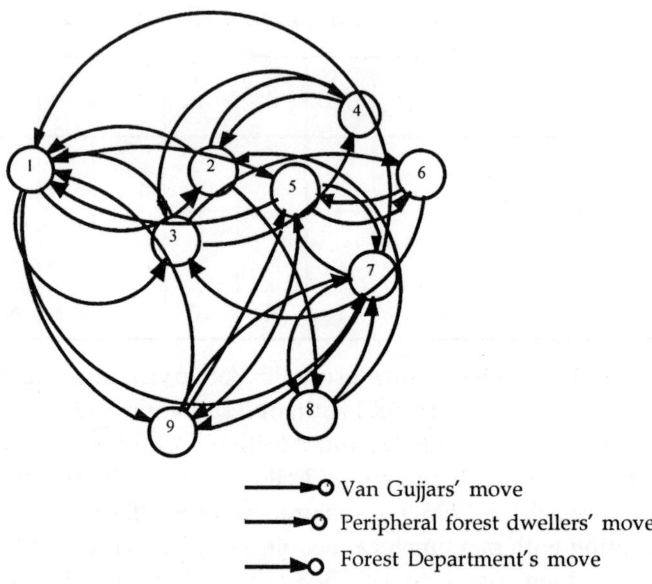

Fig. 3. State transition graph (Phase I-intermediate stage).

Intermediate to Complete Game Stage (Second phase :1996-2008)

In the third stage of the conflict, many national and international actors took their respective roles. As an effort of IPT, in 1996, the WII launched a project called 'Building Partnerships for Biodiversity Conservation in RNP' with the help of an international donor agent, 'Ford Foundation' and this continued till March 2000. This project provided to create a participatory platform where all the stakeholders were able to share their views. Another major initiative was taken by the Van Gujjars in 1998. Through RLEK, they went to the Human Rights Commission and alleged the human rights violation against them inside the RNP. The issue came to the interest of the media, like the newspapers, a BBC film team as well as a team from a large German magazine Stern. In this way the images of the Gujjars became more global even if the people themselves stayed in a forest.

We have modelled this game incorporating the same players as noted in the first phase of the conflict but their options and preferences have changed from the previous period due to the other actors' compliments. Now the Van Gujjars have several options available which strengthen their survival issue. The Forest Department has also shifted their preferences to the resource rights negotiation issue with the peripheral forest dwellers. There are a total of six options available to the players. These are, staying in the park, appealing to the NHRC, making a proposal for CFMP (Van Gujjars), exercising the rights of natural resources (Peripheral forest dwellers), and rehabilitating the Gujjars, negotiating with the peripheral forest dwellers (Forest Department) (Table 5). There are potentially 18 feasible distinct states to consider in this conflict. However some of the states are mutually exclusive or option dependent which subsequently reduces the number of feasible states (Table 6). Like the Van Gujjars stay in the park and the fact that the Forest Department rehabilitates them, both are mutually exclusive. The state 17 is a strong equilibrium under all the stability concepts and the state 5 is stable under GMR and SMR stability concepts , and 11 is stable under GMR, SMR and SEQ concepts. The equilibrium 17 represents the negotiation scenario among the players which took place partly during this period.

Table 5: Players and their options (Phase II).

Players and their options	Status Quo State
Van Gujjars	
1. Staying in the park	Y
2. Appealing to the NHRC	Y
3. Making a proposal for CFMP Peripheral forest dwellers	Y
4. Exercising the rights of natural resources Forest Department	Y
5. Rehabilitating the Gujjars	Y
6. Negotiating with the peripheral forest dwellers	Y

Table 6: Feasible states of the conflict in phase II.

Options \ States		1	2	3	4	5	6	7	8	9	10	11	12	13	14	15	16	17	18
Van Gujjars	1	N	Y	Y	Y	Y	N	Y	Y	Y	Y	N	N	N	Y	Y	Y	Y	N
	2	N	N	Y	N	Y	N	N	Y	N	Y	N	N	N	N	Y	N	Y	N
	3	N	N	N	Y	Y	N	N	N	Y	Y	N	N	N	N	N	Y	Y	N
Peripheral forest dwellers	4	N	N	N	N	N	Y	Y	Y	Y	Y	N	Y	Y	Y	Y	Y	Y	Y
Forest Department	5	N	N	N	N	N	N	N	N	N	N	Y	Y	N	N	N	N	N	Y
	6	N	N	N	N	N	N	N	N	N	N	N	N	Y	Y	Y	Y	Y	Y

Many international actors played their perspective roles as a supporter, facilitator, donor, mediator, and arbitrator and thus the network has expanded with the new strategies and options (Fig.4). The WII with the support of a donor agent has influenced the decision maker's actual state of ranking in this mediation process, but it was project based mediation for a stipulated time. Within this time, many conflicts had been resolved and a participatory platform evolved as a result of this mediation. The player's coping capacity also enhanced and trust building among the stakeholders was another achievement in this mediation process.

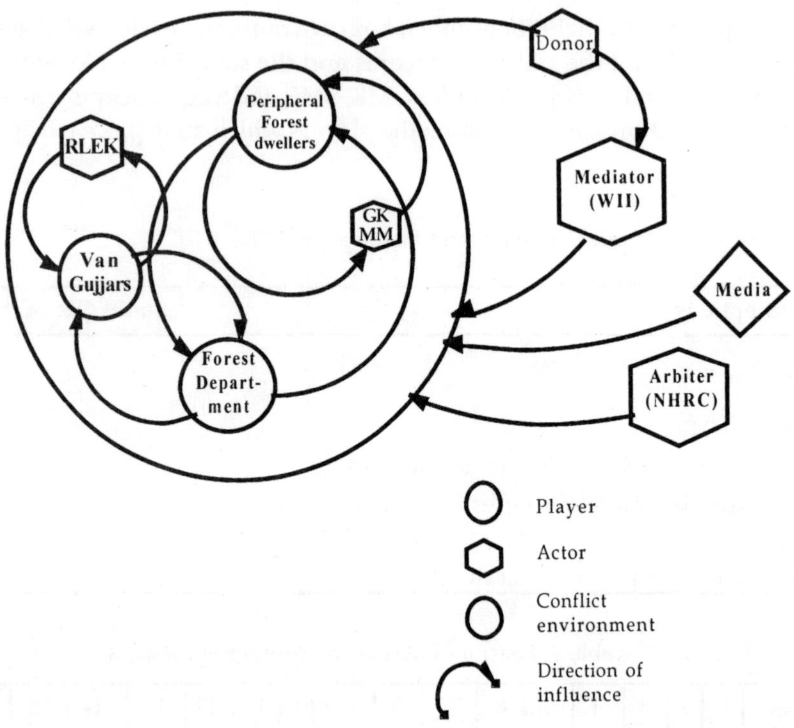

Fig. 4. Social network in the intermediate to complete game stage (Phase II).

As an intermediate player, the Van Gujjars and the peripheral forest dwellers along with their supportive players have common moves in this game. In this phase, the Van Gujjars have more options due to the external actor's competence. For example, alone they are not able to appeal to the NHRC (National Human Rights Commission). The proposal for community forest management is also possible only due to the RLEK intervening. The peripheral forest dweller's option is also shifted from claiming rights to the exercising rights due to constant efforts from the GKMM side. Thus player`s representability and knowledge enhanced as a process of network formation in a game. Table 7 shows the different reachability and payoff functions in this negotiation phase. Figure 5 represents the possible move of the players in the state transitional graph which is enhanced by the external actor interventions.

In 2006, the Forest Right`s Bill passed which further strengthened the Van Gujjars and the peripheral forest dweller's survival issue. Several meetings were held at the national level where not only the Gujjars and the forest dwellers currently from the RNP took part in these meetings but several forest dwellers from other places also participated. In this way, they were in the process of forming a network at different levels incorporating different actors to whom they were directly or indirectly linked. In this process the Van Gujjars and the peripheral forest dwellers were empowered by the external actors to become complete players in this ongoing game.

Table 7: Reachable lists and payoffs: RNP conflict (Phase II).

State	Van Gujjars	Van Gujjars along with the supportive actor		Peripheral forest dwellers along with the supportive actor		Forest Department	
K	$S_1\ (k)$	$S_1\ (k)$	$P_1\ (k)$	$S_2\ (k)$	$P_2\ (k)$	$S_3\ (k)$	$P_3\ (k)$
1	2	2,3,4,5	4	6	3	11,3,4,5	12
2	1	1,3,4,5	7	7	5	Ø	9
3	1,2,4	1,2,4,5	13	8	4	Ø	5
4	1,2	1,2,3,5	10	9	6	Ø	3
5	1,2	1,2,3,4	16	10	7	Ø	7
6	7	7,8,9,10	5	1	8	12,13,18	1
7	6	6,8,9,10	8	2	11	14	13
8	6,7	6,7,9,10	14	3	13	15	10
9	6,7	6,7,8,10	11	4	12	16	6
10	6,7	6,7,8,9	17	5	14	17	4
11	Ø	Ø	1	12	15	1	8
12	Ø	Ø	2	11	16	6,13,18	2
13	14	14,15,16,17	6	Ø	1	6,12,18	17
14	13	13,15,16,17	9	Ø	2	7	15
15	13	13,14,16,17	15	Ø	9	8	18
16	13,14	13,14,15,17	12	Ø	10	9	16
17	13,14	13,14,15,16	18	Ø	17	10	14
18	Ø	Ø	3	Ø	18	6,12,13	11

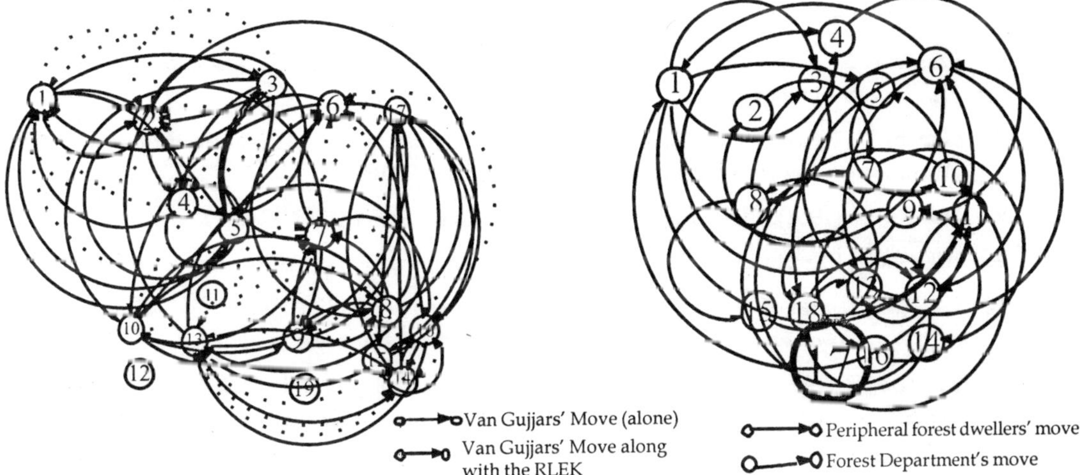

Fig. 5. State transition graph (Phase II).

Conclusion

Here, an attempt has been made to categorize the player's capacity status and to analyze the process of capacity building over a period of time in a game implicitly attained by the respective social networks joined by the actors. Based on the field visits in the Rajaji National Park area, it is found that the State Government did underestimate the possible risks of a forced resettlement policy. The creation of a national park without a sustainable livelihood alternative to the Van Gujjars and peripheral forest dwellers, ultimately leads to a win-lose situation. The different phases of the conflict and negotiation are discussed here, including the initial stage (where some players are null), the initial confrontation phase (a null player becomes an intermediate player), and the complete game phase (player may be intermediate or complete).The evolution of player's strategy in a game in conjunction with social network approach is analyzed by using GMCR model, which may give methodological development of GMCR model. This modelling and analysis shows that the forced displacement and disruption of a forest people`s livelihood cannot be a sustainable solution in a park management policy.

References

1. Ahuja, S.P. (1981): "A Socio-Economic study of the Gujjars," Centre for Planning and Action, New Delhi, *Unpublished Mimeo.*

2. Anon (1973): *Management plan for Rajaji Sanctuary* (1973-74 to 1982-83).

3. Bhardwaj, A. K,Baroda, R, and Misra, B.K. (2002) : "Building partnerships for biodiversity conservation- a collaborative project with Ford Foundation in Rajaji National Park",*Wildlife Institute of India.*

4. Badola, R. (1980): "Attitudes of local people towards conservation and alternatives to forest resources: A case study from the lower Himalayas," *Biodiversity and conservation* 7, 1245-1259.

5. Dogra, B. (2004): Parks and people save Wildlife but Do Not Displace People, published *by Dogra, B., C-27, Rakkshakunj Paschim Vihar New Delhi* 110063.

6. Fraser, N.M., and Hipel, K.W. (1984): *Conflict Analysis Models and Resolutions,* New York, NY: North - Holland.

7. Gooch, P. (1998): *At the Tail of the Buffalo; Van Gujjar Pastoralists between the Forest and the World Arena,* Department of Sociology, Lund University.

8. Hardin, G. (1968): "The Tragedy of the commons", *Science,* 162:1243-1248.

9. IPT (2002): "Preliminary Report on the Rajaji National Park", 2002.

10. Ives, Jack D, and M. Burno (1989): *Path towards a clearing: Radical empiricism and ethnographic enquirey, Bloomington and Indianapolis*: Indiana University press.

11. Krishna, S. (1996): *The Environment Discourse in India; New Directions in Development* in T.V.Sathyamurthy (Ed.) "Class Formation and Political Transformation," Vol.4, Delhi, Oxford University Press.

25

Ferti-irrigation
Potential for Wastewater Reuse in Agriculture

J. S. Chauhan, Bineet Singh, Anuraag Mohan and J. P. N. Rai

Introduction

With the growing crisis for water and the declining freshwater resources, the utilization of wastewater for agriculture has posed a new challenge for environmental management. Wastewater has always been a low cost option for farmers who go in for irrigated agriculture in water scarce regions of the world. Irrigation with treated/untreated industrial effluent is a relatively new practice, since it is seen (a) as a low cost option for wastewater disposal, (b) as a reliable, assured and cheap source of water for irrigated agriculture, especially in water starved arid and semi-arid parts of tropical countries, (c) as a way of keeping surface water bodies less polluted, and also (d) as an important economical resource for agriculture due to its nutrient value as it contains a significant concentrations of organic and inorganic nutrients, for example, nitrogen and phosphate. There is an ample irrigation potential for recycled water, containing nutrients, to be used as a fertilizing source in agriculture. Soil microorganisms have been observed to have increase metabolic activity when sewage effluent is used for irrigational purposes (Meli et al., 2002; Ramirez-Fuentes et al., 2002). However, the safe utilization of wastewater for irrigation requires the use of a proper treatment and several precautionary measures are to put in place, as the use of this water may cause environmental and human health hazards (Buechler and Scott 2006; Minhas and Samra 2004; Bradford et al., 2003). When the treatment is not adequate, an application of wastewater on land might cause various environmental problems, like groundwater contamination (bacteriological and chemical), soil degradation and the contamination of crops grown with polluted water (McCornick et al., 2004 and Scott et al., 2004).

Geographical Background of Experimental Site

Gajaraula is the district of Jyotiba Phule Nagar, Uttar Pradesh, situated at 29°, 4'N latitude, 77°,46'E longitude with an altitude of 237 m above the mean sea level which is 100 km from

Delhi, on NH-24 towards Lucknow. It is an industrial area running a distillery industry with the capacity of 300 KL alcohol/day, for the last 35 years. The effluent after secondary treatment, is put to use for ferti-irrigation on an annual basis with the rate of about 225 m^3 ha^{-1} as pre-sown irrigation. The climate of the region is semi-arid subtropical, with dry hot summers and cool winters, an average annual rainfall of about 800 mm, 75 % of which is received during the monsoon season (July to September). The ground water hydrology of this region is characterized by unconfined and semi confined aquifers including limestone and shale at a depth of about 20-25 m below ground level. The properties of the soil from the experimental site were sandy loam, organic carbon (%) 0.56, total Nitrogen (%) 0.03, pH 7.4, Ca^{+2} 1498 kg/ha, Mg^{+2} 430 kg/ha, Na^{+2} 152 kg/ha and SAR 4.89.

Samples and Analytical Procedure

Sample Description:

The ground water samples were collected from downtown Gajaraula and its surrounding area on a monthly basis in the year of 2005-2006.The depth from where the samples were extracted ranged from 60-70ft. The experimental samples were collected in polyethylene bottles (600 ml capacity) and were stored at 4^0 C until further analysis. Samples were analyzed for the physico-chemical characteristics (pH balance, Ca^{+2}, NO_3> , Cl>, BOD and Zn, Fe) according to the standard method given by the American Public Health Association, Washington, DC (APHA, 1998). All chemical analysis of the samples were performed by the Ecotechnology Laboratory Department of Environmental Science, G.B. Pant University of Agriculture and Technology Pantnagar, Uttarakhand. The Biochemical Oxygen Demand (BOD) was determined using the 5 day's incubation method, recently after the sampleswas collected . Some samples were acidified with concentrated. HNO_3 for the analysis of heavy metals (Fe and Zn) using an Atomic Absorption Spectrophotometer (AAS). Ca was determined by a Flame Photometer (Systronics 128, ASE Ltd) while NO_3^- was determined by a UV-VIS Spectrophotometer (UV-5704 ECIL).The remaining parameters were done by the Cl^- the Idometric method.

Result and Discussion

The average monthly physico-chemical composition of the ground water of the ferti-irrigated area at four sites is shown in Tables 1-4.The analytical result shows that groundwater is slightly alkaline in nature as the pH balance ranges between 7.1-7.4.In all four sites the pH balance was well within the safe limits (6.5-8.5).

The results indicate that the concentration of nitrate varied between 33-60 mg/L. The values during the winter seasons were higher than the limit (45mg/L). This may be because in summer, the microbial degradation is at its maximum and in rainy seasons, a dilution of ground water occurs but during the winter season, both of these activities are low. In spite of these two reasons, the use of fertilizer may also be one important source of nitrate in groundwater.

The value of the BOD ranged between 1.7-3.5 mg/L, higher during the winter season for the same reason as for nitrate. According to the Indian standard, the drinking water should have a BOD of less than 2 mg/L. The concentration of chloride fluctuated between 131-230mg/L which are below permissible limits i.e.250 mg/L. The value of calcium was also under limits and ranged between 41-72mg/L.

Table 1: Physico-chemical properties of the ground water sample taken from the ferti-irrigated agriculture land (SiteA1).

Parameter	Monsoon season	Winter season	Summer season	Permissible limit (IS: 10500)
pH	7.3	7.3	7.2	6.5-8.5
Cl^- (mg/l)	168.4±12	184.1±9	180.1±15	250
NO_3^- (mg/l)	34.2±	40.6±2.1	37.0 ±1	45
BOD (mg/l)	1.8±0.2	2.6±0.1	2.4±0.2	<2
Ca (mg/l)	42.4±3	50.5±6.2	59.75±5	75
Zn (mg/l)	1.86±0.2	1.89±.01	2.0±0.1	5.0
Fe (mg/l)	0.34±0.02	0.40±0.03	0.43±00.1	0.3

Table 2: Physico-chemical properties of the ground water sample taken from ferti-irrigated agriculture land (SiteA2).

Parameter	Monsoon season	Winter season	Summer season	Permissible limit (IS: 10500)
pH	7.2	7.2	7.3	6.5-8.5
Cl^- (mg/l)	167.2±9.1	185.4±11	200.3±6	250
NO_3^- (mg/l)	33.3±3	47.7±3	36.8±5	45
BOD (mg/l)	1.8±0.1	2.4±0.3	2.0±0.2	<2
Ca (mg/l)	46.4±5	58.8±5.3	43.0±2.2	75
Zn (mg/l)	1.81	1.83±0.13	1.90±0.15	5.0
Fe (mg/l)	0.33±0.02	0.43±0.02	0.46±0.02	0.3

Table 3: Physico-chemical properties of the ground water sample taken from ferti-irrigated agriculture land (SiteA3).

Parameter	Monsoon season	Winter season	Summer season	Permissible limit (IS: 10500)
pH	7.2	7.3	7.3	6.5-8.5
Cl^- (mg/l)	131.9±10	196.3±8.4	218.5±16	250
NO_3^- (mg/l)	35.6±3	56.1±5.2	47.39±4.1	45
BOD (mg/l)	2.1±0.2	3.05±0.5	2.5±0.5	<2
Ca (mg/l)	55.30±3.2	69.14±5.2	71.39±7.1	75
Zn (mg/l)	1.86±0.2	1.85±0.1	2.09±0.1	5.0
Fe (mg/l)	0.32±0.01	0.44±0.04	0.44±0.03	0.3

Table 4: Physico-chemical properties of the ground water sample taken from ferti-irrigated agriculture land (SiteA4).

Parameter	Monsoon season	Winter season	Summer season	Permissible limit (IS: 10500)
pH	7.3	7.1	7.4	6.5-8.5
Cl^- (mg/l)	199.8±16	207.8±12.1	229.6±21.3	250
NO_3^- (mg/l)	45.0±2.4	59.2±6.2	48.5±4.2	45
BOD (mg/l)	2.2±0.6	2.9±0.4	3.0±0.2	<2
Ca (mg/l)	57.35±5.2	61.77±4.3	70.19±9.1	75
Zn (mg/l)	1.94±0.1	1.87±0.09	2.09±0.8	5.0
Fe (mg/l)	0.34±0.01	0.41±0.02	0.43±0.02	0.3

Heavy metal Zinc ranged between 1.80-2.1 mg/L, which is below the permissible limit of 5mg/L, but for Iron, the concentration was above the limit 0.3mg/L throughout the year ranging between 0.30-0.47 mg/L. Most of the parameters are above the limits which make the groundwater unsuitable for drinking. The data shows that during the rainy season the value of selected parameters was low as compared with the summer and winter season. This is due to the dilution by rain water. The monthly changes in the parameters are shown in **Fig.1-6**:

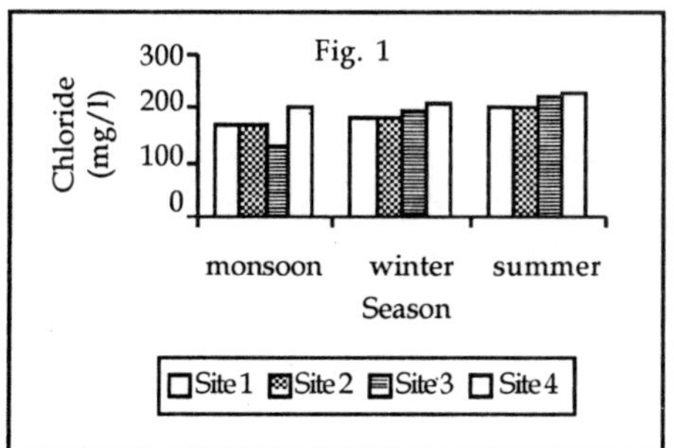
Fig. 1
Chloride (mg/l)
300
200
100
0
monsoon winter summer
Season
Site 1 Site 2 Site 3 Site 4

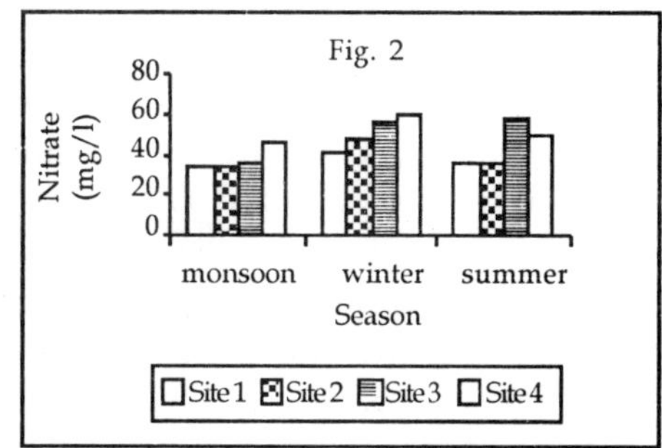
Fig. 2
Nitrate (mg/l)
80
60
40
20
0
monsoon winter summer
Season
Site 1 Site 2 Site 3 Site 4

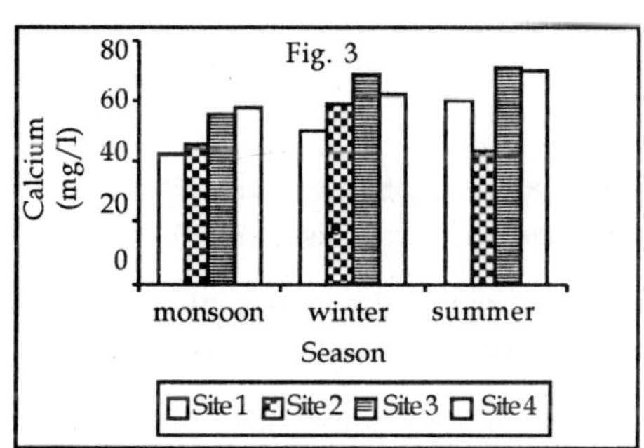
Fig. 3
Calcium (mg/l)
80
60
40
20
0
monsoon winter summer
Season
Site 1 Site 2 Site 3 Site 4

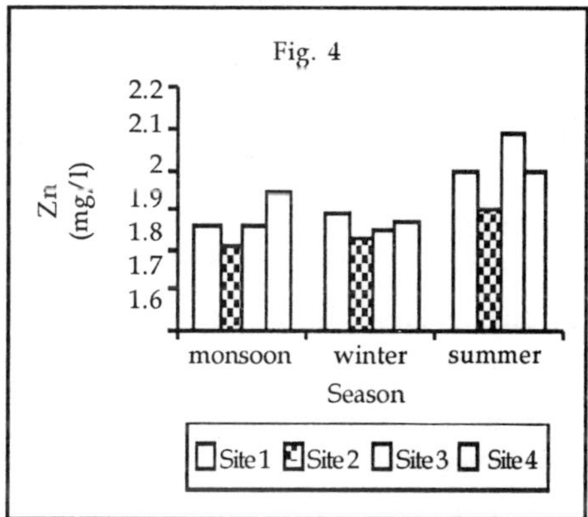
Fig. 4
Zn (mg/l)
2.2
2.1
2
1.9
1.8
1.7
1.6
monsoon winter summer
Season
Site 1 Site 2 Site 3 Site 4

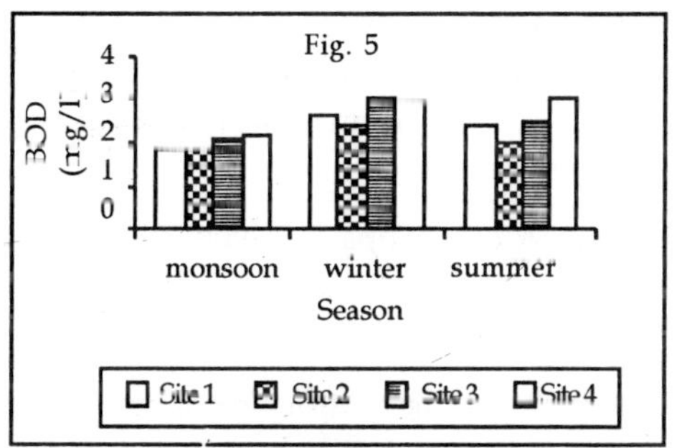
Fig. 5
4
3
2
1
0
monsoon winter summer
Season
Site 1 Site 2 Site 3 Site 4

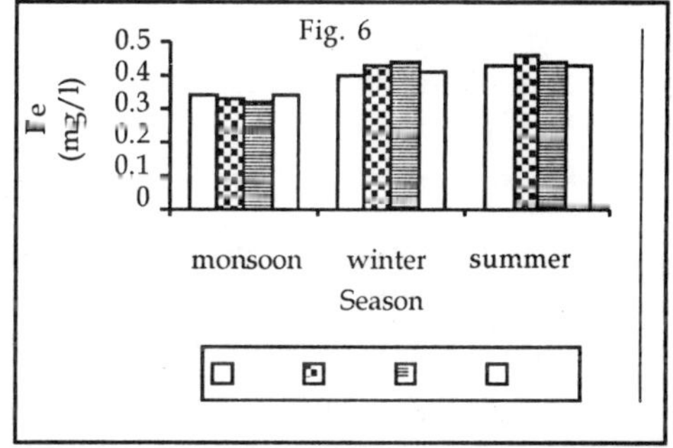
Fig. 6
Fe (mg/l)
0.5
0.4
0.3
0.2
0.1
0
monsoon winter summer
Season

Fig. 1 - 6

The selected parameters in this study show fluctuation with the seasons this reminds us to take precautions for a better result. Ferti-irrigation is an important approach for water reuse but properly treated effluent should be used for this purpose to protect the soil and ground water quality. Chonker et al .(2000) observed that the use of Post-Methanation Distillery Effluent (PMDE) should be discontinued intermittently for one to two crop seasons in order to avoid the deteriorating effects on the soil and groundwater quality. Another approach to control the groundwater pollution, is the dilution of PMDE so as to bring down its BOD to 1000mg/L before its application in the standing crops of rice and wheat for boosting up their productivity and improving the soil quality (Pathak et al., 1999).

Conclusion

The study indicated that ferti-irrigation is a relevant approach but it is important to treat the effluent in such a way that it could not pose a threat to living beings in the present or in the future. All the parameters should be kept within permissible limits so that the groundwater quality and soil properties can be maintained.

References

1. Bradford A, Brook R and Hunshal C S, (2003). "Wastewater Irrigation in Hubli-Dharwad, India: Implications for Health and Livelihoods", Environment and Urbanisation, **15(2)**, 157-70.

2. Buechler S and Scott C, (2006). Wastewater as a controversial contaminated yet coveted resource in South Asia. Occasional paper 36, Human Development Report Office, UNDP.

3. Chonkar PK, Datta SP, Joshi HC and Pathak H, (2000). Impact of industrial effluent on soil, health and agriculture-Indian experience: Part-1. Distillery and paper mill effluent. J. Sci. indst. Res. **59** 350-361.

4. CPCB (2001). "Pollution Control Acts, Rules, and Notifications issued There under"', Fourth Edition, New Delhi: Central Pollution Control Board, Ministry of Environment and Forests, Government of India, 358-359.

5. McCornick P G, Hijazi A and Sheikh B. (2004). "From Wastewater Reuse to Water Reclamation: Progression of Water Reuse Standards in Jordan", in Scott CA, Faruqui N I and Raschid-Sally L, (eds.), "Wastewater Use in Irrigated Agriculture: Confronting the Livelihood and Environmental Realities", Wallingford, UK; CAB International.

6. Meli S, Maurizio M, Belligno A, Bufo SA, Mazzatura A and Scopa A, (2002). Influence of irrigation with lagooned urban wastewater on chemical and microbial soil parameters in a citrus orchard under Mediterranean condition. *Sci. Total Environ.* **285**, 69–77.

7. Minhas PS, and Samra JS, (2004). "Wastewater Use in Peri-Urban Agriculture: Impacts and Opportunities", Central Soil Salinity Research Institute, Karnal, India.

8. Pathak H, Joshi HC, Chaudhary A, Chaudhary R, Kalara N and Dwivedi M K, (1999). Soil amendment with distillery effluents for wheat and rice cultivation, Water, Air and Soil pollut. **113**, 133-140.

26

Double Jeopardy

A Corollary of Negligent Action by Man

TANVI ARORA AND NIDHI KAUSHAL

Introduction

The purpose of industrial development of any region is to provide opportunities of better living and employment for the people. While industrial development almost inevitably creates more employment in the region, the possibilities of adverse effects on the environment also increase if these adverse effects are not properly contained or reduced to a minimum. Thus there occurs a situation in which the material goods increase but the quality of life deteriorates. In the past, environmental aspects of industrial developments were not taken into account seriously, as they were believed to be inevitable and almost necessary for the economic development but this development had another side too, the darker one. With this industrial development and progress came the devastating problem of pollution. This is one of the greatest global malices which is most widespread and it needs an immediate action as a cumulative effort by the world community. A pollutant is any material substance that poses any threat, directly or indirectly, to human welfare and which results from a direct or an indirect effect of human actions. This is definitely a definition with a human bias. It ignores the perspective of other species. A pollutant so defined is dangerous and thus a pollutant, not necessarily bad because of any inherent qualities and not because it is at the wrong place, at the wrong time, or in the wrong quantities. Here "wrong" is an evaluative content. No object is pollutant because it exists. Pollutants may be gases, and thus without fixed shape or volumes, or fluids, without fixed shapes, or solids.

We can simply say, that the presence of any substance in our environment, be it land, soil, air or water, is not in itself a problem but what matters is the quantity that is present there. Examples at this could be like certain gases which are generally present in the atmosphere like carbon dioxide and carbon mono oxide which are very essential for human subsistence but do prove to be fatal when their quantity increases from their natural percentage and cause problems like greenhouse effect etc.

An international Environmental movement, for all purpose, had its beginning in 1972, the year of the Stockholm Conference. After the Stockholm Conference of 1972, even the erstwhile underdeveloped countries have realised that the environmental degradation can be disproportionately more than economical development unless suitable safeguards are not provided from the beginning. It has been felt also that the effects of pollution in all of its aspects may not remain limited to the boundaries of developed and developing nations. The hazards of Greenhouse effects and the depletion/disruption of the ozone layer of the world atmosphere have become more real than just postulations. In India, our environmental thinking took its clue from the developed countries and perceived the preservation of the threatened species - both flora and fauna. Later, two areas relating to the prevention of any further degradation and depletion of basic natural resources and life support systems of land, water and vegetation, were identified. The need to preserve the country's production base and to combat industrial pollution and insanitation in the interest of public health has been felt. Institutional arrangements such as the National Committee for Environmental Planning and Coordination were set up in 1972 which was followed a little later by the creation of the Central Pollution Control Board. Environmental degradation affects developing countries more fundamentally than it does the developed world. It is universally recognised, in developing countries, that while economical development is an essential process to erase poverty and hunger, at the same time, it is equally important to protect the environment from pollution at regional as well as at national and global levels. As such, effective measures are called for at all levels of production, to combat pollution and to save the environment from degradation.

In India, our efforts to provide to a vast and growing population, with food, and comforts, could be sustained in the long run, only if we protect and preserve our environment from further degradation. New areas have been brought under industrialisation after the Independence (of the country) as per the policy of the National Govt. for balanced regional development. With the establishment of a few large mineral based industries like steel, power, cement, aluminium and coal complexes during the past three decades, the industrialisation process has gained momentum. Large numbers of industrial units both in the medium, small scale and ancillary sectors has been set up at different locations.

The major occupation of the people in our state is still agriculture. The region is endowed with rich mineral resources such as coal, bauxite, dolomite, iron ore etc., and forest wealth. This region has been more or less untouched by modern industry till recently. Its industrial development can be traced from the establishment of a public sector steel plant and at various places the setting up of coal/aluminium projects and thermal power projects, all in the public sector. These industries along with the pharmaceutical industries have created a havoc in the environment. India has the following merits attributed to its name:

- The Indian fertilizer industry is the fourth largest in the World.
- It is the largest manufacturer of pesticides in Asia, second only to Japan
- The Indian Pharmaceutical Industry is the largest in the developing World.

Menace of Chemicals in the Industrialized Era

The chemical industries have also led to the degradation of the environment. Combustion of coal and other solid fuels can produce smoke (containing polycyclic aromatic hydrocarbons - PAH) and sulphur dioxide besides other agents such as those also produced by: Combustion of liquid petroleum products which can generate carbon monoxide, oxides of nitrogen and other agents. Industry and incineration can generate a wide range of products of combustion such as oxides of sulphur and nitrogen, polycyclic aromatic hydrocarbons, dioxins etc. Combustion of any fossil fuel generates varying amounts of particulate matter. It also adds to the environmental burden of carbon dioxide - an important "greenhouse" gas but in these low concentrations it does not affect human health directly. The combustion of fuel can generate also hazardous substances in other ways, besides by chemical oxidation, such as by liberating benzene (from the "cracking" of petrol) or lead (from leaded petrol). Some of the primary pollutants such as nitrogen dioxide can, under the influence of UV light generate secondary pollutants notably ozone (an allotrope of oxygen). Find out more about air quality in relation to these substances.

Undoubtedly thousands of deaths have resulted from acute pollution episodes (e.g. the smogs in large cities in the early 1950s). Nowadays some people e.g. asthmatics can be adversely affected by excursions in levels of urban air pollution (notably ozone) in some major cities. What is still unclear is the extent to which urban airborne pollution in the majority of cities complying with current air quality guidelines, contributes to ill health, i.e. whether the air quality guidelines are stringent enough, to protect all the population.

Health effects of concern are asthma, bronchitis and similar lung diseases, and there is good evidence relating to an increased risk of symptoms of these diseases with an increasing concentration of sulphur dioxide, ozone and other pollutants. Moreover, there is increasing evidence to suggest that pollution from particulate matter at levels hitherto considered "safe" is associated with an increased risk of morbidity and mortality from cardiopulmonary diseases especially in people with other risk factors (such as old age, or heart and lung disease). These concerns are the subject of a great deal of research throughout the world. Although high occupational exposures to exhaust fumes especially from diesel, and to benzene does increase the risk of some cancers, reliable direct evidence of an increase of a cancer risk to the population at large from the lower levels to which they are exposed, is lacking.

Incineration can also generate hazardous substances if substances not best suited for disposal by incineration are "disposed" of in this way or if the incineration is carried out at too low a temperature. Products of combustion and other harmful airborne pollutants can arise also within the home. Thus nitrogen dioxide generated by gas fires or gas cookers can contribute to an increased respiratory morbidity of those living in the houses. Certain modern building materials may liberate gases or vapours such as formaldehyde at low concentration but which might provoke mild respiratory and other symptoms in some occupants. Modern building standards for asbestos in buildings are such that the resulting airborne fibre concentrations are so small as not to present any risk at all of asbestosis. However some estimates suggest that perhaps one extra death per year might result in the UK from asbestos related cancer as a result of non-occupational exposure in buildings. The image shows an asbestos body i.e. an asbestos fibre which has been coated by ferruginous protein during its residence within the human lung.

Special local environmental exposures can arise for example in communities exposed to drifting pesticide sprays containing say, organophosphates. Some natural phenomena such as volcanic eruptions can present serious risks to health. Fortunately they are rare but can be catastrophically dangerous both for human life as well as the flora and fauna in the vicinity.

Following are a few chemicals to whom we are exposed, unaware of the harm they cause with the passage of time. The exposure may be occupational or non occupational and they are in time fatal or may cause serious mal-functioning in the body:

Water can be an important source of chemical hazards. It can leach lead from pipes especially if the water is soft. There is good epidemiological evidence that this can have a relatively small but measurably harmful effect especially on the neurological function even at levels hitherto considered "acceptable". Other adverse effects can arise from chemicals added to the water.

Chlorinated water has probably saved millions of lives. Some concern has been raised about possible increased cancer risks in association with chlorinated water but there is as yet no proof that a causal association between the two exists. Fluoride added to water reduces the risks of caries but can also have unwanted effects such as mottling and yellowing of the teeth and fluorosis is a great problem in a state like Rajasthan.

Nitrate in water usually arising from fertiliser leaching. It can increase the risk of methaemoglobinaemia (blue babies) in bottle fed infants but this is extremely rare. Although pesticides can and do leach into water, there is no evidence that the current standards for water quality are inadequate in this respect, but most standards are based on evidence other than human epidemiology which in this context is extremely difficult to conduct. Beyond the point of supply further problems in drinking water quality may result. Thus for example water tanks containing lead may increase the burden of this metal in the water.

Deposition of solid hazardous waste can result in harmful substances leaching into water supplies, becoming airborne or being swallowed or otherwise absorbed directly (for example because of children playing on the sites). If the sites are well contained to prevent leaching into water supplies and segregated from human activity then the risk to human health is usually immeasurably small. However where the position of disposal sites and their contents are unknown and houses are proposed to be built on them or they are to be developed in other ways, extensive prior investigation may be needed in an attempt to estimate health risks.

Due to many chemicals which are used in one way or another for any purpose, the environment is impaired and can harm the beings living in that environment. They cause numerous diseases which ultimately wreck the environment and the life of the humans. Some of the diseases which are caused by the chemicals are:

Inorganic Mercury (metallic mercury and inorganic mercury compounds) enters the air from mining ore deposits, burning coal and waste, and from manufacturing plants.

It enters the water or soil from natural deposits, disposal of waste and volcanic activity. Methyl mercury may be formed in water and soil by small organisms called bacteria. Methyl mercury builds up in the tissues of fish. Larger and older fish tend to have the highest levels of mercury. Exposure to mercury could damage the brain, kidney and developing foetus. Effects on brain functioning may result in irritability, shyness, tremors, change in vision or hearing and memory problems.

Exposure to **Chromium** occurs from ingesting contaminated food or drinking water or breathing contaminated workplace air. In air, chromium compounds are present mostly as fine dust particles which eventually settle over land and water. Chromium can attach strongly to soil and only a small amount can dissolve in water and move more deeply into the soil to underground water.

Exposure to **Cadmium** happens mostly in the workplace where cadmium products are made. The general population is exposed from breathing cigarette smoke or eating cadmium contaminated foods. Cadmium damages the lungs, can cause kidney disease and may irritate the digestive tract.

Exposure to higher levels of **Arsenic** than average levels, occur mostly in the workplace or near hazardous waste sites, or in areas with high natural levels of arsenic content. At high levels, inorganic Arsenic can cause death. Exposure to lower levels for a long time can cause a discoloration of the skin and the appearance of small corns or warts.

Lead is a heavy, low melting, bluish-gray metal that occurs naturally in the Earth's crust. However, it is rarely found naturally as a metal. It is usually found combined with two or more other elements to form lead compounds. The main target for lead toxicity is the nervous system, both in adults and children. Long-term exposure of adults to lead at work has resulted in a decreased performance in functions of the nervous system. Lead exposure may also cause weakness in fingers, wrists, or ankles. Lead exposure also causes small increases in blood pressure, particularly in middle-aged and older people. Lead exposure may also cause anaemia.

The Remuneration for Industrial Advancement

Though the exposure to these chemicals for a reasonable time span causes serious diseases, a sudden and outsized exposure to certain chemicals may prove immediately to be fatal and leave the complete human race of that area in misery for generations to come. Large scale industrial releases with a serious acute effect was in the Bhopal gas leak case (India). Various smaller scale events occur such as leaks from road tankers, or fires in warehouses and factories or refineries and these may also be lethal for many lives and also impair the environment. There have been many such industrial accidents till now in India but the gravest amongst them all was the Bhopal gas tragedy in which even after decades of court cases and arguments and investigations, though compensation has been paid to many of the victims, it is not enough and there is still a strong sense of injustice that lingers in the air. Though a compensation of nearly 470 million USD has been called for, it is undoubtedly a small amount based on the long term health consequences of exposure and the number of people affected. More than twenty years of passiveness has taken its toll. Many are calling it the world's biggest humanitarian disaster. Indirectly it has lead to massive unemployment, destitution and widespread psychological problems in the people. Even till now it is a bio-hazardous zone polluting the environment.

The Union Carbide has issued the facts of the disaster on their official website. They have given an account right from the very first day they established themselves in India till the date including the compensation they have paid and the charity work they have done in the following chronological order:

Union Carbide India Limited (UCIL) was established in **1984**, when Union Carbide Corporation (UCC) became one of the first U.S. companies to invest in India. UCIL shares were publicly traded on the Calcutta Stock Exchange. UCIL was a diversified manufacturing company, employing approximately 9,000 people and operating 14 plants in five divisions.

The Bhopal plant was built in the late **1970's** and was owned and operated by UCIL, an Indian Company in which Union Carbide held just over half of the stock. Indian financial institutions and thousands of private investors in India owned the remainder of the stock. The plant produced pesticides for use in India to help the country's agricultural sector increase its productivity and contribute more significantly to meeting the food needs of one of the world's most heavily populated regions.

In 1984

On **Dec 3** the ill-fated day shortly after midnight in the early hours of December 3, 1984, on what was a bracing winter morning, mixed with the winter breeze, was a highly toxic grey cloud that was emerging from the Union Carbide 'C' factory. This poisonous substance, stored in tank number 610 of the factory was later found to be Methyl Isocynate (MIC), which had got contaminated with water. According to experts, MIC is considered to be an extremely reactive chemical and is used to produce insecticides. When water got mixed with this MIC, an exothermal chemical reaction started which resulted in a lot of heat being produced. As the pressure in the tank built up beyond safe levels, the safety valve burst open violently and the gas leaked. As around forty tons of this gas spread through the city, there was no alarm of any kind to warn the inhabitants of this populous town. Since the gas leaked out from a 30 meter chimney, it was not high enough for the people to escape the effects. Later studies have shown that the effect of this toxic gas was especially harsh because of the high moisture content in the gas, which when exposed, started evaporating and being a heavy gas, the gas started moving downwards. The movement of the wind was also such that the gas spread through the city much faster than it otherwise would have.

Within hours, the streets of Bhopal were littered with human corpses and the carcasses of buffaloes, cows, dogs and birds. An estimated 3,800 people died immediately, mostly in the poor slum colony adjacent to the Union Carbide plant. Local hospitals were soon inundated with patients, a crisis further complicated by a lack of knowledge of exactly what gas was involved, what its effects were and what the possible cure could be. Since the incident took place on a cold night when most of the people where indoors, they woke up with a burning sensation in their eyes. They rushed outdoors only to breathe greater concentrations of the gas and in panic as they ran, breathing even greater volumes of the gas, ultimately choking them to death. Eventually the death toll rose to more than 20,000 people with more than 5,00,000 people being affected directly and indirectly and many more thousands of families were permanently affected for generations.

On **Dec 4** as soon as the Word of the disaster was received at Union Carbide headquarters in Connecticut, the Chairman and CEO Warren Anderson, together with a technical team, departed to India to assist the government in dealing with the incident. Upon arrival, Anderson was placed under house arrest and urged by the Indian government to leave the country within 24 hours. Union Carbide organized a team of international medical experts, as well as supplies and equipment, to work with the local Bhopal medical community. The UCC technical team began assessing the cause of the gas leak.

On **Dec 14** Warren Anderson testifies before Congress. He stresses UCC commitment to safety and promises to take action to ensure that a similar incident "cannot happen again."

In 1985

In **February** Union Carbide establishes a fund for victims of the tragedy — the (UCC) Employees' Bhopal Relief Fund — that collects more than $120,000. UCC sends more medical equipment to Bhopal. UCC launches a disaster programme to study the effects of over-exposure to MIC.

The Government of India (GOI) enacts the **Bhopal Gas Leak Disaster Act** that enables the GOI to act as the legal representative of the victims in claims arising from or related to the Bhopal disaster.

The UCC Technical team reports that a large volume of water was introduced into the MIC tank and triggered a reaction that resulted in the gas release. Independently, a committee of experts for the Indian government arrives at the same conclusion. They claim that the gas leak was not an accident but rather was it an intentional act done by someone who had the knowledge about the procedure to handle the storage tank. **April** UCC offers $5 million in relief for victims before the U.S. District Court, bringing the total to date to $7 million. The Government of India rejects the UCC offers of aid for the Bhopal victims. In **June** the UCC funds the participation of Indian medical experts in meetings to obtain information and the latest medical treatment techniques for victims. In **July** Additional Analysis Core samples confirm that water triggered the reaction, which led to the gas release.

In 1986

In January 1986 the Union Carbide offers $10 million to the Indian Government for building a hospital to aid the victims in Bhopal. In **March** Union Carbide proposes a settlement amount of $350 million that will generate a fund for Bhopal victims of between $500-600 million over 20 years. Plaintiffs of U.S. attorneys endorse the amount. In **May** U.S. District Court Judge transfers all Bhopal litigation to India. Decision is appealed.

In 1987

In India the court rules that UCIL is a separate entity, owned, managed and operated exclusively by Indian citizens in India. The Government of India closes and razes the Bhopal

Technical and Vocational Training Centre built by Arizona State University after determining that the Union Carbide Corporation supplied funds for the project. In **August** the UCC offers an additional $4.6 million in humanitarian interim relief for immediate rehabilitation of Bhopal victims.

In 1988

Right from January to December, litigation in India continued arguments and appeals took place before the Indian Courts regarding compensation for the victims. In November, the Supreme Court of India asks the Government of India and UCC to reach a settlement, and tells both sides to "start with a clean slate."

In 1989

The Supreme Court of India directs a final settlement of all Bhopal litigation in the amount of $470 million, to be paid by March 31, 1989. Both the Government of India and Union Carbide accept the court's direction. UCC pays $420 million; UCIL pays the rupee equivalent of $50 million (including $5 million of interim relief previously paid). Within 10 days of the order, UCC and UCIL make full payment of the $470 million to the Government of India. In **May,** the Supreme Court, in a lengthy opinion, explains the rationale for the settlement and emphasizes that the compensation levels provided for in the settlement are substantially higher than those ordinarily payable under Indian law. In **December,** the Supreme Court upholds the validity of the "Bhopal Gas Leak Disaster Act of 1985" that authorized the Government of India to act on behalf of the Bhopal gas leak victims.

In 1990

In the complete year, Hearings are held throughout the year on activist petitions to overturn the settlement agreement. In **November** the State Government of Madhya Pradesh submits to the Supreme Court of India the completed categorization of the claims of all of the victims. The State determines that, in addition to the victims who suffered various levels of disabilities, the incident resulted in 3,828 deaths. In **December,** the Court concludes a review of petitions seeking to overturn the settlement.

1991

In **October** 1991, the Supreme Court of India upholds the civil settlement of $470 million in its entirety and sets aside a portion of settlement that quashed criminal prosecutions that were pending at the time of the settlement. The Court also:

- Requires the Government of India to purchase, out of the settlement fund, a group medical insurance policy to cover 100,000 persons who may later develop symptoms;
- Requires the Government of India to make up any shortfall, however unlikely, in a settlement fund;
- Gives directions concerning the administration of a settlement fund;
- Dismisses all outstanding petitions seeking a review of the settlement; and

- Requests UCC and UCIL to voluntarily fund capital and operating costs of a hospital in Bhopal for eight years, estimated at approximately $17 million, to be built on land donated by the state government.

The UCC and UCIL agree to fund the hospital, as requested.

After that the UCC sold its shares to another company with the permission of the Indian government ant the funds generated were used to build and run the Bhopal hospital. According to the company, they have done enough charitable work for comforting the people of Bhopal who were made victims of one of the world's worst chemical disasters.

Even two decades later, more than a few lakhs of people are still suffering from the debilitating effects of the gas which includes respiratory problems, cancer, congenital birth defects, blindness and many other diseases. Every year since then, scores more are still dying in Bhopal from the various after effects. Some of the symptoms of Methyl Isocynate contamination include cough, dyspnea or disorder of the lungs, chest pain leading to acute lung failure, cardiac arrest and death. It has resulted in many children being born with genetic defects and mutations and mental retardation. It has also had a long term impact on the reproductive cycle of affected women and the quality of their breast milk.

Besides the effects on people, according to environmentalists, the impact it has had on the ecology of that area is also far reaching. There are still hundreds of tonnes of toxic waste alone, which could lead to a continuous poisoning of the soil as well as the ground water. Some areas in and around that area are still so polluted that someone entering that area is likely to lose consciousness in less than ten minutes. The Union Carbide factory closed down their operation in Bhopal following the tragedy, but they did not do a proper clean up of the site which is a bio-hazardous zone even today. This lapse has resulted in, what many environmentalists claim, a slow and sustained pollution of the area within and around the closed factory.

The truth is that the investigations into the tragedy showed that there were many shortcomings at all levels. The Union Carbide factory did not have much information about the safe storage of these highly toxic gases. The medical fraternity did not have the requisite knowledge of how to deal with such a kind of contamination and on this scale. There was a lack of co-ordination between the factory and emergency services. There were not many trained professionals in that factory. Cost cutting had also had its impact on the safety of the plant, its employees and the people living around the plant. The plant was also in a densely populated area of the city which went against most known norms.

The disaster did pave the way for much stricter international standards for environmental safety, preventative strategies to avoid similar accidents and a better state of preparedness to meet future industrial disasters. In India, a number of changes were made in the Indian Factories Act and environmental legislation. There is a much better understanding of the fact that industries need to apply good process safety management systems and have efficient and safe handling and storage capacities of individual reactive chemicals. Following the disaster, environmental awareness and activism in India has increased tremendously. It serves as a warning to developing nations to create the right balance between human, environmental and economical status on the path to industrialization.

Suggestive Conclusion

The dependence of the present day society on chemical technology is of unimaginable proportions. This addiction subsists without challenge till disaster strikes. The following named disasters have brought to the fore the need for effective legal regulation of the handling of hazardous substances. The necessity for the safe management of hazardous substances and the safe disposal of hazardous industrial waste has time and again been put before the humanity in the form of various disasters resulting from the negligence of man himself. Despite various legislations being made and amended, time to time there have been still many industrial chemical hazards in the country since 1985. In Cochin in 1985 Hexacyclo-pentadiene gas leaked which caused injuries to nearly 200 people. In 1988 in a fire in an oil refinery in Bombay, 35 people lost their lives and 16 were seriously injured. In 1989 in Bhatinda because of the leakage of ammonia, nearly 500 people were badly injured. In Nagothane in 1990, Ethane and propane gas leaked in which 32 people died and 22 were injured. In 1997 in Vishakhaptnam a fire in a refinery where LPG gas leaked, took the lives of 60 people and 31 were injured. In 1991 explosion in an explosive factory in Vellore. In 2003, 25 people lost their lives and 3 were badly injured.

The various changes required in the legislation are as follows:

- The implementation of a Process Safety Management System based on PSM standards developed must be made mandatory for all industries covered under the Chemical Accidents (Emergency Planning, Preparedness and Response Rules), 1996. The enforcement of legislation by the Indian authorities must be made effective by training the law enforcers in the latest developments in risk prevention, inspection and managerial system audit techniques.
- The Regional Labour Institutes who impart training for Safety Officers employed in hazardous industries should include Process Safety Management and reactive chemical hazards in their curriculae. Specialised training in Chemical Disaster Management should be made mandatory for all members of the four tier crisis groups formed under the Chemical Accidents (Emergency Planning, Preparedness and Response Rules), 1996. A refresher training programme for the members on the latest crisis management techniques must be implemented.
- Courses like Disaster Management and Crisis Management should be given importance so as to have adequate officers to deal with such situations if any contingency arises. Even the engineers who take up the stream of industrial or chemical engineering should also be taught the basic knowledge of legal requirements of the safety measures in an industry. This should make them aware of legal provisions that are mandatory for running an industry or factory.
- More emphasis should be given to the safety of workers working in the industry or the factory and adequate relief should be made for the compensation to the workers who are victims of a chemical hazard or sufferers of a disease due to exposure to such a chemical.
- Policies for handling media communication during Crisis Management should be developed for the four crisis groups formed under the Chemical Accidents (Emergency

Planning, Preparedness and Response Rules), 1996. Training on "communicating during emergencies" should be made mandatory to the personnel of the crisis committees.

The safety regulations, governing employment of contractors in hazardous chemical plants need to be strengthened. The Government operated Technical Training Institutes should include Process Safety Training for those personnel who will be employed in Chemical plants.

Even more stricter rules should be made for the industries dealing with hazardous chemicals. Not only new laws are necessary but also the effective implementation of already existing law is lacking. There is a grave need of proper inspection of the safety measures in the already existing industries so as to avoid any other future disasters from taking place in our country.

There is a need to bring in a few reforms in the industries also. The industrialists should also realize their social responsibility in order to avoid any future accidents. For this they should:

- Have a system to update and maintain Process Safety Information needs to be implemented.
- Contractor safety management systems must address the enforcement and accountability of contractors in the safety of their workers. The safety training requirements for contractors working in hazardous areas of the plants must be defined and the contractor/employer should be held accountable for the safety performance of his employees.
- The investigation of incidents should account for human factors also. Sharing of the lessons learnt from past chemical plant incidents should be carried out through an affable "industry- government initiative".
- Industry - Institution interaction should be strengthened and the employees should be warned of consequences of their mistakes. This could be done by providing proper training to all the employees on how they should act in a distasteful contingent situation.

There is a grave need to bring some essential changes in the legislation as well as a few efforts are to be made on part of the industrialist for their social and moral responsibility. It is high time now, both for legislators and the industrialists, to work in consonance to combat this peril of hazardous substances and find out some safer alternatives.

References

1. Bell Stuart and Mcgillivray Donald; "*Environmental Law*"; Oxford University Press; 2006.
2. Divan Shyam, " *Envrironmental Law And Policy In India*", Oxford University Press, 2002.
3. Leelakrihnan P, "*Environmental Law in India*", Lexis Nexis Butterworths, 2005.
4. Malik Sumeet; "*Environmental Law*"; Eastern Book Company; Lucknow; 2008.
5. Speth Gustave James; "*Global Environmental Challenges-Transaction to a Sustainable World*"; Orient Longman Pvt. Ltd.; New Delhi; 2005.

6. Tiwari R.K,"*Global Environmental Policies*", ABD Publishers, Jaipur, India, 2007.
7. Verma Bihari Sawalia; "*Environmental Law Pollution and Management*"; University Book House P. Ltd.; Jaipur; 2007.
8. Wolf and Standley, "*Environmental Law*" Cavendish Publishing Ltd, 2003.
9. www.unioncarbide.com/Bhoal.
10. www.irastimes.org/Bhopal_gas_tragedy_htm.
11. www.rse.org/publishing/currentawareness.
12. www.oakridge.doe.gov/emergency/publicinformation.

27

Wetland Ecology
An Overview of the Kanjli Wetland

DR MANJIT SANDHU

Introduction

Wetlands are those landscapes, which remain wet for at least a part of the season essential to supporting a peculiar type of vegetation. The most characteristic features of these places is the presence of hydric soils which having been saturated with water and develop anaerobic growing conditions in the upper part. The development of such conditions is directly related to various environmental factors like precipitation, stratigraphy, topography, soil permeability, plant cover, frequency and duration of inundation or soil saturation etc. Wetlands also represent the transitional position between the deep aquatic places and the dry/terrestrial areas and thereby support a varied spectrum of vegetation and fauna. Wetlands have developed from geological, hydrological, meteorological and biological processes and interactions over a long period of time. The process which formed some natural wetlands stopped long ago, so some scientists regard them as fossil landscapes. These ecosystems vary according to their origin, geographical location, water regime, chemistry, dominant plants and soil or sediment characteristics.The Kanjli Wetland is an extremely important ecosystem in the region. It supports a diverse kind of food chain and food webs, helps in water recharging and discharging, improves water quality, reduces flooding, etc.

Study Area

The Kanjli Wetland is located about 4 km from the city of Kapurthala on the west of the Kali Bein, an important tributary of the river Beas. Geographically it is situated at 31°25' north latitude and 75°22' east longitude at an elevation of 210 metres above the mean sea level. Kanjli Lake came into formation with the construction of a small barrage during 1870. The lake is thus a fresh water permanent feature. The soils are mainly alluvial in nature, sand, clay and loam.The maximum depth of water varies from 10 feet to 25 feet depending upon the season and the water inflow.

The area falls in the semi-arid zone. The average annual rainfall in the region is around 620 mm extending from July to mid October. The temperature ranges from an average of 6 °C, occasionally dropping below the freezing point of water in winter to a maximum of 45 °C in summer (Verma *et al.*, 1994). The catchment area is mainly under agriculture. Kali Bein ultimately joins the Harike Wetland downstream after covering a distance of about 20 kms.

Objectives

The present study paper is structured to elucidate with the following objectives:

1. To provide information on the ecology of the lake and its catchment area, the biology of its flora and fauna, the impact of its environmental factors on the lake system and the socio-economic implications of the use of the lake resources.
2. To generate a database in terms of landuse/ landcover, extent of water spread and its seasonal variations and turbidity levels of lake water using multidate data.
3. To identify the hydrological and ecological values of the Kanjli Wetlands.
4. To suggest adequate measures for the conservation and management of the Kanjli Wetlands.

Data Base and Methodology

The present study is based on the visual interpretation of the IRS-IA LISS-II multidate data (pre monsoon-March 1993 and post monsoon-October 1992) in the form of false colour composites (FCC) generated from bands 2, 3 and 4 following the land use classification system proposed by the Space Application Centre Ahmedabad. Permanent features like major settlements, roads and canals have been traced from survey maps of India. Various websites regarding literature and data have also been consulted.

Results and discussion

According to the Punjab remote sensing centre, Ludhiana, an area of 5150 hectares is under the Kanjli Wetlands, out of which 209 hectares is covered by swamp or marsh and 779 is seasonally waterlogged. The lakes and ponds cover 9.5 hectares while 29 hectares are covered by the Oxbow Lakes and cut off meanders. The area under wasteland is 55.9 hectares while 123 hectares is covered with forests. Crop land (double crop) constitutes 3082 hectares in addition to seasonally waterlogged area of 779 hectares which is also used for paddy cultivation. Plantation and build up land covers 66 hectares and 281 respectively.The Sandy area is 436 hectares while land with or without shrubs is 61 hectares. The soils are mainly alluvial in nature consisting of sand, clay and loam. The maximum depth of water varies from 10 to 25 feet, depending upon the season and the water inflow.

Turbidity

In this study the qualitative turbidity of the Kanji Lake has been recorded based on the hue as manifested of false colour composite for pre and post monsoon seasons of 1992 and 1993 The turbidity classification is based on a system proposed by SAC, Ahmedabad Table 2.

Table 1: Area under various landuse categories of Kanjli wetland ecosystem.

Map Symbol	Landuse category	Area in(Hectares)
1.1	Built up land	280.8
2.1	Crop land (double)	3082.5
2.2.	Fallow land	2.1
2.3	Plantation	66.3
3.1	Forest	122.4
4.1	Salt affected	71.9
4.3	Land with or Without scrub	61.0
4.4	Sandy area	436.0
5.1.1	Lakes/ponds	9.5
5.1.2	Ox bow lakes/cut off meanders	29.0
5.1.3	Water logged seasonal	779.0
5.1.5	swamp/ Marsh	209.5
	Total	5150.0

Source: Punjab Remote Sensing Centre, Ludhiana

Table 2: Classification of water bodies based on turbidity

Turbidity level	Map symbol	Hue on FCC
Low	L	Dark blue
Moderate	M	Medium blue
High	H	Light blue/Whitish blue

Source: Punjab Remote Sensing Centre, Ludhiana

The study revealed that the Kanjli Lake qualifies for the low turbidity class during pre monsoon and the moderate turbidity class during the post monsoon season, indicating the regimentation of the lake during post monsoon season. (Verma *et al.*, 1994)

Monitoring of Water Spread

The water spread turbidity for the pre and post monsoon season has also been monitored. The study revealed that the post monsoon extent of Kanjli Lake was 3.79 hectares whereas the pre monsoon spread was 3.50 hectares. The water spread in the post monsoon season is more because it also receives rain water from the Black Bein and many seasonal rivulets coming down from the Shiwalik Hills. During the monsoon, the flow of the Black Bein is considerable and many a time it overflows its banks. The area abounds in a number of abandoned channels which get activated mostly during the monsoon (Verma *et al.*, 1994). Most of the torrents end up in shallow depressions. Disposition of these depressions along the river Beas are indicative of the old abandoned beds of the Beas. The extensive growth of water hyacinth has been observed during both the seasons which is posing a big problem to the ecological status of the Kanjli Lake.

Ecological values

Ecologically,the Kanjli Wetland is very important. It supports such a diversity of life forms. Various species of mammals, fishes, birds, other vertebrate fauna, microfauna and large species populations of plants are important features of this wetland. It supports deep water, shallow water, mesic as well as xeric features. The food chain is basically of the grazing type. The abiotic components of this ecosystem are sunlight, pH balance inorganic salts, nutrients and dissolved gases. The organic matter accumulates at the bottom and mainly comes from the death and decay of plants and animals. Producers are autotrophic plants and some photosynthetic bacteria. These are mainly the rooted submerged, floating and emergent hydrophytes like Typha sp., Eleocharis sp., Sagittaria sp., Nymphaea sp., Potamogeton sp., Vallisnaria sp., Eichhornia sp., Lemna sp.etc. and minute, floating or suspended lower plants like filamentous algae, diatoms, chlorococcales and flagellates. The primary consumers at Kanjli are herbivores. These include mollusks, crustaceans, rotifers, some insects and fish. Detrivores feed upon plant remains and organic matter. Besides, some mammals such as buffaloes, cows, etc. also visit the lake and feed on marginal rooted macrophytes. Some birds also feed on some hydrophytes. The secondary consumers are carnivores, feeding on insects, mollusks, rotifers and crustaceans. Some insects and carnivorous fishes feed on crustaceans, rotifers and mollusks. The tertiary consumers are some snakes and birds which feed on small fishes and insects. The upper most consumer level is occupied by man and fish eating and scavenger birds. The organic matter which accumulates at the bottom of the lake and forested wetland area is decomposed by a variety of heterotrophic mircrobes-bacteria and fungi.

Hydrological values

The major uses of wetlands are, that these are traditional sources of water supplies for drinking and irrigation purposes. Still, river water is the major source in the state and adjoining areas and helps in ground water recharging. Unabated reclamation and drainage of our natural wetlands is showing an impact on the depleting ground water sources in the state, thereby compelling the state Govt. to think of even adopting highly cost intensive artificial recharging means. Kali Bein is a permanent rivulet. The Bein in general and Kanjli Lake in particular act like an important water sponge, discharging and recharging the water. Excess water during rainy seasons from the adjoining agricultural crops gets discharged into the Kali Bein. Its importance as a discharging drain becomes more significant when it helps by taking away excessive rainwater from sensitive crops like wheat, potato, etc. It also serves as an important source for agriculture. At the same time, it also helps in flood management. The ground water is fast receding in many districts of the Punjab. Year after year the dugwells as well as the tubewells are deepened to take out water for irrigation. But the observations around the Kanjli Wetland show that the ground water table is stable as compared with the rest of the state. The Bein is thus playing a vital role in enriching the ground water thereby helping the nearby population, which is dependent on ground water for irrigation, industries and drinking supplies, for the easy abstraction of water. Pressure on underground water is also somewhat relieved as a number of farmers do direct abstraction of water from the Kali Bein, as it is very economical. A new tubewell has been installed in the middle. A centrifugal pump at the bottom had remained under 10-15' of deep water earlier and with the continuously reducing water table, this well became dry. Now it is further deepened to make the pump work properly.

Conservation and Management

The values of the wetlands in the landscape and their benefits for humankind are increasingly recognized yet economical development continues to destroy or degrade wetland systems. It is accepted that wetlands are functioning in a larger ecological entity. Their management and conservation programmes must, therefore, address the entire systemic processes functioning in the landscape as a whole to ensure maintaining the sustainability. Various factors have to be taken into account for both short and long term measures to prevent any further loss and improve their ecological character. A truly holistic approach needs to be implemented after optimising all the system qualities. Efforts to conserve Kanjli Wetland, which is one of national wetlands, have been continuing for the last few years. It is, however, observed that intensive efforts need to be made to restore the ecological character of this wetland. PSCST, therefore, proposes to continue conservation measures for the Kanjli Wetland in coordination with various executing departments in the State. Details of all the activities are given below:

Afforestation

Tree cover in wetland area provides suitable microhabitats for diversity of fauna. Besides, the spawning of fish takes place preferably under the shade of trees in aquatic ecosystem. However, the status of the tree cover area in the wetlands is dwindling. Thus efforts are needed to balance the ecosystem by providing more greenery by way of planting diverse kinds of native trees like species of Acacia, Terminalia, Syzygium, Salix, Pongamia, Morus, Azadirachta, Casuarina, Delonix, etc. To extend the area under green cover around the Kanjli Wetland, the Dept. of Forest and Wildlife, Punjab plans to take up plantation in another 10 hectare area during the next five years at a cost of Rs. 7.00 lac.

Wildlife Conservation

Wetlands are the important repositories of the diversity of wild genetic resources and are extremely important from a long-term ecological point of view but as the wetlands are shrinking the biological resources are also under stress. The wildlife at the Kanjli Wetland is also suffering loss due to one reason or the other. To conserve wildlife resources, the Wildlife Dept. of Punjab proposes to take up conservation measures like the protection of an area by repairing damaged fenc already erected around the wetland and by erecting new barriers. Besides, the Dept. plans to put up some wooden nests to facilitate the multiplication of birds. To avoid any disturbance to the wildlife, it is also planned to put up wooden hideouts for the explorers of nature wetlands. These activities shall require an assistance to the tune of Rs. 6.35 lac. Recent experiments in some western countries show that the landing of some important birds in wetlands also depends upon the clues and signatures supporting the occurrence of some related birds in that habitat. Since birds are an important ecological component of any ecosystem the results of such experiments may help in artificially encouraging the landing of birds. Punjab State Council for Science & Technology, therefore, proposes to install a suitable number of plastic birds initially at Ropar and Kanjli Wetland marshes. For this purpose Rs. 1,00,000/- will be required.

Control and Management of Water Hyacinth

The Kanjli Wetland is infested with the world's worst weed i.e. the water hyacinth. So far manual operations have been adopted to bring this weed under control. However, the lake gets reinfested with this weed within no time. To safeguard the ecological character of this ecosystem, it is planned to take up integrated measures of both physical removal by using a conveyor belt mechanical system and control through biological means. The aim of this activity is to establish a sustainable long term capacity for maintaining control of the water hyacinth. The control programme would rely on a manual method for a rapid short term control in restricted areas, and biological agents for a long term control. The biological control programme would initially rely on the release of two weevil species that have been found effective world wide and have already been imported, reared and released into the Harike Ecosystem. These species of weevils are Neochetina bruchi and N. eichorniae which are complimentary in their action. The possibility would also be explored for supplementing the weevils later by releases of moth Sameodes albiguittalis if found appropriate. At present no funding estimates are indicated under this project separately as the Comprehensive Proposal for the control of water hyacinth from catchment drains of Harike Wetland have already been included under the Harike Wetland project. However, to take up the physical removal of weed from the Kanjli ecosystem area, an amount of Rs. 9.50 lacs shall be required for five years.

Water Quality Monitoring

The Punjab Pollution Control Board has studied the water and sludge quality of the Kanjli Wetland area and has reported that the water of this lake generally conforms to Class 'B'. But the quality degrades even to Class 'D'. One of the important recommendations is to keep vigil on the level of pollution for which the regular monitoring of the lake water must be continued. This shall help to elucidate the nature and dynamics of the lake ecosystem on a long term basis. PPCB proposes to continue the water quality monitoring programme during the next five years for which an estimated amount of Rs. 16.00 lacs shall be required.

Conservation of Fisheries

The importance of wetlands has also been linked to the productivity of varous fish species. Besides, the diversity of fish available in a particular ecosystem determines the ecological status and functional value of that particular ecosystem. While the reports show that there are 17 species of fish existing in the lake water of Kanjli, the degrading water quality may exterminate most or even all of these species in time to come if curative measures are not initiated. Therefore, a programme aiming at restoring and sustaining the survival of all the species available in this lake has been planned. The programme would address the continuing pressure by introducing more fish species in the lake but would do so by avoiding the unforeseen effects of exotic introductions. With this view the Dept. of Fisheries would take up necessary steps at the Kanjli Wetland for which an estimated amount of Rs. 24.95 lacs shall be required.

Research Studies

This programme aims to provide information on the ecology of the lake and its catchment, the biology of its flora and fauna, the impact of environmental factors on the lake system and the socio-economic implications of the use of the lakes resources. Research programmes orientated in this direction shall contribute towards improved ecological efficiency, greater biodiversity, and an ecological balance in the lake system. To analyse the biotic components, the foodchain sequence in our wetlands and the potential threats to these places and their components, and to make long-term conservation strategies, the research studies on aquatic ecosystems of the Punjab are being promoted by the State Science & Technology Department. Certain future programmes for wetland conservation will definitely depend upon the research database. Studies on biodiversity of this wetland and limnological parameters besides habitat characteristics and an economical valuation of the Kanjli Wetland resources are priority areas of research as are described hereunder:-

a) Hydrology & productivity: Detailed studies need to be carried out to study the impact of this wetland on the hydrogeology of the area. Economical productivity linked with this issue needs to be evaluated and projected.

b) Fisheries & the sustainable use of wild life Population: Due to the heavy pressure on the wetland areas on account of various factors like the encroachment for agriculture, pollution, etc. the impact on faunal populations is catastrophic. It is clear that unless solid argument based on hard scientific data is presented for maintenance of these sites, this effort is likely to continue, hence the need of investigation in this area. The fisheries research programme would have five sub-programmes: Studies of fish biology and biodiversity conservation, aquaculture, socio-economics, database establishment and fish stock assessment.

c) Traditional human use : Wetland conservation practices can be successful only if their social impact is conducive to their use by the people inhabiting that ecosystem. It is, therefore, important that a social impact analysis of the developmental versus the conservational projects be carried out along with environmental impact analysis of various human activities initiated in the wetland area.

d) Flora & Fauna : Detailed taxonomic studies of plant and animal species of this wetland need to be carried out. This will help also in identifying the endemic species, if any, of this region which will invite particular attention for conservation.

A substantial amount of Rs. 10.00 lac for five years will be required for conducting these studies. The research projects can be initiated depending upon the availability of funds.

Public Awareness

The best conservation and management of wetland ecosystems can be ensured if the public participates in these programmes. It is possible only if the public be aware of the importance of such eco-systems. Awareness can be created through the mass-media, educational material, camps etc. Voluntary Organizations can play an important role in translating scientific ideas to public opinion. The informed general public can then become a potent force in developing sound wetland management policies. The public awareness activities would require funds amounting to Rs. 13.75 lac during the next five years.

PPCB (Punjab Pollution Control Board) has recommended the following measures :

1. Intensive afforestation activity is required to prevent the seepage and runoffs from the nearby field. A rich tree cover, besides acting as the lungs of the ecosystem will provide adequate space for the nesting of some bird species too.

2. Weed clearing, manually or by dredging, is frequently required. Steps should be taken to prevent the people from making the lake a dumping site.

3. Proper level of water must be maintained in the reservoir to save the biotic life of the lake in acute summers.

4. Deforestation should be strictly prohibited in the catchment area along the Kali Bein.

5. The villages along the Kali Bein feeding the Kanjli Lake must not discharge their sullage into the Kali Bein. The Village Panchayats may use Canal Technology for use of sullage for irrigation purposes.

6. The farmers to be educated to use the least amount of chemical fertilizer and pesticide and as far as possible to switch over to bio-fertilizers and bio-pesticides.

Conclusion

From the above discussion it can be concluded that wetlands are the lifeline of an ecosystem. These are invaluable components of nature.The Kanjli Wetlands, which are located on the Kali Bein (a tributary of the river Beas) fulfill a large number of hydrological and ecological functions which provide habitat, food, fodder for many animals, reduce flooding, help in self purification of water, regulate water and add to the many recreational features. The major threats to the Kanjli Wetlands are the prevalence of a wasteland concept, the association of wetlands with diseases, flooding hazards, a general lack of public awareness for the wetlands conservation and weed growth etc.

References

1. Anonymous (1988). Directory of Wetlands in India, Ministry of Environment and Forests, new Delhi.
2. Deptt. of Wildlife, Govt. of Punjab 1993. A Checklist of Birds of Punjab.
3. Hand, B.K. (1993). Management and Control of Aquatic Weeds in Kanjli Lake, District Kapurthala (Punjab), NEERI, Nagpur.
4. Ladhar S.S. (1995) Inventory and Ecological Status of Wetlands and Lake Ecosystems of Punjab.
5. Punjab Pollution Control Board, (1993). Kanjli Wetland - A report on status of water quality. Patiala.
6. Punjab State Council for Science & Technology (1992): Comprehensive Management Plan (Blue Print) for Harike and Kanjli Wetland Ecosystems.
7. Punjab State Council for Science & Technology (1998): Comprehensive Conservation and Management Plan (for Ninth Five Year Plan) for Kanjli Wetland.
8. Punjab State Council for Science & Technology (2000). Integrated Plan for Conservation & Management of Kanjli Wetland.
9. Sharma, B.R. (1984). Punjab District Gazetteers. Kapurthala. Revenue Deptt. Punjab.
10. Verma, V.K., Chopra, R., and Sharma P.K. (1994). Kanjli Wetland Ecosystem - Its Conservation and Management, Punjab Remote Sensing Centre, PAU Campus, Ludhiana.
11. Wetlands of India, Space Application Centre (ISRO), Ahmedabad (1998)

28

Natural Hazards And Their Management

NIVEDITA DWIVEDI

Introduction

Natural disasters have accounted for the destruction of the economical and social infrastructure. They have also resulted in environmental degradation. During the past decade, losses due to the environmental depreciation have increased manifold. Losses from natural disasters will continue to increase if we do not shift towards proactive solutions. After the Rio Conference of 1991 we are committed not only to the protection and preservation of the environment but also to the conservation of the same. Agenda 21 of the Conference envisaged that steps should be undertaken at the global platform to address this pressing need of the hour. Disaster reduction is both an issue for consideration in any Sustainable Development agenda and a cross cutting issue relating to the social, economical, environmental and humanitarian sector. There has been a colossal loss of lives and property due to these natural and man made disasters. Disasters are as old as human history but the dramatic increase and the damage caused by them in the recent past have become a cause for national and international concern. Over the past decade, the number of natural and manmade disasters has climbed inexorably. From 1994 to 1998, reported disasters on average were 428 per year but from 1999 to 2003, this figure went up to an average of 707 disaster events per year showing an increase of about 60 per cent over the previous years. The biggest rise was in countries of low human development, which suffered an increase of 142 per cent.

Natural Hazards: Definition and Types

The discussion on various terminologies has helped us in having a basic understanding of Disaster Management. However, each hazard has its own characteristics. To understand the significance and implications of various types of hazards, we must have a basic understanding about the nature, causes and effects of each hazard type and the mitigation measures that need to be taken up. In this chapter, we will discuss earthquake, tsunami, landslide, flood, cyclone and drought. The following hazards that we normally face in our country, namely:

Earthquake as a Menacing Disaster:

An Earthquake could be termed as a natural holocaust which results in the deaths of many people. An earthquake is the sudden shaking of the earth's crust. The impact of an earthquake is sudden and there is hardly any warning, making it impossible to predict an earthquake which is one of the most destructive natural hazards.[1] The Tsunami which occurred on 26th December of 2004 was triggered by an earthquake measuring 8.1 on the richter scale. Such a powerful quake was powerful enough to completely annihilate the human population in those areas where it held its grip. They may occur at any time of the year, day or night, with sudden impact and little warning. Houses were rattled like a pack of cards within the blinking of an eye.

Tsunami: Triggered by Earthquake has Colossal Repercussions

The term Tsunami has been derived from a Japanese term Tsu meaning 'harbor' and nami meaning 'waves'. Tsunamis are popularly called tidal waves but they actually have nothing to do with the tides. These waves which often affect distant shores, originate by rapid displacement of water from the lake or the sea either by seismic activity, landslides, volcanic eruptions or large meteoroid impacts. The sea water is displaced with a violent motion and swells up, ultimately surging over land with great destructive power. The effects of a Tsunami can be noticeable and even destructive.[3]

a) International Tsunami Warning Systems: Shortly after the Hilo Tsunami (1946), the Pacific Tsunami Warning System (PTWS) was developed with its operational centre at the Pacific Tsunami Warning Centre (PTWC) near Honolulu, Hawaii. The PTWC is able to alert countries several hours before a Tsunami strikes. The warning includes the predicted arrival time at selected coastal communities where the Tsunami could travel in a few hours. A Tsunami watch is issued with subsequent arrival time to other geographical areas.[4]

b) Regional Warning Systems: It usually use seismic data about nearby earthquakes to determine if there be a possible local threat of a Tsunami. Such systems are capable of giving warnings to the general public in less than 15 minutes. Apart from the tide gauge, a Tsunami can be detected with the help of radar. The 2004 Indian Ocean Tsunami recorded data from four radar positions and recorded the height of the tsunami waves two hours after the earthquake. It should be noted that the Satellite observations of the Indian Ocean Tsunami would not have been of any use in delivering warnings as the data took five hours to process. It was by pure chance that the Satellites were overhead at that time. However, in future it is possible that the space-based observation might play a direct role in any Tsunami warning.

Flood

A flood is a state of a high water level along a river channel or on the coast that leads to the inundation of land, which is not usually submerged. Floods may happen gradually and may take hours also or even happen suddenly without any warning due to a breach in the embankment, a spill over, heavy rains etc. There are different types of floods namely: flash

[1] Retrieved from www.nicee.org on 12 August, 2008

[2] Retrieved from www.imd.ernet.in/sectionseismo/static/welcome.htm

[3] http://ioc.unesco.org/itsu/

[4] Retrieved from http://www.tsunami.org

flood, riverine flood, urban flood, etc. Flash floods can be defined as floods which occur within six hours of the beginning of heavy rainfall, and are usually associated with cloud bursts, storms and cyclones requiring rapid localized warnings and immediate response to reduce damage. Wireless network and telephone connections are used to monitor flood conditions. In case of flash floods, warnings for timely evacuation may not always be possible.[5]

Flood Management: Need for a Comprehensive Policy

In India, systematic planning for flood management commenced with the Five Year Plans, particularly with the launching of the National Programme of Flood Management in 1954. During the last 48 years, different methods of flood protection with the reference to the structural, as well as to the nonstructural adjustments, have been made. They have been adopted in different states depending upon the nature of the problems and local conditions. Structural measures include storage reservoirs, flood embankments, drainage channels, anti-erosion works, channel improvement works, detention basins etc. and non-structural measures include flood forecasting, flood plain zoning, flood proofing, disaster preparedness etc. The flood management measures undertaken so far have provided a reasonable degree of protection to an area of 15.81 million hectares throughout the country.[6]

Drought

A drought is either an absence or deficiency of rainfall from its normal pattern in a region for an extended span of time leading to a general suffering in the society. It is interplay between demand that people place on a natural supply of water and a natural event that provides the water in a given geographical region. The state of Kerala which receives more than 3000 mm of rainfall every year is declared a drought affected area since it is insufficient to cater to need of the two good crops.[7]

Application of Information Technology in Disaster Management

Information Technology has converted the bipolar world into a polarized world by facilitating the dissemination of knowledge in no time. Artificial impediments in the transfer of information are being diluted slowly but steadily. It is in this perspective that it has assumed a very important role in monitoring, predicting and assessing the magnitude of a natural disaster so that precautionary steps can be taken. As the maxim says "prevention is better than cure". The United States has a very well developed sophisticated tool as far as predicting the point of initiation and magnitude of any natural disaster in any place. It requires a coordinated effort at the administrative law level to put this system in proper place. The major goal of the U.S.

---

[5] Retrieved from www.nih.ernet.in

[6] www.ndmindia.nic.in

[7] www.drought.unl. edu

Geological Survey (USGS) is to reduce the vulnerability of the people and areas most at risk from natural hazards. Natural disaster has played a major havoc. During the past four decades, natural hazards such as dust storms, severe storms and tropical cyclones, droughts, floods, earthquakes, wildland fires, volcanic eruptions and oil spills have caused major losses in human lives and livelihoods.

The prime emphasis is on risk management and disaster mitigation which can be done with the help of the modern informational and technological tools only. Risk is frequently defined as the product of the probability of a hazard and the vulnerability of a group or community. The probability of a hazard can be calculated by looking at the historical data of a region. This is a multidimensional concept where all the dynamics associated with it should be understood in order to comprehend the magnitude of the situation and find an efficacious remedy for the same.

Though it is not possible to avoid completely the natural disasters, the sufferings can be minimized by creating proper awareness of the likely disasters and their impact by developing a suitable warning system, disaster preparedness and management of disasters through the application of information technology tools.

The changing trends have opened up a large number of scientific and technological resources and skills to reduce disaster risk. The IT tools are discussed below-

GIS and Remote Sensing

The GIS provides a tool for an effective and efficient storage and manipulation of remotely sensed data and other spatial and non-spatial data types for both scientific management and policy oriented information. This can be used to facilitate the measurement, mapping, monitoring and modelling of a variety of data types related to natural phenomena. The specific GIS application in the field of Risk Assessment is: Hazard mapping to show earthquakes, landslides, floods or fire hazards.[8] These maps could be created for cities, districts or even for the entire country and Tropical Cyclone Threat Maps are used by meteorological departments to improve the quality of the tropical storm warning services and quickly communicate the risk to the people likely to get affected by a cyclone.

Remote sensing makes observations of any object from a distance without coming into actual contact. Remote sensing can gather data much faster than ground based observation and can cover a large area at one time to give a synoptic view. Remote sensing comprises Aerial Remote Sensing which is the process of recording information, such as photographs and images from sensors on aircraft and Satellite Remote Sensing, which consists of several satellite remote sensing systems can be used to integrate natural hazard assessments into development planning studies. These are: Landsat, SPOT Satellite, Satellite Radar System, and Advanced Very High Resolution Radio.

Some applications of GIS and Remote Sensing in various disasters are as follows:-

---

[8] Gisdevelopment.net

Internet: In the present era of electronic communication, the internet provides a very useful platform for disaster mitigation communications. The launching of a well defined website is a very cost-effective means of making an intra-national and international presence felt. It provides a new and potentially revolutionary option for the rapid, automatic and global dissemination of disaster information. A number of individuals and groups, including several national meteorological services, are experimenting with the Internet for real-time dissemination of weather observation, forecasts, satellite and other data. In the most critical phase of natural disasters, electronic communication has provided the most effective and in some instances, perhaps the only means of communication with an outside country.

Warning and Forecasting System: An advance system of forecasting, monitoring and issuing early warnings plays the most significant role in determining whether a natural hazard will assume alarming proportions or not. The countries have the following forecasting systems:

(a) Indian Meteorological Department (IMD): IMD provides cyclone warnings from the Area Cyclone Warning Centres (ACWCs) It has developed the necessary infrastructure to originate and disseminate the cyclone warnings at appropriate levels. It has made operational a satellite based communication system called the Cyclone Warning Dissemination System for direct dissemination of cyclone warnings to the cyclone prone coastal areas. The IMD runs operationally a Limited-area Analysis and Forecast System (LAFS), based on an Optimal Interpretation (OI) analysis and a limited area Primitive Equation (PE) model, to provide numerical guidance.

(b) National Remote Sensing Agency (NRSA): Long term drought proofing programmes on the natural resources of the district have been helped greatly by the use of satellite data obtained by NRSA. Satellite data can be used very effectively for mapping and monitoring the flood inundated areas, flood damage assessment, flood hazard zoning and past flood surveys of river configuration and protection works.

(c) Seismological Observations: Seismological observations in the country are made through a national network of 36 seismic stations operated by the IMD, which is the nodal agency. These stations have collected data over long periods of time.

(d) Warning System for Drought: The National Agricultural Drought Assessment and Management System (NADAMS) has been developed by the Department of Space for the Department of Agriculture and Cooperation, and is primarily based on the monitoring of the vegetation status through the National Oceanic and Atmospheric Administration (NOAA) Advanced Very High Resolution (AVHR) data. The drought assessment is based on a comparative evaluation of satellite observed green vegetation cover (both area and greenness) of a district in any specific time period, with that of any similar period in previous years.

(e) Flood Forecasting: Flood forecasting and warnings are issued by the Central Water Commission (CWC) Ministry of Water Resources. These are used for alerting the public and for taking appropriate measures by concerned administrative and state engineering agencies in flood hazard mitigation services. Information is gathered from the CWC's vast network of forecasting stations on various rivers in the country.

(f) Cyclone Tracking: Information on cyclone warnings is furnished on a real-time basis to the control room set up in the Ministry of Agriculture, Government of India. High-power Cyclone Detection Radars (CDR's) that are installed along the coastal belt of India have proved to be a very useful tool to the cyclone warning work. These radars can locate and track approaching Tropical Cyclones within a range of 400 km. Satellite imagery received from weather satellite is extensively used in detecting the development and movement of Tropical Cyclones over oceanic regions, particularly when they are beyond the range of the coastal radars. The existing mode of dissemination of cyclone warnings to various government officials is through high priority telegrams, telephones, telex and fax.

(g) Catastrophe Risk Monitoring System (CRMS): This involves managing risk information for the acquisition of reinsurance facilities and Catastrophe (CAT) cover, the company, through the Risk Engineering and Risk Management departments, developed the Catastrophe Risk Monitoring System.

CRMS in Natural Hazard and Risk Assessment

Utilizing the system for natural hazards and risk assessment, enables us to plot the risk being insured over various natural and geologic hazard maps. Subsequently, the system generates natural hazard assessment reports which include hazards brought about by an earthquake, typhoon, flood, volcanic eruption or landslide. The hazard susceptibility rating is analyzed and rated according to the grading levels of high, moderate, low and none. The rating system provides risk engineering analysts and underwriters of a better understanding of the degree of exposure involved and other factors that influence the exposure levels present in a particular property being assessed against the natural hazards. However, not all risks located in "high" hazard areas should be treated as "high risk" or unacceptable risk, without considering the engineering measures implemented and the physical conditions of the property. Apart from the natural hazard information in the database, the CRMS also includes in its records risk engineering information related to the physical characteristics of the property such as building height, age, type of construction, etc. Engineering measures such as seismic design, type of structural frame, etc. also form part of the overall risk assessment prior to the acceptance or declination of the risk.

Financial Arrangements for Natural Disasters in India

Natural Disasters are huge economic burdens on developing economies such as India. Every year, huge amounts of resources are mobilized for rescue, relief and rehabilitation works following natural disaster occurrences. The Central Government plays a major role as far as the mobilisation of financial resources is concerned. A scheme called Calamity Relief Fund (CRF) has been constituted for each state with contribution from the Central and State Government to undertake the relief and rehabilitation measures. This enables the states to manage and provide for calamity relief on their own by drawing upon the resources available with a fund constituted for that purpose, separately for each state. In addition to the CRF, a National Fund for Calamity Relief (NFCR) has been created to deal with hazards of rare severity managed by a National

Calamity Relief Committee (NCRC). The State Governments are required to submit memoranda for this purpose giving details of damage and destruction and the cost of relief and rehabilitation. On receipt of these memoranda, the Government of India decides on an individual basis whether a Central Team is required to be deputed to assess the situation.

Administrative Structure of Disaster Management in India: Management and Control

The Department of Agriculture and Cooperation (DAC) in the Ministry of Agriculture, Government of India, is the nodal department for all matters concerning natural disaster's relief at the Centre. The National Contingency Action Plan (CAP) facilitates the launching of the relief and rescue operations without delay. There are various committees at the national level for Disaster Management such as the Cabinet Committee for the effective implementation of relief measures in the wake of a natural calamity; National Crisis Management Committee at the national level headed by the Cabinet Secretary who is in charge of various types of disasters and supporting ministries as members; Crisis Management Group reviews various measures required for dealing with a natural disaster, and coordinates activities with the Central ministries and the State Governments pertaining to disaster preparedness and relief and obtains information from nodal officers on measures relating to the above.

Possible Risk Reduction Measures

1. Public Awareness and education: If the community is aware of the do's and don'ts, then half of the problems can be solved. These include awareness on the availability of safe drinking water, water conservation techniques, agricultural drought management strategies like crop contingency plans and the construction of a rain water harvesting structure. Awareness can be generated by the print, electronic and folk media.

2. Drought Monitoring: It involves a continuous observation of the rainfall situation, availability of water in the reservoirs, lakes, rivers etc., and comparing the result with the existing water needs in various sectors of the society.

3. Water supply augmentation and conservation through rainwater harvesting in houses and farmers' fields increases the content of water available. Water harvesting by either allowing the runoff water from all the fields to a common point (e.g. Farm ponds) or allowing it to infiltrate into the soil where it has fallen (in situ) (e.g. contour bunds, contour cultivation, raised bed planting etc.) helps to increase the water availability for a sustained agricultural production.

4. Expansion of irrigation facilities reduces the drought vulnerability. Land use based on its capability helps in the optimum use of land and water and can avoid the undue demand created due to its misuse.

5. Livelihood planning identifies those livelihoods which are least affected by the drought. Some such livelihoods include the increased off-farm employment opportunities, the collection of non-timber forest produce from the community forests, raising goats, carpentry etc.

6. Drought planning: The basic goal of drought planning is to improve the effectiveness of preparedness and response efforts by enhancing monitoring, mitigation and response measures.

7. Planning would help in effective coordination among state and national agencies in dealing with the drought. The components of a drought plan include a establishing a drought taskforce which is a team of specialists who can advise.

Conclusion

It is observed that advancement in Information Technology in the form of the Internet, GIS, Remote Sensing, Satellite communication, etc. can help a great deal in the planning and implementing of hazard reduction. For a maximum benefit, new technologies for public communication should be made use of and natural disaster mitigation messages should be conveyed through these measures. GIS can improve the quality and power of analysis of natural hazard assessments, guide developmental activities and assist planners in the selection of mitigation measures and in the implementation of emergency preparedness and response action. Remote Sensing, on the other hand, as a tool can contribute very effectively towards the identification of hazardous areas, monitor the planet for its changes on a real time basis and give an early warning to many impending disasters. Communication satellites have become vital for providing emergency communications and timely relief measures. Integration of space technology has an input into natural disaster monitoring and mitigation mechanisms are critical for hazard reduction. It is absolutely necessary to create awareness amongst the public as well as the decision makers for allocating resources for appropriate investments in information technology. Awareness and training in Information Technology in a much greater measure is required to develop human resources, particularly in the developing countries, who chronically suffer from natural disasters.

Disasters usually occur in well-defined areas, even though the community does not know the coping mechanism for the disaster. The disaster mitigation programmes must be extensively taken up covering various aspects at a national level to minimize the disaster damage. There should be a greater emphasis on the development of new technologies in disaster mitigation. Disaster preparedness and awareness is the only effective way of mitigating the impact of future disasters.

References

1. Application of RS and GIS in Damage Assessment and Rehabilitation of 26th December 2004 Great Indian Ocean Tsunami Event in Car Nicobar Island, India (Map Middle East 2005) **Arun Kumar**
2. Disaster management (Map India 2000) — **D. P. Rao**
3. Information technology and natural disaster management in India (ACRS 2000) — **Dr. Alok Gupta**
4. Remote Sensing and Geographical Information System for natural disaster management (Map India 2002) — **Samir Kumar Banger**

29

Decentralised Natural Resource Management
Key Issues and Implications for Development

RAMA AND NAVDEEP KUMAR

Introduction

Development has been seen as not only an instrument to increase production, but also to remove poverty. Public policy in India has for a long time appreciated that access to natural resources is crucial to local livelihood strategies. The majority of the poor in India are to be found in rural areas. The livelihoods they pursue are diverse, but the management of common pool resources is a principal component for many. Improvements in decentralised natural resource management can contribute substantially to their livelihoods. Many of the rural poor depend directly on shared natural resources, yet they often live in ecologically marginal areas and have limited and insecure rights to natural resources. In recent times, environmental concerns have come to the fore at the international level as well as in the agendas of the national governments. One of the concerns is how are we to manage our natural resources at a local level and above. Perceptions of a downward spiral of natural resource degradation, of the inability of natural resource users to organise themselves adequately in order to reverse degradation, and of the limited effectiveness hitherto of the state in resource-use planning and service provision in relation to natural resource management, have prompted shifts in public policy towards more local and more integrated management of natural resources. Natural resource management and its use is of interest to the promoters of decentralization and local democracy, because they are a source of revenue and power, and therefore a potential legitimacy for new local government authorities. Whether, however, the transfer of natural resource powers within or into the local institutional landscape will promote or undermine representatives, accountable and equitable processes depend strongly on which authorities are being entrusted with powers over nature. The decentralisation agenda has however led to changes in the institutional arrangements for managing shared natural resources. Through partnership models, and indirectly through the Panchayati Raj, communities have been given some autonomy in deciding priorities for natural resource management, funds to develop natural resource assets and guidelines to promote community mobilisation. These decentralisation initiatives represent major achievements in challenging the previous dominance of line department control over all aspects of natural resource management. The objective of sustainable, equitable and decentralised natural resource management is however far from being realized.

Rationale for Decentralisation of Natural Resource Management

Decentralization, a process through which powers, responsibilities and resources are devolved by the central state to lower territorial entities and regionally/locally elected bodies, increases efficiency, participation, equity, and environmental sustainability.The support for decentralization is based less on any proven success than on an ideological conviction related to the importance of local involvement and self-determination in the developmental process. There is however, a growing realism about the strong centralising forces within a policy and bureaucracy that inhibits the meaningful transfer of access and control over natural resources. Development aspirations have fuelled man to compete and cooperate - creating different paradigms of development as societies evolve. In the structured modern society, positioned within the nation state, these aspirations find common coalescing points around class, caste and gender aspirations at the community level. Each group within the community defines its own developmental needs based on the existing socio-political equations and then negotiates with the national state and the other forces such as the market, using different strategies. While this is the process from below, the dominant process drowning out this natural process is that of Planned Development interventions of the state that are supposed to include and incorporate the aspirations of the people. Decentralised natural resource management needs to be understood in the context of the political settlements at three levels. The formulation of the policies and legal framework at the central level, policies and operational guidelines at the state level and institutional mechanisms and interpretation of the policies at the local level. In terms of planned development, this interface between the community and State as the major actors, determines the sustainability of development.

In India, there is a growing awareness about the way we manage our rich tropical resources which are depleting at a fast rate. The Chipko movement is an indicator of what people can do to protect their habitat from destruction by urbanisation and industrialisation. However, the local institutions, which have been at the cutting edge of protecting natural resources have been weakened over a period of time for various reasons. Policy has focused principally on institutional frameworks conferring rights, responsibilities and roles in decentralized natural resource management. In India, two formal institutional systems have been identified as having the legitimacy and potential to enhance rural livelihoods:

Partnership Models: In the last decade there have been significant moves towards formal natural resource management partnerships between the public administration and local user groups. The two most institutionally evolved are the Joint Forest Management (JFM) and the Watershed Management (WM).

Local Government Reform: A Constitutional Amendment passed in 1993 aimed to strengthen local government, collectively called the Panchayati Raj Institutions, at District, Block and Village levels. Village level Panchayats have become responsible for preparing plans for the management of natural resources within their boundaries.

Policies that aim to change the structure of rights and control over natural resources are essentially political. Property rights are claims and assets that have been politically negotiated and defended. These rights are not only tangible claims over the resources themselves, but are also rights over the institutional structure for natural resource management. The distribution of rights over natural resources in India and the institutional structure for natural resources management were politically negotiated in the following main periods:

- **Colonial (1790 to 1930):** The proprietary, managerial and revenue-raising rights over the most valuable natural resources were vested in the state. Community access to NR for subsistence purposes was permitted.
- **Post-Independence (1947 to 1956):** The state maintained colonial property rights and administrative structures intact. Centralised control was justified as necessary to direct a programme of development on behalf of the nation. The line department approach to natural resource management was developed during this period.

These periods of political contestation over natural resource rights and management, resulted in the centralization that rejected local claims and demands. Current decentralization policies have not actually changed the structure of rights or the distribution of benefit streams from the natural resources themselves. The basic political settlement over natural resources remains unchallenged despite the apparent momentum of the agenda for decentralization. The right to manage valuable resources and raise revenue from these, an issue that was politically contested during the colonial period, remains with the state. The natural resource currently being considered in programmes for decentralization are mainly degraded common land and forest resources that have, since colonial times, been earmarked for community subsistence purposes.

It is now that the need is felt, on the one hand, for strengthening rural institutions like the Panchayats, as is evident from the 73rd Constitutional Amendment Act and the consequent passing of various state panchayat acts as part of the decentralisation efforts in India. Various studies on natural resources in rural areas, on the other hand, show an increasing strain on or depletion of these resources. One of the reasons, apart from population pressures and a market driven economy, is the lack of institutional mechanisms or inadequate powers to these institutions to protect and regulate the use of natural resources **(Blair, 1996).**

Decentralised natural resource management as a public policy objective emerged in response to pressures on particular political settlements. These manifest in the policy objectives, assumptions and ideologies on which they are based, the balance of power between interest groups and the distribution of rights – also constrain the achievement of decentralised issues. The political settlement also influences the distribution and operation of de jure and de facto rights over natural resources and the practical steps that can be taken to achieve decentralised natural resource management. Opportunities for improved natural resource management will be affected by the political settlement and the institutional/political systems. A *Gram Panchayat* is likely to be under pressure from a range of different interest groups, but our primary interest is in how such opportunities are articulated at the local level and how they interact with local interest groups.

For many reasons, natural resource management is particularly well suited to decentralization and local democratic control.

- Unlike sectors such as health and education, natural resources are a direct source of wealth as well as a target for investment. Thus, natural resources can help finance both development and local governance.
- Because most rural people in developing countries rely on natural resources for their livelihoods, democratic local governance requires popular input in decisions about natural resources management and use.
- Effective management of diverse natural resources with multiple uses requires a specific local knowledge. Controlling access to natural resources often generates overlapping claims and its conflicts that must be settled locally.

Decentralised Natural Resource Management and Development

Under the rubric of decentralization governments across the developing world are also transferring environmental managerial responsibilities and powers from central government to a variety of local institutions. These reforms aim to increase popular participation to promote more equitable and efficient forms of local environmental management. The key to effective decentralization is increased democratical participation in local public decision making. About 60 developing countries are decentralizing some aspects of their natural resource`s management **(Agrawal, 2002).** However, most current decentralization reforms are characterized by an insufficient transfer of powers to local institutions, under tight central-government oversight. Often, these local institutions do not represent and are not accountable to local communities. Nonetheless, the limited decentralization experiments that have taken place in various locations provide some important lessons. Virtually all developing countries are undertaking some type of reform to decentralize public decision-making. Under decentralization reforms, power is transferred from central government to institutions and actors at lower levels of political and/or administrative authority. The rationale behind decentralization is that these reforms foster increased efficiency and equity in developmental activities. By virtue of their proximity to the people they serve, democratic local institutions are likely to have access to better information about local conditions and better understanding of local needs and aspirations and to be more easily held accountable by local populations.

Decentralization requires both power transfers and accountable representation. To identify appropriate and sufficient powers to transfer, principles of power distribution, called environmental subsidiary principles, would be of great use. Such principles could be developed to guide the division of decision-making, rule-making, implementation, enforcement, and dispute-resolution powers among levels of government and among institutions at each level. Security of power transfers also matters. Local representatives remain accountable and subject to central authorities when their powers can be given and taken at the whim of central agents. Secure powers and accountable representation go together, yet most decentralization reforms establish only one or the other. A partial explanation is that many central government agents fear, and therefore block, decentralization. To date, the potential benefits of decentralization remain unrealized because governments have not enacted the necessary laws, or where decentralization laws do exist, they have not been implemented. Nevertheless, even partial decentralizations have borne some positive social and environmental outcomes. These include environmental standards, policies to improve equity, civic education, dispute resolution, and legal protections for activist organizations.

The potential of decentralization to be efficient and equitable depends on the creation of democratic local institutions with significant discretionary powers. But there are few cases where democratic institutions are being chosen and given discretionary powers. Ironically, a backlash is already forming against decentralizing powers over natural resources. Environmental agencies in Uganda, Ghana, Indonesia, Nicaragua, and elsewhere have argued that too much decentralization has caused damage or overexploitation **(Bazaara, 2002; Resosudarmo, 2002; deGrasi, 2002; Latif, 2002).** These calls to re-centralize control over natural resources are premature.

Before decentralization can be judged, time is needed for it to be legislated, implemented, and taken in effect. Firstly, a locally accountable representation with discretionary powers must be established. Then, accompanying measures must be identified to assure that environmental protection, justice, and freedom from conflict can exist. To encourage the decentralization experiment and test the conditions under which it yields the benefits that theorists and advocates promise, decentralization must be fully tested, monitored and evaluated.

Developmental policy in India has long appreciated the importance of environmental - poverty linkages in determining developmental outcomes. The majority of the poor in India are rural people and are particularly dependent on natural resources for their livelihoods. They often live in areas of high ecological vulnerability and relatively low levels of resource productivity and have limited and insecure rights over productive natural resources. These combined factors are significant forces contributing towards the vulnerability of rural livelihood strategies. Much of the debate over development strategies in the last decade has therefore turned around the question of how poverty, vulnerability and access to natural resources are linked and which policies can contribute towards sustainable rural livelihoods.

A number of developments in the 1990s served to further the decentralization agenda. In the economical domain, a new set of policies were put in place which departed from the mixed economy model and visualized a greater participation for the private sector. Simultaneously, with the precarious situation of public finances, there has been a move to restrict the role of the state to core functions, leaving everyday management of many services in the hands of non-state sectors such as NGOs and/or beneficiary groups and user committees. This move has the support of both influential donor bodies and the NGO sectors in India, though the reasons for support vary. With respect to natural resources, watershed programmes have been established as a major form of intervention for sustained and equitable utilisation of resources to be managed jointly by the public administration and local user groups. Similarly, a Circular issued by the Ministry of Environment and Forests in 1990 provided guidelines for Joint Forest Management between local communities and the Forest Department. Politically, an entirely unrelated development - Constitutional Amendments providing legal sanction for establishing *Panchayats* as the third tier of self-government - include natural resource management amongst the responsibilities of local government. These various moves towards decentralized natural resource management have not developed in synergy with each other and the *Panchayati Raj* in particular did not develop with a particular focus on natural resource management.

Decentralization is of great interest to environmentalists because they reshape the institutional infrastructure for future local natural resource management—potentially establishing institutions for a sustainable and equitable community representation and inclusion. Natural resources play a special role in local democratization because local populations rely on them for their daily livelihoods and governments rely on them as a source of wealth, but if allocated to nondemocratic institutions, environmental powers can play a counter productive role also. Decentralized natural resource management with its decisions can, conversely, be a fulcrum for democratic change. Local representative bodies need powers over resources that affect their constituencies in order to become legitimate actors around which civil society and citizens rally for justice, sustainable livelihoods and economical improvement.

Conclusion and Recommendations

Despite the diversification of livelihoods, the rural poor remain dependent on natural resources and frequently oppose the existing political settlement. Decentralised institutions have provided a means for ascendant agrarian classes to access centrally allocated resources and contribute towards more strategic voting patterns; however this mobilisation has little connection with natural resource-related demands. The way forward, given these divergent *trends,* is a more strategic consideration of the political and ecological constraints of decentralisation. In many contexts, and for many of the rural poor, wage labour in natural resource management programmes will be part of a stepping-stone to other perhaps non-local activities. This would represent the beginnings of an agenda for decentralized natural resource management based on local natural resource based demands. There is a grassroots demand for centrally allocated resources, which even if it be not related to natural resource management policy it can be used to improve the effectiveness of service delivery to decentralized units. A fundamental change in the distribution of rights and access to the natural resources themselves is probably not a politically feasible objective. However, a strategic decentralisation agenda would recognise not only the constraints on a decentralization imposed by the existing political settlement, but it would recognise also when and how this settlement could be challenged at the margins.

References

1. Agrawal, Arun and Jesse C. Ribot (1999), "Accountability in Decentralization: A Framework with South Asian and African Cases," *Journal of Developing Areas* Vol. 33, Summer 1999, pp. 473-502.

2. Conyers, Diane (1990), "Decentralization and Development Planning: A Comparative Perspective," in P. de Valk and K. H. Wekwete (eds.) *Decentralizing for Participatory Planning: Comparing the Experiences of Zimbabwe and Other Anglophone Countries in Eastern and Southern Africa.* Aldershot: Avebury Press.

3. Ellis, F. (2000), *Rural Livelihoods and Diversity in Developing Countries,* Oxford: Oxford University Press.

4. Farrington, J., Turton, C. and James, A.J. (1999), *Participatory Microwatershed Development in India: Challenges for the 21st Century,* New Delhi and Oxford: Oxford University Press.

5. Gadgil, M. and Guha, R. (1992), *This Fissured Land: An Ecological History of India,* Delhi: Oxford University Press.

6. Jodha, N. (1986), 'Common Property Resources and the Rural Poor in Dry Regions of India', *Economic and Political Weekly,* 5 July.

7. Kothari, A., Singh, N. and Suri, S. (eds) (1996), *People and Protected Areas: Towards Participatory Conservation in India,* New Delhi: Sage Publications.

8. Nelson, N. and Wright, S. (eds) (1995), 'Participation and Power', in N. Nelson and S. Wright (eds) *Power and Participatory Development,* London: Intermediate Technology Publications.

9. Oyugi, Walter O. (2000), "Decentralization for Good Governance and Development" *Regional Development Dialogue* 21(1):3-22, Spring 2000.

30

Disposal of Industrial Sludge of Wazirpur, Delhi

Effect of pH balance and Cation Exchange Capacity on Available Calcium and Magnesium

SUTAPA BOSE, GURMEET SINGH, A. K. BHATTACHARYYA AND A.L. RAMANATHAN

Introduction

Industrial sludge disposal is an important aspect of waste disposal in this century. Soil is one of the major sinks of toxic metal as well as nutrients. Before the disposal of any kind of sludge, characterization is an important phase to minimize the risk on the environment. Municipal sewage sludge generally contains higher concentrations of heavy metals such as Cd, Cu, or Pb etc., than are found in soils (Chaney, 1980; Alloway, 1995a, b). The factors that generally affect the chemistry of soil nutrients and heavy metals and their uptake by organisms are the pH balance, organic matter and toxic conditions; among these, the pH balance is considered to be the most important and easily manageable one (Förstner, 1991). The soil pH balance influences the availability and plant uptake of micronutrients. Liming on soil offers an approach for minimizing the risk of food chain contamination by reducing the plant uptake of sludge-born heavy metals (Jackson and Alloway, 1991; Smith, 1994). The sludge can be a valuable fertilizer as it is a good source of P and N, organic matter, and micronutrients (Ferrier et al., 1996 and Bramryd, 2002).

Calcium and magnesium occur abundantly in soil and major macro nutrients for the growth of plants. An excess of lime causes calcium antagonism (Mayers et al., 1988). Kinraidas and Parker (1987) showed that cations (Ca^{2+}, Mg^{2+}, Na^{+} and K^{+}) improved the aluminum toxicity in the wheat plant. Liming of acidic soil showed the greatest potential to release the exchangeable cations (Adams, 1984). Rhue and Mansell (1988) showed that CEC increased with the increase in the pH balance. Wazirpur industrial sludge consists of both macro and micro nutrients with higher concentrations of heavy metals (Bose et al., 2007; Bose and Bhattacharyya, 2008). The major polluting units are electro plating, pickling-rolling and textile industries. The sludge and solid waste generated from these industries are dumped by the road side. In the present study, we characterized the sludge to explore the possible disposal of acidic industrial sludge.

Material and Methods

Sample Collection and Processing

The study site, the Wazirpur industrial area, is located in the northwest part of Delhi, India. Samples were collected from different locations of the industrial area for each season (summer, monsoon and winter) from an open dumping site and roadside dump in accordance with the standard methods. The two sampling sites for soil were the Jawaharlal Nehru University (JNU) campus and the Chhattarpur farmland. The JNU soil is free of any kind of agricultural or industrial activity. The JNU is covered by thick greenery with rich flora and fauna. The soil collected from the Chhattarpur farmland has already been exposed to fertilizers, pesticides and many other pollutants. Soil samples were collected from 5 different places from the JNU as well as from Chhattarpur and were homogenized separately. Sampling was done once during the study period.

Immediatly after the collection of sludge and soils, the pH balance Electrical Conductivity (EC), Water Holding Capacity (WHC) and Moisture Content (MC) were measured and the remaining samples were kept for drying at room temperature. The air-dried sludge samples of each season were ground and passed through a 2 mm sieve and homogenized to make a representative sample. Following the same methods, other soil samples were processed separately.

Experimental Bag Preparation

Sludge was treated with two different doses of lime (0.5% and 1%). These sludges were then mixed with the JNU and Chhattarpur soil separately with different proportions (10%, 20% and 30%). 100g of each sample of sludge was amended and lime treated soils were kept in polythene bags to initiate the experiment. The experimental bags were kept in a BOD incubator at 28 ^{0}C maintaining 50% moisture of WHC for 120 days. A sate of control soil and sludge were also kept throughout the experiment maintaining the same environmental conditions.

Physico-Chemical Analysis

One set of polythene bag was removed from the BOD incubator to carry out the further physico-chemical analysis at the intervals of 0, 10, 20, 30, 45, 60, 90 and 120 days of incubation.

The soil samples were analyzed by the following methods: pH, EC, WHC and MC by Jackson (1973), Organic carbon (OC) by Walkley and Black (1934), CEC by direct distillation method (Salter and William, 1967), available calcium and magnesium by ammonium acetate extract method (Hess, 1972).

Data Analysis

Eight different physico-chemical parameters of incubated soil were monitored after each harvest. Each set of data was arranged to execute two sets of 2-factor ANOVA (Analysis of Variance) ($p<0.05$) as follows: (a) Keeping sludge amendment constant, days of incubation and lime treatment were taken as two factors and (b) Keeping lime treatment constant, days of incubation and sludge amendment were taken as two factors. The above exercises were performed for Chhattarpur soil and JNU soil separately.

Correlation was performed in between different physico-chemical parameters of soils by using SPSS, version 10.

Results and Discussion

General Properties of Control Soil and Sludge

The physico-chemical analysis of control soils and pure sludge showed a significant variation of all the parameters (Table 1). The MC, WHC and EC were higher in sludge. The sludge was acidic (pH-4.4) in nature with higher OC (3.2%). CEC was also found to be higher in (12.7 meq $100g^{1-}$) homogenized sludge. Control soils were slightly alkaline in nature and the value was higher in the case of Chhattarpur (pH-8.6) than the JNU soil (pH-8.3). Both the OC and CEC were higher in Chhattarpur soil than in the JNU soil (Table 1). In the Chhhattarpur soil, the available calcium was moderately higher (53.4 µg g^{1-}) than in the JNU control soil (47.3 µg g^{1-}) whereas in the case of available magnesium, the concentration was higher in the JNU (36.9 µg g^{1-}) than in the Chhattarpur soil (31.4 µg g^{1-}).

General Properties of Incubation Study

The pH balance decreased with the increasing percentage of sludge application in soils (Table 2) whereas it increased with the lime treatment. The OC was also enhanced with an increasing percentage of waste application but decreased with an lime treatment (Data not shown). The liming of soil decreased soil organic carbon (Chan and Heenan, 1999). The biosolid

Table 1: General physico-chemical properties of the pure sludge and control soils (mean ± sd).

Parameters	Sludge	JNU Soil	Chhattarpur Soil
pH	4.4±0.03	8.37±0.04	8.66±0.03
EC (mS cm^{1-})	1.9±0.002	0.10±0.001	0.15±0.001
WHC (%)	39.0±0.2	32.0±0.3	37.5±0.2
MC (%)	3.5±0.05	1.45±0.03	3.05±0.02
OC (%)	3.2±0.04	0.34±0.05	0.72±0.01
CEC (meq $100g^{1-}$)	12.7±0.13	10.76±0.16	11.86±0.15
Available Ca (µg g^{1-})	53.21± 4.21	53.4±4.1	47.3± 3.83
Available Mg (µg g^{1-})	28.93±1.85	36.9±2.43	31.4±2.11

application to soil increased the organic matter (Franco-Hern-andez et al., 2003). The organic carbon continuously decreased in waste amended Chhattarpur soil, with the incubation time. From table 3 it is clear that the lime treatment and sludge application increased the CEC values in both soils and with time it increased till 45 days of incubation and after that got stabilized till 120 days of incubation.

Changes of Available Calcium and Magnesium

Table 2: Changes of pH in soils amended with industrial sludge in different days of incubation (mean ± sd).

	0	10	20	30	45	60	90	120
C-0-0	8.90±0.05	8.40±0.04	8.39±0.05	8.32±0.08	8.16±0.05	8.30±0.07	8.20±0.08	8.18±0.09
C-10-0	7.87±0.03	7.70±0.03	7.74±0.04	7.70±0.05	7.56±0.04	7.75±0.08	7.75±0.07	7.62±0.08
C-10-0.05	7.88±0.04	7.73±0.04	7.79±0.03	7.72±0.06	7.57±0.05	7.78±0.05	7.77±-.09	7.63±0.08
C-10-1.0	7.96±0.05	7.82±0.04	7.84±0.03	7.77±0.05	7.62±0.07	7.78±0.05	7.82±0.04	7.67±0.07
C-20-0	7.44±0.03	7.39±0.05	7.45±0.05	7.40±0.07	7.22±0.05	7.42±0.04	7.46±0.07	7.27±0.08
C-20-0.5	7.55±0.05	7.47±0.03	7.55±0.04	7.53±0.05	7.34±0.05	7.53±0.05	7.58±0.05	7.46±0.07
C-20-1.0	7.62±0.03	7.56±0.04	7.64±0.04	7.63±0.06	7.49±0.07	7.62±0.04	7.61±0.06	7.52±0.04
C-30-0	7.06±0.02	7.05±0.04	7.08±0.05	7.04±0.04	6.72±0.07	6.84±0.06	6.87±0.07	6.66±0.06
C-30-0.5	7.27±0.04	7.25±0.05	7.32±0.03	7.30±0.05	7.05±0.03	7.14±0.06	7.20±0.07	7.08±0.06
C-30-1.0	7.60±0.05	7.43±0.04	7.48±0.05	7.44±0.04	7.27±0.05	7.44±0.05	7.53±0.05	7.32±0.07
J-0-0	8.33±0.04	8.37±0.5	8.26±0.06	8.14±0.04	8.20±0.07	8.29±0.06	8.16±0.07	8.21±0.09
J-10-0	7.58±0.04	7.84±0.04	7.75±0.03	7.72±0.05	7.87±0.06	7.87±0.03	7.84±0.05	7.89±0.06
J-10-0.5	7.65±0.03	7.85±0.03	7.80±0.06	7.78±0.08	7.93±0.08	7.89±0.06	7.85±0.08	7.90±0.07
J-10-1.0	7.82±0.04	7.88±0.04	7.79±0.07	7.79±0.06	7.91±0.04	7.90±0.07	7.84±0.09	7.92±0.07
J-20-0	7.48±0.05	7.69±0.03	7.63±0.03	7.57±0.06	7.74±0.07	7.70±0.06	7.70±0.07	7.79±0.06
J-20-0.5	7.56±0.04	7.71±0.03	7.67±0.04	7.61±0.05	7.74±0.03	7.72±0.06	7.71±0.06	7.81±0.08
J-20-1.0	7.83±0.05	7.82±0.02	7.70±0.05	7.68±0.04	7.76±0.05	7.75±0.05	7.71±0.06	7.82±0.07
J-30-0	7.38±0.03	7.52±0.04	7.54±0.04	7.52±0.07	7.63±0.04	7.62±0.07	7.57±0.05	7.72±0.09
J-30-0.5	7.46±0.04	7.60±0.03	7.56±0.05	7.56±0.06	7.64±0.05	7.61±0.07	7.58±0.06	7.73±0.08
J-30-1.0	7.84±0.05	7.76±0.05	7.68±0.05	7.60±0.08	7.66±0.05	7.63±0.06	7.62±0.07	7.64±0.08

Figure 1 showing that available calcium increased with an increasing percentage of both sludge and lime application in both soils. With time, the available calcium increased till 30 days of incubation and after that it continuously decreased with time. There was a significant variation of both sludge application and lime treatment with days of incubation in both soils (ANOVA at

Table 3: Changes of CEC (meq 100g[1]) in soils amended with industrial sludge in different days of incubation (mean ± sd).

	0	10	20	30	45	60	90	120
C-0-0	11.90±0.16	10.45±0.10	9.26±0.10	10.92±0.12	11.16±0.13	9.10±0.13	9.00±0.1	9.13±0.14
C-10-0	10.81±0.12	12.01±0.11	11.53±0.11	12.40±0.14	9.90±0.11	9.10±0.14	9.04±0.12	9.03±0.13
C-10-0.05	11.05±0.14	11.69±0.12	11.92±1014	13.59±0.16	10.60±0.14	9.82±0.12	9.25±0.12	9.17±0.15
C-10-1.0	10.50±0.11	11.37±0.11	11.92±0.15	13.91±0.15	11.24±0.14	10.44±0.11	9.91±0.14	9.62±0.11
C-20-0	11.58±0.10	10.78±0.12	11.26±0.16	12.22±0.14	12.69±0.15	11.33±0.14	10.63±0.11	10.38±0.16
C-20-0.5	11.90±0.13	11.10±0.11	12.46±0.16	14.30±0.17	12.78±0.14	11.71±0.14	10.91±0.13	10.61±0.14
C-20-1.0	12.06±0.15	11.26±0.13	12.70±0.14	13.98±0.18	13.81±0.16	12.16±0.15	11.06±0.12	10.94±0.14
C-30-0	12.75±0.13	12.74±0.12	12.27±0.15	12.84±0.16	11.95±0.13	8.64±0.13	10.15±0.14	9.75±0.16
C-30-0.5	13.07±0.11	13.06±0.12	13.32±0.11	13.25±0.12	12.92±0.15	11.39±0.17	10.47±0.14	9.98±0.12
C-30-1.0	12.99±0.16	12.90±0.12	13.48±0.15	13.24±0.14	13.89±0.17	12.35±0.13	11.30±0.16	10.56±0.15
J-0-0	10.78±0.11	9.92±0.11	8.71±0.16	9.72±0.11	10.28±0.13	9.32±0.11	9.26±0.15	9.13±0.15
J-10-0	10.11±0.13	9.85±0.10	8.45±0.11	8.96±0.16	9.47±0.15	9.53±0.16	9.51±0.13	9.14±0.14
J-10-0.5	10.95±0.11	11.36±0.12	11.45±0.15	11.25±0.12	11.79±0.16	11.03±0.15	10.54±0.15	10.47±0.15
J-10-1.0	11.32±0.15	11.65±0.11	11.84±0.16	11.52±0.11	11.23±0.11	10.94±0.15	10.36±0.13	10.21±0.16
J-20-0	10.89±0.12	11.23±0.15	11.37±0.16	11.58±0.13	11.25±0.15	10.95±0.17	10.73±0.12	10.35±0.14
J-20-0.5	11.05±0.14	11.54±0.13	11.65±0.14	11.36±0.14	11.19±0.14	10.74±0.14	10.42±0.15	10.15±0.16
J-20-1.0	11.88±0.13	11.95±0.12	11.46±0.15	11.04±0.11	10.74±0.15	10.53±0.15	10.32±0.16	10.26±0.14
J-30-0	11.68±0.11	11.84±0.13	11.95±0.16	11.36±0.14	11.19±0.17	10.84±0.11	10.32±0.11	10.21±0.15
J-30-0.5	11.95±0.18	12.11±0.13	12.38±0.14	12.09±0.14	11.85±0.14	11.47±0.14	11.19±0.14	10.88±0.14
J-30-1.0	12.11±1.16	12.38±0.14	12.15±0.16	11.94±0.11	11.57±0.12	11.25±0.13	10.94±0.15	10.81±0.13

p<0.05%). In case of available magnesium, the concentrations enhanced with a sludge application but 1% lime application decreased the concentration of available magnesium. High concentrations of calcium reduced the availability of magnesium in soils (Maynard et al., 1979). A high dose of liming generally decreases the concentrations of other basic cations in soil which are found in the present study also (Curtin et al., 1995). Table 4 shows that there was a negative correlation between the pH balance and the available calcium and magnesium but a strong positive correlation between CEC and available calcium and magnesium.

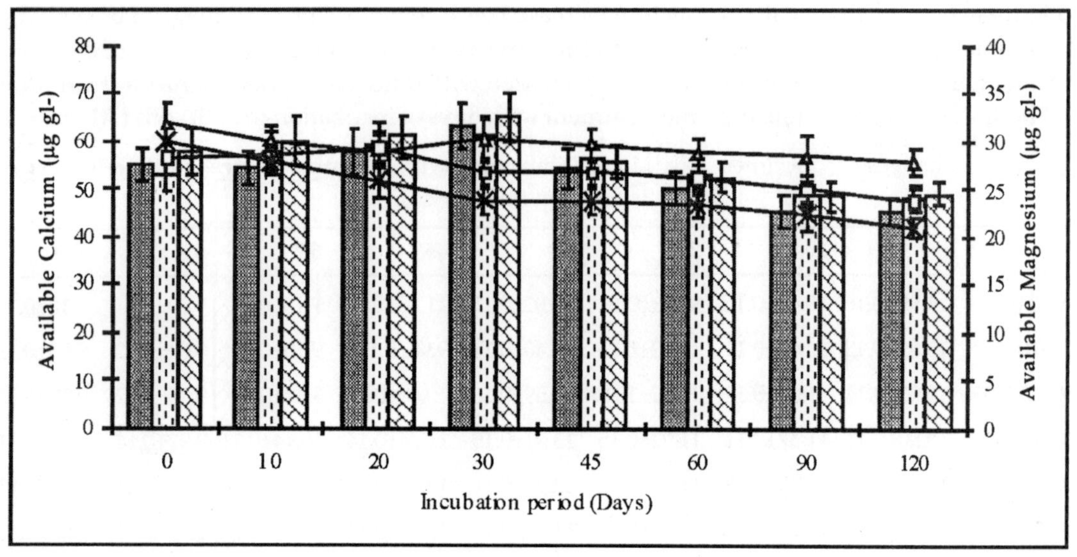

(a): Chhattarpur soil with 10% sludge

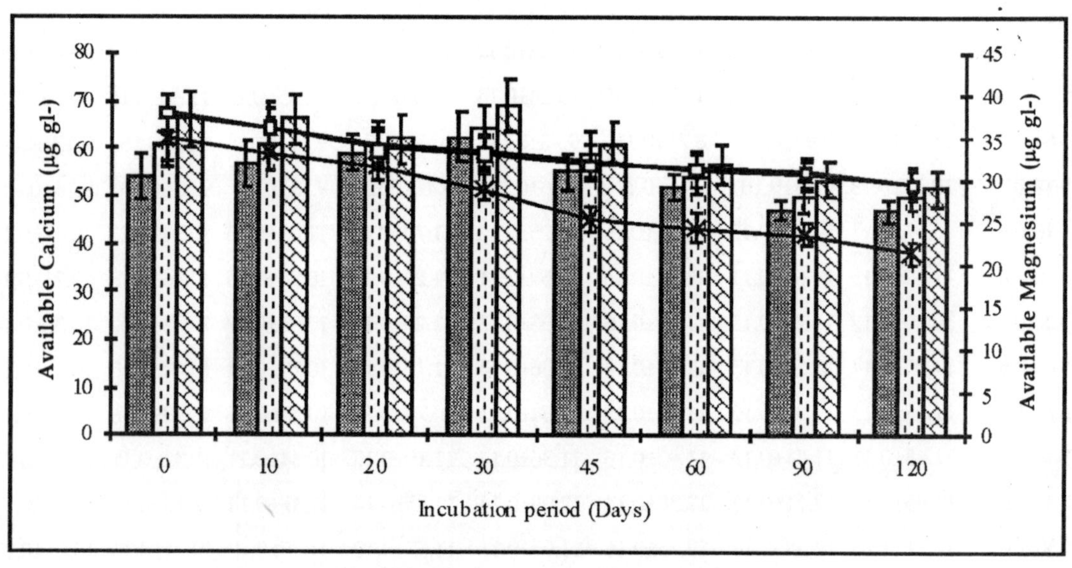

(b): Chhattarpur soil with 20% sludge

Ca-0L	Ca-0.05L	Ca-1.0L
Mg-0L	Mg-0.05L	Mg-1.0L

Ca: Available Calcium; Mg: Available Magnesium; 0L: 0% Lime; 0.5L: 0.5% Lime; 1.0L: 1% lime

Fig. 1. Concentration of available calcium and magnesium (µg g^{1-}) in sludge amended soil in different days of incubation.

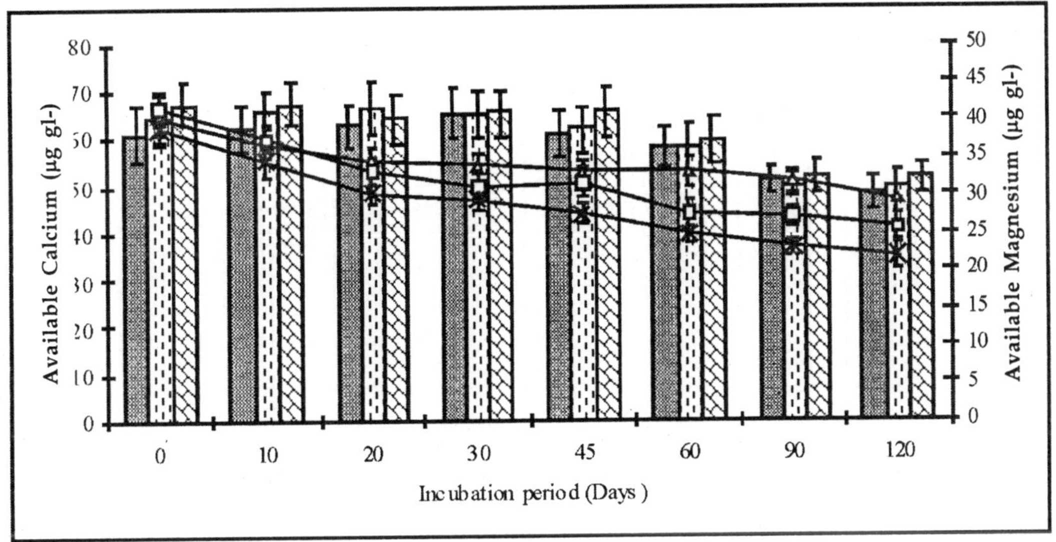

(c): Chhattarpur soil with 30% sludge

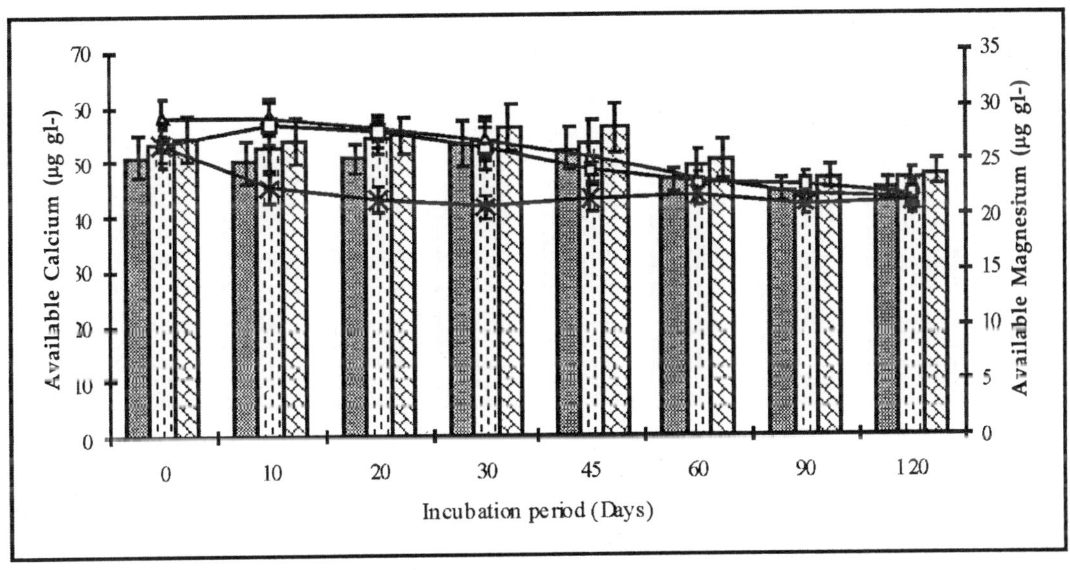

(d): JNU soil with 10% sludge

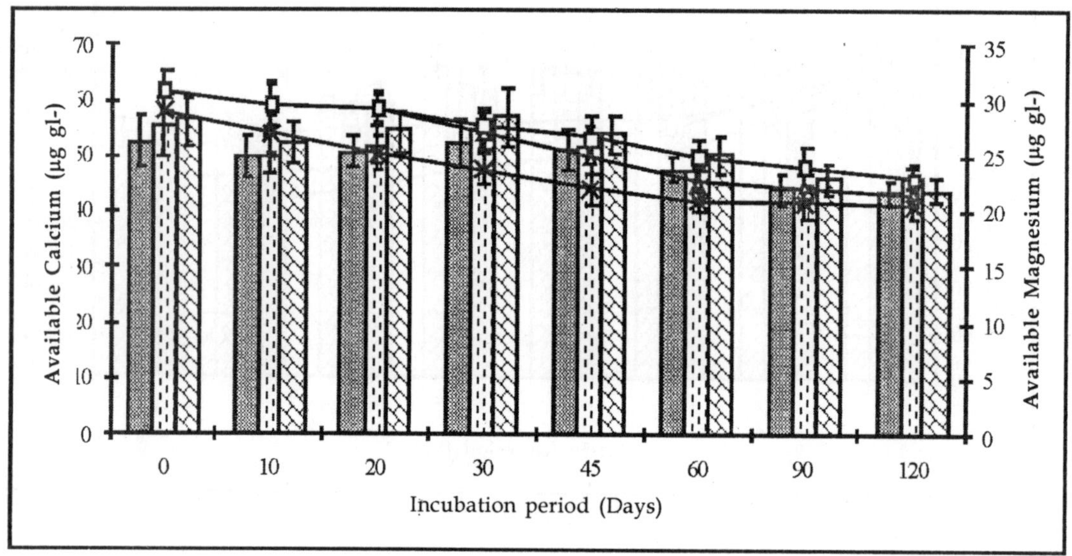

(e): JNU soil with 20% sludge

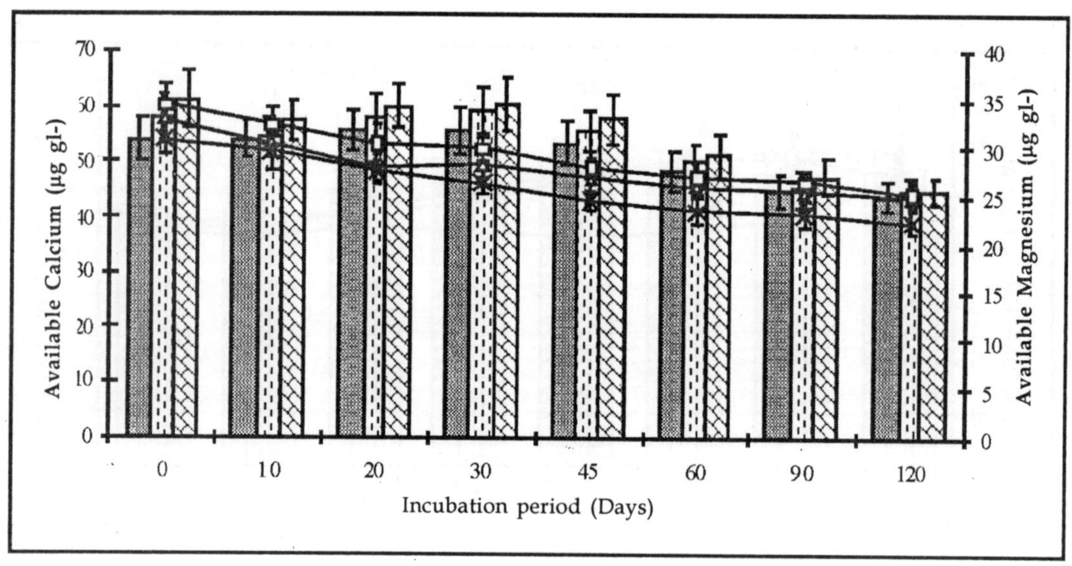

(f): JNU soil with 30% sludge

Conclusion

Both the calcium and magnesium in soils as well as the sludge were higher with higher CEC values. The present study showed that the concentrations of available calcium and magnesium increased with the increasing percentage of sludge application whereas the soil's pH balanced decreased with the sludge application. The concentrations of available calcium and magnesium

Table 4: Correlation coefficient (r) of various parameters studied in the different amendments of industrial sludge and soil, available calcium and magnesium in different days of incubation (mean ± sd).

	Ca	Mg	pH	OC	CEC
Chhattarpur Soil					
Ca	1.00				
Mg	0.52	1.00			
pH	-0.29	-0.34	1.00		
OC	0.09	0.19	-0.04	1.00	
CEC	0.83	0.39	-0.25	0.19	1.00
JNU Soil					
Ca	1.00				
Mg	0.60	1.00			
pH	-0.57	-0.60	1.00		
OC	0.47	0.04	-0.31	1.00	
CEC	0.72	0.55	-0.53	0.55	1.00

increased significantly ($p<0.05$) with both sludge and lime treatments (except 1% lime treatment) which indicated that calcium showed an antagonistic effect on magnesium. The concentrations of both calcium and magnesium also increased till 30 days of incubation and after that they the slightly decreased and got stabilized. The pH balanced showed a negative correlation ($R^2 > 0.7$) with available calcium and magnesium but CEC showed positive correlation. The present study indicated that 0.5% lime treated 10% sludge amendment can be a better option for safe land disposal of this kind of industrial sludge.

References

1. Adams, F. 1974. Soil solution. p. 441-481. In. E.W.Carson (ed) The plant root and environment. Univ. of Virginia Press, Charlottesville.

2. Alloway, B.J. 1995a. Heavy Metals in Soils, 2nd Edition. Blackie and Son Ltd, Glasgow, pp. 25-34

3. Alloway, B.J. 1995b. The Origins of Heavy Metals in Soils. In Alloway, B.J. (Ed.), Heavy Metals in Soils, second ed. Blackie Academic and Professional, Glasgow, pp. 38-57.

4. Bose, Sutapa, Bhattacharyya, A. K., 2007. Heavy metal accumulation in wheat plant grown in soil amended with industrial sludge. Chemosphere, 70 (2008) 1264–1272.

5. Bose, Sutapa, Rai, Vivek., Bhattacharyya, A. K., Ramanathan, A.L., 2007. Translocation of metals in pea plants grown on various amendment of electroplating industrial sludge. Bioresour. Technol. 2007 doi:10.1016/j.biotech.2007.08.020.

6. Bramryd, Impact of sewage sludge application on the long-term nutrient balance in acid soils of Scots pine (*Pinus sylvestris*, L.) forests, *Water Air Soil Pollut.* **140** (2002), pp. 381–399.

7. Chan. K.Y., Heenan, D.P., 1999. Lime induced loss of soil organic carbon and effect on aggregate stability. Soil Sci. Soc. Am. J. 63, 1841-1844.

8. Chaney, R.L. 1980. Health risk associated with toxic metal in municipal sludge. In: Bitton, G., Damron, B.L., Edds. G.T., Ann. Arbor Science, Ann Arbor, MI, USA, pp. 59-83.

9. Curtin, D. Smillie, G.W. 1995. Effects of incubation and pH on soil solution and CEC ratios. Soil Sci. Soc. Am. J. 59: 1006-1011.

10. Ferrier R.C., Edward A.C., Dutch J., Wolstenholme R., Mitchell D.S., Sewage sludge as a fertilizer of pole stage forests: short-term hydrochemical fluxes and foliar response, *Soil Use Manag.* **12** (1996), pp. 1–7.

11. Förstner, U., 1991, Interaction at the soil colloid – soil solution interface. in: G. H. Bolt et al., (Eds.), NATO ASI series, Kluwer Academic Publishers, Dordrecht, The Netherlands, pp. 543–582.

12. Franco-Hern_andez Olivia, Alba Natalia Mckelligan-Gonzalez, Ana Maria Lopez-Olguin, Fabiola Espinosa-Ceron, Eleazar Escamilla-Silva, Luc Dendooven. 2003. Dynamics of carbon, nitrogen and phosphorus in soil amended with irradiated, pasteurized and limed biosolids. Bioresource Technology 87, 93-102.

13. Hess, P. R., 1972. A Text Book of Soil Chemical Analysis, Chemical Publishing Co., Inc., New York, pp. 197–299.

14. Jackson A.P., Alloway B.J., 1991. The bioavailability of cadmium to lettuce and cabbage in. soils previously treated with sewage sludges. Plant and Soil 132, 179–186.

15. Jackson, M.L. 1973. Soil Chemical Analysis Ed. II. Printice Hall of India. New Delhi. Jacoby, E. 1961. Pl. Soil. 15:74.

16. Kinraids, T.B. Parker. 1987. Cation amelioration of aluminum toxicity in wheat. Plant Physiol. 84: 546-551.

31

Developing Orissa as an Eco-Tourism Destination A Case Study on Chilika Lagoon

DILIP KUMAR DAS

Introduction

The State Orissa is one of the very few states in India which has something to provide to each and every kind of tourist. The State is endowed with a culturally rich heritage, majestic monuments, beautiful beaches, sprawling Chilika Lake, captivating wildlife, exquisite handicraft, traditional tribes, classical and folk dances and music and above all, a hospitable and peace loving people.

The dynamic topographical and vegetational strength of Orissa have combined to extract some of the most stunning destinations in the state. The breathtaking beauty and sublimity of the flora and fauna of Orissa are enormously charming and enchanting.

The state is famous for the breeding of the Garihal crocodile, white Tiger, Olive redlay turtle etc. The state has a paradise of birds in Chilika Lagoon, which is the largest brackish water lake in Asia.

Objectives

- To study the Eco-Tourism potentials of Orissa.
- To study the concept of Eco-Tourism.
- To study the Eco-Tourism potential of Chilika Lagoon.
- To study the role played by different Organizations to develop Chilika as an Eco-Tourism destination.

Eco-Tourism in Orissa

Orissa's varying topography, from the wooded Eastern Ghats to the fertile river basin, has proven ideal for the evolution of compact and unique ecosystems, thereby creating such treasure troves of flora and fauna that even seem inviting to many migratory species of birds and reptiles.

With Eco-Tourism in Orissa, one will get to see all the shades of the diverse ecological system that reside within the state of Orissa. Eco-Tourism in Orissa may revolve around water bodies or beaches or national parks and wildlife sanctuaries alone or, it can be a combination of all these features that make Orissa such as enticing choice as a destination for eco travel and tours.

Orissa has a tremendous eco-tourism potential. Out of the total land mass, 37% is forest area. There are 18 sanctuaries and 2 National Parks along with the largest brackish water lake of Chilika, a Ramsar Site. The destination which can be developed as an eco-tourism destination and get financial assistance includes Chilika (the largest lake in Asia), Bhitar Kanika (the 2nd largest mangrove forest in India), Satkosia Gorge, Hirakud, Nrusingnath-Harishankar, Badrama (Ushakothi), Barbara Forest, Koraput and Deokund.

Major Eco-Tourism Destinations of Orissa

Bhitar Kanika National Park is famous for its second largest mangrove ecosystem. The bird sanctuary in **Chilika** (Asia's biggest brackish water lake) and the tiger reserve and waterfalls in the **Simlipal National Park** are an integral part of any eco tour of Orissa. The **Gharial Sanctuary at Tikarpada** and the Olive Ridley Sea Turtles in the **Gahirmatha turtle sanctuary** also feature on the list of avid nature watchers. The city wildlife **sanctuaries of Chandaka** and **Nandan Kanan** are a must visit for the lessons they teach in conservation and the revitalization of a species on the brink of extinction. Bhitar Kanika is the **second largest Mangrove ecosystem** in India and is so unique in its bio-diversity that it has become the focus of many conservation projects and a popular tourist destination for people in search of an adventurous and exciting challenge. Located on the deltas created by three rivers and the sea in the Kendrapara district of Orissa, Bhitar Kanika will leave you spellbound by its gloriously enchanting flora and fauna. Around **60 to 70 evergreen mangrove trees** are found in the region that gives the Bhitar Kanika Wildlife Sanctuary a distinct identity from the hundreds of wildlife sanctuaries and national parks that dot the land of diversity - India.

Spread over a staggering 672 sq km of area, the core area within the **Bhitar Kanika Wildlife Sanctuary** amounting to 145 sq km was declared as the **Bhitar Kanika National Park** in 1998 after the sanctuary status was bestowed on this unique ecosystem in 1975. On your tour to Bhitar Kanika, you will also get to see **170 species of birds also** including the eight magnificent subspecies of Kingfisher, Open billed Storks, Sea Eagles, Kites, Sand Pipers, Darters, Whistling Teals and Seagulls especially at the **Baga Gahana** in the Bhitar Kanika Wildlife Sanctuary.

The chief attractions from the animal world are the world famous **Olive Ridley Sea Turtles** that come to nest at **Gahirmatha**. The Crocodiles, King Cobra, Pythons, Wild Pigs, Rhesus Monkey, Sambars and Spotted Deer are other creatures that you can spot as you cut through the salty marshes that became the mangroves of India, the pride of our nation. Of the many islands in Bhitar Kanika Wildlife Sanctuary, **Dangmal** is the most prominent one that you can visit on your tour to Bhitar Kanika for its population of **salt-water crocodiles**.

Set amidst the **Chandaka Forests** in Khurda on 4.4 sq km of area, Nandan Kanan is an amalgamation of a **wildlife sanctuary, an animal zoo, a botanical garden,** has the **Kanjia Lake,**

amusement park and **nature trails**. There are some interesting trivia related to Nandan Kanan, Orissa. It happens to be the only zoo where a tigress checked in voluntarily in 1967 when tiger population was near extinction. Nandan Kanan also happens to be the first captive-breeding centre for Gharials and a sanctuary for white tigers that too were rescued from the brink of extinction. You too can see these endangered species on your tour to the Nandan Kanan in Orissa. Besides the **34 white tigers** that are thriving in captivity, there are other endangered species (68 in total) that are protected within the wildlife sanctuary and zoo in Nandan Kanan. These species include three species of **Indian Crocodiles, Asiatic Lion, Lion tailed Macaque, Nilgiri Langur, Indian Pangolin** and the **mouse deer**. There are several species of birds (81), fishes and reptiles within the wildlife sanctuary in Orissa that will keep you occupied on your tour to Nandan Kanan.

Spread over an area of 1435 sq km, **Gahirmatha Turtle Sanctuary** has been a preferred place for the Olive Ridley sea turtles that travel across oceans from as far as the South Pacific to breed on the sautéed sands of Gahirmatha. The Orissa State Government along with the sincere efforts of international and regional NGOs has been able to create a safe habitat for the giant turtles to prevent their extinction. This has been possible by adhering to strict legislature that bans the fishing trawlers and clamps down on the nearby industries. For Tikarpada's strategic location midway on the 22 km stretch of the world famous **Satkosia Gorge** makes it a popular tourist destination for wildlife and adventure sports enthusiasts. Tikarpada offers a stunning view of the Satkosia Gorge that is apt for **white water river rafting, fish angling, treks and game sighting**.

Tikarpada, on the **Satkosia Gorge**, offers a spectacular view of the stumbling, tumbling, crashing and splashing Mahanadi River as it cuts through the densely forested Eastern Ghats with sheer force and raw power on this 22 km stretch that is a haven for water sport's enthusiasts; Dry and moist **deciduous forests** interspersed with moist peninsular **Sal woods** make for the dense forest that house a compact eco-system of which humans are rarely a part. The Satkosia Sanctuary, accessible from Boudh and Nayagarh, is a stronghold of chiefly for the cat species - **tigers** and **leopards** with **elephants, guars, sambars, spotted deers, nilgai, choushingha, sloth bears and wild dogs** thrown in as preys. In Tikarpada, one can trail animals or visit the **Gharial** Sanctuary that was established to reintroduce the species in the Mahanadi River ecosystem and increase their numbers to an acceptable level. You can also check out the **crocodiles, freshwater turtles** and **snakes** at the Tikarpada Sanctuary.

Simlipal, about a 2,750-sq km expanse of forestland, in the Mayurbhanj district, is one of the most important wildlife parks not only in Orissa but also in India. Specially chosen to be one of the Tiger Reserves identified by Project Tiger to handle the onerous task of conserving India's fast depleting Tiger population, Simlipal has over 95 tigers. Within its bounds are elephants, mugger crocodiles and numerous reptiles abounding there. Over 230 species of birds have made their home amongst its forest and waterways. Apart from the wonderful wildlife, tourists get an excellent bonus of lush valleys and forestlands. The Barehipani Waterfall (399 meters) and Joranda Fall (150 meters) are worth visiting as are the mugger crocodiles at Jashipur, one of two entry points to Simlipal. The other one is Lulang, fully equipped with the Forest Lodge for Orissa Tourism.

Chilika Lagoon

It is the biggest lagoon on the Indian sub continent. The size of the lagoon fluctuates from 1165 sq. km in the rainy season to 904 sq. km in the summer. Fresh water runs from a fresh water basin around 32 rivers and saline water runs from the ocean and makes it brackish water, which supports an extraordinary productive eco-system.

The lake wintering site for presents itself as a 211 species of migratory birds from far Asia, including the Caspian Sea, Lake Baikal, and Siberia. The lagoon is also only one of the two lagoons of the world that is the home for the Irrawady dolphins, the other being Songkhala in Thailand.

Chilika Lagoon, being the "hotspot" of bio-diversity, is the largest brackish water Lagoon in the Indian Subcontinent, covering an area of 1100 sq. km. with an average length of about 64 km. and average width of 13.4 km. On account of its rich bio-diversity, the lagoon has been designated as a "Ramsar Site" in the year 1981. Chilka Lake is actually an estuarine lagoon shallow throughout its spread. The lake is connected to the sea by a 29 km. long irregular channel with several small sandy and empirical islands.

Its part freshwater and part saltwater character , very high productivity and the preserve of a variety of habitats in and around the lake allow the proliferation of an amazing number of species. Chilika is one of the terminuses on the migratory flyways and some of the largest congregations of aquatic birds in India can be seen here, particulaly in winter.

A brackshaw water lagoon that sprawls along the coast of Orrisa, Chilika attracts the largest concentration of migatory waterfowl found anywhere on the Indian sub continent. It is also famed for its fishrey resources. It harbours an assemblage of marine brackish water and fresh water biota, a number of which are now listed on the endangered, threatened and vulnerable categories. On account of its rich biodiversity Chilika was designéd as a Ramsar site in the year 1981. While the marsh tract of Nalabanda within the lake is a notified as a priority site for conservation and management by the Ministry of Environment and Forests, Government of India.

Role of Different Organisations to Promote/Restore Eco-Tourism in Chilika Lagoon

Different Governmental and Non Governmental Organizations in tandem with some international organizations are working for the conservation and preservation of the Chilika Lagoon, flora and fauna. The most prominent among them includes the Chilika Development Authority, Wetland International South Asia, Zoological Survey of India, National Remote Sensing Agency (Dept. of Space, Govt. of India) , Hyderabad, XIMB, Bhubaneswar, IITTM, Bhubaneswar etc.

Some of the major programmes included the Orientational Programme on Eco-Tourism for the boatmen at Satpada in sept 2001. The main objectives of the programme include

1. Enhance the knowledge of the boatmen as a tourist resource of Chilika.
2. To develop their skills in handling the tourists.
3. To create awareness for the wise use of lagoon resources.

The expected outcome of the programme was

The negative impact of tourism on lagoon will be minimised.

The environmental guideline will be followed by tourists and boatmen.

- Tourists will get correct information about the ecosystem of the lagoon including the Irrawady Dolphin and Birds.
- Tourist flow will increase to the lagoon so that the economical life of the people will be improved.

Tourist Arrivals in Orissa / Chilika

Year	Domestic	% Change	Foreign	% Change	Total	% Change
1998	28,61,788	1.2	33,101	(-) 5.6	28,94,889	1.1
1999	26,91,840	(-) 5.9	25,758	(-) 22.2	27,17,598	(-) 6.1
2000	28,88,392	7.3	23,723	(-) 7.9	29,12,115	7.2
2001	31,00,316	7.3	22,854	(-) 3.7	31,23,170	7.2
2002	34,13,352	10.1	23034	0.8	34,36,386	10.03
2003	37,01,250	8.4	25,020	8.6	37,26,270	8.4
2004	41,25,536	11.5	28,817	15.2	41,54,353	11.5
2005	46,32,976	12.3	33,310	15.6	46,66,286	12.3
2006	52,39,896	13.1	39,141	17.5	52,79,037	13.1
2007	59,44,890	13.4	41,880	7.0	59,86,770	13.4

Chilika (Barkul)	2,60,600	403	2,61,003	2,69,100	445	2,69,545	2,71,300	493	2,71,793
Chilika (Satapara)	84,880	790	85,670	95,390	814	96,204	1,33, 3,80	843	1,34,223

Sources: Dept. of tourism, Govt. of Orissa.

Orissa's Share in India Tourist Arrival

Year	India(in Nos.)	Orissa(in Nos.)	Share
2003	27,26,214	25,020	0.92
2004	34,57,477	28,817	0.83
2005	39,18,610	33,310	0.85
2006	44,47,167	39,141	0.88
2007	49,77,193(P)	41,880	0.84

Sources: Dept. of tourism, Govt. of Orissa

Conclusion

The travel and tourism sector has entered the take off stage and it is going to scale a great height in the near future. The eastern region, particularly Orissa, has emerged as a frontrunner in the growth chart. The tourism potential of the state of Orissa is very high, so it is growing every day, every month and every year with a steady pace. Keeping this in mind and the growth promise, the people of Orissa, travel agencies, tour operators and other tourism related organizations, including the Government should not be complacent. At a time when expansion looks assured in the travel and tourism sector, it calls for some hard thinking.

1. Has Orissa realized its optimum potential in this sector?
2. Has the State Government done enough in promoting eco-tourism in the state?
3. Has the private sector made an adequate contribution to develop eco-tourism in the State?
4. What are the priorities of the State Governments?
5. Has the Central Government extended a helping hand?

It does not need any serious analysis to say that despite their immense potential, Orissa, including all eastern regions, does not figure so prominently in the tourism map of India. Internationally, eastern India, particularly Orissa, is yet to make on a true mark on the number of domestic and foreign visitors (tourists) visiting Orissa but and its neighbouring state has been on the rise in the last few years. The rising trend may yield some satisfaction.

A comparison with other states and regions in India shows that the eastern region and particularly Orissa, has failed to measure up to its potential. Although there are several reasons for that, one of the main reasons being is that, while the other states are doing an all round publicity to attract tourists, Orissa is lagging behind in its visibility campaign. No doubts, this requires huge spending. The State Government has to take the lead. It must allocate a higher publicity budget to reach potential tourists and traveller from all over the world and lure them to put Orissa and other eastern regions on their itinerary.

It is correct to say that India has emerged recently as a prime destination for foreign tourists. There is no reason why Orissa will not get its due share in the tourism and travel sector. The state has a number of reasons to have a benefit in a location as well as a variety of destinations with availability advantages. Location wise, it is very near to Kolkata which is the gateway to the Asia Pacific Region and again it is the connecting point between the eastern and south Indian state. Destination wise, Orissa has the benefit of having monuments like Konark, Jagannath Temple, and the largest brackish water lake like the Chilika Lake, abundance of wildlife flora and fauna etc., Buddhism and Jainism monuments etc.

It is true that nearly ten years ago , the major cities of the state of Orissa were lagging behind in providing good tourist infrastructure but the situation has changed. Now Orissa can boast of several world class hotels, better roads and transport facilities (systems) along with its Information Technology and Telecommunications Network.

References

1. CDA, (2005), Monitoring Report.

2. Chilika Newsletter.

3. CWPRS, (1992), Mathematical Model Studies, Chilika Lake.

4. Das N. K., Das R.C. (1998), "Environmental Survey of Chilika" The pride of Wetland Heritage, Orissa Environment Society, Bhubaneswar.

5. Lenka S.K. (2002), "An approach to community based eco-tourism planning for Chilika Lagoon", Proceedings of International Workshop on Sustainable Development of Chilika Lagoon, 12-14 Dec'1998, CDA, Orissa.

6. Pattanaik, A.K., (2003), Photo diversity of Chilika lake, Utkal University, Orissa.

7. Statistical Bulletin, 2007, Department of Tourism, Government of Orissa.

8. www.orissatourism.gov.in Orissa Tourism Websites.

9. www.chilika.com websites.

32

Environmental Thermodynamics and Renewable Energy

Dr. Mukesh Kumar

Introduction

Mankind uses different forms of energy such as light, heat and electricity every day. Any natural phenomenon like creation, propagation and destruction is nothing but a change in the form of energy. Energy production, transformation, transport, and the end use have important impacts on the earth's environment. Our environment's twin components (matter and energy) are never independent, but complementary to each other interrelated through the famous Einstein relation : Energy = matter mass change × Velocity of light ^{2} ($E = MC^2$). It is the thermodynamics field of physics that describes and correlates the physical properties of macroscopic systems of matter and energy. A fundamental concept of thermodynamics is that of "system" vs. "surroundings". This concept is particularly important to us because "surroundings" is here synonymous with "environment.". The total behaviour of this system cannot be understood without reference to the surroundings, with which it may exchange both energy and matter. The state of an equilibrium system can be described in terms of such measurable properties as temperature, pressure, and volume , which are known as thermodynamic variables. Other variables , such as density specific heat, compressibility etc are required to produce a more complete description of a system and its relationship to its environment. When a macroscopic system moves from one state of equilibrium to another a thermodynamic process is said to take place. Some processes are reversible and irreversible. It is the laws of thermodynamics which not only govern the nature of all thermodynamic process but also place limits on them.

Thermo-dynamical Limit

The first law of thermodynamics simply expresses the fact that energy is always conserved. Any process must yield as much energy, albeit in different forms like heat, sound etc, as was put into it. Thus, the total number of calories in the useful and non-useful output produced by a machine must equal the input energy-also in calories-placed in the fuel tank.

The second law on the other hand is the very antithesis of conservation, since it expresses the impossibility of constructing a perpetual motion machine. It is the spontaneous creation of entropy or disorder that drives the process. Entropy is to consider it as an index of disorder or the absence of order. Disordered or high entropy states occur with the highest probability because there are relatively more ways to achieve them, so the total entropy of any system plus surroundings of any thermodynamically possible independent process always increases. Any such process does not require help from an outside energy source to be thermodynamically spontaneous. If the total entropy change for any thermodynamically possible process is negative, it is impossible in practice unless outside energy is brought to bear and any independent process that is possible must be thermodynamically spontaneous, which, in this sense, means any process that does not require help from an outside energy source. The second law states that in such a process the total entropy (of system plus surroundings) always increases. If the total entropy change for any conceivable process is negative, we can be sure that it is impossible in practice unless outside energy is brought to bear.

There is another index known as "free energy" which simultaneously incorporates both the energy and entropy of the system. Thermodynamically free energy refers to the amount of work that can be extracted from a system. Since the free energy of a fresh product is always more than its degradation products, so it turns out to be a convenient way to characterize all kinds of pollutants.

It is showing that all possible real processes are within the limits imposed by the laws of thermodynamics, and have some impact on the environment.

Renewable Energy and Thermodynamics

The development, basic need of mankind requires energy input. According to the first laws of thermodynamics, energy efficiency is defined in terms of a percentage of energy transferred for a useful purpose. The second law on the other hands limits the efficiency of all practical systems i.e. a 100% efficient practical system is not possible. Hence the input energy can be utilized in two ways :

- Work done : useful output
- Waste : useless output degraded environment

The waste can significantly increase the energy (i.e. temperature) of a portion of the environment, resulting in pollution. So there will always be some unwanted waste which contributes to environmental degradation. Hence it is worthless to discuss a totally pollution free environment. It does not mean that we can 't control environmental degradation, but what we can do is that we can minimize it to such an extent that it remains under the limit of tolerance and does not harm us. Hence a choice of energy resource can play a major role in minimizing environmental degradation because development is a basic need of mankind. A suitable choice of an energy resource must favor nature's thermodynamical equilibrium which is an indicator of a healthy environment. Today, energy resources such as coal, petroleum etc. which are limited, also cause environmental damage as a result of mining, shipping, processing etc. All this results in a disturbance in the thermodynamical equilibrium, causing various calamities like earthquakes, tsunamis etc. Not only has this energy demand of society been growing day by day either due to a rise in population or increasing per capita energy consumption, but it is as a result of an ever rising desire for a higher living standard.

In keeping with the above views, if we stress natural resources such as the sun, water, heat, wind, plant waste products etc, we can solve our problems of environmental degradation as well as our energy needs to a wider extent, because these natural resources are constantly replenished and will never run out. Therefore these resources are called renewable. Most of the renewable energy resources come directly or indirectly from the sun, which makes life possible on earth. The following table gives the principal sources of renewable energy :

Energy Source	**Principal Involvement**
Solar Energy	Manifested by the sun in the form of light and heat and its radiation can be converted to electricity on the basis of its photoelectric effect.
Wind Energy	Natural conditions of climate and geography due to the sun derive the wind, whose energy is captured with wind turbines.
Hydro Energy	Water is a product of evaporation caused by the wind and the sun's heat. Runoff from higher elevations to sea level can be used to generate electricity.
Biomass Energy	The rain and sunlight cause plants to grow. They decay and form biodegradable waste. Firewood, animal dung and biodegradable waste from cities and crop residue are the source of energy when these are burnt.
Geothermal Energy	Derived from hot dry rocks, magma, hot water springs, natural geysers, etc.
Ocean Energy	The temperature difference between the surface of the ocean and its depth caused by sunlight can be used also to produce electricity.

The choice of a renewable resource depends on its availability, technological appropriateness and socio-cultural acceptability. These resources are also important because they not only satisfy our demand for energy but also help in maintaining a thermodynamical equilibrium in the environment.

Hence renewable energy technologies are clean sources of energy that have a much lower environmental impact than conventional energy technologies.

Conclusion

The renewable energy seems to be the Energy for our next generation and provides energy security for us. The use of renewable energy as a thermodynamical entity in itself does not offer a solution but the integration of thermodynamics into renewable energy hinges on a limit of environmental impacts. It is concluded that the potential usefulness of renewable energy results in a substantial solution to environmental problems.

References

1. Anon. (1989). Energy and the environment, France: OECD-International Energy Agency.
2. Ibrahim Dincer, (2000). Thermodynamics, Energy and Environmental Impact, Energy Sources, 22:723–732.
3. Importance of Renewable source of energy, (2005). ICEDCO proceeding, 1.
4. Kumar Mukesh & Parashar, G.K. " Look at Energy for Sustainable Development in 21st century", Peace and Development Digest, Feb-April, 2002, 41-46.
5. Rosen, M. A., and Dincer, I.(1997). On energy and environmental impact. *Int. J. Energy Res.* 21: 643–654.
6. Saha M. N. and Srivastava B. N.(1950). A treatise on heat,The Indian Press, 3rd edition.
7. Wepfer,W. J., and Gaggioli, R.A. (1980). *Thermodynamics: Second law analysis*, ACS Symp. Ser. 122, Washington, DC, pp. 77–92.

33

Physico-chemical Analysis of the Wastewater from a Pulp and Paper Mill in the Tarai Area of Uttarakhand

AKANKSHA RASTOGI, VIR SINGH, UMA MELKANIA,
RK SRIVASTAVA AND ANITA SHARMA

Introduction

The rapid pace of industrialization that results in the generation of liquid, gaseous and solid waste is affecting and is bound to affect the quality of water. Water pollution is referred to as the degradation of the water quality as measured by the biological, chemical and physical criteria and it is one of the major concerns of humanity during the rapid process of industrialization, and this state of the environment is responsible for the major causes of most of the ills which humanity has to face. Water pollution is also set to cripple phenomenally the whole life on the planet in a number of ways which are already becoming more and more conspicuous.

The pulp and paper industry is the major industry of our country. At the same time it is also a major source of industrial pollution. It has been categorized as one of the twenty most polluting industries in India (Nampoothery and Sashidharan, 1976; Roald, 1977). The Ministry of Environment and Forest, Government of India, has categorized the pulp and paper industry as one of the most polluting industries (MOEF, 1998). The heavy demand for paper in the country is also necessitating the proliferation of this industry. In 1951, there were only 17 paper mills in the country producing 0.13 million tonnes of paper per annum. The number of paper mills has gone up to 106 in 2002, producing 1.9 million tones of paper per annum (Verma, 2004).

Our rivers, unfortunately, are getting increasingly polluted. This is a matter of great environmental concern. Polluted rivers are slowly poisoning the land, livestock and the human populations. The ill-health of the rivers amounts to the ill-health of the people. The continuous disposal of human excreta and industrial wastewater/ effluent directly into rivers and streams is the major cause of water pollution today.

The Gola river, having its origin in the Kumaun Himalayas, is a rain-fed river. Having flown into mountains for several kilometers, the river descends down into the plains where it

[1] Department of Microbiology

starts getting polluted due to rampant stone quarrying in the course of the river as well as due to the drainage of channels full of waste material into the river but, the major pollution load is contributed by the wastewater of the Lalkuan-based Century Pulp and Paper Mill. Ram Chandra *et al.* (2006) has revealed that after the confluence of the pulp and paper mill waste into the Gola River, it has produced 20–30 times the pollution load of BOD, COD, TDS, TSS, sulphate, chloride, sodium, nitrate, potassium, lignin and phenol after mixing with the pulp and paper mill waste with the river water in all seasons. Further, it has induced the bacterial growth by increasing the most probable number value of *E. coli* which was 1.57×10^4, 1.6×10^4, 1.37×10^4 and the SPC count was 1.68×10^4, 1.64×10^4, 1.67×10^4/100 ml during summer, monsoon and the winter respectively.

Flowing rivers are capable of purifying themselves and getting rid of a high degree of pollution load themselves. The purification process, however, depends on a number of factors, such as the speed of the water flow, the amount of the organic matter in the effluents, the nature of the chemicals and heavy metals present in the effluents, etc. When a river flows in mountain terrain, its speed is quite high and it ought to purify itself at a somewhat shorter distance than if it flows in the plains with a lesser speed.

The Gola river is drained with the wastewater from the pulp and paper mill in the plain areas where the speed of the river flow is very slow. Thus, the possibility of water purification with the passage of distance and time, is also very remote. The degree of the pollution, of course, is likely to be varying with the distance gradient. The pollution load at distance gradients in this small tributary of the Gola river has been studied through the evaluation of the physical-chemical properties of the water flowing into this tributary. An attempt has been made to provide mitigation measures of the water pollution also thanks to the contamination of the pulp and paper mill effluent.

Materials and Methods

Location of the Pulp and Paper Mill and Outlet of Wastewater

The Pulp and Paper Mill is located about eight kilometers northeast of the Pantnagar University at the township of Lalkuan (Uttarakhand). The wastewater of the mill flows out into a drainage channel locally called the Kichha Naala that passes through the villages of Bindu Khatta, Jawahar Nagar, Shantipuri, Anandpur, Kanakpur and Chhinki and finally, after covering about an 18 km distance, joins the river Gola. Before it merges into the Gola river, the Kichha Naala passes through green fields of the villages affecting crops, underground water sources and social life.

Sample Collection

The samples of water receiving effluent were collected in clean plastic containers. The first sample was collected from near the point of effluent discharge in the drainage channel. For the first five kilometer`s distance of the channel, samples were collected along the gradient of every half km. The subsequent samples were collected at every one km distance of the channel.

Physico-chemical Analysis

APHA (1995) and WHO (1996) recommendations were followed for analysing physico-chemical parameters of the water samples collected from different distances of the drainage channel outside the factory. The temperature of the water sample was recorded on the spot in ^{0}C with the help of a mercuric thermometer immediately after the collection of the sample. The pH balance of the water sample was measured by an electronic pH balance metre. The colour of the water sample was observed with naked eyes and compared with the standard colour chart.

The total suspended solids (TSS) were determined by centrifuging the weighed sample of water and then the sediments were dried off at 105^{0}C for 2 minutes to get the final weight. The following formula was used to determine the TSS:

TSS = [total sediments (mg)/total water sample (ml)] x 1000

The total dissolved solids (TDS) of the water samples were determined as the residue left after evaporation of the filtered sample. 100 ml of the sample was filtered through a Whatman No. 42 filter paper, and the filtrate was evaporated in a pre-weighed dish and dried to a constant weight at 180^{0}C. The increase in weight represented the total dissolved solids.

TDS (mg/l) = [(weight of dry residue, mg)/ (sample volume, ml)] x 1000

The conductivity of the water sample was determined with the help of a digital conductivity metre. The turbidity of the water sample was determined by the digital Nephloturbidity metre.

The dissolved oxygen (DO) of the water sample was determined by the DO metre. The biological oxygen demand (BOD) was measured by the Azide Modification of Iodometric method as described in APHA (1995). The chemical oxygen demand (COD) was measured according to the method described in Standard Methods for the Examination of Water and Wastewater (APHA 1995). The chloride content of the water samples was determined by Argenometric method as described by APHA (1995).

Results and Discussion

The quality of the water along with the gradient of the drainage channel with the load of polluting effluent from the Pulp and Paper Mill, as indicated by its physico-chemical characteristics, has been presented and discussed in this Chapter. Water samples during three consecutive months (February to April 2008) were collected from different sites of the channel. The first sample was taken from a few meters away from the point where the effluent is drained into the channel. For the first five kilometers' length of the effluent channel, samples were collected after every half kilometre. Then water samples were collected after every kilometre of the wastewater channel.

The wastewater samples were analysed for their physico-chemical characteristics in the laboratory of the Department of Environmental Science. The colour of the water carrying the pulp and paper mill effluent was noted down based on the visual perception at the site of the collection.The temperature of the collected water was immediately noted down. The dissolved oxygen (DO) was analysed within the first two hours of collection, just after the samples were brought to the laboratory. The results of all the physico-chemical parametres of the effluent-mixed water samples have been summarized in Table 1.

Colour

The colour of the water receiving the mill effluent was dark brown at the point of entry into the channel. This colour persists almost throughout the whole flow of the water in the channel. Foam in the water is seen near the origin, which is also witnessed at certain points where the water falls a few feet down on its journey along the channel. However, towards the last phase of the effluent-laden water along the gradient of the Kichhaa Naala, the colour of the water appears somewhat dark grey.

The dark brown to dark grey colour of the water receiving the mill effluent was due to heavy amounts of lignin that was extracted during the process of the pulp and paper making. The uses of dyes, bleaching agents, etc. are the other causes of this colour. The dark grey colour of the effluent-carrying water towards the last few kilometres of the channel before its finally getting drained into the Gola River might be due to a mixing of organic humus in the soil.

In many instances, colour is a quick and easy yardstick by which the pollution level is assessed. The major sources of coloured effluent are from textile, dyestuff industries, particularly where the process of bleaching, dying, printing and finishing in textile operations impart huge amounts of colour effluent. Besides these, industries, pulp and paper mill, sugar distilleries, tanneries, etc. also contribute to water pollution (Sharma and Kaur 2000).

Prakash (1975) stated that the organic colouring material in water stimulates the growth of many aquatic microorganisms, some of which are directly responsible for the production of odour in water. The WHO (1996) reported that colour in drinking water is usually due to the presence of coloured organic acids (humic and fulvic) associated with a humus fraction of soil and colour producing substances, which are not harmful to health.

Table 1: Physico-chemical analysis of channel water carrying pulp and paper mill with effluent pollution load.

Parameter	Unit	Range of value (min. - max.)	Average	S.D.
Temperature	^{0}C	15.6 – 25.2	19.04	0.540964
pH	value in no.	7.5 – 8.5	7.71	0.048297
Turbidity	NTU	34 - 298	83.5	1.159128
Conductivity	msm^{-3}	950 - 1185	1094.37	2.990419
Dissolved oxygen (DO)	Ppm	0 – 6.7	3.67	0.462663
Total suspended solids (TSS)	mgl^{-1}	395 - 580	428.33	13.01555
Total dissolved solids (TDS)	mgl^{-1}	1180 - 1460	1301.37	15.44847
Bio-chemical oxygen demand (BOD)	mgl^{-1}	65 – 300	154.65	15.72552
Chemical oxygen demand (COD)	mgl^{-1}	189-812	381.71	28.71882
Chloride	mgl^{-1}	128 - 686	294.67	37.45029

Temperature

Temperature is an indicator of the thermal pollution of water. Due to thermal pollution, many undesirable organisms start appearing and proliferating in water bodies, a situation that leads to the spoilage of the water quality and which ultimately seriously affects the aquatic life. The temperature of the water at the two sites near the points of receiving effluent was 23.1 and 24.5^{0}C. A stream with such a hot water might affect the micro-climate and also impact the physico-chemical characteristics as well as the aquatic environment of the main river, the Gola River.

The pH Balance (p German potenz-power. H Chemical Symbol for Hydrogen)

The pH balance value of the effluent channel water varied from 7.50 to 8.5. It means that the channel water receiving effluent was slightly alkaline. There is no specific trend in the pH balance values as we proceed from the point of origin to the point of meeting the channel with the Gola river. The pH balance value is one of the simplest and most important indicators of water quality. The pH balance value of water depends on the composition of the water and the nature of the construction material used in the water distribution system. The chemical composition of the effluent is also one of the critical factors affecting the pH balance value of the water. The nature of the chemicals used during the pulp and paper making is decisive of the pH balance value of the water in which mill effluent is received. Kumar (2007) has reported a pH balance value of 9.28 of the effluent from the same paper mill. This value suggests that the pulp and paper mill effluent before mixing into the water was highly alkaline. In our case, a lesser value of the pH balance value than 9.28 was attributable to the mixing of the effluent into the water of the channel. The WHO Working Group (1986) reported that the exposure of human beings to water with extreme pH balance values results in an irritation to the eyes, skin and mucous membranes.

Turbidity

Turbidity is the cloudiness or haziness of a fluid caused by individual particles (suspended solids) that are generally invisible to the naked eye, similar to smoke in the air. The measurement of turbidity is a key test of water quality. Fluids may contain suspended solid matter consisting of particles of many different sizes. Some suspended materials are large/ heavy enough to settle down rapidly in the bottom of a container if a liquid sample is left undisturbed (the settleable solids). Very small particles will settle only very slowly or not at all if the sample is regularly agitated or the particles are colloidal. These small solid particles cause the liquid to appear turbid (http://en.wikipedia.org/wiki/Turbidity). Turbidity varies from 52.8 NTU to 298 NTU. The highest value of the turbidity (298 NTU) was recorded near the site of the channel where the pulp and paper mill effluent get mixed with the channel water. Turbidity gives us an idea about the tolerance to hardness due to anionic surfactants, e.g., sodium dodecyl sulphate (SDS) and linear alkyl benzene sulphonate - sodium salt (LABS). The turbidity often varies linearly with the degree of hardness (ppm) of the water. This linear relationship between the turbidity and the hardness can be effectively used for the estimation of the hardness causing ions with good reproducibility (Homendra and Devi, 2004).

The higher the turbidity level, the higher the risk of developing gastrointestinal diseases in humans. This is especially problematic for immune-compromised people. Viruses and bacteria can become attached to the suspended solids. The suspended solids interfere with water disinfection with chlorine because the particles act as shields for the viruses and the bacteria. Similarly, suspended solids can protect bacteria from the UV sterilisation of water (http://en.wikipedia.org/wiki/Turbidity). A high turbidity level can block light from reaching the lower depth of water bodies, which can inhibit growth of submerged aquatic plants and subseq uently affect other species dependent on those plants, such as fish and other water species.

Electrical Conductivity (EC)

EC values of the channel water receiving pulp and paper mill effluent vary from 950 to 1209 ms/cm^3. At the point of entry of the effluent in the channel, the EC value was 1185 whereas towards the end of the channel before it merges with the Gola river, the EC value was 1183 ms/cm^3. Kumar (2007) has reported EC value of 1196 ms/cm^3 of the effluent from the same pulp and paper mill. Electrical conductivity is the manifestation of the dissolved salts and is an indicator of water pollution, which has been found pretty high in the present study indicating a high degree of water pollution due to pulp and paper mill effluents.

Dissolved Oxygen (DO)

DO is a vital indicator of the general health of an aquatic ecosystem. Extremely low or zero DO concentrations are indicative of aerobic conditions and reflect an imbalanced aquatic ecosystem which might be ghastly for the higher life-forms. Bad odour in the water and other aesthetic nuisances are other consequences of a low DO concentration in a water body.

The DO concentration in this study reveals that the pollution level at the sight where the effluent was fed into the channel was quite high. As the water got more diluted and proceeded on its journey, the oxygen went on dissolving in the water. At certain sites, the DO value was a bit higher as the water in the channel falls down with a greater speed helping more dissolution of oxygen in the water. However, in some of the sites, the speed of the water in the channel was quite slow which would not favour a higher DO value of the water. More DO value need not necessarily support an aquatic environment if the pollutant level is pretty high, which is evident from the fact that no fish or other aquatic forms were visible in the channel water.

Total Suspended Solids (TSS)

TSS is an important water quality measurement. It includes all particles suspended in water which will not pass through a filter. Suspended solids are present in sanitary waste water and many types of industrial wastewater. The TSS of the pulp and paper mill effluent before being received into the channel water was reported to be 5223 mgl^{-1} (Kumar 2007). Nemade and Srivastava (1997) have reported 610 to 1010 mgl^{-1} TSS of the effluent of the pulp and paper mill in the Satpura hills.

TSS figures in this study were lower than this which might be attributable to the dilution factor. Chakravarthi *et al.* (1995) and Singh *et al.* (1996) also reported higher TSS of the effluent from different pulp and paper mills (2790, 2670 mgl^{-1}, respectively), but Kamlakar *et al.* (1981) reported TSS of 170-200 mgl^{-1} of the effluent from a pulp and paper mill based in Lalkuan which is less compared with those obtained in this study. Earlier, Saxena *et al.* (1979) found that the TSS value of the effluent from the integrated pulp and paper mill was 503 mgl^{-1}, which corroborates with the figures obtained in this study. The variation, apart from other factors, might also be attributable to the inherent factors associated with pulp and paper manufacturing processes, such as the type and amount of the material used, etc.

Water with a TSS value over 150 mgl^{-1} usually appears dirty. As the TSS value increases, a water body begins to lose its ability to support a diversity of aquatic life. Suspended solids absorb heat from the sunlight which increases the water temperature and subsequently decreases the level of dissolved oxygen. Some cold water species such as trout are especially sensitive to changes in DO. Photosysnthesis also decreases since less light penetrates the water.

Total Dissolved Solids (TDS)

The term TDS denotes the inorganic salts, such as Ca, Mg, Na, and K cations and carbonate, chloride, sulphate and nitrate anions (WHO 1996). The WHO has specified the highest desirable value for total solids as 500 mg/ l in potable water. Higher value of TDS can be related with solid waste deposits.

TDS values vary from 1180 to 1460 mgl^{-1}. At the point where pulp and paper mill effluent is fed into the channel, the TDS value was 1460 mgl^{-1}. At 0.5 km, the TDS value was 1250. At 1.0 km the value increases to 1200 mgl^{-1}, which again decreases to 1180 at 1.5 km. In this way, the TDS near the point at which the channel merges with the Gola river was recorded to be 1399 mgl^{-1} at 18 km. The highest value of 1460 mgl^{-1} was recorded near the source. Before mixing in the water, the TDS of the pulp and paper mill at Lalkuan was found to be 7789 mgl^{-1} (Kumar 2007), which is many times higher than the figures derived in this study. Rao and Shruthi (2002) have reported TDS in water samples in the range of 620-690 mg/l in the river water of Hyderabad. Our values are higher than these values. Adak and Purohit (2001) reported 87.3 to 190 mg/l TDS in the surface and ground water quality status in Mandiakudar (Orissa). If we compare our values with these, a very serious nature of the water pollution due to the mixing of pulp and paper mill effluent in a water body comes to the fore.

Biochemical Oxygen Demand (BOD)

Water pollution by organic waste is measured in terms of the biochemical oxygen needed by bacteria in decomposing the organic waste present in the water. The BOD is a measure of oxygen required by aerobic decomposers for the biochemical degradation of organic materials (e.g., biodegradable materials) in water. It is expressed in mg of oxygen per litre of water. The higher value of the BOD indicates a low DO content of the water. Polluted water will continue to absorb oxygen for many months, and it is not practically feasible to determine this ultimate oxygen demand. Hence, the BOD of water during five days at 20^{0}C is generally taken as the standard demand, and it is about 68 percent of the total demand. A 10 day BOD is about 90 percent of the total demand.

Nemade and Srivastava (1997) recorded a BOD of 365 mgl^{-1} from the effluent of the pulp and paper mill in the Satpura hills, a figure which is comparable with that obtained in this study. Kamlakar *et al.* (1981), Chakravarthi *et al.* (1995), Singh *et al.* (1996), Baruah and Das (1998) and Kumar (2007) have studied the BOD of different pulp and paper mill effluent. Their values are also comparable. The type and amount of the raw material (plant biomass), overall organic matter load in a flowing water body, in addition to the DO value of the water, are the major factors affecting the BOD of a water body.

Chemical Oxygen Demand (COD)

This method offers a more complete estimate of the organic matter content. It is a better mode of measuring a pollution load in water. The COD is the measure of oxygen equivalent to the requirement for oxidation of the total organic matter present in water (Sharma, 2006). In other words, it is the measure of oxygen required to oxidize the organic matter, which cannot be oxidized by microorganisms due to its highly recalcitrant nature. Pollutant imparting colours also increase the COD and BOD (Kaphaliya, 2007).

The COD values reported in earlier publications can be compared with those obtained in this report. Kamlakar *et al.* (1981) have reported COD values of 3280 to 3296 mgl^{-1} of the Century Pulp and Paper Mill based at Lalkuan. These values are far higher than those of ours. Verma (2004) has cited 1200-3100 mgl^{-1} COD of paper mill effluent from the same pulp and paper mill. These figures are also higher than those reported in this research.

Chakravarthi *et al.* (1995) have shown a COD value of 3015 mgl^{-1} of the effluent from the Shri R.R. Paper Mill Nuzvid. Singh *et al.* (1996) and Baruah and Das (1998) estimated that the COD of the effluent of two pulp and paper mills, viz., Shreyans Paper Mill, Punjab and Naugaon Paper Mill Gauhati which were 580-805 and 680 mgl^{-1}, respectively. These figures are comparable with those being reported in this research work. Nemade and Srivastava (1997) have reported 798-1455 mgl^{-1} COD of the effluent of a pulp and paper mill in the Satpura hills. The lower side value is comparable with that of ours.

Lower values of COD in this study as compared with most of the other studies are perhaps due to the fact that in this case the effluent was mixed with channel water. The COD value depends on the organic matter as well as the inorganic matter present in a water body. The higher the COD than the BOD is attributable to this fact. The trend shows that as the effluent-fed water advances towards the Gola river, the COD values keep on decreasing. However, towards the terminal point, no difference in the COD was recorded.

Najafpour *et al.* (2006) have reported that the BOD of the effluent from a food canning industry was around 5100 mg/l and the COD was around 5000 mg/l. This high value of COD and BOD is because the industry is a fish canning industry and due to this, lots of organic matter is present in the wastewater which results in high BOD and COD values. The COD of the bakery industry as reported by Shin *et al.* (1990) was around 24000mg/l while that reported by Keenan and Sabelnikov (2000) for the same industry was 13400mg/l. These COD values are also higher than those reported in this work.

Chloride

Salts like carbonates, bicarbonates, chlorides, sulphates and nitrates of calcium, magnesium, sodium, potassium, iron and manganese, etc. are dissolved in natural waters. The high content of dissolved solids increases the density of water and influences osmoregulation of fresh water organisms. They reduce the solubility of gases (like oxygen) and the utility of water for drinking, irrigational and industrial purposes. Here, we have evaluated only chloride. The finding of chlorides is often used as an indicator of water pollution. Chlorine practically occurs in all waters and waste waters and is usually a major inorganic constituent. The discharge of agricultural, industrial and domestic waste water can contribute to the presence of chloride in natural waters.

The importance of chloride as an important anion has been pointed out by Mitra (1982). Krishna Murthy and Bharati (1997) studied the concentration of chloride in the river Kali in Karnataka at four different stations and observed low values of chloride during the winter months. Sahota and Gill (1997) noticed higher levels of chloride in a study of pollution levels in different rivers. Gupta *et al.* (2006) determined the concentration of chloride during his study of the pollution impact on the hydrobiology of the river Nakatia at Bareilly.

The chloride concentration values of the water samples from the pulp and paper mill effluent in our case are significantly higher than those reported in these studies carried out on less polluted rivers. Nemade and Srivastava (1997), however, found chloride concentration in the effluent from a pulp and paper mill in the Satpura hills ranging from 663 to 1385mgl^{-1}. The lower value of the chloride concentration in this case is comparable with some of our figures.

Comparison Between Wastewater and Inland Surface Water Standards

The physico-chemical characteristics of the water samples collected from the pulp and paper mill drainage channel were compared with the standards of values – the highest permissible values – so that the severity of the load of pollution in the water body in which the effluents are being poured, could be estimated.

Table 2: Physico-chemical parameters compared with those of inland surface water.

Parameter	Inland surface water*	Average values of Pulp and Paper Mill drainage channel water	Pollution status over standard figures
Total suspended solid (TSS) (mg/l)	100	1301.37	13 times more
Total Dissolved Solids (TDS) (mg/l)	2100	1301.37	Within range
pH balance Value	5.5-9.0	7.71	Within range
Temp.	shall not exceed 40ºC in any section	19.01	Within range
BOD (mg/l)	30	154.65	5 times more
COD (mg/l)	250	504.12	2 times more
Chlorides(mg/l)	1000	291.67	Within range

*Source: Garg (1996) based on CPCB (1995)

If the standard values of inland surface water, as provided by the Central Pollution Control Board (1995), as elaborated by Garg (1996), are compared with the average values determined in this study, then it was found that while the temperature, the pH balance value, the TDS and chloride values were within the prescribed range of the sample water from the pulp and paper mill drainage channel, then the COD was recorded of twice that of the permissible value. The BOD and TSS values of the water carrying effluent were recorded 5 to 13 times more than the prescribed higher limits of inland surface water, respectively (Table 2).

The TSS value of all of the samples from the drainage channel ranged from 395 to 580, which means that even the lowest TSS recorded along the gradient of the channel was about 4 times higher than the standard set for inland surface water.

References

1. Adak, M.D, and Purohit, K.M. 2001. Status of surface and ground water quality of Mandiakudar: Part I. Physico-chemical Parameters. J. Poll. Res. 20(1): 103-110.

2. APHA (American Public Health Association). 1995.Standard method for the examination of water and waste water. 17th Ed.Washington, DC.4: 4. 45-4.67.

3. Baruah, B.K. and Das, M. 1998. Paper mill effluents as health hazards to cattle and man: *Environment and Ecology* 16(1): 230-232.

4. Chakravarthi, K.R., Signan, M., Rao, K.S. 1995. A correclation study on physicio-chemical study of paper mill effluent, Nuzvid. *Indian J. of Environ. Prot.* 16: 46-49.

5. Garg, S.K. 1996. *Sewage Disposal and Air Pollution Engineering*. Khanna Publishers, Delhi.

6. Gupta, Neelima, Verma, V.K. and Gupta, D.K. 2006. Pollution impact on the hydrology of River Nakatia at Bareilly. In Kumar, A. (ed.) *Ecobiology of Polluted Waters*. Daya Publishing House, New Delhi, 82-90.

7. Homendra, Naorem and Devi, Ch. Indira. 2004. Turbidity studies on mixed surfactant systems in hard water: A new method for estimation of water hardness. *Indian Journal of Chemical Technology*, 11 (6): 783-786. http://en.wikipedia.org/wiki/Turbidity

8. Kamlakar, J.A., Sharma, D. and Melkania, U. 1981. Effect of paper and pulp effluents on the growth and development of maize and sunflower. *Ind. J. Environ. Studies* 8: 1-9.

9. Kaphaliya, Bhumija. 2007. *Assessment of Rotatory Biological Contactor (RBC) for Pollutant Removal from Effluent of Dabur India Limited*. M.Sc. Thesis. GB Pant University of Agriculture and Technology, Pantnagar.

10. Keenan and Sabelnikov, A. 2000. Biological augmentation eliminates grease and oil in Bakery wastewater. *Water Environment Research*, 72(2): 141-146.

11. Krishna Murthy, S.R. and Bharati, S.G. 1997. A study on concentration of chloride of the river Kali near Dandeli, Karnataka (India). *J. Environ. Poll.*, 4(1); 9-15.

34

Global Environmental Problems and Solutions

Mrs. Promila Kaushal

Introduction

Until recently, concern about the environment revolved almost exclusively around local and national problems. With globalization, these local problems have now transformed themselves into international issues. Over the past two decades, scientists have increasingly focussed attention on more far-reaching environmental threats, such as global warming, ozone depletion, acid rain, water and air pollution, hazardous waste, smog and rain forest destruction. These issues relate closely with each other physically and socially as well. Global warming, also known as the greenhouse effect, by far is the most important and globally discussed environmental issue. Another important environmental problem, is the depletion of the ozone layer mainly due to the excessive release of chlorofluorocarbons. Yet another important global environmental problem, which unlike other environmental problems is something which people do not think often about, is the generation of the large amount of hazardous waste. The formation of acid rain, mainly by airborne acidic pollutants is yet another major issue that demands immediate attention. There is also an environmental problem of smog, which in many areas around the world has reached extraordinary levels. The world today suffers, apart from these 5 major environmental problems, many more issues which will exacerbate if remedial measures are not taken in time and if this be done, there is no disputing the fact that our future generations will inherit a healthier and a happier earth.

Smog

We, as humans, can live a few days without food and water, but can live only a few minutes without air. The fact that an active adult inhales 10,000 to 20,000 liters of air each day, or 7 to 14 litres every minute, highlights a critical point in the fight for clean air. Smog is a kind of air pollution. The word smog is a combination of the words smoke and fog. The term was invented by a Glasgow public health official, Dr. Henry Antoine Des Voeux. Smog causes a smoky dark atmosphere to arise over cities. It decreases visibility, and creates a haze throughout the area. In many areas around the word, smog has reached extraordinary levels. Some governments have reacted quickly with severe measures in response to the problem. Classic smog results from large amounts of coal burning in an area and is caused by a mixture of smoke and sulfur dioxide. Modern smog does not usually come from coal but from vehicular and industrial emissions that are acted on in the atmosphere by sunlight to form secondary pollutants that also combine with the primary emissions to form photochemical smog.

Causes

Smog is caused by many factors. The smog that enters the atmosphere consists of over 100 chemicals, many coming from different sources. Particulates present in smog include carbon monoxide, dirt, soot, dust, and ozone. To create a real smog effect, sunlight, hydrocarbons, and nitrogen oxides have to mix together. Major producers of smog include automobiles, fires, waste treatment, oil production, industrial solvents, paints and coatings, car engines, especially diesel engines, as well as gas stations. Today, the smog problems created by cars are becoming increasingly severe. Numerous studies have monitored smog throughout the world. Some of the world's dirtiest cities have millions of inhabitants, all of whom are threatened by the smog. Modern Los Angeles suffers severely from smog, as London did in the 19th century. These two areas released certain chemicals into the air and created a foggy atmosphere. In London, fog levels have now fallen far below those of years ago. The Environmental Protection Agency now measures levels of smog and regulates smog producers.

Effects

Unlike other problems, which may be harder to understand and visualize, smog creates many immediate harmful health effects. It can cause anything from minor pain to deadly diseases such as lung cancer. The most acute effects of smog are related to the respiratory system. Some components of smog such as nitrogen dioxide, sulfur dioxide, and ground-level ozone are found to have caused damages to the mucociliary system responsible for cleaning the air tracts. As a result, the lung's ability to resist disease is reduced, and illnesses, such as bronchitis and emphysema, can be aggravated. Consequently, these air pollutants can not only decrease lung function, elasticity, and capacity by as much as 5%, but they can lead also to the premature aging of the lungs. The adverse effects of smog are not limited to humans alone. As it turns out, plants are perhaps more sensitive to air pollutants than humans. Entering leaves of plants from the stomata during normal gas exchange, both ground-level ozone and PAN can cause discoloration, damage, and loss of leaves-reducing photosynthesis by as much as 50%. Plants also become more vulnerable to attacks by pests, disease, and other environmental disasters. Consequently, the plant's ability to store food, grow, and reproduce is hindered. Yet, other damages can be seen including the corrosive effects of Sulfur dioxide on metal and stone, damaging machinery and industrial instruments as well as destroying buildings, statues, and monuments.

Solutions

Smog can be decreased by limiting those processes that create it. In countries where huge amounts of smog are produced, action is being taken to reduce smog levels.

Governments are combating smog in several ways. Laws are encouraging producers of automobiles to develop cars that produce less smog, and chemical companies are being watched over and restricted from producing certain harmful substances. In addition to national solutions which often deal with large plants that produce smog, local and individual efforts are underway as well. In Denver, Colorado, the second most polluted US city after Los Angeles, several innovative measures have been taken in an attempt to decrease smog. The government has requested that people not drive to work at least for one day a week, as well as encouraging the use of oxygenated fuels and experiments with fuels that create less smog. Los Angeles' city council came up with a long list of measures aimed at reducing smog. They decided to require carpooling, offer free bus services, and create many environmentally-friendly regulations for homes.

Global Warming

On June 23, 1988, James Hansen, the director of the Goddard Institute at NASA, told the Senate Committee on Energy and Natural Resources that global warming is a reality and it is extremely dangerous. Global warming, also known as the greenhouse effect, immediately received international attention. Scientists, environmentalists, and governments around the world took an interest in the subject. It is called the greenhouse effect because the gases that are gathering above the earth make the planet comparable to a greenhouse. By trapping heat near the surface of the earth, the greenhouse effect is warming the planet and threatening the environment. Current fears stem largely from the fact that global warming is occurring at such a rapid pace. Models are predicting that over the next century, the global temperature will rise by several degrees.

Causes

Global warming has a variety of causes. One of the largest factors contributing to global warming is the general problem of overpopulation and its many effects. The greater number of people consume more energy, drive more cars and create larger amounts of garbage. All these factors increase the global warming problem. Though having an atmosphere is important, the greenhouse effect may be making it excessively thick. The levels of gases covering the Earth have soared with industrialization and developed countries now produce about 75% of greenhouse gases. The most common gas is carbon dioxide, accounting for about 50% of all greenhouse gases. Other gases, including methane, CFCs, nitrogen oxides and ozone, also contributing to forming the greenhouse layer. Because these gases are produced by so many important and common processes, limiting their production to prevent global warming will be difficult. As the population increases and Third World countries begin to use greater amounts of energy, the problem may expand rather than contract.

Effects

To know just what the effects of global warming will be in the future is extremely difficult. Scientists use computer models to study the effects of global warming. These computer models have been fairly consistent in predicting general future trends, but often differ greatly when looking at the specifics. If temperatures do indeed rise significantly, the most important result would be that some portion of the polar icecaps would melt, raising global sea levels. The rise in sea levels would be disastrous for some places. Islands would disappear; meaning millions of inhabitants would have to relocate. Flooding would occur along coastlines all over the world, displacing more people and ruining cropland. Warmer sea surface temperatures will fuel more intense hurricanes. Forests, farms and cities will face troublesome new pests and more mosquito-borne diseases. Disruption of habitats such as coral reefs and alpine meadows could drive many plant and animal species to extinction. In the case of major global warming and melted icecaps, some countries might simply cease to exist. Global warming, if uncontrolled, could cause a major catastrophe.

Solutions

The threat of global warming is among the most important of all modern environmental problems. There are a variety of ways of dealing with it, each attempting to combat one of the many causes of global warming. The problems that cause global warming include overpopulation, deforestation, ozone depletion, garbage dumping, and many others. Certain laws and treaties are aimed at reducing the emission of pollutants that result in global warming. In 1988, the International Conference on the Changing Atmosphere drew scientists and decision makers from 48 countries. Taxing the emissions and encouraging people to take environmentally friendly action through activities as planting trees will help to combat the problem of global warming to a certain level. Education is a key method for reducing the greenhouse effect. Widespread media attention to the global warming problem is also increasing awareness. This is causing both individuals and governments to act more responsibly towards the environment.

Hazardous Waste

In addition to releasing gases and particles into the atmosphere, humans produce waste that is dumped on the environment. Often, this waste is hazardous and dangerous to both nature and human life. Industries and individuals continue to be largely unaware of this major environmental problem. The level of this dangerous waste is continuing to grow. Individuals often throw out goods without realizing that they are headed for a landfill and could be dangerous for the environment. No matter where people put these hazardous waste materials, there is always a chance that they could find their way into the ground, and eventually into our bodies. Unlike many other environmental problems, waste creation is something people do not often think about. In the future, people may have to reduce not only their generation of hazardous waste, but also their consumption of many products that end up in a landfill.

Causes

Hazardous waste is produced both on a huge scale by major industries and on a relatively tiny scale by individuals. No matter where it comes from, waste can be dangerous. One of the main causes of the abundance of hazardous waste is that people do not realize the problems associated with its disposal. It is simply removed and sent to a landfill and it is often assumed that the problem ends there. Industries have displayed quite often an unwillingness to find ways to deal with hazardous waste because of the expenses associated with it. Many industries and governments create crude landfill sites to store waste, and often just dump waste chemicals into nearby water bodies. Chemicals used for industrial processes often create dangerous forms of waste. The amount of these chemicals has risen heavily in the past, as the world entered the industrial revolution. Over 80,000 different chemicals are used in industries worldwide. Often, it is difficult and expensive to get rid of these chemicals and to store them in a way that does not endanger human life or the environment. Obviously, not all of these chemicals are dangerous, but many are and they do create serious problems. Around the world, hundreds of millions tons of hazardous waste are produced annually.

Effects

Every year, large amounts of hazardous waste cause increasing health problems. There are over 80,000 chemicals in existence, and many are used commonly in industrial processes. Insufficient research has been done to provide data on the effects of every chemical. Often, these chemicals mix together, and the combinations of these chemicals affect human health. To compound the problem created by a lack of knowledge, 1,500 new chemicals are invented every year and many are introduced into industrial processes. In 1989, a school in New Jersey had to be closed because students there had suffered excessive exposure to chromium. It was later learned that large amounts of chromium had been dumped nearby, and had blown over to the school area. Often, the lack of knowledge and uncertainty about which chemicals are dangerous reduces the possibilities of restricting their use.

Solutions

Hazardous waste has created many problems and dangers that have not gone unnoticed. Despite the fact that the problem receives less attention than many other environmental threats, some successful solutions to the problem of hazardous waste have been suggested and used. The hazardous waste can be controlled through input and output controls. The government can increase regulations on the disposal of hazardous waste to ensure that problems do not occur. It could limit the amount of waste industries are allowed to produce also or provide incentives to create less waste. After hazardous waste has been created, there are several actions that can be taken. Industries can break down chemical compounds into less dangerous forms, or store waste in ways that protect the environment from being exposed to the waste. Not only major industries but individuals as well must form a part of the solution. They can choose not to buy those products which require the production of hazardous waste, attempt to influence policymakers, and produce less hazardous waste themselves. Experts say that waste can be reduced by at least one-third using existing technologies and methods. Some countries, including many in Europe, are working to reduce waste levels. Rather than cleaning up or storing waste more carefully, one method of reducing the hazardous waste problem may be to simply stop producing much of it.

Acid Rain

The term acid rain refers to what scientists call acid deposition. "Acid rain" is a broad term referring to a mixture of wet and dry deposition (deposited material) from the atmosphere containing higher than normal amounts of nitric and sulfuric acids. Since the Industrial Revolution, emissions of sulfur dioxide and nitrogen oxides into the atmosphere have increased. Acid rain was first found in Manchester, England. In 1852, Smith found the relationship between

Typical hazardous wastes
generated by selected manufacturing industries

Wastes	Industry
Strong acids and bases Reactive waste Ignitable waste Discarded commercial chemical products	Chemistry
Tanning liquor and effluent treatment containing chromium Dyestuffs and pigments containing dangerous substances	Leather and textile
Paint waste containing heavy metals Strong acids and bases Cyanide waste Sludges containing heavy metals	Metal
Ignitable and corrosive waste Ink waste, including solvents and metals Photography waste with heavy metals solutions	Paper and printing
Heavy metal dusts and sludges Ignitable waste Solvents Strong acids and bases	Cleaning and cosmetic
Ignitable waste Spent solvents Paint waste	Furniture and wood
Paint waste Ignitable waste Spent solvents Acids and bases	Vehicle maintenance shops
Animal waste (not always hazardous) Cleaning waste CFCs (refrigerants)	Food and beverages

Sources: UACPA, 2002; Commission Decision 2001/118/EC on the European List of Wastes (2001).

acid rain and atmospheric pollution. Though acid rain was discovered in 1852, it wasn't until the late 1960s that scientists began widely observing and studying the phenomenon. Acid rain is caused mostly by emissions due to human activity of sulfur and nitrogen compounds which react in the atmosphere to produce acids. Acid rain moves easily, affecting locations far beyond those that let out the pollution. As a result, this global pollution issue causes great debates between countries that fight over polluting each other's envir onments. The levels of acid rain vary from region to region, e.g. Factory pollution from East Germany denuded the needles of the Fir Trees in the Black Forest in Southern Germany in 1981.

Wet Deposition: Wet deposition refers to acidic rain, fog, and snow. If the acid chemicals in the air are blown into areas where the weather is wet, the acids can fall to the ground in the form of rain, snow, fog, or mist. As this acidic water flows over and through the ground, it affects a variety of plants and animals. The strength of the effects depends on several factors, including how acidic the water is; the chemistry and buffering capacity of the soils involved; and the types of fish, trees, and other living things that rely on the water.

Dry Deposition: In areas where the weather is dry, the acid chemicals may become incorporated into dust or smoke and fall to the ground through dry deposition, sticking to the ground, buildings, homes, cars, and trees. Dry deposited gases and particles can be washed from these surfaces by rainstorms, leading to increased runoff. This runoff water makes the resulting mixture more acidic. About half of the acidity in the atmosphere falls back to earth through dry deposition.

Causes

For many years, there was considerable debate and disagreement over what caused acid rain. Recent scientific work, however, has helped to clarify this. The principal cause of acid rain is sulfur and nitrogen compounds from human sources, such as electricity generation, factories and motor vehicles. Coal power plants are one of the most polluting plants. The gases can be carried hundreds of kilometers in the atmosphere before they are converted to acids and deposited. Though human causes are primarily responsible for acid rain, natural causes exist as well. Fires, volcanic eruptions, bacterial decomposition and lightning also increase the amount of nitrogen oxide greatly on the planet. Once the tiny pollutant molecules have entered the atmosphere, they can travel for thousands of miles. Eventually, the particles will combine with other compounds to produce new, often harmful, chemicals. Acid rain comes down to the earth in the form of rain, snow, hail, fog, frost, or dew. Once it reaches the ground, the acidity in the substance can harm and even destroy both natural ecosystems and man-made products.

Effects

Acid rain is having harmful effects both on people and on the natural ecosystems of the world. Scientists today are convinced that acid rain is severe in many areas, and that it is having an adverse effect on the environments of those locations. The problem of acid rain is rapidly spreading because it is caused mainly by industrial processes, automobiles, and power plants, those countries that are developed have the most severe acid rain problems. However, as the undeveloped nations begin to industrialize, acid rain will increase greatly. Soil biology can be seriously damaged by acid rain. Some tropical microbes can consume acids quickly but other microbes are unable to tolerate low pH balance and are killed. The enzymes of these microbes are denatured by the acid. Acid rain can also cause damage to certain building materials and historical monuments. This is since the sulfuric acid in the rain reacts chemically with the calcium compounds in the stones (limestone, sandstone, marble and granite) to create gypsum, which then flakes off. Determining just how much the planet is being hurt by acid rain is very difficult because the ecosystems that it affects are so diverse and complex. Acid rain's effects are destructive and long lasting. Though scientists have studied lakes, streams, and many other natural ecosystems to prove its negative effects, acid rain continues to be produced and is increasing in many parts of the world.

Solutions

Modern science has proven that acid rain is a dangerous and highly destructive problem. As a result, various ways to limit acid rain have been invented, and some are now being used. Debate over acid rain and ways of preventing it have raged between environmentalists and corporations. There are many ways that power plant companies can reduce acid rain creation. They can use coal with a low sulfur content, they can remove the sulfur from smoke their plants release and they can limit processes known to generate high levels of acid rain. Policy makers and environmental experts are now looking into the best methods to limit acid rain. Environmentalists advocate the installation of sulfur cleaning scrubbers in factories, washing sulfur out of coal, and finding new methods of burning coal. Power plant operators are looking for less expensive solutions to the problem. Individuals can help by conserving energy or driving their cars less often. Governments can pass laws restricting pollution levels, or can use a variety of methods such as tradable emission permits to reduce acid rain.

Table 1. Showing The Greatst Contributes of Acid Rain

Air Pollutant	% that mobile sources contribute to Acid Rain	% that other sources contribute to Acid Rain
Volatile organic compound	37%	63%
Nitrogen oxide	49%	51%
Carbon monoxide	81%	19%
Particulate matter	27%	73%

Ozone Layer Depletion

Ozone, composed of three molecules of oxygen bonded together, forms a protective barrier in the Earth's upper atmosphere. The greatest concentration of ozone molecules, about 90 per cent of all found on the planet, is found about 15 miles (25 km) above the Earth's surface in the stratosphere. This concentration is what scientists refer to as the ozone layer. Ozone shields the Earth from harmful ultraviolet (UV) radiation that damages all living things on the planet. The decrease of stratospheric ozone was first reported in 1974 and the decrease was quickly linked to the increasing presence of a class of man-made compounds called CFC's or chlorofluorocarbons. Antarctica was an early victim of ozone destruction. A massive hole in the ozone layer right above Antarctica now threatens not only that continent, but many others that could be the victims of Antarctica's melting icecaps. Scientific models of the atmosphere are being constructed in order to assist scientists in looking for other factors in Ozone depletion, evaluate their importance and predict what may happen to our atmosphere in the future.

Causes

Only a few factors combine to create the problem of ozone layer depletion. The production and emission of CFCs (chlorofluorocarbons), is by far the leading cause. In recent decades, various human activities have released ozone-destroying chemicals into the atmosphere. Of particular importance are halogen atoms — chlorine and bromine. Chemicals released into the atmosphere by industrial practices include chlorocarbon compounds (such as CCl_4 and CH_3Cl_3), chlorofluorocarbon compounds, CFCs, (such as $CFCl_3$ and CF_2Cl_2), and halon compounds (such as CF_3Br and CF_2ClBr). Chlorocarbon compounds are used primarily as industrial solvents, degreasing compounds, and CFC precursors. The CFCs are used as working fluids in refrigeration and air conditioning systems, as foam-blowing agents, and — through the 1970s — as aerosol propellants. The halons are used as fire suppressants. Once in the stratosphere, all of these chlorine- or bromine-containing halocarbon compounds are broken apart by solar ultraviolet radiation, releasing their chlorine or bromine atoms to initiate ozone destruction. Each chlorine atom can initiate a cycle that can destroy up to 100,000 ozone molecules. Bromine atoms are even more efficient destroyers. Chlorofluorocarbons were first created in 1928 as non-toxic, non-flammable refrigerants, and were first produced commercially in the 1930's by DuPont. In 1974, Sherwood Rowland and Mario Molina followed the path of CFCs. Their research proved that CFCs were entering the atmosphere, and they concluded that 99% of all CFC molecules would end up in the stratosphere. Only in 1984, when the ozone layer hole was discovered over Antarctica, was the proof truly conclusive. At that point, it was hard to question the destructive capabilities of CFCs.

Effects

Even minor problems of ozone depletion can have major effects. Every time even a small amount of the ozone layer is lost, more ultraviolet light from the sun can reach the Earth. Every time 1% of the ozone layer is depleted, 2% more UV-B is able to reach the surface of the planet. UV-B increase is one of the most harmful consequences of ozone depletion because it can cause skin cancer. The increased cancer levels caused by exposure to this ultraviolet light could be enormous. The EPA estimates that 60 million Americans born by the year 2075 will get skin cancer because of ozone depletion. About one million of these people will die. In addition to cancer, some research shows that a decreased ozone layer will increase rates of malaria and other infectious diseases. According to the EPA, 17 million more cases of cataracts can also be expected. The environment will also be negatively affected by ozone depletion. The life cycles of plants will change, disrupting the food chain. Effects on animals will also be severe and are very difficult to foresee. Oceans will be hit hard as well. The most basic microscopic organisms such as plankton may not be able to survive. If that happened, it would mean that all of the other animals that are above plankton in the food chain would also die out. Other ecosystems such as forests and deserts will also be harmed. The planet's climate could also be affected by the depletion of the ozone layer. Wind patterns could change, resulting in climatic changes throughout the world.

Solutions

The discovery of the ozone depletion problem came as a great surprise. Now, action must be taken to ensure that the ozone layer is not destroyed. Because CFCs are so widespread and used in such a great variety of products, limiting their use is hard. Also, since many products already contain components that use CFCs, it would be difficult if not impossible to eliminate those

CFCs already in existence. The CFC problem may be hard to solve because there are already great quantities of CFCs in the environment. CFCs would remain in the stratosphere for another 100 years even if none were ever produced again. Despite the difficulties, international action has been taken to limit CFCs. With the depletion of the ozone hole and the potential for further extensive damage, the global community came together to craft a policy solution. The United Nations Environment Programme convened international negotiations to protect the ozone layer. This series of meetings to study and develop solutions to the ozone problem resulted in overcoming major obstacles and developing concrete goals and actions for phasing out the ODS (Ozone Depleting Substances). In addition, the policy developments that occurred as a result of the Montreal Protocol blazed a path for technological improvements to develop ozone-friendly chemical substitutes and processes. The Montreal Protocol on Substances that Deplete the Ozone Layer was created under the Convention for the Protection of the Ozone Layer. On January 1, 1989 the Protocol became effective, having been ratified by 29 countries representing 82 percent of the world's consumption. As of December 2002 a total of 184 countries have ratified the 1987 Protocol.

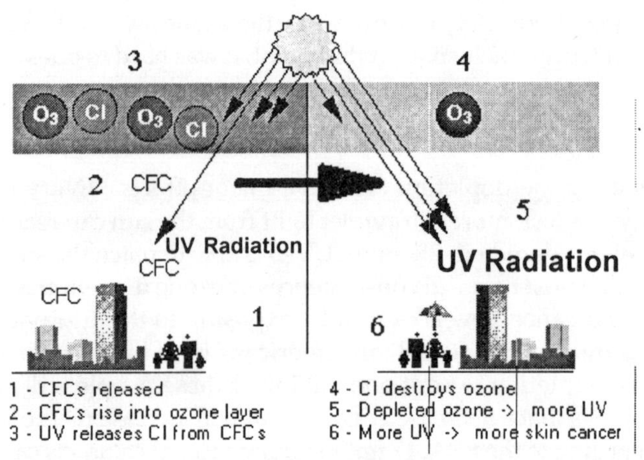

Conclusion

Concerns about the deteriorating global environment and its long-range implications have become a major issue now. Better technologies are required almost always for communities to make a transition to a healthier environment. But "better" technologies do not necessarily have to be "high-tech" or costly. Better technologies are those that allow a country to prevent environmental deterioration, rather than to contend with its consequences. Responsibility for managing the global environmental problems ultimately rests in the hands of the various governments, businesses, scientific bodies and communities themselves. With improved understanding of the global environmental issues and a suitable set of laws and regulations, most nations will be able to overcome these problems. It is time to act now otherwise the dawn of technology will lead to the sunset of humankind.

References

1. Global Environmental Governance, Foundations of Contemporary Environmental Studies, James Speth, Peter Haas.

2. Miller, Jr., George Tyler (2002). Living in the Environment: Principles, Connections, and Solutions (12th Edition). Belmont: The Thomson Corporation, p. 423.

3. Owen B. Toon and Richard P. Turco, "Polar Stratospheric Clouds and Ozone Depletion," Scientific American (June 1991).

4. Rodhe, H., et. al. "The Global Distribution of Acidifying Wet Deposition." Environmental Science & Technology. v. 36 no. 20 (October) p. 4382-8.

5. Seinfeld, John H.; Pandis, Spyros N (1998). Atmospheric Chemistry and Physics - From Air Pollution to Climate Change. John Wiley and Sons, Inc.

6. World Meteorological Organization, Scientific Assessment of Ozone Depletion: 1994 (Global Ozone Research and Monitoring Project - Report No. 37, Geneva, Switzerland, 1995).

35

Electrocoagulation and Caaco Reactor for the Treatment of Domestic Wastewater

S. Ambika and Dr. G. Sekaran

Introduction

Wastewater generation and its management have become vital issues in sustainable development. In India, according to the CPCB, 2006 report, the per capita water consumption is from 200 to 300 lit per day. It is estimated that 22,900 million lit per day (MLD) of domestic wastewater is generated from urban centres, against 13,500 MLD industrial wastewater generations. As per the updated status, out of 22,900 mld of wastewater generated, only about 5,900 mld (26%) is treated before letting out, the rest i.e., 17,100 mld is disposed of untreated.

Twenty-seven cities only have primary treatment facilities and forty-nine have primary and secondary treatment facilities. The level of treatment available in cities with existing treatment plants in terms of sewage being treated, varies from 2.5% to 89% of the sewage generated. Treated or partly treated or untreated wastewater is disposed of into natural drains joining rivers or lakes or used on land for irrigation/ fodder cultivation or disposed of into the sea or a combination of these by the municipalities. The mode of disposal in 118 cities is indirectly but ultimately into the rivers/ lakes/ ponds/ creeks; in 63 cities to the agricultural land; in 41 cities directly into rivers and in 44 cities, it is discharged both into rivers and on to agricultural land.

The conventional technologies generally followed in India for the treatment of domestic wastewater consist of many combinations of primary, secondary and tertiary treatment unit operations (CPCB, 2001). Among them, the best combination has been able to achieve a substantial reduction in dissolved organics (BOD, COD) but the absolute removal of bacteria is impossible. In certain instances, it has been observed that pathogenic microorganisms have multiplied during wastewater treatment processes rather than decreasing in concentration and thus the treated wastewater still contains a significant number of enteric bacteria (Koivunen et al., 2003).

Source of Domestic Wastewater

The samples used in this present study were carried out from the Central Treatment Plant in the Central Leather Research Institute at Adyar in Chennai-20. The fresh samples were collected daily in the early morning for analysis and an operational purpose. The wastewater was screened to remove the floatable solids. It was allowed to stand for a few minutes to remove the grit particles. Experimental studies were carried out as per Standard Methods for the Examination of Water and Wastewater as laid down by the 18th ed. American Water Works Association and the Water Pollution Control Federation and the characteristics of raw wastewater in this present study are as shown in Table 1.

Table1: Raw Waste Water Characteristics.

S.No	Parameters	Range
1	pH	7.200-7.555
2	Total Alkalinity	220-230 mg/l as $CaCO_3$
3	HCO_3	110-120 mg/l as $CaCO_3$
4	COD	736-808 mg/l
5	BOD	250-270 mg/l
6	TOC	367-380 mg/l
7	Sulphate	114-148 mg/l
8	Sulphide	16-24 mg/l
9	Total Solids	1100-1200 mg/l
10	Dissolved Solids	990-1100 mg/l
11	Suspended Solids	100-110 mg/l
12	VFA	115-126 mg/l
13	Total count	30 – 120 x 10^7 CFU

Designing of Unit Process

Electrocoagulation

A rectangular rigid – polyethylene container was used as the electrocoagulation unit (EC) in this study. Cathodes and anodes were made of iron and the anode had a diameter of 6 cm and a length of 13 cm while the cathode was a hollow rectangular container having a thickness of 2mm with an external length and breadth of 13.2 and 13.4cm. A volume of 2.6 litres of wastewater was fed to the reactor for the electrocoagulation process. Direct current power supply was connected to the electrodes. The system permitted the monitoring of the electrical parameters i.e voltage and current density provided. Air supply was provided using an air compressor.

Dual Media Sand Filter

A dual media sand filter (DMSF/SF) with a diameter of 13 cm and a height of about 40 cm was used. It consisted of a 2.5 cm layer of gravel (diameter 10 mm) separated by a 2.5 cm layer of gravel (diameter 5 mm) and was followed by a 10 cm layer of coarse sand (diameter 1 mm) 10 cm layer of medium sand (diameter 0.6 mm) and a 5 cm layer of granular activated carbon (diameter 3 mm), avoid ratio of about 0.75. The top of the sand filter was closed to create sufficient pressure to filter the water. The electrocoagulated sample was distributed onto the surface of the top gravel layer through a polyurethane tube (inner diameter 8 mm) perforated with holes of 0.8mm diameter. The filtered wastewater was collected from the outlet provided at the bottom. This dual media sand filter was used as a pretreatment for the CAACO reactor.

Caaco Reactor

The reactor used in this study had a total volume of 5.31 lit and a working volume of 4 lit, with dimensions of a 13 cm diameter and a height of 40 cm. It consisted of a 5 cm layer of gravel (diameter 10 mm) separated by a 6 cm layer of gravel (diameter 5 mm). A layer of coarse sand (diameter 5 mm) of depth 7 cm was placed inside. The reactor was filled with mesoporous activated carbon to a bed height of 4 cm. The size of the carrier particles and dimensions of the CAACO reactor used in this study were arbitrarily chosen for the ease of operation. The oxygen required for the oxidation of organics in wastewater was supplied in the form of air through an air diffuser placed in the carbon bed at a pressure of 0.6 kg/cm^2. The dual sand filtered sewage was distributed onto the surface of the carbon bed via a Polyurethane tube (8 mm) perforated with 4mm diameter holes. The sand filtered sewage was fed to the distributor using a peristaltic pump (Watson Marlow). Treated sewage was drained from the base of the filter through a 5 mm wide slit which was open to the atmosphere. The immobilized cell reactor was cleansed by pumping at least two void volumes of sand filtered water before each sewage sample was tested. One void volume of treated wastewater was discarded during the test run. Two types of carbon i.e. coconut shell and rice husk carbon had been used in this experiment and it was prepared in the CLRI laboratory through a phosphoric acid activation as reported elsewhere (John Kennedy et al., 2005). Both the carbons were sieved to the size of 600 ì. The characteristics of rice husk and coconut shell carbon are in (Table 2 and 3). Mesoporous activated carbon was used as the carrier matrix for the immobilization of the Bacteria. Carbon of 600 ì size was placed into the raw wastewater which was free from suspended solids. Immobilized cells were examined by scanning the electron microscopy (SEM).

Table 2: Characteristics of Rice Husk Activated Carbon.

S.No	Parameters	Values
1	Carbon (%)	48.45
2	Hydrogen (%)	0.7
3	Nitrogen (%)	0.1
4	Ash content (%)	42.61
5	Bulk density (gm/ml)	0.405
6	Moisture content (%)	3.8
7	Ash content (% by mass)	40
8	Matter soluble in water (%)	0.428
9	Matter soluble in acid (%)	3.908
10	pH	6.66
11	Decolorizing powder (mg/g)	52

S.No	Parameters	Values
12	Phenol number (mg/g)	3.18
13	Ion exchange capacity (meq/g)	0.015
14	Surface area BET (m^2/g)	420

Table 3: Characteristics of Coconut Shell Activated Carbon.

S.No	Parameters	Values
1	Ash content (%)	3.0
2	Bulk density (gm/ml)	0.565
3	Moisture content (%)	14.5
4	Methylene Blue (mg/g)	1.203
5	Iodine Value	0.094
6	Apparent density (g/cc)	0.743
7	Specific bulk volume (ml/g)	1.769
8	Phenol number (mg/g)	0.025
9	Specific void volume (ml/g)	0.636
10	Void volume (ml)	4.5

Performance Study of Unit Process

Electro Coagulation

In the electro chemical cell, the reduction (at anode) of metal ions forms new centres for larger, stable, insoluble complexes that precipitate as complex metal ions. This technology removes metals, colloidal solids and particles, and soluble inorganic pollutants from aqueous media by introducing highly charged polymeric metal hydroxide species. These species neutralize the electrostatic charges on suspended solids and oil droplets to facilitate the agglomeration or coagulation and the resultant separation from the aqueous phase. The treatment prompts the precipitation of certain metals and salts.

Effect of Current

EC is a complicated process involving many chemical and physical phenomena that use consumable electrodes to supply ions into the wastewater stream. The oxidation becomes stable at the point of current. The effect of the current had been studied by varying the current from 0.1 – 0.4 A, keeping the voltage constant and the relationship drawn from the obtained experimental values. The optimum reduction of COD and BOD was attained at the current of 0.2 A.

Effect of Voltage

The increment in the applied potential increased the speed of exchange of the electrons and it accelerated the reaction of the oxidation of the biodegradable organic matter. The nature of wastewater decided the optimum voltage required for its treatment. In this study. It is clearly indicated that at 5 V, the optimum reduction of both COD and BOD was obtained.

Effect of Reaction Time

As the reaction time increased, the current destabilized more dissolved colloidal particles and altered the charge on suspended particles permitting their coagulation, floatation and separation. Here the experiment was conducted for different time intervals, at a constant current of 0.2A and a voltage of 5V, and from that we got the optimum reaction time as 15 min.

Dual Media Sand Filter

The objective of using a DMSF for this present study was to remove the suspended solids from the electrocoagulated effluent so that clogging of the CAACO reactor was avoided.

Optimization of Flow Rate

The flow rate of effluent applied to the DMSF was arbitrarily fixed on the basis of ease of operation. The increase in the flow rate of wastewater from 10 $l/m^2/h$ to 100 $l/m^2/h$ to the filter decreased the contact time and the contact area. Here, for this dual media sand filter, shows how the removal of suspended solids was decreased from 88% to 60%, as the flow rate increased from 10 $l/m^2/h$ to 100 $l/m^2/h$ and the optimum flow rate was taken as 40 $l/m^2/h$.

Caaco Reactor

The CAACO reactor is a hybrid system having biological and chemical oxidations integrated in a single reactor packed with an activated carbon based catalyst of a low surface area. The CAACO reactor has the basic feature that the bacteria is immobilized in a carbon matrix. This system has been abbreviated as CAACO because it involves the immobilization of Chemo Autotrophic Bacteria (which uses sulphate as the energy source) in activated carbon & uses oxygen for oxidation of organics in the wastewater.

Effect of Bed Height

The bed heights were employed as 4, 8, 12 cm and the percentage removal of BOD and COD were increased with the bed height. This may be due to having more contact time and contact area. As the contact area increases, the exchange of degradable solids to the voids of carbon increase and result in a further oxidative destabilization. As the biodegradable solids increase the more will be the reduction of COD and BOD.

Effect of Flow Rate

It is known that as the flow rate (Q) increases, the water velocity through voids in the carbon bed reduces the exchange between the carbon particles and the mobile water. This affords a more intimate and longer contact time between the media and bacteria in the wastewater leading to an enhanced bacterial adsorption and a higher purification. Because of the decrement in the flow rate, the efficient removal of both COD and BOD had been attained, because of an increment in the contact time. As the flow rate was increased from 130 ml/h to 530 ml/h, the percentage removal of COD and BOD were decreased for all the three carbons.

Performance Evaluation of Mode

From the performance evaluation study of unit processes, it was taken that the flow rate for the DMSF as 40 l/m²/h, optimum voltage, current and reaction time was kept as 5V, 0.2A and 15 min for the electro coagulation unit and the flow rate with the bed height was kept as at 130 ml/h, 12 cm for CAACO reactor, and varying the carbon nature of the CAACO reactor, this experimental study was evaluated.

Effect of Caaco Carbon Nature

The electrocoagulated and sand filtered effluent was collected and passed through the CAACO reactor at a flow rate of 130 ml/h through a bed height of 12 cm for rice husk activated carbon (RH) and coconut shell activated carbon (CS) and a mix of these two carbons (MXD). This mode removed 98.899% of COD, 99.988% of BOD and 99.977% of bacteria for coconut shell carbon, 98.957% of COD, 99.999% of BOD, 99.988% of bacteria for mixed carbon, 98.989% COD, 100% BOD and 99.998% bacteria for rice husk carbon. The COD remaining in wastewater was reduced to 32 mg/l and 24 mg/l and 16 mg/l from 792 mg/l of raw wastewater for the coconut shell, mixed and rice husk carbon. Electrocoagulation removed 56% of COD and 54% of BOD the DMSF removed 30% of COD and 33% of BOD.

References

1. CPCB, 2001. Inspection of sewage treatment plants in Uttranchal, Uttar Pradesh, Bihar and West Bengal. Report of Central Pollution Control Board submitted to the Honorable Supreme Court of India.

2. CPCB, 2006. Report of Central Pollution Control Board submitted to the Honorable Supreme Court of India.

3. John kennedy, L., Mohan Das, M., Sekaran, G., 2004. Integrated biological and catalytic oxidation of organics/inorganics in tannery wastewater by rice husk based mesoporous activated carbon—Bacillussp. Carbon 42, 2399–2407.

4. Koivunen, J., Siitonen, A., Heiononen-Tanski, H., 2003. Elimination of enteric bacteria in biological-chemical wastewater treatment and tertiary filtration units. Water Research 37, 690–698.

5. Kumar, A. G., Sekaran, G., Swarnalatha, S., Rao, B. P. (2005) ,Immobilized reactor for rapid destruction of recalcitrant organics and inorganics in tannery wastewater. Journal of Environmental Sciences, 2005 (Vol. 17) (No. 4) 681-685.

6. Sekaran. G, K. Ramani, A. Ganesh Kumar, B. Ravindran, L. John Kennedy and A. Gnanamani, Oxidative destabilization of dissolved organics and E. coli in domestic wastewater through immobilized cell reactor system. Journal of Environmental Management, Volume 84, Issue 2, July 2007, Pages 123-133.

7. Sekaran, G., Gnanamani, A., Ganeshkumar, A., Shanmugasundaram,K.A., Rajamani, S., Ramasami, T., 2001. Tunable aerobic technology for treatment of wastewater discharge from industries. Environmental Pollution Control Journal 5 (1), 32–37.

36

Prolactin and Cortisol As Biomarkers in Ammonium Sulphate Induced Toxicity on *Catla Catla*

MATHAN RAMESH, CHOKKALINGAM KAVITHA AND YSUDAS THANGAM

Introduction

Ammonia is the principal nitrogenous waste produced by fish (Russo, 1985; De Croux *et al.*, 2004) and may become a limiting factor for the growth and even the survival in intestine culture systems using high densities of fish and restricted water exchanges (De Croux *et al.*, 2004). Ammonia is the main end product of nitrogen's metabolism in teleost (Foster and Goldstein, 1969; Foss *et al.*, 2004), and most teleost fish are highly sensitive to ammonia toxicity (Handy and Poxton, 1993). Ammonia can significantly reduce growth, and can adversely affect different organs and functions (Linton *et al.*, 1997; Foss *et al.*, 2003 a, b, 2004; Lemarie *et al.*, 2004). Stress effects in teleost fish have been classified as primary and secondary.The primary affect the centre of the neuroendocrine changes that appear at the systemic level; secondary effects often follow neuroendocrine stimulation (Mazeaud and Mazeaud, 1981). Stress stimulates the secretion of pituitary hormones as prolactin and adrenocorticotropin (ACTH) and is formed and as a result the ACTH stimulates the synthesis and release of cortisol, the major corticosteroid formed from the interrenal cells in fish. The secretion of the steroid hormone cortisol by the interrenal tissue is a characteristic reaction of teleost fish to almost all forms of environmental stress (Donaldson, 1981) and it is a key hormone mediating many compensatory morphological and physiological adjustments in stressed fish. Prolactin with cortisol is one of the main osmoregulatory hormones in fish maintaining the plasma electrolyte levels mainly by controlling the permeability of the gill epithelium (Clark and Bern, 1980). These hormones can be altered by exposure to xenobiotic chemicals and the alteration of circulating levels of hormones can provide information on the acute and sublethal effects of many chemicals. Hence in the present study, an attempt has been made to investigate whether these hormones can be used as biomarkers to primary stress effects caused by ammonium sulphate toxicity.

Materials and Methods

Specimens of *Catla catla*, a fresh water fish belonging to the family cyprinidae (Hamilton) of either sex were selected for the present study. Specimens of *Catla catla* (average weight of 6.5g and 7.8cm length) were procured from the Tamil Nadu Fisheries Development Corporation Ltd., (Bhavani sagar, Tamil Nadu, India) and stocked in a large cement tank (6′ x 4′ 3′) disinfected with potassium permanganate and washed thoroughly prior to the introduction of the fish (to prevent fungal infection). The fish were fed *ad libitum* daily with rice bran and ground nut oil cake. In order to avoid the accumulation of metabolic waste and to ensure the oxygen supply, the water was changed daily. After acclimatization, the fish with an average length of 6-7 cm and weighing 4-5 g were selected and transferred to the clean glass aquaria (75 x 35 x 37 cm). Feeding was withheld for 24 h before the commencement of the experiment to keep the experimental animals more or less in the same metabolite state.

The physico chemical features of the tap water were estimated as per APHA (1998) and are as follows: Temperature: 25.0 ± 2.0°C; pH: 7.2 ± 0.1; Dissolved Oxygen: 6.2 ± 0.02 mg/L; Total alkalinity: 175.0 ± 10.00 mg/L; Total hardness: 18.0 ± 0.5 mg/L; and Salinity: 0.6 ± 0.01 ppt. The analytical grade ammonium sulphate was purchased from Qualigens Fine Chemicals, Glaxo India Limited, Coimbatore, India and was used for the evaluation of its toxicity to the fish *Catla catla*. Preliminary toxicity tests were carried out to find the median lethal tolerance limit of fish to ammonium sulphate over 24 h. For determining LC 50 concentration, separate 10 litres circular plastic tubs of water capacity were taken. Then, different concentrations of ammonium sulphate were added to different tubs. Then, 10 fish were introduced into each tub. A control tub with 10 litres with a water and 10 fish was also maintained (no toxicant). The mortality/survival of fish in the treatment tubs was recorded after 24 h. The concentration at which a 50% mortality rate of fish occurred after 24 h was taken as the medium lethal concentration (LC 50) for 24 h, which was 99.88 ppm. The LC 50 concentration for 24 h was calculated by the probit analysis method of Finney (1978), with a confident limit of a 5% level.

For acute toxicity studies, four tubs of 15 L capacity were taken with 10 litres of water. The pH balance of the water was maintained at 7.2 ± 0.1. Then, LC 50, 24 h concentration of ammonium sulphate (99.88) was added to each tub and 10 healthy fish from the stock were introduced into each tub. Four similar replicates were maintained. For control groups, a circular plastic tub of 15 L capacity was taken with 10 L of water with a normal pH balance of 7.2 ± 0.1. Then 10 healthy fish were selected from the stock and introduced into the tub and no toxicant was added. At the end of 24 h, live fish from control and experimental tubs were taken and sacrificed for blood chemistry studies. A minimum of 20 fish per treatment, 5 replicates per treatment and 20 fish per replicate were used for acute studies. Care was taken to avoid stress during sampling.

For sub lethal toxicity studies a glass aquaria (100 liter capacity) was taken and filled with 90 litres of water. The pH balance of the control and experimental work was maintained at 7.2 ± 0.1. Then 1/10th of value of the LC 50 24 h concentration of ammonium sulphate (9.98 ppm) was added to the tank (Sprague, 1971). Subsequently 90 healthy fish were introduced into the tank. Four similar replicates were maintained. The water was changed daily in order to avoid accumulation of faecal matter and excess feed and was renewed with the toxicant. A separate control was maintained by stocking 90 fish in a glass tank without adding toxicant. Fish were fed *ad libitum* everyday. Water was changed daily. Experiments were conducted for a period of

35 days with a 7 days sampling frequency. No mortality was observed during the experimental period. Upon completion of the stipulated exposure period of 7, 14, 21, 28 and 35 days, 20 fish were taken out and sacrificed without anesthetizing for further analysis. After the removal of the fish at various intervals of time, the volume of the experimental and control media were adjusted to maintain a constant density of fish per unit volume of water.

Fish from the control and experimental water tank were sacrificed and blood was drawn by cardiac puncture using a plastic disposable syringe fitted with a 26 gauge needle. The syringe and needle were prechilled and moistured with heparin (Beparine^R heparin sodium, IP 1000 IU ml^1 derived from beef intestinal mucosa containing 0.15% w/v chlorocresol IP preservative), an anticoagulant manufactured by Biological E Limited, Hyderabad, India. It was transferred into small vials, which were previously rinsed with heparin and a sample was centrifuged at 10,000 ppm for 20 min. to separate the plasma, which was used for the plasma cortisol and prolactin estimation. The plasma cortisol was estimated by the method of Tietz (1986) and the plasma prolactin level was estimated following the method of Engvall (1980) and Uotile *et al.* (1981). The significance of treated fish was tested using the student's '*t*' test (Campbell, 1981). The significance of the sample means that the control and the ammonium sulphate treated fish were tested by using the student's '*t*' test.

Results

The controlled fish cortisol level was 2.3 ± 0.152 ng/ml and when the fish were exposed to an acute concentration of ammonium sulphate, the cortisol level was 5.94 ± 0.093 ng/ml giving 158.20 percent increase over that of the control group. Similarly the prolactin level was also increased in the ammonium treated fish, recording a percent increase of 64.29 at the end of 24 h period (Fig. 1).

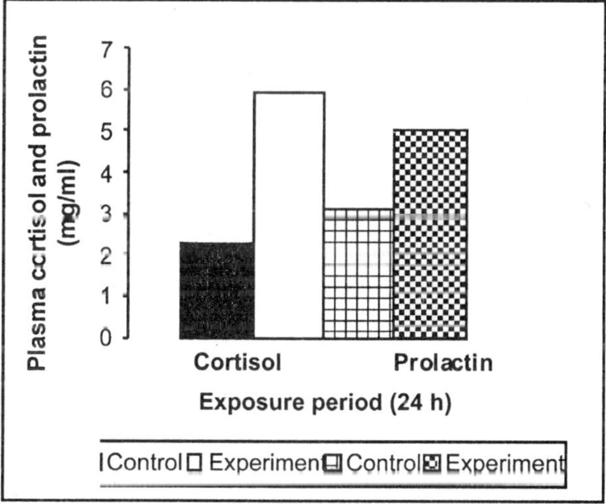

Fig.1.

During the sublethal treatment both the cortisol and prolactin levels were increased as the exposure period extended, registering a maximum percent increase of 69.59 and 183.77 at the end of the 35th day, respectively (Fig. 2 and 3). Statistical analysis indicates that all the values were significant at the 5% level except the plasma cortisol level at the end of the 35th day during sublethal treatment.

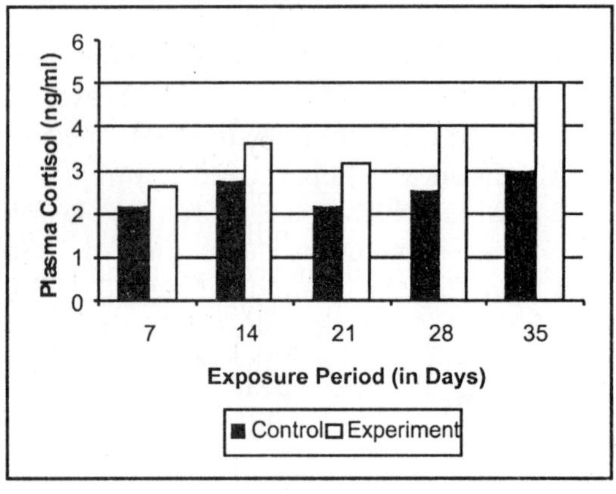

Fig. 2.

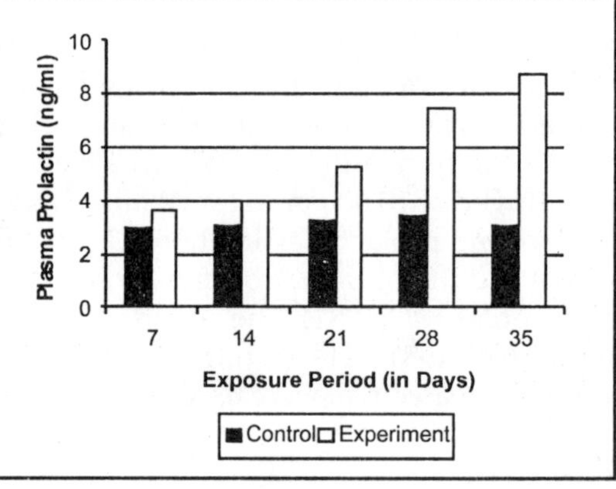

Fig. 3.

Discussion

According to Wlasow and Dabrowska (1990) toxicity of the ammonia to fish is well known, but less attention has been directed to cyprinidae regarded as more resistant to poisons. In fresh water environments, ammonia exists in two forms, ionized ammonium $(NH_4)^+$ and unionized ammonia (NH_3). Unionized environmental ammonia is toxic, probably because the gill membrane is permeable only to the molecularly dissolved form. A high ambient of ammonia in a fish production unit is usually associated with high densities and/or reuse of water, both putting a considerable strain on the water resources, thus a reduction in growth might be expected in such circumstances. In general, the increased stocking density is reported to have a negative effect on the feeding and growth in fish (Holm *et al.*, 1990; Bjornsson, 1994). Be that as it may, due to increased social interactions or to a reduced water quality (Foss *et al.*, 2004). accute ammonia intoxication is most likely to occur in situations lacking a water exchange, such as during accidental stops in the water supply (or) transport of fish in closed systems (Knoph, 1996). The behaviour described for acute ammonia intoxicated fish indicates a toxic effect of ammonia on the central nervous system (Knoph, 1996). The primary acute toxic action of ambient ammonia exposure in fish could be that internally accumulated ammonia impairs cerebral oxidative energy metabolism and results in a depletion of a high energy phosphate compound in the brain and is thought to be the mechanism of acute ammonia intoxication in mammals

The endocrina response to pollutants is an integral part of the homeostatic physiological process activated in response to environmental stresses including pollutants. Fish are known to respond to environmental pollutants by way of showing alterations in the serum hormonal levels (Thomas and Khan 1997). Plasma cortisol levels are the most commonly used stress indicators in fish because of the rapid elevation that occurs in response to various stresses such as handling, confinement, poor water quality and a wide variety of toxicants (Wendelaar Bonga 1997, Mustafa *et al.*, 2000; Ramesh *et al.*, 2007). In fish, cortisol plays a major role in the regulation of the hydromineral balance and metabolism and its role in the stress response in fish has been well documented (Wendelaar Bonga 1997; Ramesh *et al.*, 2007). Tomasso *et al.* (1981) reported that the release of corticosteroids into the circulation is brought about by two methods; firstly, as in the case of handling, the animal perceives an external threat or disturbance and responds physiologically to meet the threat; secondly, the fish apparently is not threatened or stressed as long as the chemical remains in the environment; however, when the chemical is allowed to enter the animal, corticosteroids are released into circulation and corticosteroid release, in this case, is probably a response to a physiological dysfunction brought about by the toxin.

Elevation in plasma cortisol concentrations is a widely used indicator of stress in fish and its levels have been shown to increase rapidly under an array of stressful conditions (Wendelaar Bonga, 1997). According to Wendelaar Bonga (1997) an elevation of plasma cortisol is the most widely used indicator of stress in fish; during acute stress, plasma cortisol levels rise rapidly a few minutes after exposure and return to normal levels within one or more hours; when the stress is chronic, cortisol levels may remain elevated, although well below peak levels and such cortisol responses have been reported for many fish species and after many different treatments ranging from handling and disturbances, heavy metals, organic pollutants, rapid temperature changes and acid waters, to confrontations with predators (Brown, 1993). In the present study, during acute and sublethal treatment the elevated level of cortisol responded to a generalised stress and this response was related to the duration of the exposure. Schreck and Lorz (1978) suggested that the early rise in cortisol was the result of the recognition of the fish to noxious substances in the water and they further equated this to the alarm phase of Selye (1950). During the sublethal treatment the initial rise of cortisol (Alarm phase) appeared to be a direct response of the fish, as a result of a part of the potentially harmful substance in the water. The maintenance of an elevated level during the following days apparently referenced a resistant phase during which time, the animals tried to counteract the observed physiological changes. Tomasso *et al.* (1981) reported that the ammonia exposure has resulted in an increasing plasma cortisol level correlated to the ammonia concentration and the exposure time in the freshwater fish species.

Johnson (1973) observed the endocrine control of the hydromineral balance in teleosts and they reported that an elevated cortisol level is probably the result either to create the abnormal chloride and ATPase level or to the process of trying to restore the values to normal, since corticoids have been implicated in electrolyte balance and gill ATPase activity. Schreck and Lorz (1978) reported a significant increase in the plasma cortisol level in coho salmon *Oncorhynchus kisutch* when exposed to cadmium, copper and several metals, which may be due to the presence of metals or potential harmful substances in the ambient water. Elevation in plasma cortisol levels also triggers osmotic and ionic regulation along with prolactin by increasing branchial Na^{+} K^{+} ATPase and Ca^{2+} ATPase activities (Laurent and Perry, 1990).

Prolactin is a member of the family of adenohypophysial hormones and it has been termed a "jack of-all-trades"with more than 80 different hormonal activities ascribed to it (Nicoll and Bern, 1971; Ramesh *et al.*, 2007). Prolactin is one of the main osmoregulatory hormones in fish maintaining the plasma electrolyte levels mainly by controlling the permeability of the gill epithelium. Wendelaar Bonga and Pang (1991) reported that the main function of prolactin in fish is the inhibitory control of the permeability of the integument to water and ions in a freshwater environment. Synthesis and release of the hormone are stimulated by a reduction in the water osmolarity or, in some species, water calcium concentration and other instances that affect the integumental permeability, such as acid water and some pollutants (Wendelaar Bonga, 1997). Flik *et al.* (1989b) observed that the reduction in the gill permeability by an increased response of prolactin in cadmium treated fish clearly indicates the maintenance of a stable Na^+ and water content since prolactin has been shown to decrease bronchial efflux and osmotic water influx. In the present study the increased prolactin response under acute and sublethal ammonium sulphate exposure may be a step to re-establish ionic disturbances. In fresh water fish, prolactin has a hypercalcemic action through the stimulation of the active Ca^{2+} uptake *via.*, the gills (Flik *et al.*, 1989 a).

From the present study, it is concluded that the ammonium sulphate, a nitrogenous fertilizer, is toxic both in acute and sublethal concentrations. The plasma hormones may be used as biomarkers against ammonium sulphate toxicity in aquatic ecosystems.

References

1. APHA (American Public Health Association), 1998. Standard methods for the examination of water and wastewater, 20th edition. *American Public Health Association.*, Washington, DC.
2. Bjomsson, B. 1994. Effects of stocking density on growth rate of halibut, *Hippoglossus hippoglossus* L. reared in large circular tanks for three years. *Aquaculture.*, 123: 259-270.
3. Brown, J. A. 1993. Endocrine responses to environmental pollutants. In: 'Fish Ecophysiology'. (Eds.), Rankin, J.E. and Jensen, F.B. *Champman and Hall.*, London. 276-296.
4. Campbell, R.E. 1981. Statistics for biologists. 2nd ed. Cambridge, London. 66.
5. Clark, W. E. and Bern, H. A. 1980. Comparative endocrinology of prolactin. In:
6. De Croux, P., Julieta, M. and Loteste, A. 2004. Lethal effects of elevated pH and ammonia on juveniles of neotropical fish *Colosoma macropomum* (Pisces, Caracidae). *J.Environ. Biol.*, 25(1): 7-10.
7. Donaldson, E. M. 1981. The pituitary-interrenal axis as an indicator of stress in fish. In: 'Stress in Fish'. (Ed.), Pickering, A. D. *Academic Press.*, London.11-47.
8. Engvall, E. 1980. In: Methods in Enzymology. Vol 70 (Eds), Van Vunakis, Hand Langono, J. J. *Academic Press* Inc., New York, USA. P.419.
9. Finney, D. J. 1978. In: 'Statistical Methods in Biological Assay'. 3rd ed., *Griffin Press,* London, UK. 508.
10. Flik, G., Fenwick, J. E. and Wendelaar Bonga, S. E. 1989a. Calcitropic actions of prolactin in North American eel, *Anguilla rostrata* (Le Suer). *Am. J. Physiol.,* 257: R74-R79.
11. Flik, G., Van der Velden, J. A., Seegers, H. e. M., Kolar, Z. and Wendelaar Bonga, S. E. 1989b. Prolactin cell activity and sodium fluxes in tilapia, *Oreochromis*

37

Global Warming
A Brief Analysis

SANGEETA BUNGALIA

Introduction

Global warming is a problem that has just recently come to the forefront of world affairs within the last 18 to 20 years. We have known that this problem was not only possible, but likely, but nothing has really been done. The origin of global warming is often disputed, and is being debated at the world level today. Whatever the causes may be, historians believe that this is a problem at least 100 years in the making. Since the Industrial Revolution, we have been on a fast track to pollute the earth to a way-of-life altering extent. We are only beginning to see the results of that today. Most scientists base their research on proxy data; ancient sources such as carving, and historical records of past earth climatology and the average sea level. They then compare the historical data with what we are experiencing today. Our recorded data can extend back only so far, but the consensus is that a shift is ongoing. In this field, global warming is the greatest crises ever collectively faced by human kind unlike other crises. It is global in nature, threatens the very survival of civilization, and promises to throw up only losers over the entire international socio-economical fabric. The reason for such a potential apocalyptic scenario is simple. Climate changes of geological proportions are occurring over time-spans as short as a single life time.

Environmentalists are quick to claim that many global warming skeptics have accepted funding from oil and coal companies, that they represent a distinct minority opinion among the world's scientists. Their arguments about misinterpreted data and faulty computer modeling were once valid but are now obsolete. Many economists are of the opinion that making a transition from fossil fuels to renewable energy will become costlier the longer it is delayed, and that the agricultural benefits of warmer temperatures will be limited to the northern hemisphere. Crops in the developing world, meanwhile, would be decimated (Long, 2005). The phenomenon of global warming is basically anthropogenic and is primarily due to the massive consumption of fossil fuels and secondly to the depletion of tropical rain forests. The predominant forces behind these human activities are economical and any policy or institutional measures to arrest the process of atmospheric disequilibrium effectively will have to take into account the economical, social and political implications.

The natural Global Warming effect which is necessary for the life of human beings, animals, plants and for other natural processes is in order but the man made green house effect will make this earth the worst place in which to survive in the future. The panic situation can be observed by the rising sea levels which are caused by the inflow of water from melting glaciers and polar ice sheets and by thermal expansion, which not only adversely impacts on our human shelter but also on the coral reefs, which provide a rich economical resource for fisheries, recreation, tourism and coastal protection.The situation is not better in agriculture, Health, food supply, fresh water resources, natural ecosystems such as forests and socio-economic systems are even economically related. The increasing global warming has increased the frequency of droughts, high rainfall, water scarcity, shift in forest types, reduction in food production, the threat to biodiversity, and health infections.

Global warming has resulted in a loss of biodiversity, has adversely affected the plant species that produce fruits, flowers, nuts, leaves and other valuable products and many of the species and livelihoods of millions of forest-dependent communities.

Global warming is expected to affect countries differently. Production in developed countries with relatively stable populations, such as the United States, may increase, whereas crop yields are likely to decrease in developing countries with increasing populations. Many of these countries are located in arid and semi-arid regions, where drought and famine already pose challenge to agriculture. The problem is getting worse, and the disparity between the developed and developing nations will likely increase as global temperatures rise. The International Community has taken steps to confront the problem of global warming. These include forming the IPCC, as well as drafting the 1992 United Nations Framework Convention on Climate Change (UNFCCC), which urged signatory nations to reduce greenhouse emissions to 1990 levels by 2000 (Long, 2005).

Historical Perspective of Global Warming

We know that the current problem of Global Warming is the result of human intervention in the natural process of a lifecycle. Nature has similarly warmed the earth over different periods. Nature has warmed the earth over a long period whereas we are destined to do it in a shorter period. We are accelerating the process of warming the earth. The time that has passed can be identified as being either an ice age or a period between two ice ages which is called an interglacial period. The interglacial is a warmer period. We are presently in the middle of an interglacial period, which began about 10,000 years ago and is expected to last for another 10,000 years. Going from an ice age to an interglacial period, the earth has suffered a temperature rise of not more than 5°C and that is about the same rise as a greenhouse century is expected to cause. Despite some cooling that occurred in the beginning of twentieth century and in the decade of 1940-50, there is a clear trend that the average earth temperature has risen by about 0.3° to 0.6°C between 1860 and 2000. The average temperature of 1992 was lower than those of 1990, 1991, 1994, 1995. With these disturbing factors and other minor interventions it is broadly agreed that in the last 160 years, definite global warming has taken place because of carbon dioxide addition. This is pure human intervention, which is currently not abating. The last ice age existed about 20,000 years ago. This period is marked by the accumulation of snow several kilometers deep and shallow oceans. The sea level was 90 metres lower than what it is today.

During the gradual rise in the temperature as the ice sheets move to the north, the forest pattern changes. The trees cannot migrate like human beings, animals or birds. While individual trees cannot migrate the forests where the trees grow, can creep to follow the changing climate. Hard wood trees will replace the balsam firs, broad-leaved plants would take over from grasses and grassland would replace maple trees. Enough time is available for pollen to be carried by winds and birds.

It will be worthwhile to ascertain how carbon dioxide varied during the period of all these temperature changes over glacial/ interglacial cycles. The ice deposited in the Antarctica and Greenland have provided us with such evidence. Since the massive ice dome deposited on the south polar continent and Greenland is heavily compressed under accumulating snow over the past several thousand years, they have now become ideal places to find ice samples dating back in the any time of past. Near the bottom of the ice sheets in Greenland and Antarctica, there lies snow, which might have fallen half a million years ago. It must be remembered that this ice is the compressed, state of snow, which has ample air in its pores. Before the industrial era and for much of the present interglacial period, the carbon dioxide content of the atmosphere was about 280 parts per million (ppm). This 280 ppm figure is comparable with the carbon dioxide composition seen in the previous interglacial period (120,000-130,000 years ago). Scientists have found that over the 80,000 to 90,000 years in which an ice age builds, carbon dioxide tracks in temperature have revealed variations fairly closely, reaching extremes at the last glacial maximums of 80,000 to 140,000 years ago. Another trace greenhouse gas, methane, is also found to track the temperature quite closely over the past two glacial periods. The overall result was that the earth's temperature increased with a build up of carbon dioxide concentration and decreased with their decline, going back to at least 160,000 years. As it happens, the earth is now in a warm cycle which actually peaked about 6,500 years ago, and the previous maximum occurred about 120,000 years ago. This parallel movement of carbon dioxide and temperature in historical records supports the greenhouse theory, and it is reasonable to expect the two to increase together in figure, as fossil fuel emissions drive the carbon dioxide upward (Mubeen, 2007).

Green House Effect and Global Warming

Theories of global warming were not new only to the late 20th century. In the 19th century, French scientist Jean-Baptiste-Joseph Fourier became the first person to envision earth as a giant greenhouse whose atmosphere traps the radiant heat from the sun, warming the planet and giving life to all organisms inhabiting its surface. About 70 years later, a Nobel prize-winning chemist from Sweden, Svaute August Arrhenius, became the first to suggest that the massive consumption of fossil fuels was capable of raising the temperature of the atmosphere (Long, 2005). The concept of global warming first entered the general public's consciousness during the unusually hot summer of 1988, when James Hansen of the National Aeronautics and Space Administration's Goddard Institute for Space Studies warned that the earth's temperature was steadily rising. Most scientists specializing in climate studies agreed that the trend was at least partially caused by carbon dioxide emissions from industrial activities. The United Nations, alarmed by this and similar revelations, established the Intergovernmental Panel on Climate Change (IPCC) by the end of 1988 to assess the impacts of global warming and suggest strategies by which nations could curb carbon dioxide emissions (Long, 2005).

The United Nations Framework Convention on Climate Change (UNFCC) defines climate change as "a change of climate which is attributed directly or indirectly to human activity that alters the composition of the global atmosphere and which is in addition to natural climate variability observed over comparable time periods." Climate change is primarily influenced by the total stock of Greenhouse Gases (GHGs) in the atmosphere and not by annual GHG emissions. Naturally occurring greenhouse gases include water vapour, carbon dioxide, ozone, methane and nitrous oxide and together create a natural greenhouse effect. However, human activities are causing greenhouse gas levels in the atmosphere to increase. Chlorofluorocarbons (CFCs) and hydrochlorofluorocarbons (HCFCs) are halocarbons that contain chlorine, while halocarbons that contain bromine are referred to as bromofluorocarbons (Mishra, 2004).

The naturally occurring greenhouse gases allow incoming ultraviolet solar radiation to pass through relatively unimpeded, but partially absorb and re-emit outgoing infrared terrestrial radiation. This natural process raises the earth's average temperature from 18°C to +15°C, and hence is vital for life on earth. The twentieth century witnessed the development of the greenhouse problem, which threatens to change climate in an unprecedented manner. The greenhouse problem is created due to the excessive accumulation of greenhouse gases in the atmosphere.

The estimate provided by the Intergovernmental Panel on Climate Change (IPCC) shows that a business as usual scenario will lead to an increase in the global mean temperature of about 1°C above the present value by the year 2025 and 3°C before the end of the next century. There are many greenhouse gases which could adversely affect the world's climate (Table 1).

Table 1: Contribution to Global Warming by Greenhouse Gases and Human Activities (% of Global Warming).

Sector	Carbon dioxide	Methane	Ozone	Nitrous oxide	CFC	% of warming by sector
Energy Direct	35	3	–	4	–	42
Energy Indirect	–	1	6	–	–	7
Deforestation	10	4	–	–	–	14
Agricultural	3	8	–	2	–	13
Industrial	2	–	2	–	20	24
% of warming by gas	50	16	8	6	20	100

Source: Agarwal, 2004

The atmosphere acts as a greenhouse for the earth, letting through incoming light but shuffling heat. An increased amount of certain gases increases the atmosphere's ability to block heat which leads to warmer temperatures and climate change. Solar energy arrives in the form of short wavelength radiation and some of the radiation is reflected away but, on a clear day, most of it passes straight through the atmosphere to warm the earth's surface. The earth gets rid of energy in the form of long wavelength infrared radiation. But most of the infrared radiation emitted by the earth's surface is absorbed in the atmosphere by water vapour, carbon dioxide, methane, nitrous oxide and chloroflurocarbons (greenhouse gases), making it difficult for the surface to radiate energy directly into space. Instead energy is transported by air currents and clouds high into the atmosphere, where radiation takes over and sheds the energy into space. This is fortunate for us, because if the surface could radiate energy into space unhindered, the earth would be more than 30°C colder than it is today; a bleak and barren prospect. Man made emissions disturb this equilibrium. A doubling of the concentration of long lived greenhouse gases would, if nothing else changed, reduce the rate at which the planet can shed energy to space by about 2 per cent. Because it would not affect the rate at which energy from the sun is absorbed, an imbalance will be created between the incoming and outgoing energy. 2 per cent may not sound like much, but over the entire earth it would amount to trapping the energy content of some 3 million tons of oil every minute (Agarwal, 2004).

Scientists now recognize that the temperature of the earth's surface depends on a balance of incoming radiation from the sun (solar radiation) and an outgoing radiation from the surface of the earth (terrestrial radiation). Only a small amount of the heat energy emitted from the planet's surface passes through the atmosphere back into space. The majority is absorbed by molecules of carbon dioxide, water vapour, methane, nitrous oxide, chlorofluorocarbons (CFCs), and ozone, collectively known as greenhouse gases because they are much more efficient at reflecting or trapping radiation than other gases. This trapped radiation contributes to the energy radiated back down to warm the earth's surface and the lower atmosphere (Long, 2005).

Responsible Factors for Global Warming

Climate change occurs externally (from extra-terrestrial factors – solar output, earth-sun geometry, and stellar dust) or internally (from ocean, atmosphere and land atmospheric chemistry, atmospheric albedo, surface albedo, ocean heat change, continental drift, mountain building and volcanic activity) through any one of these components. For example, an external change may involve a variation in the sun's output which would externally vary the amount of solar radiation received by the earth's atmosphere and surface. Internal variations in the earth's climatic system may be caused by changes in the concentrations of atmospheric gases, mountain building, volcanic activity, and changes in the surface or atmospheric albedo.

Main factors affecting climate change are the following:

1) Variation in the earth's orbital characteristics
2) Volcanic eruptions

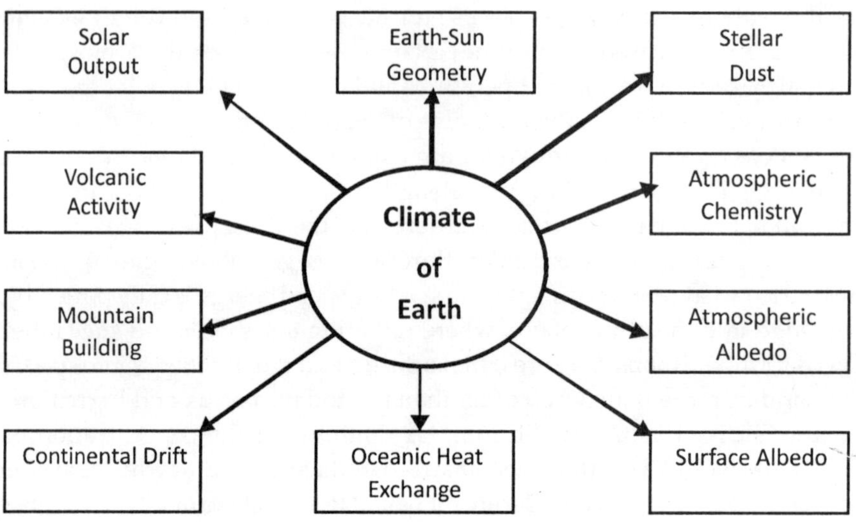

Fig. 1. Natural factors affecting climate change.

3) Variations in solar output
4) Atmospheric variations or greenhouse gases (Figure 1).

Variations in the Earth's Orbital Characteristics

The Milankovitch theory suggests that normal cyclical variations in three of the earth's orbital characteristics is probably responsible for some past climatic change. The basic idea behind this theory assumes that over time these three cyclic events varied the amount of solar radiation that is received on the earth's surface. The first cyclical variation, known as eccentricity, controls the shape of the earth's orbit around the sun. The orbit gradually changes from being elliptical to being nearly circular and then back to elliptical in a period of about 100,000 years. The greater the eccentricity of the orbit, the greater the variation in the solar energy received at the top of the atmosphere between the earth's close and farthest approach to the sun. Currently, the earth is experiencing a period of low eccentricity. The difference in the earth's distance from the sun is responsible for approximately a 7 per cent variation in the amount of solar energy received at the top of the atmosphere. When the difference in this distance is at its maximum (9%) the difference in solar energy received is about 20 per cent.

The second cyclical variation results from the fact that, as the earth rotates on its polar axis, it wobbles like a spinning top changing the orbit timing of the equinoxes and solstices. This effect is known as the procession of the equinox. The procession of the equinox has a cycle of approximately 23,000 years. The third cyclical variation is related to the changes in the tilt of the earth's axis of rotation over a 41,000 years period. During the 41,000 years cycle the tilt can deviate from approximately 22.5 to 24.5 degrees. At the present time, the tilt of the earth's axis is 2.5 degrees and when the tilt is small, there is less climatic variation between the summer and winter seasons in the middle and high latitudes. Winters tend to be milder and summers cooler. Warmer winters allow for more snow to fall in the high latitude regions. When the atmosphere is warmer it has a greater ability to hold water vapour and therefore more snow is produced at areas of frontal or orographic uplift. Cooler summers cause snow and ice to accumulate on the earth's surface because less of this frozen water is melted. Thus the net effect of a smaller tilt would be a more extensive formation of glaciers in the polar latitudes.

Periods of a larger tilt result in a greater seasonal climatic variation in the middle to high latitudes. At these times, winters tend to be colder and summers warmer. Colder winters produce less snow because of lower atmospheric temperatures. As a result, less snow and ice accumulate on the ground surface. Moreover the warmer summers produced by the larger tilt provide additional energy to melt and evaporate the snow that fell and accumulated during the winter months. Glaciers in the polar regions should be generally receding with other contributing factors being constant, during this part of the cycle. Historical evidence suggests that the Milankovitch cycle exerts its greatest cooling and warming influence when troughs and peaks of all three cycles coincide with each other.

Volcanic Eruptions

Climatologists have noticed a connection between large explosive volcanic eruptions and short-term climate change. The dust emitted into the atmosphere from large volcanic eruptions was responsible for the cooling by partially blocking the transmission of solar radiation to the earth's surface. However, measurements indicate that most of the dust thrown into the atmosphere returned to the earth's surface within six months.

Stratospheric data suggests that large explosive volcanic eruptions also eject large quantities of sulphur dioxide gas which remains in the atmosphere for as long as three years. The ejected sulphur dioxide gas reacts with water vapour commonly found in the stratosphere to form a dense optically bright haze layer that reduces the atmospheric transmission of some of the sun's incoming radiation.

Variation in Solar Output

Until recently, many scientists thought that the sun's output of radiation was varied only by a fraction of a per cent over many years. However, measurements made by satellites equipped with radio waves in the 1980's and 1990's suggested that the sun's energy output may be more variable than was once thought. Measurements made during the early 1980's showed a decrease of 0.1 per cent in the total amount of solar energy reaching the earth in just over an 18 months time period. If this trend were to extend over several decades, it could influence the global climate. Numerical climate models predict that a change in the solar output of only 1 per cent per century would alter the earth's average temperature by between 0.5-1.9°C (Agarwal, 2004).

The Greenhouse Gases

The 1990 IPCC report (Houghton et al., 1990) and subsequent reports identified the main greenhouse gases that have increased since pre-industrial times and that would have contributed to global warming. Carbon dioxide is the most important absorber of long-wave radiation. A spectacular rise in carbon dioxide can be seen and is some 25 per cent greater now than in pre-industrial times. Methane is produced by anaerobic processes which occur in a variety of settings. Natural wetlands such as bogs and swamps emit methane. Termites also emit methane in significant quantities. Both these natural sources can be directly influenced by human actions through land use changes. They may also be affected indirectly through climate change. The emissions of nitrous oxide form part of the global nitrogen cycle. It is a complex cycle and consequently there are great uncertainties in the estimations of emissions from both natural and anthropogenic sources. The main natural source of atmospheric nitrous oxide is thought to be soil. The ocean is also a significant source of nitrous oxide. The main sink is in the stratosphere. Anthropogenic sources of nitrous oxide are predominantly from agriculture and the use of fertilizers which grew significantly during the second world war. A small but significant percentage of both nitrate and ammonia based fertilizers can be converted into nitrous oxide. Nitrous oxide is increasing by a rate of 0.2 to 0.3 per cent per year.

The halocarbons that have received most attention of late are the chlorofluorocarbons (CFCs). This group of chemicals are entirely synthetic, developed commercially in the early 1930s. Their original use was as a refrigerator liquid but they rapidly expanded into other areas. The reason for their widespread use is that they were seen as absolutely safe, non-reactive and non-toxic. Like nitrous oxide, they require the higher energy of sunlight that is to be found in the stratosphere to break them down. The photochemical reactions, together with other processes in the stratosphere, are released from chlorine that can attack and deplete the ozone layer. Stratospheric ozone gases transported into the troposphere is one of the tropospheric ozone gases. Tropospheric ozone is also formulated by reactions between various other gases. These gases are nitrogen oxide (NO), nitrogen dioxide (NO_2), carbon monoxide (CO), Methane (CH_4) and non-methane hydrocarbons (NHMC). All these precursor gases are not greenhouse gases themselves but we need to be aware of increasing their anthropogenic sources because of the implications for changing the amount in the tropospheric ozone.

Aerosols are not greenhouse gases but are included in this section to emphasize their importance to the radiation balance of the earth. Tropospheric aerosols have either a direct or indirect effect on the radiation balance. The direct effect is principally through the absorption or reflection of solar radiation. The indirect effect is the modification of cloud optical properties and their life times. Both of these effects depend heavily on the aerosol's size and chemical composition (Drake, 2000).

Major Threat of Global Warming

Forest Resources

Climate is probably the most important determinant of vegetation patterns and has a significant influence on forest distribution, species dominance, plant productivity and in general, the ecology of the forests. Global Warming has the potential to impact adversely on the natural ecosystem such as forests and the socio-economic systems such as food production and fishing. The scientific evidence suggests that projected climate change is likely to lead to an increased water scarcity, increased droughts and famine, high rainfall events, threat to biodiversity, shifts in forest types, reduction in food production in dry tropics with an increased risk of hunger and flooding due to a sea level rise. Some of the impacts are irreversible such as the loss of biodiversity and the wetlands.

Forest ecosystems are highly vulnerable to climate change. According to IPCC reports, even with a modest global warming of 1-2°C, most forest ecosystems will be impacted through changes in the forest species composition, biodiversity and plant productivity. In fact, currently available scientific literature suggests that the unprecedented warming observed in the recent decades has already made an impact on forest ecosystems such as a pole-ward and an upward shift in ranges of plant, insect, bird and fish species. Further, plant flowering, bird arrival and dates of breeding and flowering are observed to be occurring earlier than before in the seasons. According to IPCC reports, forest ecosystems are likely to be subjected to a significant disruption under projected climatic scenarios at the global level. The impact of climate change will be additional to the current threats to forest ecosystems and biodiversity, further increasing their vulnerability. Large quantities of carbon dioxide could be released into the atmosphere during the transition from one forest type to another, due to high mortality rates. Initially under lower levels of warming, plant productivity and wood production may be increased due to the increased concentration of carbon dioxide in the atmosphere. Currently, forest ecosystem appear to be storing increasing quantities of carbon due to biomass productivity gains. However, this may not continue for long and, by the middle of the current century, forests could be a net source of carbon dioxide due to climatic change impacts.

Loss of Livelihood

There is a large dependence of local communities and economy on forest resources. The projected changes, in particular the loss of biodiversity, are likely to affect adversely the plant species that produce fruits, flowers, nuts, leaves and other valuable products and many of the species may become extinct leading to a loss of livelihood for millions of forest-dependent communities in the world in general and developing countries in particular. Increased biomass production, due to carbon dioxide fertilization, during the initial decades of the current century may have a positive impact on the swan timber, industrial wood and fuel wood supply. There could be a market surplus of wood during the medium term. A large market surplus of timber or industrial wood may also decrease the prices and may affect afforestation adversely and reforestation programmes, especially on private or farm land. However, in the long term, the projected higher levels of warming may lead to a reduction in the biomass stock and timber supplies in the markets. Climate change could cause irreversible damage to unique forest ecosystems and biodiversity, rendering several species extinct. Forest ecosystems require a long response time to adapt to climate change. Climate is projected to change at a faster rate than the capacity of the forest ecosystems and plant species to adapt and rejuvenate.

Retreat of the Glaciers (Severe Threat)

Global Warming is shrinking glaciers all over the world. Receding glaciers are visible signs of the impact of global climate change. We can see this is the Himalayan range of mountains stretching in an arc from Afghanistan in the west to Myanmar in the east. The youngest chain of mountain sages is also home to some of the world's loftiest mountain peaks, which have been the cynosure of the adventurer for centuries. The Himalayan ecosystems are one of the most fragile ecosystems in the world which are under severe threat due to the rapid expansionist approach of humans and related developmental activities. The changes in climate variability have led to a rapid retreat of mountain glacier systems, which are considered the lifeline of river basin and ecosystems. Scientific studies have shown that 67 per cent of glaciers are retreating at a startling rate in the Himalayas as a result of various factors including climate change. The same threat is growing for the Rocky, Andes, Ural and Alaska mountain ranges. Mount Shastra's glaciers are receding and, researchers say that the 4.7 billion cubic feet of ice on its flanks could be gone by 2100. For the glaciers to remain at their current size, Shasta would have to receive 20 per cent more snowfall for every 16 degree celsius increase in temperature.

Oceans

The most prominent ocean threat from global warming is a possible sea level rise caused by the inflow of a huge water mass from melting glaciers and polar ice sheets, and by thermal expansion. Nearly 50 per cent of the world population lives in coastal zones. In the United States, the figure is 53 per cent, with more people moving into the 17% of land in coastal zones each year. Areas vulnerable to rising sea levels include coastal cities such as New York, New Orleans, delta regions in Bangladesh, Egypt, the United States, and elsewhere; the Netherlands and low-lying islands in the Pacific and other oceans. In Bangladesh, where about 7 per cent of the habitable land is less than one meter above sea level, substantial amounts of good agricultural land could be lost. This would constitute a serious blow to a nation in which half the economy is based on agriculture and 85 per cent of the population relies on agriculture for its livelihood.

Higher seas are likely to increase damage from storm surges and accelerate coastal erosion, which could threaten coastal development, transportation infrastructure and tourism. Another potential impact is loss of estuaries, wetlands, and mangrove swamps. The most alarming prospect of sea level rise is the possibility that low lying island nations, particularly those situated on coral alolls, could disappear altogether. Coral reefs have been adversely affected also by the warming sea. Nearly 500 million people around the world live within 100 kilometers of coral reefs, which provide a rich economical resource for fisheries, recreation, tourism, and coastal protection. Coral reefs are one of the largest storehouses of marine biodiversity. Corals have difficulty adapting to warmer water, putting them under stress and causing them to expel the algae that live within them. The human cost of global warming and rising seas will soon make 70,000 people homeless.

Fresh Water Resources

A warming climate is likely to decrease the snow packs, which are a natural water storage system in mountainous regions around the globe. Although precipitation is likely to increase in some regions, more of it will fall in the form of rain, causing the snowpack to develop later and melt earlier. As a result, the peak stream flow will occur earlier in the spring, reducing summer flows in streams and rivers. This will increase competition for water supplies, not only for communities, but also between such needs as agriculture and other sectors. Water quality and quantity will also suffer. More frequent heavy precipitation events will likely flush more sediments and agricultural contaminants into rivers and lakes, thereby degrading the water quality. Excess nutrients from agricultural fertilizers washed into lakes by heavy rains, combined with warmer water can cause algae blooms on the lake surface. These blooms deplete the ecosystem of oxygen thereby harming other organisms. Flooding can also overload waste water systems, sewage treatment facilities and landfills, increasing the risk of contamination of the drinking water supplies, reducing summertime stream flow and on the other hand, reducing water quantity and quality by increasing the salinity.

Russian and American scientists have discovered that the rising temperature of the world's largest lake, located in frigid Siberia shows that this region is responding strongly to global warming. The lake contains 20 per cent of the world's fresh water, and it is large enough to hold all the water of the United States Great Lakes. It is the world's deepest lake as well as its oldest at 25 million old, it predates the emergence of humans. Africa has always been predicted to be the continent that will be worst hit by global warming and climate change. Could these predictions be coming true? Extreme rains and floods have made a very wet summer in Africa, and there is no end in sight to the downpours that are swallowing towns and forcing over a million to flee their homes in at least 20 countries. Since June 2008, Uganda, Sudan, Ethiopia and Kenya have had hundreds of thousands of people uprooted from their homes. Scores have died since West Africa has seen its worst floods in years, with 300,000 fleeing the earth coloured waters of northern Ghana. Meanwhile, forecasts by African Meteorologists say the rains have yet to peak. October may be the worst month to come in this very wet year.

Health Effects of Global Warming

Human health is intricately bound to weather and the environment. Climate plays a central role in maintaining the balance between predators and prey – a balance that is being altered by global warming in a way that could tip the scales in favor of the disease – transmitting pests and pathogens that predators had here to fore kept in check. Global warming will have grave consequences for human health and it already appears to be a major factor in the alarming spread of infections diseases such as malaria, dengue, fever and meningitis. The spread of infections diseases has accelerated not only because the world is warming, but the nighttime temperatures are rising faster than the day time temperatures. This has had particularly disturbing implications for human health because the range of many disease transmitting insects is limited chiefly by nighttime temperature because there is less relief at night. Summer heat waves are also claiming more fatalities around the globe and can be expected to pose an even more serious risk, particularly for children and the aged, as the future temperatures continue to rise;

The WWF study notes that diseases like Malaria and dengue fever are affecting new and less disease-resistant populations as warmer conditions allow mosquitoes to survive over a wider area and at higher attitudes. Dengue, a potentially fatal disease for which there is no vaccine, blanketed South America in 1995. It has been recorded in Northern Argentina, Australia and now infects Asia.

WWF believes that while the Kyoto protocol was a small step forward, a five per cent reduction in the emission of carbon dioxide, the principle effect of global warming, is not nearly enough to mitigate the most serious extreme weather conditions such as floods which may contribute to the spread of water borne diseases by overloading the waste water systems, sewage treatment facilities and landfill. Increased runoff can transport contaminants also from agriculture and mine failings into supplies of drinking water. Aggravated respiratory disorders increase because of warming weather. Global warming has affected human health also by prematuring boys and girls which can be a major cause of population growth. Death rates, particularly among the very young, the aged, and the very old as well as the poor can double or triple during days of unusually high temperature and humidity.

Agricultural Sector

World agriculture faces a serious decline within this century due to global warming unless emissions of carbon dioxide and other greenhouse gases are substantially reduced from their rising path, and developing countries will suffer much steeper declines than higher income countries, according to a new study by a senior fellow at the centre for Global Development and the Peterson institute.

Developing countries, many of which have average temperatures that are already near or above crop tolerance levels are predicted to suffer an average of a 10 to 25 per cent decline in agricultural productivity by 2080, assuming a so-called "business as usual" scenario in which greenhouse gas emissions continue to increase, according to the study. Rich countries, which typically have lower average temperatures, will experience a much milder or even a positive average effect, ranging from an eight per cent increase in productivity to a six per cent decline. Individual developing countries face even a larger decline. India, for example, could see a drop of 30 to 40 per cent. Some smaller countries suffer what could be described only as an agricultural productivity collapse. The Sudan, already wracked by Civil War fueled in part by failing rains, is projected to suffer as much as a 56 per cent reduction in agricultural production potential, and Senegal, a 52 per cent fall. China, further from the equator that most developing countries, could escape major damage on average, although its south central region could be in jeopardy. The picture is similar in the United States, with a projected reduction of 25 to 35 per cent in the south east and south western plains but a significance increase in the northern states. Overall, the agricultural production of the entire world is projected to decline from levels otherwise reached by between 3 and 16 per cent by the 2080s as a consequence of global warming. The damages would continue to deepen in the following century in the face of still greater warming.

Global Warming and the World Economy

Global warming is forcing the world to change the way it does business. According to a new report: a more sustainable global economy is emerging as countries and companies move to compact the challenges posed by climate change. Huge amount of money are pouring into clean energy projects, carbon trading and environmental and energy hedge funds, says the annual state of the world 2008 report from the World Watch Institute (WWI) an independent research organisation. Some of the world's biggest companies have announced a breakthrough in environmental initiatives in the past two years and in a surprising U turn, huge corporations in America were actually pressing the U.S. Congress to pass laws regulating greenhouse gas emissions something that would have been unthinkable even two years ago. Companies have also woken up to the fact that they could make money actually out of becoming more environmentally friendly. The chemical giant Du Pont had cut its greenhouse gas emissions by 72 per cent below 1991 levels by 2007, saving £ 1.5 bn. Another sign of dramatic change was the 575 environmental and energy hedge funds which had sprung up in the last few years. Clean technology was new the third most popular destination for venture and capital behind the internet biotechnology and 54 banks, representing 85 per cent of the global private project finance capacity, have endorsed the equator principles, a new international standard of sustainability investment.

The World Bank had calculated that 39 countries had lost five per cent or more of their wealth because of unsustainable forest harvesting, depletion of non-renewable resources and damage from carbon emissions. For 10 countries, the decline ranged from 25 to 60 per cent. The report calls for major reforms of government policy to steer investment away from destructive activities such as the extraction of oil and gas and toward a new generation of environmentally sustainable industries if the global economy collapse is to be averted. In the study of Jonah Goldberg, it is found that the earth got about 0.7°C warmer in the 20th century while it increased its GDP by 1800 per cent by one estimate. How much of that 0.7° can be laid at the feet of that 1800 per cent is unknowable, but let's stipulate that all of the warming was the result of our prosperity. That is still an amazing bargain. Life expectancies in the United States increased from about 47 years to about 77 years. Literacy medicine, leisure and even in many respects, the environment have improved mightily over the course of the 20th century at least in the prosperous west.

Global Initiatives

The World Climate Conference (WCC) which took place in Geneva in 1979 was not 'a specialist meteorological conference', but was called by the WMO to examine the relationship between on the one hand climate, and on the other, human activities and the environment. The WCC set out to assess current climatic knowledge and reach a better understanding of the ways in which climatic variability affects our activities and the environment.

1980 – The First Villach Conference (Austria)

The first International gathering of experts on the role of CO_2 in climatic variation took place in November 1980 in Villach under the auspices of the United Nations Environment Programme

(UNEP), the World Meteorological Organisation (WMO), and the International Council for Science (ICSU).

The report of the World Climate Programme (WCP-1981) concluded that:

- Because of the lack of certainty, the development of a programme for controlling atmospheric CO_2 levels and the prevention of impacts upon society would be premature.
- Priority should be given to the establishment of a solid scientific basis for viewing the problem, always bearing in mind that "agreement (was needed) on some basic issues."
- Emissions, however, due to deforestation and changing land use were deemed insufficient to provoke climate change but fossil fuel reserves were considered sufficient to have an effect on the environment if their exploitation continued at current rates.

1985 - Climate Change Conference and the Politics of Development, Villach, Austria

The WMO, UNEP and ICSU organised the second Villach Conference 'to assess the evolution and the role of increased carbon dioxide and other relatively active constituents of the atmosphere on climate change and its associated impacts. The conference also firmly supported the idea of a link between greenhouse gases and climate change. Major themes were the increase in average temperatures and the rise in sea levels. This conference concluded with the following points:

- Quantities of certain trace gases (mainly CO_2, N_2O, CH_4, O_3 and CFCs) are increasing in the troposphere.
- The role of greenhouse gases other than CO_2 is already as important as that of CO_2 in climate modification.
- The most advanced general circulation models show a rise in the mean surface temperature of between 1.5°C and 4.5°C for a two-fold increase in CO_2 concentration. A two-fold increase is considered possible over decades and may well be reached by 2030.
- Global warming of between 1.5°C and 4.5°C will lead to a rise in sea levels of 20 to 140 cm. Significant melting is not expected in the western Antarctic during the next century.

The International Geosphere-Biosphere Programme

This International Geosphere-Biosphere Programme (IGBP), also known as 'Global Change', brought into the 'Earth system' not only the atmosphere and oceanic hydrosphere but also the continental and marine biosphere, the land and the life forms which these milieux support. New communities of scientists (Pedologists, ecologists, biologists, chemists) stepped into climate research, as biogeochemical cycles were integrated in the earth-atmosphere - ocean biosphere system (Leroux, 2005). On the international level, the United Nations was sufficiently alarmed by the warning about global warming to form the Intergovernmental Panel on Climate Change (IPCC) under the auspices of the WMO and the UNEP in November 1988. Based in Geneva, this group of 2500 prominent climate scientists was given the task of assessing the science on climate change, including causes, impacts and possible responses. For some, the IPCC became the undisputed global authority on all matters pertaining to climate change.

The IPCC released its First Assessment Report in 1990. Researchers scrutinized all available temperature studies and reiterated the familiar observation that the average surface temperature of the planet had increased by about 0.6°C over the preceding century. Although the scientists involved were unable to determine whether this increase was caused by human induced climate change or natural variability, they did conclude that a doubling of pre-industrial revolution carbon dioxide levels would likely occur near the middle of the 21st century, causing an increase in the average global temperatures by as much as 4.5°C.

The IPCC Second Assessment Report was published in 1995, providing a new benchmark of international scientific consensus that became the IPCC's second report, Scientists increased their ability greatly to distinguish between natural and human influences on climate, in particular by accounting for the release of sulfate aerosols in computer simulations of the climate. These calculations resulted in a better match between the simulations of climate change and actual changes, an improvement that led the report's authors to conclude that "the observed warming tend is unlikely to be entirely natural in origin" and that "the balance of evidence suggests that there is a discernible human influence affecting the global climate." The Third Assessment Report, released in 2001, to conclude that "an increasing body of observations gives a collective picture of a warming world and other changes in the climate system." The Third Report studied not only the past to determine patterns of human activity including climate change but also looked ahead in an attempt to predict how these patterns would play out and affect humans in the future. The IPCC experts concluded that not only the emissions of carbon from the combustion of fossil fuels to be the primary influence on future carbon dioxide levels, but were projected to increase from 360 parts per million measured in the 1990's to 540 to 970 ppm by 2100 (Long, 2005).

United Nations Framework Convention on Climate Change and the Rio Earth Summit

The convention on climate change introduced 'universal citizenship', the principle of equal access for all to the enjoyment of the environment. One preamble in particular echoed the Vienna Convention (1985) and the Montreal Protocol (1987) on the protection of the ozone layer, and previous UN Resolutions on the Environment and Development (1989), on the protection of World Climate (1988-1991), rising sea levels (1989) and desertification (1989) and particular emphasis was given to:

- The worrying and 'harmful effects' of climate change;
- 'Increased average warming' resulting from a heightened greenhouse effect;
- The fact that 'climate change forecasts harbour a great number of uncertainties'; and
- The signatories 'resolving to preserve the climatic system for present and future generations'.

The UN Conference on Environment and Development (UNCED) had the slogan 'The world in our hand'. As was the case 20 years earlier in Stockholm, there was a parallel 'global forum' of local organisations, a forum for industries looking to the progressive environmental involvement of large groups, and representatives of 760 non-governmental organisations

(NGOs). This coming together of NGOs on the subjects of environment and development had been preceded in 1991, in Paris, by a meeting of more than a thousand NGOs, whose manifesto was entitled 'Ya Wananchi' (in Swahili Children of the Earth). The forum held that the earth is the common property of all of us, and they established a lyrical 'Earth Charter' the flavour of which was given by this extract from the preamble: 'We the people, planet and animals, rains and oceans, airs of the forests and tides of the oceans, honour the earth, dwelling place of all living beings. Let us cherish the beauty and diversity of life...' From this conference came the proposition for the signature of the UNFCCC, which came into force two years later (Leroux, 2005).

In June 1992, delegates from more than 160 nations met at a United Nations Conference on Environment and Development (UNCED); also known as the Earth Summit in Rio de Janerio, Brazil, to address global environmental problems. After a week of negotiations, summit participants adopted Agenda 21, an action plan that called for improving the quality of life on a global scale in the 21st century by using natural resources more efficiently protecting global commons, better managing human settlements and reducing pollutants and chemical waste.

The UNFCC which entered into force on March 21, 1994, committed industrial nations to a voluntary goal of returning carbon dioxide emissions to 1990 levels by 2000 and providing technical and financial assistance to developing and transitional nations (Long, 2005).

The Kyoto Protocol

From December 1 to December 11, 1997, nearly, 6000 United Nation's delegates from more than 160 countries met in Kyoto to negotiate what would become known as the Kyoto Protocol to the Framework Convention on Climate Change. The Question of who would pay for the protocol's stated goals - agreeing on legally binding targets and timetables for reducing greenhouse gas emissions, developing new energy sources and making existing energy production more efficient, divided delegates into opposing groups. Developing countries pointed their fingers at wealthy nations like the United States and those in Europe, blaming them for causing most of the greenhouse emissions during the past century and insisting that they should shoulder most of the burden of correcting the problem. Developed countries countered that cuts in emissions would hurt their economies, which would in turn affect the world economy.

The resulting Kyoto Protocol committed 38 industrialized and former Eastern bloc countries to reducing their combined greenhouse gas emissions by at least 5.2% from 1990 levels by 2008 to 2012. Developing countries meanwhile, were committed to continuing their efforts to monitor and address greenhouse emissions but exempt from legally binding requirements to do so. The Protocol included several controversial loopholes designed to help developed nations reduce the cost and difficulty of achieving emissions targets. These included emission trading, which allows developed countries to increase their emission caps by purchasing part of another country's Kyoto allocation: joint implementation, which allows developed nations to earn credits for projects implemented with developing nations. Wealthy nations are also allowed to subtract from their emission calculations the amount of carbon dioxide removed from the air by trees and other carbon sinks. Although some nations with high emissions would have refused to sign the protocol without the inclusion of these loopholes, discussion of a new system such as emission trading, would operate and was deferred to later meetings (Long, 2005).

Recent Initiatives

In 1995, the second IPCC evaluative report appeared, stating that 'cumulative observations suggest a discernible human influence on the global climate'.

In 2001, IPCC's group I resumed, adopted in Shanghai in January and claimed that 'observations to date present a picture of a world in the grip of warming and other changes in the climatic system'. In 2002, 10 years after Rio, the global Summit on Sustainable Development in Johannesburg was held. This second earth summit was inconclusive, but Russia, China and Canada made promises, on the ratification of the Kyoto Protocol. In 2003 in Moscow, Russia refused to ratify the Kyoto Protocol in the short term, principally because of 'uncertainties of global climate change observations and simulation modelling' (Leroux, 2005). Two weeks of International climate takes marked by bitter disagreements and angry accusations culminated on 16 December 2007, in a last-minute U.S. compromise and an agreement to adopt a blueprint for fighting global warming by 2009. Now comes the hard part. Delegates from nearly 190 nations must fix goals for industrialized nations to cut their greenhouse gas emissions while helping developing countries keep their own emissions and adapt to rising temperatures.

Negotiations also will consider ways to encourage developing countries to protect their rapidly dwindling forests - which absorb carbon dioxide.

Those gathering on the resort island of Bali were charged with launching negotiations to replace the Kyoto Protocol which expires in 2012. What they decide in the next two years will help determine how much the world warms in the decades to come. In a series of pivotal reports this year, a U.N. network for climate change and other scientists warned of severe consequences from rising seas, droughts, severe weather, species extinction and other effects - without sharp cutbacks in emissions of the industrial transportation and agricultural gases blamed for global warming. To avoid the worst, the IPCC said, emissions should be reduced by 25% to 40% below 1990 levels by 2020. Greenhouse and other heat trapping gases should be reduced at least by half by 2050, they added.

Conclusion

Climate change is the most important global environmental challenge facing humanity with implications for food production, natural ecosystems, water supply and health. The unequivocal warming of the climatic system is now evident from observations of increase in global average temperatures, widespread melting of snow and ice and the rising world average sea level. The impacts of global warming are being felt now across many parts of the world and critical ecosystems and livelihoods are being affected. Developed nations may possess the economical and technological resources to protect themselves from sea level rise by building walls and other constructions to divert water but developing and poorer countries, including Bangladesh and small islands of the Maldives in the Indian Ocean and the Marshall Islands in the Pacific, will likely be at the mercy of the advancing water. The situation is also similar in agriculture, food and water supply, forest resource and health. Because advanced countries have better resources for saving themselves with the help of innovative technology and science for a short time, the devil of global warming will not leave them for a longer period. Global warming could inflict worldwide disruption as great as was caused by the two world wars and the great depression. The threat of global warming is indeed upon us and if we are to save this beautiful planet, the world community should take collective and meaningful initiatives for the present and future generations to come. There is a dire and urgent need that world scientists, governments, environmentalist, policy makers and communities come forward and formulate a long-term strategy to mitigate the global warming impacts.

References

1. Agarwal, S.K. (2004). *Global warming and climate change.* New Delhi: APH Publishing Corporation.
2. Budyko, I.I., Ronav, A.B. and Yanshin, Y.L. (1987). *History of the Earth's Atmosphere.* Tucson: The University of Arizona Press.
3. Drake, Frances (2000). *Global warming.* London: Arnold.
4. Hansen, J., Sato, M. and Ruedy, R. (1995). Long term changes of the diurnal temperature cycle: implications about mechanism of global climate change. *Atmospheric Research* 37, 175-209.
5. Houghton, J.T., Jenkins, G.J. and Ephraums, J.J. (eds.) (1990). *Climate change: the IPCC scientific assessment.* Cambridge: Cambridge University Press.
6. Houghton, J. T. (1994). *Global warming: the complete briefing.* Oxford: Lion Publishing.
7. Houghton, J.T., Callander, B.A. and Varney, S.K. (eds.) (1992). *Climate change 1992: the supplementary report to the IPCC scientific assessment.* Cambridge: Cambridge University Press.
8. Idso, S.B. (1998). "CO_2-induced global warming: A skeptic's view of potential climate change." *Climate Research* 10, 69-82.
9. IPCC (2007). *Climate change 2007: The physical science basis,* Summary for Policymakers. http://www.ipcc.en.
10. Leroux, Marcel (2005). *Global warming myth or reality?* U.K.: Springer.
11. Long, Douglas (2005). *Global warming.* New Delhi: Viva Books Pvt. Ltd.
12. Mishra, A. (2004). *Global climate change.* Delhi: Authors Press.
13. Mitchell, J.F.B. et al. (1990). "Equilibrium climate change and its implication for the future" in Houghton, J.T. et al. (eds.), *Climate change: The IPCC Scientific Assessment.* Cambridge University Press.
14. Mubeen, A. (2007). *Our earth environment.* New Delhi: Galgotia Publications Pvt. Ltd. NRC (1994). *Solar influences on global change.* Board on global change commission on geosciences, environment and resources, National Research Council. Washington, DC: National Academy Press.

15. Oppenheimer, M. (1998). "Global warming and the stability of the west Antarctic ice sheet", *Nature* 393, pp. 325-332.
16. Parker, E.N. (1999). "Solar Physics - sunny side of global warming". *Nature* 399, 416-7.
17. Pittlock, A.B. and Salinger, M.J. (1982). "Toward regional scenarios for a CO_2-warmed earth". *Climate Change* 4, 23-40.
18. Rao, Prakash (2007). "Himalayas: Retreat of the Glaciers", *The Hindu Survey of the Environment*, pp. 19-29.
19. Sathaye, Jayant (2007). "Policy responses", *The Hindu Survey of the Environment*, pp. 7-12.
20. Stern Review (2006). *The economics of climate change, Executive summary*. London: Cambridge University Press.
21. The Hindustan Times (2008). "Growing glaciers", *The Hindustan Times Newspapers*, July 10, Delhi.
22. WWF Report (2005). *An overview of glaciers, glacier retreat and its subsequent impacts in Nepal, India, China*. WWF Publications, p. 68.
23. http://www.msnbc.msn.com/id/15828892.

38

Water Assessment of Bhambarde Water Reservoir (Khanapur Tahsil)

ALAKA A. PATIL AND N. S. CHAVAN

Introduction

Small reservoirs occupy a unique position in limnology and offer immense scope for enhanced fish production by adopting extensive aquaculture techniques [Kaushal and Sharma 2001] since the quality of water effects aquatic lives in many ways and it must be of good quality for the healthy survival of organisms. Water quality can have a great influence on the ability of the growth of aquatic plants and animals in a stream, pond or lake (Paka and Narsing Rao, 1997).The quality of water resources usually depends on its physical, chemical and biological characteristics. The normal range of these characteristics indicates a good water quality. The surface water on land is the most easily accessible source of water for human needs including aquaculture, agriculture and to industries. Today, due to the rapid urbanisation and industrialization, the fresh water bodies are polluted by the discharge of municipal and industrial waste (Swaminathan and Manonmani, 1997).

Bhambarde Lake is a small man-made water body surrounded by fields. In future, there is a threat of degradation to the water quality of this water reservoir due to fertilizers and pesticides. Therefore the assessment of the water quality of Bhambarde is an important aspect in relation to the water supply to various human activities. Still today there is no sufficient base line data about physico- chemical parameters of the Bhambarde water reservoir hence the present work has been undertaken to study the water quality monthly and monitor various physico- chemical parameters from August 2006 to July 2007.

Materials and Methods

The study area was visited monthly and surface water samples were collected by using samplers (Plastic containers of 5 litres size) from three sampling of the sites of the Bhambarde water reservoir. Site I lies near the dam's earthen embankment. Site II is much influenced by human activities such as cloth, buffalo, and automobile washing and Site III was near the feeder's canal which recharges the water in the reservoir.

Some physical and chemical parameters such as light, transparency, water temperature and dissolved oxygen were determined in the field, during the visits given for the collection of the water samples. For the physico- chemical parameters such as electrical conductivity, total alkalinity, hardness, magnesium, calcium, chloride, residual chlorine, free CO2, total dissolved solids etc. the water samples were collected and analysed in a laboratory. The analysis of the physico chemical parameters were carried out by following the standard method as described by APHA (1985).

Results and Discussion

The results of physico-chemical parameters of Bhambarde Lake are summarized in Table No. 1, 2.

Many workers have given a different range of temperatures of air and water for various water bodies around the Maharashtra State. Goel *et.al.* (1988) has recorded a water temperature

Table 1: Air and water temperature (degree celsius) of Bhambarde reservoir from August 2006 to July 2007.

Months	Sites	Air Temp °C	Water Temp °C	Light penetration cm	Odour
Aug. 06	B1	24.7	23.8	26	OL
	B2		23.7	26	OL
	B3		23.8	27.1	OL
Sept 06	B1	27.2	25.0	45.4	OL
	B2		24.8	46.2	OL
	B3		25.1	48.1	OL
Oct. 06	B1	31.1	28.8	60.1	OL
	B2		28.9	78.5	OL
	B3		28.8	62.3	OL
Nov. 06	B1	24.8	25.1	52.1	OL
	B2		24.8	52.8	OL
	B3		25.0	50.6	OL
Dec. 06	B1	24.2	23.1	56.5	OL
	B2		23.1	58.4	OL
	B3		23.2	71.5	OL
Jan. 07	B1	26.1	24.2	47.1	OL
	B2		24.8	47.6	OL
	B3		24.7	40.5	OL
Feb. 07	B1	27.3	24.1	48.1	OL
	B2		24.7	49.6	OL
	B3		24.6	48.1	OL
Mar. 07	B1	31.5	25.0	45.5	OL
	B2		25.2	45.5	OL
	B3		25.4	47.5	OL
Apr. 07	B1	32.1	25.2	22.6	OL
	B2		25.1	21.4	OL
	B3		25.4	20.8	OL
May 07	B1	34.3	27.1	12.4	OL
	B2		27.5	11.6	OL
	B3		27.6	10.2	OL
Jun. 07	B1	32.3	26.6	12.5	OL
	B2		26.7	12.4	OL
	B3		26.3	11.6	OL
July 07	B1	27.6	24.2	21.4	OL
	B2		24.1	21.6	OL
	B3		24.0	22.1	OL

Table 2: Physico-chemical parameters of Bhambarde Lake.

Parameters → Months ↓	Sites	pH	EC µmhos/cm	Total Alkalinity mg/l	Hardness mg/l	Cal mg/l	Mg mg/l	Chlorides mg/l	Do mg/l	TDS mg/l	CO2 mg/l	Residual clorine
Aug.06	B1	7.9	0.489	110	156	22.44	31.66	32.66	5.14	240	2.1	Nil
	B2	8.0	0.476	114	162	22.44	30.69	34.08	5.24	235	1.8	Nil
	B3	8.0	0.458	120	154	21.64	30.20	29.82	5.23	224	1.9	Nil
Sept 06	B1	8.2	0.428	116	138	23.24	33.61	28.42	6.04	265	1.2	Nil
	B2	8.3	0.443	125	142	24.04	34.10	29.82	6.26	285	1.1	Nil
	B3	8.2	0.405	128	136	24.04	32.64	26.98	6.26	280	1.3	Nil
Oct. 06	B1	8.3	0.382	135	138	18.43	35.56	26.98	5.82	250	0.9	Nil
	B2	8.4	0.368	128	142	18.43	35.07	25.56	5.73	220	0.8	Nil
	B3	8.4	0.389	130	148	16.03	34.59	25.56	5.83	298	0.8	Nil
Nov.06	B1	8.0	0.341	135	134	17.63	31.18	25.56	4.85	296	0.5	Nil
	B2	8.2	0.322	139	138	16.83	32.15	24.14	4.75	265	0.6	Nil
	B3	7.9	0.302	135	123	16.03	31.66	26.98	5.03	298	0.4	Nil
Dec.06	B1	8.3	0.304	189	106	13.62	30.20	24.14	4.22	220	0.4	Nil
	B2	8.3	0.312	210	110	6.41	29.71	24.14	4.43	211	0.5	Nil
	B3	8.4	0.303	210	118	4.0	29.23	21.34	4.42	220	0.4	Nil
Jan.07	B1	8.4	0.346	215	152	23.24	30.69	24.14	4.63	265	0.6	Nil
	B2	8.5	0.372	235	164	14.42	30.20	26.98	4.63	273	0.6	Nil
	B3	8.5	0.361	238	162	15.23	31.18	25.56	4.81	285	0.4	Nil
Feb.07	B1	8.5	0.415	235	206	24.84	31.66	29.82	5.03	269	0.5	Nil
	B2	8.6	0.466	251	210	23.24	32.15	31.24	5.02	302	0.3	Nil
	B3	8.6	0.453	250	252	24.04	32.15	31.24	5.03	280	0.2	Nil
Mar.07	B1	8.6	0.612	160	260	29.65	32.64	34.08	5.23	310	0.2	Nil
	B2	8.5	0.637	172	265	24.45	34.10	35.05	5.31	340	0.3	Nil
	B3	8.5	0.616	180	277	24.45	33.61	34.08	5.33	376	0.2	Nil
Apr.07	B1	8.6	0.668	175	262	30.46	34.59	44.02	6.24	339	0.2	Nil
	B2	8.6	0.623	165	266	29.65	35.07	41.18	6.24	385	0.3	Nil
	B3	8.7	0.615	170	284	29.65	34.59	35.51	6.04	396	0.1	Nil
May07	B1	8.7	0.689	148	336	36.26	35.07	42.62	6.62	455	0.3	Nil
	B2	8.6	0.694	145	345	34.26	34.10	38.34	7.04	448	0.2	Nil
	B3	8.6	0.691	140	342	34.46	39.95	34.08	7.25	466	0.1	Nil
Jun.07	B1	8.5	0.530	172	318	32.06	33.61	41.18	6.04	302	0.4	Nil
	B2	8.6	0.595	175	332	32.86	36.54	35.53	6.33	318	0.4	Nil
	B3	8.4	0.523	173	288	32.86	31.18	34.08	6.24	325	0.5	Nil
July 07	B1	8.0	0.443	148	200	30.46	30.20	34.08	6.24	270	0.3	Nil
	B2	8.1	0.476	145	212	29.65	30.69	32.66	6.35	289	0.4	Nil
	B3	7.9	0.398	135	214	29.65	31.66	32.66	6.41	242	0.2	Nil

range from 23°C to 35°C for the Kalamba Lake and 23.5°C to 37°C for the Ambedkar tank.The wohar reservoir in Aurangabad showed an annual range of water temperature from 11.8°C to 30.8°C (Ahmed and Krishnamurthy 1990). Goel *et.al.* (1991) has recorded the minimum water temperature to be 23°C in December and a maximum value of 33°C during April. Bhosale *et.al.* (1994) has recorded the water temperature range of 25°C to 30°C for different water bodies from the Sangli District. Kadam (1999) has recorded a water temperature range of 27.2°C to 30°C for the Rankala Lake in Kolhapur. Sathe *et.al.* (2001) has recorded the range of air and water temperature range as 25°C to 37°C and 24°C to 31°C for the Ped reservoir from the Sangli District.

In the present investigation the season wise analysis showed that the average air and water temperature in this reservoir was maximum during summer, comparatively less during the monsoon season and least during the winter season.

In the present investigation, the water temperature fluctuated between 23.1°C to 27.6°C. The minimum temperature was recorded during the month of Dec.2006 at all the sampling sites. The maximum temperature was recorded during the months of May 2007 at all sites. This result shows no analogy with results given by Singh (2000) in the Oxbow lake.

The penetration of light in the water depends largely on optical properties, which are influenced mainly by particulate impurities present in it. In the present study, seasonal variation in light transparency was observed. The minimum light transparency was observed during the month of May 2007. The maximum light transparency was observed during the winter season.

The pH balance of the Bhambarde water reservoir was alkaline and it ranged from 7.93 to 8.7. Gaur *et al.* (1995) has recorded the lowest pH balance value in winter and the highest in summer.

Electrical conductivity is nothing but the capacity of a solution to conduct an electrical current. In the water in the Bhambarde reservoir, the EC was reported in the range of about 0.304 to 0.694 umhos/cm. The higher values were observed during May 2007 and values decreased gradually up to Dec.2006. Similar results were reported by Pushpendra and Madhyastha (1994).

In the present investigation, Total Alkalinity was higher and ranged between 110 to 251 mg/ l and there was a fall in the total alkalinity value in the month of August 2006, and it may be due to the rainfall. Similar opinions have been expressed by Jain *et a* (1996). Bath and Kaur (1998) have given the range of total alkalinity as 105 to 250 mg/l for the Harike reservoir in the Punjab. Singh (1998) has recorded 68.00 to 82.00 mg/l total alkalinity in Himachal Pradesh. The monsoon minima and winter maxima of alkalinity was reported by Kumar *et.al.* (1996).

The Hardness of the water in the Bhambarde reservoir was at its maximum during the summer months. The range of hardness found was 106.0 to 345 mg/l . Bath and Kaur (1998) have given the range of 80.0 to 230.0 mg/l and 105.0 to 250.0 mg/l from the Harike reservoir (Punjab, India). Shaikh et al (1997) reported the maximum hardness during the summer seaeon. Saify *et.al.* (1986), Rao and Mahmood (1995) have also recorded a higher hardness level in summer and lower in winter, which is in agreement with the present findings.

The range of Calcium was 4.0 to36.26 mg/l. It was recorded at a minimum during Dec.2006 and a maximum during May2007. Seethapathi (1996). Swaranlatha and Rao (1998) have reported 10.0 to 34.5 mg/l calcium in the Banjara Lake.

In the present investigation, the minimum concentration of Magnesium (29.23mg/l) was recorded in the month of Dec.2006 and the maximum concentration of Magnesium.(39.95 mg/l) was recorded in the month of May 2007. Goel *et. al.* (1988) has reported the range of magnesium content as 2.7 to 14.1 mg/l for the Kalamba lake and 2.43 to 39.36 mg/l for the Ambedkar tank.

In the present investigation, the maximum Cl values (44.02 mg/l) were observed when the water level was low in April 2006 and the minimum (21.34 mg/l) was observed during Dec.2006. Similar results were reported by Swaranlatha and Narsing Rao (1998).The increase in the Cl content may be due to the increased temperature and evapo-transpiration of the water body. The chloride values observed in the present investigation showed a definite pattern of seasonal variation being higher in summer and lower in winter. The chloride concentration reached its maximum during summer when the water level was low. The chloride concentration decreased steadily through the monsoonal season and reached its minimum in winter. Such a condition was also observed by Saify *et.al.* (1986), Gaur *et. al.* (1995), Swarnalatha and Rao (1998) and Nair (2000). The researchers reported that a rise of chlorides may be due to an increased summer temperature and evapo-transpiration. The chloride content in the Residency Tank at Kolhapur varied from 12.8 to 33.7 mg/l (Goel and Chavan 1991). Sinha and Sinha (1993) have given the annual range of the chloride content to be 49.42 to 89.44 mg/l in the fresh water pond of Bihar.The residual Cl content in the Bhambarde Lake was absent throughout the year. Dissolved oxygen is an important indicator of water quality. The dissolved oxygen in Bhambarde Reservoir has shown seasonal variation. The oxygen level was decreased during the winter months. In May, a high oxygen level was recorded at 7.25 mg/l. Lower values of oxygen 4.22 mg/l were observed during Dec..2006, Ahmed and Krishnamurthy (1990) have recorded maximum DO in summers and a minimum in the monsoon season. The low DO value during summer was also due to an enhanced decomposition activity at a higher temperature Kumar (1995), Rao *et.al.* (1995) has given similar observations, going in full agreement with the present investigation.

The Total Dissolved Solids values ranges between 220 mg/l during Oct. and Dec. 2006 to 466 mg/l. during May 2007 Sathe *et. al.* (2000) has given the range of TDS as 260 to 4550 mg/l and 150 to 1300 mg/l for Siddhewadi and Ped reservoirs respectively.

References

1. Abraham, C. M.; "Environmental Jurisprudence In India" Martinus Nijhoff 1999
2. D. McGoldrick, 'Sustainable Development and Human Rights: An Integrated Approach' 45 International and Comparative Law Quarterly (1996)
3. Global Environmental Outlook, United Nations Environment Program (UNEP), Oxford University Press, 1999.
4. Ministry of Environment and Forests, Government of India, "Policy Statement for Abatement of Pollution", , February 26, 1992.
5. Leelakrishnan, P. ;"Environmental Law In India", 2nd Edition Eastern Book Company, 2004

39

Mosquito Control and Water Treatment Using Nanobioballs

A Nanobiotechnological Approach

Abdul A Rahman, Kantha D Arunachalam,
Raghuram Vandanapu and Pratyusha Mandapati

Introduction

In India, lentic and lotic systems are facing the problem of eutrophication and the accumulation of industrial waste. Further, lentic systems face the problem of desiccation and organisms that are living complete their life cycle and contribute organic matter which gets accumulated in the substratum in the form of humus.

The process of accretion (settlement) of organic material in the pond bottom takes place throughout the year unlike in the river channels where it is desilted. Such a method is not followed in the pond because of size and stagnation of water. The organic materials accumulated in the bottom get decomposed gradually during the summer season and the decay of organic material produces a bad odour and causes green colouration due to micro algae.

Thermal stratification in the system takes place at different seasons of the year which in turn causes changes in the physical and chemical parameters in the water. This is reflected in the composition in the organic matter in the substratum. The bottom organic material decomposes due to biotic (microbes) and non-biotic (temperature) factors and it floats in the form of an organic pollutant. This probably attracts the other organisms either as a food or as a niche to breed.

The aim of the present project is to study the traces of the organic material which floats on the surface of water and to record the organic material present in the bottom of the pond which undergoes biodegradation due to microbes. In the present study, silver nanoparticles were synthesized using neem leaves, the fungi *Aspergillus flavus* and silver nitrate. Nanobioballs were introduced into the lentic water and the result of the study is presented.

Review of Literature

Currently, there is a growing need to develop environmentally benign nanoparticle synthesis processes that do not use toxic chemicals in the synthesis protocol. Using plants for synthesis of nanoparticles could be advantageous over other environmentally benign biological processes by eliminating the elaborate process of maintaining cell cultures. It can also be suitably scaled up for large-scale synthesis of nanoparticles. (Shiv Shankar et. al., 2004). Agricultural biomass was used to reduce Cr(VI) to Cr(III) ions , indicating that biological methods can be very efficient in decontaminating polluted water and soil polluted with heavy metal ions(Gardea et al., 2000). Through an elaborate screening process involving a number of plants we observed that Neem leaves were potential candidates for rapid synthesis of silver and gold nanoparticles. Biologically synthesized silver nanoparticles have many applications such as waste water treatment. Zero valent iron nanoparticles and poly vinyl alcohol membranes embedded with silver nanoparticles are used for treating industrial waste water, surface water and ground water (Chadha et al., 2008). The antibacterial affect of biologically synthesized silver nanoparticles was found more potent when compared with chemically synthesized silver nanoparticles in cleaning the pond bottom and surface water (Govindharaju et al., 2008).

Materials and Methods

The surface water of the pond was collected and sieved with a micron filter. Similarly, the bottom water and the organic material present in the bottom were sampled using a drudge sampler.The temperature of the water in the bottom was also recorded using an electronic thermometer.

The composition of the substratum was observed using under water lightning during the night and visually during the day time and the samples were analyzed microbiologically.

The silver nanoparticles used in the nanobioballs are synthesized using both *Aspergillus niger* and a neem extract.

Materials used for the synthesis of silver nanoparticles using a neem extract are silver nitrate ($AgNO_3$), and neem (*Azadirachta indica*). Neem leaf broth was prepared by taking 20 gm of thoroughly washed and finely cut *A. indica* leaves in a 500 ml Erlenmeyer flask with 100 ml of sterile distilled water and then boiled for 2 min and finally decanted.

For the reduction of Ag^+ ions, 5 ml of neem leaf broth was added to 45 ml of 10^{-3} M aqueous $AgNO_3$ solution. UV–vis spectra were recorded as a function of the time of reaction on a spectrophotometer operated at a resolution of 1 nm.

For the present study, an astatic pond present in the premises of SRM University, Chennai and a similar pool in Taj Connemara, Chennai were selected for the study. The physical chemical parameters were recorded. However, the biological characters are different in these two water bodies. For treating the pond bottom, a treatment method was devised. The material used for this study is known as nanobioballs. These were prepared in the laboratory using silver nanoparticles, zeolite, bacteria, jaggery and clay material and each nanobioball weighs 100 grams. For one cubic meter of pond water one nanobioball is used and depending upon the volume the number of nanobioballs can be increased. During the first week the effect of nanobioballs on the water quality, particularly on the pond bottom, was recorded.

The microbiological aspect of the biodegradation of the organic material in the bottom were studied by sampling the bottom organic material and comparing with it the surface water for the availability of the trace organic material. The reason is that the bottom material get decomposed due to the temperature. The nanobioballs is a technique employed to treat the bottom of the pond and making the substratum free from organic pollution or by eutrophication. All these results were recorded and are presented.

The nanobioballs are designed with clay materials which help them to sink to the bottom of the pond. For the preparation of the clay material, care was taken to avoid organic material as it will interfere in the process. The chemical used for the nanobioball is zeolite used in the purification (more correctly softening) of water. Water in some localities contains salts of Ca, Mg and Fe present in the earth. Such water is "hard" or diluted or difficult to lather. The common name for this complex compound is sodium aluminium silicate. When hard water is passed through filters containing Zeolite, the salts of Ca and Mg get absorbed and sodium salts are released in exchange. In the present study, a special type of zeolite which is natural has been used for the preparation of nanobioballs.

The chemical is to dissolve in the bottom water column thus helping to reduce the turbidity of the water and make the water transparent to absorb solar radiation. The bacteria are encapsulated in nanobioballs which contain a nutrient rich medium. The nanobioballs before introducing are exposed outside so much so that a fungus develops and this fungus helps to protect the nanobioballs from cracking. The bacteria used ferments the organic material present in the water. Thus the organic material in the bottom is completely oxidized and mineralized making the water free from odour, traces of floating organic material and development of green algae. Indirectly mosquito breeding in this stagnant water is controlled.

After one month of the introduction of the nanobioballs, the water and bottom samples were sampled and a periodical observation was made on the water quality and the biodegradability of organic material was recorded and the result is presented.

Results and Discussion

The formation of the metal nanoparticles by the reduction of aqueous metal ions during exposure to the broth of *Aspergillus niger* may be easily followed by UV-vis spectroscopy. It is well known that silver nanoparticles exhibit as yellowish-brown in water, and these colours arise due to the excitation of surface plasmon vibrations in the metal nanoparticles.

It is observed that the surface plasmon resonance band occurs at a wavelength of 450 nm which is the characteristic of silver and it steadily increases in intensity as a function of the time of reaction without any shift in the peak wavelength. Thus it confirms the formation of the silver nanoparticles.

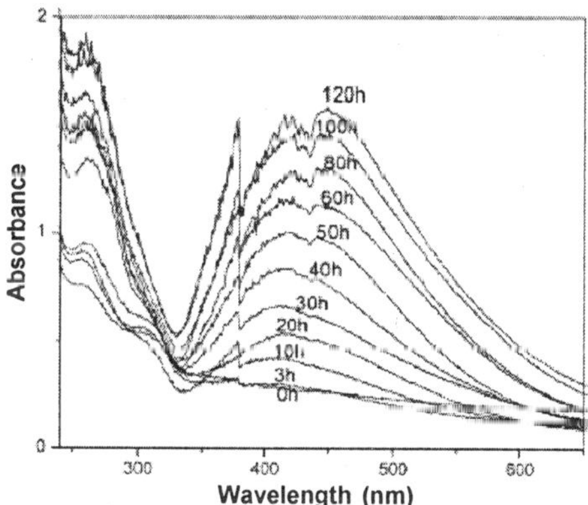

Fig. 1. UV-vis spectra recorded as a function of time of reaction of an aqueous solution of 10^{-3} M $AgNO_3$.

The silver nanoparticles have also been synthesized using neem extract. The reduction of the metal ions occurs fairly rapidly; more than 90% of the reduction of Ag^+ is completed within 4 hours after the addition of the Neem leaf broth to the metal ion solutions. In earlier studies on the synthesis of silver using bacteria and fungi, the time required for completion of the reaction (i.e., complete reduction of the metal ions) ranged from 24 to 120 h and is thus rather slow. This is one big drawback of the biosynthetic procedures that needs to be focussed on if they are to compete with chemical methods for nanoparticles synthesis. The sharp fall in reaction time from a few days to a couple of hours observed for the broth of Neem leaves is a significant advance in attempts toward achieving this goal, for silver nanoparticles. The metal particles were observed to be stable in solution even 4 weeks after their synthesis. By stability, we mean that there was no observable variation in the optical properties of the nanoparticles solutions with time.

Reduction in Turbidity

After the introduction of the nanobioballs in a pond at the SRM University and Cooum river in Chennai, the study indicated that the nanobioballs were found to treat the substratum of the pond where the organic materials are accumulated. The pH balance of the water was reduced from 7.8 to 7.2 and similarly the turbidity of the surface water was greatly reduced from .02 to .00 NTU. A comparison between a lily pond and an astatic pond indicated that it is the water quality coupled with the pond substratum which are to be important factors playing a role on the decayed organic material in the form of traces floating on the surface of the water and these are the criteria for attracting the mosquito. The pond bottom in these two ponds was cleared with the nanobioballs which are responsible for metabolizing the organic materials into minerals. The absence of organic trace materials on the surface of the pond suggests that the mosquitoes were not attracted. This again confirmed the absence of mosquito larvae in the water sample during the period of study.

Conversely the mosquito breeds in the organically contaminated medium thus making a way for the larval production. This observation was verified with the kitchen waste water sump. It is not only due to stagnation but also due to prolonged days of retaining the waste. Hence, anaerobic conditions resulted in the multiplication of mosquito population in the anaerobic chamber of waste water collection system.

Physical Parameters

Parameter	Cooum Sample Without Nanobioball	Cooum Sample with Nanobioball
Colour	Blackish Gray	Light Mud colour
Ph	7.8 to 8.0	7.0 To 7.2
Odour	Rotten Smell	Mild Fermentation Smell In 1st Week and then Odour Less
Turbidity	More	Less
Microbial Colonies	Many Colonies Of Different Bacteria	Even Colonies

Conclusion

The present study indicated that nanobioballs, which are under patent, are functioning as good material for pond bottom treatment. The surface water quality and the reduction of the transparency of the water helped to increase the dissolved oxygen content. The pH balance and turbidity of water was maintained after the introduction of nanobioballs. The ripples on the surface water were free from organic materials particularly on the brink of the pond and no mosquito larvae were recorded during the study period.

Acknowledgement

We thank the Chairman, Chancellor, SRM University for providing facilities to carry out the work and the assistance of Mr. Gopala Krishnan, Mr. Shiva Raman, SRM University, Nanotechnology Research Center, is gratefully acknowledged.

References

1. A.P. Philse, D. Maas, Langmuir 18 (2002) 9977.
2. Chadha, Tandeep Singh and M.Vidhya, Water purification: A nanomaterial approach. International conference on nano science and technology organized by IGCAR Kalpakkam India, 2008.
3. D.P.E. Dickson, J. Magn. Magn. Mater. 203 (1999) 46.
4. D.R. Lovley, J.F. Stolz, G.L. Nord, E.J.P. Phillips, Nature 330 (1987) 252.
5. J.L. Gardea-Torresdey, K.J. Tiemann, V. Armendariz, L. Bess-Oberto, R.R. Chianelli, J. Rios, J.G. Parsons, G. Gamez, J. Hazard. Mater. 80 (2000) 175.
6. K.Govindharaju, V.Kiruthiga, V.Ganesh Kumar and G.Singaravelu, Extracellular synthesis of silver nanoparticles by a marine alga, sargassum wightii grevilli and antibacterial effects. International conference on nano science and technology organized by IGCAR Kalpakkam India, 2008.
7. K. Simkiss, K.M. Wilbur, Biomineralization, Academic Press, New York, 1989.
8. S. Mann (Ed.), Biomimetic Materials Chemistry, VCH, New York, 1996.
9. S. Mann, Nature 365 (1993) 499.
10. S. Shiv Shankar, Akhilesh Rai, Absar Ahmad and Murali Sastry Rapid synthesis of Au, Ag, and bimetallic Au core–Ag shell nanoparticles using Neem (*Azadirachta indica*) leaf broth, Journal of Colloid and Interface Science 275 496–502, 2004.

40

Environmental Crisis in South Asia
Regional Planning Under SAARC

SHVETA DHALIWAL

Introduction

After the end of the cold war there has been an urge to redefine the national security and build up a comprehensive view of it[1]. The thrust of the comprehensive view of security has been to secure social, economical and environmental dimensions along with securing the boundaries of the state[2]. The traditional concept of security surrounded along defending territory and the political integrity of a country. The state was responsible for defending its sovereignty and integrity and armed forces were assigned to this duty[3].The state alone had to perform this responsibility as there were no such other institutions which could share it[4]. With the end of the cold war and the decreasing importance of geo-strategic considerations, the national security is being viewed in a comprehensive perspective. While there is no denying of the fact that the military dimensions of security are relevant, there is an added emphasis on the non-military dimensions of security. It is not sufficient to secure the territory and the sovereignty of the State. It is equally important to secure the people and his surroundings. It is in this perspective that a comprehensive view of national security has emerged. It may be noted here that the comprehensive national security approach is a deviation from the state centric view of security. Japan was the first country to talk about the comprehensive approach to national security[5].

---

[1] See: Barry Buzan, "Rethinking Security after the Cold War", *Nordic Journal of International Studies*, vol. 32, No. 1, March 1997, pp. 67-70, Also see: B. Weston (ed.), *Alternative Security: Luring Without Nuclear Detterance*, Westview Press, Boulder, 1990. pp. 263-268.

[2] Barry Buzan, the Logic of Anarchy, Columbia University Press, New York, 1992, pp. 34.

[3] Ibid. Also see for a detailed discussion of the conventional view of national security, M.P. Leffer, "The American Conception of National Security and the Beginning of the Cold War 1945-48," American Historical Review, vol. 89, 1984, pp. 246 281.

[4] Narottam Gann, "Environmental Security: An Appendage to Geo-political World Order of the United States" BIISS Journal, vol. 24, No. 3, July 2003, p. 428.

[5] Robert W. Barnett, Beyond War: Japan's Concept of Comprehensive National Security, Washington, 1984, pp. 89-91.

The comprehensive view of national security is based on the notion that it is not the state alone which needs security but the people, the resources and the socio-economical structures within the state also as these all need to be secured. In fact, now it is strongly believed that the security of the state is meaningless unless the people are secure. Therefore, some scholars have tried to define national security in terms of human security. The concept of human security gives the impression that the securing of the human beings should not remain confined to the state boundaries. The comprehensive view of national security obviously includes social, economical, environmental security along with the security of the state. The environmental security has become an important dimension of the comprehensive national security. The environmental security as a concept was officially mentioned for the first time, in the General Assembly of the UNO in 1987[6]. Since then, it has become a significant aspect of security studies both in theoretical and empirical contexts. It has been widely accepted that the indiscriminate attitudes of the people and the governments towards the environment, the self-interest, over exploitation of resources, etc., have caused scarcity of resources and their fast depletion as well as the degradation of the environment. This has caused conflicts and violence among and between the states[7]. The scarcity of resources may give rise to a conflict for the remaining resources. Therefore, there is a need to secure the environment. The security of the environment needs a positive attitude towards it. Thus, environmental security may be defined as the avoidance of negative linkages between human activities and the environment.

Environmental Issues in Asia

The Asian environment is both complex and diverse, containing a great variety of terrestrial and marine habitats and ecosystems that extend across a number of climatic zones. This environment is under great pressure and is experiencing many threats to its longer-term viability and sustainability. These threats include population growth, continuing rapid urbanization and industrialization, widespread poverty, abuse and mismanagement of natural resources, and inadequate and ineffective institutional structures and laws for environmental protection and resource management. It is a region of great contrasts possessing some of the least densely populated regions in the world and also many of the world's largest cities. Amid the poverty of much of Asia there are pockets of great affluence with patterns of consumption matching and sometimes exceeding those found in much of the United States and Europe[8], Asia includes the two most populous countries in the world — China and India — which together account for 38% of the global population. The region's population grew from 2.17 billion people in 1972 to 3.51 billion in 2000. In the future, the largest increases in population will occur in the relatively poor economies of South Asia where the population is expected to increase from 1,340 million

---

[6] Our Common Future, UCED, Oxford University Press, Oxford, 1987, p. 99.

[7] See for details, F. Thomas and Homer Dixon, Environment, Security and Violence, Princeton, NJ, 1999:48. Also see, Paul F. Diehl and Nils Potter Gleditsch (eds.) Environmental Conflict, Westview Press, Boulder, 2001, p. 45. Also see: Michael Dobkowski and Isidor Wallimann (eds.), On the Edge of Scarcity: Environment, Resources, Population, Sustainability and Conflicts, Syracuse University Press, Syracuse, 2002.

[8] Hills, P. and R. Welford. Ecological modernization as a weak form of sustainable development in Hong Kong. International Journal of Sustainable Development and World Ecology, 2002, pp. 315-331.

in 1997 to 1,737 million in 2015. Bangladesh, China, India, Indonesia and Pakistan account for one-half of the global annual population growth. Most countries have youthful populations. Some 30% of Asia's population is below 15 years of age[9].

Over the period up to 2015 the region's population is expected to grow by approximately 700 million, despite a significant reduction in population growth rates during this period. Environmental protection is both urgently needed in the region but at the same time difficult to achieve. Economical growth has traditionally been put before the environment, and increasing people's living standards and consumption ahead of achieving real sustainable development. Clearly, as a major actor in societies, businesses have a role to play. Indeed, in some cases businesses might have to take a lead because of inept and corrupt leadership within some governments. Businesses need encouragement and incentive to do this however.

There is a need for policy intervention that can encourage and guide companies to search of new innovations in environmentally beneficial directions and help create a self reinforcing process in which additional research for new technical solutions follow environmental pathways.

The Concept of Environmental Security

The notion of environmental security underlines the need to explore and propagate inter-linkages between resource use and environmental degradation because the environment can be properly protected and managed only when the urgency behind it is understood. In this context environmental security can be viewed as an effective measure towards sustainable development[10]. Since environment can be a cause of conflicts, violence and a threat to peace and stability, securing the environment would mean, in a broader perspective, removing the causes of environmental conflicts, as well as, the causes of environmental scarcity. This would require sustainability of the biotic resources of the earth and it is possible through environmental security[11]. Thus, environmental security means ordering and managing the resources and the biosphere activities. It is related to the establishment of a proper human-nature relationship.

Features of Environmental Concerns in South Asia

The South Asian region is a compact geo-ecological zone with several geographical variations ranging between high Himalayan regions to maritime zones. South Asia is comprised of eight developing countries with India, the largest, sharing borders with five of them. All except the island nations of Sri Lanka and the Maldives share land borders with India. Nepal and Bhutan are landlocked. A region of nearly 1082 sq. kms, South Asia is characterized by Indo centricity. India forms borders with almost all the countries of South Asia but no other countries form

[9] Welford, R. and P. Hills. 2003. Ecological modernization, environmental policy and innovation: Priorities for the Asia-Pacific region. International Journal of Environment and Sustainable Development, 2003, pp. 2, 3,324-340.

[10] See, Abul Kalam, "Environment and Development: Widening Security Frontier and the Quest for a New Security Framework in South Asia," BIISS Journal, vol. 19, No. 2,1989:122-23.

[11] Shaukat Hassan, "Emerging Environmental Concerns in South Asia" in Dipankar Banerjee (ed.) Security Studies in South Asia, Change and Challenges, Manohar, Delhi, 2000, p. 28.

borders with each other. India is the largest of the countries of the region. Its size, population, resources, economical development, scientific and technological advancement and military strength is heavily disproportionate in comparison with the other countries of the region. India alone holds 76 per cent of the land area. Its population is three times more than the combined population of the rest of the countries of the region. It contains 78 per cent of the total GNP of the region. This kind of asymmetry in terms of size and resources is a source of numerous problems in the region including the sharing and managing resources of the region. Such a situation also accelerates conflict over resources[12]. The South Asian states do not synchronize with the eco-geographical region due to the artificial divisioning of the state into different regions. India, Pakistan and Bangladesh emerged as independent countries out of one geographical unit. As a result these independent states share a common geography. Therefore, mutual sharing and conflict over resources are obvious. It also necessitates the development of a common approach to environmental security. However, the attention demanded by increasing internal problems and conflicting political, economic and social interests between countries confine environmental issues and problems primarily to the realm of 'low politics' The three major river systems of South Asia - The Indus, the Ganges and the Brahmaputra, are shared by most of the countries of the region. It is, therefore, obvious that they also share the hazards emanating out of these river systems. Nepal and Bhutan are land locked countries and Sri Lanka and the Maldives are island countries. This asymmetrical incongruity between the states of the region accounts for many of the disputes and conflicts. It can be said on the basis of the above brief overview that the very nature of the South Asian region is prone to various kinds of environmental issues and problems.

Population Pressure : One of the main drivers behind environmental scarcity in South Asia is population growth. The region is among the most densely populated in the world.

Bangladesh with a population of 141 million will have twice that number by 2050. Pakistan's current population of 159 million will reach 295 million by 2050[12, 13].

Deforestation: Expansion of farmlands in order to feed the growing population inevitably leads to increasing encroachment on forests and on marginal lands. It is estimated that 25-30 per cent of greenhouse gases released each year is caused by deforestation[14] and South Asia contributes a huge percentage of it.

Land Degradation: In the case of Bangladesh and Bhutan, per capita unit land resources are well below the world average of 0.26 hectares[15].

Water: Fortunately, none of the countries of South Asia are yet in the "water stress" stage[16].

---

[12] Human Development in South Asia 2003, Oxford University Press, Karachi, 2004, p.193.

[13] Population Reference Bureau, 2004 *World Population Data Sheet,* p.1.

[14] http://www.fao.org/newsroom/en/news/2006/ visited on 18th August 2008.

[15] http://www.fao.org/docrep/V4350E visited on 21st August 2008.

[16] A country can be in water stress stage when the water supply is between 600-1000 person per flow unit [p/fu; 1 fu=1million cubic meters]. Also see: http://www.unesco.org/science/waterday2000/water_use_in_the_world.htm

However, quantitative supply problems are increasing. Estimates indicate that India will enter the 'stress zone' by 2025 and Pakistan and Sri Lanka shortly after 2025[17].

Despite the grim situation of the environmental health of the region there is some ray of hope. The South Asian region has some well-established regional institutional mechanisms addressing environmental concerns, particularly the South Asian Association for Regional Cooperation which is dedicatedly working for the upliftment and improvement of the region.

Need for a Regional Approach on Environmental Issues

The environment related problems and their implications are regional issues as the countries of the region in most of the cases share them. It is true that there is a growing awareness on environmental issues in almost all the countries of South Asia in the last few years[18]. The individual countries have persuaded environment friendly policies in certain sectors. Attempts have been made towards reforestation, flood control, controlling desertification, etc.

However, there are two issues:

1. Some of the measures taken for environmental management and protection have not been effective as the sources of environmental degradation lies in some other country.

2. All the countries of the region are not conscious about environmental protection at the same scale. Their excessive dependence on natural resources, lack of alternative sources, scarcity of capital resources and technical know-how has proved to be a serious bottleneck in making adequate efforts towards environmental protection.

A common approach to securing the environment at the regional level may involve the following aspects:

(1) Sharing of knowledge and expertise regarding population control measures, policies and programmes.

(2) Cooperation for development and poverty eradication.

(3) Regularization of inter-state migrations, evolving a regional framework for controlling, repatriation and rehabilitation of refugees.

(4) Establishment of a system of disaster management and disaster preparedness at the regional level.

(5) Exchange of knowledge and researches on seismic tremors, earthquakes, landslides, their causes and possibilities.

[17] World Resources 2002-2004, World Resource Institute, Washington, DC, 2003, pp.141-143.

[18] B.C. Upreti, "Comprehensive National Security in India: A View from Western India" in Comprehensive National Security for India, Delhi Policy Group, New Delhi, 2002, p. 22.

(6) Evolving common flood control measures and development of a regional flood warning system.

(7) Common measures can be taken up for increased agriculture productivity, treatment of salinity, development of cyclone warning system, reforestation, development of water resources, air pollution control system, etc.

All these measures can be covered within the framework of a Regional Environmental Security Treaty. Such a treaty will provide an institutional basis for the growth of a common approach to environmental protection and management in South Asia. The South Asian Association for Regional Cooperation (SAARC) can take a lead in this regard and prepare the necessary background for a regional environmental security treaty. The SAARC can further consolidate its environmental protection measures. Because it is through regional cooperation alone that many of the environmental related issues can be settled[19].

Steps Taken by SAARC for Environmental Security in South Asian Region

Keeping the guidelines of environment security in view SAARC has taken steps in almost all the directions mentioned above.

SAARC - An Overview

The process of establishing regional cooperation in South Asia initiated in May 1980, was by itself a watershed of great significance. The main goal of the Association is to accelerate the process of economical and social development in member states, through joint action in the agreed areas or cooperation.

The first significant step in the evolution of regional cooperation in South Asia was the meeting of the Foreign Secretaries of the seven countries in Colombo in early 1981, which was followed subsequently by the Foreign Ministers' meeting in New Delhi in 1983, where the Integrated Programme of Action (IPA) was formally launched, through the adoption of the Declaration on South Asian Regional Cooperation (SARC). Two years later, on 8 December 1985, SAARC was born in Dhaka, with the signing of the Charter of the Association by the Heads of State or Government of member states during their first Summit. This was seen as a clear manifestation of the peoples of South Asia, to cooperate with each other in the search for solutions to their common problems.

---

[19] Ashok Swain, Environmental Cooperation in South Asia" in Ken Conca and Geoff Daberke (eds.), Environmental Peacemaking, Woodrow Wilson Centre Press, Washington, 2002, p. 111.

Four-Tier Structure

As cooperation within the SAARC framework took concrete shape, with a definite purpose, a number of key decisions were taken. The Institutional framework of the organization was thus outlined giving regional cooperation an institutional shape. Cooperation was formalized within a four-tier structure and a permanent Secretariat was established. From the early days, the Heads of State or Government remained the highest authority of SAARC activities at the top, followed by the Council of Ministers, the Standing Committee, and the Technical Committees, each body meeting at least once a year.

The Three-Tier Mechanism

As a follow-up to this commitment at the highest level, a three-tier mechanism has been established within the SAARC framework for the exchange of information on experiences of SAARC countries in poverty alleviation schemes.

The three-tier consists of:

(1) Group of Secretaries concerned with poverty eradication and social development,

(2) Finance and Planning Secretaries, and

(3) Minister of Finance and Planning.

Steps Taken by SAARC towards Environmental Security of South Asia

During the first decade of SAARC, several other important meetings took place in specific contexts. A number of SAARC Ministerial Meetings have been held, to focus attention on specific areas of common concern and have become an integral part of the consultative structure. Two Ministerial level Meetings were held at Shillong in 1986 and at Islamabad in 1990 to discuss the environmental concerns of South Asia.

The Sixth SAARC Summit at Colombo commissioned the Independent South Asian Commission on Poverty Alleviation to address the various aspects of this most formidable problem. The report of the Commission was presented on the eve of the Seventh SAARC Summit and it agreed on a South Asian consensus on poverty eradication through this consensus. The SAARC leaders have committed to accord a high priority and pledged to overcome this challenge through the implementation of an Agenda of Action which would inter-alia, include a strategy of social mobilization, policy of decentralized agricultural and human development.

In order to give further impetus to the issue of poverty eradication in the region, SAARC designated 1995 as the "SAARC Year of Poverty Eradication".

A SAARC Regional Fund (SRF) was also established with the aim of financing those activities / programmes, which remain unimplemented due to financial constraints.

During the Eighth SAARC Summit it was decided to establish a South Asian Development Fund (SADF).

The Association has designated specific SAARC years to focus particular attention on important thematic issues of great social significance and to underscore the importance of action needed in specific areas.

In addition to initiatives in these vital areas, SAARC has established four Regional Centres, the first being SAARC Agricultural Information Centre (SAIC) in Dhaka followed by SAARC Tuberculosis Centre (STC) in Kathmandu, SAARC Meteorological Research Centre (SAARC) in Dhaka and the SAARC Documentation Centre (SDC) in New Delhi.

Building bridges among the peoples of the region has been one of the prime objectives of SAARC.

The SAARC Audio Visual Exchange (SAVE) Programme, the SAARC Chairs, Fellowships and Scholarships Scheme, the SAARC Youth Volunteers Programme and the SAARC Visa Exemption Scheme are some of the important initiatives taken in this regard.

It has entered into cooperative arrangements through signing MOUs and Agreements with several regional and international organizations including UNCTAD, ESCAP, UNICEF, APT, UNDP, and UNDCP[20].

SAARC Environmental Ministers met in Colombo from 30 October to 1 November 1998 for their fourth annual Conference under the chairmanship of Nandimithra Ekanayake, MP, Minister of Environment and Forestry of Sri Lanka, and adopted a common environmental programme for the region as a follow up on the SAARC Action Plan on the Environment[21].

In the latest 15th Summit SAARC has adopted a 41 point Colombo Declararion on collective regional efforts in food, energy, terrorism, trade, climate change and connectivity on 3rd August 2008.

Environmental Security of South Asia Under SAARC: Some Suggestions

After the end of the cold war there has been much debate on the comprehensive approach to national security. It is widely accepted that the national security has to be viewed in a wider perspective. The environmental security constitutes a significant dimension of the comprehensive national security. The environment has to be viewed in a wider perspective where human and non-human living beings are also important along with the nature. The environment and the living organs are closely interlinked. Hence, environmental security must take into consideration a balanced and sustained inter-relationship between the two.

In South Asia, environmental issues have become significant in the overall framework of security due to the high population growth, excessive dependence on nature, uneven infra-structural development, poverty, under-development and a fragile ecology. While there is

[20] Batra, Hemant, SAARC, South Asian Publishers, Gurgaon, 2002, pp. 1-7.

[21] SAARC NEWSLETTER, VOL.IX, NO.11, November 1998.

an urgent need to take measures for environmental protection, a regional approach alone can be fruit bearing because of eco-geographical inter-linkages and interdependence in the region. Therefore, along with the strengthening of SAARC a Regional Environment Security Treaty can be suggestive. Given the socio-political realities of the South Asian region, the conflictual relations between the states of South Asia, complexities, identity crisis, over consciousness about resources, big-power, small-power angularities and the slow progress of SAARC and its ineffectiveness in many cases, the realization of the goal of a Regional Environment Security Treaty is not an easy task. There are several constraints but it is not a difficult task if there be mutual confidence, trust and understanding between the countries of the region.

It has to be realized that the environmental security in South Asia is possible through a regional approach only. Therefore, the efforts made by the individual countries need to be coordinated in a regional framework.

Author Ramesh Thakur has described the existing cycle of poverty, environmental degradation and lack of development in South Asia.[22]

The Author also proposes a new connection between all the above factors on which regional planning for environmental security in South Asia could be based.

A vision is efficacious to the extent that it can be concretized. This requires bringing to bear the new consciousness of South Asian cooperation to undertake five specific policy actions for our new perspective on economical development:

(1) Region without Boundaries

Visa restrictions should be eased to allow citizens of each country of South Asia to travel freely to enjoy the natural beauty of the region, and to participate in the social and cultural events of the various countries of South Asia. Tourism alone could make a major contribution to the GDP growth of the region. It would at the same time be pro "poor growth" since it would generate employment and incomes for a wide range of social groups. Such travel and social interaction would help in the rediscovery of the shared civilizational values of South Asia, and help build more pluralistic societies to strengthen democracy in the region.

(2) South Asia Health Foundation (SAHF)[23]

Health is a major trigger that pushes people into poverty and keeps productivity at a low level

---

[22] Ramesh Thakur and Oddny Wiggen, South Asia in the World, United Nations University Press, NewYork , 2004, p.207.

[23] Wignaraja, Ponna, Hussain, Akmal, Sethi, Harsh and Wignaraja, Ganeshan, 1991. "Participatory Development, Learning from South Asia". United Nations University, Oxford University Press, Karachi, p. 24. Also see: Akmal Hussain: South Asia Health Foundation, included in 'Promoting Cooperation in South Asia', An Agenda for the 13th SAARC Summit, (ed.) Rehman Sobhan, The University Press Limited, Bangladesh, 2004.

in South Asia[24]. Therefore provision of high quality preventive and curative health facilities would be a strategic intervention for poverty reduction, human development and economical growth in the region. It is proposed that a South Asia Health Foundation may be instituted with the following objectives:

(i) To set up district level General Hospitals of the highest international standards in selected districts of each of the countries of South Asia.

(ii) Each SAHF hospital would have a network of high quality basic health units and also reproductive and child health care clinics. The latter would provide pre natal and post natal care to mothers, family planning services and basic pediatric services to infants.

(iii) Each SAHF hospital would initiate community-based campaigns for hygienic drinking water, sanitation, immunization and control of epidemics.

The doctors and staff of the SAHF hospitals in a particular country could be drawn from other South Asian countries to signify the commitment of South Asians to each other. The healing and humanity in these hospitals would stand as a living symbol of both the promise and fulfillment of South Asian cooperation.

(3) South Asia Education Foundation

A South Asia Education Foundation may be instituted on the basis of a private-public partnership with contributions from multi lateral donor agencies. The purpose of the foundation would be to establish a network of schools as well as universities of the best international standards to help develop the knowledge base to prepare South Asia for its leadership role in the new world that is taking shape. The network of universities could enable students and researchers to interact intensively across international boundaries in South Asia and create a community of scholars that could produce new knowledge in the natural and social sciences[25].

(4) Implementing SAFTA

Free trade between India and Pakistan will provide not only substantial economical gains for the people of both countries but will also set in motion a powerful dynamo of enlarging the constituency for peace at the political level. Free trade in agricultural commodities will help stabilize seasonal price fluctuations, and prevent the associated real income losses to farmers. Free trade in capital and intermediate goods will lower the incremental capital output ratios, thereby enabling higher GDP growth for given levels of investment. Free trade in consumer

---

[24] Akmal Hussain, et.al., UNDP, Pakistan National Human Development Report 2003, Oxford University Press, Karachi, 2003, pp. 175-176.

[25] On the line of United Nations University the SAARC has come up with the Idea of SAARC University to be established at New Delhi, India. This was declared in the 14th Summit of SAARC, held at New Delhi, 2008.

goods and services will mean substantial welfare gains particularly for the middle class, lower inflation rates and improved income distribution in both countries. Given the asymmetry in the size of the two economies and the futility of war, it would be counter productive for Pakistan's national interests to leverage free trade as a device for resolving political disputes. Political disputes would be best resolved through the current composite peace process. The gains from free trade could play a synergistic role in accelerating the peace process.

(i) Private Sector Joint Venture Infrastructure Projects

India, Pakistan and Bangladesh should cooperate closely in establishing gas pipelines in South Asia for transporting gas from Iran, Qatar and Turkmenistan and even Myanmar. Specifically the ongoing official negotiations on transporting oil and gas from Iran through Pakistan to India should be brought to an early and successful conclusion. To strengthen the mutual inter dependence between India and Pakistan the earlier proposals like transporting diesel fuel from Panipat to Lahore, by Mr Manishanker Iyer, should also be taken up quickly. In the context of developing energy markets of these resources, power trading in the region calls for the establishment of high voltage interconnections between the national grids of the countries of the region.

(ii) Facilitating regional and global joint venture projects for developing new ports along both the western and eastern seaboard of South Asia, and at the same time up-grading existing ports to the highest international standards.

(iii) Facilitating regional investment projects in building a network of airports, together with cold storage and warehouse facilities that could stimulate not only tourism but also the export of perishable commodities such as milk, meat, fish, fruits and vegetables.

These initiatives could be part of the new policy paradigm.

(5) Restructuring Growth for Rapid Poverty Reduction

Economical growth must be not only accelerated but restructured in such a way that its capacity to alleviate poverty is enhanced for given growth rates of GDP. In this context of achieving pro poor growth, three sets of measures can be undertaken at the country as well as the regional levels:

(i) Joint venture projects need to be undertaken to accelerate rapidly growth of those sub sectors in agriculture and industry respectively which have relatively higher employment elasticities. These sub sectors include the production and regional export of high value added agricultural products such as milk, vegetables, fruits, flowers and marine fisheries[26].

(ii) Regional network of support institutions in the private sector can be facilitated for enabling small scale industries of the region to grow.

(iii) A SAARC Fund for vocational training may be established. The purpose of this Fund would be to help establish a network of high quality vocational training institutes for the poor.

---

[27] Akmal Hussain: A Policy for Pro Poor Growth, paper in: Towards Pro Poor Growth Policies in Pakistan, A joint publication of PIDE-UNDP, Islamabad, 2003, pp. 13.

Conclusion

If South Asia is to play a leadership role in the new world that is taking shape, then it must undertake specific initiatives within a new policy paradigm for pursuing peace, overcoming poverty and protecting the life support systems of the planet. However this requires that governments move out of a mindset that regards an adversarial relationship with a neighbouring country as the emblem of patriotism, affluence of the few at the expense of the many, as the hallmark of development, individual greed as the basis of public action, and mistrust as the basis of interstate relations. We have arrived at the end of the epoch when we could hope to conduct our social, economical and political life on the basis of such a mindset.

This is on historic moment when the people of South Asia have recognized that they have a new tryst with destiny. They are affirming that their security and well being lies not in inter-state conflict but in peace and cooperation. Let the governments hearken to the call of their people.

References

1. Agarwal, A. & Narain. (2000).*Dying Wisdom*. India: Centre for Science and Environment Publication.
2. Anonymous (1995).*Monitoring of Water Table, Drainage Trial and Demonstrations, Command Area Development (IGNP)*. India: Report published by Comissioner, CAD, IGNP.
3. Barrett, F.A. (1982).*The 18th Century Antecedents of Medical Geography* in Environment and Health by Rais Akhtar, 1991. Delhi: Ashish Publishing House.
4. Chaklin, A.V. (1980).*Some results and prospects of the activities of the working group on "the geography of health" under the aegis of the International Geographical Union* paper published in Social Science and Medicine, Vol. 15 D, Issue-I, Feb. 1981.5-7.
5. Christophers, S.R. et.al. (1959).*How to do a Malaria Survey*, Health Bulletin No. 10.

41

Treatment of Hazardous Heavy Metals Wastewater Using Treated Granular Activated Carbon (GAC)

AJAY KUMAR MEENA, MADHUP SHRIVASTAVA, M.D. GUPTA AND CHITRA RAJAGOPAL

Introduction

Industrial, agricultural and domestic wastes pollute water bodies with heavy metals, which reach tissues through the food chain. The toxicity of heavy metals to aquatic organisms has been a subject of interest to biologist for many years. Absorption of trace metals onto natural particulate matter can play a role in determining trace metal speciation in many aquatic systems. Among different types of pollution, the industrial waste constitutes the major source of various kinds of metal pollution in natural water. The important toxic metals i.e. Cd, Hg, Pb, Cu, Cr, Ni, Mn, Zn, As, Co, Ag, Au, Sn, V, Sb, Bi, Ce, Ga, Pt, and Fe etc finds its way to the water bodies through waste water from such industries as metal plating industries of cadmium, nickel, batteries, pigment, stabilizers, alloys paint, metallurgical, tannery, chemical manufacturing, mining, pulp and paper, oil refining, electrical, rubber processing and fertilizers [1,2]. The major sources of heavy metals

Table 1: Heavy Metals Employed in Major Industries.

Industries	Cd	Cr	Cu	Hg	Pb	Ni	Zn	Mn	Fe
Pulp, paper mills	-	√	√	√	√	-	-	-	√
Mining	√	√	√	√	√	√	√	√	√
Organic chemicals	√	√	-	√	√	-	-	√	√
Petrochemicals	-	-	-	√	√	-	-	-	-
Paint industries	-	-	-	-	√	-	-	-	-
Alkaloids, chlorine and inorganic chemicals	√	√	-	√	√	√	-	-	√
Fertilizers	√	√	√	√	√	-	-	-	-
Petroleum refining	√	√	√	-	√	√	-	√	-
Basic steel works foundries	√	√	√	√	√	√	√	√	√
Non ferrous metal works	√	√	√	√	√	√	√	-	-
Motor vehicle, air craft plating finishing	√	√	√	√	√	-	-	-	-
Flat glass, cement, asbestos	-	√	-	-	-	-	-	√	-
Textile mill products/ Printing	-	√	-	-	-	-	-	-	√
Leather tanning finishing	-	√	-	-	-	-	-	-	-
Stream generator power plants	-	√	-	-	-	-	-	-	-
Electroplating	-	√	√	√	√	√	√	-	√
Storage battery, electrical appliances	√	-	√	-	√	√	-	√	-

contamination of effluents/ wastewater are the industries, which are listed in Table 1.

The pollution of water resources due to the indiscriminate disposal of heavy metals has been causing worldwide concern for the last few decades. It is well known that some metals can have poisonous or harmful effects on many forms of life.

This problem has received considerable amount of attention in recent years. One primarily concern is that marine animals which can readily absorb those heavy metals in wastewater and directly enter the human food chains present a high health risk to consumers.

Exposure to hexavalent chromium causes dermatitis, allergic skin reaction and gastro intestinal ulcers. Chromium (VI) a tetratogen is also carcinogenic. Severe mishaps like "Minamata tragedy" due to mercury poisoning have increased the awareness about mercury toxicity. The toxic effects of mercury depend on its chemical form and the route of exposure. Methyl mercury [CH_3Hg] is the most toxic form and it affects the immune system, alters genetic and enzyme systems, and damages the nervous system. Methyl mercury is particularly damaging to developing embryos. Elemental mercury causes tremors, gingivitis, and excitability when vapours are inhaled over a long period. Ingestion of other common forms of mercury, such as the salt $HgCl_2$, damages the gastrointestinal tract and causes kidney failure. Lead is toxic to the central and peripheral nervous system as well kidney dysfunction. Chronic exposure to manganese may cause "Manganese psychosis" an irreversible brain disease. "Manganese pneumonia" results from inhalation exposure to manganese. Cadmium in toxication includes hypertension, respiratory disorder, damage to liver and kidney. Intake of large quantities of copper salts may caused haemolysis, hepatotoxic and nephrologic effects. High dosage of copper may cause lung cancer. Long-term exposure to iron salts cause "Sidderosis" and cancer. Large doses of zinc cause gastrointestinal disorder including vomiting and diarrhea. Acute poisoning of Ni (II) causes headache, dizziness, nausea and vomiting, chest pain, tightness of the chest, dry cough and shortness of breath, rapid respiration, cyanosis and extreme weakness. Waters containing heavy metals are environmentally persistent and toxic. Heavy metals are generally refractory and cannot be degraded or detoxified biologically. Hence, it is a challenging task for the industrialists and the environmentalists for the safe and effective disposal of wastewater containing heavy metals [3].

In view of the toxicity and in order to meet regulatory safe discharge standards, it is essential to remove heavy metals from wastewaters/ effluents before it is released into the environment. A number of technologies have been developed over the years to remove toxic metal ions from water. Conventional methods for the removal of heavy metals include precipitation, coagulation/ flocculation, ion exchange, reverse osmosis [4,5], complexation / sequestration, electrochemical operation and biological treatment [6].

Application of above-mentioned methods becomes economically unviable for the removal of heavy metals at lower concentrations. Adsorption, as compared to other methods, appears to be a simple attractive process in view of its high efficiency, easy handling and cost-effectiveness as well as the availability of different adsorbents. In addition, the recoveries of pure metal for recycle as well as reuse of the adsorbent are the added advantages. Adsorptive treatment using non- conventional adsorbents, such as agricultural and industrial solids wastes, have been used for the removal of heavy metals [7-12]. Moreover, the removal of metal ions from their solutions in the presence of agricultural materials may be due to the adsorption on surface and pores, and also to complexation by these materials. In the present work, our search for a cheap, readily available and effective adsorbent material has identified GAC as a potentially attractive adsorbent for the treatment of heavy metal contaminated wastewater after pre-treatment with 0.5% of Na_2S. The main objective of this study was to investigate the feasibility of using treated GAC for the maximum removal of above metal ions from wastewater at optimised process parameters such as initial concentration, adsorbent dose, contact time and pH.

This paper includes the results of studies on waste water samples analysis and treatment. The samples were collected from wastewater drains at selected sites. The waste water samples collected from sites were analysed in the laboratory for the parameters such as (Color, Odor, Turbidity, Conductivity, Total Dissolved Solids, Salinity, Acidity, Alkalinity, Total Hardness, Chloride, Fluoride, Cyanide, Sulfate, Nitrate, Total Organic Carbon, Chemical Oxygen Demand, Biological Oxygen Demand, Hg, Pb, Cd, Cr, Cu, Fe, Mn, Zn and Ni. It was found that the value/ concentrations exceeded the permissible limit for drinking/ discharge water and is really a matter of serious concern as human beings are using this water.

There is increasing concern about the quality of ground water, as there are the major source of drinking water in most of the places in this country and elsewhere. Quality is affected by introduction of chemicals and biological materials due to various industrial and domestic activities into the subsurface environment through quantitative interference with natural flow pattern, through various combinations of these. In general ground and surface water contain some naturally dissolved salts, which are introduced through a contact of the water moving in the hydrological cycle with various rocks and soil minerals.

Among man-made sources of pollution, industries serve as major sources of chemicals. Most of these sources are localized or point sources. Some wastes are internationally disposed to the system viz., injection wells, and seepage, recharge or infiltration pits. More often pollution occurs due to leakage from evaporation ponds, holding or oxidation ponds, buried waste, land fills or deep well waste disposal activities. The ground water in many parts of country is contaminated with heavy metals like Pb, Al, Cd, Cr, Cu, Mn, Fe and Zn etc. It has been reported that continuous usage of groundwater has rendered the land barren with poor yield since the soil has turned hard and impervious. This requires treatment before it can be used for domestic/ agricultural purposes.

Material and Methods

Instrumentation

All the chemicals were used of analytical reagent grade and were obtained from E. Merck. Batch experiments were conducted using different optimised parameters of granular activated carbon. They were shaken with 100 ml contaminated waste water sample at constant temperature in stopper bottles in a vibrating shaker at a speed of 125 rpm for 48 hrs. The samples were filtered by 41No Whatman filter paper and the concentration of heavy metals in the untreated and treated sample were determined by GBC AA-932 Atomic Absorption spectrophotometer using graphite furnace/ air acetylene flame. The minimum detection limit was equal to or less than EPA requirement. Three standard solutions with concentrations of metal ions in the linear range of the instrument were used to construct each calibration curve. During analysis of the samples for heavy metals concentration, those samples in which the concentration of heavy metals is observed beyond the linear range of the references were diluted to appropriate concentrations. All measurements were repeated three times and those results in which the standard deviations were found greater than 0.1 mg/l were not accepted.

The pH measurements were performed with a controlled pH analyser (LABINDIA). The pH meter was standardized using buffer solutions of pH values: 4.00, 7.00, 9.00 and 12.00.

Micromeritics ASAP 2010 make surface area analyzer and a mechanical shaker of WIDSONS SCIENTIFIC make was used for all the adsorption experiments for agitating the sample for a desired contact time.

Adsorbent

Preparation of treated GAC

The untreated GAC has poor adsorptive removal efficiency for heavy metal ions because it lacks appropriate chemical functional groups on its surface. Chemical treatment is essential to introduce a suitable functional group (S^{2-}, SH^{-}) on its surface for the improvement in adsorption capacity.

99.5 gm of GAC (coconut based) is immersed for 24 hrs in minimum quantity of distilled water containing 0.5 gm of Na_2S. The mixture was heated almost to dryness and then dried in an

Table 2: Characteristics of the Treated GAC.

S. No.	Parameters	Value
1.	pH	Alkaline
2.	Conductivity (μS cm^{-1})	102
3.	Salinity	0.0
4.	Bulk density (g/ml)	0.48
5.	Moisture (%)	4
6.	BET surface area (m^2/g)	1200
7.	Iodine number	950
8.	CCl_4 %	50
9.	Hardness number %	95
10.	Ash content %	9.0
11.	Particle size (mesh)	8 -20
Elemental analysis (weight % of the element)		
1.	Carbon	66.0
2.	Hydrogen	3.5
3.	Nitrogen	0.331
4.	Oxygen	29.1
5.	Sulphur	0.58
6.	Carboxylic functional group (meq/ g CA)	0.105
7.	Lactonic acid functional group (meq/g CA)	0.003
8.	Phenolic functional group (meq/g CA)	0.006

oven for 4 hrs at 110° C. The dried sample was washed with distilled water several times till it gave negative test for sulphide. The washed sample was again dried at 110° C for 4 hrs and stored in a dessicator for use. The characteristics of the GAC used in experiments are given in the Table 2.

Coconut shell based granular activated carbon named ACG – 50 procured from Active Carbon Ltd., Hyderabad, India. Determination of C, H, N and S were performed with an Elementar analyser GmbH.

To study the variation in concentration of hazardous heavy metal ions and other parameters, waste water samples from eight different places were collected.

To collect the waste water samples in passive polythene bottles the bottle was capped just after collection of water. For the determination of Cu (II), Hg (II), Cd (II), Pb (II), Zn (II), Ni (II), Mn (II) and Fe (II) a portion of the samples was taken and to avoid precipitation of iron a few drops of HCl were added in it then it was concentrated.

Results and Discussion

Most of the untreated industrial wastewater from the scattered units was carried out through major natural drains. The effluents have high pH (alkaline), COD, conductivity, TDS, chloride, sulphate, iron, cadmium, chromium, Zinc and lead.

Table 3: Wastewater sample analysis parameters site – S1.

S. No.	Parameters	Waste water (S1)	Permissible limits of Ground water	Discharge limits Wastewater
1.	pH	8.52	6.5-8.5	6 – 9
2.	Colour Hazen unit	Pinkish	5	-
3.	Odour	Unpleasant	Unobjectionable	-
4.	Turbidity NTU	287	5	-
5.	Conductivity ms/μs	23	-	-
6.	TDS mg/l	13100	1000	2100
7.	Salinity %	0.8	-	-
8.	Acidity mg/l	-	-	-
9.	Alkalinity mg/l	-	200	-
10.	Total hardness mg/l	328	300	-
11.	Cl^- mg/l	280	250	1000
12.	F^- mg/l	0.19	1	2
13.	CN^- mg/l	0.00	0.05	0.2
14.	SO_4^{2-} mg/l	200	200	1000
15.	NO_3^{2-} mg/l	27.5	45	-
16.	COD mg/l	1800	250	250
17.	BOD mg/l	29	30	30
18.	TOC mg/l	215	-	-
19.	TIC mg/l	245	-	-
20.	TC mg/l	450	-	-
21.	N_2 mg/l	32	-	100

Table 4: Results of treated and untreated wastewater samples

Metal ions	Untreated Sample (S1)	Treated with GAC (S1)	Untreated Sample (S2)	Treated with GAC (S2)	Untreated Sample (S3)	Treated with GAC (S3)	Untreated Sample (S4)	Treated with GAC (S4)	Permissible limits of Ground water	Discharge limits of Waste water
Pb(II) mg/l	0.3	0.001	0.51	0.001	0.04	0.001	0.22	0.001	0.05	0.1
Cd(II) mg/l	0.17	0.001	2.15	0.001	0.03	0.001	2.03	0.01	0.01	2.0
Cr(VI) mg/l	0.21	0.001	0.03	0.01	0.19	0.01	6.1	2	0.05	0.1
Hg(II) mg/l	0.009	0.00	0.029	0.001	0.002	0.001	0.028	0.001	0.001	0.01
Cu(II) mg/l	3.81	1.41	0.09	0.04	3.03	0.01	3.18	0.08	0.05	3.0
Fe(II) mg/l	1.1	0.9	4.06	0.6	3.2	0.5	4.63	1.2	0.3	3.0
Mn(II) mg/l	0.016	0.001	0.19	0.001	0.4	0.001	0.4	0.001	0.1	2.0
Ni(II) mg/l	2.775	0.0175	0.89	0.001	0.91	0.001	2.5	0.001	0.01	2.0
Zn(II) mg/l	0.04	0.001	4.00	0.001	0.34	0.001	7.53	0.001	5.0	5.0

Table 5: Results of treated and untreated wastewater samples

Metal ions	Untreated Sample (S5)	Treated with GAC (S5)	Untreated Sample (S6)	Treated with GAC (S6)	Untreated Sample (S7)	Treated with GAC (S7)	Untreated Sample (S8)	Treated (S8)	Permissible limits of Ground water	Discharge limits of Waste water
Pb(II) mg/l	0.198	0.001	0.34	0.001	0.104	0.001	0.32	0.001	0.05	0.1
Cd(II) mg/l	0.14	0.001	0.008	0.001	0.011	0.001	0.002	0.001	0.01	2.0
Cr(VI) mg/l	0.15	0.06	0.25	0.1	2.41	0.02	0.120	0.1	0.05	0.1
Hg(II) mg/l	0.003	0.001	0.02	0.001	0.002	0.001	0.001	0.001	0.001	0.01
Cu(II) mg/l	0.198	0.1	0.32	0.1	0.098	0.05	0.263	0.1	0.05	3.0
Fe(II) mg/l	3.239	0.21	3.5	2	3.096	0.08	3.078	1	0.3	3.0
Mn(II) mg/l	0.271	0.001	0.5	0.001	0.5	0.001	0.55	0.001	0.1	2.0
Ni(II) mg/l	0.46	0.001	0.24	0.001	0.63	0.001	0.89	0.001	0.01	2.0
Zn(II) mg/l	4.31	0.001	3.8	0.001	0.38	0.001	5.1	0.001	5.0	5.0

The ground water quality of the region was studied to ascertain the contamination from industrial wastewater. The study area lies along the drains. High conductivity, TDS, hardness and heavy metal rich effluents mainly from textiles, dyes and engineering industries have caused damage to both the drains and wells. The concentrations of heavy metal ions in untreated and treated waste water samples, collected from different selected sites are given in the Tables 4 & 5.

The analysis showed at site for wastewaters that conductivity 23.3ms and TDS 13150 mg/l. At certain sites, the parameters like total hardness, alkalinity, turbidity, fluoride, COD and heavy metal ions also indicated significantly higher values given in the Table 3. The waste water was not fit for domestic use and its utility value for agriculture is also questionable. This requires treatment before it can be used.

Conclusion

It is seen from the results that on treatment with treated GAC the levels of all the heavy metals contaminants is reduced to below permissible levels and in some cases, to below desirable levels. There is an appreciable reduction in Magnesium, Cadmium, Chromium, Lead, Nickel and Zinc bringing all of them within permissible levels, Copper and Iron within desirable levels.

Waste water used for human in domestic and agriculture needs treatment for removal / reduction of toxic heavy metals to below permissible levels. From the studies undertaken, treated granular activated carbon of the specified grade is seen to be single suitable adsorbent for treating the waste water contaminated with a contamination of heavy metals.

Acknowledgement

The authors are very grateful to Director CFEES, for providing all facilities and encouragement for carrying out this work. The authors are also grateful to Director CCRAS, for permitting to attend the conference.

References

1. Bingau P., Lonsdale H., Pinho M., Eds. Synthetic membranes: science, engineering and application, NATO ASI series, series C: mathematical and physical science, vol. 181. D. Ridelo Publishing Company, Dordrechet (1986).
2. Chandel C.P.S., Sharma D. K., Jangir, J.P. and Gupta, C.M. "Studies in quality of water in and around Jaipur Part - I Trace elements". IWWA Vol. 20 (3) (1988) 257.
3. Daneshar N., Salari D. and Aber S., J Hazardous Materials,B94 (2002) 49.
4. Hartiger L., hand buch der Abwasser - und Recycling technichs Munchen, Wien : Carl Hanser Verlag, (1991).
5. Hasar H., J Hazardous Materials, B97 (2003) 49.

6. Kiffs R. J., General inorganic effluents, In : Surveys in industrial wastewater treatment - manufacturing and chemical industries. Ed. D- Barnes, C. F. Forster and S. E. Hrudey. Vol. 3, Ch. 1,Lonngman, New York, NY. (1987).
7. Kadirvelu K., Thamaraselvi K. and Namasivayam C., Separation and Purification Technology. 24 (2001) 497.
8. Meena A.K., Mishra G.K., Rai P.K., Rajagopal C. and Nagar P.N., Journal of Hazardous Materials, Vol. 122 (1-2), (2005) 161-170.
9. Namasivayam B. and Ranganathan K. Environ. Technol. 16, (1995) 851.
10. Parivish (Report) CPCB, Delhi. Page 16-17.
11. Perisamy K. and Namasivayam C. Chemosphere, 32 (1996) 769.
12. Yu Bin, Zhang Y., Shukla A., Shukla S. and L. Dorris Kenneth, J Hazardous Materials,B84 (2001) 83.

42

Isolation and Characterization of Halotolerant *Penicillium* Species from Hyper-saline Environments

SUHAGIYA, V. J. AND RATNA TRIVEDI

Introduction

Cellular adaptation to extreme environmental conditions, such as high-saline environments, is a fundamental biological process needed for survival and growth of organisms (6,11,19,). Osmotic stress is caused by large concentrations of either salts or nonionic solutes in the surrounding medium; this results in dehydration of cells (2,14,20,25,). Salinity is a major limiting factor in agricultural productivity (14) and is of concern in the food and medicinal industries (3, 9,10,12,17,18,19,21,).

Fungi, are well known for their ability to adapt to environments of high osmolarity by intracellular accumulation of species of neutral, low-molecular-weight compounds which maintain positive turgor pressure (2, 4, 5). These compatible solutes can accumulate up to molar concentrations without greatly interfering with the normal functions of intracellular enzymes; these solutes may protect enzymes and other cellular components from high salt concentrations (1, 24 and 25).

Much attention is given to heavy metal pollution because metals cannot be decomposed by *in situ* biological means (13). Micro-organisms have been used at low costs to remove metals from effluents (2), with fungi known to be more tolerant to metals than bacteria or actinomycetes8, and the *Penicillium* spp. being prominent (3, 5) among these. Further, although the genus *Penicillium* has been studied and used for metal tolerance/removal, it has not been examined with respect to halophilic/ halotolerant species possessing metal resistance.

Methods and Materials

Sample Site: Surface lake sample were collected in plastic containers disinfected with alcohol. Samples were collected from the surface at a depth of 0 to 1 m from Sambhar and Didvana lakes of Rajasthan during October, 2007.

Isolation of Fungi: The isolates were spot-inoculated onto CDA containing NaCl concentrations of 0, 5.0, 10.0, 15.0, 20.0, and 25.0% (w/v) and assessed for growth in terms of colony diameter at RT up to 7 days for three sub-cultures. The isolates were then spot-inoculated on S-CDA containing 0–10 mM Pb^{2+} as $Pb(NO_3)_2$, or 0–5.0 mM Cu^{2+} as $CuSO_4.5H_2O$, or Cd^{2+} as $3CdSO_4.8H_2O/Cd(NO_3)_2$ $.4H_2O$ and monitored for growth as above.

Amylase assay: Amylase activity was assayed by using soluble starch as a substrate by the modified method of Fuwa: 2 ml of 2% soluble starch in 25 mM tris(hydroxymethyl) aminomethane (tris)-hydrochloride buffer (pH 7.0) containing 2 M NaCl was mixed with 1 ml enzyme solution. After incubation at 50°C for 10 min, a 0.2 ml portion of the 0.167 mM I_2-KI solution. The optical density at 700 nm was measured in a spectrophotometer. Hydrolysis of 0.1 mg soluble starch in 1 min was defined as 1 U of enzyme activity. In some experiments, reaction pH and temperature of enzyme assayed were made.

Results and Discussion

Penicillium spp. were seen to be one of the predominant groups amongst the halotolerant fungi from the hypersaline lakes of Rajasthan, with all twelve *Penicillium* isolates obtained showing high halotolerance. Tolerance to 25% NaCl by *Penicillium* spp. and the presence of halotolerant, have also been reported. Further, some of the cultures showed halophilic nature, distinguished by the requirement of hypersaline conditions for growth, while even minimal addition of NaCl slowed down the growth rate of halotolerant species. Optimal growth of some isolates at salt concentration of 2% or more indicated these isolates to be of marine origin A total of twelve isolates were obtained from the samples screened, among which six belonged to the genus *Penicillium*. All penicillia showed extreme halotolerance: A2, A5, A6 had maximum tolerance at 25% NaCl, A3 and A4 had tolerance at 15% NaCl, and A1 20% NaCl.

Decrease in growth with respect to increasing concentrations of saline up to 25% NaCl was gradual in A1, A2, A3 and A6, while a rapid 50% biomass reduction was observed in the remaining isolates from the salterns with every increase in salt concentration. There was also a lag in growth as well as a decrease in sporulation in all isolates with an increase in salt concentration. The action pattern of the enzyme on amylase and soluble starch was examined after every 24 hrs. The effect of % NaCl concentration on the enzyme activities are shown in (Figure-2). The optimum concentration of % NaCl was around 15 and stable at 20-25%.

Enzymes from those halophilic organisms which have so far been described have salt requirements greater than those of corresponding enzyme from either nanhalophilic organisms. In general, halophilic enzymes are denatured at low salt concentration, specially in the complete absence of salt. By and large, enzymes from halophilic organisms either maintain activity at high salt concentrations or are most active at their normal intracellular salt concentration.

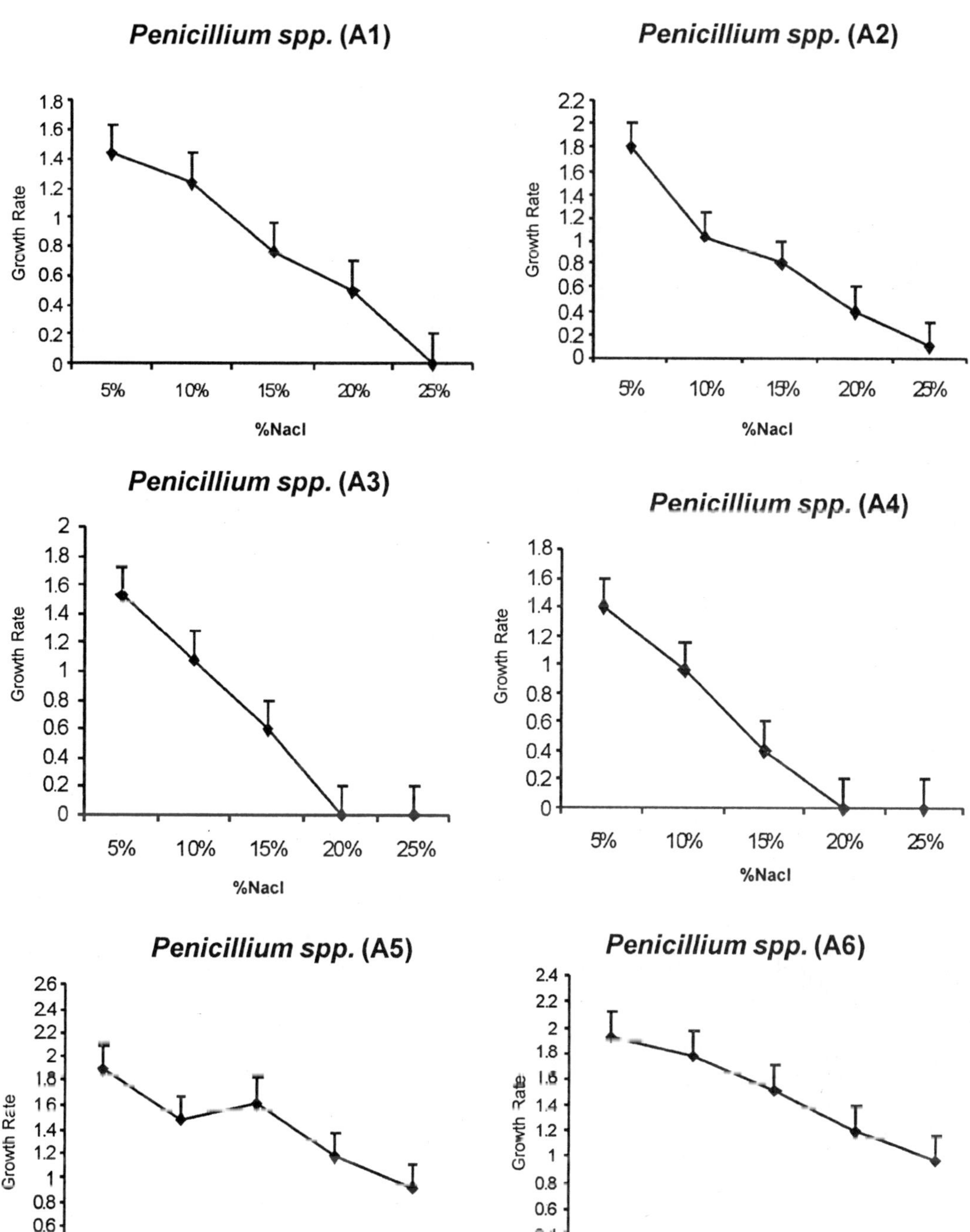
Penicillium spp. (A1)
Growth Rate
%Nacl
5%
10%
15%
20%
25%
Penicillium spp. (A2)
Growth Rate
%Nacl
Penicillium spp. (A3)
Growth Rate
%Nacl
Penicillium spp. (A4)
Growth Rate
%Nacl
Penicillium spp. (A5)
Growth Rate
%Nacl
Penicillium spp. (A6)
Growth Rate
%Nacl

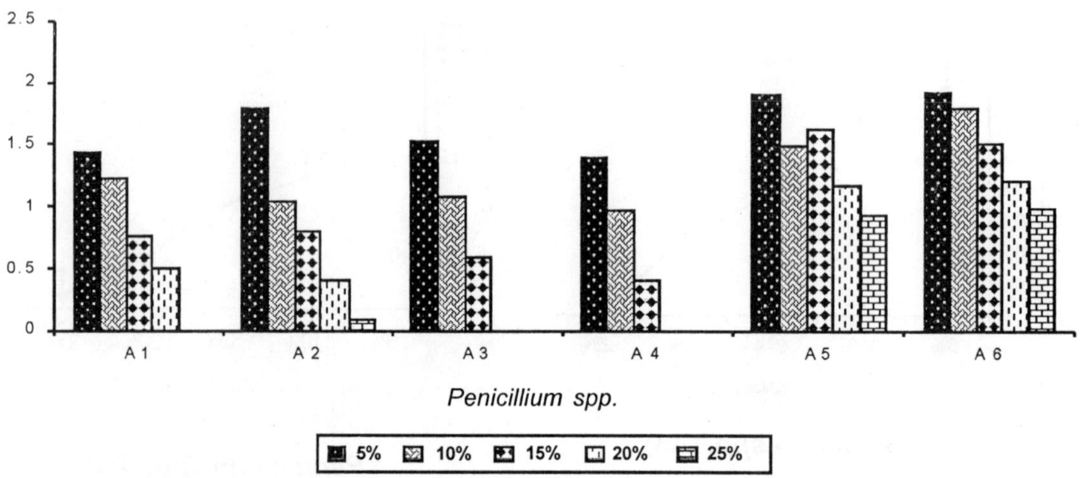

Fig. 1. Growth of Penicillium spp. in presence of % 5, 10, 15, 20 & 25 NaCl concentration.

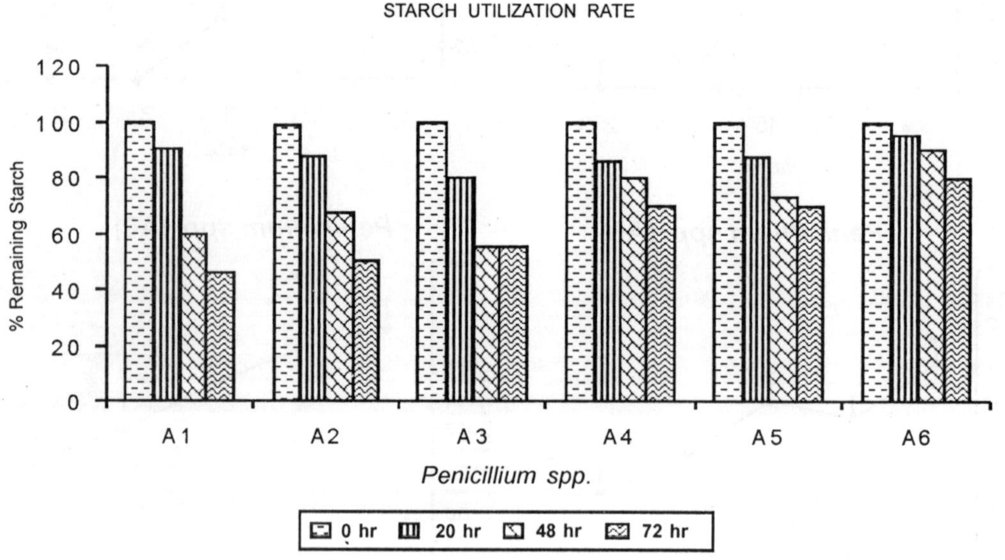

Fig. 2. Effect of %NaCl concentration on the enzyme activities.

Conclusion

It is generally observed that *Penicillium* species survive in environments containing high concentrations of carbohydrates, protein degradation products, and salts. The data presented here show that *Penicillium* survives and grows at a reduced rate in an environment containing 25% NaCl cultures have a limiting concentration of glucose; this limits the quantity of glycerol that it can generate for its osmoprotection. The diversity of micro-organisms in hypersaline environments is of growing interest. Organisms able to grow under extreme environments offer good potential as indicators of pollution and as biosorbents, and in applications for bioremedial measures. Many natural geological formations, such as petroleum reserves, are associated with hypersaline brines. Industrial processes also use salts and frequently release brine-effluent into the environment. These extremely halotolerant *Penicillium* species that are able to grow at high concentrations of salt as well as in its absence, while also possessing high resistance to heavy metals, could be used as agents for abatement of metal pollution in hypersaline conditions or in waters of fluctuating salinity, as well as in non-saline environments.

References

1. Arakawa, T., and Timasheff, S.N., (1985). The stabilization of proteins by osmolytes. Biophys. J. 47: 411–414
2. Bloomberg, A., and Adler, A. (1992). Physiology of osmotolerance in fungi. Adv. Microb. Physiol. 33: 144–212
3. Blunden, G., and S.M. Gordon. (1986). Betaines and their sulphonio analogues in marine algae. Prog. Physiol. Res. 4: 39–80.
4. Brown, A.D. (1978). Compatible solutes and extreme water stress in eukaryotic micro-organisms. Adv. Microb. Physiol. 17: 181–241
5. Brown, A.D. and Simpson, J.R., (1972). Water relations of sugar-tolerant yeasts: the role of intracellular polyols. J. Gen. Microbiol. 72: 589–591.
6. Da Costa, M.S., Duarte, J.C. and Williams, R.A.D. (ed.). (1989). Microbiology of extreme environments and its potential for biotechnology. Elsevier Science Publishers Ltd., Essex, England.
7. Fourest, E., Canal, C. and Roux, J.C., *FEMS Microbiol. Rev.*, 1994, 14, 325–332.
8. Gadd, G.M., *New Phytol.*, 1993, 124, 25–60.
9. Glaasker, E., Konigs, W. N. and Poolman, B. (1996). Osmotic regulation of intracellular solute pools in Lactobacillus plantarum. J. Bacteriol. 178: 575–582.
10. Hollaender, A., Aller, J. C., Epstein, E., San Pietro, A. and Zaborsky, O. R. (ed.). (1979). The biosaline concept: an approach to the utilization of underexploited resources. Plenum Press, New York
11. Ingraham, J. (1987). Effect of temperature, pH, water activity, and pressure on growth, p. 1543–1554. *In* F. C. Neidhardt, J. L. Ingraham, K. B. Low, B. Magasanik, M. Schaechter, and H. E.

Umbarger (ed.), Escherichia coli and Salmonella typhimurium: cellular and molecular biology. American Society for Microbiology, Washington, D.C.

12. Ko, R., Smith, L.T. , and Smith, G.M., (1994). Glycine betaine confers enhanced osmotolerance and cryotolerance on *Listeria monocytogenes.* J. Bacteriol. 176: 426–431.

13. Laws, E. A., Aquatic Pollution, John Wiley, The Netherlands, 1993, 2nd edn, pp. 351–415.

14. Le Rudulier, D., Strom, A.R., Dandekar, A.M., Smith, L. T. and Valentine, R. C. (1984). Molecular biology of osmoregulation. Science 224: 1064–1068

15. Natarajan, K.A., Subramaniam, S. and Modak, J. M., In *Biohydrometallurgyand Environment Toward the Mining of the 21st Century, Process Metallurgy Series 9A, Elsevier, Amsterdam,* 1999, pp. 351–361.

16. Niu, H., Xu, X.S., Wang, J.H. and Volesky, B., *Biotechnol. Bioeng.,* 1993, 42, 785–787.

17. Pitt, J.I. (1975). Xerophilic fungi and the spoilage of foods of plant origin, p.273–307. *In* R. B. Duckworth (ed.), Water relations of foods. Academic Press Ltd., London, United Kingdom.

18. Potts, M. (1994). Desiccation tolerance of prokaryotes. Microbiol. Rev. 58: 755–805

19. Rains, D.W., Valentine, R.C., and Hollanender, A. (ed.). (1980). Genetic engineering of osmoregulation: impact on plant productivity for food, chemicals and energy. Plenum Press, New York, N.Y.

20. Rhodes, D., and Hanson, A.D. (1993). Quaternary ammonium and tertiary sulfonium compounds in higher plants. Annu. Rev. Plant Mol. Biol. 44: 357–384.

21. Smith, L.T. (1996). Role of osmolytes in adaptation of osmotically stressed *Listeria monocytogenes* grown in liquid media and on processed meat surfaces. Appl. Environ. Microbiol. 62:3088–3093.

22. Tan, T. and Cheng, P., *Appl. Biochem.Biotechnol.,* 2003, 104, 119–128.

23. Vieira, H.S.F. and Volesky, B., *Int. Microbiol.,* 2000, 3, 17–24.

24. Wyn Jones, R.G. (1984). Phytochemical aspects of osmotic adaptation. Recent Adv. Phytochem. 18: 55–78.

25. Yancey, P., Clark, M., Hand, S., R. Bowlus, and Somero, G., (1982). Living with water stress: evolution of osmolyte systems. Science 217:1214–1222.

43

Physio-chemical Status of Some Fresh Waterbodies of the Hassan District, Karnataka

DR. B.S. RAVIKUMAR

Introduction

Fresh water has been rightly described as the very basis of life. Unfortunately during these days, the fresh water resources have never remained the same as they were earlier as a consequence of the urbanisation, industrialization, and population explosion. These fresh water resources have become dumping place for all that waste generated by human activities. Although a good amount of ecological work on the fresh water resources has been carried out both in first attempt to temperate and tropical climate, a little is known about the Wetland ecosystem of Karnataka (India), particularly in Hassan Dist. It is with this background the present study was carried out and infact, it is the investigate on the ecology of wetland ecosystems of Hassan District.

Description of the Study Area

Hassan District is located between 12°31′ and 13°33′ North and 75°33′ and 76°38′ East. Its greatest length from north to south is 129 kms (80 miles) and its greatest breadth is 116 kms (72 miles). Its has an area of 6,850 sqkm (2,650 sq miles).

One of the most striking features of plateau are the many dammed lakes or ponds used to conserve available moisture. The dam at Gorur near the confluence of the Yagachi and Hemavathy generated a reservoir.

Hassan district shows a wide range of climatic conditions. The temperature at the foot of the ghat is higher than that on the plateau. Temperature reading from Hassan indicates that December is generally the coldest month with mean daily minimum temperature of 14°C and mean daily maximum of 27°C. The temperature rises in early March and hot summer follows with April being the hottest month with a mean daily maximum of 35°C and a mean daily minimum of 20°C. The overall mean annual rainfall reported for Hassan District is 104.07 cm (41 in.)

Four fresh waterbodies were selected for the present investigation and they include Kandali, Sathyamangala, Hunasinakere and Makanakere lakes. All situated within a radius of 10 kms of Hassan City. Except Kandali and Sathyamangala the other two receive sewage from the city.

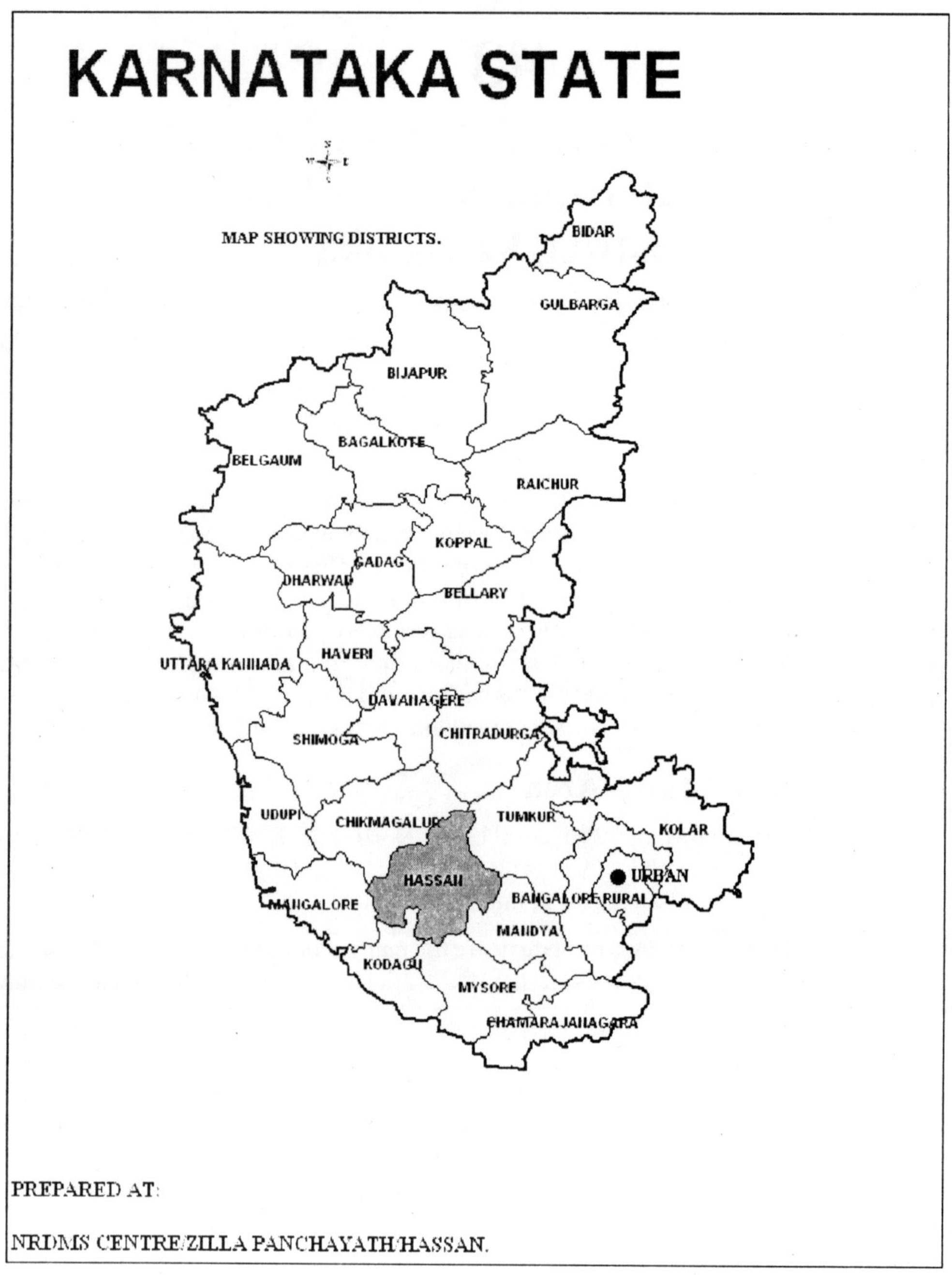

Table: 1

S.No.	Parameter	Kandali Lake			Makanakere Lake			Hunsinakere Lake			Sathyamangala Lake		
		Average of first year 2006-07	Average of second year 2007-08	Total average 2006-2008	Average of first year 2006-07	Average of second year 2007-08	Total average 2006-2008	Averave of first year 2006-07	Average of second year 2007-08	Total average 2006-2008	Average of first year 2006-07	Average of second year 2007-08	Total average 2006-2008
1	Air Temp°C	27.49	27.5	27.5	28.2	28.8	28.5	28.3	28.3	28.3	29.3	29.3	29.3
2	Water Temp°C	25.35	24.68	25.07	21.1	26.7	26.7	27.19	26.79	26.99	28.6	28.7	28.4
3	pH	7.89	7.83	7.86	8.4	8.4	8.4	8.2	8.22	8.21	7.8	7.8	7.8
4	electrical conductivity uM	132	136.5	134.25	392	353.6	372.6	246.5	255.2	250.85	138.5	137.5	138
5	Turbidity NTU	22.2	21.67	21.94	18.12	20.46	19.2	21.99	21.99	21.99	24	22.15	23.06
6	Rainfall in mm	55.48	85.86	70.68	55.48	85.86	70.68	55.48	85.86	70.68	55.48	85.86	70.68
7	Free CO2	14.45	14.17	14.32	18.22	17.62	17.92	16.50	13.94	15.27	13.2	12.9	13.07
8	Dissove O2	7.36	7.5	7.14	5.68	5.6	5.64	5.74	5.82	5.78	7.75	7.9	7.8
9	Carbonate	0.83	0.81	0.82	2.7	2.9	2.8	2.45	2.71	2.58	0.32	0.55	0.43
10	Bicarbonate	88.49	85.81	84.15	97.56	98.5	97.52	96.52	98.5	97.52	91.02	93.6	92.3
11	Total hardness	50.42	52.88	51.6	56.14	53.13	54.64	58 96	50.43	50.19	51.02	48.93	49.08
12	Calcium	37.91	38.09	38	38.73	40.33	39.48	40 71	41.26	40.94	38.04	37.78	40.93
13	Magnesium	17.27	18.13	17.7	10.73	12.32	11.53	14 38	14.26	14.32	17.07	18.02	17.54
14	Sodium	12.52	12.85	12.09	13.49	11.70	12.63	15.46	15.9	15.68	8.15	7.07	7.61
15	Potassium	5 94	6.58	6.25	661	776	7.19	8.21	6.3	7.26	7.12	5.43	6.27
16	Chlorides	63.47	60.3	61.89	109.2	84.79	96.79	176	169.6	172.8	59.84	61.16	60.5
17	Sulphates	113.84	111.5	112.67	187.5	162.1	174.8	137.1	161.7	149.4	105.02	109.38	107.2
18	Diss. Organic matter	0.71	0.94	0.83	1.106	1	1.03	1.16	1.14	1.15	0.76	0.81	0.79
19	Free ammonia	0.037	0.039	0.38	0.29	0.27	0.28	0.04	0.04	0.04	0.03	0.04	0.03
20	Nitrate	5.47	5.24	5.36	5.15	5.18	5.17	5.75	5.65	5.7	5.21	5.42	5.32
21	Nitrile	0.155	0.147	0.151	0.200	0.212	0.209	0.283	0.252	0.268	0.262	0.252	0.257
22	Phosphate	0.3	0.31	0.31	0.43	0.4	0.41	0.35	0.34	0.35	0.06	0.06	0.06
23	Silica	2.06	1.72	1.89	1.77	1.76	1.77	1.81	1.57	1.69	2.61	2.74	2.67
24	Iron	0.078	0.078	0.078	0.08	0.07	0.08	0.07	0.07	0.07	0.08	0.09	0.09
25	Total Solid	915	858	886	996	972.9	984.4	960.5	938.08	949.3	921.6	880	900.8
26	BOD	2.71	3	2.86	11.25	10.42	10.84	10.71	10.39	10.55	3.12	3.12	3.12
27	COD	22.26	23.07	22.66	40.62	44.7	44.12	38.79	36.01	30.4	23.59	23.99	23.79z

Materials and Methods

Water sample for chemical analysis were collected at an interval of 30 days for a period of two years (Feb. 2006 to Jan. 2008). Most of the factors were analysed immediately after return to the laboratory. While, few factors such as temperature of air and water, pH and Dissolved oxygen were examined at the spot of collection. Standard methods were employed for the estimation of Physicochemical factors (APHA 1995).

Results and Discussion

Table 1 shows the yearly and two yearly average values of Physico Chemical parameters of four fresh waterbodies.

The colour of the water was darkish in the case of Makanakere as it receives sewage, bluish green in Hunasinakere due to Cyanophycean bloom and it was muddy in colour in 'Sathyamangala lake as a consequence of escavation activities, However, the water was clear in respect of Kandali lake.

Temperature

Temperature of the water bodies often have an impact on their chemical concentration. In the present study the behaviour of air and water temperature do not show marked differences as is evidenced by the data recorded in table 1.

In the present investigation temperature of water ranged from 20.1°C in Makanakere and 33.6°C in Sathyamangala lake and air temp. ranged from 22.2°C at Kandali lake to 34.5°C at Sathyamangala lake.

In all the lakes, interestingly summer months registered maximum temperature. A similar observation has been made by Zafar (1955) and Munawar (1970), Mishra and Yadav (1978) and Mir and Kachroo (1990).

Carbonates, Carbon dioxide, Biocarbonates and pH

A close correlation among carbonate, bicarbonate, calcium, pH and free carbondioxide has been observed in the present study. Rao, (1955) indicated an inverse relationship between and are inversely proportional to bicarbonates. Unni (1985), Zutsi and Khan, (1988); Swarnalatha and Narasinga Rao (1993) and Sinha, (1995). The observations made in present study are essentially similar.

Calcium, Magnesium, Potassium and Sodium

It is found that in all the four lakes calcium is invariably greater than other cations while potassium stands at the least (Table 1). Even when the seasonal values are considered, absolutely no change in the position of these two cations observed. (in general, the behaviour of ionic composition is essentially similar to the observations made by Rodhe's (1949). Dakshini and Gupta (1974), Sharadendu and et al (1991) have also made a similar observations.

Dissolved Oxygen and Carbon Dioxide

The values of DO in the present study ranged between 5.64 mg/l in Makanakere and 7.80 mg/l in Sathyamangala lake while those of Co_2 remained between 13.07 mg/l in Sathyamangala lake and 17.92 mg/l in Makanakere apparently revealing are inverse relationship between the two. Such conclusions have also been arrived at by Swarnalatha and Narasinga Rao (1993). Seasonally the behaviour of dissolved oxygen and free Co_2 are rather irregular.

BOD and COD

BOD values remained always high in Hunasinakere and Makanakere which receive sewage. It ranged between a minimum of 2.86 mg/l in Kandali lake and a max. of 16.84 mg/l in Makanakere lake. Similarly the COD values were found to be relatively high in Makanakere and Hunasinakere concomitantly revealing the high degree of pollution in them. Seasonwise both the parameters were high during summer season. It has been consistently noticed BOD and COD showed inverse relationship.

Chlorides

In the present study chlorides varied from a min. of 60.50 mg/I in Sathyamangala lake and max. of 172.80/rig/l in Hunasinakere lake. It reached its peak during summer and monsoon season in all the lakes. Verma and Shukla (1968) and Sinha (1995) are of the opinion that waterbodies receiving sewage invariably contain higher amounts of chloride revealing that polluted waterbodies are rich in chloride concentration, which is also true in the present study. For instance, Makanakere and Hunasinakere registered relatively higher amount of chlorides indicating they are organically polluted when compare to Kandali and Sathyamangala lakes which are not contaminated.

Phosphate

The role of phosphate in biological productivity in aquatic systems is note worthy. Hutchinson (1957), long ago, have concluded that the amount of phosphate increases due to sewage contamination in waterbodies. In the present study, concentration of phosphate varied from 0.049 mg/l in Satyamangala and 1.007 mg/l in Makanakere lake. By and large, Makanakere and Hunasinakere showed relatively higher amount of Phosphate suggesting that the phosphate is sewage driven in these two lakes.

Sulphates

Conc. of sulphates fluctuated from min. of 60.48 mg/l in Sathyamangala lake and max. of 290.1 mg/l in Makanakere. Makanakere exceptionally registered very high amount of sulphate revealing that it is highly polluted. Zutshi and Khan (1988) have stated that polluted waters are always rich in sulphate.

Organic Matter

The amount of DOM ranged between a min.of 0.24 mg/l and max. of 1.81 mg/l in Kandali lake. It is very interesting to note that oxidisable organic matter was exceptionally high in Kandali lake which does not receive any sewage water from the adjoining area. The probable reason for this is the increased rate of decomposition. Phytoplankton composition is also responsible for the increased quantum of DOM. Fogg, (1960) has also of the same opinion.

Iron and Silica

It has been observed that silica occurred in a very low concentration and varied from a min. of 0.90 mg/l in Makanakere and max. of 3.95 mg/l in Sathyamangala lake. Seasonally, it was high during winter and low during summer months. In the present investigation, Iron was never exceeded 0.16 mg/l and ranged from min. 0.02 mg/l in Satyamangala lake and max. 0.16 mg/l in Kandali lake.

Summary

The foregoing revealed that Makanakere and Hunasinakere are highly polluted and at the verge of extinction while Kandali and Sathyamangala lakes are under ecological stress. Hence the following strategies suggested for their conservation.

1. A settling basin has to be constructed at the entry part of runoff waters into the lakes to prevent silt and nutrient rich water from entering the lake.
2. Soil conservation measures are to be taken at the earliest in the catchment area to control soil erosion.
3. The strategy to be adopted must include: catchment area treatment and water management at the basin land to control siltation, enhancing water holding capacity and to improve the water quality.
4. The participation of local communities should constitute an important component of any strategies.
5. The integration of social and ecological dimension which are inter-related and interdependent for sustainable management of the waterbodies should be the focus of the strategy.
6. The emphasis should be on preventive measure rather than on curative measures.
7. Some major problems which require immediate attention include:

   - Control of encroachment
   - Sewerage system in the city
   - Weed control
   - Increase in water circulation- Monitoring
   - For proper environment management of the lakes, it is imperative to undertake a systematic study involving scientific inputs from various desciplines. Such studies should be conducted for other lakes of the district also.

   The data generated during the study reveals that the conditions of water-bodies is rapidly becoming desperate. A number of lakes are being converted into ecological slums. Hence, remedy for the survival of one of the greatest gifts of nature is desperately needed.

References

1. APHA, 1995. American Public Health Association, Standard methods for the examination of water and waterbodies, 19th ed. Washington.

2. Mishra, G.P. and Yadav, A.K. 1978. "A comparative study of physico—chemical characteristics of river and lake water in central India. Hydrobiologia, 59.3:275-278.

3. India. Thesis accepted for degree of Ph.D., by the Osmani University, India.

4. Rodhe, W. 1949. The ionic composition of lake waters. Proc. mt. Ass. Linmmnol. 10:377—386.

5. Shardhendu and Ambasht R.S. 1991. Impact of urban surroundings on some limnological characteristic of tropical aquatic ecosystem. Acta Hydrochim, Hydrobiol. 19(4) :399-410.

6. Sinha, S.K. 1995. Potability of some rural pond's water at Muzaffarpur (Bihar) - A note on water quality index poll. Res14(1) :135—140.

7. Verama, S.R. and Shukia G.R. 1968. Hydrobiological studies on a temple tank "Devikund" in Deoband (U.P.), India, Environmental Health. 10:177-188.

8. Zutsi, D.P. and Khan, A.V. 1988. Eutropic gradient in the Dal lake, Kashmir, Indian J. Environmental Health, 30(4) 348-356.

44

Free-Living Nitrogen Fixing Bacteria Isolated from Wild Type Bambusa Species

SHARMA, P. AND DESAI P.B

Introduction

The environment in the rhizosphere is determined by three things: plants, soil, and organisms. The three factors related to plants that are important to rhizosphere health are nutrition, structure and rhizodeposition, or the material transfer from roots to soil. The three soil factors that affect the rhizosphere are moisture level, structure, and nutrients. The three organism factors that affect the rhizosphere are growth, interactions, and nutrient supply (Curl, 1986).

A main predisposing determinant of rhizosphere microorganism colonization is the spermosphere's colonization by microorganisms. The spermosphere is the area surrounding a germinating seed (Lynch, 1990). If the germinating seed has a large microorganism population, the plant is likely to have a large microorganism population as well.

Microorganism colonization happens in two phases. First, the bacteria around the germinating seed get pushed downward as the roots extend through the soil. This would account for the lower population of microorganisms on the roots that are furthest down. Next, the microorganisms multiply and compete for survival when the population reaches the limits of the ecological niche (Lynch, 1990).

There are four main kinds of interactions that occur when two or more organisms live in the same area. The first is commensalism, or symbiosis, which is an interaction that "promotes the growth of individuals within the populations." Commensalism implies that one organism benefits from the presence of another organism, but the second organism is neither benefiting from or being harmed by the first organism. The second is competition, or antibiosis. The third, which rarely occurs, is neutralism, and the fourth is mutualism (Curl, 1986).

Materials and Methods

Experimental Design

Five plants were randomly chosen from three different areas. The bacteria assembled that grew in two N-free media soil sample adhering to root surface were considered as rhizosphere (R), from the root cortex as the endorhizosphere (ER).

Isolation of free-living N_2 fixation strains. The collected plants were placed in plastic pots and kept at 5°C until sample proceeding. The roots used for endorhizosphere (ER) were washed, surface disinfected (700ml-1 ethanol for 1 min, washed three times in sterile distilled water), dried with sterile absorbent paper and crushed throughout in saline solution (8.5 gl-1 NaCl). One gram of each sample was suspended in 9 ml sterile saline solution and tenfold serial dilution was performed for each suspension obtained with the roots. One hundred-microliter aliquots of the 10^{-4}-10^{-7}dilution were inoculated in two N-free culture media: Burk's (Wilson & Knight, 1952), that uses glucose as the C source, and Nfb media that uses malate as a C source (Nitrogen Deficient semisolid malate media -NDSM), (Doberiner and Day, 1976). The plates were inoculated in duplicated at 28°C for 7 days under low O_2 condition. The number of colonies was assessed on the third and seventh days of incubation (Andrade et al.,1997a). The colonies grown in the two N-free media were counted, isolated and grouped according to the morphological similarities of the cells and colonies and biochemical characterization (Andrade et al., 1997b). Effect of pH was studied for most dominated organisms of all the plates.

Result and Discussion

Nutrient supply by insects in the field was relatively low, since less than 50% of the plants had insects captured in their leaf-traps in the summer (data not shown); however, plant vigor was high. Bacterial populations, evaluated by the log CFU g sample-1 were similar in both C source were tested. The population in the endophyllosphere (EP) was statistically lower than from the other parts of the plant (Turkey's test, 5%), in both Nitrogen Deficient Semisolid Malate Media (NDSM) and Burk's media. Isolates were classified in morphological, colonical and biochemical indices, the morphological analysis showed 90% strains were gram negative and 10% strain were gram variable.

Table 1: Characterization of Isolated organisms.

Test	AE07	AE08
Gram reaction	- ve	-ve
Motility	motile	motile
Phenol	-	-
Glycerol	+	+
Mannitol	+	+
Rhamnose	+	+
Meso inositol	+	+
Trehalose	+	+
Succinate	+	-
Propionate	+	-
Raffinose	+	+
Butanol	-	-
Sorbitol	+	+
Malonate	+	-
Peroxidase	+	-
Oxidase	+	+
Urease	-	-
Cysteine	-	-
Thiosulfate	-	-
Nitrate Reduction	+	+

Table 2: Growth on various carbon sources.

Substrate	AE07	AE08
Fructose	+	+
Glucose	+	+
Acetate	+	-
Lactate	+	-
Sucrose	+	+
Maltose	+	+
Lactose	+	+
Xylose	+	+

Bacterial populations were higher outside (phyllosphere and roots) than inside (endorhizosphere) of the plants. However, the diversity was higher in bacteria isolated from inside than from outside the plants. It is possible that the hostile environment outside the plants limits bacterial growth. Few microorganisms would be adapted to the acidic and nutrient-limited conditions, established a low level of competitiveness, therefore few adapted individuals would prevail and show enhanced growth. On the other hand, the more favorable conditions inside the

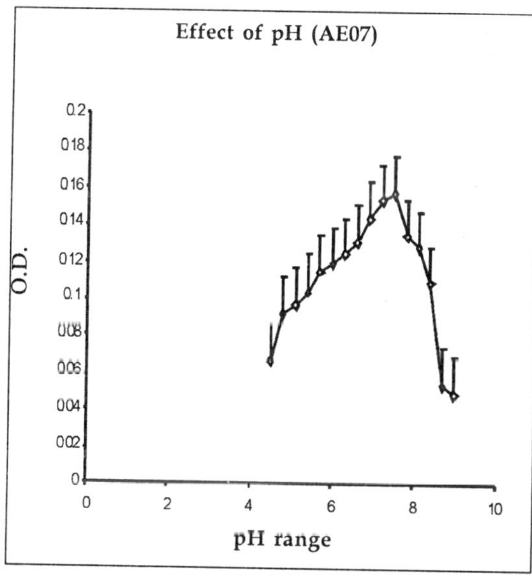

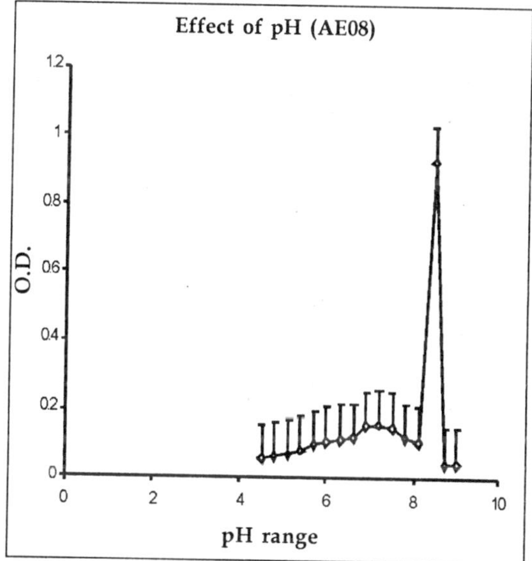

Fig.1. Effect of pH: determined effect of pH on exponential growth shown graphically from the mean OD_{600} of duplicate liquid culture.

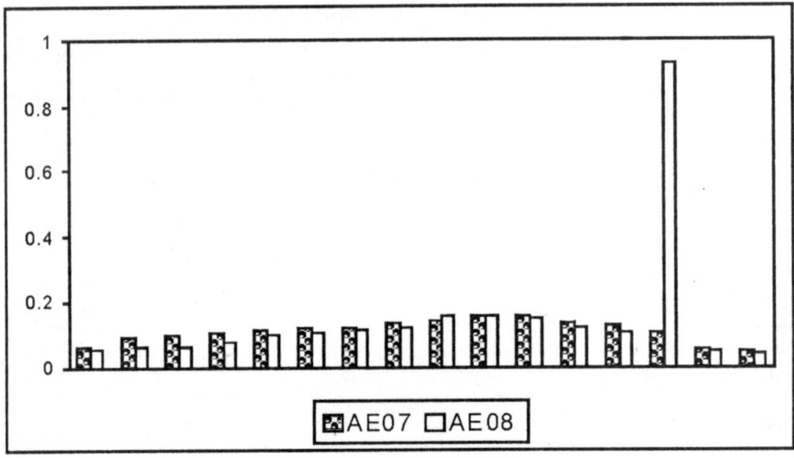

Fig. 2: Comparative analysis of effect of pH on AE07 & AE08: Isolates AE07 and AE08 had optimum alkaline pH 7.5 and minimum 4.5 where osmotolerant AE08 shown growth maximum at 8.4 pH.

plant would result in greater diversity, but the higher competition among these microorganisms would result in a lower number of individuals of each established strain.

Conclusion

Isolated organisms were classified as N_2-fixing organisms according to their functional diversity. Diazotrophic bacteria belonging to enterobacteria family were isolated from the rhizosphere of the Bambusa spp. and roots of the plants. The diversity of bacteria in association with Bambusa spp. describe in this study may be related to some of the strategies that this plant uses to survive in localities very poor on nutrients. However, the dependence that the plants have on these diazotrophic bacteria needs to be assessed, and quantification experiments are in progress.

The bacteria associated with Bambusa spp. roots and leaves are submitted to a strong selection pressure, both because the plant is not a legume and also because it grows in a nutrient-poor habitat where very few plants survive. Free living N_2-fixing bacteria adapted to these stress conditions may show great potentials for the use as inoculants, in crops as irrigated rice or in programs of recovery of degraded areas that suffer from periodic flooding such as river banks.

References

1. Andrade G, Esteban E, Velasco L, Lorite MJ, Bedmar EJ (1997a). Isolation and identification of N_2-fixing microorganisms from the rhizosphere of Capparis spinosa (L.). Plant Soil 197:19–23
2. Andrade G, Mihara KL, Linderman RG, Bethlenfalvay GJ (1997b). Bacteria from rhizosphere and hyphosphere soils of different arbuscular mycorrhizal fungi.Plant Soil 192:71–79.
3. Balota EL, Lopes ES, Hungria M, Dobereiner J (1999). Occurrence of diazotrophic bacteria and arbuscular mycorrhizal fungi on the cassava crop. Pesqui Agropecu Bras 34:1265–1276.

4. Barraquio WL, Revilla L, Ladha JK (1997). Isolation of endophytic diazotrophic bacteria from wetland rice.Plant Soil 194:15-24.

5. Do¨ bereiner J, Day JM (1976). Associative symbiosis in tropical grasses, characterization of microorganisms and dinitrogen fixing sites. In: Proceedings of the 1st international symposium of nitrogen fixation. Washington State University Press, Pullman.

6. Elbeltagy A, Nishioka K, Suzuki H, Sato T, Sato YI, Morisaki H, Mitsui H, Minamisawa K (2000). Isolation and characterization of endophytic bacteria from wild and traditionally cultivated rice varieties. Soil Sci Plant Nutr 46:617-629.

7. Estrada-De Los Santos P, Bustillos-Cristales R, Caballero-Mellado J (2001). Burkholderia, a genus rich in plant associated nitrogen fixers with wide environmental and geographic distribution. Appl Environ Microbiol 67:2790-2798.

8. Fernandes MF, Fernandes RPM, Rodrigues LD (2001). Diazotrophic bacteria associated to coconut palms in a coastal lowland region in Sergipe State, Brazil. Pesqui Agropecu Bras 36:1509-1517.

9. Gough C, Vasse J, Galera C, Webster G, Cocking E, De´narie´ J (1997). Interactions between bacterial diazotrophs and non-legume dicots: Arabidopsis thaliana as a model plant. Plant Soil 194:123-130.

10. Perica MC, Berljak J (1996). In vitro growth and regeneration of D. spatulata Labill. on various media. Hortic Sci 31:1033-1034.

11. Wilson PW, Knight SC (1952). Experiments in bacterial physiology. Burguess, Minneapolis, pp 49.

45

Genetically Modified Crops

AMIT GUPTA AND RITESH AGGARWAL

Introduction

Genetically modified crops, more accurately called genetically engineered foods, are foods that have had their DNA altered through genetic engineering. Unlike conventional genetic modification that is carried out through conventional breeding and that have been consumed for thousands of years, GE foods were first put on the market in the early 1990s. The most common modified foods are derived from plants: soybean, corn, canola, and cotton seed oil.

Controversies surrounding GM foods and crops commonly focus on human and environmental safety, labeling and consumer choice, intellectual property rights, ethics, food security, poverty reduction, and environmental conservation.

Origination of Genetically Modified Crops

The first commercially grown genetically modified whole food crop was the tomato, which was made more resistant to rotting by Californian Company Calgene. A variant of the Flavr Savr was used by Zeneca to produce tomato paste which was sold in Europe during the summer of 1996.

The attitude towards GM foods drastically changed after outbreaks of Mad Cow Disease weakened consumer trust in government regulators, and protesters rallied against the introduction of Monsanto's "Roundup-Ready" soybeans. The next GM crops included insect-resistant cotton and herbicide-tolerant soybeans both of which were commercially released in 1996. GM crops have been widely adopted in the United States. They have also been extensively planted in several other countries (Argentina, Brazil, South Africa, India and China) where the agriculture is a major part of the total economy. Other GM crops include insect-resistant maize and herbicide-tolerant maize, cotton, and rapeseed varieties.

Economic and Political Effects

- Some opponents of current genetic engineering believe the increasing use of GM in major crops has caused a power shift in agriculture towards Biotechnology companies, which are gaining more control over the production chain of crops and food, and over the farmers that use their products, as well.
- Many proponents of some current genetic engineering techniques believe it will lower

pesticide usage and has brought higher yields and profitability to many farmers, including those in developing nations. A few genetic engineering licenses allow farmers in less economically developed countries to save seeds for next year's planting.

- In August 2003, Zambia cut off the flow of Genetically Modified Food (mostly maize) from UN's World Food Programme. This left a famine-stricken population without food aid.
- In December 2005 the Zambian government changed its mind in the face of further famine and allowed the importation of GM maize. However, the Zambian Minister for Agriculture Mundia Sikatana has insisted that the ban on genetically modified maize remains, saying "We do not want GM (genetically modified) foods and our hope is that all of us can continue to produce non-GM foods."
- In April 2004 Hugo Chávez announced a total ban on genetically modified seeds in Venezuela.
- In January 2005, the Hungarian government announced a ban on importing and planting of genetic modified maize seeds, although these were agreed authorized by the EU.
- On August 18, 2006, American exports of rice to Europe were interrupted when much of the U.S. crop was confirmed to be contaminated with unapproved engineered genes, possibly due to accidental cross-pollination with conventional crops. The U.S. government has since declared the rice safe for human consumption, and exports to some countries have since resumed, but in the past years more crops have started to cross-pollinate which leaves a problem that is yet to be solved.

Advantages of GM Foods

The world population has topped 6 billion people and is predicted to double in the next 50 years. Ensuring an adequate food supply for this booming population is going to be a major challenge in the years to come. GM foods promise to meet this need in a number of ways:

- **Pest resistance:** Crop losses from insect pests can be staggering, resulting in devastating financial loss for farmers and starvation in developing countries. Farmers typically use many tons of chemical pesticides annually. Consumers do not wish to eat food that has been treated with pesticides because of potential health hazards, and run-off of agricultural wastes from excessive use of pesticides and fertilizers can poison the water supply and cause harm to the environment. Growing GM foods such as B.t. corn can help eliminate the application of chemical pesticides and reduce the cost of bringing a crop to market.
- **Herbicide tolerance:** For some crops, it is not cost-effective to remove weeds by physical means such as tilling, so farmers will often spray large quantities of different herbicides (weed-killer) to destroy weeds, a time-consuming and expensive process that requires care so that the herbicide doesn't harm the crop plant or the environment. Crop plants genetically-engineered to be resistant to one very powerful herbicide could help prevent environmental damage by reducing the amount of herbicides needed. For example, Monsanto has created a strain of soybeans genetically modified to be not affected by their herbicide product Roundup. A farmer grows these soybeans which then only require one application of weed-killer instead of multiple applications, reducing production cost

and limiting the dangers of agricultural waste run-off.

- **Disease resistance:** There are many viruses, fungi and bacteria that cause plant diseases. Plant biologists are working to create plants with genetically-engineered resistance to these diseases.
- **Cold tolerance:** Unexpected frost can destroy sensitive seedlings. An antifreeze gene from cold water fish has been introduced into plants such as tobacco and potato. With this antifreeze gene, these plants are able to tolerate cold temperatures that normally would kill unmodified seedlings.
- **Drought tolerance/Salinity tolerance:** As the world population grows and more land is utilized for housing instead of food production, farmers will need to grow crops in locations previously unsuited for plant cultivation. Creating plants that can withstand long periods of drought or high salt content in soil and groundwater will help people to grow crops in formerly inhospitable places.
- **Nutrition:** Malnutrition is common in third world countries where impoverished peoples rely on a single crop such as rice for the main staple of their diet. However, rice does not contain adequate amounts of all necessary nutrients to prevent malnutrition. If rice could be genetically engineered to contain additional vitamins and minerals, nutrient deficiencies could be alleviated. For example, blindness due to vitamin A deficiency is a common problem in third world countries. Researchers at the Swiss Federal Institute of Technology Institute for Plant Sciences have created a strain of "golden" rice containing an unusually high content of beta-carotene (vitamin A). Since this rice was funded by the Rockefeller Foundation, a non-profit organization, the Institute hopes to offer the golden rice seed free to any third world country that requests it. Plans were underway to develop a golden rice that also has increased iron content. However, the grant that funded the creation of these two rice strains was not renewed, perhaps because of the vigorous anti-GM food protesting in Europe, and so this nutritionally-enhanced rice may not come to market at all.
- **Pharmaceuticals:** Medicines and vaccines often are costly to produce and sometimes require special storage conditions not readily available in third world countries. Researchers are working to develop edible vaccines in tomatoes and potatoes. These vaccines will be much easier to ship, store and administer than traditional injectable vaccines.
- **Phytoremediation:** Not all GM plants are grown as crops. Soil and groundwater pollution continues to be a problem in all parts of the world. Plants such as poplar trees have been genetically engineered to clean up heavy metal pollution from contaminated soil.

Future Developments

Future envisaged applications of GMOs are diverse and include drugs in food, bananas that produce human vaccines against infectious diseases such as Hepatitis B, metabolically engineered fish that mature more quickly, fruit and nut trees that yield years earlier, and plants that produce new plastics with unique properties. While their practicality or efficacy in commercial production has yet to be fully tested, the next decade may see exponential increases in GM product development as researchers gain increasing access to genomic resources that are applicable to organisms beyond the scope of individual projects. Safety testing of these products will also at the same time be necessary to ensure that the perceived benefits will indeed outweigh the perceived and hidden costs of development. Plant scientists, backed by results of modern comprehensive profiling of crop composition, point out that crops modified using GM techniques are less likely to have unintended changes than are conventionally bred crops.

Are genetically modified plant foods safe to eat?

Foodstuffs made of genetically modified crops that are currently available (mainly maize, soybean, and oilseed rape) have been judged safe to eat, and the methods used to test them have been deemed appropriate. These conclusions represent the consensus of the scientific evidence surveyed by the International Council for Science (ICSU) and are consistent with the views of the World Health Organization (WHO).

However, the lack of evidence of negative effects does not mean that new genetically modified foods are without risk. The possibility of long-term effects from genetically modified plants cannot be excluded and must be examined on a case-by-case basis. New techniques are being developed to address concerns, such as the possibility of the unintended transfer of antibiotic-resistance genes.

Genetic engineering of plants could also offer some direct and indirect health benefits to consumers, for instance by improving nutritional quality or reducing pesticide use.

Scientists recommend that food safety assessment should take place on a case-by-case basis before genetically modified food is brought to the market. In such assessments, foodstuffs derived from genetically modified plants are compared to their conventional counterparts, which are generally considered safe due to their long history of use. This comparison considers to what extent different foodstuffs can cause harmful effects or allergies and how much nutrients they contain.

Consumers may wish to select foods on the basis of how they are produced, because of religious, environmental, or health concerns. However, merely indicating whether a product is genetically modified or not, without providing any additional information, says nothing about its content nor about possible risks or benefits. International guidelines are being developed for labelling genetically modified foods.

GM Crops Effect on Environment

Agriculture of any type has an impact on the environment. Genetic engineering may accelerate the damaging effects of agriculture, have the same impact as conventional agriculture, or contribute to more sustainable practices.

Growing genetically modified or conventional plants in the field has raised concern for the potential transfer of genes from cultivated species to their wild relatives. However, many food plants are not native to the areas in which they are grown. Locally, they may have no wild relatives to which genes could flow.

Moreover, if gene flow occurs, it is unlikely that the hybrid plants would thrive in the wild, because they would have characteristics that are advantageous in agricultural environments only. In the future, genetically modified plants may be equipped with mechanisms designed to prevent gene flow to other plants.

A controversy has arisen about whether certain genetically modified plants (which are insect resistant because they carry the Bt gene) could harm not only insect pests but also other species such as the monarch butterfly. In the field, no significant adverse effects on non-target species have so far been observed. Nonetheless, continued monitoring for such effects is needed.

Genetically modified crops may have indirect environmental effects as a result of changing agricultural or environmental practices. However, it remains controversial whether the net effect of these changes will be positive or negative for the environment. For example, the use of genetically modified insect-resistant Bt crops is reducing the volume and frequency of insecticide use on maize, cotton and soybean. Yet the extensive use of herbicide and insect resistant crops could result in the emergence of resistant weeds and insects.

The broad consensus is that the environmental effects of genetically modified plants should be evaluated using science-based assessment procedures, considering each crop individually in comparison to its conventional counterparts.

Implications of GM-Technologies for Animals

Animal feeds frequently contain genetically modified crops and enzymes derived from genetically modified micro-organisms. There is general agreement that both modified DNA and proteins are rapidly broken down in the digestive system.

To date no negative effects on animals have been reported. It is extremely unlikely that genes may transfer from plants to disease-causing bacteria through the food chain. Nevertheless, scientists advise that genes which determine resistance to antibiotics that are critical for treating humans should not be used in genetically modified plants.

As of 2004, no genetically modified animals were used in commercial agriculture anywhere in the world, but several livestock and aquatic species were being studied. Genetically modified animals could have positive environmental impacts, for example through greater disease resistance and lower antibiotic usage. However, some genetic modifications could lead to more intensive livestock production and thus increased pollution.

GM Crops and Climate Change

When GM crops first came on the scene, they were promoted as a vital tool for feeding a growing world population from a limited supply of agricultural land. In recent years, they have been equally likely to be presented as a key weapon in the race to tackle the problems of climate change.

On the one hand, GM crops are claimed to help mitigate climate change by reducing carbon emissions from agriculture – by reducing the need for mechanised ploughing, fertiliser applications and pesticide spraying.

On the other hand, transgenic crops, with traits like drought-tolerance or the ability to use nitrogen more efficiently, are proposed as vital tools to enable farmers to adapt to a warmer, drier climate. Finally, genetic engineering of crops, including trees, is put forward as an important step towards making them more valuable as, and easier to process into, sustainable biofuels that will help us to reduce our dependence on fossil fuels.

In this area, arguments about GM agriculture overlap with wider debates about the environmental impacts of biofuel production, trade-offs between food production and energy supply, and issues of risk, uncertainty and equity in relation to the causes and consequences of climate change.

Developing Countries' Experiences with GM Crops

Transgenic varieties of cotton, genetically modified to produce an insecticidal toxin, were commercialised in China, India and South Africa more than half a decade ago. In these countries, smallholders as well as larger-scale farmers have been growing the GM varieties. More recently, a small number of South African smallholders have begun growing GM, insect-resistant maize – a subsistence food crop. Some of these farmers have gained significant economic advantages from the new crops, while others have complained about their performance.

The experiences of these smallholder farmers have been the focus of intense scrutiny from policy-makers, aid donors, the media, farmers' groups and NGOs, and the subject of contentious claims and counter-claims from supporters and opponents of GM agriculture. Mainstream agricultural economists have produced a number of peer-reviewed econometric studies which appear to show that the adoption of GM crops has produced widespread benefits for large- and small-scale farmers alike. Farmers' organisations, NGOs and independent commentators in both North and South, however, have published accounts and analyses which suggest that GM crops are a risky proposition for the poorest and most vulnerable farmers, such as those farming marginal lands without the benefit of irrigation and dependable sources of credit.

After several years of controversy, academic studies have begun to emerge which give a more rounded picture of smallholders' experiences with GM crops. There is growing concern, in North America as well as in China and India, about the appearance of technical problems with the GM crop model, such as the resurgence of formerly "secondary" pests that are wiping out the economic advantages of GM, insect-resistant cotton in China. Supporters of GM technology argue that the next generation of crops will overcome these problems and more directly address the needs of smallholder farmers, provided they are not stifled by regulation or consumer opposition.

Criticisms against GM Foods

Environmental activists, religious organizations, public interest groups, professional associations and other scientists and government officials have all raised concerns about GM foods, and criticized agribusiness for pursuing profit without concern for potential hazards, and the government for failing to exercise adequate regulatory oversight. It seems that everyone has a strong opinion about GM foods. Even the Vatican and the Prince of Wales have expressed their opinions. Most concerns about GM foods fall into three categories: environmental hazards, human health risks, and economic concerns.

Environmental Hazards

- **Unintended harm to other organisms:** Last year a laboratory study was published in Nature showing that pollen from B.t. corn caused high mortality rates in monarch butterfly caterpillars. Monarch caterpillars consume milkweed plants, not corn, but the fear is that if pollen from B.t. corn is blown by the wind onto milkweed plants in neighboring fields, the caterpillars could eat the pollen and perish. Although the Nature study was not conducted under natural field conditions, the results seemed to support this viewpoint. Unfortunately, B.t. toxins kill many species of insect larvae indiscriminately; it is not possible to design a B.t. toxin that would only kill crop-damaging pests and remain harmless to all other insects. This study is being reexamined by the USDA, the U.S. Environmental Protection Agency (EPA) and other non-government research groups, and preliminary data from new studies suggests that the original study may have been flawed. This topic is the subject of acrimonious debate, and both sides of the argument are defending their data vigorously. Currently, there is no agreement about the results of these studies, and the potential risk of harm to non-target organisms will need to be evaluated further.
- **Reduced effectiveness of pesticides:** Just as some populations of mosquitoes developed resistance to the now-banned pesticide DDT, many people are concerned that insects will become resistant to B.t. or other crops that have been genetically-modified to produce their own pesticides.
- **Gene transfer to non-target species:** Another concern is that crop plants engineered for herbicide tolerance and weeds will cross-breed, resulting in the transfer of the herbicide resistance genes from the crops into the weeds. These "superweeds" would then be herbicide tolerant as well. Other introduced genes may cross over into non-modified crops planted next to GM crops. The possibility of interbreeding is shown by the defense of farmers against lawsuits filed by Monsanto. The company has filed patent infringement lawsuits against farmers who may have harvested GM crops. Monsanto claims that the farmers obtained Monsanto-licensed GM seeds from an unknown source and did not pay royalties to Monsanto. The farmers claim that their unmodified crops were cross-pollinated from someone else's GM crops planted a field or two away. More investigation is needed to resolve this issue.

There are several possible solutions to the three problems mentioned above. Genes are exchanged between plants via pollen. Two ways to ensure that non-target species will not receive introduced genes from GM plants are to create GM plants that are male sterile (do not produce pollen) or to modify the GM plant so that the pollen does not contain the introduced gene. Cross-pollination would not occur, and if harmless insects such as monarch caterpillars were to eat pollen from GM plants, the caterpillars would survive.

Another possible solution is to create buffer zones around fields of GM crops. For example, non-GM corn would be planted to surround a field of Bt GM corn, and the non-GM corn would not be harvested. Beneficial or harmless insects would have a refuge in the non-GM corn, and insect pests could be allowed to destroy the non-GM corn and would not develop resistance to B.t. pesticides. Gene transfer to weeds and other crops would not occur because the wind-blown pollen would not travel beyond the buffer zone. Estimates of the necessary width of buffer zones range from 6 meters to 30 meters or more. This planting method may not be feasible if too much acreage is required for the buffer zones.

Human Health Risks

- **Allergenicity:** Many children in the US and Europe have developed life-threatening allergies to peanuts and other foods. There is a possibility that introducing a gene into a plant may create a new allergen or cause an allergic reaction in susceptible individuals. A proposal to incorporate a gene from Brazil nuts into soybeans was abandoned because of the fear of causing unexpected allergic reactions. Extensive testing of GM foods may be required to avoid the possibility of harm to consumers with food allergies. Labeling of GM foods and food products will acquire new importance, which I shall discuss later.
- **Unknown effects on human health:** There is a growing concern that introducing foreign genes into food plants may have an unexpected and negative impact on human health. A recent article published in Lancet examined the effects of GM potatoes on the digestive tract in rats. This study claimed that there were appreciable differences in the intestines of rats fed GM potatoes and rats fed unmodified potatoes. Yet critics say that this paper, like the monarch butterfly data, is flawed and does not hold up to scientific scrutiny. Moreover, the gene introduced into the potatoes was a snowdrop flower lectin, a substance known to be toxic to mammals. The scientists who created this variety of potato chose to use the lectin gene simply to test the methodology, and these potatoes were never intended for human or animal consumption.

On the whole, with the exception of possible allergenicity, scientists believe that GM foods do not present a risk to human health.

Economic Concerns

Bringing a GM food to market is a lengthy and costly process, and of course agri-biotech companies wish to ensure a profitable return on their investment. Many new plant genetic engineering technologies and GM plants have been patented, and patent infringement is a big concern of agribusiness. Yet consumer advocates are worried that patenting these new plant varieties will raise the price of seeds so high that small farmers and third world countries will not be able to afford seeds for GM crops, thus widening the gap between the wealthy and the poor. It is hoped that in a humanitarian gesture, more companies and non-profits will follow the lead of the Rockefeller Foundation and offer their products at reduced cost to impoverished nations.

Patent enforcement may also be difficult, as the contention of the farmers that they involuntarily grew Monsanto-engineered strains when their crops were cross-pollinated shows. One way to combat possible patent infringement is to introduce a "suicide gene" into GM plants. These plants would be viable for only one growing season and would produce sterile seeds that do not germinate. Farmers would need to buy a fresh supply of seeds each year. However, this would be financially disastrous for farmers in third world countries who cannot afford to buy seed each year and traditionally set aside a portion of their harvest to plant in the next growing season. In an open letter to the public, Monsanto has pledged to abandon all research using this suicide gene technology.

Role of Government in Regulating GM Foods

Governments around the world are hard at work to establish a regulatory process to monitor the effects of and approve new varieties of GM plants. Yet depending on the political, social and economic climate within a region or country, different governments are responding in different ways.

In Japan, the Ministry of Health and Welfare has announced that health testing of GM foods will be mandatory as of April 2001. Currently, testing of GM foods is voluntary. Japanese supermarkets are offering both GM foods and unmodified foods, and customers are beginning to show a strong preference for unmodified fruits and vegetables.

India's government has not yet announced a policy on GM foods because no GM crops are grown in India and no products are commercially available in supermarkets yet. India is, however, very supportive of transgenic plant research. It is highly likely that India will decide that the benefits of GM foods outweigh the risks because Indian agriculture will need to adopt drastic new measures to counteract the country's endemic poverty and feed its exploding population.

Some states in Brazil have banned GM crops entirely, and the Brazilian Institute for the Defense of Consumers, in collaboration with Greenpeace, has filed suit to prevent the importation of GM crops. Brazilian farmers, however, have resorted to smuggling GM soybean seeds into the country because they fear economic harm if they are unable to compete in the global marketplace with other grain-exporting countries.

In Europe, anti-GM food protestors have been especially active. In the last few years Europe has experienced two major foods scares: bovine spongiform encephalopathy (mad cow disease) in Great Britain and dioxin-tainted foods originating from Belgium. These food scares have undermined consumer confidence about the European food supply, and citizens are disinclined to trust government information about GM foods. In response to the public outcry, Europe now requires mandatory food labeling of GM foods in stores, and the European Commission (EC) has established a 1% threshold for contamination of unmodified foods with GM food products.

GM Products: Benefits and Controversies

BENEFITS

- **Crops**
  - o Enhanced taste and quality
  - o Reduced maturation time
  - o Increased nutrients, yields, and stress tolerance
  - o Improved resistance to disease, pests, and herbicides
  - o New products and growing techniques
- **Animals**
  - o Increased resistance, productivity, hardiness, and feed efficiency

- o Better yields of meat, eggs, and milk
- o Improved animal health and diagnostic methods

- **Environment**
- o "Friendly" bioherbicides and bioinsecticides
- o Conservation of soil, water, and energy
- o Bioprocessing for forestry products
- o Better natural waste management
- o More efficient processing

- **Society**
- o Increased food security for growing populations

CONTROVERSIES

- **Safety**
- o Potential human health impact: allergens, transfer of antibiotic resistance markers, unknown effects Potential environmental impact: unintended transfer of transgenes through cross-pollination, unknown effects on other organisms (e.g., soil microbes), and loss of flora and fauna biodiversity

- **Access and Intellectual Property**
- o Domination of world food production by a few companies
- o Increasing dependence on Industralized nations by developing countries
- o Biopiracy—foreign exploitation of natural resources

- **Ethics**
- o Violation of natural organisms' intrinsic values
- o Tampering with nature by mixing genes among species
- o Objections to consuming animal genes in plants and vice versa
- o Stress for animal

- **Labeling**
- o Not mandatory in some countries (e.g., United States)
- o Mixing GM crops with non-GM confounds labeling attempts

- **Society**
- o New advances may be skewed to interests of rich countries.

WHO's role in GM Foods

WHO will take an active role in relation to GM foods, primarily for two reasons:

(1) on the grounds that public health could benefit enormously from the potential of biotechnology, for example, from an increase in the nutrient content of foods, decreased allergenicity and more efficient food production; and

(2) based on the need to examine the potential negative effects on human health of the consumption of food produced through genetic modification, also at the global level. It is

> clear that modern technologies must be thoroughly evaluated if they are to constitute a true improvement in the way food is produced. Such evaluations must be holistic and all-inclusive, and cannot stop at the previously separated, non-coherent systems of evaluation focusing solely on human health or environmental effects in isolation.

Work is therefore under way in WHO to present a broader view of the evaluation of GM foods in order to enable the consideration of other important factors. This more holistic evaluation of GM organisms and GM products will consider not only safety but also food security, social and ethical aspects, access and capacity building. International work in this new direction presupposes the involvement of other key international organizations in this area. As a first step, the WHO Executive Board will discuss the content of a WHO report covering this subject in January 2003. The report is being developed in collaboration with other key organizations, notably FAO and the United Nations Environment Programme (UNEP). It is hoped that this report could form the basis for a future initiative towards a more systematic, coordinated, multi-organizational and international evaluation of certain GM foods.

Are there implications for the rights of farmers to own their crops?

Yes, intellectual property rights are likely to be an element in the debate on GM foods, with an impact on the rights of farmers. Intellectual property rights (IPRs), especially patenting obligations of the TRIPS Agreement (an agreement under the World Trade Organization concerning trade-related aspects of intellectual property rights) have been discussed in the light of their consequences on the further availability of a diversity of crops. In the context of the related subject of the use of gene technology in medicine, WHO has reviewed the conflict between IPRs and an equal access to genetic resources and the sharing of benefits. The review has considered potential problems of monopolization and doubts about new patent regulations in the field of genetic sequences in human medicine. Such considerations are likely to also affect the debate on GM foods.

Public Debate on GM Foods in Other Regions of the World

The release of GMOs into the environment and the marketing of GM foods have resulted in a public debate in many parts of the world. This debate is likely to continue, probably in the broader context of other uses of biotechnology (e.g. in human medicine) and their consequences for human societies. Even though the issues under debate are usually very similar (costs and benefits, safety issues), the outcome of the debate differs from country to country. On issues such as labelling and traceability of GM foods as a way to address consumer concerns, there is no consensus to date. This has become apparent during discussions within the Codex Alimentarius Commission over the past few years. Despite the lack of consensus on these topics, significant progress has been made on the harmonization of views concerning risk assessment. The Codex Alimentarius Commission is about to adopt principles on premarket risk assessment, and the provisions of the Cartegena Protocol on Biosafety also reveal a growing understanding at the international level.

Most recently, the humanitarian crisis in southern Africa has drawn attention to the use of GM food as food aid in emergency situations. A number of governments in the region raised concerns relating to environmental and food safety fears. Although workable solutions have been found for distribution of milled grain in some countries, others have restricted the use of GM food aid and obtained commodities which do not contain GMOs.

Avoiding Genetically-Manipulated (GMO) Food Ingredients

In North America, all soy that is labeled "organic soy" is guaranteed to not be genetically-manipulated and not be treated with herbicides. Look for soy products and ingredients (e.g., tofu, tempeh, miso, soy sauce, soy milk, etc.) which are organic. All other soy ingredients are almost always genetically-manipulated and herbicide-treated. The same is true for canola, corn, dairy products and potatoes. Look for organic corn, potato and dairy ingredients at your local health food store. Check the ingredients labels carefully. It may be best to avoid canola altogether because it is rarely organic and is usually chemically-treated as detailed by world expert, Udo Erasmus. Outside of Europe and Asia it may not be possible at this time to avoid genetically-manipulated ingredients 100% of the time, but it is a good idea to avoid them when possible. The List of Companies Pledging to Remove GMO Ingredients is another very useful resource.

Health Hazards

There are a number of compelling reasons to completely avoid genetically-manipulated and herbicide-treated food ingredients from soy, corn, canola, dairy and potatoes. Children should be particularly careful to avoid such non-organic food ingredients.

Scientists attending the Open-ended Working Group on Biosafety of The UN-Convention on Biological Diversity (13-17 October, 1998) implored "all governments to use whatever methods available to them to bar from their markets, on grounds of injury to public health, Monsanto's genetically manipulated (GM) [herbicide-resistant] Roundup-Ready (RR) soybean." Non-organic soy ingredients are made with Roundup-Ready soybeans.

A recent experiment conducted by independent expert Dr. Alpad Pusztai in the United Kingdom has shown that genetically-manipulated foods can, when fed to animals in reasonable amounts, cause very gradual organ damage and immune system damage.

The food used in the experiment was genetically-manipulated potatoes. Two sets of potatoes were grown in the same pot and greenhouse:

1) a genetically-manipulated variety altered to produce a non-toxic "GNA lectin", and
2) a normal variety of potato. The normal potato was fed to animals with no adverse effects. The genetically-manipulated potato caused gradual organ damage and immune system damage.

A separate followup experiment conducted by Dr. S.W.B. Ewen, a Senior Pathologist at the University of Aberdeen, has confirmed that it was not the "GNA lectin," but toxic or infectious by-products of the genetic manipulation process led to the immune system damage and organ damage in the animals fed genetically-manipulated potatoes. Because it was not the lectin in the potatoes, but the genetic manipulation process itself which led to toxicity, similar results might be seen in animals or humans fed genetically-manipulated soy, canola, and corn over a long period of time (i.e., years or decades).

There were initial reports of flaws in the research when government agencies audited the Dr. Pusztai's preliminary notes. But since that time, over 20 top scientists around the world have peer-reviewed the Final Report and stated that the conclusions are justified. Parts of these experiments conducted by Dr. Pusztai and Dr. Ewen were recently published in the scientific journal, The Lancet. Most of The Lancet reviewers deemed it acceptable research for publication.

A couple of reviewers and other scientists and organizations receiving biotech money have been critical of the research. They have made the following statements (paraphrased below):

"Raw potatos should not have been fed to the animals in the experiment." However, the animals eating non-genetically manipulated raw potatos did fine. It was only the genetically manipulated food which caused health problems.

"Too few animals were used." Initial objections of The Lancet's statistician reviewer were satisfied. Enough animals were used to show a statistically significant difference between the test group and control group.

"There was an inadequate control group." This is a non-specific criticism. The experiment wasn't perfect. But the only difference between the two groups of animals was that one group ate genetically manipulated foods and the other didn't.

"One cannot take the results of this experiment and apply it to all genetically manipulated foods." The only difference was the genetic manipulation of the potatos. The same hazards may or may not be found in genetically manipulated soy, canola, etc. It is prudent to assume that all genetically manipulated ingredients have the same slow toxic effects until long-term, independent research can be conducted on each genetically manipulated crop.

On ocassion, news reports of flaws in the research are mistakenly repeated, but almost independent scientists who have seen the Final Report of Dr. Pusztai's research and are aware of the results of Dr. Ewen's research agree that the conclusions are justified.

News Report on Dr. Pusztai's Research Interview with Dr. Pusztai Summary of the Peer-Review by Researchers Confirming Research by Dr. S.W.B. Ewen (Scroll Down to Text).

There are several differences between the normal breeding process and the artificial genetic manipulation process. One key difference is the use of highly-infectious viruses for artificial genetic manipulation as a promoter to switch on the introduced gene. One commonly-used virus is a highly-infectious form of the Cauliflower Mosaic Virus (CaMV). (The form of CaMV virus found in normal foods is not highly-infectious and cannot be absorbed by mammals.) The dangers were described in detail by reknowed geneticist Dr. Mae-Wan Ho in a meeting on March 31st 1999 at the invitation of UK Environment Minister, Michael Meacher. Additional scientific information about the dangers presented by infectious promoter viruses such as CaMV are described by Dr. Mae-Wan Ho and Dr. Joe Cummins, Emeritus Professor of Genetics, Department of Plant Sciences, University of Western Ontario. Finally, a recent scientific report by Molecular Biologist, Angela Ryan provides further concerns regarding the use of the CaMV virus to create genetically-manipulated foods.

Another key difference between normal breeding and artificial genetic manipulation is that the genetic manipulation greatly increases the risk that the plant (e.g., soy) will develop toxic or allergy-causing compounds. Such unexpected changes have already been shown to occur in some genetically-manipulated crops.

The insertion of a new gene can sometimes alter the synthesis of chemicals in the plant. Such an alteration can lead to the change in existing chemical compounds in the plant (including a possible significant increase in existing levels of toxic compounds) or the development of new toxic or allergy-causing compounds. There would be no way to predict these effects in advance and it would be difficult to test for these effects without many years of careful, independent research on human test subjects. Gradual toxic effects could occur over weeks, months, years, or even decades and society would not be aware of the health damage until it was too late.

Genetic Manipulation industry representatives often point out that such unexpected hazards could be seen when breeding plants. This is true. However, the evidence demonstrates that there is a much greater likelihood of these unexpected toxic and allergic effects from genetically-manipulated plants/food ingredients.

Another major risk from genetically-manipulated foods is the possibility that regular exposure to foreign DNA and RNA material inserted into these artificial foods could cause allergic reactions or autoimmune diseases. Recent scientific research has shown that fragments of DNA from genetically-manipulated food ingredients can be detected in the brains of animals fed these food ingredients. Dr. Sharyn Martin, Ph.D. discusses the evidence that DNA and RNA fragments can cause adverse immune system reactions including autoimmune disorders in Immunological Reactions to DNA and RNA.

Scientists in the United Kingdom measured a 50% increase in soy allergies in one year. They believe that the increase in soy allergies may be caused by the increase use of genetically-manipulated soy ingredients.

Finally, some genetically-manipulated crops are changed so that they produce their own high levels of pesticides. For example, genetically-manipulated "Bt" crops have been shown to emit very high levels of toxins. Plants genetically-manipulated to produce Bt toxin produce at least 1000 times more Bt toxin per acre than does a heavy application of Bt directly on the plants. This may lead to problems with long-term ingestion of such foods (such as non-organic corn and corn-based sweeteners). Other hazards related to crops manipulated to produce their own pesticides are discussed in more detail by Dr. Joseph Cummins, Professor of Genetics in "Plant-Pesticides in GE-food: A Potential Health Risk". Even if the genetically-manipulated plant does not produce its own pesticides, it has been shown conclusively in scientific research that the herbicides used on some of these non-organic, genetically-manipulated plants (e.g., soy, canola, corn) are extremely toxic and can cause birth defects.

Worldwide Condemnation of Genetically-Manipulated Crops/ Foods

In many other countries, reknowned scientists, medical trade organizations and government officials are detailing the known health hazards and potential health hazards from genetically-manipulated food ingredients. For example, in the last several months, a top UK Scientist has warned about potential hazards from genetically-manipulated foods, the British Medical Association (BMA) has called for a ban on genetically-manipulated foods and the French President and German Chancellor listed genetically-manipulated foods under "Global Threats" at a recent summit meeting. Top scientists in Asia and other parts of the world are speaking out as well. This has caused many manufacturers and grocery stores chains all around the world (outside of North America) to ban genetically-manipulated food ingredients. In order to keep up with news from around the world, please read through the following compilation of news articles.

Corporate Public Relations (PR) Strategies

The multinational companies trying to sell genetically-manipulated foods (Monsanto, Dupont, Novartis, Agrevo [Hoechst and Schering]) have spared no expense in their public relations campaign. They have sometimes been successful in getting newspaper and magazine articles or television shows created to help promote genetically-manipulated crops. In addition, these multinational companies give huge sums of money to dietetic associations, farming and seed associations, grocery associations, and PR organizations (e.g., IFIC) in order to obtain help in propogating PR statements to the media and general public. Common PR statements include:

1. "Genetic Engineering is exactly like breeding and has been done for hundreds of years."

As described above, artificial genetic manipulation of plants/food ingredients is different from breeding and has significant hazards associated with it including toxicity hazards seen in recent research.

2. "Careful tests by the FDA, EPA, and the U.S. Department of Agriculture have proven that these ingredients are safe." (Alternative: "We have the strictest regulatory process in the world"!)

These government agencies have not conducted, nor required any significant safety testing. Scientists around the world are calling for a moratorium on genetically-manipulated food ingredients and long-term, independent human studies lasting many years before these food are allowed for sale on the market. Because these government agencies are ignoring the hazards of genetically-manipulated foods, a very large alliance of scientists, consumer groups, environmental groups, and religious groups are suing the U.S. Food and Drug Administration.

3. "Europe and Asia are not making scientific evaluations of the issue, but relying on emotional arguments."

Many of the top scientists around the world are speaking out about the hazards of genetically-manipulated crops/food ingredients. A small selection of these scientists have signed the following referenced document calling for a moratorium on genetically-manipulated crops. These are independent scientists who do not receive money from companies researching, creating or selling these genetically-manipulated crops and food ingredients. When U.S. officials make these sorts of public comments (quoted above), they are insulting much of the population of Europe and Asia and perhaps will strengthen the desire of European and Asian countries to avoid imports of food ingredients from the United States and Canada.

4. "Genetically-manipulated crops are safer because less pesticides and herbicides are used."

In fact, recent research has shown that farmers growing genetically-manipulated crops use, on average, an equal amount or more pesticides than farmers growing non-genetically-manipulated, non-organic crops.

5. "Farmers are Reaping Rewards of Growing Genetically-Manipulated Crops."

Farmers are being victimized as well. Evidence of problems they are experiencing include:

- o Research showing reduced yields from genetically-manipulated crops.
- o More money spent on herbicides and pesticides for genetically-manipulated crops.
- o Potential of reduced farm land values.
- o Possible lawsuits and intimidation from Monsanto.
- o Increased costs in order to segregate their crops
- o Risk of possible permanent damage to their soil by growing genetically-manipulated crops.

The scientific journal Nature (September 9, 1999) has reported that some farmers are considering class-action lawsuits because the seed and chemical companies (e.g., Monsanto) were misrepresenting their products as benign. The Washington Post reported (September 18, 1999):

"American farmers planted [gene-altered crops] in good faith, with the belief that the product is safe and that they would be rewarded for their efforts," the American Corn Growers Association said in a statement last week. "Instead they find themselves misled by multinational seed and chemical companies and other commodity associations who only encouraged them to plant increased acres of these crops without any warning to farmers of the dangers associated with planting a crop that didn't have consumer acceptance."

Wheat farmers should prepare to avoid these genetically-manipulated seeds when they come on the market in the next year or two.

6. "Genetically-Manipulated crops have the potential to produce "functional foods" with extra nutrients and drugs which can save lives!"

The reality is that these nutrients or drugs can be taken separately when needed. The high cost of drugs is largely due to drug companies trying to recoup the millions of dollars of research money spent and is rarely due to high production costs. The costs of developing a drug-producing, genetically-manipulated plant is quite high. The costs of drugs will remain high wheather they are genetically-manipulated into plants or not. Therefore, these drugs and nutrients can be produced without genetic manipulation as been the case in the past. It is also important to keep in mind that Alternative Medicine techniques are now beginning to replace the use of pharmaceuticals in some cases of disease treatment.

Originally, the corporate PR strategy was to say that genetically-manipulated crops would help "feed the world." But when it was pointed out that the world grows 1-1/2 times the amount of food needed to feed the population, that the problem was food distribution, and that genetically-manipulated crops have reduced yields, the companies changed their PR to say that genetically-manipulated crops will grow drugs and save lives.

There is a very serious danger of pollen from these manipulated crops infecting normal crops of the same species or of different species leading to the unintentional ingestion of drugs by the general population. Pollen can travel a very long way from fields to infect other crops. In addition, scientists are concerned that accidental inhalation of pollen from these genetically-manipulated plants might lead to adverse health effects in some people.

References

1. Ewen SW, Pusztai A. (1999) Effect of diets containing genetically modified potatoes expressing Galanthus nivalis lectin on rat small intestine. Lancet 354:1353-4.
2. Enserink, M. (1998) Institute copes with genetic hot potato. Science 281.1184
3. Enserink, M. (1999) Preliminary data touch off genetic food fight. Science. 1999 283:1094-5
4. Pusztai A, Ewen SW, Grant G, Peumans WJ, van Damme EJ, Rubio L, Bardocz S. (1990) Relationship between survival and binding of plant lectins during small intestinal passage and their effectiveness as growth factors. Digestion 46 Suppl 2:308-16.
5. Carlini CR, Grossi-de-Sa MF (2002) Plant toxic proteins with insecticidal properties. A review on their potentialities as bioinsecticides. Toxicon 40:1515-39.
6. Down RE, Ford L, Bedford SJ, Gatehouse LN, Newell C, Gatehouse JA, Gatehouse AM (2001) Influence of plant development and environment on transgene expression in potato and consequences for insect resistance. Transgenic Res. 10:223-36.
7. Kozukue N, Misoo S, Yamada T, Kamijima O, Friedman M (1999) Inheritance of morphological characters and glycoalkaloids in potatoes of somatic hybrids between dihaploid Solanum acauleand tetraploid Solanum tuberosum. J. Agric. Food Chem. 47:4478-83.
8. Lee, K and Tyler, R. International scientists raise concerns over genetically modified food. http://www.wsws.org/articles/1999/feb1999/food-f17.shtml
9. Kumar, K.S. Kavi and Jyoti Parikh, (1998) —"Climate change impacts on Indian agriculture: The Ricardian approach". in Dinar et.al., Measuringthe impacts of Climate Change on Indian Agriculture, World Bank Technical Paper No.402, 1998.

46

Biosynthesis of Silver Nanoparticles Using White Rot Fungus

PREETI VERMA, RASHMI SANGHI, ASHISH SRIVASTAVA AND SADHNA PURI

Introduction

Research in nanotechnology mostly deals with the synthesis and stabilization of various nanoparticles by physical and chemical processes. Currently, there is a growing need to develop an eco-friendly process for nanoparticle synthesis and hence the focus turned towards 'green' chemistry and bioprocesses. The work on the use of microorganisms to synthesize advanced nanoscale materials is sporadic. Presently, the potential of bio-organisms ranges from simple prokaryotic bacterial cells to eukaryotic fungus and even live plants. It is well known that some microbes such as bacteria [1], yeast [2], fungi [3] and algae [4] are able to adsorb and accumulate metal and can be used in the reduction of environmental pollution and also for the recovery of metals from waste.

Nature of Problem

Most of the synthetic methods based on the use of organic solvents and toxic reducing agents like sodium borohydride and N,N-dimethylformamide. All these chemicals are highly reactive and pose potential environmental and biological risks. So, need to develop environmentally benign nanoparticle synthesis processes that do not use toxic chemicals in the synthesis protocol. With the increasing interest in the minimization/elimination of waste and adoption of sustainable processes through green chemistry, the development of biological, biomimetic and biochemical approaches is desirable.

So in this laboratory, we have focused on the use of fungi in synthesis of silver nanoparticles by optimizing the parameters. Herein, we report a simple method for synthesis of protein capped silver nanoparticles.

Study Area- Nanotechnology

Methodology

The white rot fungal strain Coriolus versicolor (MUCL) was obtained from IMTECH, Chandigarh. Erlenmeyer flasks of the capacity 150 ml was used for growing the fungal mycelia. It contained 50 ml of the growth medium, consisting of 5 g/l Malt Extract Powder and 10 g/l glucose.

The fungal mycelium and the growth medium in which the fungus was harvested were separately challenged with silver nitrate solution ($AgNO_3$). The reduction of silver was monitored by using the UV-Vis spectral analysis. In order to optimize the reduction process variation in the parameters such as: pH, and conc. of $AgNO_3$ were made. Under alkaline conditions at room temperature, the color changes with time from colorless to light pink, reddish brown and finally to dark brown with increasing intensity were observed within 60 minutes and were indicative of the formation of Ag nanoparticles both intracellularly on fungal mycelium and extracellularly in media. At alkaline conditions, the absorbance band was at 420 nm in Ag/fungal mycelium solution as well as in Ag/media solution indicating the formation of silver nanoparticles.

The average size, morphology, and structure of particles were determined by AFM, XRD and UV/Visible absorption spectrophotometry. Fourier transform infrared study disclosed that the amino groups were bound to the particles, which was accountable for the stability of nanoparticles.

Major Findings

The fungal proteins under different experimental conditions played a significant role in reducing, and capping of the so formed Ag^0 particles. The coordination behaviors between amino groups in fungus and Ag ions are responsible for the stabilization of the silver nanoparticles.

Conclusion

This study demonstrated the synthesis of stable silver nanoparticles using the fungus, *C. versicolor*. Under alkaline conditions, the reaction was much faster and could be easily conducted at room temperature. High stability of the nanoparticles and storage at ambient conditions are the main attraction of using *C. versicolor* fungus over other conventional methods reported.

References

1. Beveridge T. Y., Murray, R.G. E. J. Bacteriology 141 (1980) 876.
2. Huang, P., Juang, C. P., Morehart, K., Allen, L. Water Res., 24 (1990) 433.
3. H. Niu, Xu, X. S. and Wang, J. H. Biotech. Bioengg., 42 (1993) 785.
4. Volesky, (ed.) Biosorption of Heavy Metals, 139–172. Boca Raton, FL: CRC Press, 1990.

47

Ecology and Human Survival
Theoretical Orientations

JASLEEN KEWLANI

Introduction

The increasing realization of the vitality of environment and its issues, has led to emergence of 'environmentalism', "which means ideologies and practices which inform and flow from a concern with environment" (Pepper, 1986, p.13). In context of contemporary environment crisis, environmental science takes a prenatal position, since it deals with the application of knowledge gained with the help of ecology for managing environment, along with its various off-shoots. Environment can be natural as well as man-made. Natural environment consists of air, water, soil, land, forests, wildlife, etc. and man-made environment which includes housing, technology, transportation, settlement, utilities, etc. To know, what type of link exists between these two forms of environment and what are the effects of this inter-linkage, (positive or negative), is one of the major aims of this research? The environmental studies are very much related with Botany, Zoology, Chemistry, Pedology, Geography, Climatology, Oceanography, Geomorphology, Sociology, Political Science, Economics, Management, etc. Since environment and man are the primary concerns of environmental studies, all the subjects related with these aspects have relationship 'Controller' of life and living styles of human beings (Saxena, 2006). Environmental studies are the need of the hour because with an indepth understanding of environment; firstly various facets and problems of survival are interpreted in authentic terms and secondly, a strategic planning can be made. To have complete analysis of environment and ecology there is a need to refer to various ecological perspectives, which have been given by prominent environmentalists, sociologists and geologists. These ecological perspectives forward sundry approaches which have been used till date for rendering ecological analysis or environmental studies.

Ecological Perspectives

While analyzing ecological issues, two perspectives came forward; (1) "Reformist Ecological perspective". Reformist ecological perspective is also known by the name of "Shallow Ecological Perspective"; and (2) "Deep Ecological perspective". The difference between these two perspectives, didn't lie in the 'ends' but in the 'means' which were adopted to achieve those ends. Though target of both of these ecological perspectives is environmental protection, but the ideology and means to manage or reconcile environmental destruction are distinct. The reformist ecology targets to reform and control the worst which has gone with the environmental entities of nature, i.e. air, water, land, etc. It refers to several social movements, which were a product of man's quest to improve the degenerating environmental quality. Environment has always been considered an important part of one's life, hence the goal of all such movements initiated by reformist ecologists, was to change society for 'better living'. Along with the motive of changing environment's scene, criteria for survival remained intact; According to Reformists, any alternate process must not attack the premise of the "dominant social paradigm", which expresses the mental image of social reality that guides expectation in society. This dominant social paradigm, according to reformist ecologists consists of basic values, culture and heritage of masses, which is deep, rooted in their social survival entangled with their relative environmental circumstances and ecological surroundings. Hence, they believe that environment must improve but it should not be accompanied with any alteration in basic dominant socio-cultural paradigm of individuals (Merchant, 1996).

On the other hand, "Deep Ecological Perspective" forwards an altered mode of discussion, posing an absolutely contrary notion to that of the Reformist Ecological Perspective. The norms and tendencies of the Deep Ecology Movements are not derived calculatively from ecology or induction, rather from the knowledge and attributes gained by the researchers working in ecological domain. The contents and their understanding require an ability to construct a conserver society. When Reformist Ecology failed to protect environment and ecology from further deterioration, Deep Ecological Perspective began functionally crucial. Arne Naess (1989) was the founder of this school of ecological thought who thinks that 'Environmental Crisis' is the 'Crises of Consciousness'. Arne Naes has been an environmentalist who stressed on "Ecological Egalitarianism' as a reflexive component of Deep Ecological perspective. Ecological Egalitarianism implied that all individuals have equal rights to live and blossom in an intuitively clear and obvious value axiom. This assertion supported that Deep Ecology is forcefully normative in nature. It is ecophilosophical not mere ecological. In addition to this view, Naes talk of Principles of 'Diversity' and 'Symbiosis'. According to him 'diversity' enhances the potentialities of survival and the chores of new modes of life; and 'Symbiosis' tends to reduce the multiplicity of kinds of forms of life and create integration within the communities of the same species. This helps to maintain equilibrium which glibs the survival of individuals. Infact Deep Ecology and its supporters support the fight against economic, cultural, military invasion and domination which leads to degradation of environmental quality.

His thought was strengthened by Eckersley (1995), who added dimension of social justice and human emancipation alongwith a change in the way of thinking about the natural world. These ideas were further strengthened by Carlos Castaneda. Carlos Castaneda (1971), says that it is a challenging task for modern man to acquire and develop understanding of Deep Ecology because it requires a major perceptual shift of man's nature. Further, Deep Ecology gained popularity in Native Americans during 1960-1970s. These Native Americans had 'separate realities' which were entangled to their life style and closely linked with environment around them. In fact Castaneda aimed at understanding how did these tribes of Native Americans cope with the changes occurring due to technological innovations and advancements in their natural environment. According to him, the modern western man can not understand these 'separate realities', which owe their origin to the basic norms of the tribes. In reaction to Castaneda views about Deep Ecological Perspective, Robert Orustein (1996) forwarded his views that the Western trained and even those who are a 'seeker' are by their culture almost unprepared to understand the esoteric traditions constituting the separate realities. This counter response shows that Castaneda's work on Deep Ecology had been critically appraised due to his undermining of the modern man's perceptual ability to interpret the importance of environment.

Another imminent component of Deep Ecology is Rama Chandra Guha (1996) who stated that Deep Ecology shows man's arrogance and his ecological hubris, which puts environment at the top of apex of life choices. This perspective according to Guha depicts a transition from anthropocentric to a biocentric approach of man. Anthropercentric approach is a 'human' centred approach and biocentric approach interprets human as only one of the elements in the ecosystems but doesn't attribute indispensability to his existence. In simple terms, anthropocentric approach gives importance to human as an element of study but biocentric approach gives cardinal emphasise to ecology and environment. According to Guha any form of intervention in nature and its paradigm should be guided primarily by the need to preserve biotic integrity rather than by the needs of humans: Guha upheld a statement that Deep Ecology encourages political militancy not negotiations and advances philosophical arguments not aesthetic notions. This statements infact makes the comparison between reformist and Deep Ecological Perspectives more ocular. In simple terms, Deep Ecological Perspective is fundamentally normative in nature, providing importance to ethics determine the attitude of individuals. According to Pojman (2000), if environment is to be protected, a deep rooted, normative as well as an attitudinal approach is to be adopted, which ought to be objective in nature.

Another sociologist named Bill Devall (1996) further elaborated cleared the contents of Deep Ecological Perspective. According to him, usable instruments of Deep Ecological Perspectives are local autonomy, decentralization of power, steady scale economy and a radically changed social structure. The word 'radical' was specifically stressed by Devall. He provided alternate terminology for 'Deep Ecology'. He used some terms like 'Radical Sociology' & 'Revolutionary Ecology'. He upheld that Deep Ecology Perspective was a reaction to the successes and excesses of the implementation of the dominant social paradigm and its assumptions. This 'dominant social paradigm' reflects mental image of social reality that guides the expectation in a society. The Reformist Ecology didn't intend to alter the dominant social Paradigm which was attacked by normative strategy of Deep Ecology later. The 'Dominant Social Paradigm' comprises of the social fabrics including kinship and family structure; naturalistic tendencies of a society; and modes of adapting to the recently occurring social changes. Deep Ecological Perspective aims at improving environmental quality and checking further degradation of environment by attacking the fundamental nature of this paradigm, because it needs a shift of normative aspect of human attitude. When environmental degradation has reached a drastic extent, an abrupt and a strong action is needed to manage it. Keeping this assertion in view, Deep Ecology becomes the most functional tool to formulate the required management strategy. In all, a stress is laid to understand those cultural, religious and social values that related man to his environment and made a social binding on the individual to protect the environment. The major emphasis will be on empowerment, social justice, class differentiation and struggle against resource depletion and environmental pollution. As Deep Ecology encompasses various aspects of various lives, it is important to discuss holistic approach.

Other than the above discussed ecological perspectives, another theory has been very prominent in environmental studies, i.e. "System Theory". Moving towards the importance of a holistic approach to analysis; 'System Theory' is of a great relevance for environmental studies. The conception of development has changed and the new concept of development as a process incorporates various fields of life together. Living organisms cover a wide range of phenomenon including individual organisms, social systems and ecosystems. Hence Systems theory becomes vital. "Common framework and language for biology, psychology, medicine, economics, ecology and many other sciences, a framework in which the so urgently needed ecological perspective is explicitly manifest" (Merchant 1996). System theory assumes that all the aspects of life together formulate a system, which is to be regularized in order to attain an 'all over development". This theory implies (i) shift from part to the whole, (ii) shift from structure to the process of maintenance (iii) shift from objective to epistemic science; which aims at clearly defining the ecological concepts (iv) shift from "building" to "network" as a metaphor of knowledge and (v) shift from truth to approximate description, which reinforces human dominance as an 'observer' who identifies various objects of nature and describes them. Imminent supporters and contributors of the theory are; Heisenberg (1971), who wrote a book titled "Physics and Philosophy" and his another book titled "Der Teil Und Ganze" (1970), states that nature is also exposed to questions. Capra (1985) while taking an interview of Geoffrey Chew, reproduced Chew's views in one of his intellectual productions and explains Chew's idea that understanding of nature needs to be undertaken entirely through self-consistency, because environment as a subject cannot be reduced to any fundamental entities. There are no fundamental equations or fundamental symmetries in environmental understanding. Environment as a physical reality is seen as a dynamic web of interrelated events related to socio-cultural systems as well. Therefore, these interrelated events need a cognitive understanding for an absolute interpretation of the social world. Thomas Kuhn (1970) also finds system theory of also of great importance and states in his theory of Scientific Revolution that changes of Paradigms occur in discontinuous, revolutionary breaks, called 'paradigm shifts'. Keeping this alternation in view, it can be said that the modern world recognizes, paradigm shift in physics as an integral part of a much larger cultural transformation. Einstein Albert (1949) has also presumed a similar view to Kuhin that no fundamental theoretical foundation exist in physics and rich its understanding. Hence, an amalgamated approach is needed which is catered by System Theory. The motive of explaining "system theory" and its components is not to add one more theoretical perspective, but to reaffirm that all the aspects of life are inter-woven and make a system in all. This research aims at analyzing that how far this System Theory has been accepted and applied and how far has it been internalized in the process of development and legislative procedure, along with the effects in case of non-adoption of a system approach in the procession towards growth.

Theorists like Boserup further produced theories on environment with 'Gender Dimension' as the cardinal emphasis. This theory further forwarded a novel impetus to the already existing theories on Ecology; because prior to it, there was no theory dealing with environment or any other allied concept through the gender dimension. Boserup in 1970 produced a work titled, "Women's role in economic development", and held that women are an imminent part of gendered division of labour, participating in economic development. This book was considered as a catalyst for the growth of a body of literature on Women's role in development. In addition to Boserup's theory, Brenda Cranney (2001) stressed upon one aspect of social reproduction, which is sexual or social division of labour in home and in farm work. Sexual division of labour refers to a division created by cultural and social norms and not by biological difference. An encapsulation of research findings show that all societies develop a sexual division of labour that varies across countries, cultures and history, thereby implying that there is nothing natural or biological in such division (Beneria and Roldan 1987; Kelkar and Nathan 1991; Rogers 1981; Rubin 1975). On the other hand, Cranney Brenda aimed at analyzing women's contribution to production and social reproduction, which is necessary to determine what labour women perform for the family and how and why specific tasks are allocated. Both in primitive and in more developed communities, traditional division of labour in both farms and families, in usually considered natural, being sexually determined. The persons of a specific community may feel that in other communities, there exist different ways of determining division of labour (dividing the work burden among sexes), which even they state as 'natural' basis of division of labour (Boserup, 1970). Anyhow, women's work does not happen in a vacuum. It is influenced by capitalistic development, which in turn influences the dynamics of family life. Linking all these thoughts and facts with the main theme of the research, it is evident that environmental degradation affects females, their livelihood and their household chores up to a large extent. Specifically feminist context, deforestation affects the availability of the forest products like fuel wood, food, etc. and also the time required to collect these products. This very phenomenon increases the work load for women and decreases household nutrition (Venkatestwara, 1995). A study carried out by Brenda, in mountain region of Himachal Pradesh proves that deforestation doubles the women's work load. The women of this area identify water and the forests as two single most important factors in their daily work and life that consumes their most of the time. They still consider water supply as a secondary issue to forests as in falls, winters and early springs, their water needs are met but the forests affect every aspect of their life everyday. Women collect two types of wood; for fodder and for fuel consumption. Fodder consists of branches of specific trees that produce leaves suitable for animals to eat. Fodder is usually collected twice a day as the leaves need to be fresh for the cows to eat. The branches are once thrown in the cow yards and after the leaves are eaten, the twigs are used for fuelwood in chullah (Cranney Brenda, 2001).

A study conducted by Cranney Brenda states that women go and collect these products from forests and when deforestation occurs women's burden of work gets intensified in terms of time and energy. A common complaint of women of Himachal Pradesh has been that they had to travel from 1 to 10 kilometers to collect wood. The weight of the load varies from 10 to 40 kilos which is in inappropriate connotation with each woman's stamina and potential. Eventually if not immediately, the incident has alarming effects on women's general health latently. Not only health, but education which the strongest wheel of future development of women, also suffers. Girl child is eliminated from her school and is imposed upon to share the household burden of the mothers because after deforestation they spend about 8-10 hours a day on walking to the forests and coming back after collection of the forest products required for household maintenance. Another content to be considered in context of women's relation with development and her importance in growth paradigm is 'Ecofeminism'. Contributions have been made by liberal, socialist and radical ecofeminists. Liberal ecofeminists aim at redistributive policy changes and do not at all recommend a full-fledged restructuring of the whole set ups. On the other hand, socialist feminists want equal representation of women in government and non-government organisation (Berman, 1993). Another ecofeminist perspective is Radical ecofeminism which asserts that women have a spiritual and biological link to the non human world and of course are closer to nature posing a 'divinity factor', as compared to other gender.

Conclusion

Many changes have occurred in Indian society, which further lead to reformulation of innumerable social structures. In the continuous process of alternations, development and its conception have taken a turn. A sociologist cum environmentalist 'Tolba' gave a definition of Development in 1978 and said that development (i) pre-supposes new direction for growth (ii) should have implications for all the countries i.e rich as well as poor and (iii) it must incorporate environment dimensions also. But paradoxically, with increasing development the issue of environmental degradation has further aggravated (Aggrawal and Dubey 2002). In India also, earlier the economic analysis used to be purely economic in nature and environmental assessment was never a part of this evaluation scheme. Perhaps, it could be termed as "International Fallacy". But accounting for the available natural resources, incorporating environmental criteria has become crucial (Kulshreshtra, Singh 2000; Ghazala, 2001). In recent years noticeable deforestation has occurred in sub mountainous zone of Punjab. The reasons have been euphemistically quoted by the government. The government states that economic growth is a credential for human growth and development, which virtually leads to excessive deforestation to establish more and more industries and to construct more dams to cater to the power needs of the industries. This phenomenon forwards an assertion that economic development and approaches to it, lead to degradation of environmental domain in context of both, its quality as well as its quantity.

References

1. Agarwal, Arun (2001). "Common Property, Forest Management and Indian Himalaya" in Contribution to Indian Sociology, Vol. 35, No. 2., May 2001. Sage Publication, New Delhi (pp. 181).

2. Agarwal, Arvind (2007), "Globalization, Development and Environmental Degradation: A Human Rights Perspective", in Human Rights, Development and Environmental Law - An Anthology, by Satish, C., Shastri, Bharat Law Publications, Jaipur.

3. Aggarwal, Anil and Sunita Narain (1996). The First Citizen's Report 1982, Centre for Science and Environment, New Delhi, (pp. 57-59).

4. Aggarwal, S.K. & Dubey, P.S. (2002). Environmental Controversies, APH Publishing Corporations, New Delhi, (pp. 293-305).

5. Beneria, Lourdes and Roldan Martha (1997), The cross roads of class and genders, The University of Chicago Press, London.

6. Berman, Tzeporah (1993), Towards an integrative Ecofeminist praxis, Canadian Women Studies, Canada.

7. Bhargava, Gopal (2004). "Environmental Challenges and Sustainable Future" in Employment News Weekly, Vol. XXVIII, No. 51, New Delhi, (pp. 40).

8. Bhattacharya, B. (2000). "Environment and Trade; some issues" in Environmental Management and Audit by Rao P. Sasi Bhushana and Rao R. Mohana, Deep and Deep Publications Pvt. Ltd., New Delhi.

9. Boserup, E. (1970), Women's role In economic development, "Gower Publishing Company Ltd, Great Britain.

10. Brown, R. Lester and Orient Longman (2002), "Ecology over Economics", in Down to Earth, April 30, Vol. 10, No. 23, (p. 56).

11. Capra Fritjof (1985), "Bootstrap Physics: A conversation with Geoffrey Chew's", in A passion for physics : Essays in Honor of Geoffrey Chew, Finkelstein and Chung-I Tang, Philadelphia.

12. Castaneda, Carlos (1971), A Separate Reality, Simon and Schuster, New York.

13. Chahal, S.K. (1994). Environment and world life; towards a New Paradigm, Ashish Publishing House, New Delhi.

14. Chauhan, I.S. and Arun Chauhan (1998). Environmental Degradation; Socio economic consequences, Rawat Publications, New Delhi.

15. Clayton, M.H. Anthony and Radcliff Nendals (1996). Sustainability; A System Approach, Earth scan publication Ltd., London.

16. Cranney, Brenda (2001), Livelihood and Environment - Local Enviroment and lived Experience - The mountain Women of Himachal Pradesh, Sage publications, New Delhi.

17. Das Gupta, Partha et al. (1994). "The Environmental resource base and Human Welfare" in Population Economic Development and the Environment; The Making of our common future by Kieslling Kersten Lindell and Landberg Hans, Oxford University Press, London.

18. Devall, Bill (1996), "The Deep Ecological Movement", Ecology, by Clayton Merchant, Rawat Publication, New Delhi, (pp 125-140).

19. Dhaliwal, G.S. (1998), Fundamentals of environmental sciences, Kalyani Publishers, New Delhi.

20. Dryze, K John S. and David Schlosbeeg (1998), Debating the Earth - the Environmentalism Politics Reader, "Oxford University Press, New York, (p. 356-358).

21. Eckersley, Robyn (1995), Market ,the state and the environment: towards integration, Macmillion Press, Melbourn.

22. Einstein, Albert (1949), Philosopher - Scientist, Library of living philosopher, Evanston.

23. Faizi, S. (2001), "A Diverse Bill", Down to Earth, May 15, Volume 9, No. 24, (pp. 50-52).

24. Ghazala, Shahabbudin (2001), "Forest Fragmentation, that's what is causing bio-diversity Losses", Down to Earth, 15th January 2001, Vol. 9, No. 16, (pp. 24-25).

25. Ghosh, Sancheeta (2007), "Concern for Environmental degradation in India's Planning: A Review", in Population and Announcement Linkages by C.P. Prakasan and R.B. Bhagat, Rawat Publishers, Jaipur.

26. Gibbon, David, et al., (1995), "Sustainable Development a challenge for Agriculture" in People and Environment by Morse Stephen and Stocking Michael, UCL Press, London.

27. Gill, M.S. (1991), Spatial Pattern - A Socio-ecological Analysis. Natural Book Organization, New Delhi.

28. Guha, Ramachandra (1996), "Radical Environmentalism: A Third-World Critique", in Ecology by Clayton Merchant, Rawat Publication, New Delhi.

29. Gupta, S.P. (2007), "Environment, Sustainable Development and Tradition" in Urbanization Development and Environment by V.S. Phadke and Swapna Banerjee Guha, Rawat Publication, New Delhi, (p., 18).

30. Gupta, Sunita (2000), Global Environment Sarup and Sons Publications, New Delhi.

31. Hanningam, A. Johan (1997), Environmental Sociology - A Social constructional perspective Routledge Publishers, London, (pp. 146-162).

32. Hazra, Arnab Kumar (2001), "Community Based Forest Management (Review)", Down to Earth, Vol. 10,No. 3, June.

33. Heisenberg, Werner (1970), "Der Teil Und Ganze", Harper and Row, New York.

34. Heisenberg, Werner (1971), Physics and Philosophy, Harper and Row, New York.

35. Iyer, G. (1996), Sustainable development-ecological and socio-culture dimensions, Kay Kay Printers, New Delhi.

36. Kadikoli, Gopal & Rabindra Nath (1996), "Forestry as Carbon Sink in India" in Environment and Development by Rathore M.S., Rawat Publications, New Delhi.

37. Karkara, G.S. (2000), "Environmental Law", Central Law Publication, Allahabad.

38. Kayasthas, S.L. (1992), "Environment and Development - Emerging Perspectives and Imperatives" in Development and Sociology-Essays in Honour of Prof. Mohammad Shafi Rawat Publications, Jaipur, (pp. 39-57.)

39. Kelkar, G. and Nathan D. (1991); "Gender and Tribe", Kali For Women, New Delhi.

40. Kellywich and Gravich Sarah (1995), "Global warming and Development" in People and Environment by Morse Stephen and Stocking Michael. UCL press, King's Lynn and Guilford Press, England.

41. Khanna, P & Babu Ram (2000), "Environmental Education of Economic growth" in Environmental Management and Audit by P.Rao Sasi Bhushana and Rao P. Mohana, Deep and Deep Publications, New Delhi.

42. Kothari, Ashish (2000), "India's Bio-Diversity Bill comes under security", in Down to Earth, Vol. 9, No. 13, p. 24.

43. Kuhn, Thomas (1970), The Structure of Scientific Revolution, Chicago Press, Chicago.

44. Kulhreshtha, A.C. and Singh Gulab (2000), "System of National Accounts and Environmental Accounting" in Environment Management and Audit by Rao P. Sasi Bhushana and Rao P. Mohana, Deep and Deep Publication, New Delhi.

45. Kumar, Arvind (2002), Environmental Pollution and Agriculture Efficient offset Printer, New Delhi, (pp. 477).

46. Lee, A. James (1985), The Environment, Public Health and Human Ecology; considerations for Economic Development, The John Hopkins University Press, London.

47. Lodha, R.M. (1996), Environment and Industry - An Alarm Shiva Publishers, Udaipur.

48. Majid, Hussain, Sajit Hussain Sayed Zaidi (1996), Environmental Management in India Manak Publication, New Delhi, (pp. 75-94).

49. Martell, Luke (1994), Ecology and Society - an introduction, polity press, Great Britain, (p.23).

50. Mehrotra, A. & R.K. Suri (1994), Remote Sensing for Environment and Forest Management, Indus Publishing Company, New Delhi, (p. 94).

51. Merchant (1996), Ecology, Rawat Publication, New Delhi, (pp. 120-281).

52. Milton, Kay (1993), Environmentalism- The view from Anthropology, Routledge Publishers, London, (pp. 178-180).

53. Mishra, R.P. (1995), Environmental Ethics – A dialogue of cultures, Concept Publishing Company, New Delhi.

54. Mitra, Amit (2000), "Joint Forest Management; Case Study" in Environment and Audit by Rao P. Sasi Bhushana and Rao P. Mohana, Deep and Deep Publications Pvt. Ltd., New Delhi, (pp. 102).

55. Mohanty, Naragyan Rabi (1998), "Environment and Development Search for an alternative paradigm" in Sociology of Environment by Pawar and Patis, Rawat Publication, New Delhi, (pp. 76-88).

56. Moosvi, Ali Raza (2000), "Rural Development through Joint Forest Management- A case study" in "Community Participation in Natural Resource Management" by Mishra G.P. & Bajpai B.K., Rawat Publications, Jaipur, (pp. 286-289).

57. Naess, Arne (1989), Ecology, Community and Life Style, Cambridge University Press, Cambridge.

58. Negi, S.S. (1994), India's forests, Forestry & wild life, Indus Publishing Company, New Delhi.

59. Orustein, Robert (1976), The Mind Field, Octagon Press, New York.

60. Patanaik, Naba Kumar & Rao Bhushana P. Sasi (2000), "Environmental Education for 21st Century" in "Environment, Management and Audit" by Rao P. Sasi Bhushana and Rao P. Mohana; Deep and Deep Publication Pvt. Ltd., New Delhi.

61. Pepper, David (1996), Modern Environmentalism, an introduction, Routledge Publishers, New York.

62. Peter and Calvert, Susan (1999), The South, the North and the Environment, Biddles Ltd, Guilford and King's Lynn Printers, London.

63. Pojman, Louis P. (2000), Global Environmental Ethics, May field Publishing Company, London, (pp. 176-186).

64. Prasad, NLNS (2000), "Role of NGOs in Environmental Conservation" in Environmental Management and Audit, by Rao Bhushana P. Sasi Bhushana and Rao P. Mohana, Deep and Deep Publication, New Delhi.

65. Punalikar, S.P. (2000), "Inferences between Development and Environment; A Micro narrative on Tribal society in Gujarat", in Resource Management and contours of Development, by Barik B.C., Rawat Publications, New Delhi, (pp. 70-72).

66. Raju, A. Jagganath (2000), "Sustainable Development CCD" in Environment Management and Audit, by Rao P. Sasi Bhushana & Rao Mohana, Deep & Deep Publication & Pvt. Ltd., New Delhi.

67. Rao, P.K. (2001), Sustainable Development – Economics and Policy Blackwell Publishers, U.S.A., (pp. 43-45).

68. Rathore, M.S. (1996), "Environment and Development" Areas of conflict and convergence" in Environmental Development, by Rathore M.S., Rawat Publication, Jaipur, (pp. 15-45).

69. Reddy, Narayan (2002), Building capacities for Sustainable Development, Kanishka Publishers & Distributors, New Delhi.

70. Relan, M., Arora (2007), "People, Parks and Wildlife: Towards Co-Existence", in "Human Rights, Development and Environmental Law - An Anthology", by Satish, Co., Shastri, Bharat Law Publication, Jaipur.

71. Robertson, R. (1992), "Globalization: Social Theory and Global Culture", Sage Publishers, London.

72. Rogers, Barbare (1981), The domestication of woman, Tavistock Press, London.

73. Roy Burman B.K. (1995). "Peoples perception of Nature" in Environmental Ethics – A dialogue of Cultures, by Mishra. R.P., Concept Publishing Company, New Delhi.

74. Rubin, G. (1975), "Traffic in Women," in Toward an Anthropology of Women, Monthly Review Press, New York.

75. Salgara, S.A. and Iyer M.P. (1993), "Environmental Chaos," in Environmental Ruin, The Crisis of Survival," by Lodha R.M. Indus Publishing company, New Delhi.

76. Saxena, H.M. (2006), "Environmental Studies", Rawat Publishers, New Delhi.

77. Saxena, N.C. (1996), "Policy and Issues in Forestry" in Environment and Development, by M.S. Rathore M.S., Rawat Publication, New Delhi, (pp. 88-116).

78. Shafi, Mohammad and Mehndi Raza (1992), Forestry Ecosystems of the world, Nice Printers, New Delhi.

79. Shastri, Madhu and Rajesh, Gaur (2007), "Environmental Priorities in India" in "Human Rights, Development and Environmental Law - An Anthology", by Satish, Co., Shastri, Bharat Law Publication, Jaipur.

80. Sheth, Pravin (1997), Environmentalism – politics, Ecology of Development, Rawat Publications, New Delhi, (p.55).

81. Shiva, Vandana (1991), Ecology and the politics of survival, Sage Publications, New Delhi.

82. Singh, R.B. (2002), Human Dimensions of sustainable development, Rawat Publications, New Delhi.

83. Singh, Uma Shankar (2003), "Fighting Forest Fires" in Environment Management and Audit, by Rao P. Bhushana and Rao. Mohana, Deep and Deep Publication Pvt. Ltd., New Delhi.

84. Sinha (1997), Human Health and Environment, A.P.H. Publishers, New Delhi.

85. Smil, Vandev (1933), Global Ecology – Environmental Change and Social Flexibility, Routledge Press, New York.

86. Smith, Keith (1996), Environmental Hazards, 2nd edition, Routledge, New York.

87. Speth, Gustave, James (2004), "Global Environmental Challenges - Transitions to a Sustainable World", Orient Longman, New Delhi.

88. Venkateshwaran, Reddy (1995), Environment Development and the Gender Gap. Sage Publication, London, (pp. 54-80).

89. Verma, J.S. (2006), "The New Universe of Human Rights, Universal Law Publishing Co. Pvt. Ltd., Delhi.

90. Vyas, S. Vijay (1996), "Environmental Policies and Policy Implementation in India" in Environment and Development, by M.S. Rathore Rawat Publication, Jaipur.

48

NGO's Building our Society
Lifelong Solution for Environmental Issues

UMENDRA DUTT, MRS. RANJEETA AND DR (MRS.) RAKHI JUNEJA

Introduction

Non-government organizations have proved their role in the sustainable development at national as well as international level. There protest and campaigns resulted in drastic changes in various fields such as public health, human rights, environmental issues. Development signifies improvement from some inconsistent or undesirable state to desirable one in any field of the social living. Disasters hamper the development processes. These disasters can be war, floods, earthquakes or due to environmental imbalance. NGO plays an important and crucial role in the rehabilitation process. These organisations actually supplement the efforts made by the government where they try to reach at the grass root level and provide relief to the disaster affected people. Their primary role is to provide public awareness among through the mass media , joint action programmes at national or international levels and to provide their services in a non discrimination way. They are the people who help in rebuilding the community.

Growth of NGO's in the recent years with a mission to address various environmental issues is acknowledgeable. There has been growing environmental awareness among the communities and individual and the reason behind this awareness is due to the campaigns and education programmes run by the major NGO's concerned with the environment. Such organisations are working to foster grass root based approaches to the protection and preservation of the region's environment. These include non-governmental organizations (NGOs) at the international, regional and national levels, as well as groups concerned with the empowerment of marginalized sections of society, such as women, indigenous peoples, and youth groups, and other community based organizations. These public groups are increasingly contributing efforts towards sustainable development through the participation, demonstration, projects, advocacy, and research and monitoring with cooperation and networking with other NGOs and government departments. Our research paper is also based on the work carried out by our organisation in promoting of environmental knowledge awareness in the society [2].

Current Status and Trends

Community based organisations have played important role in the management of the common properties or so called as assets such as water resources, forests, environment and biodiversity. Their Role was reduced drastically by the government organisation but recently there has been re-emergence of such organisations having youth, women, farmers and businessmen. They have played an important role in raising environmental concerns, developing awareness of environmental issues and promoting sustainable development. Encouraging public participation in environmental management awareness of environmental issues and promoting sustainable development. The encouragement of the public participation in the environmental management through the legislation in recent years has also enhanced the role of the NGO's and major groups. Many developing and developed countries have made rules to promote the creation of such community based organisations working for environmental issues [1]. Like in Malaysia the constitution recognizes the rights of the people to participate in the protection of natural resources and environment. Such constitutions amendments are present in other countries such as Australia, South Africa, Europe and North America.

The role and activities of the major public interest organisations are constantly changing due to the various social and political changes which actually alter their work for example in Pakistan when the military rule was imposed then all the NGO organisations were banned due to emergency and the some who were allowed their credibility was questionable. Financial restrictions have caused the group to cease the regular publication of its investigative reports. Despite this financial setback, the work of NGOs has won considerable credibility and appreciation in the region, which can be evidenced by the growing partnerships with government. For instance, NGOs and major groups have substantially increased their involvement in policy related playing a key role in assisting government agencies to meet the requirements of environmental management.

In recent years, the range of activities undertaken by environmental NGOs and other major groups has broadened. They now undertake a much wider range of activities than simply raising environmental awareness and/or acting as pressure groups. Their activities now include environmental monitoring; promoting environmental education, training and capacity-building; implementing demonstration projects; conducting advocacy work in partnership with the government; and the promotion of regional and international cooperation on environment. Many also get involved in the practical management of conservation areas, and promote community or individual action and campaign for greater accountability on the part of the government and corporate sector. The majority of NGOs in the region now works concurrently on environment and development, thus acknowledging that environmental problems are embedded in economic and social systems [4].

The stronger believes that NGOs and government agencies can work together in a complementary relationship that has become stronger and credibility the NGOs have acquired from the successful campaigns has created strong and growing public support for new advocacies, for example in case of the Punjab there are many NGOs who are operating for various social causes now all the NGOs are associated with each other like in March 2008 we called for a workshop on special training methods for environmental awareness then many other NGOs have also participated such as NGO for AIDS awareness, women health , child labour. Hence emergence of NGOs with very strong technical backgrounds this plays a substantial role in the formation of public opinion. At the regional and international level there is evidence of an increasing networking of NGOs and other major groups. At these levels, they are concerned with the sharing of experiences, influencing discussions and policy-making of regional and international inter-governmental bodies and raising concern over the globalization process.

Roles and Activities

NGOs have emerged as major players and partners in both development and conservation activities in the region. At the community level, they are in the front line in providing assistance in the acquisition of basic needs and amenities; in identifying issues, raising awareness, and providing information to grassroots communities in articulating the communities' problems and needs and bringing these to the attention of those who can affect change; in defending both the environmental and developmental rights of communities and building the capacity of communities to manage their natural resources and in dealing with sustainable development concerns [5]. NGO's work at the national level focuses mainly on the policy work and plays a vital role in the identification of the weakness and gaps in the current policy and legal frameworks, information gathering and educating public, private and government sector.

Awareness and Campaigning

These groups carry out environmental awareness raising and campaigning locally and nationally. Our organisation Kisan Virasat Mission has organised many state level events such as student symposia, workshops, seminars and invited talks. We have got reorganisation national for our work in mobilising the public opinion regarding the environmental issues. Our organisation is just three years old and we have about 300 formal and 1200 informal members. Scientific and technical NGOs are assisting in bridging the gap between science, policy makers and the citizenry [7]. Their research and education work is proving a vital addition to the decision and policy-making process.

In India, for instance, the Centre for Science and Environment publishes 'Citizen's Reports on the Environment' which focuses on specific environmental issues, such as urban pollution, and flood management. Written in nontechnical languages, these reports enable the general public to better understand the issues. Many of the more established NGOs in the region work on major national campaigns using a range of promotion activities, from grassroots awareness-raising, through to lobbying and media campaigns

Monitoring and Reporting

Our missions are based on the research which focus on the monitoring specific environmental issues as at the local level public interest organisations can keep track of the critical issues on the continuing basis. Like for example NGO's complement about the work of government institutions can cooperate with law enforcement authorities. Various sub-activities are given below.

Reporting

Reporting has emerged as the very important constituent of the activities of an NGO. Many NGOs produce the reports weekly on the environmental issues. Recent trends emerged as NGO's cooperate with each other and prepare a collective report every week. Example in India the Centre for Science and Environment publishes Citizen's State of Environment Report. In many instances, these broad assessments are supplemented by specialized reports that facilitate debate on key environmental issues, promote public awareness and encourage active community participation in environmental protection. In addition to State of the Environment Reports, Investigative Reports on the specific environmental issues are also increasing in the region.

Monitoring

Environmental monitoring and reporting by NGOs have contributed substantially to environmental Protection across the region. At the national or regional level, NGO monitoring can track the effectiveness of legislation, and investigate issues such as the movement of hazardous waste, the migration of species, the trade in endangered or restricted animals or plants or research on the state of rivers, forests or other ecosystems. NGOs use this type of work to influence practical actions, and to develop campaign strategies or propose policies [8]. For Example in Punjab the government has implemented a scheme for primary school students called as the mid day meal scheme. Now we received complaints regarding the irregularities in the overall process followed for mid day meals, then we formed a committee who will particularly look into this issue where we decided to conduct survey and monitor the neighbouring schools to actually see the reality. Our monitoring job has alarmed those official who are negligent in their jobs hence fear of NGO's helped in proper execution of the mid day meal scheme.

Journalism

Environmental journalism can play a vital role in creating market reactions in the international stock markets. It has now been felt that economies of many developed countries respond to the environmental news. Environmental journalism has helped in addressing the critical issues easily. Example U.S. and Canadian stock markets have shown markets react significantly to environmental news.

Research

Advent of the newer challenges to our ecosystem has actually resulted in the need for new strategies for handling such issues. Research has been emerged as a scientific tool and panacea for all such problems. Since last few years we have been facing issues like waste management, water management, pollution control etc. Now research into the possible causes and solutions is very important. New NGOs are emerging in the region to promote knowledge and awareness of these issues, while more established NGOs are responding to the new challenges by re-focusing their research efforts. For example, in India, the Centre for Science and Environment (CSE) was instrumental in convincing 28 selected pulp and paper mills to provide data similar to the USEPA's "toxic releases" database. Our organisation has started a mission for training people regarding the improved genetic crops in the state of Punjab which require lesser water and less fertilizers for the growth, now for carrying such mission it becomes very important that we should first collect all the information regarding the genetically improved crops, benefits and disadvantages and this is only possible through the research.

Education and Training

Education needs to be regarded investment as this plays a vital role in the economic growth of any country which transforms into an asset in the coming future. Education is the sources of knowledge, values, skills which are necessary for the development and building of any nation. Education helps in achieving the goals which are laid in advance. Environment education end goal is transformation of the environment according to the nature's law. It is the comprehensive study which includes all the relationships between the humans and their impact which is independent field of study. Environment education starts from school level and prevalent at higher level of our education systems i.e. universities and research institutes. Generally we call this as nature study and conservation education but all are same as the principle behind all of them is to save the environment for artificial changes brought by us. Environmental education is both theoretical and practical as it is learning how to manage and improve the relationship between human society and the environment in an integrated and sustainable way [9].

Training Objectives

1. Development of educational/teaching materials and aids in the formal education sector to encourage non-governmental organizations, mass media and other concerned organizations for promoting awareness among the people at all levels.
2. To promote environment education through existing educational/scientific/research institutions and to ensure training and manpower development in environment education and to mobilize people's awareness for the preservation and conservation of environment.
3. The program conducted/initiatives launched as part of this scheme are categorized under Formal and Non-Formal sectors where the programs under Formal Environmental Education are Environment Education in School System, Environmental Appreciation Courses, Environmental concepts in Management and Business Studies while the programs under Non-Formal Environmental Education are National Environment Awareness Campaign (NEAC), Eco-clubs (NGC), Mass Awareness.
4. Develop mechanisms and institutions for enhancing outreach activities through Nature Clubs of India, Eco-clubs and Interpretation programs to Increase the presence and influence of environment education in formal education system at the primary and higher levels through policy advocacy with the Central Boards and the National Council for Education and Research Training.
5. To develop a comprehensive teacher training programs that includes recapitulation and implement environment sensitization programs or modules for key target groups.
6. To advocate research on EE in the formal education to enhance impacts on policies related to increased focus on EE and to Integrate ESD into the training of India's future educators through National EE Guideline implementation.

NGO and Government Partnership

Government and NGO partnerships are being encouraged in a number of ways. In some countries laws exist to ensure community and major group's participation in developing regional and

Fig. 1

national policies and plans. In some countries laws exist to ensure community and major group's participation in developing regional and national policies and plans. For example, in Thailand, the 1992 Environment Act delegates the work on environmental management to provincial and local authorities, and encourages people's participation through environmental NGOs. As countries put into practice formal policies requiring public participation in decision-making, the influence and potential political power of NGOs increases.

Funding Support

Many governments in the region provide or facilitate, funding to strengthen NGO activities in environmental protection and natural resource conservation. Governments, donors and NGOs have also joined together to form endowment funds to support environmental projects. Examples are in Bhutan (Bhutan Trust Fund for Environmental Conservation), Indonesia (Indonesian Biodiversity Foundation or *Yayasan KEHATI*), and the Philippines (Foundation for the Philippine Environment). Many Countries have special funds based on contributions from the government and the private sector was established to provide assistance for the global environmental conservation activities of NGOs.

Validation of Environmental Information

The validation of information forms the basis for successful collaboration between governments, NGOs, community representations and other stakeholders, including project proponents, the private sector, the scientific community and the press and broadcast media. In circumstances where NGO/ major groups are formally involved in inter-agency bodies (i.e. Councils for

Sustainable Development) and in public consultation processes, as in the Sri Lanka, India, the Philippines, Pakistan and many other countries, information exchange and dialogue are the continuous process that allows ongoing verification and clarification between parties, thereby facilitating progress and reducing the need for conflict resolution.

Resources and Environment Management

The revival of the community involvement in management and policy issues, many public interest groups have become involved in community-based field projects. Community participation in the management of resources and the environment and the work of public interest groups is increasingly involved in finding practical solutions to social problems. Development of the environmental NGOs, environment governance structure has been reorganised. The research is intended to develop sound protocols which will help in preserving the environment. The procedures for this development lie in the form of exchange of programs such as seminars, workshops where awareness is raised among the students , facilities, rural and urban people regarding the ever increasing issues related to the environment. The emergence of the environmental NGO's in the modern society as an independent sector has been fascinating phenomena in environmental governance. The environmental activities carried out by these organisations are environmental education and guidance, participation in the environmental policy making and implementation, training sessions , holding invited talks by the eminent people from the field of environmental studies, organising workshops on the current trends and issues. An integrated effort is required for addressing the environmental planning, management and action. A more confronting interdisciplinary, cooperative, coordination and public participation are the important components in the process of sustainable development. Various educational institutes have been opened across the national and international boundaries to address such issues. These help by providing training to public and private industry professional, NGO's, Students regarding the environmental issues [10].

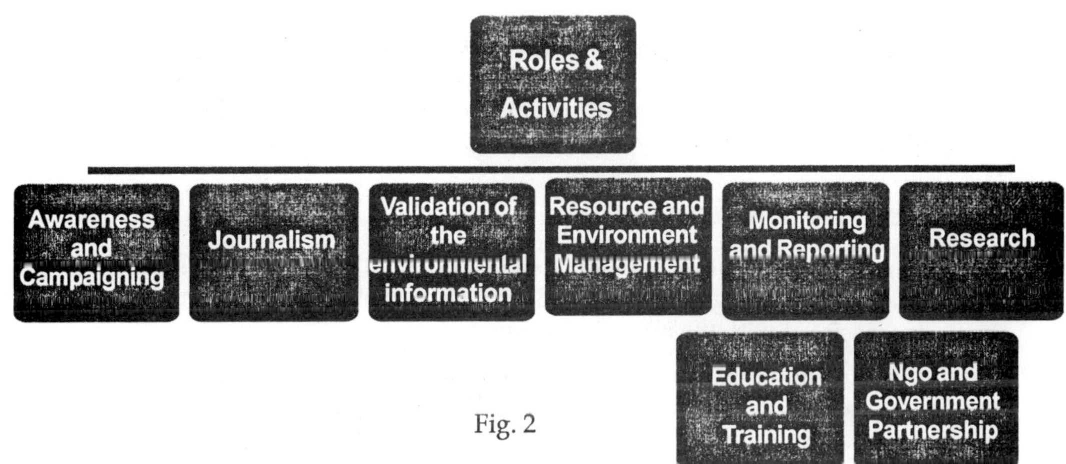

Fig. 2

Our Organisation

The Kheti Virasat Mission - KVM is a non-profit conscious civil society organization established in March 2005 and registered as a trust with head office at Jaitu town of district Faridkot Punjab,

India. KVM is working in the field of sustainable agriculture, conservation of natural resources, environmental health and eco-sustainable technologies. KVM undertakes policy debates, issues of WTO and globalization, activities of environmental education, awareness and advocacy, youth activities for environment and sustainable development. Apart from this KVM has also built cross section alliance through networking with other civil society groups, activists, and experts. KVM is working to promote sustainable - ecological agricultural practices, conservation and regeneration of natural water resources and to re-establish the traditional wisdom and practices related to water. Umendra Dutt is Executive Director of Kheti Virasat Mission. Dr Rakhi Juneja is active member of this mission and chaired many invited talks and workshops on Public and Environmental Health. Mrs Ranjeeta is a high school teacher through profession but she is leading personality in the field of education. She has actively participated in all the awareness programs organized by the Virasat Mission. All the three authors have done a wonderful job and this paper is result of their hard work.

Our Objectives

1. To elaborate and discuss the common characteristics of our ecology system, it's functioning in the given socio-economic, socio-cultural, political settings.
2. Highlight the crucial factors responsible of environmental reforms and take the challenges encountered to develop an efficient environmental system for the human community.
3. Act as a catalyst in bringing the local initiative and community participation in the overall improvement of our ecosystem.
4. To develop the civic and environmental consciousness among the public and private organisations that is directly or indirectly related to the environment.
5. Work for betterment of the civic standards, environmental protection to build cleaner and healthier environment.
6. Provide service to all the segments of the society which include rich and poor, women , children , youth, urban and rural people through the missions such as women empowerment mission, use of environment friendly pesticides , medical camps, training for farmers for using genetically improved crops.

Our Role in the Environment

1. Educating the school, college and universities students about the various environmental issues that are widening at alarming rates such as global warming, pollution, health hazards associated with the misuse of ecology.
2. To support the initiates taken by the central and state government in protecting our environment and motivate research on different measures to be taken to solve environmental problems.
3. To promote the idea of buying only environment friendly products i.e. the products that are safe for our ecology and environment.
4. Training programs specifically for farmers where the experts from agriculture universities are called to explain the benefits of genetically improved crops that require lesser fertilizers and pesticides hence help in building better environment.

Initiatives by the Kisan Virasat Mission

1. Use of Eco Friendly Pesticide
2. Environmental Awareness Camps
3. Pollution Control Programs
4. Environment Health Associate Activities
5. Environmental Education Advocacy

Conclusion

This research paper is based on the overall functioning of the NGO's in any area of operation. We have tried to explore the multidisciplinary approach followed by them in addressing environmental issues. The public concerns for environment related issues have increased among people of every country. Our studies have reflected that number of the public interest and communities involved in the environmental activities have increased. These NGOs have also increased the scope and diversity of such activities. Current studies show that their number has shoot up to 10000 which was just 1200 in 1992 Earth summit. In addition, the increase in the range of their activities reflects not only the increasing professionalism with which major groups are fulfilling their obligations and responsibilities, but the greater recognition and credibility accorded to them by national governments, regional and international organizations. We hope that this research report will help the research community to understand the ever expanding public interest and community organisation role in the solving environmental issues.

References

1. Carolyn Stephenson, What are Non-governmental Organizations?< http://www.beyondintractability.org/essay/role_ngo/>
2. Chitra, A. Role of Ngo's in protecting Environment and Health.
3. Environment Education Division< http://envfor.nic.in/divisions/ee/ee.html.
4. Environmental Education Materials: Guidelines for Excellence Workbook Bridging Theory & Practice< http://www.naaee.org/npeee/workbook.pdf
5. Iraj Malk Mohammadi , The Role of Environmental Non-Governmental Organizations in Natural Resources Management Extension (Case Study in Iran)< http://www.scipub.org/fulltext/ajes/ajes13221 229.pdf
6. Mohua Guha Environmental Education: A pathway for sustainable Development< http://iipsenvis.nic.in/nlv2n4d05/envi_edu.pdf
7. Partnership with NGO and private sector for improving health of urban poor< http://uhrc.in/downloads/Presentations/Siddhaarth_Surat_2006.pdf.
8. Sundar Vadaon , Role of NGO's in Environmental Conservation and Development < http://www.karmayog.org/startanngo/startanngo_16320.html.
9. The rise and role of NGOs in sustainable development< http://www.bsdglobal.com/ngo/roles.asp.
10. Vennila Govindaswamy, Importance of Environmental Education for Sustainable Development.

49

Use of Vermi-Composting in Ecological Sanitation System

S. B. Nimbalkar, Dr. P. H. Sawant and Dr. R. A. Hegde

Introduction

According to reports, around 2.6 billion of the 6 billion on the planet have no access to any form of basic sanitation. Sanitation is a critical issue as it is linked to both human health and dignity. Poor sanitation is leading directly to a decline in the quality and quantity of available water resources, and the problem is now finally being treated with a greater degree of seriousness than ever before. This was highlighted during the World Summit on Sustainable Development in Johannesburg, 2002, where the existing Millennium Development Goals (MDG's), adopted by the UN in New York in September 2000, were expanded to include the sanitation target of halving the proportion of people without access to sanitation in 1990 by the year 2015.

In many cities, towns and rural areas of the world today people live and raise their children in highly polluted environments. Urban and peri-urban areas in developing countries are among the worst polluted and disease ridden habitats of the world. Much of this pollution, which leads to high rates of disease, malnutrition and death, is caused by a lack of toilets and inadequate sanitation services. The lack of sufficient or adequate services is a result of many factors, including: inadequate financial resources, insufficient water, lack of space, difficult soil conditions and limited institutional capabilities. As cities expand and populations increase, the situation will grow worse and the need for safe, sustainable and affordable sanitation systems will be even more critical.

Ecological Sanitation (EcoSan) can be an approach to improve sanitation and recovery nutrients from human excreta and urine. The approach has been implemented in developing countries. Ecological Sanitation (EcoSan) regards human excreta as a resource to be recycled rather than as a waste to be disposed off. Recycling returns nutrients to soils and plants reduce the need for chemical fertilizers and restores good soil organisms to product plants. The problems raised by the decreasing quality and quantity of fresh water resources are becoming increasingly seriously

The education system has to prepare students to think about urine, faeces and grey/black water as resources. Emphasis has to shift from the simple disposal to the hygienisation of contaminated flow streams, and to resource conservation and safe reuse. Today all over the water crisis is being observed. This water crisis is in part a direct result of the failure of the current sanitation paradigm.

Outside of the cost considerations, conventional water-borne sanitation systems have further fundamental shortcomings as water is used to transport the wastes and they have high water consumption and hence making them unsuitable in the long-term for regions with water scarcity. In many places this has already led to an over-exploitation of the limited renewable water resources. Clean drinking water is too precious a resource to be flushed down the toilet and the use of flush toilets in areas where the water supply only operates for a few hours per week clearly manes no sense.

Much of this pollution, which leads to high rates of disease, malnutrition and death is caused by a lack of toilets and inadequate sanitation services. The lack of sufficient or adequate services is a result of many factors including : inadequate financial resources, insufficient water, lack of space, difficult soil conditions and limited institutional capabilities. The concept of Ecological Sanitation (EcoSan) toilets can be achieved where the water crisis is severe.

Concept

"Ecologically sustainable sanitation" or "EcoSan" for short, is defined as an approach to sanitation which respects ecological integrity, conserves and protects freshwater, promotes healthy living, and recycles nutrients from human excreta for agricultural ideally, EcoSan system enable the complete recovery of all nutrients from faeces, urine and grey water to the benefit of agriculture, and the minimization of water pollution. At the same time they ensure that water is used economically and is reused to the greatest possible extent, particularly for irrigation purposes. An even broader understanding of the term could also include the use, storage and infiltration of rainwater, treatment and recycling of solid organic wastes, minimization of the energy input for wastewater disposal and utilization of the energy content of solid and liquid wastes. EcoSan systems offer appropriate and sustainable solutions for different circumstances and demands. They permit acceptable and affordable sanitation for poor and rural areas, as well as for high-income areas and industrialized countries. EcoSan, however, this is not true. As long as the sanitation system is sustainable (environmentally and economically), it can be called an EcoSan system.

All in all, EcoSan represents a new basic understanding of wastewater handling in which faeces and urine are not considered as pollutants but instead as useful resources. In nature, there is no waste. All products of living things are used as raw materials by others as part of a cycle.

EcoSan offers a solution to sustainable sanitation provision as it aims at providing improved sanitation by sanitizing the excreta and re-using it in agriculture. The purpose of sanitizing and re-using excreta is to reduce contamination of the natural environment such as rivers and ground water; it also ensures that the valuable nutrients in the sanitized excreta are used for food production.

Limitations of Conventional Waste - Water Management Systems

Although increasing criticism has been leveled at conventional forms of central wastewater management systems for ecological and economic reasons, those systems i.e. a combined system with post connected multistage wastewater treatment facilities, are widely used all around the globe today. figure 1 schematically illustrates the main limitations of conventional wastewater management systems such as:

- Unsatisfactory purification or uncontrolled discharge of more than 90% of wastewater worldwide;
- Pollution of water bodies by organics, nutrients, hazardous substances, pathogens, pharmaceutical residues, hormones, etc;
- Severe environmental damage and eutrophication of the water cycle;
- Consumption of precious water for transport of waste;
- High investment, energy, operating and maintenance costs;
- Frequent subsidisation of prosperous areas, and neglect of poor settlements;
- Loss of valuable nutrients and trace elements contained in excrement through their discharge into water bodies;
- Impoverishment of agricultural soils, and increased dependence on chemical fertilisers;
- Predominance of combined central systems, resulting in problems with contaminated sewage sludge;
- Linear end-of-pipe technology.

Also, where there is no sewer network to transport the sewage, and also no access to take out the sludge through vacuum vehicles, which are provided by Municipal Corporations, poor practices

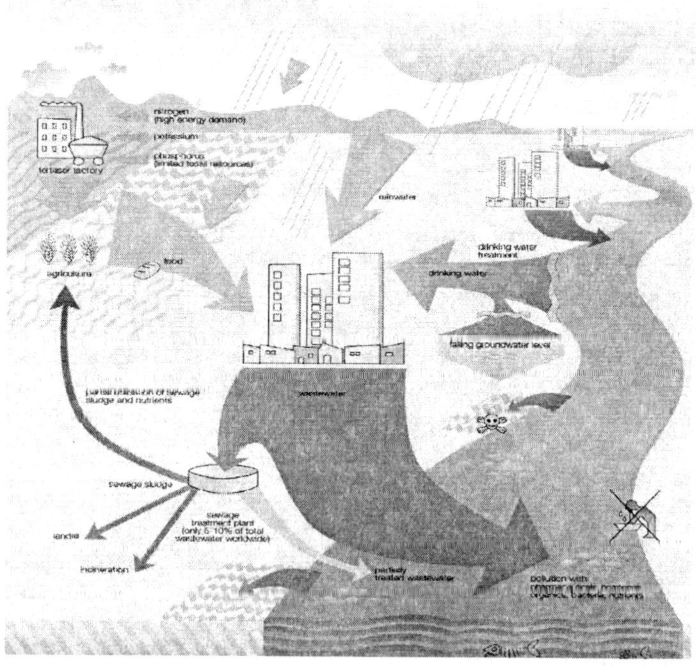

Fig. 1. Limitations of Conventional Wastewater Management System.

are adopted like removal of the sludge manually. This seems very inappropriate, that the human excreta is removed by another human manually. Four photographs given below describes the story of the poor practices.

Advantages of EcoSan concept

Photographs : Manual removal of Human Excreta.

To overcome drawbacks of the so called "end-of-the-pipe" sanitary systems and manual removing systems, which are based on the modern misconception that human excreta are simply wastes with no useful purpose and must be disposed of, and in order to meet the MDGs and achieve sustainability in the field of sanitation a new paradigm is needed. Ecological sanitation, or "ecosan" for short, is this new paradigm in sanitation that recognises human excreta and water from households not as a waste but as resources that can be recovered, treated where necessary and safely used again. Tailored to local needs, ecological sanitation systems, ideally, enable a complete recovery of nutrients in household wastewater and their reuse in agriculture. In this way, they help preserve soil fertility and safeguard long-term food security, whilst minimizing the consumption and pollution of water resources.

EcoSan is a holistic approach to sanitation and water management, representing a break with the too often poorly performing end-of-pipe technologies of the past, and recognising human excreta and domestically used water as a resource that should be made available for reuse. As an integrated alternative, a hallmark of ecosan is its interdisciplinary approach that goes beyond the narrow disciplines of domestic water supply and technological considerations to address issues such as agriculture, sociology, hygiene, health, town planning, economics and small business promotion, institutional administration, and so on. Such an approach also makes a large contribution to the integrated management of water and other natural resources. Figure 2 illustrates the main advantages of ecosan systems such as:

- Improvement of health by minimizing the introduction of pathogens from human excrement into the water cycle;

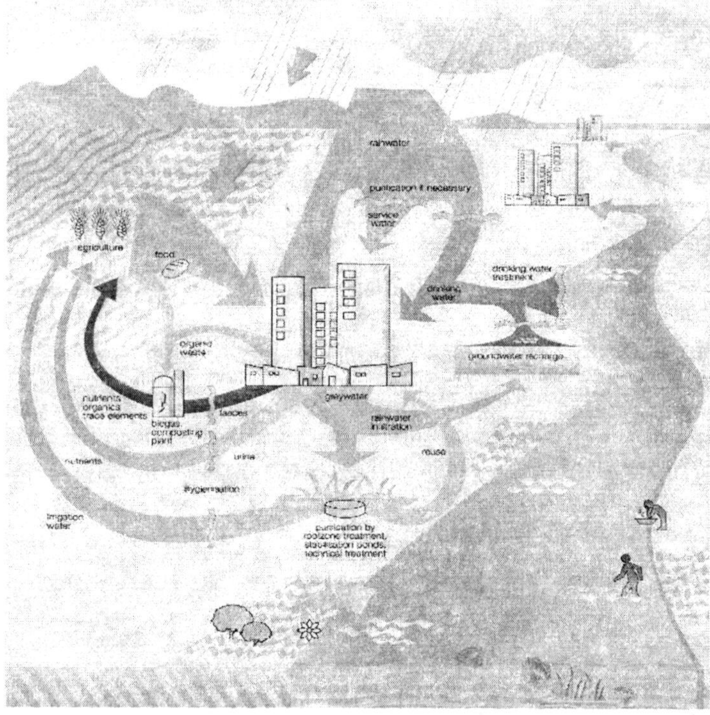

Fig. 2. Advantages of Ecological Sanitation System.

- Promotion of recycling by safe, hygienic recovery and use of nutrients, organics, trace elements, water and energy;
- Resource conservation, through lower water consumption, substitution of chemical fertilisers and minimisation of water pollution;
- Preference for modular, decentralised partial-flow systems for more appropriate cost-efficient solutions;
- Possibility to integrate on-plot systems into houses, increasing user comfort, and security for women and girls;
- Contributes to the preservation of soil fertility;
- Improvement of agricultural productivity and hence contributes to food security;
- Promotion of a holistic, interdisciplinary approach (hygiene, water supply and sanitation, resource conservation, environmental protection, urban planning, agriculture, irrigation, food security, small-business promotion,);
- Material-flow cycle instead of disposal.

Technologies in Use for EcoSan Projects

- Dehydrating toilets with urine diversion (also called dry urine diversion toilet);
- A waterless toilet with one or two vaults that are used alternately and urine diversion pedestals or squatting pans;
- Composting toilets,
- Vacuum systems,
- Anaerobic treatment with biogas production,
- Membrane technology,
- Aqua culture,
- Constructed wetlands

Each of the above technology has its application as per the prevailing site conditions.

Design of Proposed EcoSan System for a Idgaon Village

At present, majority of households in rural India is a huge slum with inhabitants of different caste, religion and race, did not have their own toilets and residents had access to open seating practices. As the lack of toilets is only one indication of the appalling living conditions for many thousands of slum dwellers, particularly women, the establishment of a public toilet centre was considered to be a matter of very great urgency.

The following aims are set into consideration to choose the EcoSan toilet for Idgaon.

- Improving living conditions in the slum, minimizing the risk of disease spreading during monsoon flood periods and increasing women's security;
- Recycling of nutrients and organics due to the collection, treatment and reuse of urine and faeces for production of fertilizer and compost, respectively;
- Generation of income for the development of the slum by charging for the use of the toilet, selling of fertilizer;
- Finally changing attitudes of people and encouraging them to consider human urine and faeces as a valuable resource.

Basic Data for Dimensioning and Layout

1. 90% of the total number of residents uses the community toilet for defecation.
2. Residents use toilet thrice for urination.
3. The toilet used all 365 days a year.
4. 2 litres of water used for hand washing.
5. Human waste :-

   Urine –500 Lit/year ≈ 1.4 Lit/day/capita

   Faeces –50 Lit/year ≈ 0.14 Lit/day/capita

Technology Suggested

To overcome unhygienic conditions related to malfunctioning of the main wastewater disposal facility and to meet the needs of extension of the locality, a sanitation concept comprising the treatment/reuse of human excreta with earthworm composting;

Composting Toilets

The technology suggested for this particular project is the vermi composting type toilets.

Vermicomposting is the process by which organic materials are converted into humus with the use of specific types of earthworms that breakdown the organic materials. There are some species that can consume organic materials very rapidly and disintegrate them into very fine particles by passing them through a grinding. The earthworms species: Eisenia fetida and Eisenia andrei are most commonly used for the vermicomposting. They derive their nourishment form microorganisms that grow upon the organic materials. At the same time, they promote further microbial activity in the residuals so that the faecal matters or "casts" that they produce, is much more fragmented and microbial active than what the earthworms consume. During this process, the important plant nutrients in the organic material-particularly nitrogen, potassium and calcium are released and converted through the microbial action into forms that are much more soluble and available to plants than those in the parent compounds. This technology is used most widely in Australia, while a lot of dry sanitation systems are getting local worms that help degrading without having them especially introduced to the system. The very important role of worms in EcoSan is not yet well known.

This is an easy way to recycle human excreta. Worm composting, or vermiculture, requires very little work, produces no offensive odors, and helps plants thrive. Only a few things are needed to make good worm compost.

The best kinds of worms for composting are "red worms," or "red wigglers." They are often found in old compost piles, but are different from the earthworms would normally find in the ground (Figure 3). These worms have a big appetite, reproduce quickly, and thrive in confinement. They can eat more than their own weight in food every day. Vermiculture can be a lucrative economic activity for rural women.

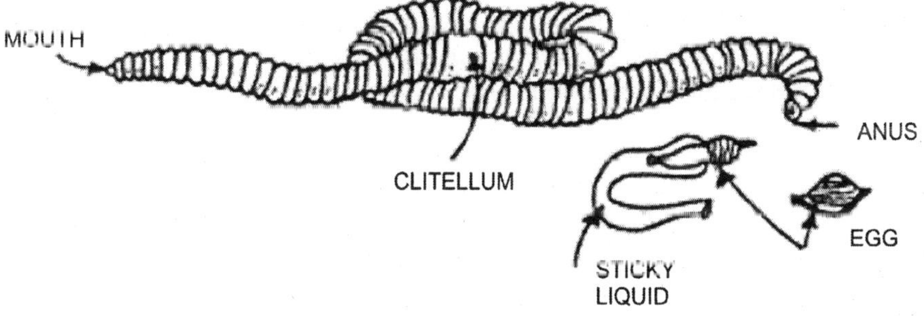

Fig. 3. Earthworm.

Cost-revenues Analysis

In connection with the phasing-out of the project at Idgaon and the intended up scaling of the eco-friendly sanitation project a cost-revenues analysis based upon expenses required construction of the EcoSan system in Idgaon village and assumptions in regard to capital costs, operation & maintenance requirements, the fertilizer equivalent of human excreta and use of the biogas.

The findings of cost revenue analysis, indicate that running a large scale eco-friendly sanitation project, which is relying on a pump and haul service system for collection and transportation of source-separated flowstreams, can be economically viable under certain conditions (e.g. optimizing frequency of service runs, collection of user fees, reuse of biogas as a substitute to LPG, reuse of recyclates).

Conclusion

The very idea that excreta are waste with no useful purpose is a modern misconception. It is at the root of the pollution problems which result from conventional approaches to sanitation, particularly flush-and-discharge. In nature there is no waste: all the products of living things are used as raw materials by others. Recycling sanitized human urine and faeces by returning them to the soil serves to restore the natural cycling of life-building materials that has been disrupted by our current sanitation practices. Further, the energy efficiency of this process is greater the more locally this recycling takes place.

Nutrients recovered from human excreta can be used to enhance the productivity of horticulture and agriculture in home gardens and farms, in urban as well as rural areas.

Composting is not the only way of treating excreta without water, but it is the only way to transform human waste into earth. Humidity is necessary and therefore the significance of composting toilet systems is more suitable to humid than to dry climates. The described project will give important results for operating and maintaining and what can be improved to make composting toilet systems more acceptable, even for both climates. The separation and collection of urine make drying of faeces possible. Only small changes are necessary, to transform a composting toilet system into a drying toilet system.

The problem is, to develop systems on a low cost level with a high standard of hygiene and function. Therefore, it is necessary to have projects like this in developing country like India, because they give orientation and experiences for users, research institutes and authorities for further development. Nevertheless, there are many situations in every village in India, where hygienic conditions have to be improved.

References

1. ACTS Project Proposal: ACTS eco-friendly public toilet center.
2. Agricultural Marketing Information Network - AGMARKNET (2006). http://agmarknet.nic.in/cmm2_home.asp?comm=Banana&dt=27/01/2006.
3. Calvert, P. (2004). Ecological Solutions to Flush Toilet Failures, EcoSolutions.

4. Dipl Ing. Martin Wafler (2006). Report on Case Studies of ecosan Pilot Projects in India, Version 1.
5. Ecological sanitation (1998), published by Department for Natural Resources and the Environment Swedish International Development Cooperation Agency.
6. Ministry of Small Scale Industries, Government of India (2006) http://www.laghu-udyog.com/publications/traderep/erode/erode2.htm.
7. Patel, I. (2003). Technical Options for Sanitation (1st edition).
8. WHO/UNICEF (2004). Meeting the MDG Drinking water and Sanitation target: A Mid term Assessment of Progress, WHO/UNICEF Joint Monitoring Programme for Water Supply and Sanitation (JMP) Report.

50

Use of Negative Ion Liberating Compounds in Preventing Marine Biofouling

VIKRANT H. BHATT, HIRAK A. BISWAS, SHEELA D. KAMAT, GAURI S. DHAMDHERE

Introduction

About 71% of earth's surface is covered with water, nearly 99% of which is sea water [1]. Typical aquatic environments include oceans, estuaries, salt marshes, lakes, rivers, ponds, rivers springs [2].

Most major classes of earth's organisms are primarily or exclusively marine [3]. More than one million species are estimated to inhabit in seas. [4]

Marine habitats are considered to be robust when dealing with disturbances such as climate changes and glaciations measured over millions of years. The environment includes splashing sea water, high velocity of sea water pumps, pipings or high speed vessels and simple immersion [2].The environment is further complicated by variations in salinity, dissolved oxygen, biological organisms and contaminations. Surface water systems such as open intake sea water, river and lake, brackish as well as industrial waste water feeds usually have a relatively high biological activity [1]. Marine organisms are both useful as well as harmful. Despite their variety of uses the harmful effects caused by these marine organisms and resulting in heavy economic losses cannot be overlooked. One such harmful effect that has produced a lot of concern is 'Bio-fouling of Metals'.

A variety of metals and their alloys are widely used for construction purposes. The properties of tensile strength, malleability and ductility make metals ideal construction materials. Thus a variety of metals such as iron, copper, nickel, aluminum and their alloys are widely used in marine construction. Amongst the various alloys of iron, carbon steel is most widely used for ship building and construction of marine equipment. Despite its uses, iron, steel and their alloys are not particularly resistant to corrosion. Marine corrosion thus includes deterioration of structures and vessels immersed in sea water, corrosion of machinery and piping systems that use sea water for cooling and other industrial purposes. The corrosion of metals is affected by several factors including salinity and chlorinity, temperature, dissolved oxygen, dissolved carbon-dioxide, pH, pollutants, influence of biological organisms [2].

The idea that there might be a biological root to corrosion problems has been explored for over a century. Biological influences were first considered to be potential cause for corrosion in metals as early as 1891 by Garret. Since that time many mechanisms have been proposed and many different forms of biologically induced corrosion have been discovered. Biologically induced corrosion (BIC) can occur in relatively inaccessible parts of a system. As one might suspect, almost every form of biologically induced corrosion is actually some form of localized attack [5]. Microbial induced corrosion (MIC) is also major area of concern when it comes to biofouling. It causes Deposit Formation, Tubercle Formation, Bioconcretions, Embrittlement, Pitting, Premature Failure, Reduced Heat Transfer, Reduced Production, Destruction of Iron Piping, and Catastrophic Failure (17, 18 and 19).

'Biofouling or biological fouling is the undesirable accumulation of microorganisms, plants, algae, and animals on submerged structures in contact with water for a period of time.' It is reported that there are 600 kinds of adhesives and as many as 1,300 kinds of creatures that are the cause of fouling on the ship bottom. First bacteria start sticking and grow up to hundreds of microns for several days.

The process of bio-film formation begins immediately upon immersion of metal in liquid environment. It begins with deposition of 'primer' coat of natural, high polymer film which is complete within first two hours of immersion.

The second step is the selective binding of short rod shaped bacteria to the primer which can occur within next 4 hours to 8 days depending upon temperature and depth [6]. After about 3 days of exposure the material surfaces are dominated by 'prosthecate' micro-organisms which reproduce, grow and secrete slimes. Taking advantage of secure anchorage and nutrient rich organic film attached organisms escape from starvation and continue to reproduce. Meanwhile, attachment of new organisms of diverse character (rod-shaped, spherical and filamentous) continues to grow on original conditioning film. As filamentous appendages of early colonizers continue to grow, attachment of algae, spores, diatoms and inorganic particles are observed. At this stage, usually after a week of first exposure, larvae forms of sessile organisms and barnacles are also observed (16). Material at this stage is slimy, fibrous mat. Optical flow and heat transfer properties of solid material is seriously degraded. In locations away from sunlight, where algal growth is limited, film becomes completely overlaid with silt and other mineral deposits.

Bio-films are rarely homogenous. Sometimes they provide only spotty coverage of metal surface. Even when they provide complete coverage, their thickness and composition may vary.

Aims and Objectives

Bio-fouling leads to many problems and economic losses. Biofouling results in corrosion of metals used for construction. Biofouling on the hull of ships reduces the streamline flow thereby reducing speeds and increasing fuel consumption by upto 50%. The increased fuel consumption leads to increase in global warming levels (7).

There are variety of methods used for prevention of biofouling each having its own drawback. Use of biocides (5) is toxic to marine life and to paint workers. Tributylin, a patent antifoulant causes masculinization of female gastropods and deformation of oyster shells. Antifouling paints also release toxic ions in the water which are hazardous. Copper and silver are extensively used in antifouling paints but these metals are toxic to barnacles (8). Other methods are not as effective.

The aim and objective is to study biofouling and improve the efficiency of paints by addition of negative ion liberating compounds. This is a potential antifouling strategy in the initial stages of bio-fouling as the bacterial cell surface is negatively ionized. They repel when the material in concern is covered with weak negative ions. This repelling action causes marine creature repellent phenomenon and brings about an antifouling effect without use of hazardous substance (9). This method is non-toxic to marine life.

Materials and Methods

i) Sample: We collected marine water samples from different sites from surface and from a depth of 12 feet. The sampling sites were Ferry's Wharf, Versova Creek and Juhu Beach. Samples of Biofilm were also scraped from ship's hull and transported in fresh sea water.

ii) Media: For enrichment of Iron oxidizing bacteria, Thiobacillus broth was used whereas for isolation, thiobacillus agar was used. The media were sterilized before use.

Thiobacillus Broth Media composition - Formulation g/liter - Ammonium sulphate 0.4, Calcium chloride 0.25, Ferrous sulphate 0.01, Magnesium sulphate 0.5, Monopotassium phosphate 4.0, Sodium thiosulphate 5.0. and Agar- 12.5 gram were added to prepare Thiobacillus Agar (14).

Zobell's Medium composition- Formulation g/Liter- Sodium Chloride 19.45, Bacti Agar 15.00, Magnesium Chloride, anhydrous 5.90, Sodium Sulfate 3.24, Peptone 5.00, Calcium Chloride 1.80, Yeast Extract 1.00, Potassium Chloride 0.55, Sodium Bicarbonate 0.16, Ferric Citrate 0.10, Potassium Bromide 0.08, Strontium Chloride 0.034, Boric Acid 0.022, Sodium Silicate 0.004, Sodium Fluoride 0.0024, Ammonium Nitrate 0.0016, Sodium Phosphate Dibasic 0.008 (15).

Reagents

For Chemical Assay

Estimation of Fe^{+2} and Fe^{+3} was carried out by thiocyanate method using 3N potassium thiocyanate and potassium persulfate as reagents (12, 13).

For Chromatography

Whatman filter paper was used for both sugars and amino acids. Several 1% authentic sugars and amino acids served as standards.

For sugar, aniline H2 phthalate was used as developer. For amino acids, 0.2% ninhydrin was used.

For sugar, solvent system consisting of butanol:water:pyridine:toluene(10:6:6:1) was used, whereas for amino acids, phenol:water (80:20) was used. (10)

Test Samples

Test samples consisted of small carbon steel coupons were used. Ships are usually made of carbon steel hence it was chosen as test sample. Carbon steel coupons were polished by sand paper, blasted and then used.

Anti Fouling Material

Two different anti-fouling materials were used. One consisted of chromium based paint mixed with 1% Lanthanum nitrate (w/v) and other consisted of chromium based paint containing 10% quartz sand (w/v). The material was coated on coupons by spray painting following the application of primer coat.

Methods

Enrichment

The enrichment was carried out by adding 5ml of each sample to 50ml of sterile media for iron oxidizing bacteria containing 4% $FeSO_4$. Un-inoculated flasks containing sterile media were kept as control. The flasks were incubated at room temperature on shaker for 3-4 weeks and the development of encrustation on the sides of flask was studied. Following the development of encrustation (reddish brown film), a part of film and 5ml of broth from first enrichment broth was transferred to 50ml of sterile fresh enrichment broth and incubated as before (20).

After each enrichment, the sample of inoculated broth as well as encrustation on sides of flask were observed under microscope after staining with Gram's staining and monochrome staining method. Following second enrichment the samples were isolated on a sterile Thiobacillus agar plates by inverted T method and incubated at room temperature for 5-6 days. The colonies that developed following incubation were also stained and observed under microscope.

For Immersion Tests in Laboratory

Following enrichment and isolation, mass culture was built up for immersion tests.

For immersion test samples from second enrichment were inoculated into fresh sterile media for iron oxidizing bacteria containing 1% $FeSO_4$ and incubated as before. For this test, twelve 250ml flasks each containing 200ml of sterile media with 1% $FeSO_4$ were taken, 9 were inoculated with 20ml of broth from mass culture. Carbon steel coupon samples consisting of uncoated coupons(C), coupon coated with paint(P), coupon coated with paint containing 1% Lanthanum nitrate (A) and coupons coated with paint containing 10% quartz salt(B) were numbered and carefully weighed and their weights were noted. The twelve flasks were divided into three sets each containing four flasks. Each flask of set one were taken and three coupons of (P) type + one of (C) type by means of thread into each of the flask. Uninoculated flasks with coupon serve as control. The flask of set two and set three were treated similarly but only by replacing (P) coupons with (A) and (B) coupons respectively. All operations were carried out under strict anaerobic conditions and flasks were incubated at room temperature for static conditions for two months. At the end of one month, 1 flask from each of three sets were removed, the coupons removed carefully and placed in a labeled Petri dish. Each coupon was cleaned, dried and change in weight was noted by weight reduction assay (Table 3 & 4) (Figure 1 & 2).

For Immersion Tests in Field

Field immersion tests were carried out in marine waters of Ferry's Wharf. For this, eight of each coupon type was tied on four different nylon ropes. The samples were then placed in a nylon net which in turn was placed in a wire mesh. Wire mesh was secured by using nylon ropes to bind the open ends. Two such assemblies were suspended by means of a nylon rope from an iron barge into sea water at a depth of 4 -5 feet. At the end of the month, each of the four coupon type from one assembly was removed and placed in clean glass containers containing fresh sea water.

The samples were then scrapped with the help of a nylon brush in 5ml of sterile sea water. This was then serially diluted to obtain upto 10^{-10} dilutions. 0.1ml of each of these dilutions was surface spread on sterile Zobell's agar. The plates were then incubated for 24 hours and the colonies that developed were counted. A similar procedure was carried for the second assembly at the end of two months (11).

Chromatography Studies

Enrichment broth from mass culture was also subjected to chromatography techniques to identify if any organic compounds were secreted. The supernatant was filtered and its pH was adjusted to 7.2 using KOH and heavy iron precipitate was removed by boiling at 55-60°C followed by centrifugation. The supernatant was spotted on Whatman's filter paper no.1 along with 0.1% authentic sugars, resolved using butanol:water:pyridine:toluene (10:6:6:1) and developed using aniline hydrogen phthalate. Similarly supernatant was screened for amino acids using phenol: water (80:20) as solvent system and 0.2% ninhydrin as developer. The Rf values were calculated, (Table 1 & 2)(10).

Oxidation Rate Studies

For determining rate of iron oxidation, the samples from mass culture as well as from uninoculated broth were taken out at intervals of 3 days for a period of one month and the concentration of Fe^{+2} and Fe^{+3} were determined by potassium thiocyanate method (12, 13).

Results

Enrichment and Isolation

The enrichment and isolation techniques showed the presence of iron oxidizing bacteria. During incubation a reddish brown colored film began to develop on the sides of the flask after 6-7 days. A decrease in pH was observed from 3.5 to 2.5. With further incubation, the inside surface of the flask was covered with the brown film and after 18-20 days the pH of the broth was below 2. Gram staining revealed gram negative short curved rods. Monochrome staining also revealed the same. The isolation of (second) enrichment broth on Thiobacillus Agar plates revealed presence of small, circular, orange –reddish colonies following incubation at room temperature for 6-7 days. Gram and monochrome staining revealed short curved rods.

Immersion Tests

After incubation the weight was found to decrease significantly in case of control coupons in all flasks but no decrease was found in case of either of the coated coupons. Large amount of slime was found to be coating the control coupons also large amount of black precipitate was found to be adhered tenaciously to the coupons. No visible slime was seen in case of coated coupons but the surface was slimy to touch. A further incubation for 2 months caused a further decrease in weight of control coupon, the surface of the control coupon was actually found to peel off with a black precipitate found all over the coupon along with a reddish coloured slime. Small amounts of visible slime was observed in all coupons coated with paint and those coated with paint and 10% quartz sand but no visible slime was observed on coupons coated with paint containing 1% lanthanum nitrate.

Chromatography

Analysis of supernatant from enriched broth for sugar and amino acids did not show presence of any sugar or amino acid (Table 1 & 2).

Table 1: Chromatographic Test for Detecting the Presence of Amino Acids.

Amino Acid	Rf values
Alanine	5.9
Aspartate	2.5
Glycine	5.3
Lysine	4.6
Unknown	-

Table 2: Chromatographic Test for Detecting the Presence of Sugars

Sugar	Rf values
Glucose	4.0
Galactose	3.5
Maltose	1.9
Unknown	-

Oxidation of Fe^{+2}

On studying the oxidation of Fe^{+2} by potassium thiocyanate method, (21,50) it was observed that initially rate of oxidation of Fe^{+2} to Fe^{+3} was low with only 1.25μg/ml of Fe^{+3} being produced at the end of three days. However with further incubation, probably because of increase in cell numbers the oxidation significantly increases with about 175μg/ml of Fe^{+3} being produced at the end of 9 days. This was accompanied by a decrease in pH from initial 3-4 to 2-3 at end of 12 days. The oxidation of Fe^{+2} to Fe^{+3} increased rapidly with further incubation (Table 5) (Figure 3).

Field Immersion Tests

It was observed that after a period of one month, the number of viable bacteria was greatest in case of control coupons (Table 6). Visible observation of control coupon revealed the presence of not only slime layer but also presence of small attached sea weed harboring small macroscopic creatures like lobsters, crabs etc. Also the surface was covered with black precipitate and had foul smell. Observations of all the coated coupons also revealed presence of a surface slimy to touch (Figure 1).

No visible slime layers or macroscopic creatures were seen. Also the black precipitate found on control coupons was absent. The number of viable bacteria in case of coupons coated with quartz sand was higher than that of coupons coated with paint containing lanthanum nitrate. Following incubation for another month (Table 7) the uncoated coupons showed presence of significant amounts of surface film and long branching structures similar to sea weed was found attached. Reddish coloured slimy growth and green coloured matt were seen within which macroscopic marine creatures like shrimps were entangled (Figure 2). Removal of this film revealed pitting of the surface which was originally smooth. A large amount of black precipitate was released on scrapping. Visible slime developed on paint containing 10% quartz sand and small amount on paint coated coupons. No visible slime was observed on coupons coated with paint containing 1% lanthanum nitrate.

Discussion

A study was carried out on biofouling of iron in marine environment at both the laboratory and marine fields at Ferry's Wharf. The study mainly involved assessing the efficiency of negative ion liberating compounds in preventing bacterial adhesion: the first step in biofouling without causing any environmental problems.

Enrichment and isolation of iron oxidizing organisms from marine water proved to be difficult and since the obligate autotrophic nature of these organisms precludes its growth on agar media. Enrichment was obtained after several attempts. Isolation was particularly difficult and several attempts to isolate the organisms on Thiobacillus Agar failed. Further studies were therefore carried out using enrichment broth cultures. The analysis of enrichment broth (1% $FeSO_4$) supernatants by chromatography did not show presence of any organic compounds such as carbohydrates, amino acids etc. although the production of pyruvic acid was reported by Carl Schnaitman et al (1975) (10).

Further the ability of enriched culture to use 1% solutions of inorganic ferrous sulphate was measured by oxidation of iron to ferric state. Oxidation of ferrous to ferric state at initial pH

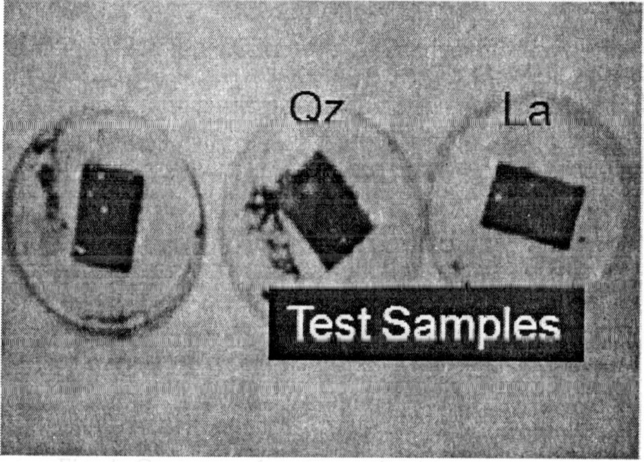

Fig. 1. Coupons after 1 month of immersion test.

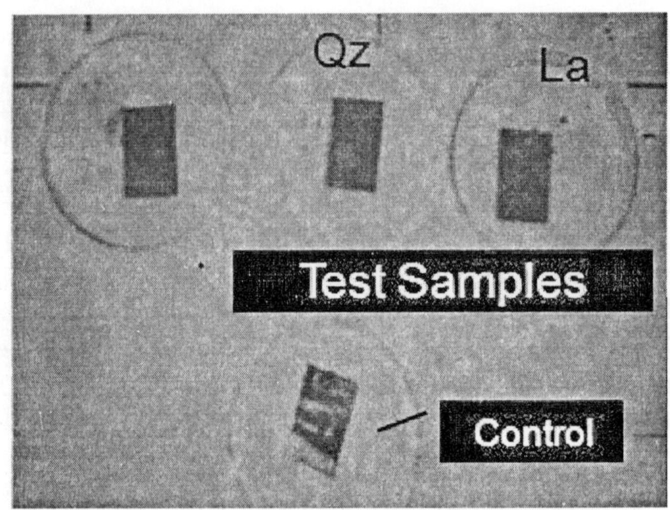

Fig. 2. Coupons after 2 months of immersion test.

In Fig. 1 and 2. Qz = Quartz sand and La = Lanthanum Nitrate.

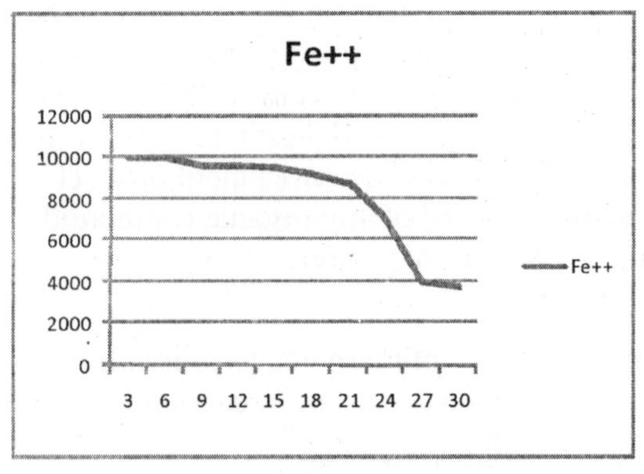

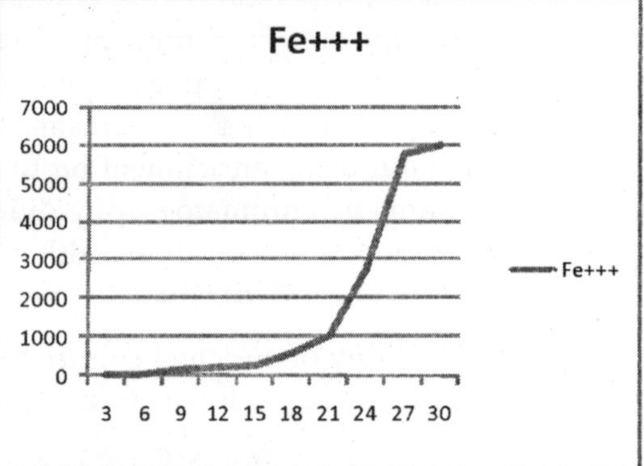

Scale = X Axis= Number of days Y Axis= Concentration of Fe++ and Fe+++ in μg/μl

Fig. 3. Concentration of Fe++ and Fe+++ against number of days.

Table 3: Results of Weight Reduction Assay after One Month.

Paint						Paint + Lanthanum Nitrate						Paint + Quartz Sand					
Control			Test			Control			Test			Control			Test		
W1	W2	W3	W1	W2	W3	W1	W2	W3	W1	W2	W3	W1	W2	W3	W1	W2	W3
			10.914	10.900	0.014				10.891	10.880	0.011				9.938	9.928	0.010
10.103	9.779	0.324	11.088	11.080	0.008	11.123	10.550	0.573	10.959	10.950	0.009	9.998	9.326	0.662	9.147	9.158	0.011
			10.334	10.328	0.006				10.708	10.700	0.008				10.034	10.020	0.014

Table 4: Results of Weight Reduction Assay after Two Months.

Paint						Paint + Lanthanum Nitrate						Paint + Quartz Sand					
Control			Test			Control			Test			Control				Test	
W1	W2	W3	W1	W2	W3	W1	W2	W3	W1	W2	W3	W1	W2	W3	W1	W2	W3
			11.084	44.023	0.061				11.023	11.000	0.023				10.198	10.180	0.018
8.361	7.547	0.814	11.021	11.008	0.013	9.923	8.990	0.933	9.000	8.992	0.008	11.121	10.098	1.023	10.159	10.150	0.009
			9.326	9.323	0.003				8.927	8.914	0.013				9.954	9.927	0.027

Where, W1 = Initial weight, W2 = Final Weight, W3 = Difference In Weight

Table 5: Estimation of Fe^{++} to Fe^{+++} by Iron Oxidizing Bacteria.

	Fe^{+++}				Fe^{+++} Fe^{+++}				Fe^{++}
pH/ No	Dilution	O.D	Conc from graph (μg/μl)	Final cons. (μg/μl)	Dilution	O.D	Conc from graph (μg/μl)	Final conc (μg/μl)	(μg/μg)
(3-4) 3	1:10	0.03	0.125	1.25	1:1000	0.25	10	10000	10000-1.25= 9998.75
(3-4) 6	Undil	0.3	10	10	1:1000	0.25	10	10000	10000-10= 9990
(3-4) 9	Undil 1:10	0.9 0.3	~ 12	~ 120	1:1000	0.24	9.75	9750	9750-120= 9360
(2-3) 12	Undil 1:20	~ 0.22	~ 8.75	~ 175	1:1000	0.24	9.75	9750	9750-175= 9575
(2-3) 15	Undil 1:80	~ 0.15	~ 6	~ 240	1:1000	0.24	9.75	9750	9750-240= 9510
(2-3) 18	Undil 1:100	~ 0.14	~ 5.5	~ 550	1:1000	0.24	9.75	9750	9750-550= 9200
(2-3) 21	1:100	0.25	10	1000	1:1000	0.24	9.75	9750	9750-1000= 8750
(1-2) 24	1:200	0.34	13.75	2750	1:1000	0.24	9.75	9750	9750-2750= 7000
(1-2) 27	1:200 1:1000	0.65 0.16	26 6.5	5200 6500	1:1000	0.24	9.75	9750	9750-5850= 3900
(1-2) 30	1:1000	0.15	6	6000	1:1000	0.24	9.75	9750	9750-6000= 3750

Table 6: Viable count on Zobell's Agar after One Month.

Dil.	Control				Paint				Paint + Lanthanum Nitrate				Paint+ Quartz Sand			
	Count/ 0.1ml	Avg. count/ 0.1ml	Avg. count/ 5ml	Count/ Cm^3 of coupan	Count/ 0.1ml	Avg. count/ 0.1ml	Avg. count/ 5ml	Count/ Cm^3 of coupan	Count/ 0.1ml	Avg. count/ 0.1ml	Avg. count/ 5ml	Count/ Cm^3 of coupan	Count/ 0.1ml	Avg. count/ 0.1ml	Avg. count/ 5ml	Count Cm^3 of Coupan
Undil.	TNTC				89				-	-	-	-	-	-	-	-
10^{-1}	57				5				-	-	-	-	-	-	-	-
10^{-2}	7	6.35	3.18	1.28	-	6.95	3.48	1.40	-	-	-	-	-	-	-	-
10^{-3}	-	$x10^4$	$x10^5$	$x10^4$	-	$x10^2$	$x10^3$	$x10^2$	-		-	-	-	-	-	-
10^{-4}	-				-				-	-	-	-	-	-	-	-

Table 7: Viable count on Zobell's Agar after Two Month.

Dil.	CONTROL				PAINT				PAINT + LANTHANUM NITRATE				PAINT + QUARTZSAND			
	Count/ 0.1ml	Avg. count 0.1ml	Avg. count 5ml	Count/ Cm^3 of coupan	Count/ 0.1ml	Avg. count/ 0.1ml	Avg. count/ 5ml	Count/ Cm^3 of coupan	Count/ 0.1ml	Avg. count/ 0.1ml	Avg. count/ 5ml	Count/ Cm^3 of coupan	Count/ 0.1ml	Avg. count/ 0.1ml	Avg. count/ 5ml	Count/ Cm^3 of coupan
Undil.	TNTC				89				9	90	450	18.000	20	200	1000	40.00
10^{-1}	TNTC				5				-	-	-	-	-	-	-	-
10^{-2}	TNTC	1.21	6.07	0.24	-	2.85	1.42	5.75	-	-	-	-	-	-	-	-
10^{-3}	93	x10^6	x10^6	x10^6	-	x10^4	x10^5	x10^3	-		-	-	-	-	-	-
10^{-4}	15				-				-	-	-	-	-	-	-	-

was found to be very slow. However, as the organisms continued to grow, the pH dropped gradually with increase in concentration of ferric ion and a corresponding decrease in ferrous concentration. At pH values between 2-3 a dramatic increase in oxidation of ferrous to ferric state which was comparable with results obtained by W.E. Razzel and P.C Trussel (1980).

Weight loss measurements performed for carbon steel coupons coated with paint containing two different negative ion liberating compounds were compared with uncoated coupons after periods of one and two months. The uncoated coupons in both cases showed variable results as suggested in the result tables and these must be statistically evaluated.

Efficiency of the effect of negative ion liberating compounds at field levels were evaluated by immersing carbon steel coated and uncoated coupons and performing viable count measurements. Control uncoated coupons cfu/ml which was much higher than two of the three types of coated coupons i.e. paint plus lanthanum nitrate, paint and quartz sand and paint alone. The average viable count for these three after a period of one month was 1.4x10^2 for coupons coated with paint whereas no count was obtained for remaining coated coupons. Similarly results for these three types of coupons after a period of two months were found to be 5.75x10^3, 1.8146x10^1, 4.036x10^1.

In each case the count was less than that of control coupons. Although both lanthanum nitrate and quartz sand liberate negative ions, lanthanum nitrate appears to be more efficient than quartz sand probably because when lipopolysaccharide containing bacteria come in contact with such a surface, specific and/or short range interactions may become predominant as compared with nonspecific, long range interaction (London Vander Waal's electrostatic and stearic intersections) and therefore LPS may facilitate the attachment of bacteria to quartz sand. A similar effect has been evaluated by E.Coli JM109 by Abu Lail et al. (2003) .

Conclusion

Biofouling is due to bio-deterioration in which fouling organisms adhere and corrode solid surfaces in marine environments. Biofouling of undersurfaces, hull and other water submerged parts of offshore structures of ships leads to increased weight and loss in speed. Biofilms formed during the process are hard to dislodge and even after cleaning of surface biofouling cycle starts again. Biofouling further results in initiation of biologically induced corrosion (BIC). BIC is an insidious form of corrosion. What makes BIC more complicated is that often microbe itself is not corroding the surface. Indirect nature microbial attack makes it more difficult to predict. Fortunately significant study has gone into these problems and a host of prevention techniques exists for combating this problem. The current project essentially evaluates the efficiency of negative ion liberating compounds as additive to chromium based paints to prolong the onset of biofouling and subsequent BIC. Negative ion liberating compounds used lanthanum nitrate and quartz sand. Quartz sand exhibits piezoelectric properties and was therefore selected for the experiments. A comparison of two compounds as additive by viable count in field studies indicated that lanthanum nitrate was more efficient as compared to quartz sand and maybe preferred as additives over quartz sand. However both lanthanum nitrate and quartz sand were found to be more effective than paint alone. These thus may be efficiently used as additives although less efficient to Lanthanum phosphate – Tourmaline – ceramic additive which prevents biofouling at field level for 8 months. A comparative study with these and other negative ion liberating compounds must however be made.

The experiments carried out at laboratory levels using enrichment broth cultures of iron oxidizing organisms gave varied results although comparatively less decrease in weight was observed for all three coated coupons. All the above results need to be evaluated statistically. However it is fair to conclude from the above results that there lays a great potential in the development of antifouling strategy that makes use of one or a combination of negative ion liberating compounds. The expected benefits seem to be enormous.

References

1. Bapuji.M., Wagh.A.B., and Wilsanad.V., (1999). "Antifouling activities of marine sedimentary invertebrates on some macrofoulers". Indian.J.Mar.Sci 28: 280-284.

2. Beech.B.I., and Gaylarde.C.C., (1989). " Adhesion of *Desulfovibrio desulfuricans* and *Pseudomans fluorescence* to mild steel structures". J.App.Bacteriol. 67:201-207.

3. Chugo Yokochi, Hideaki Nogami and Yoshiteru Tomura http://www.nmri.go.jp/main/cooperation/ujnr/24ujnr_paper_jpn/yokochi.pdf.

4. Dexter.C.S., "Asm Handbook of Corrosion", Vol 13 (893- 914).

5. Dube.H.C., Vaidya.S.Y., and Vala.A.K., (2001). "Biofouling bacteria at Bhavnagar port." Indian.J.Microbiol. 41: 315 – 317.

6. Encyclopedia Titanic http://www.encyclopedia-titanica.org/rms-titanic-biodeterioration.html.

7. Gegrke.T., and Wolfgang.S., (2003). " Interactions between microorganisms and physiochemical factors cause MIC of steel pilings in harbour (ALWC)", Conference Paper, NACE STORE,/product.asp? SKU51300% 2D03557%2DSG & Prod Name = 03557 + INTERACTIONS + BE.

8. Gomez de saravia S.G., Guiamet. S.P., and Videl H.A., (1998). "98290 Preventing MIC through microbial adhesion inhibition", Conference Paper, NACE STORE,/product.asp?SKU = 51300% 2D98290% 2DSG & Prod Name = 98290 + PERCENTING + MI.

9. Goswami D.C. and Kalita H. (1988) "Rapid Determination of Iron in Water by Modified Thiocyanate Method" DefSci J, Vol. 38, NO. 2, April 1988, pp 177-182.

10. HIMEDIA LABS. http://www.himedialabs.com/productpreparation.aspx?productcode =M789.

11. Lizama.H.M., Suzuki.I., and Tackaberry.D.P., (1989). "Competitive inhibition of ferrous iron oxidation by Thiobacillus ferroxidans by increasing concenteration of cells", J.App.Environ. Microbiol. 55(5): 1117 -1121.

12. Lundgren.G.D., and Schnaitman.C. (1985). "Organic compounds in spent medium of Ferrobacillus ferroxidans", Can.J.Microbiol. 11 : 23- 27.

13. Madigan.M.T., Martinko.J.M., and Parker.J., (1997). "Biology of organisms", Prentice Hall International Inc. eighth edition, (550).

14. Marianne Stanczak (2004). Biofouling: It's not just barnacles any more. http://www.csa.com/discoveryguides/biofoul/overview.php.

15. Marine fouling and its prevention, Contribution Number 580, from the woods hole, Oceanographic institute. https://darchive.mblwhoilibrary.org/bitstream/1912/191/23/chapter%2014.pdf.

16. Opportunities in Marine Biotechnology and Aqua Culture http://www.nal.usda.gov/bic/bio21/aqua.html.

17. Salley, A.J., (1996). " Fundamental Principals of Bacteriology", Tata McGraw Hill Publishing Company Limited, Seventh edition, (671).

18. Thierry D : Aspects of microbially induced corrosion: Papers from EUROCORR '96 and the EFC working party (EFC 22).

19. USBiological . J. Marine Research 4:42 (1941). http://www.usbio.net/technicalSheet.php?prodSku=M2405-01.

20. 10th Internation Congress on Marine corrosion and fouling: http://hdl.handle.net/1947/3822.

51

Green Synthesis of Thiophenylated Quinones using Dry Media Reaction

SARASWATI KANODIA

Introduction

Thioarylquinones are known to possess fungicida[1], antitumor[2] and antibacterial[3,4] properties. 2-Thiobenzyl-1,4-naphthoquinone, 2-thiophenyl-1,4-naphthoquinone and 2-(4-nitrothiophenyl)-1,4-naphthoquinone were found to be effective for the inhibition of Ehrlich ascites tumor in mice. Thioarylated quinones have recently been utilized effectively in the synthesis of various naturally occurring naphtho(2,3-b)furan-4,9-diones[5,6].In the past they have been prepared by the addition of thiol to 1, 4 – quinones in methanol and oxidation of the resulting substituted hydroquinone by an oxidizing agent. But this procedure has some drawbacks such as low product yields (40-60%) and longer reaction periods.

This communication deals with the concept of utilizing reagents or reactants adsorbed on an insoluble inorganic support for organic synthesis. Several classes of solids have commonly been used for surface organic chemistry including aluminas, silica gels, zeolites and clays. In the present study an attempt was made to improve upon the yields by carrying out direct thiophenylation of 1,4-quinones adsorbed on alumina with thiophenol. This procedure has the distinct advantage over the solution of the same reagent i.e. it leads to a clean, efficient and economical technology (green chemistry); safety is largely increased, work up is considerably simplified, cost is reduced and the reactivities and sometimes selectivities are enhanced without dilution.

Experimental

Reaction of 1, 4 – naphthoquinone with thiophenol

1,4-Naphthoquinone (1 mmol, 158 mg) was adsorbed on neutral alumina by dissolving it in acetone, adding the alumina and evaporating the solvent using a rotatory evaporator. To the alumina containing the adsorbed material was added thiophenol (1.1 mmol, 0.2 ml) and the reaction mixture was stirred at room temperature for half an hour. The progress of the reaction was monitored on a TC plate (silica gel, benzene). After the completion of the reaction, the reaction mixture was extracted with acetone. Acetone was evaporated under reduced pressure, the residue thus obtained was separated by preparative TLC over silica gel using petroleum ether: benzene (1:1) as a solvent to give yellow prisms (Rf value 0.79, yield 240 mg), m.p. 158°C. It was identified as 2–thiophenyl–1, 4–naphthoquinone (VIII) by its spectral data and melting point.

Al_2O_3 , PhSH

r.t. stirring

R=R^1=R^2=H	(VIII) R=SPh,R^1=R^2=R^3=H
R=CH^3,R^1=R^2=H	(IX) R=CH^3,R^1=SPh,R^2=R^3=H
R=Cl,R^1=R^2=H	(X) R=Cl,R^1=SPh,R^2=R^3=H
R=OH,R^1=R^2=H	(XI) R=OH,R^1=SPh,R^2=R^3=H
R=Br,R^1=R^2=H	(XII) R=Br,R^1=SPh,R^2=R^3=H
R=NH^2,R^1=R^2=H	(XIII) R=NH^2,R^1=SPh,R^2=R^3=H
R^1=OH,R=R^2=H	(XIV) R=SPh,R^2=OH,R^1=R^3=H

Table: Thiophenylation of Quinones.

Reactant	Product (hrs.)	Time (%)	Yield (°C)	M.pt.
I	VIII	1.5	90	158[7]
II	IX	1.0	80	109[7]
III	X	1.5	90	104[7]
IV	XI	8.0	75	149[8]
V	XII	1.5	90	132[9]
VI	XIII	4.0	85	17[14]
VII	XIV	1.5	70	143[10]

References

1. Atlamsani A. and Bregeault J.M., (1993). Synthesis, 79.
2. Bloruquist A.T. and Goldstein A., (1963). Org. Syn., Coll.Vol. 4, 838.

3. Clifford A.A. and Waters W.A., (1963). J. Chem.Soc., 3056.
4. Dalla Cort A., Mandolini L. and Panaioli S., (1988). Synth.Commun., 18(6), 613.
5. Dougherty G., (1928). J.Am.Chem.Soc., 50, 571.
6. Englinton G. and Galbraith A.R., (1959). J.Chem.Soc., 889.
7. Sharma J., (1992). Ph.D. Thesis, Delhi Univ.
8. Thapliyal P.C., Singh P.K. and Khanna R.N., (1993). Synth.Commun., 23(20), 2821.
9. Tour J.M., Pendalwar S.L., Kafka C.M. and Cooper J.P., (1906). J.Org.Chem., 57, 4786 (1992). F.Francis, Ber., 39, 3803.

52

Applications of Raman Laser and Fourier Transform-Infrared Spectroscopy in the Experimental Studies of Diseases

S. UPADYAY AND R.K. JHA

Introduction

Alterations in the lipid and protein components have been found to be responsible for the change in the Raman spectra of erythrocyte membranes upon varying pH and temperature, whereas specific changes in the C-H stretching region are reported to be related to the alterations in the integral protein environment. Earlier Steward et al. (1960) employed IR spectroscopy to determine the ethanol and carbon tetrachloride in blood, whereas Freeman (1966) used it to determine strains of tuberculosis bacilli.

Till now most of the information concerning the conformation of immunoglobulin (IgG) has come from X-ray, circular dichroism (CD) and infrared spectroscopy. It has been shown by several workers (Abaturov et al., 1969; Litman et al., 1973; Amzel and Poljak, 1979) that the immunoglobulin contains the beta-structure and irregular conformation but not the alpha- helical conformation. Abaturov et al. (1969) have reported the observed frequencies of the four amide bands of IgG, its peptide chains and proteolytic fragments. The purpose of this work is to show that laser Raman and FT-IR spectroscopies can be used to understand and characterize the conformational changes occurring at the molecular and electronic level, following perturbations caused by proliferating agents like *Mycobacterium leprae, Mycobacterium tuberculosis and Pseudomonas aeruginosa infections* (Verma and Wallach, 1975; Harvey et al., 1976; Nikkelson et al., 1978; Wallach et al., 1979; Somani, 1984). DMD is an X-linked, recessive neuromuscular disorder with an incidence of 1 in 3500 (Kumar and Bajaj, 1990). Sato et al. (1978) found marked distinction between the membrane from normal and DMD erythrocytes in terms of temperature dependence, pH dependence and accessibility to reduction by ascorbate. Wilkerson et al. (1978) suggested that DMD membranes are abnormal in terms of membrane fluidity or lipoprotein interactions. We have carried out Raman studies comparing plasma membranes from normal and DMD affected persons in region 800-1200 cm^{-1}.

Material and Methods

The blood samples from tubercular, leprous, burn and neurological cases were collected from different hospitals. Red cells were dehydrated over phosphorus pentoxide. The samples were prepared by the methods given by Fairbanks et al. (1971) and Bajaj and Khandelwal (1985). The separation of IgG was carried out by the ion exchange chromatographic technique (Wier, 1980).

Immunoglobulin samples were lyophilized and the IgG so obtained was further tested for its purity with the help of antisera (Hoechst) using the single radial immunodiffusion technique (Oucherlony, 1962). After the separation, 10mg, of the sample was dissolved, in D_2O and transferred to the sample cell container.

The infrared spectra of prepared samples were recorded with single beam Fourier Transform Infrared Spectrophotometer, (Prekin-Elmer, 1710). Raman spectra of heme proteins, immunoglobulin and erythrocyte ghosts were recorded in the 500-3000 cm^{-1} region with laser Raman Spectrophotometer (Model NR-1000) consisting of photomultiplier unit (R-464) including Argon ion laser at 514.5 nm having scanning speed of 20 cm^{-1} min^{-1} (Figures 1 and 2, for examples).

Results and Discussion

Results obtained from the FT-IR studies of normal and pathological samples demarcate specific regions for a particular type of disorder. In pulmonary tuberculosis (PTB) cases, strong signal at 3886. 3679 and 3608 cm^1 are observed in the lattice water region arising due to O-H bond, whereas in the lepromatus leprosy (LL) cases, peaks around 3461, 3445 and 3442 cm^{-1} are found in the same region. Amide B bands are found in PTB cases at 3083, 3082 and 3064 cm^{-1} appears with a shoulder at 2915 cm^{-1} in the (PTB) cases (Figure 1). In the normal group signal at the 2871 cm^{-1} band is sifted in PTB cases towards lower energy and in infected burn cases, towards higher side at 2860 cm^{-1}. Typical IR signals are observed in LL cases at 2068 and 2067 cm^{-1}.

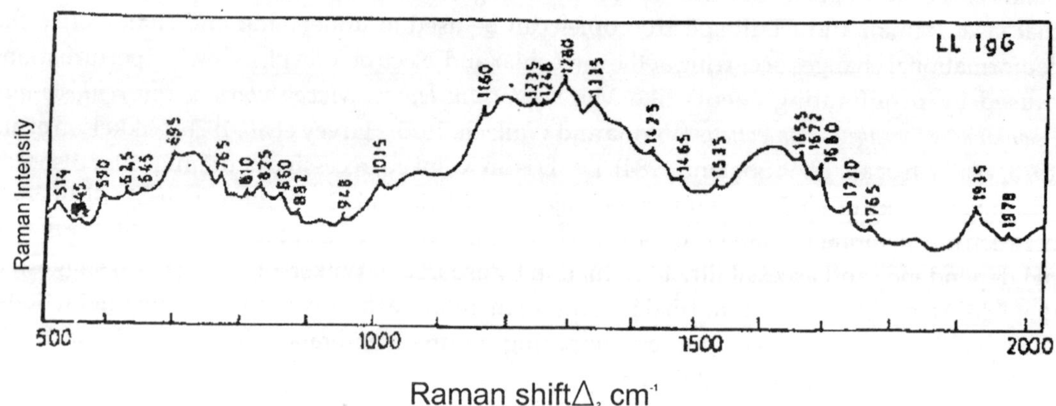

Fig. 1. Laser Raman spectrum of LL IgG in D_2O recorded from 500 to 2000 cm^{-1}

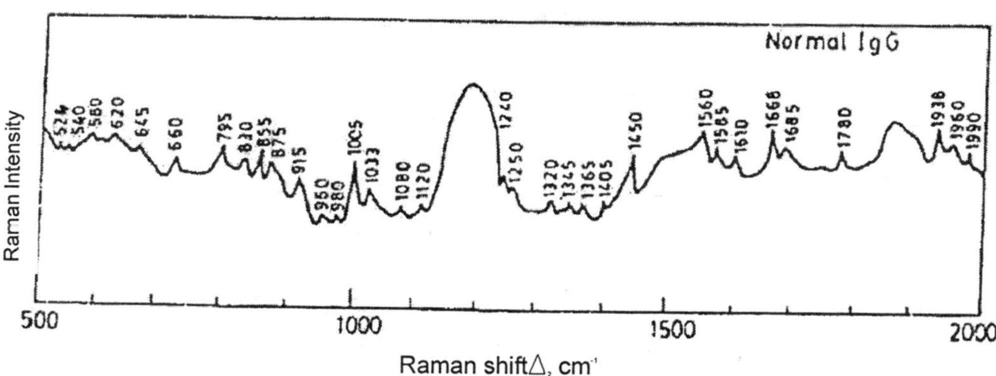

Fig. 2. Laser Raman spectrum of normal hu an IgG in D_2O recorded from 500 to 2000 cm^{-1}

Strong peaks occur in amide I, amide II region at 1640 and 1560 cm^{-1} for heme proteins of burn patients, whereas in normal samples signals are observed around 1596 cm^{-1}. In the amide IV to VI stretching region, a peculiar peak is observed at 700 cm^{-1}, whereas in the normal cases this peak is seen around 774 cm^{-1}. Heme proteins of burn patients having 30% burn surface areas with *Pseudomonas* infection exhibit infrared absorption bands at 3300 (amide A), 3100 (amide B), 1650 (amide I) and 1550 cm^{-1} (amide II). These are the characteristic bands of the -CONH group.

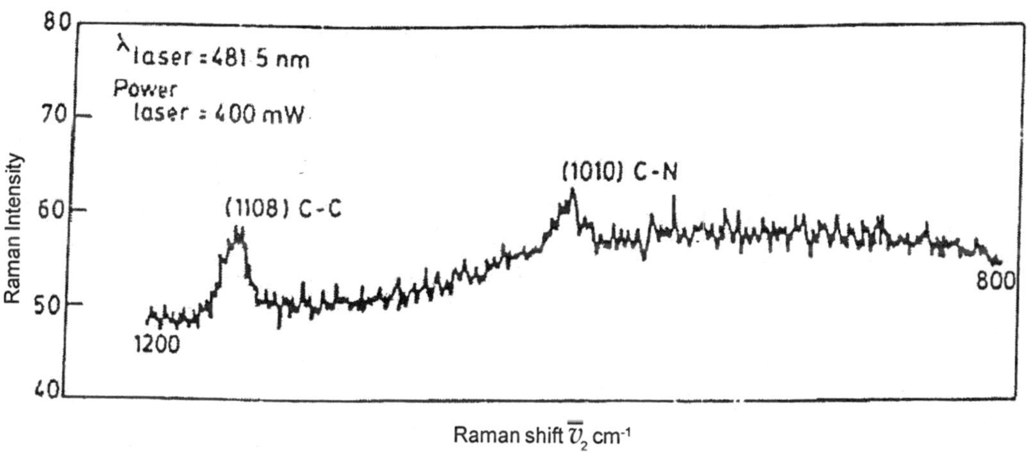

Fig. 3. Laser Raman spectrum of the serum of a DMD patient in the range 800 to 1200 cm^{-1}.

The frequency may vary from one burn case to another due to the changes in bonding between the metal and the ligand and steric restriction about the ligand, which prevent it from achieving the preferred stereochemistry. The other reasons may be weak bonding interactions, usually of the dipole-dipole type between the vibrator and its immediate environment (Clark and Hester, 1986). Fermi or other vibronic interactions with neighbouring vibrators (Maxwell and

Caughey, 1974) may shift the frequency bands also. On the other hand, the consistency of normal hemoglobin CO stretch values at 1952 cm^{-1}, over a wide range of species, demonstrates a remarkable consistency in bending site characterized over a broad span of evolution. Consquently, detection of the CO band at different frequencies in the blood represent a convenient and rapid method for the detection of abnormal hemoglobin (Aryal, 1985). The CO bands appear at 1980 cm^{-1}, in cases with 60% burns. There is clear cut distinction between the CO bands of the patients with different percentages of burns. Our results are in the line with those reported by Gross et al. (1978) stating the changes in plasma amino acids.

Raman spectra were recorded in the C-H and C-C stretching region 800-1200 cm^{-1} for DMD (Figure 3). All samples show two prominent lines at 1010 and 1158 cm^{-1}due to C-N stretch and C-C stretch respectively. It clearly shows that conformational change marker broadens and loses intensity with denaturation.

A moderate IR signal appears at 1108 cm^{-1} in grand mal epilepsy (GME) due to the O-O band, (Figure 4) which is absent in normal controls (figure 5). We notice a band at 1650 cm-1, which is typical factor needed for the identification of the alpha-helix in the LL-IgG molecule. The complexity, shape and absorption of the amide I band of secondary structure of IgG are highly heterogeneous (Kumar et al., 1988). The maximum of the band occurs at 1644 cm^{-1} and shows an irregular conformation of IgG. FT-IR studies shows that in GME amide band appear at 3319 and 3299 cm^{-1}, whereas no such bond is observed in normal samples. Similarly the S-H bands at 2683 and 2369 cm^{-1} are present in GME, whereas no such bonds are seen in normal samples; amide I and amide II bands are also found to be absent in normals but present in epileptic cases (Figure 4 and Figure 5) O-H bonds are observed in normal samples, while in majority of epileptic cases, they appear between 1803 and 1873 cm^{1}.

The four Raman lines appearing at 1110, 1340, 1410 and 1445 cm^{-1} may have contributions from the CH_2 group of cholesterol. The low intensities of these lines show the probable concentration of cholesterol in the erythrocytes. Previous studies (Aryal, 1985) on lipid metabolism following burn injury depressed following injury. Shift in the positions of the peaks in C-H stretching region and the occurrence of a doublet may be explained in terms of disturbances of protein metabolism in burns. The enhanced protein breakdown causing protein deficiency is the possible factor affecting this region.

Conclusions

It is concluded that bands arising due to O-H, N-H, C-C, P-O-C, O-O, C-H bonds are severely affected in case of PTB, whereas significant sifts in the strong signals are observed in the lattice water, amide I and metal ligands, stretching regions in LL cases. In burn cases, signals of amide B cyanoderivatives of myoglobin and methemoglobin amide I and amide II, carbide groups of aminoacid derivates and proxide compounds amide IV to amide VI group are affected in the specific regions.

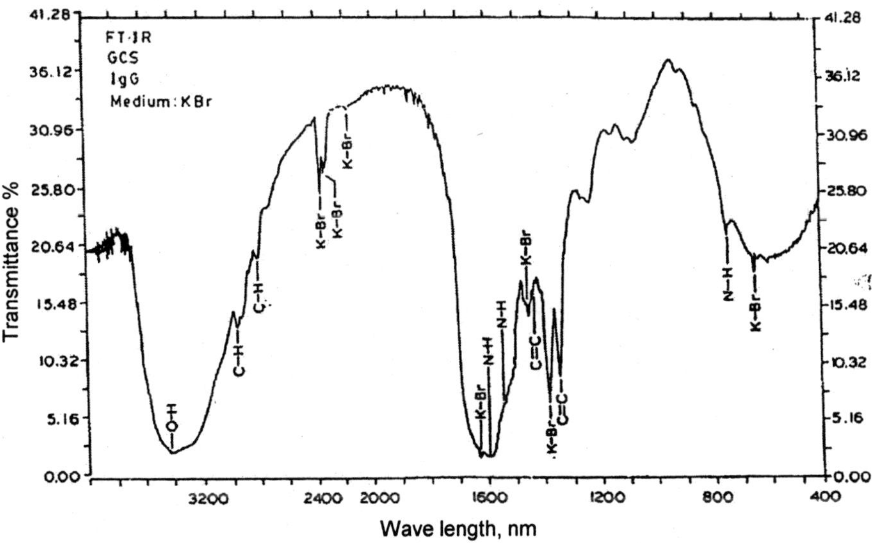

Fig. 4. FT-IR spectrum of IgG sample of epileptic (GCS) patients.

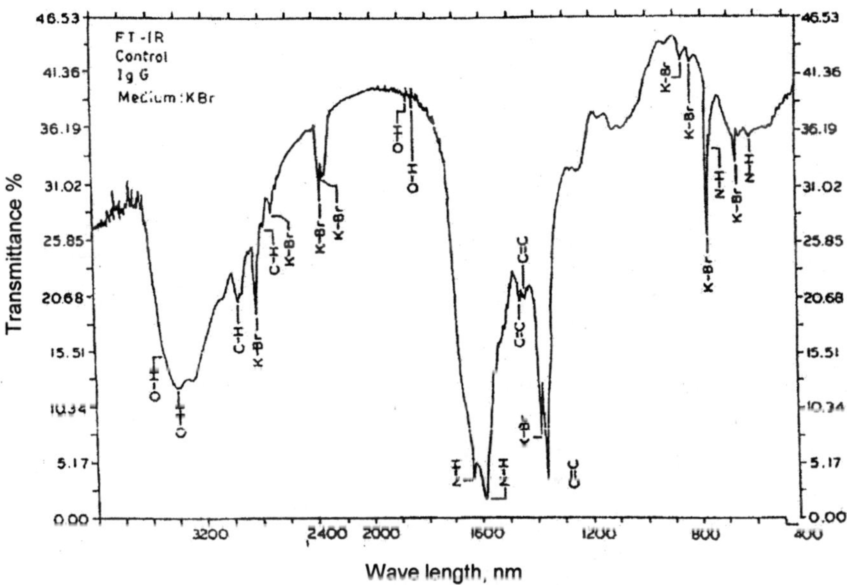

Fig. 5. FT-IR spectrum of IgG of a non-epileptic patient of 20 years. Blood group was AB^+, Hemoglobin count was 11.89 per 100 mg, the white blood corpuscle count was 7600/μl Neutrophils were 45%, eosinophils were 3% lymphocytes were 48% and monocytes were 4%.

FT-IR spectra of neurological disease samples surfacially resemble those of normals, but strong peaks in the hydrocarbon region, and the disappearance of a few normal bonds are the distinct feature of these samples.

Laser Raman spectra of IgG of LL sample show that the alpha-helical conformation is induced following the invasion of *M. leprae*, whereas irregular and antiparallel, beta-pleated sheet type of conformations are present in the normal samples. These conclusions are supported by our IR studies. Normal IGg exhibit ggt and tgt conformation, while LL IgG exhibits ggg and tgt conformation. The tyrosine moieties of normals IgG are exposed, while in LL. they remain unexposed.

Raman spectra of erythrocyte membranes show that C-C, C-H, symmetric and asymmetric CH_2 and CH_3 vibrations are impaired following thermal injuries particularly in Pseudomonas aeruginosa infection. The lines due to C-H and C_C bond may be used for the conformation of DMD.

It is concluded that FT-IR and laser Raman spectroscopic techniques can be used as important tools for understanding the pathology of different diseases at the molecular level.

Acknowledgements

The authors are grateful to the Vice Chancellor and Head of the Department of Physics & Astrophysics, University of Delhi as well as Director, F.S.L. Rohini, for providing excellent research facilities and congenial atmosphere needed for this present work.

References

1. Abaturov LV, Nozlin RS, Vengerova T L and Varshavsky Tm (1969) Biochem Biophys Acta 154 386-96.
2. Amzel L M and Poljak R J (1979) Am Rev Biochem 48 961-97.
3. Aryal S K (1985) Vibrational and magnetic resonance studies on hemoprotein and tissues afflicted with bacterial assemblies I thermal burns Ph D thesis. Delhi University.
4. Bajaj MM and Khandelwal O P (1985) Physics and chemistry of human leukemia (Delhi: Academic Publications).
5. Bajaj M M, Jha R K, Upadhyay s and Singh S, Effect of BIS load Enhancement on the DNA sequence: Impact of LSFAO on the Human chromosome 14; IVth Annual Symposium on Frontiers in Biomedical Research, Delhi 2003,p-3.
6. Clark RJH and Hester R E (1986) Advances in spectroscopy: Spectroscopy of biological systems (New York: Jpjm Wiley & Sons) Vol. 13,pp,, 1-16, 347-390.
7. Fairbanks G, Steck TL and Wallach D F H (1971) Biochem 10 2606
8. Freeman N K (1966) Advance BiolMed Phys. 4 167
9. Grores A C, Moore J P, Woolf L I et al (1978) Sugrery 83 138

10. Harvey A M, Johns R J, Owens A H and Ross R S (1976) The Principles and practice of Mediine (Engleweed Cliffs, N J: Prentice Hall). pp 535-609.

11. Kumar R and Bajaj M M (1990) Vegyan 76(2) 1.

12. Kumar S, Bajaj M M and Jai DC (1988) Current Trends in pain Research and Therapy, Muscular Skeletal Pain 3 11.

13. Litman GW, Litman RS, Good RA and Rosenberg A (1973) Biochemistry 12 2004-9.

14. Maxwell J C and Caughey MS (1974) Biochem. Biophys. Res Commun 60 1309.

15. M.M Bajaj, R. Jha, S. Singh, S. Upadhayay & V.R. Singh (2003) Severe Acute Respiratory Syndrome (SARS) and BIS Effect. Paramamitra Prakashan, New Delhi: India.

16. M.M. Bajaj K. Somani and R.K. Jha (2003) Pulmonary Tuberculosis: Biophysical Aspects, Int. Sc. Research & Welfare Organisation, New Delhi-18 India.

17. M.M. Bajaj, R.K. Jha, P. Agarwal, S.S. Agarwal and D.C. Jain, Bisneurochemistry. (2004) BIS entropy rainfall. International Conference on Recent Trends and New Directions of Research in Cybernetics and Systems Theory, IASST, Khjanapara, Guwahati, Assam, India, Jan. 1-3, p. 10.

18. M.M. Bajaj, P. Agarwal, R.K Jha, S. Upadhyay, S. Sheikhar, (2004) Topological quantum field theory of BIS effects and geometry of BIS effect and geometry of BIS loop spaces: Application in Bistramatology. International Conference on Recent Trends and New Directions of Research in Cybernetics and Systems Theory, IASST, Khanapara, Guwahati, Assam, India, Jan. 1-3, p.9.

19. Wallach DFH, Verma SP and Fookson JF (1979) Biochem Biophys Acta 559 153.

53

Knowledge, Attitude and Practice of Youth for Environment Management

TUSHTI BHARDWAJ*

"*The world today is economically richer and environmentally poorer than ever*"
Lester R. Brown, President of Washington-based World Watch Institute.

Introduction

Environment plays a pivotal role in human life as well as in the development of society. With growing technological advancement and industrialization, the purity of the environment has been threatened to an appalling extent. The increasing economic development and a rapidly growing population that has taken the country from 318 million people in 1947 (as per 1941 census) to over one billion people (2001 census) is putting a strain on the environment, infrastructure, and the country's natural resources. Industrial pollution, soil erosion, deforestation, rapid industrialization, urbanization, and land degradation are all worsening problems. Overexploitation of the country's resources be it land or water and the industrialization process has resulted in considerable environmental degradation of resources. About 80 percent of urban waste in India ends up in the country's rivers, and unchecked urban growth across the country combined with poor government oversight means the problem is only getting worse. A growing number of bodies of water in India are unfit for human use, and in the river Ganga, holy to the country's 82 percent Hindu majority, is dying slowly due to unchecked pollution.

New Delhi's body of water is little more than a flowing garbage dump, with fully 57 percent of the city's waste finding its way to the Yamuna. It is that three billion liters of waste are pumped into Delhi's Yamuna each day. Only 55 percent of the 15 million Delhi residents are connected to the city's sewage system. The remainder flushes their bath water, waste water and just about everything else down pipes and into drains, most of them empty into the Yamuna. According to the Centre for Science and Environment, between 75 and 80 percent of the river's pollution is the result of raw sewage. Combined with industrial runoff, the garbage thrown into the river and it totals over 3 billion liters of waste per day. Nearly 20 billion rupees, or almost US $500 million, has been spent on various clean up efforts (gits4u.com). Due to increased exploitation, pollution and population growth, it is estimated that in less than 200 years, 128 species of birds and 95 species of mammals have disappeared from the globe. Throughout Europe, large mammals, including the wolf, bear and other wild cats face threats from competing land users and danger of extinction. Elephants, it is estimated, would be extinct from India and Malaysia in the very near future.

The need to protect and improve the environment is so compelling for the peaceful survival of mankind and other life forms on planet Earth that it becomes the duty of every individual to protect the environment.

History of Environmental Protection in Ancient India

An appraisal of the historical background to environmental protection in India would indicate that forests & wildlife were considered as vital ingredients of the global system. Here, the entire scheme of environmental preservation was essentially duty-based. In this sense, the ancient Indian society accepted the protection of the environment as its duty to do so. Opening up the Hindu mythology, the Vedas, Puranas, Upanishads and other ancient scriptures of the Hindu religion have given a detailed description of trees, plants, wildlife and their importance to people. Kautalya's Arthashastra, written in the Mauryan period, realized the necessity of forest administration and Ashoka's 5th Pillar Edict expressed his view about the welfare of creatures in the State. Evidence from civilizations of Mohenjadaro and Harappa has further proved that the small population lived in consonance with the ecosystem and their needs maintained harmony with the environment. In Islam, there is close harmony between man and nature. However, during the Medieval period, the only contribution of Mughal emperors has been the establishment of magnificent gardens, fruit orchards and green parks, which were used as holiday resorts, palaces of retreat or temporary headquarters during the summer season. The British conquest in India brought about a plunder of natural resources coupled with a complete indifference towards environmental protection. A general survey of early environmental legislation reveals that apart from the forest laws, nineteenth century legislation also partially regulated two other aspects of Indian environment viz. water pollution and wildlife.

United Nations Conference on Human Environment

In the backdrop of some sincere efforts of tackling pollution control, for the first time, the attention of the world was drawn towards environment in the United Nations Conference on Human Environment held at Stockholm in June 1972. The Declaration on Human Environment was passed containing twenty-six principles, with the main object of overcoming environmental problems related to the development of States and to provide clean & healthy living conditions. The declaration stated that economic and social development was necessary for ensuring a healthy environment for man. This, in turn, has been called the Magna Carta on environment from which two important conclusions can be reached: (i) Man has the fundamental right to freedom, equality and adequate conditions of life in an environment of quality that permits a life of dignity and well-being; and (ii) Man bears a solemn responsibility to protect and improve the environment for present and future generation.

In the last decade, the most revolutionary step towards the preservation of the environment was the Earth Summit convened by the UN General Assembly at Rio de Janeiro from 3rd to 14th June, 1992. The Conference saw the largest gathering of world leaders ever in the history - deliberating and chalking out a blue print for the survival of the planet. The Summit was primarily held to discuss the problems of global warming, depletion of the ozone layer, deforestation, air and marine pollution and other environmentally interrelated threats facing the earth. It added a new dimension on the issues of environment and development in international negotiations. The main objective of the Summit was to find an equitable balance between the economic, social and environmental needs of present and future generations and to lay down a foundation for global partnership between developed & developing countries. The United Nations Framework Convention on Climatic Change (UN FCCC) was opened for signature at this Summit. It was formed in March 1994, and aimed stabilizing the greenhouse gas concentrations at levels that would prevent dangerous human interference with the climate system. In December 1997, in Kyoto, Japan, nations of the world took a first major step in order to protect our globe from the phenomena of global warming caused by the emission of excessive amounts of Green House Gases into the atmosphere. These nations adopted the Kyoto Protocol on Climatic Change and opted to use modern, innovative and cost-effective techniques and mechanisms to protect the environment.

In the early years of Indian independence, there was no precise environmental policy. Government tried to make attempts only from time to time as per the growing needs of the society. The period of 1970s witnessed a lot of changes in policies and attitudes of the Indian Government when its attitude changed from environmental indifference to greater sustainability and subsequently, manifold steps were taken to improve environmental conditions. The year 1972 marks a watershed in the history of environmental management in India. When the twenty-fourth UN General Assembly decided to convene a conference on the human environment in 1972, and requested a report from each member country on the state of environment, a Committee on human environment under the chairmanship of Pitambar Pant, member of the Planning Commission, was set up to prepare India's report. With the help of the reports, the impact of the population explosion on the natural environment and the existing state of environmental problems were examined. From this period onwards, the Central Government has been considered as highly environmentally active. In 1976, the Constitution of India was amended to insert a separate fundamental duties chapter. The 1980s witnessed the creation of many eco-specific organizations. The Constitution of India originally adopted, did not contain any direct and specific provision regarding the protection of natural environment. Perhaps, the framers of the Indian Constitution, at that time, considered it as a negligible problem. However, in fact it contained only a few Directives to the State on some aspects relating to public health, agriculture and animal husbandry but these Directives were and are still not judicially enforceable.

Forty-second Constitutional Amendments

Taking note of the Stockholm Conference and the growing awareness of the environmental crises, the Indian Constitution was amended in the year 1976. This gave it an environmental dimension and added to it direct provisions for the preservation of ecological and biological diversity.

Article 48A, a directive principle, was inserted into Part IV of the Constitution, reading as follows: The State shall endeavor to protect and improve the environment and to safeguard the forests and wildlife of the country. Correspondingly, an obligation was imposed on the State through Article 51 A(g) in Part IVA, which casts a duty on every citizen of India stating: It shall be the duty of every citizen of India to protect and improve the natural environment including forests, lakes, rivers and wildlife and to have compassion for living creatures.

Need of Education

Countries all over the world have been taking serious actions and passing adequate laws in protecting the environment. India, one of the most populous democracies of the world, is facing a crisis situation. The environmental conditions are deteriorating, the population is growing at a rather rapid pace, trees are cut in thousands each day, the industrial development has polluted the air as well as water and the growing number of automobiles has littered the place with noise pollution. All these degenerating factors have a tremendous impact on the social, political and economic conditions prevalent in the country. Though over the past few years efforts have been made for conserving our forests, land, water and air, better efforts are expected. Merely the enactment of laws is not sufficient. They must be adequately enforced.

The Governments of the different countries must ensure proper implementation of the environment laws. Laws cannot affect the natural processes that cause environmental changes but can and do regulate human behaviour in response to natural disasters. Individuals must themselves take care and precautions in protecting the environment. Companies, instead of relying merely on Government rules, procedures and track records whilst investing must also look to alternative institutions for guidance and look to cultural values and traditions. They must set up plants and factories in keeping with the maximum standards required for environmental protection and take care that no requirements are avoided. Though, humans have been responsible for most of the ecological imbalances, if we consider the utilitarian approach to this problem, people will protect the environment simply because it is the cardinal basis for their survival so it becomes the duty of every individual to be conscious of his or her actions to protect environment. If individuals and companies realize the importance of the environment, we can save the world from a disaster.

The present context requires the involvement of people at all levels viz. prevention, promotion and management of environment. It is well known that youth is the best resource for bringing out a change and spreading positive energy for its sustenance. The role of youth in environment management has been recognized by government too and so the environment education was made compulsory in the school curriculum. Given the urgency to protect the environment, it is important that young generation must be sensitized and educated to the environment issues, reflect an 'appropriate attitude' and 'will- to- act' as action oriented resource persons to protect and promote the environment. In this backdrop, the present research was carried out to examine the knowledge, attitude and practice level of youth about environment management.

Nature of the Problem

The present research aimed to assess the knowledge level of youth and extend its scope to examine their attitude and practice towards improvement and management of environment. This was an exploratory study with implications for practice based intervention with young generation.

Methodology

The present research was carried out in the metropolitan city like Delhi and college students formed the target of the study. The research studied a sample of 160 students drawn using non-probability sampling techniques in two stages. In the first stage, one of the colleges of the University of Delhi was selected conveniently. In the second stage a sample of 1/10th proportion of the total strength of the college (160/1600) was selected. Students who conveniently agreed to be a part of the study were given a self designed questionnaire to be filled up.

Results

Profile of the respondents

Table 1: Demographic profile of respondents.

Demographic characteristics	Number of respondents (%)
Gender	
Male	55 (34.4)
Female	105 (65.6)
Educational year	
I	59(36.8)
II	57 (35.6)
III	44(27.5)
Family type	
Nuclear	105(65.6)
Joint	55 (34.4)
Diet pattern	
Vegetarian	67(41.8)
Non-vegetarian	44 (27.5)
Mixed	49 (30.6)
Father's educational status	
Illiterate	3(1.8)
Functional literate	3(1.8)
Primary	4(2.5)
Secondary	29(18.1)
Senior secondary	31(19.4)
Graduate	59(36.8)
Post graduate	27(16.8)
Mother's educational status	
Illiterate	10 (6.3)
Functional illiterate	10(6.3)
Primary	38(23.8)
Secondary	35(21.9)
Senior Secondary	36 (22.5)
Graduate	22 (13.8)
Post graduate	9 (5.6)
Income group	
Below 5,000	21 (13.1)
5,000 -10,000	45 (28.1)
10,000-15,000	38 (23.8)
15,000-20,000	17 (10.6)
20,000 and above	41 (25.6)

The above table shows that majority of respondents (65.6%) were girls as compared to 34.4 percent of boys in the sample. This reflects that girls are keener to learn about new things. Almost equal number of respondents (36.8 and 35.6 percent respectively) participated from I and II year, but only 27.5 percent participated from III year reflecting that students are more enthusiastic or curious to learn new things in early years of college life. It may also happèn that by the time students reach final year of education in college they may become more career conscious and so focused to the same. Majority of respondents (65.6%) belonged to nuclear family whereas 34.4 percent lived in joint family system. In case of 41.8 percent of respondents family had vegetarian diet pattern, 27.5 percent non-vegetarian, while 30.6 percent had mixed diet pattern wherein few members were vegetarian while others were non-vegetarian. But taken as a whole 58 percent of families had members with non-vegetarian diet pattern. A big majority (63.6) of respondents had their father educated over and above graduation. Similarly taken as a whole 42 percent of mothers were studied above senior secondary level. The educational profile of parents shows that in majority of cases, respondents belong to educated families which expected to be aware of environmental issues. Almost 60 percent of families have their monthly income more than 10,000 rupees. The demographic profile shows that respondents belong to well educated and decent income group families.

Table 2: Contribution to recycle the paper.

Contribution to recycle the paper	Frequency (%)
Not at all	110(68.8)
Rarely	24(15)
Sometimes	18 (11.3)
Quite often	4 (2.5)
Always	4 (2.5)

Majority of respondents (68.8%) had never thought of recycling the waste paper, whereas fifteen percent (15%) of them did so only rarely. This shows that respondents never had the idea of recycling the waste paper to be reused afresh. When asked what restricted them to contribute the waste paper they shared that they don't know about the paper recycling process and lack of knowledge restricted them. They were even not aware of what can be their contribution in the paper recycling process. Respondents even did not had the idea of where is the nearby recycling unit where they can drop the waste paper. Few of the respondents shared that they did not know the importance of the same and feels it is useless. Few others shared that since plenty of new notebooks, papers and books are available in market, never faced the shortage of paper so never thought in the direction. They shared that even before responding to this questionnaire they never cared about it, it is for the first time they have the realization of the same. Few others shared that sense of laziness contributed to it.

A very few students (5%) who responded that they generally used to think about paper recycling shared it was not exactly recycling the paper rather reusing the paper for art work or decoration that they meant. They shared that television programme like "art attack", involvement with environment organization like "global climate campaign" and mother's inclination for utilizing paper for decoration motivated them at least to think about this issue.

Use of Paper

The respondents were asked to give their choice for which is the best: using one side of paper or using both sides of the paper. A very big majority (95.6%) felt that using both sides of the paper is the best option as it avoid wastage of resources, can help save papers, economical, easy to handle and so avoid trouble at the time of reading the document. Few also felt that it may also help us save trees as demand for paper will reduce the felling off the tree.

A small proportion of respondents who opted for using one side of the paper, justified that the same is required in case of preparing the practical files. Further the hand writing looks good if one side of the paper is used. It shows that somewhere during the course of education system students receive the message for using one side of the paper for beautifying the work. The need of the hour requires to check such messages and sensitizing the students for appropriate use of paper.

Table 3: Frequency of taking print on both sides of paper.

Print on both side of paper	Number of respondents (%)
Never	6 (3.8)
Rarely	20(12.5)
Sometimes	40 (25)
Quite often	35(21.8)
Always	59(36.9)

The above table shows that majority of the respondents (36.9%) always take print on both sides of the paper whereas 25 percent sometimes do the same and 21.8 percent quite often do it. On the other hand 12.5 percent of students rarely take print on both sides of the paper and 3.8 percent never use both sides of the paper for printing.

The respondents were asked what would they do with the one sided used papers. A big majority of (87.72%) responded that they will use other side of paper for rough work, whereas (12.28%) responded that they will dispose off the paper. This shows the lack of sensitivity among these students about the appropriate use of paper.

Rituals and Environment

The students were asked if they know that flowers can be used for making herbal colours. It was found that though a big majority (57%) was aware of the same but only one of them actually contributed his bit for the same. The respondent's exposure of working with the environment related organization gave him this opportunity. When respondents were asked what restricted them for contributing to herbal colour preparation, they shared that lack of knowledge, resources and time never allowed them doing so. They are not aware of the process involved in preparing herbal colours and even where to dump the waste flowers if they at times feel like contributing their bit in this direction. Few also felt that since it is time consuming process so never could think of getting engaged in such activities. Few others felt that since we do not play holi, so never cared for the same. Few reflected that by doing so they may end up harming the flowers. This shows a general sense of confusion and lack of awareness among youth about the process of herbal colour preparation.

Table 4: Ritual celebration.

Usage	Use herbal colours to Play holi (%)	Use crackers on Diwali (%)
Yes	25 (15.6)	115(72)
No	56 (21.8)	45 (28)

The above table shows that only 15.6 percent make use of herbal colours to play holi. It was seen that 49 percent stay away from playing holi. The table also reflects that 72 percent of the families use crackers to celebrate Diwali or other family occasion like marriage. This shows that majority of families in one way or another contributes to environment pollution.

Table 5: Ceremonial and river pollution.

Disposing off ceremonial waste in river	Frequency (%)
Never	38 (23.8)
Rarely	14 (8.8)
Sometimes	16 (10)
Quite often	7 (4.4)
Always	76(47.5)
NA	9 (5.6)

The respondents were asked what they do with the havan samagri or other ceremonial waste after the rituals at home. Nearly fifty percent shared that they always dispose it off in nearby river. Only 23.8 percent shared that they never throw the havan samagri or other ceremonial waste in rivers rather they either put in tulsi plants as manure, collect the same in polythene bag to either hang on a tree or throw it after few days, directly put it in dustbin, or dispose if off in vacant plot of land.

The respondents were asked if they consider themselves responsible for polluting the river. In response to the same it was found that 68.4 percent considered themselves responsible for polluting the rivers of the area. The major reasons of the same as shared by respondents were:-

- As he/she or their family members dispose off the ceremonial waste or even at times their household waste in nearby river. Few respondents shared that while doing so they never carry guilt feelings as the concern of not being the only one for doing so never let them feel guilt. Moreover our culture and custom ask us to do so therefore never have scope of carrying guilt feelings.
- Though dispose off ceremonial waste in river but no other alternative options are available. Further by doing so they packed the havan samagri in polythene and throw it in river which is more dangerous to the health of the river.
- In many cases, respondents felt that they throw garbage in drainage system which ultimately goes to river and so make them responsible for polluting the river.

- Even after knowing the harmful effects of our actions to rivers we fail to restrict ourselves and throw waste in river, so we are responsible for polluting the river.
- Since I never contribute to clean the river so in a sense I am responsible for polluting the river. Further I never take initiative for educating people to avoid polluting the river.
- We felt that since elders at home ask us to throw the religious waste in river, so it becomes our obligation to follow them.

One third of the respondents group (31.6%) did not consider themselves responsible for polluting the river as they never dispose off ceremonial waste in river. Further it is not the individuals who pollute the river rather the industries which drop the drainage system on the river side.

The respondents were asked whether a dip in Holy River purify self or it pollute the river. Majority of respondents (68.42%) felt that it purify the self as holy river is always pious and the same belief system are hold as per hindu mythology. About one third of the respondents (31.6) felt that though as per belief system it may purify the self but in end result it pollute the river. The youth were asked if they favour the immersion of brightly coloured clay idols into the river. In response to the same a big majority (72.8%) opposed the immersion of brightly coloured clay idols in river. When asked if they have taken any action against it, almost all shared that they could not take any action as they do not have the courage to oppose their elders. Moreover it may hurt the religious sentiments of many. Few others felt that nobody will listen and respect the opinion of the youngsters like us even if we attempt to do so. Respondents felt that it is a serious issue and should be banned under the government act if we want to protect our rivers. Few others expressed their apathy on this issue and shared that as we are not concerned with this ritual and we don't care about it.

Only 28.9 percent of the respondents favour the immersion of brightly coloured clay idols in the river as it is a ritual for long and we have not yet found another alternative.

Knowledge about biodegradable and non-biodegradable waste

The respondents were asked to classify a given list of waste as biodegradable and non-biodegradable waste. The table below represents their responses on the same.

Table 6: Knowledge of biodegradable and non-biodegradable items.

Item	Biodegradable (%)	Non-biodegradable (%)	Don't know (%)
Kitchen, hotels and restaurant waste	98 (61.3)	54 (33.8)	8 (5)
Waste generated from fruits and vegetable markets	99 (61.8)	49(31)	11 (6.8)
Papers	128 (80)	28(17.5)	4 (2.5)
Plastics/Polythene	51(31.9)	107(66.8)	3(1.8)
Glass and metallic contents	63 (39.4)	86(53.8)	11 (6.7)
Waste produced during construction and demolition of buildings	46(28.7)	105(65.6)	9(5.6)

The above table shows that only about 61 percent of respondents knew that kitchen, hotels and restaurant waste as well the waste generated through fruits and vegetable markets are biodegradable waste, rest almost 39 percent were either did not know it or classify it wrongly as non-biodegradable waste. Only 80 percent of respondents were sure of paper being biodegradable items, 66.8 percent of respondents knew that plastic/polythene is non-biodegradable items. Similarly 53.8 percent knew that glass and metallic and 65.6 percent knew that waste produced during construction and demolitions of buildings are non-biodegradable items.

Table 7: Dispose off household waste in biodegradable and non-biodegradable bins.

Frequency of segregating and disposing off household waste separately	Number of respondents (%)
Never	118 (73.8)
Rarely	21 (13.1)
Sometimes	10 (6.3)
Quite often	4 (2.5)
Always	7 (4.4)

The youth were asked how often do they segregate household waste as biodegradable and non-biodegradable waste and dispose off separately. In response to the same it was seen that 73.8% never segregate the household waste and dispose it separately. In order to understand the reasons of the same they were further asked if they have separate biodegradable and non-biodegradable bins in their locality. It was found that 70.2 percent of respondents did not have separate bins in their locality while 5 percent did not have any idea of the same. The respondents were further asked if their household waste is taken away by the sweeper or their family dispose off itself at the community dustbins. It was found that in 64.1% families' household waste was taken away by the sweeper while 35.9% of families dispose it off themselves at the community dustbins.

Appropriate Utilization of Resources

The youth were asked to reflect upon their consciousness about usage of resources like water and electricity. They were asked how often do they waste water for bathing/washing/watering plants and how often do they switch off the lights and/or fans when not in use.

Table 8: Utilization of resources.

Frequency of appropriate behavior	Wastage of water	Switch off lights/ fans in college when not in use	Switch off lights/ fans at home when not in use
Never	22(13.8)	3(1.8)	2(1.3)
Rarely	38 (23.8)	20 (12.5)	2(1.3)
Sometimes	62(38.8)	35 (21.9)	14(8.8)
Quite often	11(6.9)	27(16.9)	25(15.6)
Always	27(16.9)	76(47.5)	117(73.1)

The above table shows that only 13.8 percent of respondents in their reflection about the wastage of water could share that they never waste water, while the rest 86.2 percent intentionally or unintentionally waste the water to certain degree (rarely ----Always). When asked about the usage of electricity, it was interesting to learn that less than 2 percent did not care about switching off lights/fans in college or at home. While the majority was found to be careful for appropriate electricity usage but as compared to college, respondents were more careful at home since only 47.5 percent were always careful about electricity usage in college as compared to 73.1percent at home.

Concern to Nature

With a view to understand youth's concerns for nature they were asked about their response to green cover i.e. plantation, love to animals, responsibility for cleanliness, consciousness to eco-friendly actions and vehicular emission. To understand youth's love for nature, they were asked how many saplings they planted in the past 6 months.

Table 9: Saplings planted by youth.

Saplings planted	Number of students (%)
Not at all	57(35.6)
Less than 3	44(27.5)
3-5	25 (15.6)
5-10	17(10.6)
More than 10	17(10.6)

The above table shows that majority of respondents i.e. 35.6 percent never planted any sapling in the past 6 months. Percentage of respondents planted more than 5 saplings in the past 6 months was 21 percent. When asked to name any two winters and summer flowers only 5 percent of respondents could do so correctly.

Table 10: Love to animals.

Expected behavior	Yes (%)	NO (%)
Own pets	17.5	82.5
Encourage birds feed	66.7	33.3
Knowledge of any animal welfare organization	10.5	89.5

The above table shows that only 17.5 percent of respondents own pets like, dogs, parrot, pair of whit rats and fish aquarium. It was seen that 66.7 percent of respondents encourage birds feed in their courtyard. But only 10.5 percent of respondents actually knew about any animal welfare organization or nearby veterinary hospital. The youth were asked if they would find an injured animal/bird what would they do. In response to the same 34 percent of respondents shared that they would take the animal/ bird to a nearly veterinary hospital about which they were actually found to be unaware of. Fifty percent of respondents shared that they would simply ignore it, while the rest thirty percent shared that they will bring the fellow to home, offer first aid, consult with friends and/or elderly for dropping the fellow to an appropriate place. It was seen that none of the respondent ever joined any nature or environmental group.

Usage of Carry Bags

The youth were asked which bag (polythene / paper / jute/cloth) they prefer to use for carrying grocery or stationary.

Table 11: Usage of bags.

Type of bags	Number of respondents (%)
Polythene bag	70 (44)
Paper bag	7 (4.4)
Jute bag	14 (8.8)
Cloth bag	67 (41.8)

The above table shows that a big majority (44%) prefer to use polythene bags followed by 41.8 percent of those who prefer to use cloth bags. Percentage of youth using paper bag and jute bag is very rare i.e. 4.4 percent and 8.8 percent respectively. The main reasons of much usage of polythene bags as shared by respondents were easy availability, easy to handle/ manage, safe to carry, because of being comparatively cheaper shopkeepers give the same carry bag, and it gives more beautiful looks too. Similarly those who preferred to use cloth bags shared that such bags are more durable, easy and convenient to handle, comfortable to use, free of germs, reusable, big in size, washable, easy availability at home and eco-friendly in nature.

Cleanliness and Youth's Contribution

The youth were asked if they spit or ever throw waste bottles/ papers/ packets on roads. Further they were asked if they see other person doing so, did they ever ask them not to do so?

Table 12: Habit of keeping the surroundings clean.

Action for keeping	Frequency of action (%)				
the surroundings	Never	Rarely	Sometimes	Quite often	Always clean
Throw waste bottles/ papers/ packets	26.3	33.3	31.6	1.8	7
Restrict person throwing waste bottles/paper packets	34.2	25.4	32.5	3.5	4.4
Spit on roads	57.9	17.5	16.7	1.8	6.2
Restrict others to spit on road	55.7	16.7	17.5	6.2	4.4

The above table shows that 26.3 percent of respondents never throw the waste bottles/ papers/packets on road but rest i.e. 73.7 percent do so in their day to day life. It was interesting to note that a big majority 65.8 percent take initiative to restrict others for doing so. A big majority (57.9%) never spit on roads but the rest 42.2 percent do so to some extent. Approximately 45 percent of respondents take initiative to restrict others for doing so.

Youth were asked what they would like to do if they will be given a vacant piece of land in front of their house. Majority of respondents preferred to have plantation, vegetation, or developing garden there. Few others opted for developing playground, sitting arrangement for elderly, shelter to stray dogs with food and water arrangements and building a school. In two exceptional cases respondents said that he will park his vehicle there whereas the other said that he will purchase the land and construct the building.

Summary and Discussion

Over the years, it has been realized that in the race of development we have not been optimally using our environment and it has been deteriorating at high pace adversely affecting our eco-system. Countries all over the world have been taking serious actions and passing adequate laws in protecting the environment. India, one of the most populous democracies of the world, is facing a crisis situation. The environmental conditions are deteriorating, the population is growing at a rather rapid pace, trees are cut in thousands each day, the industrial development has polluted the air as well as water and the growing number of automobiles has littered the place with noise pollution. In such situation it becomes necessary to sensitize the young generation about the alarming dangers to our environment which requires an analysis of the present state of their knowledge level, their attitude and the nature of practice they are engaged in targeting the goal of environment protection and management. The findings of the present study highlight the same and set the ground to develop an intervention strategy to mould the actions of youth for bridging up the KAP gap. The findings shows that college youth never had the idea of recycling the waste paper to be reused afresh. Their lack of knowledge, publicity of the concept and the accessibility of the resources contributed to the same. Though a very big majority of youth preferred to make use of both sides of a paper as it is economical and avoids wastage but a significant proportion of youth preferred to use one side of the paper as same has been the requirement of preparing the practical files. Further it was seen that a sizeable percent of students rarely take print on both sides of the paper resulting in wastage of paper. This shows the lack of sensitivity among these students about the appropriate use of paper. This necessitates the need to consider it seriously and take up issue in schools and college to sensitize students and teachers. Youth were found to be unaware of the process involved in preparing herbal colours and even where to dump the waste flowers if they at times feel like contributing their bit in this direction. A general sense of confusion and lack of awareness among youth about the process of herbal colour preparation was observed. A big majority of respondents (68.4%) considered themselves responsible for polluting the rivers of the area. The main reasons for the same were religious sentiments, rituals, values of respecting the elders and carelessness. But one third of the respondents group felt that it is not the individuals who pollute the river rather the industries which drop the drainage system on the river side. About one third of the respondents felt that though as per belief system dip in a holy river may purify the self but in end result it pollute the river. Though a big majority was against the immersion of brightly colourd idols in river but none of them could ever take any action against it as they could never develop courage to oppose the elders and hurt the religious sentiments of people. Youth reflected lack of knowledge about the biodegradable and non-biodegradable waste. It further shows that they are not in practice of segregating and disposing the household waste separately. Moreover the sufficient resources in terms of availability of biodegradable and non-biodegradable bins were not available in all the localities. Majority was found to be careful for appropriate electricity usage but as compared to college, respondents were more careful at home. A very big majority 86.2 percent intentionally or unintentionally waste the water to certain degree. It reflects a sense of apathy to social obligation. Majority of respondents i.e. 35.6 percent never planted any sapling in the past 6 months. Only 10.5 percent of respondents actually knew about any animal welfare organization or nearby veterinary hospital. Fifty percent of respondents shared that they would simply ignore an injured animal/bird which reflects lack of love and concern to nature's gifts. Majority (44%) prefer to use polythene bags followed by those who prefer to use cloth bags because of their being more durable, easy and convenient to handle, comfortable to use, free of germs, reusable, big in size, washable, easy availability at home and eco-friendly in nature. In order to improve the environment, youth came up with a number of suggestions like-

- Educating youth about the benefits of safe environment, keep the environment clean, avoid water logging, proper drainage system, bring behavior change for disposing off the waste in biodegradable and non-biodegradable bins separately, contributing to recycle the paper and making judicious use of paper.
- Stop cutting down the trees, grow more trees, expanding the green cover, educate people on the importance trees, and provide proper space for stray cattle.
- Restrict the unauthorized factory, implementation of strict laws and setting up strict environmental norms in automobiles industries.

The findings of the study highlighted the low level of knowledge among youth about the ways for improving our environment. It reflected a general 'apathy –to- act' among the youngsters. The study emphasized the need to initiate action oriented programmes so as to encourage youth, build up their skill base and mobilize their involvement in the process of environment management.

References

1. Arora, S. and Kohli, T.P. (2005). Sustainable development and school teaching: going beyond awareness. In Arora, G.K. & Talwar, A. (ed.), Sustainable development - an interdisciplinary perspective. Research and publishing house, Delhi.
2. Arora, G.K. (1995). Environment, population and development issues in developing countries. India Quarterly, Indian Council of World Affairs, April/Sep, Vol. LI, No. 2-3, pp.97.
3. Gits4u.com . Environment management in India, surfed on 23/07/08.
4. Sinha, D.K. (1982). Some facets of eco-development. Jadavpur University Publications, Calcutta.
5. Sapra, R.K. (1987). Environment management in India. Ashish Publishing house, Vil. I and II, New Delhi.

54

Characterization and Pollutant Impact of Surface Runoff in Urban Areas

P. E. Zope and Dr. P. H. Sawant

Introduction

The sources of urban pollutants are diverse and associated with both natural and human activities. They can be broadly categorized into point sources (PS) and non point sources (NPS) pollution. Non point sources refer to the pollutants that have no readily identifiable source and are transported into a receiving water in diffused manner. Sources of this pollution include precipitation, soil erosion, accumulation and wash off of atmospheric dust, wash-off of street dust, fertilizers and pesticides, animal waste, and direct discharge of pollutants into storm sewers (Novotny and Olem, 1994) (Nazzyihah et al., 2007). The effluent of pollutants from non point source resulting from rainfall not only contains various kinds of pollutants but also carries a large pollutant load so that it exerts a great influence on receiving waters, (Whipple and Hunter, 1981, Characklis & Wiesner, 1997) (Choe et al, 2002).

The key contaminant parameters in terms of receiving a water pollution potential are total suspended solids (TSS), biological oxygen demand (BOD), bacteria, heavy metals (particularly zinc, lead and cadmium), herbicides and polyaromatic hydrocarbons (PAH). In addition, nutrients can be a problem where urban surface waters discharge to already nutrient-rich water bodies (Ellis and Mitchell, 2006).

Also heavy metals found in storm water also mostly originate from automobile use activities, including gasoline combustion, brake lining; fluids (brake fluid, transmission oil, anti-freeze, grease, etc.), undercoating, and tyre wear. Auto repairs, pavement wear, and de-icing compound use, also contribute heavy metals to storm water where eroding area soils are the major source of the particulates in the storm water (Pitt & Lalor, 2000).

Storm event sampling programmes and runoff quality analysis are fundamental for estimating pollutant mass loads in both natural and distributed ecosystems (Ellis and Jacobsen, 1996, McLeod et al., 2006, Yusop et al., 2006, Nazahiyah et al[1]., 2007).

This paper aims at the analysis of the pollutants in the surface runoff and the estimation of the pollutant loads to find out the pollutant impact and thereby it attempts to provide the basic data to establish a proper treatment process and the best managerial practice to reduce the pollutant impact at the catchment area of the Milan subway, Mumbai.

Methods

Site Description

The study site of the Milan subway is located in at the western suburb of Santacruz in Mumbai city, Maharashtra state in India. The Milan subway is the connecting part of the east and west area of the Santacruz city in Mumbai having heavy vehicular traffic.

The catchment area of the Milan subway consists of the slum area, residential area, commercial area, marble temple making shops, tabelas, recreation ground, garages, automobile workshops, open spaces and lawns. The pollutant source from the catchment area is mainly from the automobile workshops, commercial areas, and marble temple making shops, tabelas, construction sites and the slum area. The total catchment area of the Milan subway is 11.7256 ha. Table 1 shows the bifurcation of the catchment area as per land use.

Table 1: Catchment of Milan subway area as per land use.

Sr. No	Land Use	Area (M2)	Percentage
01	Commercial Area	19307.16	16.47
02	Residential Area	43125.65	36.78
03	Open Spaces & Railways area	24779.44	21.13
04	Recreational Area	4730.96	4.03
05	Road area	25313.40	21.59
	Total	117256.61	100

Climatic Conditions

The yearly mean precipitation of the Mumbai city is 2129.8 mm (FFC Report), ninety percent of which is concentrated within four months from June to the end of September.

Identification of Pollutant Sources

The concentration and the total load of pollutants are closely related to the land use, type of catchment and rainfall condition. In particular, the surface runoff generated in residential, commercial and industrial zones in urban areas is highly likely to contain hazardous material such as oil components and heavy metals as well as floating materials, and requires a proper treatment process, which should be preceded by a basic survey on the characteristics of the surface runoff. A storm event sampling programme and runoff quality analysis are fundamental for estimating pollutant mass loads in both natural and distributed ecosystems.

The identified sources of pollutants at the catchment are of the Milan subway are enlisted as under:

- ✓ Vehicular traffic and automobile workshops.
- ✓ Lawn and garden maintenance.
- ✓ Air pollution: - Fallout of suspended solids from traffic, industrial source and wind erosion.
- ✓ Municipal maintenance activities.
- ✓ Industrial and commercial activities.
- ✓ Illegal connections of sanitary services from the slum area.
- ✓ Illegal disposal of household hazardous wastes.
- ✓ Transportation spills.
- ✓ Construction activity.
- ✓ Pet faeces and litter.
- ✓ Waste from marble shops.
- ✓ Runoff from residential driveways and parking areas.

Pollution Load

The average annual pollution load can be estimated as:-

Pollution Load= EMC X runoff.

The event mean concentration (EMC) is defined as the pollutant load washed off by a storm event divided by the event runoff volume (Adam and Papa[16], 2000). A good event monitoring programme is essential where accurate estimates of pollution loads are required. However in the absence of water quality data, EMC values reported in the literature can be used as a guide to estimate the likely range of pollution load (Chiew & McMahan, 1999).

$$EMC=M/V$$

$$=\Sigma QiCi\Delta t/\ (Qi\Delta t)$$

Where, M is the total mass of pollutant over the entire event duration, V is the total volume of flow over the entire event duration (m3), t is time (min), Qi(t) is the time-variable flow (m^3/min), Ci is the time variable concentration (mg/l) and Δt is the discrete interval (min) measured during the runoff event (Nazahiyah et al., 2007). Table 2 shows the results of the storm water samples at Milan subway site.

Table 2: EMCs of storm water runoff from catchment area (Unit: mg/l).

Concentration	Pollutants							
	pH	DO	Chlorides	TSS	COD	BOD	O & G	TDS
Max	7.35	4.08	42	418	144	36	7.05	362
Min	6.62	3.06	24.03	72	40	16	4	52
Avg	7.04	3.89	34.37	312.7	59.67	18.33	5.85	245.5
Standard limit	5.5 -9.0	4	1000	100	250	30	10	2100

Pollutant Load-Runoff Relationships

The increase in pollutant mass loading during storm and subsequent flow conditions is attributed to the nonpoint source effects. The load-runoff relationship equation is:

$$L/A=x\,(Q/A)^{\beta}$$

Where, L is pollutant load (kg/ha) A is watershed area, Q is runoff (m^3/hr) and x and β are regression coefficients (Lee & Bang, 2000).

Unit Pollutant Loading Rates

The unit pollutant loading rates are calculated by the following equation:

L = 1/100(Cv x AR x EMC) ;(Choe et al.[3], 2002).

Where;

L = Unit pollutant loading rate (Kg/ha/year);
Cv = Co-efficient of runoff;
AR = Annual rainfall (mm/year);
EMC = Event mean concentration (mg/l).

In this study the value of Cv was taken 0.95, the average of the measured value during the rainfall, and that of the AR to be 2129.8 mm/yr, the yearly mean precipitation of the sampling sites. The calculated unit pollutant loading rates for the study site are summarized in Table 3. In general, the unit pollutant load of the residential area is higher than industrial area.

Table 3: Unit Pollutant Loading for catchment area of Milan subway (Unit: kg/ha/yr).

Pollutants	DO	Chlorides	TSS	COD	BOD	O & G	TDS
Unit pollutant loading	78.71	695.41	6326.28	1207	370.9	118.36	497.22

Conclusion

1. The average EMCs of the total suspended solids is 312.7 mg/l, which is very high from the standard permissible limits. The average EMC of the dissolved oxygen is marginally higher than the permissible limits and this may be due to the increased concentration of the total suspended solids.
2. The unit pollutant loading of the total suspended solids is higher than the allowable permissible limits.
3. It is necessary to reduce the pollutant impact source of suspended solids at their source only by applying the structural and non structural best managerial practices.

References

1. Brayan Ellis J and Gordon Mitchell , (2006), "Urban Diffuse Pollution: Key Data Information for the Water Framework Directive", Journal of Water and Environment, 20(01), 19-26.
2. Characklis, G.W. and Wiesner, M.R., (1997), "Particles, Metals and Water Quality in Runoff from Large Urban Watershed", J. of Environ. Eng. Div ASCE, 123(8), 753-759..
3. Choe J.S., Bang K. W. and Lee J. H. , (2002) "Characterization of Surface Runoff in Urban Areas", Water Science & Technology, 45(09), 249-254.
4. Chitale Madhavrao & Committee, (2006), "Fact Finding Committee on Mumbai Floods", State Govt Committee Report, 31-130.
5. Fulkerson Mark, Nandi Fidelia, N.and Chasar Lia, S., (2007), "Characterizing Dry Deposition of Mercury in Urban Storm Runoff", Water Air Soil Pollution, 185, 21-32.
6. Faram M.G, Hrugo K. O. and Andoh R. Y. G., (2007), "Characteristics of Urban Runoff Derived Sediments Captured by Proprietary flow through Storm Water Interceptors", Water Science & Tech, 56(12), 21-27.

7. Mitchell G.,(2005)," Mapping Hazards From Urban Diffuse Pollution; a sccrening Model to Support Sustainable Urban Drainage Planning", J. Environ. Manage. 74, 1-9.

8. Lee Jun Ho and Bang Ki Woong, (2000), "Characterization of Urban Storm Water Runoff", Wat. Res., 04(06), 1773-1780.

9. Robert Pitt and Melinda Lalor , (2000), "The Role of Pollution Prevention in Storm Water Management", Proceeding of Conference on Storm Water and Urban Water Systems Modelling, (Feb 24-25, Toronto, Ontario).

10. R Pitt, Field R. , Lalor M. , and Brown M. , (1995), Urban storm water toxic pollutants: assessment, sources and treatability, Water Environment Research, 67(03), 260-275.

11. Nazaahiyah R., Yusop Z., and Abustan, (2007), ''Storm Water Quality and Pollution Loading from an Urban Residential Catchment in Johar, Malaysia'' Water Science & Technology, 56(07), 1-9.

12. Whipple, W. and Hunter, J.V. (1981), Settleability of Urban Runoff Pollution, J. of the WPCF, 53(12), 1726-1731.

13. Zope P.E., Sawant P. H. and Jeswani Hansa, (2008), "Pollution Prevention in Urban Storm Water Management", National Conference on Sustainable Water Resources Development and Management, SWRDAM-2008, Aurangabad, page 390-396.

55

Investigating Botswana Junior Secondary Religious Education on the Extent of Creating Biodiversity and Environmental Awareness

JAMES ONYANGO AWINO

Introduction

Environmental education is one of the latest developments in Botswana's educational system that has been given impetus by its incorporation into all subjects. In 1994, the Revised National Policy on Education (RNPE) recommended infusion and integration of the following issues into the school curricula: Environmental Education, Population Family Life Education, HIV/AIDS Education and the world of work. The first efforts in incorporating environmental education in the Three-Year Junior Secondary Religious Education (RE), syllabus was in 1996 when the World Religions Approach to the Religious Education syllabus in Botswana Junior Secondary Schools was adopted.

The Junior Secondary RE syllabus of 1996 developed through efforts of various stake holders including but not limited to Botswana Christian Council, Botswana Buddhist Association, University of Botswana, RE teachers, some Heads of schools and officers of the Curriculum Development Division. The efforts of the foregoing task force members yielded five modules of the broad-based RE syllabus.

- √ The first module deals with introduction to religion, origin of the universe and humankind, religious practices and ceremonies.
- √ The second module integrates basic beliefs, teachings, intermediaries and ceremonies.
- √ The third module deals with respect for life which includes three forms of life.
- √ The fourth module integrates issues of sexuality such as the importance of the family and the role that religions play in family life, the roles of men and women and influence of any (at least) three religions on them, understanding facts about Human Immune Deficiency Syndrome (HIV/AIDS), how different religions help in controlling HIV/AIDS and assist in making AIDS victims feel accepted. It also deals with knowing the different

contraceptives used for family planning and analyze views of different religions on them.

√ The fifth module deals with issues of justice which includes but not limited to the meaning and importance of freedom, awareness of basic human rights from a religious perspective and understanding capital punishment (Republic of Botswana, 1996).

of all these five modules briefly described in the foregoing details, the third module that deals with respect for life is especially relevant to this study under the syllabus sub-heading 3.1. This part under the sub-heading "Three Forms of Life" indicates topics, general objectives and specific objectives as outlined (in Table 1).

Table 1: Three Forms of Lifer (Unit 3.1).

Topics	General Objectives	Specific objectives
Human Life	1. Know the different forms of life and appreciate human life.	1. List the three forms of life.
		2. Describe characteristics of the **three** forms of life according to various religions.
		3. Explain ways in which man is regarded as the most important of all creation according to various religions.
		4. Identify limitations of human life.
Animal Life	2. Appreciate the importance	1. List different ways in which animal life can be protected in at least three religions.
		2. Explain ways in which animal life can be destroyed.
		3. Mention **five** ways in which human beings can use animal life.
Plant Life	3. Know and understand the importance of plant life.	1. List **five** ways in which plant life can be protected.
		2. State the religious importance of plant life in at least three religions.
		3. List **five** ways in which plant life can be destroyed.
		4. Describe ways in which plant life can be used in different religions.

Objectives of the Study

The study intends to analyze the extent of creating biodiversity and environmental awareness using two intimately related environmental paradigms, the anthropocentric and ecocentric continuum. Specifically the study is meant to:

1. Find out the extent to which the objectives of the Junior Certificate RE programme syllabus covers biodiversity and environmental awareness.
2. Identify major educational implications drawn from the explication of the two paradigms.

Brief Review of Related Literature

Anthropocentric Versus Ecocentric Religious Education

- The study brings two environmental strands of thought into a relationship to provide a framework in which the extent of coverage may be captured and interpreted as illustrated in figure 1 of anthropocentric and ecocentric attitudes to environment.

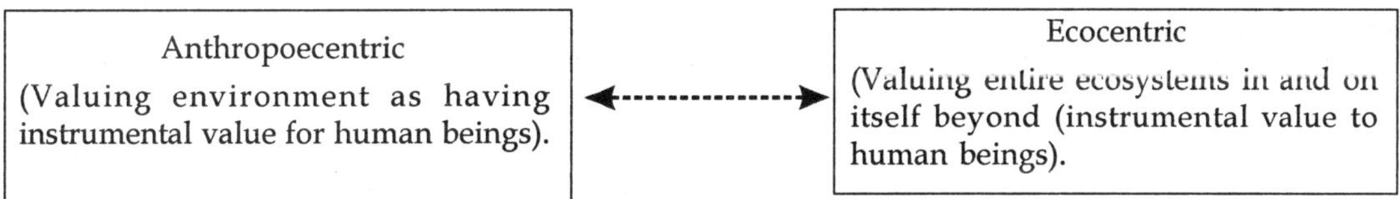

Fig. 1. Attitudes to Environment.

- Some studies have looked upon general beliefs about environmental concerns as having two dimensions that confront an anthropocentric with an ecocentric viewpoint in the person-environment relation (Amerigio, Aragones, DeFrutos, Servillano and Cortes, 2007).
- Several scholars have pointed out that amongst those with the anthropocentric motive; the human being is the centre of the relation to the environment in a parasitic relationship. But those with an ecocentric worldview or motive would be on equal terms with the environment in a symbiotic relationship. (Dunlap, VanLiere, Merring & Jones, 2000; Thomson and Barten, 1994; Milbrath, 1986; Dunlap and VanLiere, 1978)
- The first motive seems to be a dominant social paradigm which has resulted in the environmental deterioration caused by human beings by the belief that the environment belongs to human beings.

Environmental behavior

- Harm-minimization vs. Utility-maximization outlined by some scholars and in Jewish, Buddhist, Hindu and Christian philosophical traditions in their dialectical discourse e.g., the yin and yan concept (Sharma, 2006; Chowdhury and Bhattacharjee, 2002; Narayan, 1990).

- The conceptual continua indicated in Figure 1, the anthropocentric stance, where human beings appear central to the environment in terms of importance, tends to give rise to the rampant ecological devastation or degeneration of the environment because of the philosophical parochialism such idea holds (Sharma, 2006; Haque, 1989; Elkins 1989). Snauwaert (1996) maintains that such a position offers a weaker foundation for an ecologically sustainable ethic.
- The above submissions have focused our attention on both the anthropocentric and ecocentric ethics i.e. the anthropocentric ethics tend to assume that the environment is for the human beings in which the central value is the modern utilization (utility-maximization) thinking giving rise to most of the problems affecting our environment today. The latter ecocentric ethic (harm-minimization) implies compassion, respect and responsible attitude towards environment as a whole and can lead to stronger environmental sustainability.

The Role of Religious Education to Environment

- The distinction needs to be made between anthropocentric and ecocentric approaches to religious education if the environment is to be salvaged for us and future generations e.g. anthropocentric premises can lead human beings to have skewed assumption in developing curricula which reflects on humankind as the most important center of the universe. Morris (2002:581) discusses such a paradigm of consciousness by stating that it is hard to think that we are not the center of everything.
- My view is that learners should be facilitated through an adequate curriculum to avoid doctrinaire approach by being exposed to different paradigms to avoid the narrow confines of environmental knowledge. Only then shall we be able to think of ourselves as creatures living side by side with all, symbiotically, in an ecosphere.
- There are a number of initiatives that can give direction to educators who want to re-engineer and facilitate change in environmental education:

√ 1992 Earth Summit (Agenda 21) - the sustainability agenda.

√ RNPE (1994) infusion agenda – Botswana.

√ Need for a paradigm shift from the assumptions of the traditional interpretations that can create a new balance between utilitarian, ecotarian and ethicotarian philosophies of life (Webster, 2001).

√ The rise of environmentalism in 19th to 20th centuries giving environmental ethic a rational and theoretical support e.g. the Swedish environmental code adopted in 1998, the Scottish Environmental Education Council/ WWF- UK initiative (Alabaster and Blair, 2001; Ali-

Khan, 1990,1991),the Toyne Report (DfE, 1993; Willis, 1994), Education for Sustainability (Roome and Oates, 2001), the work of the Brundtland Commission (Pearce, Barbier, Markandya, Barrett, Turner and Swanson, 1991:210); Agenda 21; the International Chamber of Commerce; the Global Environment Charter of the Japan Federation of Economic Organizations; the Responsible Care Programme originated by Canadian Chemical Producers' Association.

√ Further three positions for addressing sustainability concerns are provided: compliance, stewardship and social responsibility (Roome and Oates, 2001).

If we have to attune to the proper role of education in realizing the sustainability agenda that was agreed at the 1992 Earth Summit (Agenda 21) including the RNPE (1994) infusion agenda, then our curriculum should provide considerable and informed scope for strong sustainability awareness within the syllabi frameworks. Webster (2001) in his debate on 'The Secondary Years' observes that post modernity is eroding the foundations of modern secondary schooling and the teachers who are prepared to create critical awareness should rise up to design new kinds of educational strategies that are more sanscrosanct to ecological principles. I argue that such principles can create a new balance between utilitarian, ecotarian and ethicotarian philosophies of life. Surely they do suggest the need for a paradigm shift from the assumptions of the traditional interpretations as revealed in anthropocentric approach to the environment to the ecocentric paradigm more of which can approximate the best environmental education. The most notable observation to be contributed here is that educational programmes we deal with often ignore the concerns of the non-human creation while focusing on the human centered philosophical system of values. In essence, a holistic program and ethic should be able to satisfy ecological needs in their entirety.

For example, the rise of environmentalism in 19th to 20th centuries led to a renewed interest by some philosophers in applied moral philosophy to give environmental ethic a rational and theoretical support. They tried to formulate agreed codes of conduct regulating human behavior towards nature/environmental issues. The Swedish environmental code adopted in 1998 and put in force in 1999 has fundamental environmental rules comprising almost 500 sections whose purpose is to promote sustainable development and consequently assure a healthy and sound environment for present and future generations. It stipulates that the Environmental Code shall be applied in such a way as to ensure that:

√ human health and the environment are protected against damage and detriment, whether caused by pollutants or other impacts;

√ valuable natural and cultural environments are protected and preserved;

√ biological diversity is preserved;

√ the use of land, water and the physical environment in general is such to secure a long term good management in ecological, social, cultural and economic terms; and

√ reuse and recycling, as well as other management of materials, raw materials and energy are encouraged with a view to establishing and maintaining natural cycles (The Swedish Environmental Code, 2000: 9).

Another early harbinger of greening the education sector is reported to be the Scottish Environmental Education Council/ WWF- UK initiative. This commissioned an investigation into the extent to which UK institutions of Further and Higher Education (FHE) prospectuses covered the environmental elements of their courses (Alabaster and Blair, 2001). A further initiative was done by the Committee of Directors of Polytechnics, one of which addressed institutional environmental practice (Ali- Khan, 1990) and the second of which focused on the curriculum (Ali- Khan, 1991). A more significant step was the government's role in creating an expert committee on environmental education in FHE (The Toyne Report). This met and published a report on environmental responsibility which gave environmental concerns a wider base DfE, 1993; Willis, 1994).

Roome and Oates (2001), in their study on 'Corporate Greening,' outlines the changes taking place in business, labour and education as a consequence of the ideas contained in the vision and principles of sustainable development. They have questioned the adequacy of the changes to date and the extent to which they contribute to a more sustainable society. Their ideas provide a background to discussions about education for sustainability (EFS) whose implications are threefold. First, EFS should incorporate ideas and understanding about what is currently practiced, but must go beyond positivist descriptions and explanations to strongly normative accounts of what ought to be practiced. Second, as the meaning of sustainability is continuously unfolding, a process of continuous learning requires knowledge, models of the world and values contributing to a more sustainable world. Third, EFS demands profound change in the organization, structure and practice of education equal to change required in other areas of society.

Similarly, other initiatives that provide significant response towards sustainability and improving environmental performance are: the work of the Brundtland Commission; Agenda 21; the International Chamber of Commerce; the Global Environment Charter of the Japan Federation of Economic Organizations; the Responsible Care Programme originated by Canadian Chemical Producers' Association. Further three positions for addressing sustainability concerns are provided: compliance, stewardship and social responsibility (Roome and Oates, 2001).

The foregoing initiatives provide a common theme that runs through them that sustainability goes beyond the improvement of environment performance. They are concerned with bringing environmental values into our practices and considering the needs of the future in relation to the needs of the present. We can remind ourselves of Brundtland Commission that defined sustainable development as development that meets the needs of the present without compromising the ability of the future generations to meet their own needs (Pearce, Barbier, Markandya, Barrett, Turner and Swanson, 1991:210). The ultimate intended interpretation of this concept, from economic perspective, is that the welfare of the generation alive today should not be measured by development activity if it can reduce the welfare of future generations. This is the economic Pareto Principle in the overall welfare of the society. It means that if development activity can make you better off without making anyone else worse off, then it is fair. I argue that if it can make all better off without making everything else (animate and inanimate) worse off, then it is fair.

Method

In this type of study document analysis was used to study the extent of coverage of environment issues in religious education with respect to the ecocentric and anthropocentric perspectives. Specifically, the three year Junior Secondary Syllabus was examined to guide in predicting its environmental coverage based on two cognitive components of general environmental attitudes; the anthropocentric and ecocentric motives in environmental conservation that might influence the extent of coverage. The researcher scanned through most of the relevant specific objectives to decipher the dominant paradigm for each objective: anthropocentrism or ecocentrism. Data was drawn from the Junior Secondary Syllabus and analyzed from anthropocentric and ecocentric perspectives. The interpretation was made based on frequencies obtained to establish the extent to which the two environmental paradigms are captured.

Findings And Discussions

This section provides and discusses results obtained in accordance with the already given research objectives.

The Analysis of the Extent JCRE Covers Biodiversity and Environmental Awareness.

I have employed the framework anthropocentric-ecocentric dimension to decipher the extent to which RE syllabus covers environmental issues as follows:

Table 2 presents the dominant paradigm between anthropocentric and eccentric that influenced each objective.

In specific objective 1.1, the listing of three forms of life seems to be limited to a community of living organisms without any reference to the non-living counterparts in the environment. I argue that this is partly anthropocentric. This objective could have been practiced in nature and should have satisfied the entire ecosystem. Similarly, specific objective 1.2 is also limited to three forms of life includes human beings but excludes the non-living things. For that matter, it is earthy anthropocentric.

The specific objective in section 1.3 echoes an exclusive anthropocentric approach. In this part man is depicted as the most important of all creation. The phrase "most important" seems to suggest that the non-human creation/environment lacks intrinsic worth. Such a conception in which the human element is the measure of all things may lead to dominating and exploitative attitude towards non-human environment. It can also trigger a mistreatment of it. This is strongly anthropocentric.

The specific objective 1.4 which is about identifying limitations of human life is still closer to an exclusive anthropocentric treatment. So do the specific objectives 2.1 and 3.1 which address the problem of anthropocentrism without a focus on entire environment. It still points to human protection of animal life and not at all creation.

The specific objective 2.2 and 3.3 required ways in which animal and plant life can be destroyed. These two objectives tend to instill the intrinsic worth of animals and plants, even though they fail to mention other non-human creation. For that matter, they are partly ecocentric.

Section 2.3 of the objectives requires students to mention ways in which human beings can use animal life. Similarly, section 3.4 equally requires students to describe ways in which plant life can be used in different religions. The unfolding ideas in both categories are a means of use i.e. the instrumental value of the environment for human beings. Hence appears on anthropocentric category.

Overall the dominant paradigm by counting the frequencies of the two paradigms, in table 2, is the anthropocentric belief. It is therefore clear from the findings which of the two types of scenario are covered to a greater extent. It indicates the greater presence of anthropocentric environmental belief. The findings reveal the ratio of anthropocentric to ecocentric cognitive components standing at 7:4 (64% and 36%) respectively the dissemination of which may presumably have significant consequences.

Table 2: Three Forms of Life (Unit 3.1).

Specific objectives	Descriptors/observed trend
1. List the three forms of life.	Partly anthropocentric
2. Describe characteristics of the three forms of life according to various religions.	Partly anthropocentric
3. Explain ways in which man is regarded as the most important of all creation according to various religions.	Anthropocentric
4. Identify limitations of human life.	Anthropocentric
5. List different ways in which animal life can be protected in at least three religions.	Partly ecocentric
6. Explain ways in which animal life can be destroyed.	Partly ecocentric
7. Mention five ways in which human beings can use animal life.	Anthropocentric
8. List five ways in which plant life can be protected.	Partly ecocentric
9. State the religious importance of plant life in at least three religions.	Partly anthropocentric
10. List five ways in which plant life can be destroyed.	Partly ecocentric
11. Describe ways in which plant life can be used in different religions.	Anthropocentric

Identification of Major Educational Implications Drawn from the Explication of the Anthropocentric and Ecocentric Paradigms.

The major educational implications that can be drawn from the explication of the dual-factor anthropocentric-ecocentric continua of beliefs concerning the relationship between human beings and their relation to environment include but are not limited to the following:

1. The educational curriculum should be that of curbing ecological crisis which seem to be embedded in anthropocentric inclined beliefs/attitudes in which people act as if they are the centre of the universe. The ecological crisis that such an attitude triggers engender environmental loss such as: the depletion of the ozone layer through the excessive use of chlorofluorocarbons (CFCs); looming global warming through excessive emission of greenhouse gases, loss of world's biological diversity and the loss of diverse environmental assets.

2. The educators must facilitate learners' awareness of the importance of ecocentric principle by which harm minimization to the environment (to all living and non-living things) is implied. As acknowledged by Sharma (2006: 42)".... harm minimization paradigm has implications for organizations ...based on utility maximization regardless to the damages they cause to the environment.

The two hypothesized paradigms are not to be seen as prescriptive but as a guide to developing curriculum objectives reviews that are crucial if we are to make proper transition to sustainable modes of living for us and future generations.

Conclusion

The findings of this study reveal that anthropocentrism form a major influence of the teaching and learning of environmental issues in Religious Education to a greater extent (64%) as opposed to the ecocentric elements (34%). It appears from the findings that it is the weak version of the environmental approach (anthropocentrism) that seems to be the standard practice as at now in this program. The weak version (anthropocentricism) is that the environment is only valuable in so far as they have instrumental/utilitarian value to human beings (Snauwaert, 1996). The strong version of environmental teaching and learning, 'ecocentric approach,' advances an ethical claim in which there is no division between human and non-human creation. I call this a strong version since it recognizes the importance of the environment and the web of life where no single organism is more important than the other.

The anthropocentric and ecocentric perspectives are given not as prescriptive views but as a generic guide which should be taken into account for an adequate treatment of environmental education curriculum whenever we prepare our curriculum objectives.

References

1. Alabaster, T. & Blair, D. (2001) Greening the University. In J. Huckle & S. Sterling (Eds.). **Education for Sustainability** London: Earthscan Publications Ltd.

2. Ali-Khan, S. (1990) **Greening Polytechnics.** London: Committee of Director of Polytechnics. (CDP).

3. Ali-Khan, S. (1991) **Greening the Curriculum**. London:CDP.
4. Amerigo, M., Aragones, J.I., de Frutos, B., Sevillano, V. & Cortes, B. (2007). Underlying dimensions of ecocentric and anthropocentric environmental beliefs. **The Scotish Journal of Psychology,** 10(1), 97-103.
5. Chowdhury, Subir & Sangeetha B. (Eds.) (2002) **Blending the Best of the East and West.** New Delhi: Excel Books.
6. DfE (1993) Environmental Responsibility: **An Agenda for Further Higher Education.** London: HMSO.
7. Dunlap, R. E., & Van Liere, K. (1978). The new environmental paradigm. **Journal of Environmental Education,** 9, 10-19.
8. Dunlap, R. E., Van Liere, K.D., Merting, A. G. & Jones, R.E. (2000). Measuring endorsement of the new ecological paradigm: a revised NEP scale. **Journal of Social Issues,** 5, 425-442.
9. Elkins, P. (ed) (1989). **The Living Economy: A New Economist in the Making.** London: Routledge.
10. Haque, S. (1989) **Philosophical Parochialism in theories of Development and Underdevelopment.** Los Angeles: University of Southern Africa.
11. ICC (1992) **The Business Charter for Sustainable Development,** International Chamber of Commerce, Paris
12. Milbrath, L. W. (1986) Environmental beliefs and values. In M.G. Hermann (Ed.) **Political Psychology.** San Francisco: Jossey-Bass.
13. Republic of Botswana (1994) **The Revised National Policy on Education (Government** paper No.2). Gaborone: Government Printer.
14. Republic of Botswana (1996) **Three - Year Junior Secondary Religious Education Syllabus.** Gaborone; Ministry of Education.
15. Roome, N. & Oates, A (2001) Corporate Greening. In J. Huckle and S. Sterling (Eds). **Education for Sustainability** London. Earthscan Publications Ltd.
16. Sharma, S. (2006). **Management in New Age: Western Windows-Eastern Doors.** New Delhi: New Age International (P) Ltd, Publishers.
17. Snawaert, D. (1996) **The Relevance of the Anthropocentric Debate** (Online). Available at: http://www.ed.uiuc.edu/EPS/PES-Yearbook/96_docs/snauwaert.html Accessed 19 July 2008.
18. **Swedish Environmental Code** (2000) Stockholm: Ministry of Environment.
19. Thompson, S.C.G, & Barton, M. (1994) Ecocentric and anthropocentric attitudes towards environment. **Journal of Environmental Psychology,** 14, 149-157.
20. Webster, K (2001) The Secondary Years. In J. Huckle & S. Sterling (Eds.) **Education for Sustainability.** London: Earthscan Publications Ltd.
21. WCED (1987) **Our Common Future.** Oxford: Oxford University Press.
22. Willis, K. (1994). **'A Survey' Environmental Project.** Manchester: University of Manchester.

56

Livestock as a Mainstay of Rural Economy and its Environment - A case study of Randhawa Village

SUNIL

Introduction

Livestock plays a significant role in the rural agrarian society. It not only supports the income of landless farmers but they are also used for draught power. In the rural areas, particularly India's countryside, the rural life is incomplete without livestock. Livestock like camels and bullocks are mainly reared for draught power but on the other hand sheep and goats are reared for their wool and meat. To some extent, the rural economy is dependent on milk production and that is why Bovines are the mainstay of the rural economy. Livestock are reared by both landless and the landlords. Landlords use the livestock for both the milk production and the draught power, whereas, landless rear the livestock for meat and milk production. They earn income by selling the milk and thus a degree of commercialization is the significant characteristic of the rural economy. Apart from this, the livestock have become connected with the faith and religious beliefs of the rural people. Because of the mechanization of agriculture, the role of draught animals has been reduced but in spite of that, they are useful for milk production and meat. Thus, they are the mainstay of the rural economy. This paper attempts to examine the pattern, composition, and degree of the commercialization of livestock.

Objectives:

(1) To examine the pattern of the livestock and its composition.

(2) To evaluate the livestock assets according to the social and economical status of the households.

(3) To study the yield level of bovines and its variation with respect to the social and economical status of the households.

(4) To evaluate the degree of commercialization of livestock economy.

Hypotheses:

The present study is designed to test the following hypotheses:

(1) the composition of the livestock varies with the social and economical status of the households. The proportion of goats and sheep are higher among the households having low social and economical status of the households, whereas, the households belonging to the upper and intermediary castes have better access to land resources and rear bovines.

(2) The livestock assets are larger in size in the households having a higher social and economical status.

(3) The yield level of bovines is far and away higher than the households having a higher social and economical status.

(4) The degree of the commercialization of the livestock is higher among the households having lower social and economical status as livestock is the source of living for such households.

(5) Methodology:-

The households in the village have been classified in different social and economical brackets in the distribution of livestock in the village.

The social status of the households has been defined in terms of caste hierarchy in the village.

Upper castes (Brahmin, Rajput)

Intermediary castes (Jat)

Artisan castes (Sunar, Kumhar, Chimpa, Khati, Nai)

Scheduled castes (Chamar, Nirban, Dhanak, Balmikim)

The economical categories have been defined in terms of land ownership and the size of a holding.

Landless	-	Not owning land
Marginal farmers	-	Below 5 acres
Small farmers	-	5 to 9.9 acres
Middle farmers	-	10 to 19.9 acres
Large farmers	-	Above 20 acres.

Structure of Livestock

Out of 406, 320 households in the village own livestock. Bovines constitute about 67 percent of the total livestock in the village. Buffaloes are the most important bovine which constitute about

55 percent of the total livestock. Sheep and goats constitute only about one-fourth of the total livestock in the village. Camels constitute merely about 4 percent of the total livestock and are mainly used for draught power. Bullocks and oxens constitute only about 3 percent of the total livestock. The draught animals constitute only about 7 percent of the total livestock in the village. This underlines the declining role of draught animals in the agricultural operation as these are gradually being replaced by machinery.

Livestock distribution according to Social Status:

Livestock is reared by all sections of the society in the village. About 86 percent of the artisan caste owns livestock but only 59 percent of the intermediary caste keep animals which are lowest amongst all the caste groups in the village. About 76 and 82 percent of households among scheduled and upper castes respectively, rear livestock.

Upper castes rear more buffaloes and the density of the buffaloes is higher among the artisan caste which has 20 per 10 households. Sheep and goats are mainly reared by the scheduled caste groups. They constitute about 37 percent of the total livestock among scheduled castes but the draught animals are reared mainly by the intermediary caste group who use them as draught power.

The density of cows is higher among upper caste group which is about 4.65 per 10 households while lower among the artisan castes. Upper caste groups own about 108 buffalo calves and 25 calves of cows, which is higher among all social groups.

Livestock distribution according to Economical Status:

The proportion of animal rearing households is highest among small farmers which is almost 95 percent and lowest amongst the landless households, which is 70 percent. The density of draught animals is higher among small farmers which is about 6.92 per 10 households. Small farmers have also density of sheep and goats which is 25 per 10 households. Landless households have a lesser density of all the livestocks.

Milk production:

The production of milk is the most important motive for animal rearing in the village. About 76 percent of the total animal rearing households of the village are engaged in the production of milk. The largest share in milk production comes from buffaloes.

There are 19 percent of households which have an annual yield between 1801 to 2300 litres. About 28 percent of the households have an annual yield of between 1301 to 1800 litres whereas there are only 11 percent households which have an annual yield below 800 litres. Upper caste households have such households which have annual yield of more than 2300 litres and only 3 percent of such households which have an annual yield less than 800 litres, whereas the lower castes have only 19 percent of such households which have an annual yield of more than 2300 litres and 16 percent of such households have an annual yield of below 800 litres.

According to their economical status, about 64 percent of the buffalo rearing households among large farmers have an annual yield of more than 2300 litres and about 7.0 percent have below 800 litres whereas among the landless households, about 17 percent of these households have buffalo with annual yield of more than 2300 litre and 17 percent of households have buffaloes with an annual yield at less than 800 litres.

Marketing of Milk and Its Products:

Milk and its products are mainly sold within the village. The main product sold is milk. There are about 37 percent of households in the village which sell milk and 17 percent of such households which sell mill and its products. Among the upper castes there are 45 percent of households which sell milk and its products. About 48 percent of households of intermediary caste sell milk and milk products .

About 54 percent of the households of marginal farmers sell milk and its products. There is only 21 percent of households of large farmers which sell milk and its products.

Conclusion

Randhawa is among the economically backward villages hence animal husbandry is also backward here. People rear animals mainly for their milk production and as a source of power in agriculture. About 79 percent of the households own livestock. Bovines constitute about 68 percent of the total livestock and buffaloes account for nearly 55 percent of the total livestock. The hypotheses that the composition of livestock varies with the social and economical status of households and sheep and goats are reared by low social and economic status of households is proven as the artisan castes have the higher density of buffaloes i.e. 20 buffaloes per ten households. The density of cows is higher among the upper and intermediary castes. The density of sheep and goats is higher among scheduled castes i.e. 12 animals per ten households.

The density of draught animals and bovines is higher among large farmers, but it is interesting that they refrain from rearing sheep and goats. They have a low density i.e. 1.17animal per ten households, although the hypotheses that the yield of bovines is higher among the households having higher social and economic status, is proved.

References

1. Benefit of Endosulfan in Agriculture Production: Analysis of usage information, U.S. EPA,Docket ID NO. EPA-HQ-OPP-2002-0262-0062, 2007

2. California Pesticide Use Reporting Data, California Department of Pesticide Regulation, 1997-2007, cited in pesticide use in California, www.pesticideinfo.org.

3. Toxicological profile for Endosulfan - Endosulfan Factsheet - ATSDR, US Dept of Health and Human Services, Public Health Service, Anon (1993)

4. United Nations Environment Programme and the Food and Agriculture Organization of the United Nations, Chemical Review Committee 3, March 26, 2007.

5. World Health Organization, The WHO Recommended Classification of Pesticide by Hazard, 2005.

6. World Wildlife Fund Comments on reregistration of Endosulfan submitted to Public Information and Record Integrity Branch, Information Resources and Services Division(7502c) Office of Pesticide Programme, Environmental Protection Agency, Washington Anon (Nov 12 2001)

57

Vedic Philosophy
An Environmental Approach

Dr. Rajendra Parihar

Introduction

Society and Biodiversity are the main features of nature. Geographically speaking, society is a cultural landscape, which is the outcome of human efforts. Biodiversity is physical landscape, which is natural in its origin or rather to say, God given. Therefore, society and biodiversity both are intertwined to each other in such a way that they cannot be separated.

Society develops at any geographical place due to population growth, the resource utilization pattern and the technological levels, as well as wisdom of its citizens etc. Since Indian society is one of the oldest societies in this world, therefore, it has witnessed so many ups and downs in its course of evolution.

Biodiversity basically defines the relationship between man and his environment. This relationship changes according to time and space matrices. Change is the law of nature, which comes into effect in two ways i.e. day to day gradual change and historical drastic change.

The drastic major change comes both through climatic change and the fundamental ups and down in society as well as in the biodiversity.

The fundamental changes, world society has so far witnessed are -

Agricultural revolution, Industrial revolution and presently the Communication revolution (also known as globalization).

All three major changes are called revolutions because of their effect and intensity. Agricultural, industrial and communication revolutions have changed the fundamental basic relationship of man to his environment. Human needs and greed both grow according to population size and levels of technology. Political hegemony and population pressures lead to technological inventions. The latest techniques and wisdom again lead to the natural resources utilization pattern (models) etc.

Historically speaking the food gathering society had a scattered population and used stone plus sticks as technology. The agricultural, settled society had a minimum population and a wooden plough as techniques. The industrial society had a medium population and tractor machines as technology.

Last but not least, post modern society now has an over population a super computer as the latest technical use and throw in the relationship with natural resources and has no wisdom at all. It is the real situation in which the present civilization is almost trapped.

The ray of hope or possibility of life on this planet as visualized is Vedic Philosophy only. Its environmental approach can guide us to survive with dignity because of its holistic characteristics. We have forgotten our ancestors blessing and guidelines somewhere in the process of development.

Nature of Problem

The major problems that the present society is facing are – The decline in biodiversity, unplanned population growth, environmental degradation and challenges for the sustainable social order. These problems crop up due to unviable models of development, short sightedness, a political hegemony hangover with segregated world views, a narrow approach of socio-political and economical managers of ancient, medieval and even modern role models of western culture because they have dominated almost the last five centuries in the state affairs, specially after the industrial evolution.

The approach, interaction and models of development adopted by western planners to deal with natural resources were not holistic and have created more and more dichotomies in the world i.e. western, eastern, north, south, developed, developing, forward, backward, ruler and ruled, civilized, uncivilized and so on.

This approach resulted into the disintegration of world society, ethics and spiritualism considered an outdated agenda in economical development. They have adopted the approach of "convince or confuse" to manage a world wide ignorance regime through their political and cultural hegemony. Therefore, this approach and the western perspective laid the foundation for our present problems.

Now let us look into the Vedic philosophy perspective. The framework, and this approach that is the only solution as a viable way out, is the way in which we have to deal with the biodiversity and social systems to work in such a fashion as to promote the concept of an holistic brotherhood, as "live and let live, "Vashudheva Kutumbkam" principles for the post modern global society.

Vedic philosophy emphasizes five basic elements (Panch-mahabhuta) – Earth, Water, Fire, Wind and Sky. The earth was first time utilized by King Pruthu, and that is why it is called Prithvi (earth). The earth was utilized with great dignity, respect and sacrificing in its operation.

We consider earth as a mother, not just a physical landscape. In the oldest source of literature, this Rigveda stanza explains that cordial relationship with nature :

मधुवत ऋतायतें मधु क्षरन्तु सिन्धवः
माध्वोः मा सन्तु औशधीः
मधु नक्तमुतो षासो मधुमत् पार्थिवरजः
मधु धौरस्तु नः पिरा
मधुमन्नो वनस्पतिः मधुमानस्तु सूर्यः
माध्वीःगवो भवन्तु नः

The wind, ocean, vegetation, soil, sky, sun and cow all these provide us pleasure and sustenance.

This is being well established in the Vedic literature that

"माता भूमिः पुत्रोऽहं पर्षथ्वियाः"

– अर्थवेद भूमि सूक्त

Seers says that the earth is my mother, and I am her son, we should take her help to feed us but not to exploit. In fact, the Hindu way of life is full of the literary sources which provide us an ethnic information regarding our day to day dignified relationship with mother earth and human beings.

समुद्र वसने देवि पर्वत स्तन मण्डले।

विश्णु पत्नि नमस्तुभ्यं पाद स्पर्ष क्षमस्वमे।।

Even today old people in the countryside, when they get up early in the morning, first of all pray to mother earth to forgive them because we are putting leg on you.

The resource utilization pattern and approach is also established in this stanza as a guiding principle

ऊँ ईषावास्यमिदं सर्व यत्किंचजगत्यां जगत्।

तेन त्यक्तेन भुंजीथाः मा गधः कस्य स्विद्वनम्।।

Everything is God created, god is everywhere, consumption should be with sacrifice (limit), do not indulge in any kind of theft. Plants, trees etc. are also considered as living beings, they should be protected at any cost. Hindu tradition categorises forests into three groups : First, Shrivan – for human sustenance and wealth, second, Tapovan – where the seer discovers the truth, visualize ultimate reality etc. and the third Mahavan – a huge biosphere for flora and fauna.

Vedic philosophy is a system of knowledge which emerged about 2000 years B.C. in which every element, phenomenon, and individual is considered as a part of the creation; rr~ Roe~ fl, Environmentally speaking the individual is projected as a part of nature, not a master of nature.

The real matrix of part and whole, elements and entire creation is very well explained through various schools of thought known as Darshana or philosophy, which means, "survey of all things" (Anviksiki in Sanskrit language).

The main emphasis of Vedic philosophy is on receptivity and contemplation, not the controlling or regulating of the object of study (nature) as our western thinkers hold their views.

The Nayaya, Vaisesika, Sankhya, Yoga, Mimansa and Vedanta are six basic Darshana of Indian society which have their roots in the Vedic Philosophy to deal with any problem that the present world community faces. In fact, human beings are a part of nature, not considered inherently more important than any other being to exploit the resources for their selfish ends.

These six schools of thought are also known as Astika (orthodox), literally meaning those who accept the authority of the Vedas. While those who deny the authority of the Veda are known as Nastika (heterodox) i.e. Charvaka or Lokayata (materialistic), Jainism and Buddhism etc.

Methodology

The basic methodology adopted in this state of affairs is to review the entire Vedic literature in a scientific objective analysis manner in order to get the real guidelines, and principles laid down to regulate the social order in amicable way.

The basic four human deeds as Hindu traditions have mentioned are as follows :

धर्म = Lifestyle with certain rules, regulations, limitations, rituals etc.

अर्थ = Ethnic income, hard earned money, not through illegal means

काम = Desires, realistic, reasonable and visualized

मोक्ष = Liberation from all wordly affairs, that can stop the vicious circle of eighty four lacs categories of 'Yoni' (beings).

These four human deeds must be analysed in a scientific way in the post modern society to meet the future challenges ahead.

Old people, especially in the countryside in all directions the of nation must be interviewed for their vision and indigenous approach to deal with the natural resources.

The concept of Oran (land dedicated to local deity), Gocher (land for cow grazing) of Rajasthan and Devalaya of Maharashtra must be applied in human settlements to protect the biospheres.

The Vedic philosophy concept of the four fold bodies of human beings also needs a fresh look especially for the younger generation i.e.

स्थूल शरीर = Physical structure of human being, hardware stuff.

सूक्ष्म शरीर = Software stuff of human beings i.e. Soul and Man.

कारण शरीर = Vision, knowledge etc.

महाकारण शरीर = Ignorance, Avidhya.

All these basic concepts of Vedic philosophy have to be analysed in a proper way to thresh out the present problems of global society. Therefore, primary and secondary sources are to be consulted in proper time and context.

MAJOR FINDINGS

The major findings of this academic exercise are as follows :

- Ecologically speaking, the damage which has been done, must be repaired within a time bound period.
- Globalization is a needful process in which everyone must accept and cooperate, with certain modifications, because this will ultimately lead to the new world order.
- The slogan of the day is "Back to the Vedas", has to be put in to practice at every level.
- An holistic world view is the need of the hour and the Indian Hindu way of life is the most viable solution which we have.
- An oriental development model based on non-violence, could be way out of the present global crises.
- A spiritual educational system (SES) is the need of the full job which has to be done all over the world in its proper context, right from the beginning to higher education.
- A two child norm must be implemented to check the population growth.
- A global democratic party system must be introduced to counter the narrow political hegemony concept.
- Development with dignified model of economical development is a need of the millennium to be implemented with an immediate effect based on the Vedic concept of a spiritually oriented consumption system (consume for minimum need no greed).
- The latest techniques and indigenous approach should be implemented in regional planning.
- Last but not least, "global enforcement authority", should be set up to control the world economy and democracy to relocate terrorist regimes at remote areas.
- Eradicate poverty, illiteracy and unemployment to pave the way for concept of "lcs Hkwfe xksiky dh" (all land belongs to God, who is the sole owner. Others are just trustees, and man is a part of nature, not a master to exploit resources to meet his selfish ends.

Conclusion

Society and biodiversity are integral parts of each other that have to be analysed in a proper way of investigation based on objective prevailing conditions of any phenomenon which exists on the surface of the earth. Social structure, systems and rituals are basically created by human efforts to meet out their various requirements.

The basic difference between society and biodiversity is its variations which determine the parameters of the changes. Social variations are more prominent, diverse and vary from place to place because of the variation in human races, groups based on caste, creed, rituals, are economical and political status etc. They again lead to the various types of dichotomies in the social order that have been witnessed in ancient, mediaeval and modern times while the post modern society needs a minimum variation and a maximum unity to sustain itself in the new century.

On the other hand, biodiversity is shrinking day by day due to population pressure, greed and wrong approaches to deal with natural resources. The use of the latest technology with selfish wisdom has led to the sectoral economical growth which projected socio-economic diversified models of development and disintegrated society into various groups, ultimately resulting into throat cut competition and violence, not cooperation and peace.

All these factors are solely responsible for the present crisis which human society faces. The need of the hour is an holistic world view and that is there in the Vedic philosophy of "Vasudheva Kutumbkama" meaning that the entire earth is as one family.

Therefore it is a well established fact that Vedic philosophy is a deep rooted assumption about the sharing of existence across all beings, including nature. In fact human beings are a part of nature, not considered inherently more important than any other being to subjugate the others.

Hence, "Vedic philosophy : Environmental Approach" is a key to the present global problems which society faces, having amicable solutions, a way out, a viable alternative to shorten out the universal biodiversity and the social crises with a deep philosophical foundation of vision.

References

1. Andrew Light and Holemes Roiston (ed) (2003). Environmental Ethics : An Anthology Black Well Publisher Ltd., 108 Cowley Road, Oxford, OX41JF United Kingdom.
2. Bhardwaj, O.P. (1986). Studies in the Historical Geography of Ancient India. Sandeep Prakashan, Delhi.
3. Bhargava, M.L. (1964). The Geography of Rigvedic India. Upper India Publishing House, Lucknow.
4. Budyko, M.I. (1980). Global Ecology. Progress Publishers, Moscow.
5. Deshpande M. and Hook, P. (1978). Genesis of Rignedic Retroflexion : A Historical and Sociolinguistic Investigation. Ann Arbar, Mich : University of Michigan.
6. Dobson, A. (1990). Green Political Thought Rutledge, London.
7. Edwards, L.R. (2005). Environmental Justice in America : A New Paradigm. Indiana University Press, 601, North Morton Street, Bloomington (USA).

8. Elliot, R. and Gare, A. (1983). Environmental Philosophy. Open University Press, Milton Keyens.

9. Frederick, Engels (1974). Dialectics of Nature. Progress Publishers, Moscow.

10. Geldner, K.F. (1951-57). Der Rigveda and Vol. 5. Hamdard Oriental Series, Vol. 5, 33-36. Harnard University Press.

11. Gerasimov, I.P. (1983). Geography and Ecology. Progress Publishers, Moscow.

12. Hegel (1970). Philosophy of Naure. Clarendon Press, Oxford, U.K.

13. Heywood, V.H. and Gardner, K. (eds.) (1995). Global Biodiversity Assessment, UNEP and Cambridge University Press, Cambridge, 1140 pp.

14. Johannes, R.E. (1989). Traditional Ecological Knowledge : A Collection of Essays IUCN. Gland Switzerland, 64 pp.

15. Keith, A.B. (1912). Vedic Index of Names and Subjects, 2 Vol. 5, Motilal Banarasidass, Delhi.

16. Kocchar, Rajesh (2004). The Vedic People Their History and Geography. Orient Hongman Pvt. Ltd., 1/24, Asaf Ali Road, New Delhi -2.

17. Majumdar, R.C. (ed.) (1988). The Vedic Age, Bhartiya Vidya Bhawan, Bombay.

58

Environmental Education and Awareness

ZILL-E-HUMA[1]

ENVIRONMENTAL AWARENESS AND EDUCATION

It is an illusion perceived by many contemporary educators that Environmental Education (EE) is a new phenomenon that has been highlighted due to our concern for the environment. On the contrary, it goes as far back as 1948 when the term Environment Education was first used at **International Union for the Conservation of Nature and Natural Resources** (IUCN) Conference, Paris (Disinger, J. 1983) whereas Wheeler (1985) suggests that the term first appeared in the book **Communities** by Paul and Percival Goodman, published in 1947. Concerted efforts, to define EE as a specific endeavor, began in the 1960s. These efforts were given international support at the **United Nations Conference on the Human Environment** held in Stockholm in 1972, where participating governments recommended that it be recognized and promoted internationally through the United Nations. One of the initial tasks was to develop some consensus on what EE could and should become, and to assist governments in implementing relevant programs as soon as practicable. Two major conferences (Belgrade, 1975; Tbilisi, 1977), supported by regional meetings of experts, were hosted by the newly formed UNESCO-UNEP International Environmental Education Programme. The final report of Tbilisi conference set out the goals of education clearly reflecting those already identified at Belgrade.

The provisions of the 'Tbilisi Declaration on the role, objectives and characteristics of environmental education', remain in wide international use and have sustained their role as a guiding influence over the past three decades. It defines EE as:

[1] She is the M.Phil scholar of Kinnaird College Lahore. Her area of interest is "Urban Development and Environmental Interactions". She has a master degree in Geography from University of the Punjab, Lahore and has two year teaching experience. She is the member of All Pakistan Geographical Association and Asian Population Association as well.

Environmental education is a learning process that increases people's knowledge and awareness about the environment and associated challenges, develops the necessary skills and expertise to address the challenges, and fosters attitudes, motivations, and commitments to make informed decisions and take responsible action (UNESCO, 1998).

The goals of EE are: (Tbilisi, 1978)

- To foster clear awareness of, and concern about economic, social, political and ecological interdependence in urban and rural areas.
- To provide every person with opportunities to acquire the knowledge, values, attitude, commitment and skills needed to protect and improve the environment.
- To create new patterns of behavior of individuals, groups and society as a whole, towards the environment.

Five categories of EE objectives have been outlined: (Tbilisi, 1977, Womersley, 1981; USEPA 2005)

- Awareness and sensitivity to the environment and environmental challenges.
- Knowledge and understanding of the environment and environmental challenges.
- Attitudes of concern for the environment and motivation to improve or maintain environmental quality.
- Skills to identify and help resolve environmental challenges.
- Participation in activities that lead to the resolution of environmental challenges.

EE encompasses a spectrum of approaches, such as use of the media, the Internet and other networks, participatory community programs, formal environmental content in curricula, training for industry and small to medium businesses and qualifications in areas such as environmental science, management, engineering and law.

Relevance of EE to our Everyday Lives

EE education is relevant to our everyday lives because it can ensure the health and welfare of nation by[2]: (Pandey 2005):

- Protecting human health
- Advancing quality education
- Expanding employment opportunities
- Promoting sustainable development
- Protecting natural heritage

---

[2] Report assessing environmental education in the United States and the implementation of the National Environmental Education Act of 1990. Natl. Environ. Ed. Adv. Cncl. US EPA. December 1996. 45 pp.

STRUCTURAL ELEMENTS OF EE

According to Lucas (1979), education related to Environment comprises of three core threads. These are:

Education about the environment, which is basic knowledge and focuses on students' understanding of important facts, concepts and theories.

Education *in/from* the environment involves students in direct contact with environment and using it as resource to develop awareness and concern for the environment and get first hand personal experiences with in it.

Education *for* the environment aims to promote a willingness and ability to adopt life styles that are compatible with the wise use of environmental resources. This reflects the ethical element of Environmental education.

At present, many concepts and models of EE exist; the aims of which are to determine the key elements of EE and to present the relations between them (Giolitto *et al.*, 1997; Klimov and Ukolov, 1994; Palmer, 1997, 1998; Schools' Council, 1974; Sterling and Copper, 1992; Uzzel, 1999). Each of these has its own peculiarities and differs in the number of factors, which influence EE and their relationships. The standard model widely practiced in various locations and represents the harmonious development of the three areas of EE was given by Palmer (1993a) .It attempts to explain the relationship of components of its structure and how it can be utilized for practical planning and inclusion in curricula.

Structuring environmental education for global issues

EE programs have been designed for either **infusion** into existing curricula or the **insertion** of new courses into study. **Framing**, a third alternative can be especially effective in learning about global issues (Heimlich, 1992). In the **infusion** approach, content and skills are integrated into existing courses so as to focus on that content without losing the integrity of the courses themselves. This is most often seen in elementary and middle school levels, but less in high school. Case studies have been used effectively in infusion efforts (Singletary, 1992). **Insertion,** the addition of specific courses in environmental education, tends to be used more at the high school level. **Framing** moves beyond the arbitrary boundaries of traditional disciplines by creating a framework which allows learning to be related and integrated within a student's life (Heimlich, 1992). Using this approach, educators and students can investigate, interpret, explore, manage, discover, and make decisions about global issues.

ENVIRONMENTAL EDUCATION FOR SUSTAINABILITY

Sustainable development is defined, as defined by Brundtland Commission (WCED, 1987) is "***development that meets the needs of the present without compromising the ability of future generations to meet their own needs.***"

Education for sustainability is a lifelong learning process that leads to an informed and involved citizenry having the creative problem-solving skills, scientific and social literacy, and commitment to engage in responsible individual and cooperative actions. These actions will help ensure an environmentally sound and economically prosperous future.

The UN conference on Environment and Development, The Earth Summit, 1992 set out *agenda 21*[3] for achieving sustainable development. *Agenda 21* contains forty different chapters on ways in which different social and economic sectors and activities can be reoriented to emphasize sustainable development. Chapter 36 is on 'Education, Public Awareness and Training' and carries the message that education can give environmental and ethical awareness, values and attitudes, skills and behavior consistent with sustainable development and for effective public participation in decision-making. (Palmer, 1998).

EE has the potential to significantly contribute to sustainable development by overcoming the two major education challenges of sustainable development: One to promote positive attitude and informed decisions of citizens and govt. leaders that are conducive to sustainability. The other is to teach people the benefits of integration of conservation priorities with the need for development (USEPA, 1996).

EE for sustainability focuses on six themes: (*Education for Sustainability: An Agenda for Action)*

1. Lifelong learning: The potential for learning about sustainability throughout one's life exists both within formal and non-formal educational settings.

2. Interdisciplinary approaches: Education for sustainability provides a unique theme to integrate content and issues across disciplines and curricula.

3. Systems thinking: Learning about sustainability offers an opportunity to develop and exercise integrated systems approaches.

4. Partnerships: Partnerships forged between educational institutions and the broader community is key to advancing education for sustainability.

5. Multicultural perspectives: Achieving sustainability is dependent upon an understanding of diverse cultural perspectives and approaches to problem solving.

6. Empowerment: Lifelong learning, interdisciplinary approaches, systems thinking, partnerships, and multicultural perspectives empower individuals and institutions to contribute to sustainability.

Education is a motor for change. That is why in December 2002, the United Nations General Assembly, through its Resolution 57/254, declared **The UN Decade of Education for Sustainable Development** (UNDESD) 2005-2014. It also designated UNESCO as the lead agency for the promotion of this Decade. The basic **vision** of the Decade is a world where everyone has the opportunity to benefit from education for societal transformation.

---

[3]*Agenda 21* is the internationally agreed report of the UNCED or "Earth Summit" which was held in Rio de Janeiro in June 1992 . *Agenda 21* devotes a whole chapter to the role of environmental education in relation to sustainability:

DISCUSSION

Increase in urbanization, population explosion and economic development has put a serious stress on the natural resources. Development entails use of resources and unbridled development depletes resources at a much faster rate than they can be replenished, if at all.

Technological innovations and advancements in cleaner technologies, no doubt, have a positive effect on the state of environment yet it doesn't assure sustainable use of resources until and unless there is awareness and behavioral changes. For instance, state of the art plants may treat water to a high level but it doesn't affect the consumption pattern of individuals.

The ever-increasing significant threats to the Earth's resources justify the urgent need for an informed citizenship and the need of wide scale education relating to our responsibilities towards the environment. It is in this context that the role of education and awareness cannot be over emphasized. EE is not just about learning or acquiring formal education, rather it aims at understanding the environmental issues confronting our planet, developing a mindset that nurtures a behavior towards sustainable use of natural assets and environmental friendly attitudes.

Thus 'Environmental Education' is used here in its broadest sense to include:

1. raising awareness;
2. acquiring new perspectives, values, knowledge and skills; and
3. formal and informal processes leading to changed behavior in support of a sustainable environment.

Sustainability education is not confined to formal schooling. It also occurs in a wide range of non-formal education settings at work and at home.

Currently the environmental education efforts generally fit into two categories, **Formal EE and Non formal EE.**

Formal EE consists of activities specifically taking place in educational institutions at elementary and secondary schools, colleges, universities and professional institutions while **non formal EE** includes activities in businesses, non profit organizations and any other that are not considered part of formal education system. These also include media, computer networks, zoos, museums, workplaces, and community activities etc.

One of the problems with formal education is that students graduate without actually knowing how to think in whole systems, how to develop relationships between the structural elements, to find connections; how to look at a larger picture and ultimately how to sift out information and separate the trivial from the important. The purpose of EE, thus, should be to educate people who think broadly and who understand systems, connections, patterns, and root causesery discipline.

From the review of literature and successful global case studies,it becomes apparent that EE has been expanding at all levels-primary, secondary and tertiary since long, atleast in the developed countries of the world. In the US for example National environmental education Act provides for substantial support at all levels of education. The status of EE in developing countries is far lower, despite efforts by UNESCO, UNEP and IUCN.This is primarily due to poor economic conditions and inadequate educational infrastructure.

In the context of Pakistan, the notion of EE is still in infancy. Recently numbers of educational institutions have started imparting EE at the secondary and tertiary levels. Still we have to go a long way. It is necessary that awareness and education be imparted and started from nursery level, as in developed countries. The broad aim, thus, should be to inculcate a sense of respect and responsibility towards the environment and build awareness among all age groups. Though formal education has an important role to play, when it comes to EE, the teaching and learning process must be done through a 'fun-and-learn' method, thereby generating a genuine interest for the subject in the young. In the US, e.g schools and environmental organizations are involved in providing what is called 'Experiential learning/education' in natural science and ecology to children where they are made to interact with nature. Teton Science Schools, Wyoming and Landholm Trust are two such examples where I have personally witnessed the same.

APPROACHES FOR ENVIRONMENTAL EDUCATION AND PUBLIC AWARENESS IN PAKISTAN

- Running EE programs in schools and colleges. Compulsory core module to be prepared and implemented in all Colleges/Universities and its integration into teaching programs of all undergraduate courses.

- Encouraging educational institutions (colleges/institutions) to set up environmental and nature clubs in educational institutions.

- Developing and implementing sector and theme specific environmental communications and education programs.

- Restructuring of courses at professional institutions like agricultural and engineering universities, at medical colleges, and in master's programs to include relevant environmental components.

- Conducting training and awareness building workshops for teachers. Exchange programs for visits of teachers to foreign countries and participation in International seminars with the purpose of obtaining latest technical know how.

- Developing and disseminating EE material to all segments in the society through the web, electronic and print media.

- Programs to foster increased public awareness of sustainability through a public awareness campaigns. These should employ specific examples of everyday actions that are sustainable and environmentally friendly.

- Targeting the rural population via entertainment media i.e., radio, TV in creating awareness of environmentally friendly practices especially as regard to use of chemicals in agriculture, disposal of waste, health and population issues and conservation concerns.

- Establishment of Environmental Resource centers in urban areas.

In short the essence of EE , in its broadest sense, is about empowerment and development of a sense of ownership, improving the capacity for people to address environment and development issues in their communities. It is about touching their belief's and attitudes so that they want to ***live*** sustainably and to translate their attitudes to action. This process needs to incorporate **formal education** as well as **informal education**. The world most successful programs in the 21st century will be those in which both of these elements are supported alongside each other.

References

1. Disinger, J. (1983)' Environmental Education's Definitional Problem'. *ERIC Information bulletin No.2.*Ohio:ERIC

2. Giolitto, P., Mathot, L., Pardo, A., and Vergnes, G. (1997) *Environmental education in the European Union*. Brussels, Luxembourg: ECSC-EC-EAEC

3. Heimlich, J. E. (1992) "Promoting a concern for the environment." (*ERIC Document reproduction Service Number ED 351 206*)

4. IUCN,UNEP, WWF (1991) *Caring for the Earth: A Strategy for Sustainable Living*, Gland, Switzerland: IUCN.

5. Klimov, A. V. and Ukolov, A. I. (1994) Sistema ekologicheskogo obrazobaniya [The system of ecological education]. In *Problemy sozdaniya edinoy sistemy ekologicheskogo obrazovaniya i vospitaniya v Ukraine* [The problems of the development of the universal system of ecological education], ed. V. E. Nekos, V. I. Astakhova et al., 57-58. Kharkov, Ukraine: Kharkov State University.

6. Lucas, A.M. (1979) Environment and Education: Conceptual Issues and curriculum Implications, Melbourne: Australian International Press and Publications.

7. Palmer, J.A. (1998) Environmental Education in the 21st Century, Routledge, London and New York.

8. Pandey, V. C. (2005) Environmental Education, Isha Books,Delhi110 033.

9. Singletary, T. J. (1992) "Case studies of selected high school environmental education classes." *Journal of Environmental Education, 23(4), 35-50.*

10. Sterling, S. and Cooper, G. (1992) *In Youch: Environmental Education for Europe*. Surrey, UK: WWF, Panda House.

11. UNCED (1992) Promoting education and public awareness and training, *Agenda 21*, United Nations Conference on Environment and Development, NewYork: UN .

12. US (1994) *Education for Sustainability: An Agenda for Action*, Washingon, DC 20402-9328 :ISBN 0-16-048783-8

13. USEPA (1996) Report assessing environmental education in the United States and the implementation of the National Environmental Education Act of 1990.DIANE Publishing Co.

14. USEPA (2005) *Nebraska Environmental Education Master Plan: Building Conservation and Environmental Education for the Future.*

15. UNESCO (1977) *First Intergovernmental Conference on Environmental Education Final report,* Tbilisi, USSR. Paris: UNESCO.

16. Volk, T. L., Hungerford, H. R., and Tomera, A. N. (1984) "A national study of curriculum needs as perceived by professional environmental educators." *Journal of Environmental Education, 16(1), 10-19*

17. WCED (1987) *Our Common Future* .Oxford: Oxford University Press, p.43.

18. Wheeler, K (1985)' Environmental Education An historical perspective', *Environmental education and Information,*4(2),The environmental Institute, University of Salford in Palmer, J.A. (1998) Environmental Education in the 21st Century, Routledge, London and NewYork.

Definitions of environmental education have been presented in the following documents: U.N. Educational, Scientific, and Cultural Organization (UNESCO), *Belgrade Charter* (Belgrade, Yugoslavia, 1975); *Final Report, Intergovernmental Conference on Environmental Education* (Tbilisi, USSR, 1977); The World Commission on Environment and Development (Brundtland Commission), *Our Common Future* (Oxford: Oxford University Press, 1987); North American Association for Environmental Education (NAAEE), *Defining Environmental Education: The NAAEE Perspective,* Unpublished paper, 1983; United Nations Conference on Environment and Development (UNCED), *Agenda 21: Programme of Action for Sustainable Development* (New York: United Nations, 1992); International Council for Adult Education, *7 Year Plan for Major Institutional Change, Phase II, 1996* ; National Archives, *Memorandum of Understanding on Environmental Education among the Department of the Environment Canada and the Secretariat of Social Development Republic of Mexico and the Environmental Protection Agency,* U.S. Environmental Protection Agency (Washington, DC: 1992).

59

Citizen's Voice and Public Participation in Environmental Decision

Media's Strategy and NGO's Contribution

Rajesh Das

Introduction

..."To move forward we must recognize that in the midst of a magnificent diversity of cultures and life forms we are one human family and one Earth community with a common destiny. We must join together to bring forth a sustainable global society founded on respect for nature, universal human rights, economic justice, and a culture of peace. Towards this end, it is imperative that we, the peoples of Earth, declare our responsibility to one another, to the greater community of life, and to future generations" (Preamble, Earth Charter, 2000).

The audience (people's) participation – based approach to the design of media message, helps to focus on the problems of designing audience- responsive messages in Third world. For any developmental communication, like environmental communication, the project planner or development planner first listen to the audience before beginning of message design. It is obvious that which information the people needs, in what form (media strategies or content or illustration) and by whom (representative of GO / NGO, opinion leader or people's representative) [1].Read the today's newspaper, or switch on the TV set. Global warming, toxic chemical spills, destruction of tropical rain forest, rising the sea level or poaching the wild animal- the readers or the viewers get any of the environmental topic in the daily news capsule. Human threats to the wild places and their behavioral changes, (commercialization, consumerism, global market economy), are the crucial menace to retain the sustainable development of environment. It's completely vulnerable, because it flattens the earth, not a single country or geographical area. The concept of biotic community is basic to an understanding of ecosystem; hence of ecology. A community or 'biocoenose' is an aggregate of organism, which forms a distinct ecological unit. Such a unit may be defined in terms of biotic (flora and fauna) and abiotic (air, water soil, light etc) components, (Tansley, 1935, Haeckel, 1866). Odum, 1959, Kendeigh, 1967, explained that interaction of organic and inorganic substances is the basic constrain to retain the ecobalance. The environmental activists also realized that time the importance of study of the environmental communication. "This is the way we communicate with one another about the environment powerfully affects how we receive both it and ourselves and, therefore, how we define our relationship with the nature world[2]."

Modes of Public Participation

In general, the word 'Public' means the community or the people as a whole or a group of people sharing a common interest. After McQuail, it's a general body of free citizens of a given society or some smaller geographical space. The concept of public also refers to a democratic idea (freedom or equality of rights) [Denis McQuail, 2007]. When these group (public), desire to share on a common issue, and then it may be called as the people's mobilization (through motivation) towards betterment[3]. Public participation, (in an environmental issues) encourage the ability to influence any developmental program (on environment), or decision by an individual and / or group of the citizen in favour of sustainable development of the earth. Here the group or the individual should enjoy some basic rights that create a collective approach of society for eco - balance. The participatory communication approach was conceived more than two decades ago. Since then its principles have enjoyed increasing influence over the work of development communicators. Today, these principles drive the works of a significant number of communicators from the NGOs, and, to a lesser extends, the programmes of government agencies. Participatory communication is actually a horizontal mode of information flow. In case of environmental communication it helps to share knowledge, among GOs, NGOs or other agencies on one hand and the citizens on other[4].

Table 1: Modes of Public Participation in Environmental Decision.

Legal Right	Mode of Participation	Authority	Democratic Principle
Right to Know	Written request for information; access to documents online; etc.	Right to Information Act, 2005	Transparency
Right to Comment	Testimony at public hearing; participation in the advisory committee; written comments.	National Environmental Policy Act	Direct participation
Right to Sanding	Plaintiff in lawsuit, amic us brief (third party) in lega case	Wildlife Protection Act, 1972, 2006; Indian Forest Act, 1927 etc.	Accountability

Source : Environmental Communication and Public Sphere, Robert Cox, Sage, 2006, p 85.

Generally, four different ways of participation can be observed in most development projects claiming to be participatory in nature. (Robert Cox, 2006) They are:

- Participation in implementation: People are actively encouraged and mobilized to take part in the actualization of projects. They are given certain responsibilities and set certain tasks or required to contribute specified resources.

- Participation in evaluation: Upon completion of a project, people are invited to critique the success or failure of it.
- Participation in benefit: People take part in enjoying the fruits of a project.
- Participation in decision-making: People initiate, discuss, conceptualize and plan activities they will all do as a community[5].

Participatory mode of communication, in environmental issues encourages the Subject-Subject (NGO and service -receiver), relation. Though, it was believed in earlier (50s – 60s), that development communication should follow Subject - Object relationship. Using the grassroots or local media it tries to help to create acclimate of mutual understanding between the two poles, even sub -poles under same cluster[6]. This non- linear participatory communication flow also helps to build up a multifaceted interaction of people (feedback). In this context, explaining the implication of the Quality Information Service System (QISS), Muhammad Yunis, founder of Bangladesh Grameen Bank, commented the organization (may be GOs or NGOs) distribute the required and meaningful information to the right people in the right time at the right place and in their (receiver) accessible form (Papa, Singhal and Papa, 2006). The following model shows, how the decentralization of information can protect people's participation in the local level. In a specific domain, (in the present article it is forest and forest -dwellers) information spreading as the 'fission- reaction' through opinion leader could increase the success rate of QISS[7]. This type of multidimensional information spreading approach persuades the individual motivation and empowerment towards a collective mobilization of society for sustainable development of earth.

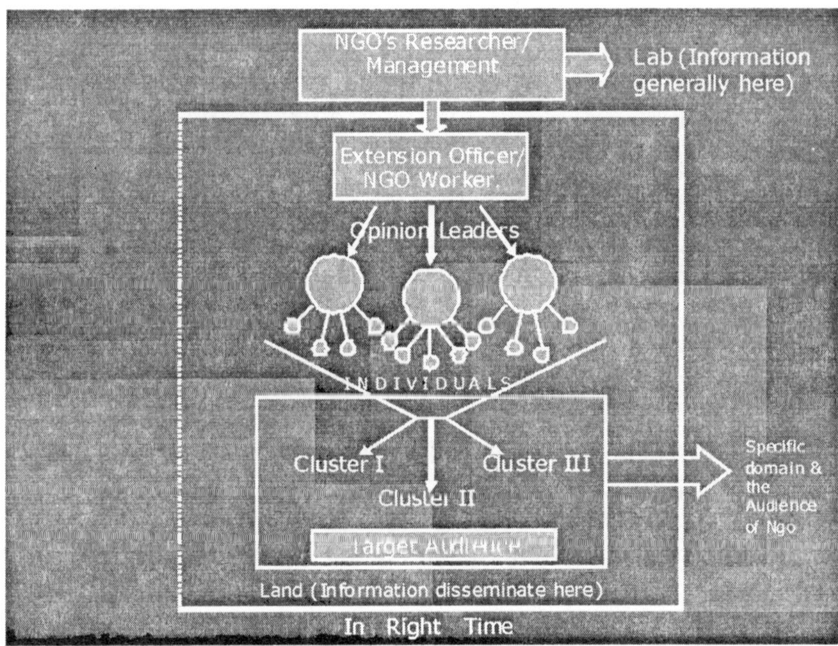

Experience from the Field: Sunderban Lifeline

The largest deltaic region of the world (recognized as the World Heritage Site, by the UNESCO, 1987), is situated at the southern part of Bengal, spreading over India and Bangladesh. During the first part of nineteenth century, two British geographers Mr. Dampier and Mr. Hodge, surveyed and marked the area of Sundarbans by an imaginary line from Sagar Island in the South and Taki in the north. The Sundarbans National Park is located in the world largest delta formed by the confluence of the rivers Ganga, Brahmaputra and Meghana. The Sundarbans Wildlife Sanctuary is the world's largest estuarine sanctuary. Islands such as Goasaba, Sandeshkali and Basanti form the northern boundary of the Sundarbans whereas on the south lies the Bay of Bengal; the Matla and Bidya Rivers form the eastern boundary and to the west side of the Sunderbans National Park is the international boundary of Bangladesh. Sundarban has extremely rich diversity of aquatic and terrestrial flora (so far, 64 pure mangroves and its associated species have been reported authentically) and fauna. Sundarban's highly productive ecosystem acts as a natural fish nursery. Sundarban Mangrove reduces the fury of cyclonic storm and prevents erosion due to tidal action. Finally, millions of people depend on Sundarban Ecosystem for their livelihood and sustenance through fishing, collection of honey and fuel wood[8].

Table 2: Sundarban- At a Glance.

Geographic Area	9630 sq km
Habitat Area	4493 sq km
Reserve Forest	4263 sq km
Sundarban National Forest	1310 sq km
Core Area of Tiger	2585 sq km
Total No. of Police Station	16
Total No. of Block	19
Population	31,20,986 (2001 Census Report)

'Sundarban Lifeline', a project run by, Nature Environment and Wildlife Society, NEWS (a leading NGO in Sundarban area, website- www.naturewildlife.org), to create awareness about Sundarban and its Mangrove forest in the surrounding villages. Their endeavor is also directed towards the economic empowerment of the local villager. The present paper covers two villages as the domain of field study, namely Sonagaon -Dulki (Goasaba Block) and Tridibnagar (Basanti Block), in South Parganags district, West Bengal. At present NEWS organizes a number of programme successfully in these villages to focus an integrated development as well as social and economic empowerment of villagers. They formed eight committees for each village and numbers of sub -committee under it, with proper representation of the local people. It helps to decentralize and participatory approach which are the basic structure of Sundarban Lifeline Project. Field Staffs (NGO members) and village committee act as an opinion leader, with proper supervision of West Bengal University of Animal Husbandry and Fisheries Sciences (WBUAFS); Department of Marine Sciences and Sociology, Kolkata University; to assist in the implementation of the project[9].

Box-1

The Project at a Glance[10]

i) Beneficiaries identified and then Self Help groups formed, livelihood materials distributed (goatery, piggery, chicken farming, fisheries, and duckery are the options provided).

ii) Livestock materials including their housing, necessary food, medicines and vaccination have been provided. Local staff of the NEWS has taken active part in buying the livestock materials as suggested by the group beneficiaries instead of disbursing cash in hand direct to the villagers.

iii) Vocational tanning camps have been organized to create awareness and involvement of local people. Leaflets and pamphlets are distributed, introducing proper training through audio visuals, practical exercises imparted on how to maintain the housings, feeding procedures and local forest resources.

iv) Initiating scientific practices and know-how of aquaculture in harmony with traditional knowledge practiced hitherto under guidance of experts associated with Department of Marine Science, Kolkata University.

v) Some of the beneficiaries in the villages have been given the responsibility to maintain the nurseries in small plots adjacent to their house, where the seedlings for roadside plantation i.e. of Subabul, Arjun, Shirish, Mahogany (Non-Mangrove plantation) are maintained and proper training imparted.

vi) Planning has been taken to plant 4000 saplings per hectare of land to restore embankments by way of plantation of mangroves (Sundari, Garan, Garjan, Genwa) along the mudflats. For development of mangrove nursery in 30 hectare, i.e. 1, 20,000 saplings, nurseries have already been developed in the villages.

vii) Regular field visits by Mangrove training expert is being made who is giving necessary training and guidance to the village women on the proper development and maintenance of the same. It is highly encouraging that women have participated enthusiastically in the nursery development process.

viii) It may be noted that at every stage planning has been done at the grass root levels after proper discussion and consultation with Panchayat Pradhans , beneficiaries and experts through group meeting.

The Audience participated enthusiastically to make it a real process of exchange of ideas.

Public Participation and Environmental Governance

Public participation practice is a growing part of environmental decision-making. The Earth Charter Initiative, 2000, (is a declaration of fundamental principles for building a just, sustainable, and peaceful global society for the 21st century) expresses this sense of environmental responsibility by stating that the improvement of democratic practices, transparency and accountability of government institutions, along with civil participation in decision making, are strongly related factors to the objectives of the protection of the environment and social and economic justice and Build democratic societies that are just, participatory, sustainable, and peaceful [Principles, I (3) and iv (13)][11]. Sundarban Lifeline is a project followed the environmental governance. It's a horizontal structure of relation and interaction among government and non-government structures. It concerns how the decisions are made, with a particular emphasis on the need for citizens, interest groups, and communities generally, to participate and have their voices heard. Therefore, the concept does not apply to the province of government alone. It is also observed how citizens take on their own responsibility and develop environmental initiatives. As an extension of the concept of environmental governance, good environmental governance is measured by the effectiveness of strategies and initiatives implemented to achieve environmental goals. These goals may be capacity building, increased access to environmental information, people's participation and justice.

In this context a sample survey (random- basis) was conducted, among 250 villagers, in Sonagaon -Dulki (Goasaba Block) and Tridibnagar (Basanti Block). There were three key sections in that study- i)the impact of environmental governance; ii) the environmental awareness among villagers and iii) the media selection for environmental campaign.(see end note). Some of the given data (from field) are enlisted here, which are very much imperative in the present paper.

Table 3: Generally Villagers Get Information on Environmental Awareness Programme, From:

	NGO Worker	Friend/ Neighbour	GOs Representative	Local Media
Male (%)	31	34	14	21
Female (%)	37	30	18	15

Table 4A: The Following Table Contains Two Groups. It was Circulated Among Respondents to Match Group A with Group B:

Group - A	Group-B
Global Warming	World Conservation Union
Deforestation	Both Plant and Animal
IUCN	Collaboration with Government
Ecosystem	Depletion of Ozone Layer
NGO	Erosion of River -Bank

Table 4B: Among the Villagers They Attempted to Match the Group. But Their Knowledge on Basic Environmental Problems or Idea of GO-NGO's Cooperation is not Satisfactory.

Score (%)	Male (130 individuals)	Female (120 individuals)
100-80	10	03
Less 80 and up to 60	32	19
Less 60 and up to 40	67	43
Below 40	21	55

No doubt it's a poor performance. Significantly, 37% and 30 % of female of the total sample of female get their required information on environment issues either from NGO or neighbour (via opinion leader), respectively. In case of male these ratio are 31% and 34%. Hence, the largest portions of mass (66%) of the local people access their information from these two sources. So to say, some problems are inherent in the present information dissemination process. Now, the next series of survey- analysis help to get an idea about the limitations of the method of interaction with stakeholders.

Table 5: Normally, GOs or NGOs Workers/ Representatives Interact with Villagers:

Frequency (%)	GOs Member	NGOs Member
Once in a Week	04	09
Once in a Month	09	17
Once in six Month	67	49
Very Rare	20	25

Table 6: Which Language/s Peers Used to Demonstrate the Problem or Interact with Villagers?

Language/s	Used by GOs /NGOs Representative (%)
Bengali	64
Bengali andEnglish	08
Bengaliand Local Languages	17
Only Local Languages	11

Table 7: Villagers are Likely to Get Information of the Following Modes/ Strategies on Environmental Awareness Programme.

Format	Likings (%)
Demonstration/Posters/Pamphlets	12
Puppetry /Street Drama	25
Slide show/Documentary	16
Group and Interpersonal Discussion with Experts	27
Radio or TV Programme in Local Languages	20

It has already been pointed out that the final element in the communication process is feedback. Schramm and Osgood (1955), in their paper ' Information Theory and Mass Communication', referred to , two –way communication circuit lays ample stress upon the feedback for making any communication effective[12]. In case of environmental communication it should provide the additional notion of a "field of experience," or the psychological frame of reference; this refers to the type of orientation or attitudes, which interactants maintain toward each other. The regular based field of experiences also help to adapt and/ or change the message design (content or medium) of environmental awareness programme by the GOs or NGOs. Because a message may have different meanings, depending upon the specific context or setting[13].

People- Participation Based Environmental Message - Idea and Implementation

In the discourse of environment the question of disseminating the content and facets of development has been a long-standing problem. In third world countries, like India such communication, generally flows from two ends - from the 'elite democracy' on the one hand and 'participatory democracy' on the other. The elite theory has also been described as bureaucratic or technical and the participatory theory as the pluralist or social democratic approach. Participatory model evokes mobilization of the populace to co-operation in developing activities and empowering of people so that they may articulate and manage their own development. The context of this form is local and community settings with individuals, group, organization or community level analysis (Melkote Srinivas, 2001)[14].Through the active social support system like mutual help and selfhelp group, the participatory model makes a social network within a focused domain.

To build up an environmental awareness, like global warming, biodiversity, ozone depletion or preserve the wild resources, among people (world wide) may consider 100% domain of the problem. And for illustration, Sundarban Lifeline (the project and problem) by NEWS is a sub domain under it. Environmental communication is the basic constrain in this domain. This type of communication reveals the pragmatic and constitutive vehicle for our understanding of the environment as well as our relationship in the natural world. Participatory mode of environmental communication, with proper representation of GOs and NGOs, facilitates to formulate an environmental public sphere[15]. It can be defined as a realm of influence on environmental issues that is created when individuals engage others in environmental communication- through conversation, argument, debate or questioning about sustainable development of environment that affects a wider community in globe. Individuals and community groups find it very difficult to participate meaningfully in environmental decision-making unless they have access to information relevant to the decision to be made. Ideally, the public should have access to the same information as the decision-maker. The goal of environmental communication is message production in support of the mass mobilization goals of the grass root organization. The GOs or NGOs take initiative this transformation. The entire system uses feedback to determine if its desired goal is reached (Mody Bella, 1991)[16].

In this context some declarations of Agenda 21 are too appropriate. The first UN Conference on Environment and Development (UNCED Earth Summit) held in Rio de Janeiro in 1992 represented a turning point in the way we look at environment and development. World leaders adopted Agenda 21, a blue print to attain sustainable development in the 21st century. Agenda 21 provides a comprehensive action programme to attain sustainable development and address both environmental and developmental issues in an integrated manner at global, national and local levels. The International Action Plan agreed at the 1992 Earth Summit has created or strengthened civil society involvement in the decision-making process. This participation by those concerned with, or affected by, proposals (stakeholders) is reflected in new forms of decision-making processes being initiated at the all levels. Chapter 14 of Agenda 21 setting out the programmes and specific actions needed to promote sustainable agriculture and rural development also, which reads, ensuring people's participation and promoting human resource development for sustainable agriculture. Within this context, a stakeholder is a group or organization who has influence in a particular area of policy or who is affected by policies. Agenda 21 identified 9 Major Groups: women; children and youth; indigenous people; NGOs; local authorities; trade unions; business and industry; science and technology, and farmers[17]. Multi-Stakeholder processes aim to bring together different 'actors' to develop a dialogue at different levels. They involve working together towards a common goal or purpose. They are based on democratic principles of transparency, accountability and participation. The result is usually a stronger partnership. Achieving sustainability requires an immense collective effort. It forms of such participation may be described as, Fission Reaction, starts from a point and then spreads the entire in a continuous process[18]. The whole process is broadly supported by required and meaningful message with individual's involvement. Bella Mody(1991), made a schematic presentation on how the people's involvement for message design will be set up. The following points are:[19]

- Learn everything about the topic/ programme / project.
- Observe the lifestyle and values of different segments of the people to help the opinion leader or peer members decide how to communicate.
- Dialogue with the people on what each segment already knows feels and does on the topic.
- Write down the objective: what people impact should be used to measure whether communication has been achieved?
- Choose which channels and what frequency of exposure are required to reach the objective the Gos or NGOs have set.
- Design a creative – persuasive strategy to package the meanings the peer members want to share.
- Write specification of every message, describing the goal, content and recommended format/ treatment.
- Pretest the creative- persuasive strategy on a sample of the audience to find out whether the chosen approach is working.
- Modify the message design according to pretest finding and then proceed with final production.
- Monitor physical exposure, attention, comprehension and implementation levels after message distribution begins.
- Evaluate whether the message is achieving its knowledge, feeling and behaviour goals.

People's participation is the sharing of information between stakeholders, in a particular domain.

Its only possible when the Quality Information Service sustains in the sphere, (in the present paper it is the villages of Sundarban). Mangrove deforestation in Sundarban river bank is a major problem. One of the major livelihood in the Sundarban people (mainly women), is to catch the shrimp under tidal water for prawn culture. When they collect the shrimp, at a same time different aquatic fauna also comes in net. Due to their ignorance they normally destroy it, and make an imbalance in brackish water fauna. In the present survey, among respondents questions were asked regarding these problems. It was tried to reveal that the information which they collect from peer members (either GOs and NGOs) how much it's able to fulfill the people's need in time. Later it was analyzed that majority of the people (88%) believe that getting information (mainly ecological) is suitable for their daily life, but due to some complexity (on content or language or terminology) the information is not useful of nearly 50% of villagers.

Table 8: Selecting People's Responsive Content

Frequency (%)	Content is Useful	Content is Timely	Information is Appropriate	Information is Simple
Male	53	54	87	23
Female	52	52	89	19

Conclusion

So to say, there are three major factors in the whole paper, communication, nature and the public sphere. Communication is the form of symbolic action. While our beliefs, attitudes and, relating to nature and environmental problems are mediated by communication. Some time it flows through group or interpersonal mood or may be local media or mass media. In this triangle, the public sphere emerges as a discursive space for communication about the environment. In the present paper, it is in Sundarban, regarding biodiversity and Mangrove deforestation. The peer members of GOs or NGOs, act as catalyst, who caters on the required information from Lab to Land. Message specification, specific measurable objectives for the message, the content of the message and mix of message delivery channels- are the stages through which the horizontal information flow can be done effectively.

It is obvious, that to flow a horizontal knowledge sharing in the grass root area, opinion leaders in various cluster (farmer, small businessman, house wife etc. in a village) could play a significant role. It is a combined structure – experts, researchers, and organization's representative and local people. To reach the objective participation is desired in each level and within the whole system at a same time. It also be secure right to information, public comment (on issue based) and right of standing which are the basic procedural rights of public participation on environmental awareness programme. In US and other developed country, the most frequently used modes of individual's people communication on environment matters are a) testimony on public hearings, b) participation on advisory panel and collaboration with other parties with an interest in an environmental decision. Citizens' Advisory Committee in an effective formula, to retain the peoples' voice in decision-making level. Its a group or panel, appointed by a government to solicit input from diverse interests in a public sphere - for example, citizens, business environmentalist and NGOs activists, about a project or problem. One more model of public participation is, community based collaboration. This is an approach to problem solving that involves individuals and representatives of affective groups, business and other agencies in addressing a short-term problem defined by the local community. It will be useful due to its group - thinking procedure, or persuasive nature. Because, community based collaboration focuses both the cognitive and non - cognitive mood of communication strategy. It's a reality, when the dissemination of information or any discussion is broadcasted with human emotion; it affects the audiences mind immediately. Through the collaboration and participation of the people, the agenda setting and following the gate keeping method of media can help immediately. Collectively, all these help to formulate an alternative public sphere within the society, where (in the focused domain) environmental programme and project run successfully through peoples' participation. A healthy environment means we are more likely to benefit from economic prosperity. In this sense, poverty eradication and the protection of the environment are interrelated[20]. The benefits of environmental protection are unlimited: we can appreciate the aesthetic beauty of nature, experience health benefits, and have some peace of mind that future generations will also have access to these benefits.

References

1. A Comparative Analysis of Public Participation and Access to Justice MICHAEL Jeffery QC, http://www.paclii.org/journals/fJSPL/vol09no2/2.
2. Chatterjee Asim Kumar, Modern Approach to Text Book of Ecology, Nirmala Library, 1999,p 9.2 -9.6.
3. Cox Robert, Environmental communication and the Public Sphere, Sage Publication, 2006, p 83-89.
4. Dey Pradip Kumar, Perspectives in Mass Communication, Kalyani Publishers, 1993, p. 28 - 32.
5. Eade Deborah, Development NGOs and Civil Society, Rawat Publishers, 2005, p. 36 - 42.
6. Environ, Vol. viii No 4, 2003, Vishal Book Centre, p 4-6.
7. Environ, Vol. x No 1, 2008, Vishal Book Centre, p 64.
8. Feather John and Sturges Paul, ed. International Encyclopedia of Information and Library Science, 2_{nd} Ed, Routledge, pp - 278-282.
9. Habermas, J. Strukturwandel, 2_{nd} Ed, Frankfurt, 1989, Translated as The Structural Transformation of The Public Sphere, Polity, Cambridge, 1989.
10. McQuail Denis (2007) Mass Communication Theory, Vistar Publication, New Delhi, p-565.
11. Melkote R. Srinivas and Steeves II Leslie, Communication for Development in the Third World, 2_{nd} Ed, Sage Publication, 2001,pp. 337-352.

12. Melkote R. Srinivas and Steeves H Leslie, Communication for Development in the Third World, 2nd Ed, Sage Publication, 2001,pp 55-57 and 234 - 240.
13. Mody Bella, Designing Message for Development Communication, Sage, 1991,p 55-60.
14. Mody Bella, Designing Message for Development Communication, Sage,1991,p 40-44.
15. Mody Bella, Designing Message for Development Communication, Sage, 1991,p 10-13.
16. Papa Michael J., Singhal Arvind , and Papa H. Wendy, organizing For Social Change, Sage Publication, 2006, p 16 -20.
17. Sanctuary Asia, Vol . xxii No 2, March / April 2002.
18. Scanlon John and Burhenne-Guilmin Francoise (eds.), *International Environmental Governance-An International Regime for Protected Areas*, 2004, p. 2-5.
19. (1992) United Nations Department of Economic and Social Affairs, Division for Sustainable Development, <http://www.un.org/esa/sustdev/documents/agenda21/english/agenda21toc.htm> (Accessed 4 November 2005).
20. www.earthsummit2002.org ,Towards Earth Summit.